SELLING TODAY

PARTNERING TO CREATE VALUE

SELLING TODAY

PARTNERING TO CREATE VALUE

seventh canadian edition

GERALD L. MANNING
DES MOINES AREA COMMUNITY COLLEGE

MICHAEL AHEARNE
UNIVERSITY OF HOUSTON

BARRY L. REECE
VIRGINIA POLYTECHNIC INSTITUTE AND STATE UNIVERSITY

H. F. (HERB) MACKENZIE
GOODMAN SCHOOL OF BUSINESS
BROCK UNIVERSITY

PEARSON

Toronto

Editor-in-Chief: Claudine O'Donnell
Acquisitions Editor: Carolin Sweig
Marketing Manager: Jessica Saso
Program Manager: Karen Townsend
Project Manager: Jessica Hellen
Developmental Editor: Charlotte Morrison-Reed
Production Services: Cenveo® Publisher Services
Permissions Project Manager: Joanne Tang
Photo Permissions Research: Dimple Bhorwal, Aptara
Text Permissions Research: Phyllis Padula, Aptara
Cover Designer: Alex Li
Cover Image: Rafal Olechowski/Fotolia

10 9 8 7 6 5 4 3 2 V0TX

Library and Archives Canada Cataloguing in Publication

Manning, Gerald L., author
      Selling today : partnering to create value / Gerald L. Manning , Michael Ahearne, Barry L. Reece, H.F. (Herb) MacKenzie. — Seventh Canadian edition.

Includes index.
Revision of: Selling today : partnering to create value / Gerald L. Manning
      ... [et al.] 6th Canadian ed. Toronto : Pearson Canada, 2013.
ISBN 978-0-13-315685-0 (pbk.)

      1. Selling—Textbooks.   I. Ahearne, Michael, author II. Reece, Barry L., author III. MacKenzie, H. F., author IV. Title.

HF5438.25.M35 2015   658.85   C2014-904175-6

ISBN 978-0-13-315685-0

Brief Contents

v

Contents

Preface

Today, the profession of selling enjoys unprecedented growth in importance as the western world completes its transition from a production-focused to a sales- and service-focused economy. There are well over a million people employed in sales positions across Canada: more than 10 percent of the workforce. This increasingly sales-oriented economy calls for a more professional and customer-oriented selling attitude. This in turn necessitates learning and teaching selling strategies and skills in a more systematic fashion. The role of sales representative is predicted to be one of the occupations in greatest demand over the next decade.

Surprisingly, those seeking a job in sales are not the only ones who will benefit from learning how to sell. In fact, almost everyone these days uses traditional sales-related activities in their professional and social lives. People use a whole assortment of selling techniques in everyday life to persuade decision makers and advance their causes. According to Daniel Pink, the author of the recent best-selling book, *To Sell Is Human*, people are using about 40 percent of their time at work to engage in what he calls "non-sales selling"—persuading, convincing, influencing, and moving others in ways that do not involve anybody making a purchase. Moreover, people across a wide variety of professions spend about 24 minutes of every hour influencing or moving others, and they consider this time investment crucial to their success.[1] Selling is increasingly becoming a master skill for success in the twenty-first century.

This paradigm shift in which selling has become an integral part of the social and business environment has coincided with another major revolution, the dramatic change in how people access information. The information age has transferred the power from sellers to customers. Today's customers can easily compare the offerings of different sellers through various online methods and choose those offerings that best suit their needs. Good word of mouth spreads more quickly through social media, and suboptimal service is punished more severely through online reviews. Today's sellers realize that creating anything but what customers value the most will result in those customers buying from the competition. A bigger realization, however, is that in this information age, even satisfied customers may not become repeat customers or provide referrals. The wide access to information makes it easier for even satisfied customers to rethink their options every time they want to make a purchase.

In order to lock their customers in and *create and deliver superior value* in times when customers have more choices and lower switching costs, salespeople are adopting a partnering style of selling to build long-term, strategic relationships with their customers. Having these long-term relationships is important, as it is more profitable for companies to retain existing customers than it is to acquire new ones. The pivotal role of a *partnering style of selling* in today's highly competitive business environment is a common theme throughout the seventh Canadian edition of *Selling Today: Partnering to Create Value*.

The primary goal of each revision of *Selling Today* is to develop the finest research-backed and most practical and applied text available in the marketplace. The revision process begins with a thorough review of several hundred articles, books, and research reports. The authors also study popular sales training programs such as Conceptual Selling, SPIN Selling, Integrity Selling, Trusted Advisor, and Solution Selling. These

---

[1] Daniel Pink, *To Sell Is Human: The Surprising Truth about Persuading, Convincing, and Influencing Others.* (NY: Riverhead Books, 2012), pp. 19–25.

training programs are used by major corporations such as Microsoft, Marriott, UPS, SAS Institute, Purolator, and Xerox Corporation. Of course, reviews and suggestions by professors and students influence decisions made during the revision process.

STAYING ON THE CUTTING EDGE: NEW TO THIS EDITION

Since our last edition, the business environment and research on professional selling have undergone significant changes. As active researchers, practitioners, and consultants in the field of selling, our primary goal is to provide an up-to-date and cutting-edge treatment of the field. The seventh Canadian edition of *Selling Today* describes what ramifications the information age has for the selling world and how sales professionals must cope with new issues arising from the information revolution with an ethical, customer-centred mindset. The most significant changes in the new edition include:

- *Greater emphasis on ethical selling.* Ethical selling is highlighted, as Chapter 3, "Ethics: The Foundation for Relationships That Create Value," has been totally revised and updated. Moved up to Chapter 3 from Chapter 5 in the sixth edition to address the many ethical lapses existing in the business world, this new material emphasizes the need for a highly ethical interaction with customers as the starting point of all relationship development if one is to build long-term, partnering-style selling relationships. Moreover, a new ethics assessment has been added to the end of the chapter, and new seventh-edition text models are used to highlight an emphasis on ethical selling.

- The seventh Canadian edition features new boxed features in many chapters. We would like to point your attention to those titled **Social Media and Selling Today, From the Field, Selling in Action,** and **Global Business Insight,** describing important cultural and economic differences for selling internationally as well as new challenges and strategies for utilizing social media in selling in today's information-driven business world. In addition, CRM boxed inserts appear throughout the text on how salespeople apply customer relationship management software to improve their partnering strategies.

- *Latest Research and Trends from Academic Journals and Trade References.* Extensive referencing of academic articles found in the *Journal of Personal Selling and Sales Management, Journal of Marketing, Harvard Business Review,* and others has been brought up to date. Topics and trends in selling garnered from numerous trade publications such as *Selling Power, ThinkSales, Value Added Selling, Sales and Marketing Management,* and *The American Salesperson,* have been integrated throughout the seventh edition.

- *New Study Guides.* These are added to maximize student learning when viewing both the Reality Selling and Adaptive Selling videos. With more video support than any text on the market, these new study guides ensure in-depth student learning.

BUILDING ON TRADITIONAL STRENGTHS

Selling Today: Partnering to Create Value has been successful because the authors continue to build on strengths that have been enthusiastically praised by instructors and students. Speaking to these strengths, *Selling Today* has become the standard for personal selling textbooks internationally, significantly exceeding all other textbooks in this area in worldwide sales. International editions of the book have been sold in over 30 different countries, including China, Croatia, Indonesia, the Netherlands, Mexico, and Spain. *Selling Today* is the premier research-backed textbook in the marketplace for personal selling.

Previous editions of *Selling Today* have evolved by tracing the trends in professional selling and highlighting the most critical areas for salesperson success. This edition provides new material on a number of evolving and important concepts.

1. **The partnering era is described in detail.** Partnership selling principles, so important to today's successful selling and marketing strategies, are presented and clearly illustrated throughout the text. Strategic alliances—the highest form of partnering—are also discussed in detail.

2. **Value-added selling strategies** are presented throughout the text. Salespeople today are guided by a new principle of personal selling: *Partnerships are established and maintained only when the salesperson creates customer value.* Customers have fundamentally changed their expectations. They want to partner with salespeople who can create value, not just communicate it. Value creation involves a series of improvements in the sales process that enhance the customer's experience.

3. **Real-world examples,** a hallmark of previous editions and a continued focus in this edition, build the reader's interest in personal selling and promote an understanding of the major topics and concepts. With opening vignettes at the beginning of each chapter that put you in the shoes of the salesperson, and role plays that allow you to utilize the skills you have learned, the real-world examples truly enrich the overall learning experience. **The Reality Selling Video Series** features successful salespeople and provides real-world examples of sales careers and presentations. Additional real selling examples have been obtained from a range of progressive organizations, large and small, such as Xerox, Hilti, UPS, Lionbridge Technologies, WFS Ltd., and more.

4. In addition to the role-play exercises and video case problems, the **Reality Selling Video Role Plays** remain an invaluable resource for instructors. Found in Appendix 1, these scenarios give students the chance to assume the role of a salesperson in selling situations that are relevant to today's competitive environment. These role-play scenarios build on what students learned in the **Reality Selling Video** sales presentations and interviews. The detailed salesperson/customer role-play scenarios use the actual products and sales positions of the salespeople who appeared in the Reality Selling Videos. Websites of the companies you will be using to role-play sales presentations are supplied so that students can learn appropriate amounts of product and company information. The Reality Selling Video interviews and sales presentations provide the necessary background and contextual information for you to use in both selecting the scenario and conducting the role play. The role plays are also specifically designed to prepare students for professional selling role-play competitions at annual college and university competitive event conventions.

5. The **knowing–doing gap,** common in personal selling classes, is closed by having you, the student, participate in the comprehensive role play/simulation "Partnership Selling: A Role Play/Simulation for Selling Today," available on the companion website to the text. You assume the role of a new sales trainee employed by the Park Inn International Convention Centre. Serving as an excellent capstone experience, this feature helps you develop the critical skills needed to apply relationship, product, customer, and presentation strategies.

6. **The Professionally Produced "Adaptive Selling Training Video Series."** This is the only custom-produced video series available for a textbook on selling. The four-part series is produced and directed by Arthur Bauer, a well-known and widely acclaimed award-winning training video professional. Concepts in the text are presented based on carefully written scripts, utilization of professional actors, and filming in real, contemporary business settings. These high-cost, professionally produced videos available to professors who adopt the *Selling Today* text are also marketed and sold to sales training directors throughout the world and used to train their salespeople in the skills critical to success in the profession of selling.

   The first video on building relationships, "Communication Styles—A Key to Adaptive Selling," describes how to use behavioural psychology to build strong, mutually rewarding relationships. Designed to be shown when presenting Chapter 5, it discusses how to avoid style bias by understanding and flexing one's style to adapt and communicate effectively with the customer's style. A Web-based style assessment exercise is designed to discover one's own preferred style. The second video, "Questions, Questions, Questions," presents a widely researched approach to discovering customer needs using the consultative model. Shown when covering Chapter 11, this video included application exercises at the end of the chapter to apply and enhance the development of this critical, consultative selling skill. Closely aligned with the four questions in the Spin Selling Model, professional actors show how each of these questions are effectively used in the sales process. The third Adaptive Selling Video titled "Negotiations—Solving the Tough Problems" supports the principles in Chapter 13 on negotiation. Using a medical equipment sales setting, professional negotiation strategies are dramatically presented for moving through the sometimes difficult process of answering customer concerns, moving the sale forward, and achieving a win-win solution. The fourth video, titled "Ask for the Order," is built on the concepts in Chapter 14, "Adapting the Close and Confirming the Partnership." This video is designed to visually and dramatically present the many methods for moving the sales process to a successful conclusion.

7. **The following high-interest boxed inserts** are updated for this edition, and new and interesting material regarding the role of social media in selling as well as global selling has been added to the social media and global selling inserts:

   ■ **From the Field.** These real-world examples explain how selling skills affect the success of persons who may or may not consider themselves salespeople.

   ■ **Selling in Action.** These concise inserts feature contemporary issues in selling to keep the readers of *Selling Today* abreast of the latest developments.

   ■ **Global Business Insight.** These brief inserts provide practical tips on how to build global relationships. Most inserts focus on a specific country.

   ■ **Social Media and Selling Today.** Informing you how social networking applies to personal selling, these succinct inserts identify how social media networks such as Facebook, Twitter, LinkedIn, and YouTube can be used effectively in the selling process.

8. **End-of-chapter summaries are organized into bullet points** corresponding to the key points that appear in the Chapter Preview of each chapter. These summaries provide

students with a review tool that can be used to understand how the concepts and themes covered are related to one another—i.e., the "big picture."

9. A **complete update** of key terms for selling appears in each chapter. These terms are boldfaced and defined throughout the text.

ORGANIZATION OF THIS BOOK

The material in *Selling Today* continues to be organized around the four pillars of personal selling: relationship strategy, product strategy, customer strategy, and presentation strategy. Moreover, in the seventh Canadian edition, we emphasize ethical selling as an important factor within which all the four strategies should be embedded. Part I, **Developing a Personal Selling Philosophy**, includes Chapters 1 and 2 and sets the stage for an in-depth study of these strategies. The first chapter provides a contemporary definition of selling and gives students the opportunity to explore career opportunities in the information age, while the second chapter describes the evolution of personal selling associated with the information revolution.

Research indicates that high-performance salespeople are better able to build and maintain relationships than are moderate performers. Part II, **Developing a Relationship Strategy**, focuses on several important person-to-person relationship-building practices that contribute to success in personal selling. The influence of ethical selling as the foundation of successful relationships is discussed in Chapter 3. Creating value with a relationship strategy is discussed in Chapter 4. Chapter 5, "Communication Styles: A Key to Adaptive Selling Today," introduces communication styles and explains how to build strong relationships with style flexing.

Part III, **Developing a Product Strategy**, examines the importance of complete and accurate product, company, and competitive knowledge in personal selling. A well-informed salesperson is in a strong position to configure value-added product solutions for customers' unique needs. The importance of having expert product knowledge as well as knowledge of competition and industry trends is discussed in Chapter 6, while Chapter 7 explains how to sell with a value-added strategy.

Part IV, **Developing a Customer Strategy**, presents information on why and how customers buy, and explains how to identify prospects. With increased knowledge of the customer, salespeople are in a better position to understand customers' unique wants and needs and create customer value in the multi-call, lifetime customer setting. Chapter 8 sheds light on consumer- and business-buying behaviours while Chapter 9 describes the strategies used to develop prospects and accounts.

The concept of a salesperson as an adviser, consultant, value creator, and partner to buyers is stressed in Part V, **Developing a Presentation Strategy**. Emphasis is placed on the need-satisfaction presentation model as well as ways to provide outstanding service after the sale. Chapter 10 introduces the concept of adaptive selling as a useful strategy to approach customers. Chapter 11 explains how to identify customer needs with a consultative questioning strategy, and Chapter 12 discusses the role of a consultative presentation in delivering value to the customers. The principles of formal negotiations as a part of a win-win strategy are discussed in Chapter 13, while Chapter 14 focuses on proper attitudes and strategies to close the sales. Chapter 15 finishes Part V by discussing the role of customer service in building sustaining profitable relationships with the customer.

Personal selling is one of the few professions that inherently require a great deal of self-discipline. Part VI focuses on managing self as well as others by discussing the four dimensions of opportunity management in Chapter 16 and the fundamentals of sales force management in Chapter 17.

Finally, this edition features Appendix 1, "Reality Selling Role-Play Scenarios," which includes 11 role-play scenarios that provide students with the opportunity to—of course—sell.

A SPECIAL NOTE TO STUDENTS ON HOW TO USE THE BOOK

This seventh Canadian edition of *Selling Today* has several new features that distinguish it from other texts. Here we offer you a few tips to make the most out of the materials presented in the new edition.

Selling is fun. That does not mean it is easy to close a deal. Each chapter in this new edition has been reorganized with the sole goal of providing you with a systematic summary of key concepts related to the topic area and ample application exercises. While there are different ways you can approach the text, we believe it is most effective to start each chapter with a concrete understanding of how the chapter fits into the big picture of selling through value creation, the overriding theme of this textbook. In this regard, we have extensively revised and updated the chapter previews, chapter summaries, key terms, review questions, and cross-references among the chapters to assist you in integrating key concepts.

Practice makes perfect. We have created numerous role-play exercises that resemble real-life selling situations. In our experience, some students may dismiss these exercises as easy. Try one of the exercises and you will see how these students could not be more wrong. Don't be mistaken—the exercises are not that difficult, but we do inject a great deal of reality into them to make them complex enough to provide you with the opportunity to hone your selling skills. So practise them with a friend, a family member, or in front of a video camera or mirror.

Finally, **observe, analyze, and think about your experiences with salespeople in everyday life**, using the concepts and themes you have learned from the text. Think about how those salespeople sell to you, or how you would do it differently if you were in their position.

We encourage you to write to us regarding your experience with this new edition.

SELLING TODAY SUPPLEMENTS

Selling Today: Partnering to Create Value, Seventh Canadian Edition, is accompanied by a complete supplements package. The instructor resources listed below are password protected and available for download via **www.pearsoncanada.ca/highered.**

Instructor's Resource Manual. The comprehensive instructor's manual includes detailed presentation outlines, answers to review questions, suggested responses to learning activities, instructions for using the case problems, and a complete trainer's guide for using the role play/simulation.

Test Item File. More than 1000 test questions—including multiple-choice, true/false, and essay questions—are provided in Microsoft Word format. The Test Item File enables instructors to view and edit the existing questions, add new questions, and generate tests. This robust test bank is also available in My Test format (see below).

My Test. The new edition test bank comes with My Test, a powerful assessment-generation program that helps instructors easily create and print quizzes, tests, and exams as well as homework or practice handouts. Questions and tests can all be authored online, allowing instructors ultimate flexibility and the ability to efficiently manage assessments at any time, from anywhere.

PowerPoint Slides. A collection of more than 200 slides—culled from the textbook or specifically designed to complement chapter content—is available.

Companion Website. The companion website (**www.pearsoncanada.ca/manning**) offers students valuable resources, including chapter quizzes and exercises, Decision-Making Mini Simulations and BizSkill Simulations, Adaptive Selling videos, role-play videos, and an online assessment tool for better understanding one's own style as well as the adaptive selling communication style of others. Sales literature and support materials for completing role plays as part of "Partnership Selling: A Role Play/Simulation for Selling Today" are also supplied on the companion website.

DVD Videos. Several new videos are available with the seventh Canadian edition that will be invaluable tools in the classroom.

Reality Selling Video Series. In response to high demand from instructors, the Reality Selling Video Series offers videos with accompanying chapter opening vignettes, case problems, and role-plays that demonstrate how recent college graduates are using their selling skills to pursue rewarding sales careers. A comprehensive listing of these videos is presented in Appendix 1.

Adaptive Selling Training Video Series. This four-video series now includes a recently added sales training video based on the content of Chapter 13, "Negotiating Buyer Concerns." Students can view the types of negotiating situations that salespeople encounter—in a classroom setting. Based on extensive research in selling organizations, students learn how to negotiate win-win solutions to overcome the price problem.

Pearson Custom Library. For enrolments of at least 25 students, you can create your own textbook by choosing the chapters that best suit your own course needs. To begin building your custom text, visit **www.pearsoncustomlibrary.com**. You may also work with a dedicated Pearson Custom editor to create your ideal text—publishing your own original content or mixing and matching Pearson content. Contact your local Pearson Representative to get started.

Learning Solutions Managers. Pearson's Learning Solutions Managers work with faculty and campus course designers to ensure that Pearson technology products, assessment tools, and online course materials are tailored to meet your specific needs. This highly qualified team is dedicated to helping schools take full advantage of a wide range of educational resources, by assisting in the integration of a variety of instructional materials and media formats. Your local Pearson Education sales representative can provide you with more details on this service program.

CourseSmart for Instructors. CourseSmart goes beyond traditional expectations to provide instant online access to the textbooks and course materials you need at a lower cost for students. And even as students save money, you can save time and hassle with a digital eTextbook that allows you to search for the most relevant content at the very moment you need it. Whether it's evaluating textbooks or creating lecture notes to help students with difficult concepts, CourseSmart can make life a little easier. See how when you visit **www.coursesmart.com/instructors**.

CourseSmart for Students. CourseSmart goes beyond traditional expectations to provide instant online access to the textbooks and course materials you need at significant savings over the print price. With instant access from any computer and the ability to search your text, you'll find the content you need quickly, no matter where you are. And with online tools like highlighting and note-taking, you can save time and study efficiently. See all the benefits at **www.coursesmart.com/students**.

THE SEARCH FOR WISDOM IN THE AGE OF INFORMATION

The search for the fundamentals of personal selling has become more difficult in the age of information. The glut of information threatens our ability to identify what is true, right, or lasting. The search for knowledge begins with a review of information, and wisdom is gleaned from knowledge. Books continue to be one of the best sources of wisdom, as are online links and videos. We provide an excellent array of support videos, such as the Reality Selling section, making the seventh Canadian edition more practical and hands-on than any other textbook in the market. Many new books, and several classics, were used as references for the seventh Canadian edition of *Selling Today: Partnering to Create Value*. A sample of the more than 40 books used to prepare this edition follows:

To Sell Is Human by Daniel Pink
The Tipping Point by Malcolm Gladwell
Integrity Selling for the 21st Century by Ron Willingham
A Whole New Mind by Daniel H. Pink
Rethinking the Sales Force by Neil Rackham and John R. DeVincentis
Business Ethics by O. C. Ferrell, John Fraedrich, and Linda Ferrell
Negotiating Genius by Deepak Malhotra and Max H. Bazerman
Blur: The Speed of Change in the Connected Economy by Stan Davis and Christopher Meyer
Close the Deal by Sam Deep and Lyle Sussman
Complete Business Etiquette Handbook by Barbara Pachter and Marjorie Brody
Effective Human Relations: Personal and Organizational Applications by Barry L. Reece and Rhonda Brandt
First Impressions: What You Don't Know About How Others See You by Ann Demarais and Valerie White
Hug Your Customers by Jack Mitchell
Keeping the Funnel Full by Don Thomson
Marketing Imagination by Ted Levitt
Marketing: Real People, Real Choices by Michael R. Solomon, Greg W. Marshall, and Elnora W. Stuart
Megatrends by John Naisbitt
Personal Styles and Effective Performance by David W. Merrill and Roger H. Reid
Psycho-Cybernectics by Maxwell Maltz
Questions—The Answer to Sales by Duane Sparks
Re-Imagine! Business Excellence in a Disruptive Age by Tom Peters
Self Matters by Phillip C. McGraw
SPIN Selling by Neil Rackham
SPIN Selling Fieldbook by Neil Rackham
Strategic Selling by Robert B. Miller and Stephen E. Heiman
The 7 Habits of Highly Effective People by Stephen R. Covey
The Customer Revolution by Patricia Seybold

The Double Win by Denis Waitley
The New Conceptual Selling by Stephen E. Heiman and Diane Sanchez
The New Professional Image by Susan Bixler and Nancy Nix-Rice
The New Solution Selling by Keith M. Eades
The Power of 5 by Harold H. Bloomfield and Robert K. Cooper
The Sedona Method by Hale Dwoskin
The Success Principles by Jack Canfield
Value-Added Selling by Tom Reilly
Working with Emotional Intelligence by Daniel Goleman
Zero-Resistance Selling by Maxwell Maltz, Dan S. Kennedy, William T. Brooks, Matt Oechsli, Jeff Paul, and Pamela Yellen

ACKNOWLEDGMENTS

Many people have made contributions to the seventh Canadian edition of *Selling Today: Partnering to Create Value*. We thank award-winning video producer Art Bauer for his creativity, dedication, and attention to detail in the production of the Adaptive Selling Today Training Video Series. We also thank Son Lam for his help and contributions with the Reality Selling Video Series, Cases, and Role-Play exercises. Throughout the years the text has been improved as a result of numerous helpful comments and recommendations by both students and faculty.

We extend special appreciation to the following reviewers: Andrea Ely, Capilano University; Don Hill, Langara College; Athena Hurezeanu, Seneca College; Frank Maloney, George Brown College; David Moulton, Douglas College; Wendy Threader, Algonquin College; Duane Weaver, Vancouver Island University.

About the Authors

Gerald L. Manning
Des Moines Area
Community College

Gerald Manning is an international author, consultant, speaker, and successful businessperson.

Professor Manning's book *Selling Today: Partnering to Create Value*, now in its thirteenth edition, is today's international number-one selling textbook on negotiations and partnering. With Chinese, Spanish, International English–Speaking, Canadian, Croatian, and U.S. editions, millions have profited from the strategies and tactics presented. He is author of four additional books on management and sales, all published by large, international publishing companies. Gerald Manning also serves as a sales and marketing consultant to senior management and owners of more than 500 businesses, including both national and international companies. He appears regularly as a speaker at national sales and management conferences, and is featured regularly in training videos on sales and management.

Professor Manning served as chair of the Marketing/Management Department of one of the leading colleges in the country for more than 30 years. In addition to his administrative duties, he has served as lead instructor in negotiations and sales. Mr. Manning received the "Outstanding Professor of the Year" award given annually by his college.

He has also applied numerous negotiation and personal selling principles and practices as owner of a very successful commercial and residential real estate investment, development and management company.

Professor Manning's speaking and classroom experience, along with his consulting, and the management of his company have provided him a unique opportunity to research, study, test, refine, and write about personal selling. With this background, and a long-term partnership-type relationship with acclaimed training video producer Arthur Bauer, the Adaptive Selling TrainingVideo Series was produced.

Dr. Michael Ahearne
University of Houston

Michael Ahearne is Professor of Marketing and C. T. Bauer Chair in Marketing at the University of Houston. He is also Executive Director of the Sales Excellence Institute (SEI). The SEI is widely recognized as the leading university-based sales institute in the world, training more than 2000 sales students, placing Ph.D. students at top research universities and working with more than 200 major corporations annually. He earned his Ph.D. in Marketing from Indiana University. He has also served on the faculty at the University of Connecticut and at Pennsylvania State University. In addition, he has lectured internationally about sales and sales management in such countries as Austria, Belgium, France, Germany, India, Italy, Spain, and Russia.

Dr. Ahearne's research has focused primarily on improving the performance of salespeople and sales organizations. He has published over 40 articles in leading journals such as *Journal of Marketing, Journal of Marketing Research, Management Science,*

Strategic Management Journal, Journal of Applied Psychology, and *Organizational Behavior and Human Decision Processes*. He was recently recognized by the American Marketing Association as one of the 20 most research-productive scholars in the field of marketing. His research has been profiled in *The Wall Street Journal, Business 2.0, Business Investors Daily, Fox News, INC Magazine*, and many other news outlets.

Before entering academia, Mike played professional baseball for the Montreal Expos and worked in marketing research and sales operations for Eli Lilly and PCS Healthcare. He actively consults in many industries, including insurance, health care, consumer packaged goods, technology, and transportation.

Dr. Barry L. Reece
Virginia Polytechnic Institute
and State University

Barry Reece is Professor Emeritus at Virginia Polytechnic Institute and State University. Prior to joining the faculty at Virginia Tech, he held faculty positions at Ellsworth Community College and the University of Northern Iowa. Over the years, he has served as visiting professor at the University of Iowa, University of Missouri, University of Nebraska, University of Colorado, and Wayne State College. He is the author or coauthor of six college textbooks that have been through a total of 40 editions since 1980.

Dr. Reece received his Ed.D. from the University of Nebraska. He has been actively involved in teaching, research, consulting, and designing training programs throughout his career. He has conducted more than 500 workshops and seminars devoted to leadership, human relations, communications, sales, customer service, and small business operations. He has received the "Excellence in Teaching Award" for classroom teaching at Virginia Tech and the "Trainer of the Year Award" presented by the Valleys of Virginia Chapter of the American Society for Training and Development.

Dr. H. F. (Herb) MacKenzie
Goodman School of Business
Brock University

Herb MacKenzie is currently Associate Professor of Marketing at the Goodman School of Business, Brock University in St. Catharines, Ontario. He has taught in the undergraduate, graduate, and executive education programs at universities in Canada, Europe, and the Middle East, and has been consulting to both private- and public-sector businesses since 1985. He has more than 15 years of industrial sales and sales management experience and has published many cases, conference proceedings, and articles in the areas of sales management, buyer-seller relationships, and distribution channel management. He has authored and co-authored more than 20 textbooks on introduction to business, personal selling, sales management, and marketing, and has edited five Canadian marketing casebooks. He has been recognized by his students as Professor of the Year and Marketing Professor of the Year and was twice the winner of the Faculty of Business Faculty Award of Excellence.

Chapter 1
Relationship Selling Opportunities in the Information Economy

Learning Objectives

After studying this chapter, you should be able to

1   Define *personal selling* and describe the three prescriptions of a personal selling philosophy.

2   Describe the emergence of relationship selling in the age of information.

3   Discuss the rewarding aspects of a career in selling today.

4   Discuss the different employment settings in selling today.

5   Explain how personal selling skills have become one of the master skills needed for success in the information age and how personal selling skills contribute to the work performed by knowledge workers.

6   Identify the four major sources of sales training.

 Reality Selling Video Series—Alex Homer/Tom James Company

Job seekers who visit websites such as Monster.ca are usually surprised to discover that sales careers represent one of the largest job-posting categories. The next big surprise comes when they discover the great variety of companies that hire salespeople. Alex Homer (see next page) is a professional clothier for the Tom James Company (**www.tomjames.com**), the world's largest manufacturer and retailer of custom-made, luxury clothing. Tom James has sales offices in Canada, the United Kingdom, France, Germany, the Netherlands, Australia, and across the United States. Each Tom James client purchases directly from one of the company's well-trained professional clothiers, who provide clients with wardrobe consultation on a variety of fashion topics such as wardrobe coordination, current trends, proper fit, pattern and cloth selection, necessary collection pieces, and attire for specific occasions. Tom James clothiers like Alex always come to their clients because appointments are conducted at the client's location of choice.

Alex Homer discovered the Tom James Company in 2007 after he placed second in a national sales competition for students. Tom James took interest in Alex, and Alex

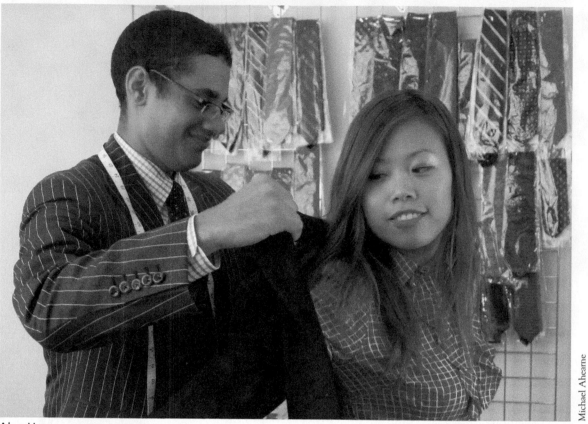

Alex Homer

decided to learn more about Tom James by participating in ride-alongs with the company's existing sales representatives. He liked it and decided to accept the job offer. Before starting to actually call on customers, Alex received training in selling, product knowledge, and prospecting. Regarding career development, Tom James offers new hires the necessary training to build a successful selling career regardless of their level of past experience. It also offers opportunities for net worth building, such as profit sharing, retirement plans, and stock plans. In 2009, 30 percent of Tom James sales professionals earned $100 000 or more in commissions, leadership pay, bonuses, and stock dividends.

PERSONAL SELLING TODAY —A DEFINITION AND A PHILOSOPHY

MOST PEOPLE ARE AWARE OF ARTHUR MILLER'S VERY SUCCESSFUL PULITZER PRIZE–WINNING 1949 stage and screenplay, and its title *The Death of a Salesman*. The reality of personal selling today is that there is a "Rebirth of the Salesperson." Between 2000 and today, when many thought the computer and Internet were causing a reduction in the need for salespeople, the number of selling jobs actually increased. Selling is one of the largest employment categories in Canada. Approximately 10 percent of the entire Canadian workforce is employed in a sales-related position, and research indicates the need for many more salespeople over the next decade. According to Neil Rackham, author of the bestselling *Spin Selling* and *Rethinking the Sales Force*, "personal selling today employs more people than any other business function—more than accounting, engineering and law put together."[1]

Strategic/Consultative Selling Model	
Strategic step	**Prescription**
Develop a personal selling philosophy	• Adopt marketing concept • Value personal selling • Become a problem solver/partner

Figure 1.1 Today, salespeople use a strategic plan based on a personal philosophy that emphasizes adopting the marketing concept, valuing personal selling, and becoming a problem solver/partner.

This ratio of salespeople to the total number in the workforce is true for many developed countries. In less developed countries such as China and Brazil, as their economies grow wealthier, the need for salespeople will increase substantially. One study done by McKinsey and Company projects that India's growing pharmaceutical industry will triple its cadre of drug representatives to 300 000 by 2020.[2]

Personal selling occurs when a company representative interacts directly with a customer or prospective customer to present information about a product or service.[3] It is a process of developing relationships; discovering needs; matching the appropriate products with those needs; and communicating benefits through informing, reminding, or persuading. The term **product** should be broadly interpreted to encompass physical goods, information, services, and ideas. Increasingly, personal selling is viewed as a process that adds value. In an ideal situation, the salesperson builds a mutually rewarding relationship, diagnoses the customer's needs, and custom-fits the product to meet those needs. Having knowledge of these customer needs will lead to higher customer satisfaction and willingness to purchase a product.[4]

Preparation for a career in personal selling begins with the development of a personal philosophy or set of beliefs that provides guidance. To some degree, this philosophy is like the rudder that steers a ship. Without a rudder, the ship's direction is unpredictable. Without a personal philosophy, the salesperson's behaviour also is unpredictable.

The development of a **personal selling philosophy** involves three prescriptions: adopt the marketing concept, value personal selling, and assume the role of a problem solver or partner in helping customers make informed and intelligent buying decisions (Fig. 1.1). These three prescriptions for success in personal selling are presented here as part of the Strategic/Consultative Selling Model. This model is expanded in future chapters to include additional strategic steps in the selling process. Chapter 2 will illustrate how the marketing concept has produced an evolving set of improvements to the sales process, moving it from peddling to value-added partnering.

EMERGENCE OF RELATIONSHIP SELLING IN THE INFORMATION ECONOMY

THE RESTRUCTURING FROM AN INDUSTRIAL ECONOMY TO AN **information economy** began approximately 50 years ago (Fig. 1.2). During this period, our economy began shifting from an emphasis on industrial activity to an emphasis on information processing. We

personal selling Involves person-to-person communication with a prospect. It is a process of developing relationships; discovering customer needs; matching appropriate products with those needs; and communicating benefits through informing, reminding, or persuading.

product Should be broadly interpreted to encompass physical goods, information, services, and ideas.

personal selling philosophy A salesperson's commitment to adopt the marketing concept, value personal selling, and assume the role of a problem solver or partner to help customers make informed and intelligent buying decisions.

information economy An economy where there is an emphasis on information processing.

Industrial Economy 1860–1960	Information Economy 1960–2020
Major advances in manufacturing and transportation	Major advances in information technology
Strategic resources are capital and natural resources	Strategic resource is information
Business is defined by its products and factories	Business is defined by customer relationships
Sales success depends on meeting sales quotas	Sales success depends on adding value

INCREASES IN RELATIONSHIP SELLING AND RELATIONSHIP MARKETING →

Figure 1.2 The age of information has greatly influenced personal selling. Salespeople today use a variety of technological tools to gather and process information of value to the customer. They recognize that information is a strategic resource and relationship skills are needed to build a conduit of trust for information acceptance.

were giving way to a new society where most of us would work with information instead of producing goods.[5] Today we live in an age in which the effective exchange of information is the foundation of most economic transactions, and the implications for personal selling are profound. We will describe the four major developments that have shaped the information economy and discuss the implications for personal selling.

Major Advances Occur in Information Technology and Electronic Commerce The information age has spawned an information technology revolution. Technology as well as globalization and speed of change influence almost everything we do.[6] Salespeople and other marketing-related players in today's information age use personal computers, mobile phones, smartphones, websites, customer relationship management (CRM) applications with cloud computing, email, instant messaging, blogging, and social media sites such as Facebook, YouTube, Twitter, and LinkedIn. Frequently referred to today as **Selling 2.0**, these information technology tools, along with innovative sales practices, are used to create value for both the buyer and seller by improving the speed, collaboration, customer engagement, and accountability of the sales process.

The explosive growth of electronic commerce and other Internet activities has changed the way we use computers. Stan Davis, futurist and co-author of *Blur: The Speed of Change in the Connected Economy*, notes that in today's information economy we use computers less for data crunching and more for connecting. These connections involve people to people, company to customer, machine to machine, product to service, organization to organization, and all these in combination.[7] The jobs of information-age workers depend on these connections. People who work extensively with information, such as salespeople, need these electronic connections to conduct their information gathering, information sharing, and information management responsibilities.

selling 2.0 Information technology tools along with innovative sales practices used to create value for both buyers and sellers by improving the speed, collaboration, customer engagement, and accountability of the sales process.

Information Is a Strategic Resource Advances in information technology have increased the speed by which we acquire, process, and disseminate information. David Shenk, author of *Data Smog: Surviving the Information Glut*, notes that we have moved from a state of information scarcity to one of information overload.[8] In an era of limitless data, informed salespeople can help us decide which information has value and which information should be ignored. Salespeople are the eyes and ears of today's marketplace. They collect a wide range of product, customer, and competitive intelligence.[9]

Business Is Defined by Customer Relationships Michael Hammer, consultant and author of *The Agenda*, says the *real* new economy is the customer economy. As scarcity gave way to abundance, as supply exceeded demand, and as customers became better informed, we saw a power shift. Customers took more control of their own destinies.[10]

On the surface, the major focus of the age of information seems to be the accumulation of more and more information and the never-ending search for new forms of information technology. It's easy to overlook the importance of the human element. Humans, not computers, have the ability to think, feel, and create ideas. It is no coincidence that relationship selling and relationship marketing, which emphasize long-term, mutually satisfying buyer–seller partnering relationships, began to gain support at the beginning of the information age. Companies such as DuPont, Kraft Foods, and General Electric have adopted a philosophy that focuses on customer satisfaction, team selling, and relationship selling.[11]

Social Media and Selling Today

Creating Customer Value with Social Media

Popular business strategies such as "Selling is a Contact Sport" and "Speed is Life" describe the value of social media in the selling process. Being immediately available to a customer is essential to a salesperson's success for many reasons, including providing information at the moment the customer needs it; responding to a customer's relationship-building contact; and obtaining and following up on leads. Instant outreach to one or more customers is also critical for high-performing salespeople. This instant contact capability empowers salespeople to quickly send notices of price changes, product modifications, product operation tips, service alerts, website updates, and invitations to business and social events.

Advances in communication technology enhance the value of salesperson availability and outreach by dramatically reducing the time required for salesperson and customer interactions. Among these advances is the category generally referred to as *social media*. Facebook, Twitter,

LinkedIn, YouTube, and smartphones are frequently identified as key components of this category.

Facebook can be used by a salesperson to expand his or her personal information that may be found on the company's website. Products or services are also found on Facebook, allowing customers and others to learn about and discuss a salesperson's offerings. LinkedIn allows registered users to maintain a list of contact details of people they know and trust in business. Smartphones and similar mobile devices allow communications to include still and moving images designed to improve recipients' understanding and acceptance of the accompanying messages.

High-performing salespeople and their organizations are well advised to carefully study the continuous advances in communication technologies and rapidly adopt the advantages they offer.[a] Playing the serious "sport" of customer contact at the fastest possible speed is now a critical necessity in a salesperson's life.

value-added selling Improving the sales process to create value for the customer. Salespeople add value when they offer better advice and product solutions, carefully manage customer relationships, and provide better service after the sale.

Sales Success Depends on Adding Value Value-added selling can be defined as a series of creative improvements within the sales process that enhance the customer experience. Salespeople can create value by developing a quality relationship, carefully identifying the customer's needs, and then configuring and presenting the best possible product solution. Value is also created when the salesperson provides excellent service after the sale. Neil Rackham, author of *Rethinking the Sales Force*, and other experts in sales and marketing say that success no longer depends merely on communicating the value of products and services. Success in personal selling rests on the critical ability to create value for customers.

The value added by salespeople today is increasingly derived from intangibles such as the quality of the advice offered and the level of trust that underlies the relationship between the customer and the salesperson. The value of these intangibles can erode with shocking speed when the customer feels deceived or discovers that the competition is able to add more value to the sales process.[12]

CONSIDERATIONS FOR A FUTURE IN PERSONAL SELLING

JOB SEEKERS WHO VISIT **Monster.ca** OR **CareerBuilder.ca** ARE USUALLY SURPRISED TO discover that sales careers represent one of the largest job posting categories. Many thousands of entry-level sales positions are listed every day. The next big surprise comes when they discover the great variety of companies that hire salespeople. Some companies, such as Procter & Gamble, Purolator, and Blackberry, are well known across Canada. But there are many smaller, more regional companies that advertise for salespeople, as well as many foreign-owned companies that have sales forces in Canada and that may be unfamiliar to people seeking sales jobs. Toronto-based BlueSky Personnel Solutions helps companies across Canada solve their human resources needs and uses field salespeople to sell its services to prospective businesses. Würth Canada is a division of Würth Group, the world's largest fastener company. It has 470 employees, and 381 of them are salespeople. They sell to small and large customers in the automotive/trucking and maintenance/metals markets across Canada.[13]

From a personal and economic standpoint, selling can be a rewarding career. Careers in selling offer financial rewards, recognition, security, and opportunities for advancement to a degree that is unique when compared to other occupations.

Wide Range of Employment Opportunities

The 500 largest sales forces in North America employ more than 21 million salespeople.[14] These companies will seek to recruit 500 000 post-secondary graduates. A large number of additional salespeople are employed by smaller companies. In addition, the number of new sales positions is consistently increasing, and sales positions commonly rank among the jobs considered most in demand.[15] A close examination of these positions reveals that there is no single "selling" occupation. Our labour force includes hundreds of different selling careers, and chances are there are positions that match your interests, talents, and ambitions. The diversity within selling will become apparent as you study the career options discussed in this chapter.

Selling Is a Life Skill

Many business students who have no intention of pursuing a career in sales will eventually have successful sales careers. Some students will begin their careers in sales and then move on—sometimes to management positions in their company. Some students will begin their careers in other areas and will find that the opportunities and benefits of being in sales will motivate them to switch to sales careers. Many students will spend their whole lives in non-sales careers, but most will find that the skills they learn from selling will benefit them throughout their working lives. As we point out in this chapter, selling skills are needed by management personnel, entrepreneurs, and professionals.

Eddie Greenspan, Canada's best-known criminal lawyer, has been practising law for more than 30 years. He has many of the personal characteristics of superior salespeople: He loves what he does and he hates to lose. While salesmanship is not a word he would ascribe to as solemn a situation as a jury trial, he says, "In a court of law, you're in the business of selling the truth. . . . You have to make the listeners believe that you believe what you are selling."[b]

While many college and university students ultimately become salespeople, often it's not their first career choice. Students tend to view sales as dynamic and active but believe a selling career will require them to engage in deceitful or dishonest practices. The good news is that old stereotypes about sales are gradually going by the wayside. Students who study the careers of highly successful relationship salespeople discover that ethical sales practices represent the key to long-term success.

Activities Performed by Salespeople

A professional selling position encompasses a wide range of tasks and, therefore, salespeople must possess a variety of skills. Figure 1.3 provides important insight about how many outside salespeople spend their time on the job. Note the time spent in administrative tasks and sales preparation. This, along with face-to-face selling and travelling time, provides a large amount of variety for salespeople. In some selling positions, such as retail selling, more time may be spent in face-to-face selling.

A salesperson representing Federal Express (FedEx) makes numerous sales calls each day in an attempt to establish new accounts and provide service to established accounts. A wide range of potential customers can use FedEx delivery services. A salesperson working for a Caterpillar construction equipment dealer may make only two or three sales calls per day. The products offered by the dealer are expensive and are not purchased frequently.

Freedom to Manage One's Own Time and Activities Because of the wide range of activities, most selling positions allow salespeople to be in control of how they use their time, decide what activities they will prioritize in their work schedules, and interact with a wide range of people. This contrasts with many careers where people are assigned to a particular location and team of people, assigned very specific tasks, and directly supervised by others. This freedom to plan activities and prioritize the use of time, not unlike that of an entrepreneur, is high on the list of why many successful salespeople have chosen sales as a career. However, the ability to manage one's time, set priorities,

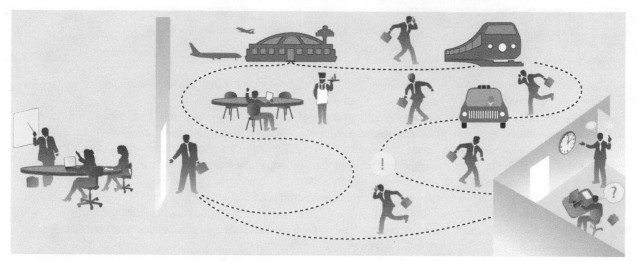

Sales is the lifeblood of any business. According to 2008 Yankee Group research study titled "Mobile CRM Tipping Point Finally Arrives," sales representatives spend their time on the following activities:

- Face-to-face selling 26%.
- Sales prep 16%
- Administrative tasks 26%
- Travel and waiting 32%

Figure 1.3 How Salespeople Spend Their Time
A professional selling position encompasses a wide range of tasks and, therefore, salespeople must possess a variety of skills.
Source: Sybase Inc., www.sybase.com/files/Thankyou_Pages/Sybase_Mobile_Solutions_for_SAP_Sales_Reps_print.pdf (accessed June 21, 2010).

and execute successfully on these priorities is critical to success in selling. We will present more on the subject of opportunity management in Chapter 16.

Titles Used in Selling Today Just as selling occupations differ, so do the titles by which salespeople are known. Many of these titles and careers are represented in the careers described in the Reality Selling Videos presented throughout the book. A survey of current job announcements indicates that companies are using titles (and abbreviations) such as these:

Account Executive (AE)	Sales Consultant
Account Representative	Business Development Representative (BDR)
Account Manager	Sales Associate
Relationship Manager	Marketing Representative
District Representative	Territory Manager
Marketing Partner	Channel Partner
Regional Accounts Manager (RAM)	National Accounts Manager (NAM)
Key Accounts Manager (KAM)	Global Accounts Manager (GAM)
Strategic Accounts Manager (SAM)	Account Development Representative (ADR)

Two factors have contributed to the creation of new titles. First, we have seen a shift from "selling" to "partnering." When salespeople assume a consulting or partnering role, the value of the relationship often exceeds the value of the transaction. Second, the new titles reflect a difference in education and skill sets needed for the sales position.[16] Both of these factors, along with the newer definition and philosophy of selling noted earlier in this chapter, have brought about the increasing use of the title "Account Manager" to describe the responsibilities of today's personnel. It is important to recognize, however, that there are still a large number of individuals employed in selling who prefer, and are proud, to be called "salespeople."

Salespeople, regardless of title, play an important role in sustaining the growth and profitability of organizations of all sizes. They also support the employment of many non-selling employees.

Above-Average Income

Studies dealing with incomes in the business community indicate that salespeople earn significantly higher incomes than most other workers. Some salespeople actually earn more than their sales managers and other executives within the organization. In fact, a successful career in sales and sales management can result in earnings similar to those of doctors, lawyers, and chief executives.[17,18] Companies' sales force expenditures are roughly three times what they spend on advertising.[19] This high level of compensation—whether from base salary, bonus, or incentives—is justified for good performance. Table 1.1 provides information on sales compensation in Canada. Executive and sales force compensation continue to climb despite uncertain economic conditions.[20]

In recent years, we have seen new ways to report sales compensation for salespeople. The Hay Group, working with C&C Market Research, developed a reporting method that tracks earnings for different types of sales approaches. Research indicates that salespeople involved in transactional sales, which generally focuses on selling products at the lowest price, also earned the lowest compensation. Sales personnel involved in value-added sales earned the highest level of compensation. These highly paid salespeople created improvements and therefore value in the sales process that enhanced the customer experience.[21]

Table 1.1 Sales Compensation, Canada, $000's

Sales Compensation, Canada $000's	Base Salary			Total Cash		
	25%ile	50%ile	75%ile	25%ile	50%ile	75%ile
Inside Sales	$33.4	$37.8	$42.9			
Sales representative	$44.6	$52.2	$61.0	$52.4	$62.7	$77.3
Sales representative (senior)	$59.6	$69.3	$80.7	$69.2	$80.0	$104.5
Key Accounts Representative	$65.5	$81.6	$95.3			
Sales Manager	$62.9	$74.8	$91.0	$69.4	$82.7	$121.2

Notes

Total cash columns show base salary plus incentive compensation for obvious incentive-driven positions.

Source: Amanda Frank, Monster Contributing Writer, "Average Salaries for Jobs in Sales," http://career-advice.monster.ca/salary-benefits/salary-information/average-salaries-for-jobs-in-sales/article.aspx, accessed February 6, 2014.

Above-Average Psychic Income

psychic income Consists of factors that provide psychological rewards; it helps to satisfy the need for recognition and security, and motivates us to achieve higher levels of performance.

Two major psychological needs common to all people are recognition and security. **Psychic income**, which consists of factors that provide psychological rewards, helps satisfy these important needs and motivates us to achieve higher levels of performance. The need for recognition has been established in numerous studies that have examined human motivation. Workers from all employment areas indicate that recognition for work well done is an important morale-building factor.

In selling, recognition will come more frequently and with greater intensity than in most other occupations. Because selling contributes so visibly to the success of most business firms, the accomplishments of sales personnel will seldom go unrecognized. Most people want to achieve some measure of security in their work. Selling is one of those occupations that usually provide job security during both good and bad times.

Opportunity for Advancement

Each year, thousands of openings appear in the ranks of supervision and management. Because salespeople work in positions of high visibility, they are in an excellent position to be chosen for advancement to positions of greater responsibility. The top executives of many of today's companies began their careers in the ranks of the sales force. Theodore Kinni, in *Selling Power*, notes, "Today's C-suites are literally bursting with sales professionals."[22] Of course, not every salesperson can become president of a large corporation, but, in the middle-management ranks, there are numerous interesting and high-paying positions in which experience in selling is a prime requisite for advancement. We present information on careers in sales management in Chapter 17.

Selling in Action

Opportunities for Women in Sales

In a world that is beginning to value diversity, we are seeing growing opportunities for women in sales. However, some misinformation concerning women in sales still exists. Four common myths follow:

Myth: Women will not relocate or stick around long enough to repay the firm's hiring and training expenses. Today, working women make up nearly half of the workforce and they have made significant gains in a wide range of traditionally male-dominated areas. About 50 percent of the working women contribute more than half of their family's income. Most of the women in this group, who also outnumber male students in many business schools today, need to work, want to work, and seek rewarding career opportunities.

Myth: Women earn significantly less in sales than their male counterparts. Although a pay gap between men and women exists in the field of sales, it is relatively small compared with the earnings gap for women who work full time in the workforce as a whole.

Myth: Buyers are less accepting of female salespeople. In the field of personal selling, perceived expertise, likability, and trustworthiness can have a major influence on purchase decisions. Women who project these qualities seldom face rejection based on gender.

Myth: Women face special problems when assigned to selling positions in foreign countries. The truth is that recent research suggests that businesswomen often enjoy a significant edge over their male counterparts when given overseas assignments.[c]

Opportunities for Women

Prodded by a growing awareness that gender is not a barrier to success in selling, business firms are recruiting qualified women in growing numbers. The percentage of women in the sales force has increased considerably. In fact, in sales and related occupations, women comprise approximately 50 percent of the workforce.[23] Although women are still relative newcomers to industrial sales, they have enjoyed expanded career opportunities in such areas as real estate, insurance, advertising services, investments, and travel services. A growing number of women are turning to sales employment because it offers excellent economic rewards[24] and, in many cases, a flexible work schedule. Flexible schedules are very appealing to women who want to balance career and family.

At Pitney Bowes, a major provider of corporate mail services, about 24 percent of the top employees are women. Many of the top salespeople are women who were formerly teachers.[25] About 20 percent of all financial advisers are women.[26]

In recent years, the labour market has become a place of churning dislocation caused by the heavy volume of mergers, acquisitions, business closings, bankruptcies, and downsizings. Personal selling careers, as well as those career areas that value selling skills, have become attractive employment options to the thousands of professionals who walk away from—or are pushed out of—corporate jobs.

EMPLOYMENT SETTINGS IN SELLING TODAY

CAREERS IN SALES INCLUDE BOTH INSIDE AND OUTSIDE SALES POSITIONS. AN **INSIDE salesperson** is one who performs selling activities at the employer's location, typically using the telephone and email. Many manufacturers and wholesalers have developed inside sales forces to take orders, make calls on customers, and provide support for outside salespeople. In some cases, the inside salespeople are called *customer service representatives* and provide a number of support services on behalf of outside salespeople.

inside salesperson
A salesperson who performs selling activities at the employer's location, typically using the telephone and email.

Inside sales can be either *inbound* or *outbound*. Inbound inside salespeople respond to calls initiated by the customer. Telemarketing is a common form of outbound inside sales that serves several purposes, including sales and service. In some cases, this includes technical support personnel who provide technical information and answer questions. Some companies utilize sales assistants to confirm appointments, conduct credit checks, and follow up on deliveries.[27] The use of telemarketing, websites, and the Internet has grown rapidly as businesses use these methods to contact potential new customers and to follow up on current small customers or customers in distant areas.

Unlike inside sales, an **outside salesperson** travels to meet prospects and customers in their place of business or residence. Information technology companies such as Hewlett-Packard and Dell employ thousands of salespeople to sell computer systems, peripherals, and integrated technology solutions to other companies, large and small. Wholesalers across Canada, such as Sysco Canada, Acklands-Grainger, and WFS Ltd. (discussed in Chapter 15), employ outside salespeople who, in addition to selling products, offer a variety of services to their customers, such as maintaining inventories, merchandising, providing promotional support, gathering and interpreting market information, extending credit, and distributing goods. In addition, many direct-to-consumer salespeople engage at least partially in outside sales—for example, financial services, life insurance, or direct sales.

outside salesperson
A salesperson who travels to meet prospects and customers in their place of business or residence.

Inside and outside salespeople for the same company often work together and rely heavily upon each other. For example, inside salespeople often prospect, generating and qualifying leads for outside salespeople to call on personally. Also, once an initial sale is made by an outside salesperson, inside salespeople are asked to provide ongoing customer contact and service, taking responsibility for meeting customer needs while being alert for opportunities to sell additional products or services.

Selling through Channels

Many times people mistakenly think of selling jobs as being limited to the interaction between the company and the end user of a good or service. However, goods and services flow from manufacturer to end user through a *channel of distribution*.

As can be seen in Figure 1.4, sales jobs exist throughout this distribution chain.[28] In fact, many of the most promising sales careers in terms of career advancement and compensation exist at the beginning of the channel flow in the form of *business-to-business*, or *B2B*, sales. **Trade selling** refers to the sale of a product or service to another member of the channel of distribution. For example, a manufacturer of household goods may employ sales representatives to sell its products to retailers. It may instead (or also) sell its products to wholesalers that warehouse the product, and in turn the wholesaler employs sales representatives to sell these and other products to retailers that the manufacturer does not want to service directly. In the latter part of the channel flow, we find retail salespeople and, in some cases, service salespeople selling to consumers. This is often referred to as *business-to-consumer*, or *B2C* sales. As you can see, selling careers may be classified in several ways.

Similar scenarios exist with industrial products where the end user is a business rather than an individual consumer and with services where the end user is either a consumer or business user. Another example of B2B sales is **missionary**, or **detail, sales.** Rather than selling directly to the end user, the missionary salesperson attempts to generate goodwill and stimulate demand for the manufacturer's product among channel members.

Career Opportunities in the Service Channel

Sales careers in service sales include both business-to-business and business-to-consumer sales. Today nearly 80 percent of the Canadian labour force is employed in some capacity in the service sector of the economy. The growth rate for the service industry is much higher than the growth rate for goods companies. Service companies provide career opportunities in a variety of settings.

- *Hotel, motel, and convention centre services.* Each year, thousands of seminars, conferences, and business meetings are held throughout Canada. Most of these events are hosted by hotels, motels, or convention centres. The salespeople, often referred to as account manager, sales manager, or account executive, employed by these firms play an important role in attracting clients to utilize these facilities. Salespeople diversify markets and upgrade services to sell room space, food, beverages, entertainment, and other services to create an attractive atmosphere for potential clients.

  Typical of the salespeople employed in this sector is Victoria Davis, part of the sales team at Holiday Inn & Suites in St. Catharines, Ontario. Victoria is the conference services manager. She must communicate effectively with customers,

trade selling Refers to the sale of a product or service to another member of the channel of distribution.

missionary, or **detail, sales** Refers to sales made when the manufacturer's salesperson generates goodwill and stimulates demand among channel members, rather than through selling directly to end users.

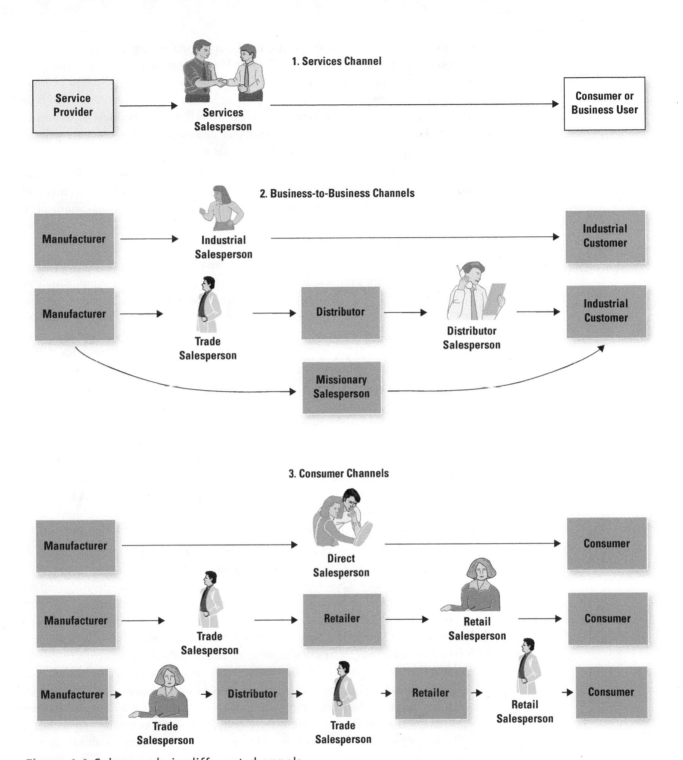

Figure 1.4 Salespeople in different channels.

completely understand their specific needs, and then ensure that the hotel delivers on any promises made.[29] You will meet Victoria again in the case at the end of Chapter 14. In the selling of hotel and convention centre sales, as well as a number of the other types of service selling, salespeople may be involved in both B2B and B2C selling, depending upon whether they are selling to a business or to an individual. Buying motives and selling strategies described in later chapters will vary considerably depending upon whether the sale is B2B or B2C.

■ *Telecommunications services.* The deregulation of telephone service resulted in considerable fragmentation within the industry and the creation of numerous new communications companies. This has led to an increased need for telecommunications salespeople. These individuals must have a thorough knowledge of their system and a good understanding of competing telecommunications systems.

■ *Financial services.* This is one of the hottest areas of sales growth. There are more than 3000 firms that provide financial services in Canada, directly employing more than 550 000 people.[30] Banks, brokerage firms, and other businesses are branching out, selling a broader range of financial planning and investment services. More and more, bank employees are involved in personal selling activities, developing new accounts, and servicing existing ones. Bank personnel are completing sales training courses in record numbers these days.

■ *Media sales.* Revenue from advertising supports the radio, television, newspaper, and magazine industries and is also a major source of profit for the Internet. Amy Vandaveer, a salesperson featured in Chapter 6, sells advertising space for *Texas Monthly.* Both local and national advertising support each of these and each must sell advertising to remain in business. In fact, newspapers and magazines generate far more revenue from the sale of advertising than from subscriptions. The wide variety of client needs and the task of meeting these needs make the work of media sales representatives interesting. Additionally, the requirement for members of the media sales staff to develop or to help the client develop commercials makes this work very interesting.

■ *Real estate.* The purchase of a home is usually the single largest expenditure in the average person's lifetime. In 2013, 457 893 homes were sold through cooperative listing systems such as MLS across Canada.[31] The purchase of commercial property by individual investors or business firms is also a major economic decision. Therefore, the thousands of Canadian real estate salespeople assume an important responsibility. Busy real estate salespeople often hire sales associates to conduct open houses or perform other tasks. Real estate salespeople must obtain listings, advertise the properties, conduct visits with potential clients, and sell properties. Pearl Paul moved to Canada from Trinidad in 1972. She decided to get into real estate sales when her husband wanted to return to his hometown—Winnipeg—in search of work. After only three years in sales, Pearl Paul became the top-selling salesperson among approximately 150 salespeople in her Royal LePage office. Honesty helped Pearl establish trust and build good relationships. The backside of Pearl's business card states, "The referral of your friends and family is the greatest compliment you can give me."[32]

■ *Insurance.* Selling insurance has always been one of the most rewarding careers in sales. Common forms of insurance sold include life, liability, fire, health, automobile, casualty, homeowner, and business. There are two broad groups of insurance salespeople. Employees of major companies such as Manulife Financial, Liberty

Pearl Paul's success comes from establishing and maintaining good client relationships.

Mutual, Sun Life Financial, or State Farm make up one group. In 2012, 13 500 insurance sales professionals were hired across Canada, down from 15 600 five years earlier. The 2013 Canadian Life Insurance Ownership Study found that only 68 percent of Canadian households have any type of life insurance, compared to 79 percent in 2006 when the previous study was conducted. Three of four Canadians indicted that they preferred to buy face-to-face, indicating opportunity for those who wish to sell in the industry.[33] Marcus Smith, whom we introduce in Chapter 2, is an excellent example of this type of salesperson who sells various insurance products but only for his company, Liberty Mutual. The second type consists of independent agents who represent a number of insurance companies. The typical independent agency sells a broad line of personal and commercial insurance services offered by many companies.

■ *Business services.* The great number of new businesses and the expansion of existing businesses have resulted in an increase in the demand for business services provided by outside contractors. Some of these services include computer programming, training, printing, credit reporting, payroll and accounting, payment processing, recruiting, transportation, and security. Many other sales careers involving the sale of services exist. The field is increasing at a rapid pace and sales positions become available in services sales every day.

Career Opportunities in the Business Goods Channel

Manufacturers employ sales and sales support personnel in a variety of different positions in outside and inside sales. Outside salespeople interact with potential customers on a face-to-face basis. Some of the categories of outside salespeople include field salespeople, sales or application engineers, and missionary or detail salespeople. Inside salespeople include customer service representatives (CSRs) who rely primarily on the telephone and the Internet to communicate with customers, to identify new prospects, and to carry out other sales activities.

- *Industrial salespeople.* Industrial salespeople include both technical salespeople (sales engineers or application engineers) and nontechnical salespeople. Sales engineers or technical salespeople sell heavy equipment, machinery, chemical products, aircraft, complex electronic equipment, and military equipment. Such salespeople must have a good technical understanding of their products and customer needs. Nontechnical salespeople generally sell office equipment; disposable goods such as adhesives, cleaners, and packaging; and office supplies.

- *Sales engineers or applications engineers.* Sales or applications engineers must possess a detailed and thorough technical knowledge of their products as well as competing products. These salespeople must be able to identify and analyze customer problems and develop solutions to these problems that meet the customer's needs. Sales engineers must be technically proficient in all aspects of their products and in communicating the merits and advantages of their products to the customer.

  Steve Tice, president of Sim Graphics Engineering Corporation, and Steve Glenn, vice president for new business development, are the primary sales engineers for the corporation.[34] Sim Graphics develops automated graphic simulation systems for use in industry, hospitals, and educational institutions. Their company utilizes customized demonstration presentations for potential customers. Many potential customers fail to understand the complexity of the systems, so demonstrations are needed to show what is actually available. On some occasions it is necessary to build and demonstrate a prototype or to make a full-blown presentation. Customers who do not understand the product will be reluctant to purchase something they don't comprehend.

field salespeople Salespeople who regularly visit face-to-face with new customers and current customers.

- *Field salespeople.* **Field salespeople** interact with new customers and current customers. They must be able to identify customer needs and requirements and to recommend the proper product or service to meet the customer's needs. Field salespeople who provide excellent service often receive information from their satisfied customers on new leads. These customers often provide recommendations to other potential customers for the field salesperson.

  Betty Robertson, president of Lyncole Industries, is also the field sales representative for her company. Lyncole sells piping and associated supplies to contractors. Betty states that following up on the installation of the equipment is very important. The contractors she sells to are potential repeat customers; it is essential to follow up and make certain that the customer is satisfied.[35]

missionary, or **detail, salespeople** Salespeople who attempt to generate goodwill and stimulate demand for the manufacturer's product among channel members, rather than selling direct to the end user.

- *Missionary salespeople.* **Missionary salespeople,** also known as *detail salespeople,* serve to develop goodwill, provide information, and stimulate demand for the manufacturer's products. A missionary salesperson does not sell the product but receives recognition for increasing the sale of products indirectly. Missionary salespeople must be able to provide technical product information and offer sound advice in areas such as credit policies, pricing, display, layout, and storage.

  Deborah Karish, a sales representative for Amgen, stresses relationship selling in her work with medical facilities while selling to both medical staff and physicians.

She had to learn the technology of her products, how they were manufactured, and how the medicines could be utilized most effectively in treating patients. She went through a pairing program with physicians to learn how the products are used. Deborah knows it is necessary to establish good relationships with the medical staff. Failing to establish good relationships generally means that the people will not work with the salesperson.

Career Opportunities in the Consumer Goods Channel

Sales careers in the consumer goods channel, referred to earlier as *B2C* selling, include both retail selling and direct selling careers. Conventional retailers face increased competition from online retailers. Consumers spend billions of dollars on Internet purchases. Traditional retailers are forced to offer customers more than products in order to compete effectively against online sellers. Well-trained salespeople can add value to the traditional shopping experience.

■ *Retail salespeople*. A large number of salespeople work in retail. Retail selling is an excellent area for gaining initial sales experience. Retail selling careers abound in a number of product areas.

   When he was still in secondary school, Chris Mckee worked on weekends and evenings washing motor homes for Ontario's largest motor home dealership—The Hitch House. Chris received his Ontario motor vehicle certification at age 18—a requirement to sell motor homes and recreational vehicles—while still a student at Georgian College. He worked his way up in the service department, parts department, and business office, and is currently a member of the sales team, where he sells motor homes ranging in price from $70 000 to more than $650 000. Chris participates in factory training programs, where he has become an expert in motor homes and their systems. He has also gained considerable experience driving RVs to trade shows, and sometimes picking them up at the manufacturer's production facilities.[36]

   Stoney Creek Furniture in Stoney Creek, Ontario, is Canada's largest furniture showroom. The company's sales associates—dedicated to superior customer service—helped the retailer recently win the National Home Furnishings Association North American Retailer of the Year. This was the first time the award was given to a Canadian retailer. The company's non-commissioned sales associates have been described as "well-trained, experienced, and among the best in the world."[37]

■ *Direct salespeople.* **Direct salespeople** are independent contractors who represent manufacturers, selling products or services directly to consumers, usually face-to-face but also via the telephone or Internet. The three largest global direct selling firms are Amway, Avon, and Mary Kay, with $2.2 billion in sales and more than 1.1 million salespeople.[38] The sales volume of these three companies equals the total estimated annual sales of Canada's 900 000 direct salespeople. Approximately two-thirds of the 75-plus companies that operate in Canada are members of Direct Sellers Association of Canada. Direct selling firms often bring goods to consumers who might otherwise not have access to them: 26 percent of customers live in rural areas, and 13 percent are over 65 years old.[39] Personal care, home/family care, wellness, and leisure/educational products, along with services such as utilities, phone, legal, etc., are the major industries represented by this form of selling.

A rapidly growing form of direct sales is network (or multilevel) marketing. In this form of distribution, manufacturers eschew advertising and other trade/promotional spending, relying instead on a large network of independent consultants or distributors to sell the product or service directly to consumers or businesses. The independent consultant builds his or her business not only through the direct sales of the product or service to consumers, but also by sponsoring new consultants to sell the company's products or services. The sponsoring consultant then earns commissions on the product/service sales generated by the new consultant, in addition to what he or she personally sells. The number of levels on which a consultant is paid varies by company, but the benefit to the consultant is the ability to leverage both his or her own efforts plus that of other consultants in his or her "downline." These types of organizations are highly reliant on socialization, communication, and cooperation between consultants for successful sales results.[40]

SELLING SKILLS—ONE OF THE "MASTER SKILLS FOR SUCCESS" IN THE INFORMATION AGE

IN HIS BEST-SELLING BOOK *Megatrends*, JOHN NAISBITT NOTED THAT "THE GAME OF LIFE in the information age is people interacting with other people."[41] With its emphasis on effective and adaptive interpersonal interaction, selling has become one of the "master skills for success in the information economy."

A study reported in Daniel Pink's *To Sell Is Human* makes a similar observation concerning what he calls the rise of "nonsales selling." He reports in his sample of 7000 individuals in the workforce:

1. People are now spending about 40 percent of their time at work engaged in nonsales selling—persuading, influencing, and convincing others in ways that don't involve anyone making a purchase.

2. Across a range of professions, people are devoting roughly 24 minutes of every hour moving others—what Pink refers to as "nonsales selling."

3. Respondents consider this moving others, that is, nonsales-selling skill set, crucial to their professional success.[42]

---

direct salespeople Independent contractors who represent manufacturers, selling products or services directly to consumers, usually face-to-face but also via the telephone or Internet.

Knowledge Workers in the Information Economy

The late Stanley Marcus, chairman emeritus of the prestigious Neiman Marcus company, said, "Sooner or later in business, everybody has to sell something to somebody." He noted that even if you are not in sales, you must know how to sell a product, a service, an idea, or yourself.[43] Marcus's views have garnered a great deal of support among observers of the information age. Today's workforce is made up of millions of knowledge workers who succeed only when they add value to information. **Knowledge workers** are individuals whose work effort is centred around creating, using, sharing, and applying knowledge. The information economy is about the growing value of knowledge, making it the most important ingredient of what people buy and sell.[44] One way to add value to information is to collect it, organize it, clarify it, and present it in a convincing manner. This skill, used every day by professional salespeople, is invaluable in a world that is overloaded with information.

As noted earlier, relationships have become more important in the information age. In many cases, information does not have value unless people interact effectively. Creating networks with social ties allows knowledge workers to acquire and provide information more successfully.[45] For example, a salesperson may possess information concerning an important new technology, but that information has no value until it is communicated effectively to an investor, a customer, or someone else who can benefit from knowing more about his product. A bank loan officer may have the resources needed to assist a prospective homeowner in reaching her dream, but in the absence of a good relationship,

knowledge workers Individuals whose work effort is centred around creating, using, sharing, and applying knowledge.

customer relationship management (CRM) Software that records in one place the extensive information necessary to understand a customer and his or her needs and expectations.

Learning about Salesforce, NetSuite, Siebel, Sugar CRM, SalesLogic, and Other CRM Systems

Many technology tools are available to today's salespeople and marketing personnel because there is so much information to manage. There is one category of software specifically designed for a salesperson's responsibilities. **Customer relationship management (CRM),** sometimes referred to as "sales automation," is software that records in one place the extensive information necessary to understand a customer and his or her needs and expectations. This type of software is becoming essential because it can be used to capture and rapidly display the information needed to work toward assuring the satisfaction of many customers at the same time. In addition to providing the basic data about a company and its products, CRM software offers information needed to build partnering relationships and add value throughout the sales process.

CRM enables its user to easily sort and store information so it can be quickly retrieved to enhance each customer contact. At a salesperson's fingertips is the name of a customer's spouse when a conversation is social. One can be quickly reminded of a buyer's favourites when

arranging lunch or golf. Product delivery and credit preferences are available should the topics be raised in an email. CRM keeps a salesperson intimately involved in a sale by identifying the customer's stage in the sales process, reminding about tasks and due dates to move the sale along, keeping track of all previous steps in the process and information shared, and displaying personal information recorded about those involved in a purchase, in order to improve relationships with them.

Leading CRM software company websites include www.Salesforce.com, www.NetSuite.com, www.Siebel.com, www.SugarCRM.com, and www.SalesLogix.com. Each of these companies supplies training videos and, in some cases, a free trial demo. Their training videos can also be accessed on YouTube. To learn about these companies, and to access their videos and free trials, visit their websites. You will learn in future chapters how CRM enhances the effectiveness of high-performing salespeople in their efforts to establish relationships, partner with, and meet and exceed their customers' needs and expectations.

communications may break down. Thus, in the information age, it becomes important for firms to create structures to encourage knowledge sharing.[46]

Individuals who have developed skills associated with careers in sales are more likely to be successful when they decide to go out on their own because, more often than not, those skills translate very well to other businesses.[47] Today, personal-selling skills contribute in a major way to four groups of knowledge workers who may not consider themselves salespeople:

- Managerial personnel
- Professionals (accountants, consultants, lawyers, architects, engineers, etc.)
- Entrepreneurs
- Marketing personnel and customer service representatives

Managerial Personnel

People working in managerial occupations represent a large group of knowledge workers. They are given such titles as "executive," "manager," or "administrator." Leaders are constantly involved in capturing, processing, and communicating information. Some of the most valuable information is acquired from customers. This helps explain the rapid growth in what is being described as "executive selling." Chief executive officers and other executives often accompany salespeople on sales calls to learn more about customer needs and in some cases to assist with presentations. Manny Fernandez of the Gartner Group, a technology consulting firm based in Stamford, Connecticut, spends more than half his time travelling on sales calls.[48] Leaders also must articulate their ideas in a persuasive manner and win support for their vision. Brian Tracy, author of *The 100 Absolutely Unbreakable Laws of Business Success*, says, "People who cannot present their ideas or sell themselves effectively have very little influence and are not highly respected."[49]

Professionals

Today's professional workers include lawyers, designers, programmers, engineers, consultants, dentists, counsellors, doctors, accountants, and many other specialized knowledge workers. Our labour force includes several million professional service providers, persons who need many of the skills used by professional salespeople. Clients who purchase professional services are usually more interested in the person who delivers the service than in the firm that employs the professional. They seek expert diagnosticians who are truly interested in their needs. The professional must display good communication skills and be able to build a relationship based on trust.

Technical skills are not enough in the information age. Many employers expect the professional to bring in new business, often referred to as **business** or **client development**, in addition to keeping current customers satisfied. Employers often screen professional applicants to determine their customer focus, ability to interact well with people, and client development skills.

Many firms are providing their professional staff with sales training. The accounting firm Ernst & Young sets aside several days each year to train its professional staff in personal selling. The National Law Firm Marketing Association recently featured Neil Rackham, author of *Spin Selling*, as keynote speaker at its national conference. The

business or **client development** Bringing in new business, from new or existing clients or customers.

Who is Jimmy Pattison? Depending on where in Canada you are located, he may or may not be well known. You might recall seeing the Pattison name underneath many billboards across this country.

However, Jimmy Pattison is much bigger than a billboard. From a humble Saskatchewan beginning, Jimmy Pattison demonstrated his entrepreneurial calling at a very early age. He started by selling packets of seeds door to door; eventually graduated to selling pots and pans, also door to door; and then, while in university, graduated to selling used cars. While a student at UBC, Jimmy Pattison would buy a used car in the evening, drive it to school the following day, sell it at a modest profit, and return home by bus. Eventually, he bought a share in his first GM dealership. Today, the Pattison Group is involved in the automotive, media, packaging, food sales and distribution, entertainment, export, and financial industries.

The Pattison Group has 35 000 employees at 473 worldwide locations, with sales of $7.5 billion. As one of Canada's richest people and the owner of Canada's third-largest private company, Jimmy Pattison describes himself as someone "having no other skills except as a salesman."[e]

Wicker Corporation, a manufacturer of equipment for the plastics industry, has initiated a program designed to motivate its researchers, engineers, and manufacturing staff members to get involved in sales. Faced with increased competition and more cost-conscious customers, a growing number of law, accounting, engineering, and architectural firms are discovering the merits of personal selling as an auxiliary activity.[50]

Entrepreneurs

Thousands of new businesses are started each year in Canada. As noted previously, people who want to start a new business frequently need to sell their plan to investors and others who can help get the firm established. Once the firm is open, owners rely on personal selling to build their businesses.

James Koch, chief executive officer of the Boston Beer Company (brewer of Samuel Adams beer), makes a strong case for personal selling. Like most new companies, his started with no customers. To get the new company established, he assumed the role of salesperson and set a goal of establishing one new account each week.

Today Koch continues to spend time on the street visiting convenience stores, supermarkets, and taverns. Competition from popular craft beers such as Fat Tire and Magic Hat, and imports such as Stella Artois and Beck's, present a major challenge. He's also trying to get the attention of young men who think of Samuel Adams as their father's beer. He readily admits that selling his beer is the most rewarding part of his job. Koch could have sold his company to a megabrewer long ago, but that option is not appealing to this wealthy entrepreneur who loves to sell.[51]

Marketing Personnel and Customer Service Representatives

Because of the close working relationships of marketing directors, product managers, marketing research specialists, warehouse and shipping specialists, and others working with customers in the marketing efforts of companies, it is imperative for these personnel to understand, and in most cases to acquire, the skills of personal selling. This generally results in a much more productive sales and marketing effort and a satisfied customer base.

The assignment of selling duties to employees with customer service responsibilities has become quite common today. The term **customer service representative (CSR)** is used to describe knowledge workers who process reservations, accept orders by phone or other means, deliver products, handle customer complaints, provide technical assistance, and assist full-time sales representatives. Some companies are teaming CSRs and salespeople. After the sale is closed, the CSR helps process paperwork, check on delivery of the product, and engage in other customer follow-up duties. In addition to increased service quality, the improved customer expertise from this process improves customer loyalty.[52]

Assigning sales duties to customer service representatives makes sense when you consider the number of contacts customers have with CSRs. When a customer seeks assistance with a problem or makes a reservation, the CSR learns more about the customer and often provides the customer with needed information. Customer needs often surface as both parties exchange information. It is important to keep in mind the advice offered by the authors of *Selling the Invisible*: "Every act is a marketing act. Make every employee a marketing person."[53]

Increasingly, work in the information economy is understood as an expression of thought. At a time when people change their careers eight or more times during their lives, selling skills represent important transferable employment skills.

LEARNING TO SELL

"ARE SALESPEOPLE MADE OR ARE THEY BORN?" THIS CLASSIC QUESTION SEEMS TO imply that some people are born with certain qualities that give them a special advantage in the selling field. This is not true. The principles of adaptive selling, listening, and customer orientation can be learned and applied by people whose personal characteristics are quite different.[54]

In the past few decades, sales training has been expanded on four fronts. These four sources of training are corporate-sponsored training, training provided by commercial vendors, certification studies, and courses provided by colleges and universities.

Corporate-Sponsored Training

Hundreds of business organizations, such as Apple Computer, IBM, Maytag, Western Electric, and Zenith, have established training programs. These large corporations spend millions of dollars each year to develop their salespeople. *Training* magazine, which conducts annual analyses of employer-provided training, indicates that salespeople are among the most intensively trained employee groups. A new salesperson preparing for a consultative selling position may spend a few months to a year or more in training. For many salespeople, the training is as close as their laptop computer. Lucent Technologies, for example, uses web-based training for about one-third of its training courses.[55]

Training Provided by Commercial Vendors

The programs designed by firms specializing in the development of sales personnel are a second source of sales training. Some of the most popular courses are offered

Table 1.2 Sales Training Offered by Commercial Vendors

Training programs provided by commercial vendors are very popular. This table introduces a few of the well-established sales training programs offered to salespeople who are interested in improving their selling skills.

Company	Training Programs	Description
Canadian Professional Sales Association www.cpsa.com	• Professional Selling • Strategic Account Management	Provides in-class and online sales training with emphasis on consultative selling and building value-based partnerships
Sales Performance International www.spisales.com	• Solution Selling • Opportunity Selling	Provides sales training based on concepts explained in *The New Solution Selling,* by Keith Eades
Integrity Systems, Inc. www.integritysolutions.com	• Integrity Selling • The Customer	Provides sales training based on concepts explained in *Integrity Selling for the 21st Century,* by Ron Willingham
Huthwaite, Inc. www.huthwaite.com	• Spin Selling Certificate • Creating Client Value	Provides sales training based on concepts in *The Spin Selling Fieldbook,* by Neil Rackham
Miller Heiman, Inc. www.millerheiman.com	• Strategic Selling • Conceptual Selling	Provides sales training based on concepts presented in *Strategic Selling* and *The New Conceptual Selling*
AchieveGlobal www.achieveglobal.com	• Professional Selling • Professional Sales	Provides the original Xerox Skills (PSS) *Professional Selling Skills (PSS)* sales training; *Course Content Coaching* has been updated
Wilson Learning Worldwide www.wilsonlearning.com	• The Versatile Salesperson	Provides updated sales training based on the original Larry Wilson *Counselor Selling Training Program*
Dale Carnegie Training, Inc. www.dalecarnegie.com	• Sales Advantage • How to Sell Like a Pro	One of the largest international training companies, providing sales training using many of the concepts presented in the Dale Carnegie books, such as *How to Win Friends and Influence People*
Richardson E-Learning www.richardson.com	Richardson Quick Skills	*Richardson QuickSkills*™ 5.0 incorporates a set of online tools that allows for improved efficiency in developing and delivering customized and tailored online sales training courses

by the Canadian Professional Sales Association, Richardson E-Learning, Acclivus Corporation, Wilson Learning Corporation, Miller Heiman Inc., Dale Carnegie Training, and AchieveGlobal (see Table 1.2.) The legendary Professional Selling Skills (PSS) course, developed in the late 1960s by Gene Keluche, is still offered by AchieveGlobal. This carefully designed course, once owned by Xerox, has been completed by millions of salespeople in Canada, the United States, and around the world.[56]

The Canadian Professional Sales Association provides professional accreditation for salespeople who complete its Certified Sales Professional program.

H.F. (Herb) MacKenzie

Certification Programs

The trend toward increased professionalism in personal selling has been the stimulus for a third type of training and education initiative. Many salespeople are returning to the classroom to earn certification in a sales or sales-related area. In the United States, many salespeople earn the Certified Medical Representative (CMR) designation. The CMR curriculum includes nearly 40 courses that are delivered to more than 9000 students. The National Automobile Dealers Association in the United States sponsors the Code of Conduct Certification program for automotive sales representatives. Both of these certification programs require extensive study of modules and the completion of rigorous examinations. The Canadian Professional Sales Association offers the Certified Sales Professional (CSP) designation to sales professionals in Canada who meet the highest standards of education, experience, and ethical conduct.

Some companies have developed their own sales training certification programs. The Pitney Bowes Certified Postal Consultant (CPC) program is designed to improve the level of assistance given to customers who want to upgrade their mail process. It is available to members of the 4000-person Pitney Bowes sales force who sell both products (postage meters) and services. Freightliner developed a certification program for its 1800-member sales force. The various courses include topics ranging from product knowledge to truck-selling skills.[57]

College and University Courses

The fourth source of sales training is personal selling courses offered by colleges and universities throughout Canada. These courses are attracting an increasing number of students interested in careers in accounting, entrepreneurship, and finance, as well as sales and marketing. Sales training has also become an important part of the MBA curriculum at several elite universities as well.[58] Although there is no formulaic answer that can be applicable to all selling situations, these courses provide students with a repertoire of skills that help them become more effective. The business community, in general, is increasingly asking for more selling skills from graduates of business programs.

REVIEWING KEY CONCEPTS

- Define personal selling and describe the three prescriptions of a personal selling philosophy.

   Personal selling occurs when a company representative interacts directly with a customer or prospective customer to present information about a product or service. Salespeople are encouraged to develop a personal selling philosophy based on three prescriptions: adopt the marketing concept, value personal selling, and assume the role of a problem solver or partner.

- Describe the emergence of relationship selling in the age of information.

   Restructuring from an industrial economy to an information economy began in the 1950s. We now live in an age in which the effective exchange of information is the foundation of most economic transactions. Salespeople use a variety of information technology tools to gather and process information of value to customers.

- Discuss the rewarding aspects of a career in selling today.

   Selling careers offer many rewards not found in other occupations. Income, both monetary and psychic, is above average, and there are many opportunities for advancement. Salespeople enjoy job security, mobility, and independence. Opportunities in selling for members of minority groups and for women are growing. In addition, selling is very interesting work, because a salesperson is constantly in contact with people. The adage "no two people are alike" reminds us that sales work is never dull or routine.

- Discuss the different employment settings in selling today.

   The text describes each of the three major career options and employment opportunities in the field of personal selling—namely, services, business goods, and consumer goods. Keep in mind that each category features a wide range of selling positions, varying in terms of educational requirements, earning potential, and type of customer served. The discussion and examples should help you discover which kind of sales career best suits your talents and interests.

- Explain how personal selling skills have become one of the master skills needed for success in the information age and how personal selling skills contribute to the work performed by knowledge workers.

   Today's workforce is made up of millions of *knowledge workers* who succeed only when they add value to information. The new economy rewards salespeople and other knowledge workers who collect, organize, clarify, and present information in a convincing manner. Selling skills contribute in a major way to four groups of knowledge workers who usually do not consider themselves salespeople: customer service representatives, professionals (accountants, consultants, lawyers, etc.), entrepreneurs, and managerial personnel.

- Identify the four major sources of sales training.

   Sales training can be acquired from four key sources: corporate-sponsored training, training provided by commercial vendors, certification programs, and courses offered by colleges and universities. Many MBA programs now include professional selling and sales management in the curriculum.

Key Terms

Review Questions

1. Explain how personal selling can help solve the problem of information overload.

2. According to the Strategic/Consultative Selling Model (Fig. 1.1), what are the three prescriptions for developing a successful personal selling philosophy?

3. List and describe the four employment settings for people who are considering a selling career.

4. What future is there in selling for women?

5. Some salespeople have an opportunity to earn certification in a sales or sales-related area. How can a salesperson benefit from certification?

6. Explain why high-performance value-added salespeople earn much more than high-performance transactional salespeople.

7. List three titles commonly used to describe manufacturing salespeople. Describe the duties of each.

8. Develop a list of eight selling career opportunities in the service field.

9. Explain why personal selling is an important auxiliary skill needed by lawyers, engineers, accountants, and other professionals.

10. List and briefly describe the four major sources of sales training.

Application Exercises

1. Examine a magazine or newspaper ad for a new product or service that you have never seen. Evaluate its chances for receiving wide customer acceptance. Does this product require a large amount of personal selling effort? What types of salespeople (service, manufacturing, wholesale, or retail) are involved in selling this product?

2. For each of the following job classifications, list the name of at least one person you know in that field:

   a. Full-time person who sells a service

   b. Full-time inside wholesale salesperson

   c. Full-time manufacturer's salesperson

   d. Full-time retail salesperson

   Interview one of the people you have listed and ask the following questions concerning their duties and responsibilities:

   a. What is your immediate supervisor's title?

   b. What would be a general description of your position?

   c. What specific duties and responsibilities do you have?

   d. What is the compensation plan and salary range for a position like yours?

   Write a job description from this information.

3. When Shelly Jones, a vice president and partner in the consulting firm Korn/Ferry International, looks into the future, he sees some new challenges for salespeople. He recently shared the following predictions with *Selling Power* magazine:

   a. Salespeople will spend more time extending the range of applications or finding new markets for the products they sell.

b. The selling function will be less pitching your product and more integrating your product into the business equation of your client. Understanding the business environment in which your client operates will be critical.

c. In the future you will have to be a financial engineer for your client. You need to understand how your client makes money and be able to explain how your product or service contributes to profitable operation of the client's firm.

Interview a salesperson who is involved in business-to-business selling—a manufacturer's representative, for example—and determine whether this person agrees with the views of Shelly Jones.

4. There are many information sources on selling careers and career opportunities on the Internet. Three examples include SalesJobsCanada.com, Monster.ca, and CareerBuilder.ca. Search the Internet for information on selling careers.

Use your search engine to find career information on a pharmaceutical representative, a field sales engineer, and a retail salesperson.

5. Sales managers are frequently asked what personal characteristics are most important to success in selling. Among the criteria often cited are sociability, aggressiveness, enthusiasm, empathy, verbal ability, and time management. Which of these do you believe are the most important? Least important? Are there important personal characteristics that are missing from this list?

↻ ROLE-PLAY EXERCISE

This role play will let you practise selling your knowledge, skills, and experience to a prospective employer. You will be meeting with a class member who will assume the role of an employer who is developing a new sales team. Prior to this interview, reflect on the courses you have completed, work experience, and other life experiences that may have value in the eyes of the employer.

You may also want to reflect on any volunteer work you have completed and any leadership roles you have held. Be prepared to discuss the personal selling skills you are developing in this course, skills you have learned in previous employment settings, and related skills you have learned in other courses you have taken, such as psychology, communications, sociology, etc.

Reality Selling Video Case Problem

Alex Homer, featured at the beginning of this chapter, works as a professional clothier for the Tom James Company (www.tomjames.com). Alex sells a comprehensive collection of high-quality attire: formal (black tie/tuxedo), business (suits), business casual (sport coats, slacks, etc.), and weekend (jeans, sport shirts, shorts, khakis, etc.). His clients are typically gentlemen and ladies who do not have time to go to the store, dislike the idea of store shopping, or have fit characteristics that present challenges for purchasing clothing "off-the-peg."

For Alex, it is important to call on existing customers as well as prospects and to be aware of the different approaches used in each type of sales call. Typically, prior to visiting with an existing customer, he puts together clothing ideas for the season that make sense for the client based on how she/he dresses and how much her/

his closet is lacking in a particular area (such as shirts or slacks). For new prospects, Alex contacts them by telephone. Realizing that cold-calling is an antiquated way of building a long-standing and fruitful sales career, the Tom James Company emphasizes the importance of referrals to build a business. Referrals tend to be easier to contact by phone and they typically purchase more in-person, due to the strength of the referrer's name. All in all, referrals remove many obstacles to turning a person who is completely unaware of one's business into a client.

According to Alex, the biggest challenge in his business is getting in front of people. This challenge stems from many possible sources: lack of time for the prospect, perceived price/value imbalance, lack of experience in in-office clothing shopping, and being perceived as a "suit" company rather than an all-inclusive clothing provider.

Especially for repeat clients, who represent 80 percent of the company's annual business, Alex Homer describes solid call preparation as key for successful selling. If the salesperson is unprepared and shows up in the client's office with a bag in hand and a "what-are-you-buying-today?" attitude, clients can sense this and become frustrated. They understand that professional clothiers provide a service and expect them to be prepared as a partner/problem solver regarding their wardrobes. As Alex puts it, "Stores provide clothing. Tom James provides a service."

When it comes to understanding the needs of a prospect, Alex follows a certain sales process: He first asks his clients what is most important to them when they go clothing shopping. For most of his clients, it is one of four things: price, quality, fit, or trend-sensitivity. Based on that, he determines what clothing the client wears during the vital parts of their business (client meetings, board meetings, trials, close-the-sale presentations, speaking engagements, and so forth). Then he asks how they would evaluate their closet (excellent, good, fair, or poor). Finally, if applicable, he finds out what it would take to make a slight improvement in their closet. (See the chapter opener on page 1 and Reality Selling Today Role Play 1 in Appendix 1 on page 425 for more information.)

Questions

1. Does it appear that Tom James and Alex Homer have a personal selling philosophy like that described in this chapter? Provide examples that support each of the three prescriptions.

2. Put yourself in the position of Alex Homer. What might be the most rewarding and the most adverse aspects of his sales job?

3. Describe how Alex uses personal selling skills in utilizing existing knowledge and gathering new information from the customer in order to advance the sales process.

4. Discuss different ways in which Alex can actively generate good customer referrals.

5. What skills are particularly important for Alex's sales job? Which of the four major sources of sales training outlined in this chapter would you recommend for acquiring those skills?

PARTNERSHIP SELLING: A ROLE PLAY/SIMULATION

(If your instructor has chosen to use the Partnership-Selling Role-Play/Simulation exercise that accompanies this text, these boxes alert you to your Role-Play/Simulation assignments. Your instructor will also provide you with needed information.)

Preview the role-play/simulation materials provided in the Student Resources section of your companion website at **www.pearsoncanada.ca/manning**. A Contents page lists appropriate page references for the activities. These materials are produced by the Park Shores Resort and Convention Center, and you will be using them in your role as a new salesperson (and, at times, as the customer) for the hotel and its convention services.

The role-play exercises begin in Chapter 6, as you begin to create your product strategy. However, in anticipation of the role play, you can begin to imagine yourself in the role of an actual salesperson. Start to think about how you can develop your personal selling philosophy. What are some ethical guidelines that you may wish to adopt for yourself? (Ethics is also the subject of Chapter 3, "Ethics: The Foundation for Relationships That Create Value.") What skills do you need to develop to become a partner with your prospective customers? (Refer to the position description in Part I.)

The Park Shores has implemented a quality improvement process. How does this affect your role as a sales representative? (Refer to the Total Quality Customer Service Glossary also in Part I.)

Chapter 2
Evolution of Selling Models That Complement the Marketing Concept

Learning Objectives

After studying this chapter, you should be able to

1   Discuss the evolution of personal selling models as an extension of the marketing concept.

2   Describe the evolution of consultative selling from the marketing era to the present.

3   Define *strategic selling* and name the four broad strategic areas in the Strategic/Consultative Selling Model.

4   Describe the evolution of partnering and the nature of strategic account management.

5   Explain how value-added selling strategies enhance personal selling.

Successful salespeople who sell financial services products—such as those employed by Manulife Financial, London Life, Sun Life Financial, or State Farm—are masters of consultative selling. Marcus Smith one of the most productive sales representatives of Liberty Mutual (**www.libertymutual.com**), uses the consultative relationship selling approach exclusively. He believes that excellence in selling starts with an in-depth understanding of what customers value most. After gaining a careful understanding of their needs, he works closely as a partner with his customers in selecting the right products that will solve their buying problems and satisfy their long-term needs.

Founded in 1912, Liberty Mutual is an important player in the highly competitive insurance market. The three pillars of the company's culture consist of behaving with integrity, treating people with dignity and respect, and providing superior products and services. Smith is a strong believer in those corporate values. Yet implementing this relationship-oriented selling approach represents a challenge, given the constraints of resources and the competitive intensity of the insurance market. Smith's strategy is simple

Marcus Smith

Michael Ahearne

yet effective: placing emphasis on tracking and forecasting market information, focusing on identifying profitable customers, and directing resources to those customers.

Smith does not start conversations with his new customers with a sales pitch. Instead, he spends time building rapport with each customer and finding some beliefs and opinions that he and his customers have in common. These icebreakers go a long way toward making customers feel comfortable sharing with Smith what their actual needs are. Then he asks permission to ask questions to fully understand his customer's unique needs. After confirming what the customer needs, he presents a balanced comparison between his offers and those of competitors. Being empathetic and honest with customers lies at the heart of his consultative relationship-selling philosophy.

MARKETING CONCEPT REQUIRES NEW SELLING MODELS

A CAREFUL EXAMINATION OF PERSONAL SELLING PRACTICES DURING THE PAST 50 years reveals some positive developments. We have seen the evolution of personal selling through several stages. The early *persuader stage* that was popular prior to the emergence of the marketing concept emphasized pushing or peddling products. At this stage, with little regard for long-term, mutually rewarding customer relationships, salespeople attempted to convince any and all market members to buy products offered. Over the years, personal selling evolved to the *problem-solver stage*, obtaining the participation of buyers in identifying their problems, which could then be translated into needs. At this stage the salesperson attempts to present products that correspond with customer needs.[1] Today, salespeople are no longer the flamboyant product "peddlers" of the past. Instead, they are increasingly becoming diagnosticians of customers' needs and problems. A growing number of salespeople recognize that the quality of the partnerships they create is as important as the quality of the products they sell. This sweeping change in personal selling models, from peddling to long-term consultative problem solving and value-added partnering, was prompted by the emergence of the marketing concept.

Table 2.1 Evolution of Personal Selling (1950 to Present)

Sales and Marketing Emphasis	Selling Emphasis
Marketing Era Begins (1950s)	
Organizations determine needs and wants of target markets and adapt themselves to delivering desired satisfaction; product orientation is replaced by a customer orientation	• More organizations recognize that the salesperson is in a position to collect product, market, and service information concerning the buyer's needs
Consultative Selling Era Emerges (Late 1960s to early 1970s)	
Salespeople are becoming diagnosticians of customers' needs as well as consultants offering well-considered recommendations; mass markets are breaking into target markets	• Buyer needs are identified through two-way communication • Information giving and negotiation tactics replace manipulation
Strategic Selling Era Emerges (Early 1980s)	
The evolution of a more complex selling environment and greater emphasis on market niches create the need for greater structure and more emphasis on planning	• Strategy is given as much attention as selling tactics • Product positioning is given more attention • Greater emphasis on account management and team selling
Partnering Era Emerges (1990 to the present)	
Salespeople are encouraged to think of everything they say or do in the context of their long-term, high-quality partnership with individual customers; sales force automation provides specific customer information	• Customer supplants the product as the driving force in sales • Greater emphasis on strategies that create customer value • Adaptive selling is given greater emphasis

Evolution of the Marketing Concept

What is the **marketing concept**? It is a principle that holds that achieving organizational goals depends on knowing the needs and wants of target markets and delivering the desired products. Under the marketing concept, customer focus and value are the paths to sales and profits.[2]

The era of marketing and the age of information began in the early 1950s (Table 2.1). A General Electric executive is credited with making one of the earliest formal statements indicating corporate interest in the marketing concept. In a paper heralding a new management philosophy, he observed that the principal marketing function of a company is to determine what the customer wants and then develop the appropriate product or service. This view contrasted with the prevailing practice of that period, which was to develop products and then build customer interest in those products.[3]

The foundation for the marketing concept is a business philosophy that leaves no doubt in the mind of every employee that customer satisfaction is of primary importance. All energies are directed toward satisfying the customer. As Peter Drucker once observed, "The customers define the business."

Although the marketing concept is a business fundamental, some companies ignore it and suffer the consequences. Ford Motor Company was a leader in quality control during the 1980s and early 1990s but then seemed to shift its focus to other areas. The result was a drop in J. D. Power and Associates' quality rankings and a drop in sales. Ford also failed

marketing concept A principle that holds that achieving organizational goals depends on knowing the needs and wants of target markets and delivering the desired products.

to stay in touch with consumer tastes.[4] With renewed insight into the marketing concept, Ford now appears to be reconnecting with its customers.[5]

Business firms vary in terms of how strongly they support the marketing concept. Some firms have gone the extra mile to satisfy the needs and wants of their customers:

■ UPS founder Jim Casey adopted the marketing concept when the company was first established. He described the firm's customer focus this way: "Our real, primary objective is to serve—to render perfect service to our stores and their customers. If we keep that objective constantly in mind, our reward in money can be beyond our fondest dreams."[6]

■ Marriott Hotels uses a blend of "high tech" and "high touch" to build customer goodwill and repeat business. Each of the 8500 sales representatives can sell the services of 10 motel brands in Marriott's portfolio. The customer with a small meeting budget might be encouraged to consider a Fairfield Inn property. The customer seeking luxury accommodations might be introduced to a Ritz-Carlton hotel (acquired a few years ago). All reservations go through the same system, so that if one Marriott hotel is full, the sales representative can cross-sell rooms in another Marriott hotel in the same city.[7]

Marketing Concept Yields Marketing Mix

marketing mix A set of controllable, tactical marketing tools that consists of everything the firm can do to influence the demand for its product. These can be organized into four sets of variables: product, price, place, and promotion.

Once the marketing concept becomes an integral part of a firm's philosophy, its management seeks to develop a network of marketing activities that maximize customer satisfaction and ensure profitability. The combination of elements making up a program based on the marketing concept is known as the **marketing mix** (Fig. 2.1). The marketing mix is a set of controllable, tactical marketing tools that consists of everything the firm can do to influence the demand for its product. The many possibilities can be organized into four groups of variables: *product*, *price*, *place*, and *promotion*.[8]

One of the four Ps shown in Figure 2.1—promotion—can be further subdivided into advertising, sales promotion, personal selling, and public relations. When a company adopts the marketing concept, it must determine how some combination of these elements can result in maximum customer satisfaction.

Figure 2.1 Each of the elements that make up the marketing mix must be executed effectively for a marketing program to achieve the desired results.

Learning Different Business Cultures

If your company is going global and you need to deal with customers from China, Brazil, Germany, or Russia, learning different ways of developing and maintaining business relationships is a must for you. Too many Canadians rely on the "time is money" belief and they take shortcuts in some key areas. For example, they often fail to take the time needed to build a relationship with the client or learn how to approach different clients with different cultures.

■ The negotiation process in China, Japan, and Latin American countries is very slow, with a lot of time spent on relationship activities.

■ In Japan, great importance is placed on relationships, and building long-term business relationships is what matters most.

■ The importance of relationships for Russians is low, and they mostly remain reserved until negotiations conclude.

■ The French approach to business interactions is formal; having etiquette is extremely important in dealing with French clients.[a]

Important Role of Personal Selling

Every marketer must decide how much time and money to invest in each of the four areas of the marketing mix. The decision must be objective; no one can afford to invest money in a marketing strategy that does not provide a good return on money invested. *Personal selling is often the major promotional method used—whether measured by people employed, by total expenditures, or by expenses as a percentage of sales.* More than 10 percent of the total workforce in Canada and the United States are employed in sales positions, and about 40 percent of them have field sales responsibility. They cost their companies well over a trillion dollars every year and represent by far the largest marketing expenditure. This is more than four times what is spent on advertising.[9]

Firms make large investments in personal selling in response to several major trends: Products and services have become increasingly sophisticated and complex; competition has greatly increased in most product areas; and demand for quality, value, and service by customers has risen sharply. In response to these trends, personal selling has evolved to a new level of professionalism. Since the beginning of the information age, personal selling has gone through three distinct developmental periods: the consultative selling era, the strategic selling era, and the partnering era.

EVOLUTION OF CONSULTATIVE SELLING

Consultative selling, WHICH EMERGED IN THE LATE 1960S AND EARLY 1970S, IS AN extension of the marketing concept (see Table 2.1). This approach emphasizes need identification, which is achieved through effective communication between the salesperson and the customer. The salesperson establishes two-way communication by asking appropriate questions and listening carefully to the customer's responses. The salesperson assumes the role of consultant and offers well-considered recommendations. Negotiation replaces manipulation as the salesperson sets the stage for a long-term partnership. Salespeople who have adopted consultative selling possess a keen ability to listen, define the customer's problems, and offer one or more solutions.

consultative selling An approach to personal selling that is an extension of the marketing concept. Emphasis is placed on need identification, need satisfaction, and the building of a relationship that results in repeat business.

transactional selling A sales process that most effectively matches the needs of the value-conscious buyer, who is primarily interested in price and convenience.

Although consultative selling is emphasized throughout this text, it is helpful to understand the role of transactional selling in our economy. **Transactional selling** is a sales process that most effectively matches the needs of the value-conscious buyer, who is primarily interested in price and convenience. Many transactional buyers are well aware of their needs and may already know a great deal about the products or services they intend to purchase. Because the transaction-based buyer tends to focus primarily on low price, some marketers are adopting lower-cost selling channels. Low-cost transaction selling strategies include telesales, direct mail, and the Internet. This approach to selling is usually employed by marketers who do not see the need to spend very much time on customer need assessment, problem solving, relationship building, or sales follow-up.[10, 11]

The decline in popularity of transactional sales approaches is due to two industry trends: the rise of e-commerce, which displaces transactional sales managed by people, and the increasing complexity of businesses. As more business supplier-related transactions are managed through portals and online bidding, businesses have a diminished demand for salespeople to manage the transactional sale.[12]

Service, retail, wholesale, and manufacturing firms that embrace the marketing concept have already adopted or are currently adopting consultative selling practices. The major features of consultative selling are as follows:

1. The customer is seen as *a person to be served*, not a prospect to be sold. Consultative salespeople believe their function is to help the buyer make an intelligent decision. They use a four-step process that includes need discovery, selection of the solution, a need-satisfaction presentation, and servicing the sale (Fig. 2.2). These customer-centred strategies will be explained in Chapters 10 to 15.

2. The consultative salesperson, unlike the peddler of an earlier era, does not try to overpower the customer with a high-pressure sales presentation. Instead, the buyer's needs are identified through *two-way* communication. The salesperson conducts precall research and asks questions during the sales call in an attempt to develop a relationship and learn as much as possible about the person's needs and perceptions.

3. Consultative selling emphasizes *need identification, problem solving,* and *negotiation instead of manipulation.* This approach is very compatible with the *problem-solver stage* of personal selling discussed in Chapter 1.[13] Helping the buyer make an informed and intelligent buying decision adds value to the sales process.

4. Consultative selling emphasizes *service* at every phase of the personal selling process. Several important research studies indicate the strong, positive impact of customer satisfaction on company profits.[14] The relationship between a seller and a buyer seldom ends when the sale is made. In most cases, customer expectations increase after the sale.

At first glance, it may appear that consultative selling practices can be easily mastered. The truth is, consultative selling is a complex process that puts great demands on sales personnel. This approach to personal selling requires an understanding of concepts and

Figure 2.2 The Consultative Sales Presentation Guide. This contemporary presentation guide emphasizes the customer as a person to be served.

principles borrowed from the fields of psychology, communications, and sociology. It takes a great deal of personal commitment and self-discipline to become a sales consultant/adviser.

EVOLUTION OF STRATEGIC SELLING

STRATEGIC SELLING BEGAN TO RECEIVE CONSIDERABLE ATTENTION DURING THE 1980S (Table 2.1). During this period we witnessed the beginning of several trends that resulted in a more complex selling environment, owing to increased global competition, broader and more diverse product lines, more decision makers involved in major purchases, and greater demand for specific, custom-made solutions. These trends will continue to influence personal selling and sales training in the age of information.

As companies face increased levels of complexity in the marketplace, they must give more attention to strategic planning. The strategic planning done by salespeople is often influenced by the information included in their company's strategic market plan. **Strategic planning** is the process that matches the firm's resources to its market opportunities. It takes into consideration all of the major functional areas of the business that must be coordinated, such as financial assets, workforce, production capabilities, and marketing.[15] Almost every aspect of strategic planning directly or indirectly influences sales and marketing.

strategic planning The process that matches the firm's resources to its market opportunities.

The strategic plan should be a guide for a strategic selling plan. This plan includes strategies that you use to position yourself with the customer before the sales call even begins. The authors of *Strategic Selling* point out that there is a difference between a *tactic* and a *strategy*.[16] **Tactics** are techniques, practices, or methods you use when you are face-to-face with a customer. Examples are the use of questions to identify needs, presentation skills, and various types of closes. These and other tactics will be discussed in Chapters 10 to 15. **Strategies**, on the other hand, are prerequisite to tactical success. If you develop effective strategies, you are more likely to make your sales presentation to the right person, at the right time, in a manner most likely to achieve positive results.

tactics Techniques, practices, or methods that a salesperson uses during face-to-face interactions with customers.

strategies The things that salespeople do as the result of precall planning to ensure that they call on the right people, at the right time, and with the right tactics to achieve positive results.

A selling strategy is a carefully conceived plan that is needed to accomplish a sales objective. Let's assume you are a sales representative employed by a pharmaceutical company. In an ideal situation, you want to establish a dialogue with the physician and learn about the types of patients she sees, diseases she treats, and challenges she faces in her practice. However, you do not want to call on busy doctors who may have no use for the drugs offered by your company. A strategy might include a careful study of the entire physician population in your territory. This analysis will help you identify those who need information about the drugs your company offers.[17] With this information, you can select the most appropriate selling tactic (method), which might be to present samples to doctors who are not currently prescribing your drug.

Strategic planning, an important element of the *problem-solver stage*, sets the groundwork for a value-added form of consultative selling that is more structured, more focused, and more efficient. The result is better time allocation, more precise problem solving, and a greater chance that there will be a good match between your product and the customer's needs.

Adaptive selling is another key element of the *problem-solver stage*. **Adaptive selling** can be defined as altering sales behaviours during a customer interaction in order to improve communication. It relates to a salesperson's ability to collect information regarding the customer's needs and respond appropriately. Adaptive selling frequently requires complex behavioural adjustments.[18]

adaptive selling Altering sales behaviours during a customer interaction in order to improve communication.

Within many companies there is little alignment between sales and marketing. In fact, a real turf war often exists between these two functions. One source of friction is *economic*. Senior management must make decisions regarding budget allocation for each function. The folks in marketing may want to spend large amounts of money on advertising to generate customer awareness of a new product. The folks in sales may feel this money would be better spent by increasing the size of the sales force.

The second source of conflict is *cultural*. Sales and marketing attract different types of people who spend their time in different ways. The marketing staff may be focused on program elements (product warranty, price, placement of the product, etc.). Salespeople, in contrast, want to focus their attention on existing and potential customers. One way to end the war between sales and marketing is to encourage more joint planning and information sharing. The leaders of both functions must try to achieve common ground in terms of philosophies and values.[b]

Many companies have discovered that specialized sales training is an effective strategy. When Microsoft wanted to build a stronger partnership with its customers, all of its 5000 sales professionals completed the Solution Selling sales training course. This training, based on concepts presented in *The New Solution Selling* by Keith Eades, helped Microsoft salespeople create greater value for its customers.[19]

The Strategic/Consultative Selling Model

When you study a value-added approach to personal selling that combines strategic planning, consultative selling practices, and partnering principles, you experience a mental exercise that is similar to solving a jigsaw puzzle. You are given many pieces of information

Salespeople who build partnering relationships are rewarded with repeat business and referrals. These relationships require a strategic approach to selling.

Konstantin Chagin/Shutterstock

Strategic/Consultative Selling Model*	
Strategic step	Prescription
Develop a personal selling philosophy	• Adopt marketing concept • Value personal selling • Become a problem solver/partner
Develop a relationship strategy	• Maintain high ethical standards • Project professional image • Manage the relationship process
Develop a product strategy	• Become a product expert • Sell benefits • Configure value-added solutions
Develop a customer strategy	• Understand the buying process • Understand buyer behaviour • Develop prospect base
Develop a presentation strategy	• Prepare objectives • Develop presentation plan • Provide outstanding service

* Strategic/consulative selling evolved in response to increased competition, more complex products, increased emphasis on customer needs, and the growing importance of long-term relationships.

Marketing Concept:
• coordinate all activities
• to create satisfied customers
• and achieve company goals.

Figure 2.3 The Strategic/Consultative Selling Model is an extension of the marketing concept.

that must form a complete picture. Putting the parts together isn't difficult, however, if you can see the total picture at the beginning. Therefore, a single model has been developed to serve as a source of reference throughout the entire text. Figure 2.3 shows this model.

The Strategic/Consultative Selling Model features five steps, each based on three prescriptions. The first step involves the development of a personal selling philosophy, which was introduced in Chapter 1. Each of the other four steps relates to a broad strategic area of personal selling. Each step makes an important and unique contribution to the selling/buying process.

Adaptive selling requires a strategic selling plan. Adaptive selling can be defined as altering sales behaviours during a customer interaction in order to improve communication. It relates to a salesperson's ability to collect information regarding the customer's needs and respond appropriately. Adaptive selling frequently requires complex behavioural adjustments.

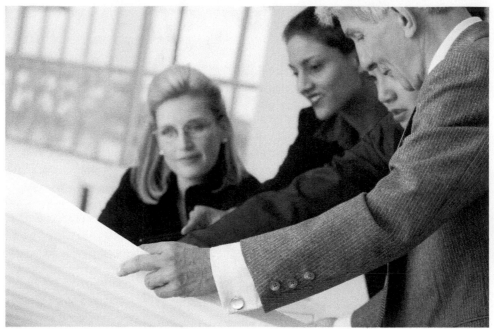

Developing a Relationship Strategy Success in selling depends heavily on the salesperson's ability to develop, manage, and enhance interpersonal relations with the customer. People seldom buy products or services from someone they dislike or distrust. Harvey B. Mackay, founder of Mackay Envelope Corporation, says, "People don't care how much you know until they know how much you care." Most customers are more apt to discuss their needs and wants openly with a salesperson with whom they feel comfortable.

relationship strategy A well-thought-out plan for establishing, building, and maintaining quality relationships.

A **relationship strategy** is a well-thought-out plan for establishing, building, and maintaining quality relationships. This type of plan is essential for success in today's marketplace, which is characterized by vigorous competition, look-alike products, and customer loyalty dependent on quality relationships as well as quality products. The relationship strategy must encompass every aspect of selling, from the first contact with a prospect to servicing the sale once this prospect becomes an established customer. The relationship strategy is an integral dimension of **relationship selling**. Relationship selling is a form of personal selling that involves securing, developing, and maintaining long-term relationships with customers.[20] Increased support for relationship selling recognizes the growing importance of partnerships in selling. The primary goal of the relationship strategy is to create rapport, trust, and mutual respect, which ensures a long-term partnership. To establish this type of relationship, salespeople must *maintain high ethical standards, which form the very foundation for long-term partnerships*. They must project a professional image with a win-win philosophy and manage their relationships by adapting their communication style (see Fig. 3.2). Chapters 3, 4, and 5 provide important information on development of the relationship strategy.

relationship selling A form of personal selling that involves securing, developing, and maintaining long-term relationships.

Some people think that the concept of *relationships* is too soft and too emotional for a business application; these people think it's too difficult to think about relationships in strategic terms. In fact this is not the case at all. Every salesperson can and should formulate a strategic plan that builds and enhances relationships.

Developing a Product Strategy Products and services represent problem-solving tools. The **product strategy** is a plan that helps salespeople make correct decisions concerning the selection and positioning of products to meet identified customer needs. The three prescriptions for the product strategy are *become a product expert, sell benefits, and configure value-added solutions*. The development of a product strategy begins with a thorough study of one's product (see Fig. 2.3) using a feature–benefit analysis approach. Such product features as technical superiority, reliability, fashionableness, design integrity, or guaranteed availability should be converted to benefits that appeal to the customer. Today's high-performance salespeople strive to become product experts. Chapter 6 focuses on company, product, and competition knowledge needed by salespeople.

Product knowledge is not the only important element of a product strategy. In fact, salespeople who are too focused on selling products often fail to identify complete solutions to the customer's problem. Stephen Covey, author of the best-selling book *The 7 Habits of Highly Effective People*, says, "Diagnose before you prescribe." If the salesperson does not deeply engage the customer and fails to diagnose the problem correctly, chances are the solution recommended may not be the best one.[21]

The development of a product strategy often requires thoughtful decision making. Today's more knowledgeable customers seek a cluster of satisfactions that arise from the product itself, from the manufacturer or distributor of the product, and from the salesperson. The "new" product that customers are buying today is the sum total of the satisfactions that emerge from all three sources. The cluster of satisfactions concept is discussed in more detail in Chapter 7.

Developing a Customer Strategy Patricia Seybold, author of *The Customer Revolution*, says we are in the midst of a profound revolution—the customer revolution. And it's bigger than the Internet revolution:

> Customers have taken control of our companies' destinies. Customers are transforming our industries. And customers' loyalty—or lack thereof—has become increasingly important. . . .[22]

Customers have become increasingly sophisticated in their buying strategies. More and more, they have come to expect value-added products and services, and long-term commitments. Selling to today's customer starts with getting on the customer's agenda and carefully identifying his or her needs, wants, and buying conditions. Salespeople who have a better understanding of customer needs are better able to produce satisfied customers who are willing to pay more![23]

A **customer strategy** is a carefully conceived plan that will result in maximum responsiveness to the customer's needs. This strategy is based on the fact that success in personal selling depends, in no small measure, on the salesperson's ability to learn as much as possible about the prospect. It involves the collection and analysis of specific information on each customer. When developing a customer strategy, the salesperson should *develop an understanding of the customer's buying process, understand buyer behaviour,* and *develop a prospect base*. The first two parts of the customer strategy are introduced in Chapter 8. Suggestions concerning ways to develop a solid prospect base are discussed in Chapter 9.

The customer strategy is dictated by the needs of the customer. For example, it's best to consider relationship formation from the customer's perspective. When a *consultative* selling approach is required, the customer strategy will usually encompass a long-term

product strategy A well-conceived plan that emphasizes acquiring extensive product knowledge, learning to select and communicate appropriate product benefits that will appeal to the customer, and configuring value-added solutions.

customer strategy A carefully conceived plan that will result in maximum responsiveness to the customer's needs.

Patricia Seybold, CEO and founder of the Patricia Seybold Group, and best-selling author of *The Customer Revolution,* says we are in the midst of a profound revolution—the customer revolution.

Source: Patricia Seybold

Patricia Seybold

relationship and ongoing collaboration. If a *transactional* approach is required, the customer strategy would not, in most cases, emphasize need assessment, problem solving, relationship building, and sales follow-up.[24]

Developing a Presentation Strategy Typical salespeople spend about 30 percent of their time in actual face-to-face selling. However, the sales presentation is a critical part of the selling process. The **presentation strategy** is a well-developed plan that includes *preparing the sales presentation objectives, preparing a presentation plan that is needed to meet these objectives,* and *renewing one's commitment to provide outstanding customer service* (see Fig. 2.3).

The presentation strategy usually involves developing one or more objectives for each sales call. For example, a salesperson might update personal information about the customer, provide information on a new product, and close a sale during one sales call. Multiple-objective sales presentations, which are becoming more common, are discussed in Chapter 10. Presale presentation plans give salespeople the opportunity to consider those activities that take place during the sales presentation. For example, a salesperson might preplan a demonstration of product features to use when meeting with the customer. Presale planning ensures that salespeople are well organized during the sales presentation and prepared to offer outstanding service.

Interrelationship of Basic Strategies The major strategies that form the Strategic/Consultative Selling Model are by no means independent. The relationship, product, and customer strategies all influence development of the presentation strategy

presentation strategy
A well-developed plan that includes preparing the sales presentation objectives, preparing a presentation plan that is needed to meet these objectives, and renewing one's commitment to provide outstanding customer service.

Sales Success Paves the Way for Young Entrepreneur

At age 19, Rosado Shaw wanted to be a salesperson, but the company she worked for wouldn't let her sell. She had recently dropped out of college and taken a job with a company that makes umbrellas and tote bags. One day she took a sick day and called on the marketing staff at a museum of natural history. The result of this impromptu sales call was a $140 000 order. She then went to the president of the company and asked, "Are you going to let me sell now, or what?" After two years in sales, Shaw moved to a rival firm, Umbrellas Plus, and acquired more experience. She eventually purchased a controlling interest in the company and turned it into a $10 million enterprise.[c]

Deborah Rosado Shaw

(see Fig. 2.4). For example, a salesperson might develop one relationship-building tactic for use during the initial face-to-face meeting with the customer, and another for use during the negotiation of buyer resistance. Another relationship-building method might be developed for use after the sale is closed. The discovery of customer needs (part of the customer strategy) will greatly influence planning for the sales presentation.

Figure 2.4 The major strategies that form the Strategic/Consultative Selling Model are by no means independent of one another. The focus of each strategy is to satisfy customer needs and build quality partnerships.

EVOLUTION OF PARTNERING

"Partnering" became a buzzword in the 1990s, and in the 2000s it became a business reality.[25] Partnering has been driven by several economic forces. One is the demise of the product solution in several industries. When products of one company are nearly identical to those of the competition, the product strategy becomes less important than the relationship, customer, and presentation strategies. In contrast, some partnerships grow out of the need for customized products or services. Many manufacturers have formed partnerships with companies that offer flexibility in terms of product configuration, scheduling of deliveries, or some other factor.

Today's customer wants a quality product *and* a quality relationship. Salespeople willing to abandon short-term thinking and invest the time and energy needed to develop high-quality, long-term relationships with customers are greatly rewarded. A strong partnership serves as a barrier to competing salespeople who want to sell to your accounts. Salespeople who are able to build partnerships enjoy more repeat business and referrals. Keeping existing customers happy also makes a great deal of sense from an economic point of view: Experts in the field of sales and marketing know that it costs four to five times more to get a new customer than to keep an existing one. Therefore, even small increases in customer retention can result in major increases in profits.[26]

partnering A strategically developed, long-term relationship that solves the customer's problems.

Partnering is a strategically developed, long-term relationship that solves the customer's problems. A successful long-term partnership is achieved when the salesperson is able to skilfully apply the four major strategies and, thus, add value in various ways (Fig. 2.5). Successful sales professionals stay close to the customer and constantly search for new ways to add value.

The salespeople at Mackay Envelope Corporation achieve this goal by making sure they know more about their customers than the competitors know. Salespeople who work for Xerox Corporation are responding to a sales orientation that emphasizes

---

Selling in Action

From Peddling to Partnering

In the middle of the last century, the peddling style of selling was fairly simple. Memorize your script, open your sample case a certain way, fire back standard responses to predictable objections, and do it over and over again until the law of averages results in making your sales goals.

Today, though, the transactional aspects of sales are disappearing. Customers and prospects with access to the Internet have as much data as (and in some cases more than) salespeople themselves do. The skills that matter the most today are strategic consulting and partnering skills. These include the ability to help customers identify new disruptive problems along with solving

established ones. Often it includes selling insights rather than products.

For example, salespeople for Dentsply International, a global supplier of dental products and services, talk to dentists about hygienists' absences from work related to carpal tunnel syndrome and similar injuries. Then they demonstrate how Dentsply's lighter, cordless hygiene equipment may reduce wrist stress. Salespeople for Aramark used insights learned from serving one market to change the way prospective customers in other segments thought about managing their businesses.[d]

Figure 2.5 Partnering is a strategically developed, long-term relationship that solves the customer's problems. A successful partnering effort results in repeat sales and referrals that expand the prospect base. The strength of the partnership increases each time the salesperson uses value-added selling strategies.

postsale service. Bonuses are based on a formula that includes not only sales but also customer satisfaction.

Strategic Selling Alliances—The Highest Form of Partnering

Throughout the past decade we have seen the growth of a new form of partnership that often is described as a **strategic selling alliance**. The goal of strategic selling alliances is to achieve a marketplace advantage by teaming up with another company whose products or services fit well with your own.[27] A strategic selling alliance, also called strategic account management, is usually led by a *Strategic Account Manager*, (SAM). The SAM's job description is to execute an enterprise-wide sales strategy for growth, profitability, customer loyalty, and customer-driven innovation. A key element of strategic account management is involving senior level management on the sales and buying teams in relationship development, product configuration, and service after the sale. Technical sales-support personnel are also an important part of the strategic account management team.

In varying degrees of account management, additional titles are used to describe the process of aligning and partnering with today's customers and clients. As described in Chapter 1, the use of the title "account manager" has become commonplace in describing this process. For example:

- The *Regional Account Manager* (RAM) is a part of a larger sales team and acts as the direct client contact and manager of a number of business accounts. These accounts usually encompass a certain territory. For example, one who works in Canada may have all the accounts she manages based in Alberta.

strategic selling alliance Alliances that are achieved by teaming up with another company whose products or services fit well with your own.

- The *Key Account Manager* (KAM) is responsible for the coordination and management of a company's prioritized accounts. These accounts may be given special treatment due to their long-term growth potential, current volume of business, global presence, or strategic fit, among other factors. Brampton, Ontario-based TFI Food Equipment Solutions has three KAMs: one who services McDonald's and major convenience store and gas retail accounts (Avondale, 7/11, Esso), one who services major fast-food accounts (Tim Hortons, Wendy's, KFC, Burger King), and one who services supermarkets and other retail chain accounts (Loblaw Companies, Sobeys).[28]

- The *National Account Manager* (NAM) is responsible for recruiting and negotiating various business transactions and signing on new regional and national retailers. This person coordinates activities providing support to the channel, which includes market and account launches, key metrics, and communications with management in departments such as Operations, Field Sales, Marketing, and Supply Chain or Logistics.

- The *Global Account Manager* (GAM) is a key account manager who is specialized on a specific product portfolio and not on a given customer or geography. This person is housed in a specific business unit, yet he or she spans the globe. A GAM is often required to speak multiple languages and understand the intricacies of many different cultures.

These account manager positions are generally not considered entry-level sales positions. They represent senior sales positions in most firms, which entry-level salespeople aspire to attain by mastering the strategic/consultative selling skills presented in this book.

Corning, a maker of glass products, has formed partnerships with several companies that need innovative glass technology. For example, Corning formed an alliance with Samsung, a Korean manufacturer of television screens. RadioShack has formed strategic partnerships with several leading consumer electronics manufacturers. This move helped the company avoid the costs of starting new divisions.[29]

The first step in building a strategic account relationship is for the SAM to learn as much as possible about the proposed partner. This study takes place long before face-to-face contact. Alliances that are formed between companies that vary greatly in such areas as customer focus, financial stability, or ethical values will likely fail.[30] The second step is to meet with the proposed partner and explore mutual benefits of the alliance. At this point the strategic account manager or salesperson is selling advice, assistance, and counsel, not specific products. Building win-win alliances requires the highest form of consultative selling. Very often, the salesperson is working with a company team made up of persons from such areas as research and development (R&D), finance, and distribution. Presentations and proposals usually focus on profit impact and other strategic alliance benefits.[31] Due to the low-cost threat of emerging nations, many western-based companies have had to develop strategic account management. Its crucial importance will vastly continue to grow.[32]

Partnering Is Enhanced with High Ethical Standards

In the field of selling there are certain pressures that can influence the ethical conduct of salespeople, and poor ethical decisions can weaken or destroy partnerships.

To illustrate, let us assume a competitor makes exaggerated claims about a product. Do you counteract by promising more than your product can deliver? What action do you take when there is a time management problem and you must choose between servicing past sales and making new sales? What if a superior urges you to use a strategy that you consider unethical? These and other pressures must be dealt with every day.

Although Chapter 3 is devoted entirely to ethical considerations in personal selling, it should be noted that ethics is a major theme of this text as a whole, with the topic interwoven throughout several chapters. The authors believe that ethical decisions must be made every day in the life of a salesperson, so this important topic cannot be covered in a single chapter.

Partnering Is Enhanced with Customer Relationship Management

Many companies have adopted some form of customer relationship management. **Customer relationship management (CRM)**, sometimes referred to as *sales automation*, is the process of building and maintaining strong customer relationships by providing customer value.[33] A modern CRM program relies on a variety of technologies to improve communications in a sales organization and enhance customer responsiveness. A variety of CRM applications will be discussed throughout the text.

customer relationship management (CRM) The process of building and maintaining strong customer relationships by providing customer value.

VALUE CREATION—THE NEW SELLING IMPERATIVE

WE HAVE DEFINED VALUE-ADDED SELLING AS A SERIES OF CREATIVE IMPROVEMENTS within the sales process that enhance the customer experience. The *information economy* will reward those salespeople who have the skills, the knowledge, and the motivation to determine how to create value at every step of the sales process.

As Figure 2.6 shows, value creation begins with an understanding of the customer's value needs. Salespeople can create value in many ways: by establishing a relationship based on trust; by carefully identifying the customer's needs; and by identifying the best possible product solution. In the case of a complex sale, understanding the customer's value needs may take a great deal of time and may involve bringing in team members who have specific technical expertise.

Creating an appealing value proposition (Part 2) requires a detailed study of the customer's value needs. If you discover that timely delivery of your product is of critical importance, you must give the customer what they want. And if you promise on-time delivery, you must back up your claims.

Communicating the value proposition (Part 3) presents another major challenge. Traditional selling has too often emphasized communicating only the value that lies in the product. The focus of the sales call has too often been the product, not creating value for the customer.[34]

Delivering value (Part 4) can be very challenging. It may require coordination of credit approval, training, installation, service, and other aspects of the sale. Of course, each element of the selling process provides an opportunity to add value.

Figure 2.6 Creating and Delivering Customer Value Model
The salesperson's role in value creation is illustrated in this figure.

Source: Solomon, Michael R.; Marshall, Greg W.; Stuart, Elnora W., *Marketing: Real People, Real Choices,* 6th Ed., ©2009, p. 23. Reprinted and electronically reproduced by permission of Pearson Education, Inc. Upper Saddle River, New Jersey.

REVIEWING KEY CONCEPTS

- Discuss the evolution of personal selling models as an extension of the marketing concept.

  The *marketing concept* is the belief that a firm should dedicate all its policies, planning, and operations to the satisfaction of the customer. Salespeople today are problem solvers who obtain the participation of buyers in identifying their problems, which can then be translated into needs.

- Describe the evolution of consultative selling from the marketing era to the present.

  The *marketing era* that began in Canada in the 1950s looked first at customer needs and wants and then created goods and services to meet those needs and wants. *Consultative selling* emerged in the late 1960s and early 1970s as an approach that emphasizes the identification of customer needs through effective communication between the salesperson and customer. The evolution of selling continued with the development of *strategic selling* and *partnering*.

- Define *strategic selling* and name the four broad strategic areas in the Strategic/Consultative Selling Model.

  Strategic selling evolved in the 1980s and involves the preparation of a carefully conceived plan to accomplish sales objectives. Strategic selling is based on a company's *strategic market plan*, which takes into consideration the coordination of all the major functional areas of the business—production, marketing, finance, and personnel. The four broad strategic areas in the Strategic/Consultative Selling Model (after the development of a personal selling philosophy) are developing a relationship strategy, developing a product strategy, developing a customer strategy, and developing a presentation strategy.

- Describe the evolution of partnering and the nature of strategic account management.

    Partnering is a strategically developed, long-term relationship that solves the customer's problems. The long-term partnership is achieved when the salesperson is able to skilfully apply the four major strategies and therefore add value in various ways.

The *strategic selling alliance*, or, as it is sometimes called, *strategic account management*, is the highest form of partnering. Strategic account management is an enterprise-wide initiative seeking the development of strategic partnering relationships with a limited number of key customers and focused on achieving long-term, significant, and measurable business.

- Explain how value-added selling strategies enhance personal selling.

    Value-added selling has emerged as a major response to the customer economy. This approach to personal selling is defined as a series of creative improvements that enhance the customer's experience. The information economy rewards those salespeople who have the skills, the knowledge, and the motivation to determine how to create value at every step of the sales process.

Key Terms

adaptive selling **35**

consultative selling **33**

customer relationship management (CRM) **45**

customer strategy **39**

marketing concept **31**

marketing mix **32**

partnering **42**

presentation strategy **40**

product strategy **39**

relationship selling **38**

relationship strategy **38**

strategic planning **35**

strategic selling alliance **43**

strategies **35**

tactics **35**

transactional selling **34**

Review Questions

1. Why is peddling or "pushing products" inconsistent with the marketing concept?

2. Describe how new models of selling emerged in response to the marketing concept.

3. Describe the importance of personal selling as a part of the marketing concept.

4. What is consultative selling? Give examples.

5. Diagram and label the four-step Consultative Sales Presentation Guide.

6. List and briefly explain the four broad strategic areas that make up the selling process.

7. Briefly describe the evolution of partnering. Discuss the forces that contributed to this approach to selling.

8. Provide a brief description of value-added selling. What economic forces have motivated companies to adopt value-added selling?

9. Briefly explain why some organizations are developing strategic selling alliances.

10. Explain why the ethical conduct of salespeople has become so important.

Application Exercises

1. Assume that you are an experienced professional salesperson. A professor who teaches at a nearby university has asked you to speak to a consumer economics class about the benefits of personal selling. Make an outline of what you will say.

2. A friend of yours has invented a unique and useful new product. This friend, an engineer by profession, understands little about marketing and selling this new product. She does understand, however, that "nothing happens until somebody sells the product." She has asked you to describe the general factors that need to be considered when you market a product. Prepare an answer to her question.

3. When Brenda Fisher received her B.Ed., she thought she would like to teach. However, a pharmaceutical firm offered her a sales position that would require her to call on doctors and pharmacists to explain her firm's product line. Describe the similarities and differences between personal selling and teaching.

4. To learn more about industry-based, global sales training programs, access www.wilsonlearning.com. Click on the "Sales Effectiveness" link and examine the content of the various sales courses offered throughout the world by this company. From this review, describe the similarities between what this company offers and the material in this chapter.

5. One of the topics frequently debated among salespeople and sales managers is whether men or women are better suited to sales positions. Where do you stand on this issue? Find support for your position and then be prepared to defend your views in class.

ROLE-PLAY EXERCISE

The purpose of this role play is to provide you with an opportunity to engage in a basic need identification exercise. You will be meeting with someone (a class member) who is preparing for an important job interview and needs to buy a pen and/or pencil. Prior to the meeting, make a list of the questions you will ask. Then pair off with the class member and ask your questions. Be sure to take notes. At the end of the interview, be prepared to recommend the most appropriate pen and/or pencil.

Reality Selling Video Case Problem

At the beginning of this chapter, you were given an introduction to Marcus Smith, who is employed by Liberty Mutual, a successful insurance company. Smith is responsible for introducing a very large number of products and services and he must always keep one eye on the competition. He must be prepared to answer questions about his own products and services and those of the competition. He must also be prepared to discuss the intricacies of the insurance terms and possible bundles of insurance policies in order to offer his customers the best value.

Like every other professional salesperson, Smith is constantly involved in learning. We now know that the principles of selling can be learned and applied by people whose personal characteristics are quite different. Most successful salespeople spend considerable time acquiring product knowledge, keeping up to date

in their industry and related industries, and learning more about their customers. Smith acquired his formal training in professional selling from the Program in Excellence in Selling while he attended university. In the insurance industry, salespeople often go through industry-related training and a formal exam to acquire a license to sell personal and property insurance. Smith also undergoes Liberty Mutual's rigorous training program, which provides courses in four concentrations: products and services, company, competition, and quoting.

Smith realizes the importance of a relationship strategy that is built on a win-win philosophy. In addition to building a strong relationship with the customer, he must be able to work effectively with others who directly or indirectly influence the sale. He shares market information with his peers periodically because a broad view of the market as a whole is crucial in the highly competitive insurance industry. The salesperson who is honest, accountable, and sincerely concerned about the customer's welfare brings added value to the sales. (See chapter opener on page 29 and Reality Selling Today Role Play 2 in Appendix 1 on page 426 for more information.)

Questions

1. Does it appear that Smith has adopted the three prescriptions of a personal selling philosophy? (See Strategic/Consultative Selling Model.) Explain.

2. What prescriptions of the relationship strategy (see Strategic/Consultative Selling Model) have been adopted by Marcus Smith? Describe why a relationship strategy is especially important in personal selling.

3. Value-added selling is defined as a series of creative improvements in the sales process that enhance the customer's experience. Describe the various ways in which Marcus Smith can create value for his customers.

4. Why would it be important for the marketing support personnel (marketing research, product management, marketing communications, etc.) employed by Liberty Mutual to understand personal selling? Can you describe any marketing support people who would benefit from the acquisition of personal selling skills?

PART I
ROLE-PLAY EXERCISE
Developing a Personal Selling Philosophy

SCENARIO

You are currently working part-time at the Best Buy store located in Three Rivers Mall. You are a full-time student majoring in marketing at Red River College. The manager of your store wants you to identify potential customers on your campus and sell Dell laptop computers to those individuals who have a need for this product.

CUSTOMER PROFILE

Theresa Feng is a full-time commuter student who lives with her parents and shares the family's one computer with her mom. Each morning she drives about 32 kilometres to the campus and spends most of the day attending classes, working in the library, and visiting with friends. She currently spends about two hours each evening on the computer at home.

SALESPERSON PROFILE

You started working at the Best Buy store shortly after graduating from high school. The store manager was impressed with your computer expertise and your friendly manner. Although you are able to sell any type of computer, you tend to specialize in laptop computers, which are ideal for college students who have mobile computing needs. Your personal computer is a new Dell laptop, which replaced your desktop computer.

PRODUCT

You sell several different laptop computers that vary in price from $399 to $1099. Each laptop is equipped with specific, easily accessible ports to interact with a variety of external components. All of your laptops offer both productivity and entertainment applications. Services offered by Dell include helpful assistance via telephone or online tutorials at **www.support.dell.com**. Dell's warranty provides service and support to be handled by the Geek Squad (**www.geeksquad.ca**), which is located in the store.

INSTRUCTIONS

For this role play, you will meet with Theresa Feng, played by another student, and determine her interest in and need for a laptop computer. Prior to meeting with Theresa, preplan your relationship strategy, product strategy, customer strategy, and presentation strategy. Chapter 2 provides a description of each strategic area. Be prepared to close the sale if you feel that the customer will benefit from this purchase.

Sales success in the new economy requires us to think of ourselves as problem solvers/partners throughout the sales process.

Chapter 3
Ethics: The Foundation for Relationships That Create Value

Learning Objectives

After studying this chapter, you should be able to

1   Explain the importance of developing a relationship strategy.

2   Describe issues that challenge the ethical decision making of salespeople.

3   Describe the factors that influence the ethical conduct of sales personnel.

4   Describe how ethical decisions influence the building of partnering relationships in selling.

5   Discuss guidelines for developing a personal code of ethics that create value.

 Reality Selling Video—Edith Botello/Mattress Firm

Edith Botello started her career as a salesperson with Mattress Firm (**www.mattressfirm. com**), one of the world's largest and most successful retailers in the specialty bedding market. Edith is currently the assistant manager of one of the company's 560 stores. She is responsible for the sales productivity, maintenance, and merchandising of the store. Within her district, she is also an in-market trainer, recruiter, and intern coordinator.

Edith believes that qualifying (the term used by Mattress Firm to describe need identification) and listening are the most important skills to be a successful salesperson in her industry. Therefore, she really tries to understand why customers come to visit her and what will make them get a great night's sleep. People come into her store with a wide variety of needs: Their bed is 20 years old; they are upgrading to a different size; they are buying a college bed; they need a bed for a guest bedroom; their current bed has dips and sags; they are going in for surgery next week and would like to recover on a supportive mattress; and so forth. Accordingly, Edith's goal is to ask the right questions so that she can sell them a solution based on their individual needs. Mattress Firm has taught Edith techniques on how to sell to different types of people. Edith believes that the main

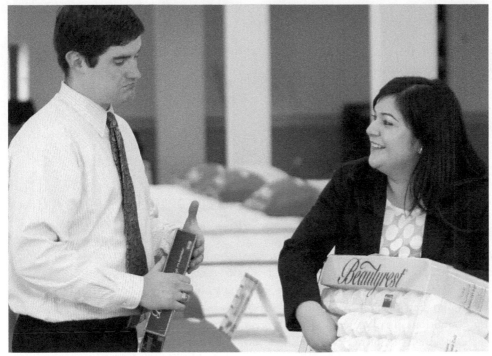

Edith Botello

reason many salespeople are successful is that they get their customers to believe in them by educating the customers and making them feel great about their purchase. Edith feels very fortunate to work for a company that values training and customer service.

Building relationships with customers is very important for Edith because people typically buy from salespeople they like and trust. One way she builds relationships is by getting to know her customers and talking to them about things that interest them. As Edith puts it, you cannot expect your customers to open up to you unless you kick things off by asking questions. Edith also makes use of testimonials to demonstrate how previous customers have resolved their needs with particular sleep products. Customers like to hear that their salesperson has experience dealing with, and finding solutions to, problems they are encountering.

DEVELOPING A RELATIONSHIP STRATEGY FOR PARTNERING-STYLE SELLING

DEVELOPING AND APPLYING THE WIDE RANGE OF INTERPERSONAL SKILLS NEEDED in today's complex sales environment can be challenging. Daniel Goleman, author of the bestselling books *Emotional Intelligence* and *Working with Emotional Intelligence*, notes that there are many forms of intelligence that influence our actions throughout life.

Emotional Intelligence

One of these, **emotional intelligence**, refers to the capacity for monitoring our own feelings and those of others, for motivating ourselves, and for managing emotions well in ourselves and in our relationships. People with a high level of emotional intelligence display

emotional intelligence The capacity for recognizing our own feelings and those of others, for motivating ourselves, and for managing emotions effectively in ourselves and our relationships.

Strategic Step

Develop a Personal Selling Philosophy

Develop a Relationship Strategy

Prescription

☑ Adopt Marketing Concept
☑ Value Personal Selling
☑ Become a Problem Solver/Partner

☐ Maintain High Ethical Standards
☐ Project Professional Image
☐ Manage the Relationship Process

Figure 3.1 Every salesperson should have an ongoing goal of developing a relationship strategy that adds value to the sale.

many of the qualities needed in sales work: self-confidence, trustworthiness, adaptability, initiative, optimism, empathy, and well developed social skills.[1]

Goleman and other researchers state that there are widespread exceptions to the rule that IQ predicts success. In the field of personal selling and most other business occupations, emotional intelligence is a much greater predictor of success.[2] The good news is that emotional intelligence can be enhanced with a variety of self-development activities, many of which are discussed in these chapters on developing a relationship strategy that results in partnering-style relationships that add value.

Information-age selling involves three major relationship challenges. The first major challenge is building new relationships. Salespeople who can quickly build rapport with new prospects have a much greater chance of achieving success in personal selling. The second major challenge is transforming relationships from the personal level to the business level. Once rapport is established, the salesperson is in a stronger position to begin the need identification process. The third major challenge is the management of relationships. Successful salespeople must manage many different relationships.[3] Salespeople must develop relationship management strategies that focus on many individuals and key groups.

In this chapter, we introduce the importance of maintaining high ethical standards as the very foundation to build long-term partnering-style relationships that create value. Chapter 4 focuses on a win-win philosophy and discusses the importance of projecting a professional image. Chapter 5, on adaptive selling, explains how an understanding of our own communication style and that of the customer can help us better manage a relationship process that adds value (see Fig. 3.1).

Issues Challenging the Ethics of Salespeople

In the field of personal selling, the temptation to maximize short-term gains by some type of unethical conduct is always present and occurs more often than in most other careers. Salespeople are especially vulnerable to unethical decision making because they are subject to many temptations. These temptations are often motivated by offers from clients, competitors, company personnel, and suppliers, and may involve personal gain on the part of the salesperson. While attractive to one or more of the stakeholders associated with the sale in the short run, they serve as the basis for the destruction of long-term relationship, product, customer, and presentation strategies. A few examples follow:

- A customer asks you to create a set of product specifications for completing a sales proposal. A new supplier of yours indicates a sizable direct cash payment would be made to you if you listed the supplier's technical data in the specifications. What would you do?

- You work with the research and development departments of the companies you call on, and therefore are trusted with confidential information about strategic new product development. One of your larger clients has asked if you could help them with a project by answering some questions about their competitor's research activities. How would you respond?

- Your competition, whom you know well, wants to meet with you to talk about a competitive bid you will be presenting. A suggestion is made that if you will bid this job a little higher than they do, they will definitely do you the same favour on the next purchase made by your customer. What should you do?

- You have visited the buyer twice, and each time the person displayed a great deal of interest in your proposal. During a recent negotiations meeting, the buyer hinted that the order might be signed if you could provide tickets to a national sporting event. Your company has a longstanding policy that gifts are not to be given under any circumstances. What do you do?

- The competition is using exaggerated claims to close the sale of its product. Should you counteract this action by using exaggerated claims of your own to build a stronger case for your product?

- A lucrative proposal you are scheduled to make will provide only a mediocre solution to your client's problem. Your client trusts you, and you know there are better solutions that are being provided by the competition that you cannot match. What would you do?

- Your sales manager is under great pressure to increase sales. At a recent meeting of the entire sales staff, this person said, "We have to hit our numbers no matter what it takes!" Does this emotional appeal change your way of dealing with customers?

- During a recent business trip, you met an old friend and decided to have dinner together. At the end of the meal, you paid for the entire bill and left a generous tip. Do you now put these nonbusiness-related expenses on your expense account?

These ethical dilemmas arise in the field of selling. How do salespeople respond? Some ignore company policy; disregard municipal, provincial, federal, and international laws; cast aside personal values and standards of conduct; and yield to the pressure. Yielding to this pressure often destroys long-term partnering relationships, and can result in fines, monetary damages, and, in some cases, prison time.

However, a large number of trusted salespersons are able to resist. They can be counted on by the various stakeholders to a sale to form highly ethical win-win relationships, fully understand the customers' buying strategies, make honest non-exaggerated claims about their product, and fully embrace a needs-based consultative presentation strategy. Therefore, in the partnering-style seller/buyer relationship, a high level of ethical decision making becomes the foundation for creating value (see Fig. 3.2).

Figure 3.2 Ethical decision making is the foundation for partnering-style relationship, product, customer, and presentation strategies.

FACTORS INFLUENCING ETHICAL DECISION MAKING OF SALESPEOPLE

A NUMBER OF IMPORTANT FACTORS INFLUENCE ETHICAL DECISION MAKING. THESE factors help sales and marketing personnel to distinguish right from wrong. Figure 3.3 outlines the forces that can help salespeople deal honestly and openly with prospects at all times.

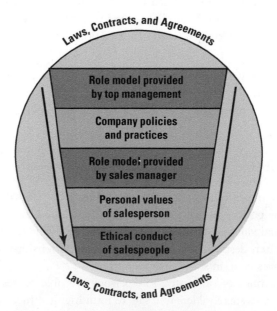

Figure 3.3 Factors Influencing the Ethical Behaviour of Salespeople
In personal selling, the temptation to maximize short-term gains by some type of unethical conduct is always present. The forces in this figure can help salespeople deal honestly and openly with prospects at all times.

Influences in a Global Economy

Ethical and legal issues that are quite complex on the domestic scene become even more complicated at the international level. International business is growing, and Canada is deeply involved in the global marketplace. Thomas Friedman, author of the best-selling book *The World Is Flat: A Brief History of the Twenty-First Century*, says today's highly competitive and global marketplace is flattening the world of international business. In order to compete with China, India, and other dynamic economics, Canadian-based companies must adopt a more aggressive global focus.[4]

Cultural Issues Today's global marketplace reflects a kaleidoscope of cultures, each with its own unique qualities. **Culture** is the sum total of beliefs, values, knowledge, ethnic customs, and objects that people use to adapt to their environment. Cultural barriers can impede acceptance of products in foreign countries and weaken interpersonal relationships. When the salesperson understands the cultural background of the foreign customer, communication problems are less likely. Many people from Asia, Arab countries, and much of Africa prefer a more indirect style of communication and therefore value harmony, subtlety, sensitivity, and tact more than brevity.[5] The customer who seems to be agreeing with everything you say may have no intention of buying your product. This person may simply be displaying polite and tactful behaviours.

Perceptions of time differ from country to country. Canadians value promptness, but businesspeople from other countries often approach meetings in a more relaxed manner. Arriving late for a meeting may not be viewed as a problem. Many companies are spending thousands of dollars to make sure that employees sent abroad are culturally prepared. Eastman Chemical Company, for example, has developed a highly successful orientation program for employees who have accepted overseas assignments.[6]

culture The sum total of beliefs, values, knowledge, ethnic customs, and objects that people use to adapt to their environment.

Legal Issues Doing business in the global marketplace continues to be an ethical minefield. Illegal demands for bribes, kickbacks, or special fees may stand in the way of successful transactions. The Canadian and U.S. governments have enacted legislation that prohibits our companies from using bribes or kickbacks to influence foreign officials. The new U.K. Anti-Bribery Act prohibits any kind of commercial bribery. Prosecution is aggressive and penalties are severe, ranging from multimillion-dollar fines for companies and jail time for individuals. But monitoring illegal activities throughout the world is a very difficult task.[7] Motorola, for example, is using software to analyze invoices and payments in order to uncover possible payoffs. Gifts from suppliers to Canadian and U.S. companies can also be a problem. Each year, United Technologies sends a letter to foreign suppliers saying "we don't want gifts."[8]

Canadian and U.S. businesses acknowledge that it is difficult to compete with organizations from other countries that are not bound by these laws. However, the International Business Ethics Institute (**www.business-ethics.org**) believes that our companies have been a very positive role model for the rest of the business world.

Influence of Sales Management Ethical standards tend to filter down from the top of an organization. Employees look to company leaders for guidance. The organization's moral tone, as established by management personnel, is the most important single determinant of employee ethics. Richard Schulze, Best Buy founder and chairman, is the

The most influential ethics spokesman at Timberland is CEO Jeffrey Swartz, a third-generation CEO whose grandfather founded the company. With pride, he points out Timberland's slogan: "Boots, Brand, Belief."

ZUMA Press, Inc./Alamy

person who must put ethics concerns on the front burner and make sure that employees stay focused on that priority. The most influential ethics spokesman at Timberland is CEO Jeffrey Swartz, a third-generation CEO whose grandfather founded the company. With pride, he points out Timberland's slogan: "Boots, Brand, Belief."[9]

In recent years, top management has often been guided by advice from professional service firms such as McKinsey & Company, Merrill Lynch and Company, and Arthur Andersen. Too often these firms are recommending strategies that result in quick, short-term gains. Alan M. Webber, who has been studying professional service firms for

Are you an active social networker? A recent study was conducted by the Ethics Resource Center that provided some important results with implications for salespeople. Do you spend more than 30 percent of your time on social network sites? Then be careful, since a recent study has shown that active social networkers see many of those activities that other people find unethical as acceptable behaviours. For example, this study found that 59 percent of active social networkers believed that "friending" a client/customer on a social network is acceptable, while only 28 percent of other workers saw it as an acceptable behaviour. Forty-two percent of active social networkers believed that tweeting or blogging negatively about your company or colleagues is also acceptable, while only 6 percent of others believed so. This divide between

active social networkers and others is crucial because if your client is from the other group, then what you think is acceptable, such as "friending" your customer on Facebook, might come across to your client as unprofessional.[a]

Another extremely important aspect of today's social media comes from the fact that what you post on these media can quickly go viral. For example, tweeting about how you used your sales savvy to close a deal can easily spread and reach your customer/other customers and project the wrong image of you and your company as people with self-interest and little customer focus. Companies these days are very cautious about the kind of messages that spread out from the inside and make sure that everything is consistent with their overall corporate image.

20 years, notes, "They want the money right now." He says, "[T]o make the most money, you actually have to believe in the product or service you offer and care for the customers or clients whom you serve."[10]

Influence of Company Policies and Practices

Company policies and practices can have a major impact on the ethical conduct of salespeople. Al Rosen, who taught accounting at York University for 30 years, says that once you are hired, you become a product of your company, and its ethics drift through you. He says, "People are telling you to forget this and that—it becomes a birds-of-a-feather atmosphere."[11] Many employees do not have well developed moral sensitivity and, therefore, need the guidance of ethics policies. These policies should cover distributor relations, customer service, pricing, product development, and related areas.[12]

Developing policy statements forces a firm to "take a stand" on various business practices. Distinguishing right from wrong can be a healthy activity for any organization. The outcome is a clearer philosophy of how to conduct business transactions. Furthermore, the efforts of salespeople can be compromised by the unethical actions of their companies. Selling products for a company that condones unethical practices is very difficult for the salesperson who maintains high ethical standards.[13]

Sun Life Financial—headquartered in Toronto, with offices in 22 countries serving millions of customers—provides its employees with a carefully worded document titled "Code of Business Conduct." Employees must affirm annually their commitment to these values. Several of these values form the foundation for a corporate culture that encourages ethical behaviour:[14]

- **Integrity** We are committed to the highest standards of business ethics and good governance.

Global Business Insight

Doing Business in China

China has entered the World Trade Organization, and its leaders have promised to tear down the barriers that have frustrated foreign business representatives for so long. This country provides a huge market for foreign brands. However, doing business in China begins with a careful study of Chinese business customs.

- Patience is critical when doing business in China. Avoid taking the initiative until you fully understand the rules.

- Business entertaining is frequently done banquet style. If you host a banquet, plan your menu carefully because foods have different meanings. You will be in complete control and no one will eat or drink until you give the signal. Toasting is a ritual in China.

- Chinese businesspeople do not make deals quickly. They prefer to spend time building relationships that will last for years. Harmony is important.

- When making introductions, the oldest and highest-ranking person is introduced first. Chinese bow slightly when greeting another person and the handshake follows.

- Gift giving is a complex process in China. Gifts should be given after all business transactions have been completed. Avoid gifts that suggest death in the Chinese culture: clocks, knife openers, and handkerchiefs, for example.[b]

- **Customer Focus** We provide sound financial solutions for our customers and always work with their interests in mind.
- **Value** We deliver value to the customers and shareholders we serve and to the communities in which we operate.

Most marketing companies provide salespeople with guidelines in such areas as sharing confidential information, reciprocity, bribery, gift giving, entertainment, and business defamation.

Sharing Confidential Information

Personal selling, by its very nature, promotes close working relationships. Customers often turn to salespeople for advice. They disclose confidential information freely to someone they trust. It is important that salespeople preserve the confidentiality of information they receive.

It is not unusual for a customer to disclose information that may be of great value to a competitor. This might include development of new products, plans to expand into new markets, or anticipated changes in personnel. A salesperson may be tempted to share confidential information with a representative of a competing firm. This breach of confidence might be seen as a means of gaining favour. In most cases this action will backfire. The person who receives the confidential information will quickly lose respect for the salesperson. A gossipy salesperson will seldom develop a trusting relationship with a customer.

reciprocity A mutual exchange of benefits, as when a firm buys products from its own customers.

Reciprocity

Reciprocity is a mutual exchange of benefits, as when a firm buys products from its own customers. Some business firms actually maintain a policy of reciprocity. For example, a manufacturer of commercial sheets and blankets may purchase hotel services from firms that use its products. Is there anything wrong with the "you scratch my back and I'll scratch yours" approach to doing business? The answer is sometimes yes. In some cases, the use of reciprocity borders on commercial blackmail. Salespeople have been known to approach firms that supply their company and encourage them to buy out of obligation. The firm may be forced to buy products of questionable quality at excessive prices. A business relationship based on reciprocity often has drawbacks, such as the ever-present temptation to take reciprocal customers for granted. A customer who buys out of obligation may take a back seat to customers who were won in the open market.

Personal selling, by its nature, promotes close working relationships. It is important that salespeople preserve the confidentiality of information they receive. Violation of this ethical responsibility will quickly erode a relationship with the customer.

Jeanette Dietl/Fotolia

Bribery The book *Arrogance and Accords: The Inside Story of the Honda Scandal* describes one of the largest commercial corruption cases in North American history. Over a 15-year period, Honda officials received more than US$50 million in cash and gifts from dealers anxious to obtain fast-selling Honda cars and profitable franchises. When the bribery became public, 18 former Honda executives were convicted of obtaining kickbacks; most went to prison.[15] In some cases, a bribe is wrong from a legal standpoint. In almost all cases, the bribe is wrong from an ethical point of view. However, bribery does exist, and a salesperson must be prepared to cope with it. It helps to have a well-established company policy to use as a reference point for what is not acceptable.[16]

Salespeople who sell products in foreign markets need to know that giving bribes is viewed as an acceptable business practice in some cultures. However, bribes or pay-offs may violate federal government legislation. Canada has the *Corruption of Foreign Public Officials Act*, and for Canadian salespeople who work for U.S. companies, the *U.S. Foreign Corrupt Practices Act* (FCPA) may also be relevant. Lucent Technologies dismissed two high-ranking executives in China after it found potential violations of the FCPA.[17]

Gift Giving Gift giving is a common practice in Canada. However, some companies do maintain a "no gift" policy. Many companies report that their policy is either no gifts or nothing of real value. Some gifts, such as advertising novelties, planning calendars, or a meal, are of limited value and cannot be construed as a bribe or payoff.

There are some grey areas that separate a gift from a bribe. Most people agree that a token of insignificant value, such as a pen imprinted with a company logo, is an appropriate way to foster goodwill. A bribe, on the other hand, is an attempt to influence the person who is receiving the gift.

Are there right and wrong ways to handle gift giving? The answer is yes. The following guidelines will be helpful to any salesperson who is considering giving gifts to customers:

1. Do not give gifts before doing business with a customer. Do not use the gift as a substitute for effective selling methods.

2. Never convey the impression you are "buying" the customer's business with gifts. When this happens, the gift becomes nothing more than a bribe.

3. When gift giving is done correctly, the customer will clearly view it as symbolic of your appreciation—a "no strings attached" goodwill gesture.

4. Be sure the gift is not a violation of the policies of your firm or of your customer's firm. Some companies will not allow employees to accept gifts at all; others place a dollar limit on a gift's value.

In summary, if you have second thoughts about giving a gift, do not do it. When you are sure some token is appropriate, keep it simple and thoughtful.

Entertainment Entertainment is a widespread practice in the field of selling but may be viewed by some people as a bribe. The line dividing gifts and entertainment from bribes is often quite arbitrary. Salespeople must frequently decide how to handle entertaining. A few industries see entertainment as part of the approach used to obtain new accounts. This is especially true when competing products are nearly identical. A good example is the cardboard box industry. These products vary little in price and quality. Winning an account may involve knowing who to entertain and how to entertain.

Entertainment is a highly individualized process. One customer might enjoy a professional football game while another might be impressed most by a quiet meal at a good restaurant. The key is to get to know your customer's preferences. How does the person spend leisure time? How much time can the person spare for entertainment? You will need to answer these and other questions before you invest time and money in entertainment.

Business Defamation Salespeople frequently compare their product's qualities and characteristics with those of a competitor during the sales presentation. If such comparisons are inaccurate, are misleading, or slander a company's business reputation, such conduct is illegal. Competitors have sued hundreds of companies and manufacturer's representatives for making slanderous statements while selling.

What constitutes business defamation? Steven M. Sack, co-author of *The Salesperson's Legal Guide*, provides the following examples:

1. *Business slander.* This arises when an unfair and untrue oral statement is made about a competitor. The statement becomes actionable when it is communicated to a third party and can be interpreted as damaging the competitor's business reputation or the personal reputation of an individual in that business.

2. *Business libel.* This may be incurred when an unfair and untrue statement is made about a competitor in writing. The statement becomes actionable when it is communicated to a third party and can be interpreted as damaging the company.

3. *Product disparagement.* This occurs when false or deceptive comparisons or distorted claims are made concerning a competitor's product, services, or property.[18]

Use of the Internet Use of the Internet offers salespeople many advantages, but it can also create a number of ethical dilemmas. For example, email abuse has become a modern-day problem because some employees forget that their employer owns the email system. Email messages that contain inflammatory or abusive content, embarrassing gossip, or breaches of confidentiality can lead to legal liabilities. A growing number of companies are developing policies that define permissible uses of their email system.[19]

Some resourceful salespeople have created their own websites to alert, attract, or support clients. The rise of these "extranets" has created some problems because they often function outside of the company's jurisdiction. What should top management do if a salesperson encourages her customers to participate in a special web auction for a backlogged product? What if the salesperson makes exaggerated claims about a new product? Every marketing firm needs to carefully monitor the development and use of extranets.[20]

The effectiveness of company policies as a deterrent to unethical behaviour depends on two factors. The first is the firm's attitude toward employees who violate these policies. If violations are routinely ignored, the policy's effect soon erodes. Second, policies that influence personal selling need the support of the entire sales staff. Salespeople should have some voice in policy decisions; they are more apt to support policies they have helped develop.

Ethical and Legal Issues with Recording CRM Data

Customer relationship management systems enable you to collect information about people with whom you maintain relationships, including the taking of notes. It is a good practice to record more than basic transaction information, such as personal details about your customers. Reviewing your observations about the customers' behaviour and your recording of their statements can help you understand them and their needs. Re-reading their comments about ethical issues can assist you in assessing the value of maintaining a business relationship with them.

To be fair, it is important to record only the facts concerning your observations, not necessarily your conclusions, especially if negative. Information in an electronic database can last a long time and, for reasons such as litigation or company acquisitions, can be "mobile." This means that others may form an opinion about your customer based on your recorded conclusions, with potential detrimental consequences for your customer. Because the customer may not be aware of the existence of the information in your database, that person does not have a fair opportunity to correct any erroneous conclusions. Another reason to carefully record only the facts is the possibility that any inappropriate information may come to the attention of the customer. For example, there are reported instances in which a customer later joined the sales organization and gained access to the customer relationship management (CRM) system.

Most CRM systems contain scheduling functions, which means that you can set aside time on your calendar to attend meetings, make phone calls, and perform tasks. The scheduling tools usually include alarms, which remind you that a deadline is approaching. The disciplined use of these features can help you get your work accomplished on time. Taking advantage of the system's reminder tools can be especially important when it involves fulfilling your commitments. The system can help you build trust by reminding you to always do what you said you would do.

Influence of the Sales Manager

The salesperson's actions often mirror the sales manager's behaviour and expectations. This is not surprising when you consider the relationship between salespeople and their supervisors. They look to their supervisors for guidance and direction. The sales manager is generally the company's closest point of contact with the sales staff. This person is usually viewed as the chief spokesperson for top management.

Sales managers generally provide new salespeople with their first orientation to company operations. They are responsible for interpreting company policy. On a continuing basis the sales manager monitors the salesperson's work and provides important feedback regarding conduct. If a salesperson violates company policy, it is usually the sales manager who is responsible for administering reprimands. If the moral fibre of a sales force begins to break down, the sales manager must shoulder a great deal of responsibility, even if it goes against "standard practice."[21]

Sales managers influence the ethical behaviour of salespeople by virtue of what they say and what they do. From time to time, managers must review their expectations of ethical behaviour. Salespeople are under continual pressure to abandon their personal ethical standards to achieve sales goals. Values such as integrity and honesty must receive ongoing support from the sales manager. The role of the sales manager will be discussed in more detail in Chapter 17.

Influence of the Salesperson's Personal Values

Ann Kilpatrick, a sales representative in the transportation industry, encountered something unexpected when entertaining a potential client. The client said, "Let's go to

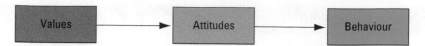

Figure 3.4 The Relationship of Values, Attitudes, and Behaviour
Values represent the ultimate reasons salespeople have for acting as they do. Values serve as a foundation for either constructive or destructive attitudes, and these attitudes serve as a foundation for ethical or unethical behaviour.

Johnny's." She was not familiar with Johnny's but, on arrival, discovered it was a raunchy bar. Kilpatrick related that she sat there for five minutes and then said, "This is not what I was expecting. This is a sleazy place. Let's go somewhere else where we can talk." She was not willing to compromise her personal values to win a new account.[22]

values Your deep personal beliefs and preferences that influence your behaviour.

Values represent the ultimate reasons people have for acting as they do. **Values** are your deep personal beliefs and preferences that influence your behaviour. To discover what really motivates you, carefully examine what it is you value.[23] Values serve as a foundation for our attitudes, and our attitudes serve as a foundation for our behaviour (see Fig. 3.4). Destructive attitudes can result in unethical behaviours, whereas constructive attitudes generally create ethical behaviours. We do not adopt or discard values quickly. In fact, the development of values is a lifelong process.

Customers have a very negative view of salespeople who lack integrity. Yet the temptation to lie about a product's features or benefits grows when you are trying to meet sales quotas. Pharmacist John Craig describes a meeting with a pushy sales representative employed by a pharmaceutical company. The salesperson emphasized the wonders of a powerful, expensive painkiller but failed to describe its side effects. Craig said, "He was very pushy at the beginning," and this behaviour revealed a character flaw.[24]

Values Conflict Values help us establish our own personal standards concerning what is right and what is wrong. Ron Willingham, author of *Integrity Selling for the 21st Century*, says, "Selling success is more an issue of who you are than what you know."[25] A salesperson's ethics and values contribute more to sales success than do techniques or strategies. Some salespeople discover a values conflict between themselves and their employer. If you view your employer's instructions or influence as improper, you have three choices:

1. Ignore the influence of your values and engage in unethical behaviour. However, even with success, inattention to values will result in a loss of self-respect, feelings of guilt, and in some circumstances legal liability.[26] When salespeople experience conflicts between their actions and values, they also feel a loss of confidence and energy.[27] Positive energy is the result of creating value for the customer. Negative energy emerges when salespeople fail to honour and embrace their ethical values.

2. Voice strong opposition to the practice that is in conflict with your value system. Take a stand and state your beliefs. When ethical infractions occur, it's best to bring them up internally and try to influence decisions made by your peers or superiors. In some cases, doing the right thing may not be popular with others. Price Pritchett, author of *The Ethics of Excellence*, says, "Not everybody will be on your side in your struggle to do the right thing."[28] However, more and more companies are celebrating employees who come forward to identify questionable conduct.

3. Refuse to compromise your values and be prepared to deal with the consequences. This may mean leaving the job. It may also mean that you will be fired.

Salespeople face ethical problems and decisions every day. In this respect they are no different from doctors, lawyers, teachers, or any other professional. Ideally, they will make decisions on the basis of the values they hold.[29]

Influence of Laws, Contracts, and Agreements

Take another look at Figure 3.3 (page 54) and notice that all of the key elements, personnel, and policies are influenced by laws, contracts, and agreements. Everyone involved in sales and marketing is guided by legal as well as ethical standards. We live in a society in which the legal system plays a key role in preventing people from engaging in unethical behaviour.

Laws The specific obligations imposed by government on the way a business operates take the form of statutes. In Canada, it is necessary for salespeople not only to know federal statutes but also to recognize that there are many provincial and territorial statutes, and that important differences exist between provinces and territories. The *Competition Act* is the major federal legislation in Canada that defines illegal practices, including price fixing, bid rigging, price discrimination, predatory pricing, double ticketing, resale price maintenance, bait and switch selling, and pyramid selling.

All Canadian provinces and territories have passed legislation that establishes a cooling-off period during which the consumer may void a contract to purchase goods or services. While the provisions of **cooling-off laws** vary from jurisdiction to jurisdiction, their primary purpose is to give customers an opportunity to reconsider a buying decision made under a salesperson's persuasive influence. In most jurisdictions, this legislation is referred to as either *The Direct Sellers Act* or *The Consumer Protection Act*.

> **cooling-off laws** Provincial and territorial laws that give customers an opportunity to reconsider a buying decision made under a salesperson's persuasive influence.

Contracts and Agreements The word *contract* may bring to mind the familiar multipage, single-spaced documents that few people seem able to understand. A **contract** is simply a promise or promises that the courts will enforce. Oral contracts are enforceable, but written contracts are preferable, as they reduce the possibility of disagreement; courts give written contracts great weight in a lawsuit. A written contract can consist of a sales slip, a notation on a cheque, or any other writing that offers evidence of the promises that the parties made.[30]

> **contract** An oral or written promise enforceable by law.

Salespeople are sometimes the legal representatives of their company and, therefore, must be careful when signing written contracts. They often oversee contracts with customers, suppliers, and resellers. A salesperson may be asked to sign an employment contract at the time he or she is hired. Most of these agreements include a noncompete clause. One of the most common clauses, a noncompete clause, prohibits salespeople from joining a competing firm for a year after they leave. Most clauses are legally binding even when an employee's position is cut. Employers see employment contracts as an effective way to protect intellectual property, customer lists, and other resources an employee might take to a competing firm.[31]

Many companies are learning that resolving legal disputes can be very costly and time-consuming. Resolving a dispute in the courts can sometimes take several years. A serious effort to prevent unethical activities can prevent costly litigation.

BUILDING TRUST WITH THE TRANSACTIONAL, CONSULTATIVE, AND STRATEGIC ALLIANCE BUYER

EVERYONE INVOLVED IN PERSONAL SELLING MUST WORK HARD TO BUILD RELATIONSHIPS based on trust. Customers are more apt to trust salespeople they believe to be ethical, leading to a much more productive partnership.[32] Although trust is an essential element of every sale, the meaning of trust changes with the type of sale.[33]

- *Trust in transactional sales*. The primary customer focus in this type of sale is trust in the product. Is the product reliable? Is the product priced as low as possible? Can the product be delivered in a timely fashion? The transactional buyer may purchase a product from a salesperson he or she does not feel totally comfortable with if it meets their purchase criteria.

- *Trust in consultative sales*. In a consultative sale, the customer focus shifts from the product to the person who sells the product. The consultative buyer is thinking, "Can I trust this salesperson to identify my problem and offer me one or more solutions?" Customers involved in a consultative sale usually do not separate the product from the person selling it. They want to do business with a salesperson who displays such positive qualities as warmth, empathy, genuineness, competence, and integrity.

- *Trust in strategic alliance sales*. The strategic alliance buyer wants to do business with an institution that can be trusted. This buyer looks beyond the well-qualified salesperson and assesses the entire organization. A strategic alliance customer will not feel comfortable partnering with a company whose values differ greatly from his or her own. Ethical accountability will greatly influence the way an alliance partner is judged and valued.

Trust exists when we strongly believe in the integrity, ability, and character of a person or an organization. Although trust is an intangible, it is at the very core of all meaningful relationships. Trust is slowly won, but can be quickly lost.[34]

Making Ethical Decisions That Build Selling Relationships

business ethics Principles and standards that guide behaviour in the world of business. They help translate your values into appropriate and effective behaviours in your day-to-day life.

Business ethics comprise principles and standards that guide behaviour in the world of business. They help translate your values into appropriate and effective behaviours in your day-to-day life. Whether a specific behaviour is right or wrong, ethical or unethical, is often determined by company leaders, customers, investors, the legal system, and the community.[35] Of course, the views of various stakeholders may be in conflict. Kickbacks and secret payoffs may be acceptable practices to the vice president of sales and marketing, yet may be viewed as unethical by members of the sales force, the board of directors, investors, and the general public.

There is no one uniform code of ethics for all salespeople as societal and relational norms can vary from person to person.[36] However, numerous business organizations, professional associations, and certification agencies have established written codes. The Canadian Professional Sales Association (CPSA), introduced in Chapter 1, requires all persons seeking to become a Certified Sales Professional to agree to abide to the CPSA Sales Institute Code of Ethics (see Fig. 3.5).

The CPSA Sales Institute Code of Ethics is the set of principles and standards that a certified sales professional will strive to adhere to with customers, organizations, competitors, communities and colleagues.

The Certified Sales Professional pledges and commits to uphold these standards in all activities.

I will:

1. Maintain honesty and integrity in all relationships with customers, prospective customers, and colleagues and continually work to earn their trust and respect.
2. Accurately represent my products or services to the best of my ability in a manner that places my customer or prospective customer and my company in a position that benefits both.
3. Respect and protect the proprietary and confidential information entrusted to me by my company and my customers and not engage in activities that may conflict with the best interests of my customers or my company.
4. Continually upgrade my knowledge of my products/services, skills and my industry.
5. Use the time and resources available to me only for legitimate business purposes. I will only participate in activities that are ethical and legal, and when in doubt, I will seek counsel.
6. Respect my competitors and their products and services by representing them in a manner which is honest, truthful and based on accurate information that has been substantiated.
7. Endeavour to engage in business and selling practices which contribute to a positive relationship with the community.
8. Assist and counsel my fellow sales professionals where possible in the performance of their duties.
9. Abide by and encourage others to adhere to this Code of Ethics.

As a certified sales professional, I understand that the reputation and professionalism of all salespeople depends on me as well as others engaged in the sales profession, and I will adhere to these standards to strengthen the reputation and integrity for which we all strive. I understand that failure to consistently act according to this Code of Ethics may result in the loss of the privilege of using my professional sales designation.

Figure 3.5 The CPSA Sales Institute Code of Ethics

Source: www.cpsa.com/institute.html. Used by permission.

With over 140 years of experience and over 12,000+ trained, the CPSA is proud to support sales professionals as they pursue sales as a respected career of choice. The CPSA Sales Institute Code of Ethics can be found online at: www.cpsa.com/csp/cspProcess/cspCodeofEthics.aspx

Influence of Character in Ethical Decision Making

character Your personal standards of behaviour, including honesty, integrity, and moral strength. Your character is based on your internal values and the resulting judgments you make about what is right and what is wrong.

integrity Part of your character; what you have when your behaviour is in accordance with your professed standards and personal code of moral values.

Today, we recognize that character and integrity strongly influence relationships in personal selling. **Character** is composed of personal standards, including honesty, integrity, and moral strength. Your character is based on your internal values and the resulting judgments you make about what is right and what is wrong. The ethical decisions you make reflect your character strength. It is a quality that is highly respected in the field of personal selling. **Integrity** is the basic ingredient of character that is exhibited when you achieve congruence between what you know, what you say, and what you do.[37] Toronto-based clinical psychologist Barbara Killinger says, "Integrity is built one small step at a time, yet it can slip away seemingly overnight."[38] In a world of uncertainty and rapid change, integrity has become a valuable character trait. Salespeople with integrity can be trusted to do what they say they will do. One way to achieve trustworthiness in personal selling is to refrain from deceiving or misleading the customer.

We are indebted to Stephen Covey, author of *The 7 Habits of Highly Effective People*, for helping us to better understand the relationship between character strength and success in personal selling. In his bestselling book, Stephen Covey says there are basic principles that must be integrated into our character. One example is to always do what you say you are going to do. "As we make and keep commitments, even small commitments, we begin to establish an inner integrity that gives us the awareness of self-control and courage and strength to accept more of the responsibility for our own lives."[39] Fulfilling your commitments builds trust, and trust is the most important precondition of partnering relationships that create value.

Colleges and universities are beginning to play a more active role in character development. Courses that focus on business ethics are becoming increasingly common and, in many business programs, at least one such course is required. Some programs prefer to include ethics as an important component of several courses. The purpose of including ethics is not simply to point out what is right and what is wrong behaviour. It is more important to ensure students can recognize ethical situations, have a framework to assess possible actions they might take, and recognize that their decisions have real consequences for both themselves and for others.

The Erosion of Character on Ethical Decision Making

Despite growing interest in business ethics, unethical behaviour has become all too common. A survey conducted by *Newsweek* suggests that the current generation of workers may be more tolerant of deception. Many of those involved in the survey did not view lying and cheating as unacceptable.[40] Employees who are involved in unethical behaviour often report that they were under pressure to act unethically or illegally on the job.

As the past decade unfolded, many large inflexible corporations were transformed into smaller, more nimble competitors. New economy thinking prevailed as business firms, large and small, worked hard to become lean, innovative, and profitable. We witnessed an almost unrelenting emphasis on earnings that was driven, in many cases, by executive greed. During this period, some of the most respected companies began to cross the ethical divide.[41]

A company cannot enjoy long-term success unless its employees are honest, ethical, and uncompromising about values and principles. Yet many employees engage in dishonest practices that erode character. The collapse of Lehman Brothers, one of the largest U.S. corporations, can be traced to a culture that emphasized risk-taking, personal ambition over teamwork, and earnings growth at any cost. The new economy depends on innovation and aggressive development of markets, but actions that weaken the moral contract with employees, customers, and shareholders can have serious consequences. Let's examine some "half-truths" that have influenced the erosion of character in ethical decision making.

- *We are only in it for ourselves.* Some critics of today's moral climate feel that the current moral decline began when society's focus shifted from "what is right" to "what is right for me." In personal selling, this point of view can quickly subtract from rather than add value to a customer relationship. Fortunately, there are many salespeople for whom integrity and self-respect are basic values. Darryl Ashley, a pharmaceutical representative for Eli Lilly Company, suspected that a pharmacist (a customer) was diluting chemotherapy drugs in order to increase profit margins. Darryl shared his suspicions with one of the cancer doctors who was purchasing the drug from the pharmacist. Tests indicated that the drug had indeed been diluted.[42]

- *Corporations exist to maximize shareholder value.* In the past, corporations were often viewed as economic and social institutions—organizations that served a balanced group of stakeholders. In recent years, analysts, stock traders, CEOs, and the media have too often focused on a single standard of performance—share price.[43] Marjorie Kelly, editor of *Business Ethics*, says, "Managing a company solely for maximum share price can destroy both share price and the entire company."[44]

  Pressure to increase "numbers" led to sales abuses at WorldCom Incorporated. Some salespeople double-booked accounts in order to make their quota and collect increased commissions. The false reporting was identified by an internal company probe and the guilty sales representatives were fired.[45] The same pressure led financial executives at Canada's Nortel Networks to report forecast revenues and earnings that were "out of touch with reality"; as a result, the company's CEO and a number of senior financial executives were fired.[46]

- *It's not wrong because everyone is doing it.* Shoshana Zuboff, contributing columnist for *Fast Company* magazine, sees widespread acceptance of wrong as normal. She points to acceptance in some industries of the belief that "It's not wrong because everyone is doing it."[47] Employees working for prominent companies such as Merck, WorldCom, Putman Investments, Tyco, and Edward D. Jones & Company have been involved in ethical lapses.[48] Most white-collar crime is committed by persons who lack character and integrity, or who had a momentary but disastrous lapse in judgment.

- *Companies need to be lean and mean.*[49] Downsizing has become a common practice even when the economy is strong. After layoffs, companies must deal with serious problems of low morale and mistrust of management. Those employees who remain after a company reduces its ranks often feel demoralized, overworked, and fearful. The stress of long hours and a faster pace can result in losses in quality and bad service that alienate customers. Richard Sennett, author of *The Corrosion of Character*, says that the decline of character strength can be traced to conditions that have grown out of our fast-paced, high-stress, information-driven economy. He states that character strength builds as we display loyalty, mutual commitment, and the pursuit of long-term goals.[50] These are the ethical qualities needed to build a foundation for strong partnering-style interactions that create value.

Character strength builds as we display loyalty, mutual commitment, and the pursuit of long-term goals. These are the qualities needed to build strong buyer–seller relationships.

Yuri Arcurs/Shutterstock

Today many business firms are struggling to align their values, ethics, and principles with the expectations of their salespeople and their customers. The process of negotiating ethical standards and practices must be ongoing. Citigroup Incorporated, the world's largest financial services firm, is working hard to move beyond regulatory scandals. Charles Prince, Citigroup CEO, wants the company to better balance its "delivering-the-numbers" culture with a long-term attention to reputation. He readily admits that "at times, our actions have put at risk our most precious commodity—the trust of our clients, the patience of our employees, and the faith of our shareholders."[51]

Can moral behaviour be taught? The National Business Ethics Survey, conducted annually by the Ethics Resource Center (**www.ethics.org**), found that 90 percent of employees said that ethics training is useful or somewhat useful to them. A growing number of students are completing business ethics courses as part of their business programs.[52]

From the Field
She Quits Her Job over Her Personal Code of Ethics

Birgitta Jonsdottir, during a recent whirlwind tour in Toronto, disclosed that she has had a varied career bouncing between her home country of Iceland and North America. The mother of three has been a nanny, a retail sales clerk, and a door-to-door salesperson, and is now a prominent member of parliament in Iceland.

Describing her short career in door-to-door selling, she says she "pushed a vacuum cleaner on an elderly couple that had never bought anything on a payment plan." As she was returning home after the sale, she had misgivings about what she had done. She realized that she used her persuasive ability for her personal benefit, selling something to someone who didn't need it. At that point, she quit and returned to Iceland.[d]

DEVELOPING A PERSONAL CODE OF ETHICS THAT ADDS VALUE

TOO OFTEN PEOPLE CONFUSE THEIR ETHICAL STANDARDS WITH LEGAL STANDARDS. They believe that if they are not breaking the law, then they are acting in an ethical manner.[53] A salesperson's personal code of ethics must extend beyond the legal definition of what is right and wrong. To view ethics only in terms of what is legally proper encourages the question, "What can I get by with?" A salesperson must develop a personal code of ethics that extends beyond the letter of the law.

Bruce Weinstein, a professional ethicist who is often introduced as "The Ethics Guy," offers sound advice on living an ethical life. He says we should do the right thing simply because it's the right thing to do. The only way you can build a loyal and growing client base is to demonstrate that you have the customers' own best interests at heart. You are trying to make things better for them. "Here is where ethics differs from the law. It demands more of us," says Weinstein.[54]

Many people considering a career in selling are troubled by the thought that they may be pressured into compromising their personal standards of right and wrong. These fears may be justified. The authors of *The Ethical Edge*, a book that examines organizations that have faced moral crises, contend that business firms have given too little thought to the issue of helping employees to function ethically within organizations.[55] Many salespeople wonder whether their own ethical philosophy can survive in the business world. These are some of their questions:

"Can a profitable business and good ethics coexist?"
"Are there still business firms that value adherence to high ethical standards?"
"Is honesty still a valued personal trait in the business community?"

In the field of athletic competition, the participants rely heavily on a written set of rules. The referee or umpire is ever-present to detect rule violations and assess a penalty. In the field of personal selling, there is no universal code of ethics. However, some general guidelines can serve as a foundation for a personal code of business ethics.

1. *Relationship comes first, task second.* Sharon Drew Morgan, author of *Selling with Integrity*, says you can't sell a product unless there is a level of comfort between you and the prospect. She encourages salespeople to take the time to create a level of comfort, rapport, and collaboration that encourages open communication.[56] Placing task before relationship is based on the belief that the salesperson knows more than the customer. Morgan reminds us that "the buyer has the answers; the seller has the questions."[57] These answers will surface only when the buyer–seller relationship is characterized by rapport and trust.

2. *Be honest with yourself and with others.* To achieve excellence in terms of ethical practices, you have to believe that everything you do counts. Tom Peters, in *Thriving on Chaos*, says, "Integrity may be about little things as much as or more than big ones."[58] It's about accuracy in completing your expense account—and resisting the temptation to inflate the expense report for personal gain. It's about avoiding the temptation to stretch the truth, to exaggerate, or to withhold information. Paul Ekman, author of *Telling Lies*, says that withholding important information is one of the primary ways of lying.[59] A complete and informative sales

Personal selling must be viewed as an exchange of value. Salespeople who accept this ethical guideline view personal selling as something you do *for* customers, not something you do *to* customers.

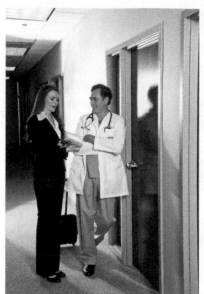

Kablonk/SuperStock

presentation may include information regarding the product's limitations. If you let your character and integrity be revealed in the little things, others will see you as someone who acts ethically in all things. Any violation of honesty, however small, dilutes your ethical strength, leaving you weaker for the big challenges you will face sooner or later.[60]

3. *Personal selling must be viewed as an exchange of value.* Salespeople who maintain a value focus are searching for ways to create value for their prospects or customers. This value may take the form of increased productivity, greater profit, enjoyment, or security. The value focus motivates the salesperson to carefully identify the prospect's wants and needs.[61] Salespeople who accept this ethical guideline view personal selling as something you do *for* customers, not something you do *to* customers. The role of the salesperson is to diagnose buyer needs and determine whether value can be created. Always be prepared to add value.

REVIEWING KEY CONCEPTS

- Explain the importance of developing a relationship strategy.

  The manner in which salespeople establish, build, and maintain relationships is a major key to success in personal selling. *Emotional intelligence*, defined as the capacity for monitoring our own feelings and those of others, for motivating ourselves, and managing emotions well in ourselves and in our

  relationships, is critical to the development of a successful selling relationship strategy.

- Describe issues that challenge the ethical decision making of salespeople.

  A selling career, more than most other careers, is frequently subjected to situations that provide short-term gain, resulting in the long-term erosion of integrity and destruction of relationships. Various stakeholders to a sale make requests and offers that are unethical and, in a number of situations, illegal. Salespeople are repeatedly challenged to make ethical decisions. Ethics, therefore, forms the foundation for partnering relationships that are developed through the salesperson's relationship, product, customer, and presentation strategies.

In the field of personal selling, the temptation to maximize short-term gains by some type of unethical conduct is always present and occurs more often than in most other careers. Salespeople are especially vulnerable to unethical decision making, because they are subject to many temptations. These temptations are often motivated by offers from clients, competitors, company personnel, and suppliers, and may involve personal gain on the part of the salesperson. While attractive to one or more of the stakeholders associated with the sale in the short run, they serve as the basis for the destruction of long-term, partnering relationships.

- Describe the factors that influence the ethical conduct of sales personnel.

At the international level, ethical and legal issues can be very complex. The global marketplace reflects a great number of cultures, each with its unique qualities. Coping with illegal activities throughout the world is also very challenging. Illegal demands for bribes, kickbacks, or special fees can serve as a barrier to business transactions.

Salespeople can benefit from the stabilizing influence of good role models. Although top management personnel are usually far removed from day-to-day selling activities, they can have a major impact on salespeople's conduct. Dishonesty at the top of an organization can cause an erosion of ethical standards at the lower echelons. Sales managers provide another important role model. They interpret company policies and help establish guidelines for acceptable and unacceptable selling practices.

- Describe how ethical decisions influence the building of partnering relationships in selling.

Character and integrity strongly influence relationships in personal selling. Unethical sales practices will ultimately destroy relationships with customers. These practices undermine trust, which is at the very core of all meaningful relationships.

Many colleges and universities are playing a more active role in character development. Character education is often integrated into courses that focus on ethics. Character is composed of personal standards of behaviour, so all of us can do things that build character. Keeping our commitments to others provides just one example of how character is built.

- Discuss guidelines for developing a personal code of ethics that creates value.

Salespeople must establish their own standards of personal conduct. They must decide how best to serve their company and build strong partnerships with their customers. The pressure to compromise one's ethical standards surfaces almost daily. The primary deterrent is a strong sense of right and wrong. Three general guidelines can serve as a foundation for a personal code of ethics:

a. Relationship comes first, task second.

b. Be honest with yourself and with others.

c. Personal selling must be viewed as an exchange of value.

Key Terms

Review Questions

1. List the three prescriptions that serve as the foundation for development of a relationship strategy.

2. Carefully review Figure 3.5, the CPSA Sales Institute Code of Ethics. Select the three standards you feel would present the greatest challenge to salespeople. Explain your choices.

3. How does business slander differ from business libel?

4. What major factors help influence salespeople's ethical conduct?

5. What are cooling-off laws? How do they protect consumers?

6. Why must a salesperson's ethical sense extend beyond the legal definition of what is right and wrong?

7. Explain why the sales manager plays such an important role in influencing the ethical behaviour of salespeople.

8. A company policy on ethics will usually cover several major areas. What are they?

9. Is it ever appropriate to give gifts to customers? Explain.

10. List and describe three guidelines used as a foundation of a self-imposed code of business ethics.

Application Exercises

Grey Issues–Ethical Decision Making in Selling Today is an assessment designed to help make more informed ethical decisions. Many of the ethical issues included in this assessment will be faced when one applies for and obtains a personal selling position. Completion of this assessment will provide an introduction to a wide range of real-life ethical dilemmas. It will stimulate in-depth thinking about the ethical consequences of one's decisions and actions.

This application exercise is a two-part assessment. Part I includes five mini-cases that introduce ethical dilemmas likely to be faced when applying for a sales position. Part II includes five ethical dilemmas that will likely be encountered in a typical sales position. Each mini-case poses four solutions. In some cases, only one solution is the correct choice; in others, more than one choice has merit. Keep in mind, however, that one solution will be the best selection from the options listed.

It is important to read the Park Shores Resort and Convention Centre Account Executive Position Description in "Partnership Selling: A Role Play/Simulation" online in the Student Resources section at **www.pearsoncanada.ca/manning** prior to taking the assessment.

Circle Your Best Choice

Part I—Mini-Case 1—Prior to the interview, T. J. McKee the Sales Manager requests a personal resume. Your current average grade in your program is 68, but it will very likely increase to 70 or higher at the end of the current semester. What should you do?

a. Indicate that your current average grade is 70.

b. Indicate that your current average grade point average is 70, but make a mental note to explain (during the interview) that it is currently 68 but will likely increase to 70 or higher at the end of the semester.

c. Indicate that your current average grade is 68.

d. Omit this information from the resume.

Mini-Case 2—Recently, you received an invitation to become a member of Alpha Phi Omega, a fraternity that honours students who have a record of outstanding service to the community. Very few students are invited to join, and the membership committee, which screens applications, occasionally rejects applications. Should you list membership in Alpha Phi Omega on your resume?

a. Do not list this membership on your resume.

b. List this membership on your resume but indicate that approval is pending.

c. Do not list this membership on the resume, but describe your community service activities.

d. List the membership on the resume without any additional information.

Mini-Case 3—During the interview, T. J. McKee requests salary information about your most recent full-time position. You believe this information may influence the starting salary offer, should you be offered the job. The Park Shores uses a commission plan with a guaranteed salary. What should you do?

a. Tactfully tell Mr. McKee that this information is personal and you would rather not discuss past earnings.

b. Provide the information as requested.

c. Provide an inflated figure in hope of receiving a higher initial salary offer.

d. Refuse to provide the information, but do tell him the amount you hope to earn if hired.

Mini-Case 4—Prior to visiting his company for the interview, you receive a letter from T. J. McKee that explains that you will be reimbursed for all travel and meal expenses. You will stay in a complimentary room at the Park Shores Resort and Convention Centre. The letter states that the daily meal expense (per-diem) is $65. The early morning flight includes a complimentary snack. You have lunch with Sara Millen, manager of the hotel, and she pays the bill. That evening you have dinner on your own at a restaurant near the hotel. The bill, including tip, is $36.25. The next morning, you take an early morning flight home and once again enjoy a complimentary snack on the plane. When you turn in your expenses, what amount of meal reimbursement should you request?

   a. Request $36.25 for the evening meal.

   b. Request $65, which is the amount available for meals.

   c. Request $41.50 in order to cover the cost of the evening meal and snacks you purchased at the hotel gift shop.

   d. Turn in no meal expenses because the amount spent was quite small.

Mini-Case 5—A large hotel and conference centre in Halifax, Nova Scotia has invited you to interview for a sales position. All expenses will be paid. You have no interest in moving to Nova Scotia, but you would enjoy visiting Halifax as you have never been to the east coast. What should you do?

   a. Accept the invitation. You need the experience that only a real interview can provide.

   b. Do not accept the invitation because you have no interest in relocating to Nova Scotia.

   c. Accept the invitation because you will have an opportunity to visit Canada's east coast.

   d. Accept the invitation and approach the interview with an open mind. Do not close the door on a job opportunity.

Part II—Mini-Case 1—On November 18, a customer requests a price quotation for a conference that will be held on March 22. This customer has scheduled two previous conferences at the Park Shores Resort and Convention Centre. You know that on December 1 the hotel will announce a special conference "package plan" that will provide this customer with a lower rate. The new rate schedule will extend from December 1 to April 1. What action should you take at this time?

   a. Prepare a price quotation for the current rate.

   b. Delay preparing the price quotation until December 1.

   c. Prepare a price quotation using the rates that will be announced December 1.

   d. Prepare a price quotation at the current price, but make a mental note to send the customer a revised quotation on December 1.

Mini-Case 2—Throughout the past several weeks, you have met with a representative of Follett Corporation on several occasions. You are anxious to book a large conference that will involve over 200 Follett employees. Every detail of the proposal has been negotiated, but the prospect seems reluctant to sign the contract. One option available is to tell the customer that room availability is limited, and any additional delays may create scheduling problems during the time period requested. In reality, business is usually very slow during the time period requested, so room availability should not be a problem. What should you do?

   a. Stop making contact with the prospect and wait for a decision.

   b. Continue to make an effort to close the sale, but do not provide any information that is not accurate.

   c. Make another call on the customer and point out that scheduling problems will likely arise if the contract is not signed now.

   d. Make another call on the customer and this time offer a significant price reduction.

Mini-Case 3—After closing a sale with a very difficult customer (the "customer from hell"), you indicated that you would follow up on a special room layout request and a minor menu substitution. During negotiations, you developed a strong dislike and distrust for this customer because of the unethical negotiation techniques he used. Because of the demands made during negotiations, and the fact that these requests were talked about after the customer signed the contract, you are thinking about forgetting the special requests and providing only the services specifically outlined in the contract. What should you do?

   a. Provide all items specified in the contract and take care of the special requests.

   b. Follow up on the special request and add additional fees to the final bill.

   c. Provide only those items specified in the contract.

   d. Contact the customer a few days before the scheduled meeting and tell him you will be unable to fulfill his special requests.

Mini-Case 4—The Park Shores Resort and Convention Centre has offered a special bonus to any salesperson who develops 10 new accounts during the current fiscal year. You need one more account to earn the bonus. Apco Equipment Corporation is considering your hotel and conference centre for an upcoming business meeting. Your contact at Apco says the meeting is tentative and may not be scheduled. One option is to offer Apco a contract with major price concessions and a liberal cancellation clause. The signed contract will qualify you for the bonus. What should you do?

 a. Make the special offer to Apco, but search for another new account in case the Apco deal falls through.

 b. Make the special offer to Apco and make every effort to close the sale.

 c. Give up the search for new accounts and enjoy a less stressful life.

 d. Pursue the Apco account, and other new accounts, but offer Apco a standard contract and no special concessions.

Mini-Case 5—When you accepted a sales position at the Park Shores Resort and Convention Centre, you signed a noncompete agreement. This agreement states that information acquired while representing the Park Shores cannot be taken to a new employer. With the press of a button on your computer keyboard, you can download a profile of all established accounts you were given at the time you started working for the Park Shores, a profile of each new account you have developed, and the name and address of all prospects that you have identified. You have been offered a sales position at a competing hotel and you are tempted to take this information with you. What should you do?

 a. Take all of this information home so it will be available when you start the new job.

 b. Take only the list of prospects you identified.

 c. Do not take any of the information because it would be covered by the noncompete agreement.

 d. Request the permission to take this information home.

ROLE-PLAY EXERCISE

This morning you met with a customer who has purchased office supplies from you for almost three years. You are quite surprised when she says, "I am prepared to place an order worth $10 500, but you must match an offer I received from a competitor." She then explains that the competitor is offering new customers a seven-day, all-expenses-paid trip to Quebec City if they place an order for more than $10 000. What would you do?

Prepare to role-play your response with another student. Review the material in this chapter, paying special attention to ways you can add value and build long-term relationships with ethical decision making.

Reality Selling Video Case Problem

Mattress Firm (www.mattressfirm.com) is one of the largest and most successful specialty bedding companies in the world. It offers sleep solutions, including conventional and specialty mattresses, as well as bedding-related products. The company has grown to become one of the largest and fastest growing mattress retailers. The company operates more than 560 stores in 38 markets nationwide and carries the top mattress brands. From the very beginning, the company set out to be a different kind of mattress retailer, focused on creating a unique shopping experience.

According to Edith Botello, featured at the beginning of this chapter, the biggest differentiator between Mattress Firm and its competitors is the sales process. As Edith puts it, buying a mattress can be overwhelming: How do you know which one is the best if all you see when you walk into a store are dozens of white rectangles? At Mattress Firm, sales reps make it simple for their customers to pick out their mattress without trying out every single bed. The process invites customers to get fitted for a mattress, just as with suits, shoes, and gowns. This is done through the company's Sleep Diagnostic System, which asks the customer a series of questions about their sleep quality and then measures their weight distribution and postural alignment. The system then recommends a type of support and eliminates 80 percent of the beds in the showroom. Taking the risk out of buying a mattress by letting the customer know what mattresses are best for them is something that only Mattress Firm offers.

How can ethical aspects of selling come into play in Edith's job as a retail salesperson? One example would be that sometimes salespeople have the opportunity to write up a sale where they would get credit but have not earned the right to do so. At times, customers shop around but eventually end up at the same store and want the same product that was offered to them previously. In such a case, the customer may request the particular salesperson who helped him or her previously. If that salesperson is not there, the new salesperson could choose to not give her/him credit. Another example might be a customer who tries to get greater price discounts by making untrue statements about a competitor's price offering or shopping around at different Mattress Firm locations in order to get the lowest possible price. In many cases, however, the salesperson will recognize this behaviour and act accordingly.

Being ethical is a core value at Mattress Firm. New hires are made aware of Mattress Firm's expectations from the beginning of their employment to ensure that they are ethical with their customers and other salespeople. Mattress Firm's Code of Conduct is a guide to the general principles that permeate the employees' relationships with customers, business partners, and, last but not least, each other. The Code goes far beyond compliance with laws and regulations. It is also a set of practical instructions to help employees in their day-to-day work. It explains, for example, how to manage potential conflicts of interest and how to report suspected violations of the rules.

At Mattress Firm, several policies and elements in the incentive compensation system exist that also help to safeguard ethical behaviour. The Standard Operating Procedure (SOP) dedicates an entire section to commission sales and how to handle different situations such as team selling, ticket trading, SPIFFS, bonuses, etc. For example, the commission system encourages sales reps to hold the line on price concessions. National sales contests are also audited to ensure ethical behaviour. The SOP and Employee Code of Conduct are housed on the company's intranet and are available to view at any time. (See the chapter opener on page 50 and Reality Selling Today Role Play 3 in Appendix 1 on page 428 for more information.)

Questions

1. Put yourself in Edith Botello's place as a sales rep selling mattresses. Can you imagine situations in your job that might challenge your ethical conduct?

2. For retailers such as Mattress Firm, what are the major areas that should be covered in a company policy on ethics?

3. Revenue-based incentive compensation plans, by their very nature, pressure sales reps to generate high sales, which might cause unethical sales practices. How could an incentive compensation system be designed that stimulates sales generation but safeguards ethical sales behaviour at the same time?

4. Image you were a salesperson for Mattress Firm, just like Edith Botello. A customer walks into your store and, after a while, shows great interest in a specific Tempur-Pedic. When it comes to the price, the customer mentions that your competitor across the street offered him exactly that mattress at a 10 percent lower price than Mattress Firm. You have some doubts that this statement is actually true, but you do not want to disgruntle the customer and compromise the sale. How would you react?

Chapter 4
Creating Value with a Relationship Strategy

Learning Objectives

After studying this chapter, you should be able to

1 Explain how partnering relationships add value.

2 Discuss how thought processes can enhance your relationship strategy.

3 Identify and describe the major nonverbal factors that shape our sales image.

4 Describe conversational strategies that help us establish relationships.

5 Explain how to establish a self-improvement plan based on personal development strategies.

RELATIONSHIP STRATEGY

ETHICS   ETHICS

PRESENTATION STRATEGY

PARTNERING TO CREATE VALUE

PRODUCT STRATEGY

ETHICS

CUSTOMER STRATEGY

 Reality Selling Video Series—Susana Rosas/ CB Richard Ellis

The salespeople who work for CB Richard Ellis (**www.cbre.com**) understand the importance of developing relationship strategies. This successful commercial real estate services company, with 24 Canadian sales offices from Halifax to Vancouver, employs more than 1800 Canadians. Worldwide, the company has 31 000 employees who work from more than 300 offices in some 50 countries. Building long-term partnering relationships with customers has helped CB Richard Ellis become so successful.

Susana Rosas (see page 77), a real estate broker at CB Richard Ellis, places a great deal of emphasis on building rapport during the first contact. She, like most other real estate professionals, knows that rapport with commercial real estate clients is of critical importance. She knows that to build relationships with clients, a good knowledge of the market is necessary but not sufficient. She has to master a multitude of skills, among which keeping an open and empathetic conversation style with her clients is the key. Above all, listening closely to everything that prospects say helps a salesperson to accurately identify their wants and needs. Furthermore, she works closely with her team members in the same collaborative manner to make sure all of those identified needs are met.

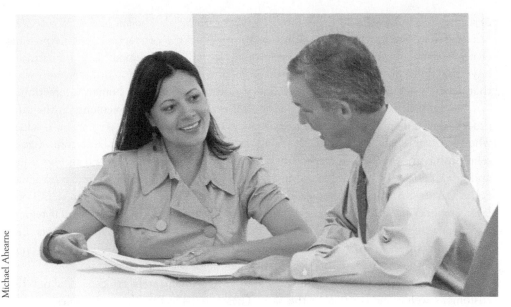

Michael Ahearne

Susana Rosas

RELATIONSHIPS ADD VALUE

RON WILLINGHAM, AUTHOR OF *Integrity Selling for the 21st Century*, SAYS THERE IS a relationship between the salesperson's achievement drive and her or his view of personal selling. Salespeople who feel a professional responsibility to create as much value for customers as possible exhibit more energy, a stronger work ethic, and a greater eagerness to ask customers for decisions.[1]

The manner in which salespeople establish, build, and manage relationships is not an incidental aspect of personal selling; in the information age it is the key to success. In the information economy, business is defined by customer relationships, and sales success

fototext/Alamy

Daniel Pink, well-known author of the best-selling *To Sell Is Human* and *A Whole New Mind,* predicts that one of the major players in the future will be the empathizer. Empathizers have the ability to imagine themselves in someone else's position and understand what the person is feeling. They are able to understand the subtleties of human interaction.

depends on adding value. Daniel Pink, author of *To Sell Is Human* and *A Whole New Mind*, says we are moving from the information age to the conceptual age. He predicts that one of the major players in the conceptual age will be the **empathizer**. Empathizers have the ability to imagine themselves in someone else's position and understand what that person is feeling. They are able to understand the subtleties of human interaction.[2]

We have defined *value-added selling* as a series of creative improvements in the sales process that enhances the customer experience. Customers perceive that value is added when they feel comfortable with the relationship they have with a salesperson. A good relationship encourage customers to feel that if a problem arises, they will receive a just and fair solution. A good relationship creates a clear channel of communication about issues that might surface during each step of the sales process. Len Rodman, CEO of a large engineering and construction company, recalls a problem in one particular region: Earnings were minimal and the person in charge, could not sell to high-tier clients. Len put a different salesperson in charge, whose strength was building relationships and, within an 18-month period, that region became one of the most profitable.[3]

The salesperson who is honest, accountable, and sincerely concerned about the customer's welfare adds value to the sale. These characteristics give the salesperson a competitive advantage—an advantage that is becoming increasingly important in a world of "look-alike" products and similar prices.

Partnering—The Highest-Quality Selling Relationship

Salespeople today are encouraged to think of everything they say or do in the context of their relationship with the customer. They should constantly strive to build a long-term partnership. In a marketplace characterized by increased levels of competition and greater product complexity, we see the need to adopt a relationship strategy that emphasizes the "lifetime" customer. High-quality relationships result in repeat business and important

Today's customer wants a quality product and a quality relationship. This means that salespeople can create value with a well-developed relationship strategy.

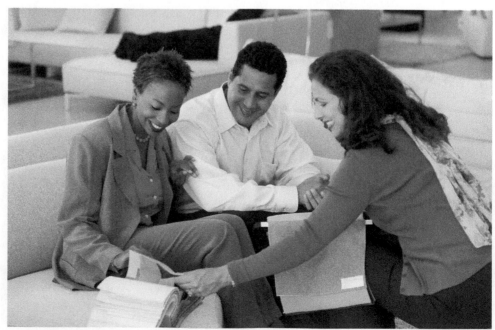

Bikeriderlondon/Shutterstock

Preparing Written Customer Communications with CRM

Exceptional CRM systems such as Salesforce.com enable you to quickly process written communications with numerous clients. One example is the form letter or email. Preparing a standard letter or template in advance lets you quickly select and send a personalized letter or email. "Personalized" means that the system will automatically add to the document the recipient's name, title, and other contact information you choose, even if the letter is going out to many recipients. Careful thought should be given to each template created so that the language reflects your win-win philosophy, your relationship strategy, and your professionalism.

Recipients of your appointment confirmations, information verifications, company or product news, or brief updates recognize and appreciate your effort to keep them informed. The written word conveys consideration and helps avoid misunderstandings and miscommunications. CRM empowers you to easily use the written word to advance your relationship building.

referrals. A growing number of salespeople recognize that the quality of the partnerships they create is as important as the quality of the products they sell. Today's customer wants a quality product *and* a quality relationship. One example of this trend is the J. D. Power and Associates customer satisfaction studies. J. D. Power conducts customer satisfaction research in several different industries; for example, the Domestic Hotel Guest Satisfaction Study measures guest satisfaction among frequent business travellers. J. D. Power conducts customer satisfaction research in several different industries.[4]

In Chapter 2 we defined *partnering* as a strategically developed, high-quality, long-term relationship that focuses on solving the customer's buying problems.[5] This definition is used in the sales training video entitled *Partnering—The Heart of Selling Today*. Traditional industrial-age sales training programs emphasized the importance of creating a good first impression and then "pushing" your product. Partnering emphasizes building a strong relationship during every aspect of the sale and working hard to maintain a quality relationship with the customer after the sale. Today, personal selling must be viewed as a process, not an event.[6]

Larry Wilson, noted author and founder of Wilson Learning Worldwide, identifies partnering as one of the most important aspects of strategic thought processes needed by salespeople. He points out that the salesperson who is selling a "one-shot" solution cannot compete against the one who has developed and nurtured a long-term, mutually beneficial partnership. Wilson believes there are three keys to a partnering relationship:

- *The relationship is built on shared values.* If your client believes that you both share the same ideas and values, it goes a long way toward creating a powerful relationship.

- *Everyone needs to clearly understand the purpose of the partnership and be committed to the vision.* Both the salesperson and the client must agree on what they are trying to do together.

- *The role of the salesperson must move from selling to supporting.* The salesperson in a partnership is actively concerned with the growth, health, and satisfaction of the company to which she or he is selling.[7]

Salespeople willing to abandon short-term thinking and invest the time and energy needed to develop a high-quality, long-term relationship with customers are rewarded with greater earnings and the satisfaction of working with repeat customers. Sales resulting from referrals also increase.

Figure 4.1 An effective relationship strategy helps high-performing salespeople build and maintain win-win relationships with a wide range of key groups.

Relationship Strategies Focus on Four Key Groups

Establishing and maintaining a partnering-type relationship internally as well as with customers is a vital aspect of selling. High-performance sales personnel build strong relationships with four groups (see Fig. 4.1):

1. *Customers.* As noted previously, a major key to success in selling is the ability to establish working relationships with customers in which mutual support, trust, and goals are nurtured over time. Research suggests that salespeople who maintain regular contact with their customers and develop sound business relationships based on mutual trust are able to drive up sales productivity.[8] Cisco Systems is one of many companies that now measure themselves by the quality of their relationships with their customers. Salespeople earn their bonuses in large part based on customer satisfaction rather than on gross sales or profit.[9]

2. *Secondary decision makers.* High-performance salespeople understand the importance of building relationships with the people who work with customers. In many selling situations, the first person the salesperson meets is a receptionist, a secretary, or an assistant to the primary decision maker. These persons can often facilitate a meeting with the prospect. Also, the prospect may involve other people in making the buying decision. For example, the decision to buy new office furniture may be made by a team of persons, including the buyer and the people who will actually use the furniture.

3. *Company support staff.* The maintenance of relationships internally is a vital aspect of selling. Support staff may include persons working in the areas of market research, product service, credit, training, or shipping. Influencing these people to change their priorities, interrupt their schedules, accept new responsibilities, or fulfill any other request for special attention is a major part of the salesperson's job. At UPS, the drivers are the eyes and ears of the sales force, so the most successful UPS salespeople nurture a relationship with the drivers in their sales territory.[10]

4. *Management personnel.* Sales personnel usually work under the direct supervision of a sales manager, a department head, or some other member of the firm's management

team. With the increasing frequency and effectiveness of team selling, the company president or CEO may accompany the salesperson on a call. Maintaining a good relationship with this person is important.

Adapting the Relationship Strategy

Ideally, the relationship strategy should be adapted to the type of customer you are working with. Chapter 2 provided a description of the three most common types of selling situations: transactional selling, consultative selling, and strategic alliance selling. Transactional buyers are usually aware of their needs and often stay focused on such issues as price, convenience, and delivery schedules. They usually know a great deal about the products or services they wish to purchase. In the transactional sale, the relationship strategy is often secondary.

In the consultative sale, however, the impact of relationships on the sale is quite important. A consultative sale emphasizes need identification, which is achieved through effective communication and a relationship built on mutual trust and respect. The consultative salesperson must display a keen ability to listen, define the customer's problem, and offer one or more solutions. The opportunity to uncover hidden needs and create custom solutions is greatly enhanced by a well-conceived relationship strategy.[11]

In terms of relationship building, strategic alliance selling is often the most challenging. Very often the salesperson is working with a company team made up of people from such areas as research and development (R&D), finance, and distribution. The salesperson must build a good working relationship with each team member. Forming an alliance with another company involves building relationships with several representatives of that buying organization.

Customers almost never buy products from someone they dislike. A salesperson who is not viewed as helpful and trustworthy will not succeed in any type of selling situation.

THOUGHT PROCESSES THAT ENHANCE YOUR SELLING RELATIONSHIP STRATEGY

INDUSTRIAL-AGE FOLKLORE CREATED THE MYTH OF THE "BORN" SALESPERSON—A DYNAMIC, outgoing, highly assertive individual. Experience acquired during the age of information has taught us that many other factors determine sales success. Key among these factors are a positive self-image and the ability to relate to others in effective and productive ways. With the aid of knowledge drawn from the behavioural sciences, we can develop the relationship strategies needed in a wide range of selling situations.

Self-Concept—An Important Dimension of the Relationship Strategy

Your **self-concept** is the bundle of facts, opinions, beliefs, and perceptions about yourself that are present in your life every moment of every day.[12] The self-concept you have today reflects information you have received from others and life events that occurred throughout childhood, adolescence, and adulthood. You are *consciously* aware of some of the things you have been conditioned to believe about yourself. But many comments and events that have shaped your self-concept are processed at the *unconscious* level and continue to influence your judgments, feelings, and behaviours whether you are aware of them or not.[13]

self-concept Bundle of facts, opinions, beliefs, and perceptions about yourself that are present in your life every moment of every day.

Phillip McGraw, author of *Self Matters*, says we often sabotage our own success by adopting limiting beliefs. These are the specific things we think about that cause us to conclude that we are not capable of achieving success. These beliefs restrict our thinking and our actions.[14] McGraw, better known as "Dr. Phil," has developed a one-sentence guide to understanding the importance of your self-concept: *The past reaches into the present, and programs the future, by your recollections and your internal rhetoric about what you perceive to have happened in your life.*[15] Past experiences and events, which McGraw describes as "defining moments," can influence your thinking for a lifetime.

How can you develop a more positive self-concept? How can you get rid of self-destructive ways of thinking? Bringing your present self-concept out into the open is the first step in understanding who you are, what you can do, and where you are going. Improving your self-concept will not happen overnight, but it can happen. A few practical approaches are summarized as follows:

1. *Focus on the future and stop being overly concerned with past mistakes or failures.* You should learn from past errors, but they should not immobilize you.

2. *Develop expertise in selected areas.* By developing "expert power," you not only improve your self-image but also increase the value of your contributions to your employer and your customers.

3. *Learn to develop a positive personal attitude.* To develop a more positive outlook, read books or listen to audio presentations that describe ways to develop a positive personal attitude.

Stephen Covey, author of *The Seven Habits of Highly Effective People*, says the ability to build effective, long-term relationships is based on character strength, not quick-fix techniques.

Epa european pressphoto agency b.v./Alamy

Consider materials developed by Daniel Pink, Harvey Mackay, Jack Canfield, Stephen Covey, Brian Tracy, Dale Carnegie, and Phillip McGraw.

Later in this chapter you will learn how to develop and initiate a plan for self-improvement. If you want to improve your self-concept, consider adopting this plan.

The Win-Win Philosophy

As noted in Chapter 2, the marketing concept is a philosophy that leaves no doubt in the mind of every employee that customer satisfaction is of primary importance.

Adding Value Builds Strong Relationships

Janssen Inc., an innovative, research-based pharmaceutical company located in Toronto, has been servicing the Canadian market for more than 50 years. Its salespeople are among the best in the industry and adhere to the values and leadership standards promoted by its parent company, Johnson & Johnson.

Dean Keating, a primary care sales representative, focuses his efforts on working to develop value-added solutions for his physician customers. Many busy physicians do not have the resources to provide additional support and education for patients with Alzheimer's disease or their caregivers, for example. Dean helps arrange the availability of nurses specially trained in Alzheimer's disease to provide this support.

Is this focus on understanding customer needs valued by doctors? As a result of this solution-oriented approach, Dean is seen as a true partner by his customers.

Today, salespeople who can demonstrate that they deliver understanding and value to their customers are able to build superior relationships. Everyone wins.[a]

Salespeople who work closely with customers are in a position to monitor customer satisfaction.

Adopting the win-win philosophy is the first step in developing a relationship strategy. Stephen Heiman and Diane Sanchez, authors of *The New Conceptual Selling*, describe the "win-win" approach as follows:

> In Win-Win selling, both the buyer and seller come out of the sale understanding that their respective best interests have been served—in other words, that they've both won. It is our firm conviction, based on thousands of selling situations, that over the long run the only sellers who can count on remaining successful are the ones who are committed to this Win-Win philosophy.[16]

The win-win strategy is based on such irrefutable logic that it is difficult to understand why any other approach would be used. The starting point to the development of a win-win philosophy is to compare the behaviours of persons who have adopted the win-lose approach with the behaviours of persons who have adopted the win-win approach (see Fig. 4.2).

Win-lose people	Win-win people
• See a problem in every solution	• Help others solve their problem
• Fix the blame	• Fix what caused the problem
• Let life happen to them	• Make life a joyous happening for others and themselves
• Live in the past	• Learn from the past, live in the present, and set goals for the future
• Make promises they never keep	• Make commitments to themselves and to others and keep them both

Figure 4.2 The starting point to developing a win-win philosophy is to compare behaviours of win-lose salespeople with those of win-win salespeople.
(Adapted from a list of losers, winners, and double winners in *The Double Win* by Denis Waitley.)

Empathy and Ego Drive

We have described the growing importance of the *empathizers*—those with the ability to imagine themselves in someone else's position and to understand what that person is feeling. A salesperson simply cannot sell well without the invaluable ability to get critical feedback from the client through empathy. When you sense what the customer is feeling, you can change pace and make whatever modifications are needed in your sales presentation.[17] Fortunately, the ability to relate to and connect with customers can be learned.

ego drive An inner force that makes the salesperson want and need to make the sale.

Ego drive is another basic quality that is of critical importance in personal selling. **Ego drive** is an inner force that makes the salesperson want and need to make the sale. Closing the sale provides a powerful means of enhancing the salesperson's ego. Research indicates that top salespeople have both the motivation to make the sale and the empathy that gives them the connecting tool with which to do it. Therefore, empathy and ego drive reinforce each other.[18]

VERBAL AND NONVERBAL STRATEGIES THAT ADD VALUE TO YOUR SELLING RELATIONSHIPS

THE FIRST CONTACT BETWEEN A SALESPERSON AND A PROSPECT IS VERY IMPORTANT. During the first few minutes—or seconds, in some cases—the prospect and the salesperson form impressions of each other that will either facilitate or detract from the sales call. Malcolm Gladwell, author of the bestselling book *Blink*, says that when two people meet for the first time, both will make very superficial, rapid judgments about the other person. This decision-making process, he argues, usually happens subconsciously in a split second (in the blink of an eye).[19]

Every salesperson projects an image to prospective customers, and this image influences how a customer feels about the sales representative. The image you project is the sum total of many verbal and nonverbal factors. The quality of your voice, the clothing you wear, your posture, your manners, and your communication style represent some of the factors that contribute to the formation of your image. We discuss

Everett Collection Inc/Alamy

Malcolm Gladwell, noted author of the best-selling book *Blink,* says that when two people meet for the first time, each in a split second, at a subconscious level, will make very superficial rapid judgements about the other person.

several forms of verbal and nonverbal communication in this chapter. Communication style is examined in Chapter 5.

Adding Value with Nonverbal Messages

When we attempt to communicate with another person, we use both verbal and nonverbal communications. **Nonverbal messages** are "messages without words" or "silent messages." These are the messages—other than spoken or written words—that we communicate through facial expressions, voice tone, gestures, appearance, posture, and other nonverbal means.[20]

Research indicates that when two people communicate, *nonverbal messages convey much more impact than verbal messages*. Words play a surprisingly small part in the communication process. Every spoken message has a vocal element, coming not from *what* we say, but from *how* we say it. The voice communicates in many ways: through tone, volume, and speed of delivery. A salesperson wishing to communicate enthusiasm needs to use a voice that is charged with energy.

As we attempt to read nonverbal communication, it is important to remember that no *one* signal carries much meaning on its own. If a person you meet for the first time displays a weak grip during the handshake, for example, don't let this one signal shape your first impression. Such factors as posture, eye contact, gestures, clothing, and facial expressions must all be regarded together.[21]

Nonverbal messages can reinforce or contradict the spoken word. When your verbal message and body language are consistent, they give others the impression that you can be trusted and that what you say reflects what you truly believe. When there is a discrepancy between your verbal and nonverbal messages, you are less apt to be trusted.[22]

nonverbal message A form of communication that has been defined as "messages without words" or "silent messages."

Influence of Your Entrance and Carriage As noted earlier, the first impression you make is very important. The moment a salesperson walks into a client's office, the client begins making judgments. Susan Bixler, author of *The Professional Image* and *Professional Presence*, makes this comment:

> All of us make entrances throughout our business day as we enter offices, conference rooms, or meeting halls. And every time we do, someone is watching us, appraising us, sizing us up, and gauging our appearance, even our intelligence, often within the space of a few seconds.[23]

Bixler says that the key to making a successful entrance is simply believing—and projecting—that you have a reason to be there and have something important to offer the client. You can communicate confidence with a strong stride, good posture, and a friendly smile. A confident manner communicates to the client the message, "This meeting will be beneficial to you."

Influence of Shaking Hands An inadequate handshake is like dandruff: No one will mention it, but everyone will notice it. The handshake is an important symbol of respect and, in most business settings, it is the proper greeting.[24] In the field of selling, the handshake is usually the *first* and frequently the *only* physical contact you make during a sales call. The handshake can communicate warmth, genuine concern for the prospect, and an image of strength. It can also communicate aloofness, indifference, and weakness to the customer. The message we communicate with a handshake is determined by a combination of five factors:

1. *Eye contact during handshake.* Eyes transmit more information than any other part of the body, so maintain eye contact throughout the handshaking process and display a pleasant smile.
2. *Degree of firmness.* Generally speaking, a firm handshake communicates a caring attitude, while a weak grip (the "dead-fish" handshake) communicates indifference.
3. *Depth of interlock.* A full, deep grip communicates friendship to the other person.
4. *Duration of grip.* There are no specific guidelines to tell us what the ideal duration of a grip should be. However, by extending the duration of the handshake we can often communicate a greater degree of interest in and concern for the other person. Do not pump up and down more than once or twice.
5. *Degree of dryness of hands.* A moist palm not only is uncomfortable to handle but also can communicate the impression that you are quite nervous. Some people have a physiological problem that causes clammy hands, and they should keep a handkerchief within reach to remove excess moisture.[25]

The best time to present your name is when you extend your hand. When you introduce yourself, state your name clearly and then listen carefully to be certain you hear the customer's name. To ensure that you will remember the customer's name, repeat it. In some cases, you will need to check to be sure you are pronouncing it properly. When appropriate, it is a good idea to write the name.

Influence of Facial Expressions If you want to identify how another person is feeling, watch facial expressions closely. The face is a remarkable communicator, capable of accurately signalling emotion in a split second and capable of concealing emotion equally

Remembering Names

In the field of personal selling, remembering a person's name is very important. To improve your ability to recall names, use one or more of these memory aids.

- *Verify the spelling.* After hearing the name, ask, "Is that Reece with a 'c' or an 's'?" Repetition helps you remember the name.

- *Ask how the person wants to be addressed.* Ask, "Should I call you Miss Thomas, Ms. Thomas, or Mrs. Thomas?" This is another opportunity for repetition.

- *Relate the name to something easy to remember.* If the person's last name is Park, connect this name with

"Algonquin Park (Ontario)" in your mind. Some aspect of appearance (hair style, eyeglasses, etc.) might serve as a connecting reference.

- *Use the name quickly.* Work the person's name into the conversation right away: "Ms. Thomas, may I ask you a few questions?"

- *Use the name frequently.* During and at the end of the meeting, work the name into the conversation: "Ms. Thomas, thank you for meeting with me."[c]

well. You can tell in a blink of an eye if your customer's face is registering surprise, pleasure, or skepticism (see Fig. 4.3). Facial expressions are largely universal, so people around the world tend to "read" faces in a similar way. It is worth noting that the smile is the most recognized facial signal in the world and it can have a great deal of influence on others. George Rotter, professor of psychology at Montclair University, says, "Smiles are an enormous controller of how people perceive you." People tend to trust a smiling face.[26] Get in the habit of offering a sincere smile each time you meet with a prospect.

Influence of Eye Contact When the customer is talking, eye contact is one of the best ways to say, "I'm listening." If you are looking across the room or at papers in your briefcase, the customer will assume you are not listening. However, prolonged eye contact can send the wrong message. A prolonged direct stare can be threatening. To avoid the prolonged stare, take fleeting glances at your notes. As the customer speaks, nod occasionally to indicate agreement or interest.[27]

Confidence   Boredom   Evaluation

Figure 4.3 Our subtle facial gestures are continuously sending messages to others.

Spending an afternoon with a customer on the golf course is part of the relationship strategy of this salesperson. Many companies support this approach to building and maintaining relationships.

Ted Levine/Corbis

Impact of Appearance on Relationships

We form opinions about people based on a pattern of immediate impressions conveyed by appearance. The clothing we wear, the length and style of our hair, the fragrances we use, and the jewellery we display all combine to make a statement about us to others—a statement of primary importance to anyone involved in selling.

unconscious expectations Certain views concerning appropriate dress.

We all have certain views, or **unconscious expectations**, concerning appropriate dress. In sales work we should try to anticipate the expectations of our clientele. The clothing worn by salespeople does make a difference in terms of customer acceptance because it communicates powerful messages. The clothing we wear can influence our credibility and likeability, thereby adding value to our selling relationships.

Most image consultants agree that there is no single "dress for success" look. The appropriate wardrobe will vary from one city or region to another and from company to company. However, there are some general guidelines that you should follow in selecting clothing for sales work. Four key factors should govern your decisions: simplicity, appropriateness, quality, and visual integrity.[28]

Simplicity The colour of your clothing, as well as the design, will communicate a message to the customer. Some colours are showy and convey an air of casualness. In a business setting we want to be taken seriously, so flashy colours should usually be avoided.

Appropriateness Selecting appropriate clothing for sales work can be a challenge. We must carefully consider the clients we serve and decide what will be acceptable to them. Many salespeople are guided by the type of products they sell and the desired image projected by their employers. Deciding what constitutes appropriate attire in today's business-casual world begins with an understanding of what it means to "dress down." **Business casual** is clothing that allows you to feel comfortable but look neat and professional. Pay close attention to the clothing your clients wear.[29] If a client is wearing a nice sport coat, a collared long-sleeved shirt, and dress slacks, don't wear khaki trousers and a short-sleeved polo shirt. In recent years, the casual dress trend has reversed at many companies, and workplace dress codes have become more formal.[30]

business casual Clothing that allows you to feel comfortable but looks neat and professional.

Quality The quality of your wardrobe will also influence the image you project to customers. A salesperson's wardrobe should be regarded as an investment, with each item carefully selected to look good and fit well. Susan Bixler says, "If you want respect, you have to dress as well as or better than your industry standards."[31]

Visual Integrity Visual presence must have a certain amount of integrity and consistency. The images you project are made up of many factors, and lack of attention to important details can negate your effort to create a good impression. Too much jewellery, a shirt that does not fit well, or shoes that are not shined can detract from the professional look you want to project. People are often extra alert when meeting someone new, and this heightened consciousness makes every detail count.[32] Many young people today have tattoos or body piercings. While these may be considered fashionable among friends, they may be problematic for salespeople as some customers will hold other views. Like dandruff on your collar or stale tobacco on your breath, they may not be mentioned, but they will most certainly be noticed, and they are likely to have a negative impact on your sales. Keep in mind that customer contact often takes place in several settings. The first meeting with a customer may take place in his or her office, but the second meeting may be on the golf course. And the third meeting may take place at a nice restaurant. The clothing you wear in each of these settings is important.

Effect of Voice Quality on Relationships

As noted previously, every spoken message has a vocal element. What we hear is greatly influenced by the speaker's tone of voice, vocal clarity, and verbal expressiveness. On the telephone, voice quality is even more important because the other person cannot see your facial expressions, hand gestures, and other body movements. You cannot trade in your current voice for a new one; however, you can make your voice more pleasing to others. How? Consider these suggestions.

1. *Do not speak too quickly or too slowly.* Rapid speech often causes customers to become defensive. They raise psychological barriers because a "rapid-fire monologue" is associated with high-pressure sales methods. Many salespeople could improve their verbal presentation by speaking more slowly. The slower presentation allows others to follow, and it allows you, the speaker, time to think ahead—to consider the situation and make judgments. Another good tip is to vary the speed of your speech, leaving spaces between thoughts. Crowding too many thoughts together may confuse the listener.[33]

2. *Avoid a speech pattern that is dull and colourless.* The worst kind of voice has no colour and no feeling. Enthusiasm is a critical element of an effective sales presentation. It is also contagious. Your enthusiasm for the product will be transmitted to the customer.

3. *Avoid bad speech habits.* Kristy Pinand, a youthful-looking 23-year old, routinely used "teen speak." For example, she described a recent promotion as "so cool." Her supervisor felt she not only looked young but sounded very young, and this image could potentially hurt her ability to win the respect of clients. She urged Ms. Pinand to select her words more carefully. Ms. Pinand heeded the constructive advice and now rehearses her remarks aloud before she calls a client.[34]

Some speech habits can make us sound poorly educated and inarticulate. At age 22, Mike White learned that his unique regional accent and colourful speech patterns created problems at work. He recognized this was a "turnoff" to some of the image-conscious people he worked with. One day, his sales manager asked him if he had his racquetball equipment with him and White replied, "Yeah, I brung it." Fortunately, White's supervisor was willing to tactfully correct his grammatical problems and help him communicate with greater clarity. Today, Mike White is CEO of a successful company and a frequent speaker at trade shows.[35]

Effect of Etiquette on Your Relationships

The study of etiquette (sometimes called *manners* or *protocol*) reveals a number of ways to enhance your relationship strategy. Salespeople who possess knowledge of the rules of etiquette can perform their daily work with greater poise and confidence. Think of etiquette as a universal passport to positive relationships and respect.

With practice, anyone can develop good etiquette without appearing to be "stiff" and at the same time win the respect and admiration of others. Space does not permit a complete review of this topic, but we cover some of the rules of etiquette that are especially important to salespeople.

1. *Avoid the temptation to address a new prospect by first name.* In a business setting, too much familiarity too quickly can cause irritation.

2. *Avoid offensive comments or stories.* Never assume that the customer's value system is the same as your own. Rough language, off-colour stories, or personal views on political issues can do irreparable damage to your image.

3. *Recognize the importance of punctuality.* Ann Marie Sabath, owner of a firm that provides etiquette training for business employees, says, "We teach people that if you're early, you're on time, and if you're on time, in reality, you're late." Showing up late for an appointment will be viewed as rudeness by most clients.[36]

4. *When you invite a customer to lunch, do not discuss business before the meal is ordered unless the client initiates the subject.* Also, order food that is easily controlled and avoid such items as ribs, chicken, or lobster.

It is likely that your sales contacts and others associated with your accounts are using social media. This means that their postings will appear occasionally on Facebook, LinkedIn, and other similar sites. Most of these online services permit you to be notified by email when such postings occur. Many entries in most social sites are frivolous, so a review of every post may be unnecessary. However, it is wise to monitor these posts carefully enough to detect important relationship information.

You may wish to make note of many of these postings in your sales database. A sales contact may mention recent activities such as events attended, hobbies, or notable experiences. Someone might make reference to an alma mater or to a friend who is well known. You can use this kind of information to add value to subsequent conversations with the person who posted. The information may give you a chance to point out interests or friends you have in common. You may also take note of issues to avoid, such as commenting on a recent varsity game your contact's school may have lost.

Your own entries on social websites can also add value to your relationship with sales contacts. Usually, you can directly comment on a sales contact's post instead of waiting until a subsequent conversation. You might comment that you agree with the entry or add helpful—and positive—information that supports the contact's comment.

5. *When you use voice mail, leave a clear, concise message.* Do not speak too fast or mumble your name and number.

6. *Avoid cell phone contempt.* Turn off the cell phone ringer any time you are with a client. Never put your phone on the table during a meal.

It has been said that good manners make other people feel better. This is true because good etiquette requires that we place the other person's comfort ahead of our own. One of the best ways to develop rapport with a customer is to avoid behaviour that might be offensive to that person.

CONVERSATIONAL STRATEGIES THAT ENHANCE SELLING RELATIONSHIPS

THE FOUNDATION FOR A LONG-TERM RELATIONSHIP WITH THE CUSTOMER IS FREQUENTLY a "get acquainted" type of conversation that takes place before any discussion of business matters. Within a few minutes it is possible to reduce the relationship tension that is so common when two people meet for the first time. This informal visit with the customer provides the salesperson with an opportunity to apply three guidelines for building strong relationships featured in *How to Win Friends and Influence People*, the classic book written by Dale Carnegie.

- *Become genuinely interested in other people.* Tim Sanders, Chief Solutions Officer at Yahoo!, says, "How we are perceived as human beings is becoming increasingly important in the new economy."[37] When you become genuinely interested in the customer, you create an experience that is long remembered.

- *Be a good listener; encourage others to talk about themselves.* Stephen Covey, the noted author and consultant, recommends empathetic listening. This requires listening with your ears, your eyes, and your heart.[38] We live in a culture in which empathic listening is quite rare. Interrupting has become all too common as people rush to fill every gap in the conversation.

The length of this conversation depends on your sense of the prospect's reaction to your greeting, how busy the prospect appears to be, and your awareness of topics of mutual interest. Keep any small-talk conversation relatively short unless your client wants to expand on it. Even then, it is important to plan a way to move the conversation to the over-riding business reason for your call. Never engage in any small-talk conversation unless you are genuinely interested in the topics brought up. If your customer shows any indication of noninterest, move immediately to the business you are there to conduct. The following three areas should be considered in developing conversation. There will often be other times during the sales call when it may be appropriate to engage in one or more of these three areas of conversation.

Comments on Here and Now Observations

Observant salespeople are aware of the things going on around them. These observations can be as general as unusual developments in the weather or as specific as noticing unique artefacts in the prospect's office. These observations often provide the basis for *small talk*, which can break the ice and speed up the building of a relationship.

Adding Value with the CARE Model

Andrew Gallan, a district sales manager for Abbott Laboratories, supervises a group of sales representatives who call on busy physicians. From many years of experience, he has discovered that what matters most to these customers is caring for them and their needs. He uses the acronym CARE to remind his sales representatives of behaviours that build long-term relationships.

Customize—Every customer is unique and requires a custom-tailored selling effort.

Appreciate—Expressing sincere appreciation is an important strategy for building a relationship with the customer.

Respond—The sales presentation should match product features with benefits to the patient base and the physician's practice.

Execute—Always follows through on your commitment to provide a valued service to your customers.

Those who adopt the CARE model are more likely to become trusted, respected, and invaluable partners to their customers.[d]

Compliments

When you offer a *sincere* compliment to your prospect, you are saying, "Something about you is special." Most people react positively to compliments because they appeal to the need for self-esteem. Your admiration should not be expressed, however, in phony superlatives that will seem transparent. Jack Canfield, author of *The Success Principles*, reminds us that everything we say to a customer produces an effect: "Know that you are constantly creating something—either positive or negative—with your words."[39]

Search for Mutual Acquaintances or Interests

A frequent mode for establishing rapport with a new prospect is to find friends or interests you have in common. If you know someone with the same last name as your prospect, it may be appropriate to ask whether your friend is any relation. Anything you observe in the prospect's office or home might suggest an interest that you and your prospect share. A strong bond often develops between two persons who share the same interest or hobby. Estate planner Frances Carlisle says her love of animals lands her many clients. Some of these clients wish to include provisions for the care of pets in their estate plans. Sometimes an unusual hobby (skydiving, mountain climbing, auto racing, etc.) is the perfect way to stand out and cultivate relationships with clients.[40]

SELF-IMPROVEMENT STRATEGIES THAT ADD VALUE

ORSON WELLES, A WELL-KNOWN AND HIGHLY RESPECTED ACTOR, ONCE SAID, "EVERY actor is very busy getting better or getting worse." To a large extent, salespeople are also "very busy getting better or getting worse." To improve, salespeople must develop an ongoing program for self-improvement (see Chapter 16). It is important to keep in mind that all improvement is self-initiated. Each of us controls the switch that allows personal growth and development to take place.

In Chapter 3, we introduced the concept of emotional intelligence, and we noted that it can be increased with the aid of self-development activities. Would you like to develop a more positive self-concept? Improve your ability to develop win-win relationships? Develop effective nonverbal communication skills? Improve your speaking voice? These relationship-building strategies can be achieved if you are willing to follow these four steps:

Step one: Set goals. The goal-setting process begins with a clear, written statement that describes what you want to accomplish. If your goal is too general or vague, progress toward achieving that goal will be difficult to observe. Next, you must identify the ways in which you plan to achieve your goal. Perseverance is the key to goal achievement.

Step two: Use visualization. To **visualize** means to form a mental image of something. The power to visualize (sometimes called guided imagery) is in a very real sense the power to create. If you really want to succeed at something, picture yourself doing it successfully. For example, spend time developing mental pictures of successful sales presentations or visualizing yourself as one of the top salespeople in your organization. Once you have formed a clear mental picture of what you want to accomplish, identify the steps needed to get there and then mentally rehearse them. The visualization process needs to be repeated over and over again.[41]

visualize Form a mental image of something.

Step three: Use positive self-talk. People with a strong inner critic will receive frequent negative messages that can erode their self-esteem. It helps to refute and reject those negative messages with positive self-talk. **Self-talk** takes place silently in the privacy of your mind—a series of personal conversations you have with yourself continually throughout the day. Just like statements from other people, your self-talk can dramatically affect your behaviour and self-esteem.[42]

self-talk Takes place silently in the privacy of your mind—a series of personal conversations you have with yourself continually throughout the day.

This salesperson has set a fitness goal. Physical fitness can be an important part of a self-improvement program.

Arne Trautmann/iStock/Thinkstock/Getty Images

Step four: Reward your progress. When you see yourself making progress toward a goal, or achieving a goal, reward yourself. This type of reinforcement is vital when you are trying to change a behaviour. There is nothing wrong with taking pride in your accomplishments.

Self-improvement efforts can result in new abilities or powers, and they give us the motivation to draw more fully on the talents we already have. As a result, our potential for success is greater.

REVIEWING KEY CONCEPTS

- Explain how partnering realtionships add value.

  The concept of *partnering* is revisited and discussed in detail. Partnering emphasizes building a strong relationship during every aspect of the sale and working hard to maintain a quality relationship with the customer after the sale. Relationship building must also include management personnel, company support staff, and secondary decision makers. Partnerships can be strengthened when salespeople use value-added relationship strategies.

- Discuss how thought processes can enhance your relationship strategy.

  An understanding of the psychology of human behaviour provides a foundation for developing relationship strategies. In this chapter, we discuss the link between self-concept and success in selling. Self-imposed fears can prevent salespeople from achieving success. The relationship strategy is built on the win-win philosophy, empathy and ego drive, and character and integrity.

- Identify and describe the major nonverbal factors that shape our sales image.

  We describe several factors that influence the image we project to customers. The image others have of us is shaped to a great extent by nonverbal communication. We may choose the right words to persuade a customer to place an order, but aversive factors communicated by our clothing, handshake, facial expression, voice quality, and etiquette miscues may prejudice the customer against us and our product or service.

- Describe conversational strategies that help us establish relationships.

  The various conversational strategies that enhance relationships are reviewed. These include comments on "here and now" observations, compliments, and the search for mutual acquaintances. Dale Carnegie's guidelines for building strong relationships are discussed.

- Explain how to establish a self-improvement plan based on personal development strategies.

  We discussed the importance of adopting strategies for self-improvement. A four-step self-improvement plan is the key to relationship building.

Key Terms

business casual **88**

ego drive **84**

empathizer **78**

nonverbal message **85**

self-concept **81**

self-talk **93**

unconscious expectations **88**

visualize **93**

Review Questions

1. How important are establishing, building, and maintaining relationships in the selling process?

2. List the four groups of people with whom sales personnel must be able to work effectively.

3. Why is *partnering* described as the highest-quality selling relationship? Why has the building of partnerships become more important today?

4. Describe the win-win approach to selling.

5. Describe the four key words that should govern our decisions regarding an appropriate set of guidelines to "dress for success" in today's sales environments.

6. How is our self-concept formed? Why is a positive self-concept so important in personal selling?

7. Describe five rules of etiquette that are especially important to salespeople today.

8. Identify three conversational methods that can be used to establish relationships.

9. Describe the meaning of *nonverbal messages*. Why should salespeople be concerned about these messages?

10. List and describe each step in the four-step self-improvement plan.

Application Exercises

1. Select four salespeople you know and ask them if they have a relationship strategy for working with customers, management personnel, secondary decision makers, and company support staff. Ask each salesperson to give you two or three specific examples of steps they have taken to build and maintain a positive relationship with their customers.

2. The partnering style of selling is emphasized throughout the book. To gain more insight into the popularity of this concept, use an Internet search engine of your choice and key in the words "partnering + selling." Notice the large number of documents related to this query. Click on and examine several of these documents to learn more about this approach to selling.

3. Complete the following etiquette quiz. Your instructor will provide you with answers so you can check your responses.

   a. On what side should you wear your name tag?

   b. Is it appropriate to drink beer from a bottle at a formal reception or dinner?

   c. When introducing a female salesperson to a male prospect, whose name should be spoken first?

   d. At the table, when should you place your napkin in your lap?

   e. Is it ever proper to comb, smooth, or touch your hair while seated at a restaurant table?

4. In October, people of the Hindu religion celebrate Diwali, the festival of lights. The festival of lights is one of the most important and most beautiful Indian festivals. Rick Saulle, a pharmaceutical sales representative employed by Pifzer, knew that one of the most important physicians he called on was Indian and would celebrate Diwali. He also knew that it is commonplace to provide sweets to Indians who celebrate Diwali. Saulle visited an Indian grocery store and purchased a plate of Indian sweets. When he presented these to the physician, the response was very positive. The doctor grabbed Saulle's hand, shook it forcefully, and sincerely thanked him for honouring this important holiday.[43]

   Canada is host to a kaleidoscope of the world's cultures, and the trend toward greater diversity will accelerate in the years ahead. Reflect on the gift given by Mr. Saulle and then answer these questions.

   a. Is it appropriate for a salesperson to give a gift to someone who is celebrating a religious holiday?

   b. In addition to giving a gift, what are some other ways to recognize a religious festival or holiday?

   c. List and describe three holidays or festivals celebrated by religions other than Christian.

5. Move quickly through the following list of traits. Use a check mark beside those that fit your self-image. Use an *X* to mark those that do not fit. If you are unsure, indicate with a question mark.

   —— I like myself.

   —— I trust myself.

   —— People trust me.

   —— I often do the wrong thing.

—— I usually say the right thing.

—— People avoid me.

—— I dislike myself.

—— I enjoy work.

—— I waste time.

—— I control myself.

—— I put up a good front.

—— I enjoy nature.

—— I use my talents.

—— I am dependent on others for ideas.

—— I feel hemmed in.

—— I am involved in solving community problems.

—— I use time well.

—— I do not use my talents fully.

—— I enjoy people.

—— I do not like myself.

—— I usually say the wrong thing.

—— I do not like to be around people.

—— I am discouraged about life.

—— I have not developed my talents.

—— People like to be around me.

Now look at the pattern of your self-assessment.

a. Is there a pattern?

b. Is there a winner or loser pattern?

c. What traits would you like to change? List them.

d. Pick the trait you would like to change the most and prepare a plan to achieve this change. Your plan should include specific goal statements.

6. It is pointed out in this chapter that clothing communicates strong messages. In this exercise you will become more aware of whether your clothes communicate the messages you want them to communicate.

a. Make a chart like the one that follows:

Item of clothing being analyzed	What I want my clothes to say about me to others	What others think my clothing says about me

b. In the first column, list the clothing you are now wearing (e.g., dress slacks, dress shoes, and sweater; athletic shoes, jeans, and T-shirt; or suit, dress shirt, and dress shoes).

c. In the middle column, describe the message you would like the clothes you have chosen to say (e.g., "I want to be comfortable," "I want people to trust me," or "I want people to take me seriously.").

d. Have somebody else fill in the third column by describing what they think your clothes say about you.

e. Compare the last two columns. Do your clothes communicate what you want them to? Do the same exercise for social dress, casual dress, business attire, and hair style.

Note: If you are currently employed, analyze the clothing you wear at work.

 ROLE-PLAY EXERCISE

This is a two-part role-play exercise. Part one involves preparation for a sales call on a new prospect you have not met previously. The primary objective of this meeting is to get acquainted with the prospect and begin the process of building a long-term relationship. You anticipate that this prospect will become a very good customer. Review the text material on thought processes that will enhance your relationship strategy, nonverbal strategies that add value to your relationships, and conversational strategies that enhance relationships. Prepare a written outline of what you plan to say and do during the first five to ten minutes of the meeting. Think of this outline as your "strategic plan." Part two involves a role play with a class member who will play the role of the prospect. Throughout the role play, try to say and do everything that was part of your plan. At the end of the role play, give your strategic plan outline to the prospect and request feedback on your performance.

Reality Selling Video Case Problem

The commercial real estate services industry is highly competitive. CBRE, the firm featured at the beginning of this chapter, offers a wide variety of services such as industrial and logistical services, real estate consulting, investment properties services, and global corporate services. When clients want to find an office space, they hold their realtor to high standards. After all, the term of a lease contract is a long one, and the stakes are high. CBRE salespeople understand the magnitude and trend of the commercial real estate market. They know that the customers are anxious to partner with someone who can be trusted to look after their best interests.

When new salespeople join the CBRE sales force, they usually work under a senior broker. The mentor helps these recruits form a professional image that appeals to the type of clientele served by the company. In the end, there is a direct link between the image projected by the salespeople and the success of the company. CBRE also adopts a team-based selling approach to ensure that the client is in good hands as the relationship between CBRE and the client develops. Susana Rosas, an experienced CBRE broker, believes that working under a mentor to learn how to process a deal with a relationship orientation is invaluable. That mentality is part of CBRE's culture and success. Susana works closely with her team members through several stages of the relationship with CBRE clients, from prospecting to post-sales follow-up. When working with new recruits and her team members, she emphasizes the following points:

- Customers notice even the little details such as the firmness of a handshake or simply the properness of an introduction.

- Salespeople at CBRE must be able to build rapport with a variety of personality types. Some customers are quiet, reserved, and somewhat guarded when expressing their views. Others are more impulsive and express their views openly. Salespeople are encouraged to alter their communication style to increase the comfort level of the customer. Susana believes that it is always important for a salesperson to gauge how his or her communication style impacts the prospect. A positive attitude is another important aspect of the relationship-building process at CBRE.

- Susana is a strong believer that salespeople should find out what customers value. Most of the time, a salesperson must come up with innovative solutions to seemingly irreconcilable needs, such as the need to have a large space to accommodate cyclical ups and downs of the customer's industry and the need for efficiency. What is the most important aspect of commercial real estate sales? Most customers do not open up and share important information until they trust the salesperson. (See the chapter opener on page 76 and Reality Selling Today Role Play 4 in Appendix 1 on page 429 for more information.)

Questions

1. Why should real estate salespeople spend time developing a relationship strategy? What might be some long-term benefits of this strategy?

2. Review the four key groups of people that the relationship strategy should encompass. List the various individuals who would fit in each group.

3. Is it ever appropriate to touch your client other than with a handshake? Explain your answer.

4. How would you behave differently when dealing with a return client versus a new client?

5. What are some precautions to take when preparing for a meeting with a foreign-born prospect?

Chapter 5
Communication Styles: A Key to Adaptive Selling Today

Learning Objectives

After studying this chapter, you should be able to

1   Discuss how communication style influences the relationship process in sales.

2   Identify the two major dimensions of the communication-style model.

3   Explain the four communication styles in the communication-style model.

4   Learn how to identify your preferred communication style and that of your customer.

5   Learn to achieve interpersonal versatility and build strong selling relationships with style flexing.

 Adaptive Selling Training Video Series
Communications Styles—A Key to Adaptive Selling

COMMUNICATION STYLES—OR BEHAVIOUR STYLES, AS THEY ARE SOMETIMES CALLED—HAVE been described as one of the most popular training topics in sales and management.

In this two-part Adaptive Selling Today training video, you'll meet Lana, a senior salesperson. While working with Ron, Sandra, and Raymond (one of her top customers, her sales team member, and her marketing manager, respectively), Lana shares what she has learned about building selling relationships with communication styles. We will learn how Lana and her team take a "No, this won't work" response from Ron and, with the adaptive selling "Platinum Rule," attempt to build a mutually rewarding relationship.

Every year publications such as *Canadian Business*, *Fortune*, and *Fast Company* feature profiles of well-known business leaders. These articles often focus on the communication styles of the executives who provide leadership in companies across North America. Who can forget Al "Chainsaw" Dunlap, who was described as aggressive, frank, opinionated,

Communication styles are a key to adaptive selling.

and impatient? He earned his nickname by ordering huge layoffs when he was the CEO responsible for restructuring companies such as Scott Paper and Sunbeam Corporation. Deborah Hopkins earned the nickname "Hurricane Debby" for the way she conducted business while holding leadership positions at Unisys, GM Europe, Boeing, and Lucent Technologies. Her demanding, ambitious, and sometimes emotional style occasionally created personality clashes. In contrast, Bill Gates is described as a quiet, reflective person who often seems preoccupied with other matters. And then there is Jeff Bezos, the founder and CEO of Amazon.com, who is often described as the happy extrovert. He seems to enjoy being with other people and often displays spontaneous, uninhibited behaviour.[1]

We form impressions of people by observing their behaviour. The thoughts, feelings, and actions that characterize someone are generally viewed as their **personality**.[2] Communication style is an important aspect of our personality.

> **personality** The thoughts, feelings, and actions that characterize someone.

COMMUNICATION STYLES—AN INTRODUCTION TO MANAGING SELLING RELATIONSHIPS

ALMOST EVERYONE HAS HAD THE PLEASANT EXPERIENCE OF MEETING SOMEONE FOR THE FIRST time and developing instant mutual rapport. There seems to be something about some people that makes you like them instantaneously—a basis for mutual understanding that is difficult to explain. On the other hand, we can all recall meeting people who "turn us off" almost immediately. Why do these things happen during the initial contact?

The impressions that others form about us are based on what they observe us saying and doing. They have no way of knowing our innermost thoughts and feelings, so they make decisions about us based on what they see and hear.[3] The patterns of behaviour that others observe can be called **communication style**. *Behaviour style* and *social style* are additional terms frequently used to describe these patterns of behaviour.

Adaptive selling, introduced in Chapter 2, is defined as altering sales behaviours in order to improve communication with the customer. It relates to a salesperson's ability to

> **communication style** Patterns of behaviour that others observe. Voice patterns, eye movement, facial expression, and posture are some of the components of our communication style.

> **adaptive selling** Altering sales behaviours in order to improve communication with the customer.

We form impressions of others by observing their behaviour. Jeff Bezos, founder of Amazon. com, is often described as the happy extrovert who frequently displays spontaneous, uninhibited behaviour. In contrast, Microsoft's Bill Gates is described as a quiet, reflective person who often seems preoccupied with other matters.

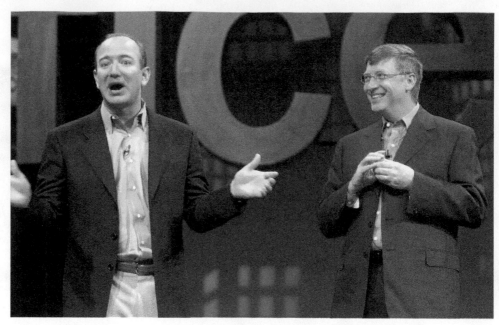

Stan Honda/Getty Images

collect information regarding the customer's needs and respond appropriately. Adaptive selling frequently requires complex behavioural adjustments.[4] Adjusting one's communication style in order to fit individual customer needs and preferences is an important element of adaptive selling.

Communication-Style Bias

Bias in various forms is quite common in our society. In fact, governments at all levels have passed many laws to curb blatant forms of age, ethnic, religious, and gender discrimination. We also observe some degree of regional bias when people from various parts of Canada meet.

The most frequently occurring form of bias is not commonly understood in our society. What has been labelled **communication-style bias** is a state of mind that almost every one of us experiences from time to time, but we usually find it difficult to explain the symptoms. Communication-style bias can develop when we have contact with another person whose communication style is different from our own. For example, a purchasing agent was overheard saying, "I do not know what it is, but I just do not like that sales representative." The agent was no doubt experiencing communication-style bias but could not easily describe the feeling.

Your communication style is the "you" that is on display every day—the outer pattern of behaviour that others see. If your style is very different from another person's, it may be difficult for the two of you to develop rapport. All of us have had the experience of saying or doing something that was perfectly acceptable to a friend or co-worker and being surprised when the same behaviour irritated someone else. However, aside from admitting that this happens, most of us are unable to draw meaningful conclusions from these experiences to help us perform more effectively with people in the future.[5]

In recent years, thousands of sales professionals have learned to manage their selling relationships more effectively through the study of communication styles. Books such

communication-style bias A state of mind we often experience when we have contact with another person whose communication style is different from our own.

as *I'm Stuck, You're Stuck* by Tom Ritchey, *People Styles at Work* by Robert Bolton and Dorothy Grover Bolton, and *The Versatile Salesperson* by Roger Wenschlag serve as good references. Many training companies offer seminars that provide enrolees with a practical understanding of communication-style theory and practice. Wilson Learning (**www.wilsonlearning.com**) offers a program entitled *The Versatile Salesperson*. This program helps salespeople develop the interpersonal skills necessary to work effectively with customers whose communication style is different than their own. Over 7 million people worldwide have completed Wilson Learning programs that focus on communication styles.[6]

Communication-Style Principles

The theory of behavioural- or communication-style bias is based on a number of underlying principles. A review of these principles will be beneficial before we examine specific styles.

1. *Individual differences exist and are important.* It is quite obvious that we all differ in terms of such physical characteristics as height, shoe size, facial features, and body build, but the most interesting differences are those patterns of behaviour that are unique to each of us. Voice patterns, eye movement, facial expressions, and posture are some of the components of our communication style. Additional characteristics are discussed later in this chapter. Research by Swiss psychoanalyst Carl Jung and others has helped us understand the importance of individual differences.

2. *A communication style is a way of thinking and behaving.* It is not an ability, but instead a preferred way of using the abilities one has. This distinction is very important. An ability refers to how well someone can do something. A *style* refers to how someone likes to do something.[7]

3. *Individual style differences tend to be stable.* Our communication style is based on a combination of hereditary and environmental factors. Our style is somewhat

---

From the Field

Some Accountants Communicate

In a famous Monty Python skit, John Cleese describes an accountant he is interviewing as dull, unimaginative, humourless, tedious, and drab, and says that while in most professions these would be considered drawbacks, not so in accounting. But the reality today is that highly successful professional accountants do not match the stereotype that Cleese describes.

Today's best chartered accountants know they must manage relationships with clients, and that means regularly communicating with them. Ruth Todd is a partner at KPMG LLP (Canada) and has been a chartered accountant for approximately 20 years. Ruth says that KPMG promotes a culture of "client service excellence," and that means staying in touch with clients so they always

know you are interested in their business and that you wish to help them find solutions that meet their needs. Some clients call Ruth on a regular basis; some almost never call. Ruth says, "I regularly go through my portfolio of clients and ensure that none get ignored. I contact some by phone, some by email, and some in person, depending on their preference. I find that when I regularly call them, many reciprocate and call me when they have a question because they know I want to help." Ruth also points out that she does not invoice a client for every phone call. She says, "If you are too focused on billing, the client will become hesitant to call for advice. You need to think about adding value and building long-term relationships."[a]

original at the time of birth; it takes on additional individuality during the first three to five years of life. By the time we enter elementary school, the teacher should be able to identify our preferred communication style. While an individual's communication style tends to remain fairly constant throughout life, adapting to different communication counterparts or the ability to "flex" can be enhanced and mastered.

4. *There are a finite number of styles.* Most people display one of several clusters of similar behaviours, and this allows us to identify a small number of behavioural categories. By combining a series of descriptors, we can develop a single "label" that describes a person's most preferred communication style.

5. *To create the most productive relationships, it is necessary to get in sync with the communication style of the people you work with.*[8] Differences between people can be a source of friction unless you develop the ability to recognize and respond to the other person's style.

The ability to identify another person's communication style, and to know how and when to adapt your own preferred style to it, can afford you a crucial advantage in dealing with people. Differences between people can be a source of friction. The ability to "speak the other person's language" is an important relationship-management skill.[9]

Improving Your Relationship Selling Skills

Anyone who is considering a career in selling will benefit greatly from the study of communication styles. These concepts provide a practical method of classifying people according to communication style and give the salesperson a distinct advantage in the marketplace. A salesperson who understands communication-style classification methods and learns how to adapt them can avoid common mistakes that threaten interpersonal relations with customers. Awareness of these methods greatly reduces the possibility of tension arising during the sales call.

The first major goal of this chapter is to help you better understand your own most preferred communication style. The second goal is to help you develop greater understanding and appreciation for styles that are different from your own. The third goal is to help you manage your selling relationships more effectively by learning to adapt your style to fit the communication style of the customer. This practice is called **style flexing**.

style flexing The deliberate adjustment of one's communication style to accommodate the needs of the other person.

COMMUNICATION-STYLE MODEL

THIS SECTION INTRODUCES YOU TO THE FOUR BASIC COMMUNICATION STYLES. ONE OF THESE will surface as your most preferred style. The communication-style model that defines these styles is based on two important dimensions of human behaviour: dominance and sociability. We look at the dominance continuum first.

Dominance Continuum

dominance Reflects the tendency to influence or exert one's will over others in a relationship. Each of us falls somewhere on the continuum.

Dominance can be defined as the tendency to control or prevail over others.[10] Dominant people tend to be quite competitive. They also tend to offer opinions readily and to be decisive, opinionated, self-assertive, and vocal. Each of us falls somewhere on the dominance continuum illustrated by Figure 5.1.

Low ────────────────────────────────── High

Figure 5.1 The first step in determining your most preferred communication style is to identify where you are on the dominance continuum.

A person classified as high in dominance is generally a "take charge" type of person who makes a position clear to others. A person classified as low in dominance is usually more reserved, unassertive, and easygoing. Dominance has been recognized as a universal behavioural characteristic. David W. Johnson developed the Interpersonal Pattern Exercise to help people achieve greater interpersonal effectiveness. He believes that people fall into two dominance categories:

1. *Lower dominance:* These people have a tendency to be quite cooperative and let others control things. They tend to be lower in assertiveness.

2. *Higher dominance:* These people like to control things and frequently initiate demands. They are more aggressive in dealing with others.[11]

The first step in determining your most preferred communication style is to identify where you fall on the dominance continuum. Do you tend to rank low or high on this scale? To answer this question, complete the Dominance Indicator form in Table 5.1. Rate yourself on each scale by placing a check mark on the continuum at the point that

Table 5.1 Dominance Indicator					
Rate yourself on each scale by placing a check mark on the continuum at the point that represents how you perceive yourself.					
I Perceive Myself as Somewhat					
Cooperative	/	/	/	/	/	Competitive
Submissive	/	/	/	/	/	Authoritarian
Accommodating	/	/	/	/	/	Domineering
Hesitant	/	/	/	/	/	Decisive
Reserved	/	/	/	/	/	Outgoing
Compromising	/	/	/	/	/	Insistent
Cautious	/	/	/	/	/	Risk-taking
Patient	/	/	/	/	/	Hurried
Complacent	/	/	/	/	/	Influential
Quiet	/	/	/	/	/	Talkative
Shy	/	/	/	/	/	Bold
Supportive	/	/	/	/	/	Demanding
Relaxed	/	/	/	/	/	Tense
Restrained	/	/	/	/	/	Assertive

represents how you perceive yourself. If most of your check marks fall to the right of centre, you are someone who is higher in dominance. If most of your check marks fall to the left of centre, you are someone who is lower in dominance. Is there any best place to be on the dominance continuum? The answer is no. Successful salespeople can be found at all points along the continuum.

Sociability Continuum

sociability Reflects the amount of control one exerts over emotional expressiveness. People who are high in sociability tend to express their feelings freely, while people who are low on this continuum tend to control their feelings.

Sociability reflects the amount of control we exert over our emotional expressiveness.[12] People who are high in sociability tend to express their feelings freely, while people who are low in this dimension tend to control their feelings. Each of us falls somewhere on the sociability continuum illustrated in Figure 5.2.

Sociability is also a universal behavioural characteristic. It can be defined as the tendency to seek and enjoy interaction with others. Therefore, high sociability is an indication of a person's preference to interact with other people. Lower sociability is an indicator of a person's desire to work in an environment where he or she has more time alone instead of having to make conversation with others. The person who is classified as being lower in the area of sociability is more reserved and formal in social relationships.

The second step in determining your most preferred communication style is to identify where you fall on the sociability continuum. To answer this question, complete the Sociability Indicator form shown in Table 5.2. Rate yourself on each scale by placing a

High

Low

Figure 5.2 The second step in determining your most preferred communication style is to identify where you are on the sociability continuum.

Table 5.2	Sociability Indicator					

Rate yourself on each scale by placing a check mark on the continuum at the point that represents how you perceive yourself.

		I Perceive Myself as Somewhat				
Disciplined	/	/	/	/	/	Easygoing
Controlled	/	/	/	/	/	Expressive
Serious	/	/	/	/	/	Lighthearted
Methodical	/	/	/	/	/	Unstructured
Calculating	/	/	/	/	/	Spontaneous
Guarded	/	/	/	/	/	Open
Stalwart	/	/	/	/	/	Humorous
Aloof	/	/	/	/	/	Friendly
Formal	/	/	/	/	/	Casual
Reserved	/	/	/	/	/	Attention-seeking
Cautious	/	/	/	/	/	Carefree
Conforming	/	/	/	/	/	Unconventional
Reticent	/	/	/	/	/	Dramatic
Restrained	/	/	/	/	/	Impulsive

check mark on the continuum at the point that represents how you perceive yourself. If most of your check marks fall to the right of centre, you are someone who is higher in sociability. If most of your check marks fall to the left of centre, you are someone who is lower in sociability. Keep in mind that there is no best place to be. Successful salespeople can be found at all points along this continuum.

As you reflect on your dominance and sociability ratings, keep in mind that self-ratings can be misleading. Many people do not see themselves in the same way that others see them. Friends and co-workers who frequently observe your behaviours may be in a better position to identify your communication style.

With the aid of the dominance and sociability continuums we can now discuss a relatively simple communication-style classification plan that has practical application in the field of selling. We describe the four basic styles: Emotive, Directive, Reflective, and Supportive.

Four Styles of Communication

By combining the two dimensions of human behaviour—dominance and sociability—we can form a partial outline of the communication-style model (Fig. 5.3). Dominance is represented by the horizontal axis and sociability is represented by the vertical axis. Once the two dimensions of human behaviour are combined, the framework for communication-style classification is established.

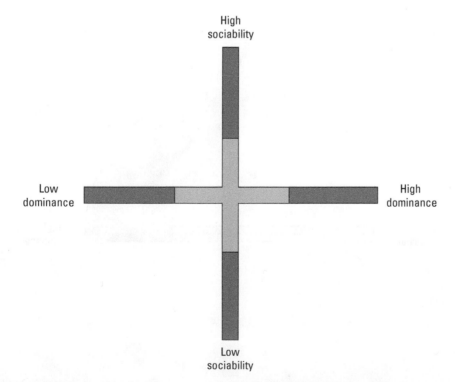

Figure 5.3 When the dominance and sociability dimensions of human behaviour are combined, the framework for communication-style classification is established.

Emotive Style The upper right-hand quadrant of Figure 5.4 defines a style that combines higher sociability and higher dominance. We call this the **Emotive style** (see Fig. 5.5). Emotive people stand out in a crowd. They are expressive and willing to spend time maintaining and enjoying a large number of relationships.[13] Television personalities Rick Mercer and Oprah Winfrey provide excellent models of the Emotive communication style. Sports personality Don Cherry and actors Jim Carrey, Mike Myers, and Robin Williams (d. 2014) also project the Emotive communication style. They are outspoken, enthusiastic, and stimulating. The Emotive person wants to create a social relationship quickly and usually feels more comfortable in an informal atmosphere. Some of the verbal and nonverbal clues that identify the Emotive person follow:

1. *Appears quite active.* This person gives the appearance of being busy. A person who combines higher dominance and higher sociability often displays spontaneous, uninhibited behaviour. The Emotive person is likely to express feelings with vigorous movements of the hands and a rapid speech pattern.

2. *Takes the social initiative in most cases.* Emotives tend to be extroverts. When two people meet for the first time, the Emotive person is more apt to initiate and maintain the conversation as well as to initiate the handshake. Emotives rate higher in both directness and openness.

3. *Likes to encourage informality.* The Emotive person moves to a first-name basis as soon as possible (too soon in some cases). Even the way this person sits in a chair communicates a preference for a relaxed, informal social setting.

Sociable	Unstructured
Spontaneous	Excitable
Zestful	Personable
Stimulating	Persuasive
Emotional	Dynamic

Figure 5.5 Key words for the Emotive style.

Figure 5.4 The Emotive style combines high sociability and high dominance.

Neil Burstyn/Agence Quebec Presse/Newscom

Emotive people, such as Rick Mercer, are stimulating, excitable, and spontaneous. Emotives generally do not hide their feelings and often express opinions dramatically and impulsively.

4. *Expresses emotional opinions.* Emotive people generally do not hide their feelings. They often express opinions dramatically and impulsively.

The Directive Style The lower right-hand quadrant of Figure 5.6 defines a style that combines higher dominance and lower sociability. We will call this the **Directive style** (see Fig. 5.7).

Directive style A communication style that displays the following characteristics: appears quite busy, may give the impression of not listening, displays a serious attitude, and likes to maintain control.

Aggressive	Determined
Intense	Frank
Requiring	Opinionated
Pushy	Impatient
Serious	Bold

Figure 5.7 Key words for the Directive style.

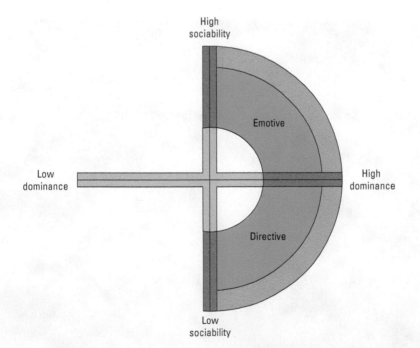

Figure 5.6 The Directive style combines high dominance and low sociability.

To understand the nature of people who display the Directive communication style, picture in your mind's eye the director of a Hollywood film. The person you see is giving orders in a firm voice and is generally in charge of every facet of the operation. Everyone on the set knows this person is in charge. While this common image of the Hollywood film director is probably exaggerated, this example will be helpful as you attempt to become familiar with the Directive style.

Many senior executives of large corporations project the Directive style, as does Kevin O'Leary of *Dragons' Den*, Canadian Prime Minister Stephen Harper, and former U.S. Secretary of State Hillary Clinton. Directives may be described as frank, demanding, assertive, and determined.

In the field of selling you will encounter a number of customers who are Directives. How can you identify these people? What verbal and nonverbal clues can you observe? A few of the behaviours displayed by Directives follow:

1. *Appears to be quite busy.* The Directive generally does not like to waste time and wants to get right to the point. Judy Sheindlin of the *Judge Judy* television show displays this behaviour.
2. *May give the impression of not listening.* In most cases the Directive feels more comfortable talking than listening.
3. *Displays a serious attitude.* A person who is lower in sociability usually communicates a lack of warmth and is apt to be quite businesslike and impersonal.
4. *Likes to maintain control.* The person who is higher on the dominance continuum likes to maintain control. During meetings the Directive often seeks to control the agenda.[14]

People who display the Directive style, such as Kevin O'Leary, like to take charge and maintain control. People who display the Directive style are generally viewed as determined, bold, and serious.

Leon Switzer/ZUMAPRESS/Newscom

The Reflective Style The lower left-hand quadrant of the communication-style model features a combination of lower dominance and lower sociability (Fig. 5.8). People who regularly display this behaviour are classified as having the **Reflective style** (see Fig. 5.9).

The Reflective person tends to examine all the facts carefully before arriving at a decision. Like a cautious scientist, this individual wants to gather all available information and weigh it carefully before taking a position. The Reflective type is usually a stickler for detail.[15] The late physicist Albert Einstein fits the description. Rex Murphy, the journalist who hosts CBC's *Cross Country Checkup*; David Suzuki, the scientist who hosts CBC's *The Nature of Things*; and CBC news anchor Peter Mansbridge, who hosts *Mansbridge One on One*, all display the characteristics of the Reflective type.

The Reflective communication style combines lower dominance and lower sociability; therefore, people with this classification tend to be reserved and cautious. Some additional behaviours that characterize this style follow:

1. *Controls emotional expression.* Reflective people tend to curb emotional expression and are less likely to display warmth openly. Bill Gates displays this personality trait.

2. *Displays a preference for orderliness.* The Reflective person enjoys a highly structured environment and generally feels frustration when confronted with unexpected events.

Reflective style A communication style that displays the following characteristics: controls emotional expression, displays a preference for orderliness, tends to express measured opinions, and seems difficult to get to know.

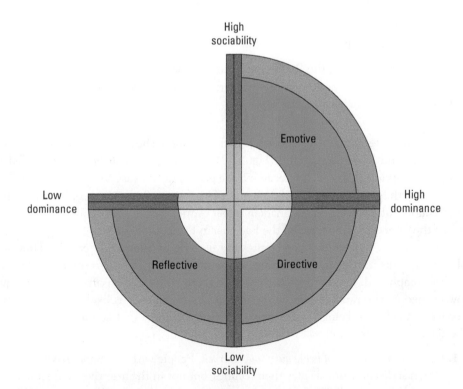

Figure 5.8 The Reflective style combines low dominance and low sociability.

Precise	Scientific
Deliberate	Preoccupied
Questioning	Serious
Disciplined	Industrious
Aloof	Stuffy

Figure 5.9 Key words for the Reflective style.

Persons with the Reflective style, such as Peter Mansbridge, tend to control their emotions and examine all the facts when making a decision.

George Pimentel/WireImage/Getty Images

3. *Tends to express measured opinions.* The Reflective individual usually does not express dramatic opinions. This communication style is characterized by disciplined, businesslike actions.

4. *Seems difficult to get to know.* The Reflective person tends to be somewhat formal in social relationships and therefore can be viewed as aloof by many people.

In a selling situation the Reflective customer does not want to move too fast. This person wants the facts presented in an orderly and unemotional manner and does not want to waste a lot of time socializing.

The Supportive Style The upper left-hand quadrant shows a combination of lower dominance and higher sociability (Fig. 5.10). This communication style is called the **Supportive style** (see Fig. 5.11) because these people find it easy to listen and usually do not express their views in a forceful manner. Entertainers Meryl Streep, Kevin Costner, Paul Simon, Julia Roberts and Canadian singer Anne Murray all display the characteristics of the Supportive style, as did the late Diana, Princess of Wales.

Low visibility generally characterizes the lifestyle of Supportive people. They complete their tasks in a quiet, unassuming manner and seldom draw attention to what they have accomplished. In terms of assertiveness, persons with the Supportive style rank quite low. Someone who ranks higher on the dominance continuum is likely to view the Supportive individual as being too easygoing. Other behaviours that commonly characterize the Supportive person follow:

1. *Gives the appearance of being quiet and reserved.* People with the Supportive communication style can easily display their feelings, but not in the assertive manner common to the Emotive individual.

2. *Listens attentively to other people.* In selling, good listening skills can be a real asset. This talent comes naturally to the Supportive person.

Supportive style A communication style that displays the following characteristics: appears quiet and reserved, listens attentively to other people, tends to avoid the use of power, and makes decisions in a thoughtful and deliberate manner.

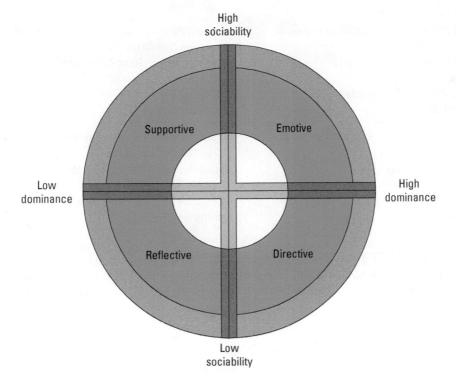

High
sociability

Supportive   Emotive

Low   High
dominance   dominance

Reflective   Directive

Low
sociability

Figure 5.10 The Supportive style combines low dominance and high sociability.

Lighthearted	Patient
Reserved	Sensitive
Passive	Relaxed
Warm	Compliant
Docile	Softhearted

Figure 5.11 Key words for the Supportive style.

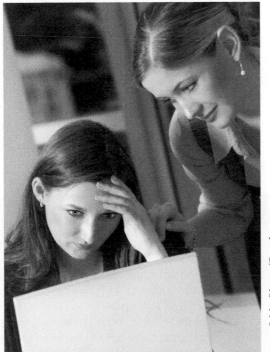

People with the Supportive communication style are usually quiet and unassuming.

Doreen Salcher/Hemera/Getty Images

Supportive (Manning/Reece/Ahearne/MacKenzie)	Emotive (Manning/Reece/Ahearne/MacKenzie)
Amiable (Wilson Learning)	Expressive (Wilson Learning)
Supportive-Giving (Stuart Atkins Inc.)	Adapting-Dealing (Stuart Atkins Inc.)
Relater (People Smarts)	Socializer (People Smarts)
Steadiness (Personal Profile System)	Influencing (Personal Profile System)
Supportive (DiSC)	Influencing (DiSC)
Reflective (Manning/Reece/Ahearne/MacKenzie)	Directive (Manning/Reece/Ahearne/MacKenzie)
Analytical (Wilson Learning)	Driver (Wilson Learning)
Conserving-Holding (Stuart Atkins Inc.)	Controlling-Taking (Stuart Atkins Inc.)
Thinker (People Smarts)	Directive (People Smarts)
Cautiousness/Compliance (Personal Profile System)	Dominance (Personal Profile System)
Conscientious (DiSC)	Dominance (DiSC)

Figure 5.12 The four basic communication styles have been used in a wide range of training programs. For comparison purposes, the approximate equivalents to the four communication styles discussed in this chapter are listed.

3. *Tends to avoid the use of power.* Whereas the Directive may rely on power to accomplish tasks, the Supportive person is more likely to rely on friendly persuasion.

4. *Makes decisions in a thoughtful and deliberate manner.* The Supportive person usually takes longer to make a decision.

Popularity of the Four-Style Model

We are endlessly fascinated by ourselves, and this helps explain the growing popularity of the four-style model presented in this chapter. To satisfy this insatiable appetite for information, many training and development companies offer training programs that present the four social or communication styles. Figure 5.12 features the approximate equivalents of the four styles presented in this chapter. Although four-style programs were initially created and marketed in the United States, they have become a global phenomenon, according to staff at Wilson Learning.[16] Inscape Publishing, the company that developed

Keeping Track of Communication Styles with CRM

Customer relationship management (CRM) software empowers a salesperson with information essential to continue a partnership. The software can be used to record, retain, and produce personal information including such factors as marital status, names and ages of children and other family members, and individual preferences, interests, and hobbies. (An astute sales organization will implement privacy policies for such personal information.) With a large customer list, before placing a call, the salesperson could quickly review the database information to refresh his or her memory about the prospect. Were any promises made during a previous call fulfilled, or are there still some issues outstanding? Were things discussed previously that now need to be followed up? This can be especially helpful when preparing to talk with someone with a specific communication style.

the DiSC learning instrument over three decades ago, reports that more that 40 million people worldwide have completed DiSC workshops.[17]

Determining Your Communication Style

You now have enough information to identify your own communication style. If your location on the dominance continuum is right of centre and your position on the sociability continuum is below the centre mark, you fall into the Directive quadrant. If your location on the dominance continuum is left of centre and your position on the sociability continuum is above the centre mark, then your most preferred style is Supportive. Likewise, lower dominance matched with lower sociability forms the Reflective communication style, and higher dominance matched with higher sociability forms the Emotive communication style.

An Online Assessment of Your Communication Style You can gain further insight into your communication style by accessing the **www.pearsoncanada.ca/manning** website and clicking on the Online Assessment of Your Communication Style link. After completing the assessment, you will be supplied with a profile indicating your most preferred communication style. You will also be presented with a profile of your secondary style. See application exercises 1, 2, 3, and 4 on page 121 for more ways to use this online assessment tool.

Of course, all of us display some characteristics of the Emotive, Directive, Reflective, and Supportive communication styles. However, one of the four styles is usually predominant and readily detectable.[18] This is your preferred style.

Some people who study the communication-style model for the first time may initially experience feelings of frustration. They find it hard to believe that one's behavioural style tends to remain quite uniform throughout life. People often say, "I am a different person each day!" It is certainly true that we sometimes feel different from day to day, but our most preferred style remains stable.

The Supportive person might say, "I sometimes get very upset and tell people what I am thinking. I can be a Directive when I want to be!" There is no argument here. Just because you have a preferred communication style does not mean you will never display the behavioural characteristics of another style. Some people use different styles in different contexts and in different relationships.[19] Reflective people sometimes display Emotive behaviour, and Emotive people sometimes display Reflective behaviour. We are saying that each person has one most-preferred and habitually used communication style. The online assessment mentioned earlier will help you identify the frequency of you displaying a secondary style.

MINIMIZING COMMUNICATION-STYLE BIAS

SALESPEOPLE OFTEN MAKE THE MISTAKE OF FOCUSING TOO MUCH ON THE CONTENT OF THEIR sales presentation and not enough on how they deliver their message.[20] Communication-style bias is a barrier to success in selling. This form of bias is a common problem in sales work simply because salespeople deal with people from all four quadrants. You cannot select potential customers on the basis of their communication style. You must be able to develop rapport with people from each of the four quadrants. When people of different styles work together but don't adapt to one another, serious problems can develop.[21]

How Communication-Style Bias Develops

To illustrate how communication-style bias develops in a sales situation, let us observe a sales call involving two people with different communication styles. Lana Wheeler entered the office of Ron Harrington, one of her large accounts, with a feeling of optimism. She was sure that her product would save Ron's company several thousand dollars a month. She was 99 percent certain that, this being her third call on Ron, the sale would be closed. Ten minutes after meeting Ron, she was walking out of his office without an order. What went wrong?

Lana Wheeler is an engaging type who is an Emotive in terms of communication style. Her sales calls are typically fast-paced. She entered Ron's office and immediately began to close the sale. Ron interrupted and told Lana he couldn't commit to her proposal. Lana appeared to ignore Ron's response and told him she could put some more figures together on pricing and then used another trial close. Ron finally told Lana, "Look, you don't understand the way I do business. We have bigger issues than additional figures. As I said, this is a 'no go' project."

Ron's communication style is Directive. He feels uncomfortable when someone is making a decision for him. He wants to maintain control and be in charge of making his own decisions. He felt tension when Lana tried to get him to make a decision on her terms. If Lana had spent more time asking questions, listening more closely, and allowing Ron to feel like the decision was his, she may have found out what "the bigger issues" were. The approach she used would have been more appropriate for the Supportive or Emotive communication style.

A salesperson who is highly adaptable can usually build rapport with customers regardless of their communication style. Style flexibility is a sales strategy that can be learned and is crucial to building partnering relationships.

Adaptive Selling Requires Versatility

versatility Our ability to minimize communication-style bias.

Personal selling has become more customer focused than ever before, so every effort should be made to reduce the tension between the salesperson and customer. Dr. David Merrill, one of the early pioneers in the development of communication-style instruments and training programs, uses the term **versatility** to describe our ability to minimize communication-style bias.[22] Roger Wenschlag, author of *The Versatile Salesperson*, describes versatility as "the degree to which a salesperson is perceived as developing and maintaining buyer comfort throughout the sales process." *Adapting* to the customer's preferred communication style can enhance sales performance.[23]

Mature and Immature Behaviour There is a mature and an immature side to each behavioural style. Let us examine the Emotive style to illustrate this point. People with this style are open, personable individuals who seem genuinely friendly. The natural enthusiasm displayed by the mature Emotive is refreshing. On the other hand, an Emotive person who is too talkative and too emotional may have difficulty building rapport with some customers; this is the immature side of the Emotive communication style.

You will recall that we used the words "industrious" and "precise" to describe the Reflective style. These are words that apply to the mature side of the Reflective person. We also used the words "aloof" and "stuffy." These words describe the immature side of the Reflective. The good news is that we all have the potential for developing the mature side of our communication style.

Strength/Weakness Paradox It is a fact of life that your greatest strength can become your greatest weakness. If your most preferred style is Reflective, people are likely to respect your well-disciplined approach to life as one of your strengths. However, this strength can become a weakness if it is exaggerated. The Reflective person can be too serious, too questioning, and too inflexible. Robert Haas, former CEO of Levi Strauss & Company, is known for extraordinary—some say obsessive—attention to detail. Those who work with him say an offhand conversation can sound like a lecture. This Reflective, however, has the ability to flex his style. Levi's employees are fiercely loyal to Haas and describe him as compassionate to a fault.[24]

People with the Directive style are open and frank. They express their true feelings in a direct manner. In most cases we appreciate candour, but we do not like to be around people who are too straightforward or too blunt in expressing their views. Steven Ballmer, former CEO of Microsoft, was known as a very demanding executive during his early years with the company. His explosive temper was legendary and he often put the fear of God into his staff members. He once needed throat surgery because he yelled so much. Later he became more diplomatic and less domineering.[25] Satya Nadella, who replaced Ballmer in 2014, is expected to manage in a more relaxed, low-key manner. When people come across as *opinionated*, they tend to antagonize others. We should avoid pushing our strengths to the point of unproductive excess.[26]

To illustrate how strengths become weaknesses in excess, let us add more detail to our communication-style model. Note that it now features three zones that radiate out from the centre (see Fig. 5.13). These dimensions might be thought of as intensity zones.

Zone one. People who fall within this zone display their unique behavioural characteristics with less intensity than those in zone two. The Emotive person, for example, is moderately high on the dominance continuum and moderately high on the sociability continuum. As you might expect, zone one communication styles are more difficult to identify because there is less intensity in both dimensions (dominance and sociability).

Zone two. Persons who fall within this zone display their unique behavioural characteristics with greater intensity than persons in zone one. The zone two Reflective, for example, falls within the lowest quartile of the dominance continuum and the lowest

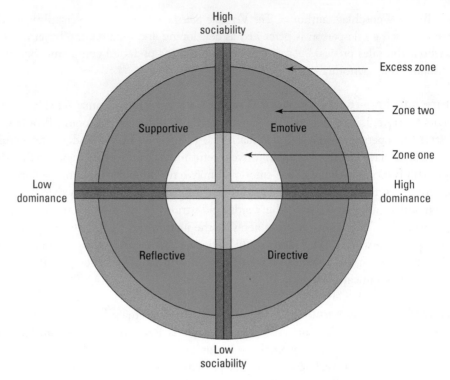

High
sociability

Excess zone

Zone two

Supportive   Emotive

Zone one

Low   High
dominance   dominance

Reflective   Directive

Low
sociability

Figure 5.13 The completed communication-style model provides important insights needed to manage the relationship process in selling.

quartile of the sociability continuum. The boundary line that separates zone one and zone two should not be seen as a permanent barrier restricting change in intensity. Under certain circumstances we should abandon our most preferred style temporarily. A deliberate move from zone one to zone two, or vice versa, is called *style flexing*.

Excess zone. The excess zone is characterized by a high degree of intensity and rigidity. When people allow themselves to drift into this zone, they become very inflexible, which is often interpreted by others as a form of bias toward their style. In addition, the strengths of the inflexible person become weaknesses. Extreme intensity in any quadrant is bound to threaten interpersonal relations.

We are apt to move into the excess zone and exaggerate our style characteristics under stressful conditions. Stress tends to bring out the worst in many people. Here are some of the behaviours that salespeople and customers may display when they are in the excess zone:

Emotive style	Expresses highly emotional opinions
	Stops listening to the other person
	Tries too hard to promote own point of view
	Becomes outspoken to the point of being offensive
Directive style	Gets impatient with the other person
	Becomes dictatorial and bossy
	Does not admit being wrong
	Becomes extremely competitive

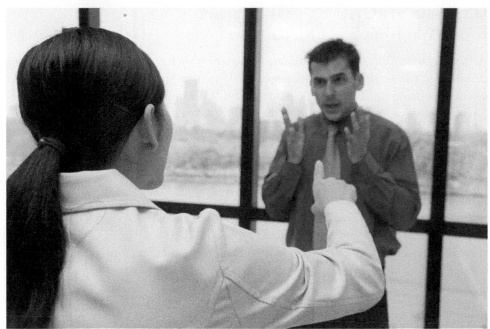

The excess zone is characterized by a high degree of intensity and rigidity. We are more apt to move into the excess zone under very stressful conditions.

Blend Images/Superstock

Reflective style	Becomes stiff and formal
	Is unwilling to make a decision
	Avoids displaying any type of emotion
	Is overly interested in detail
Supportive style	Agrees with everyone
	Is unable to take a strong stand
	Becomes overly anxious to win approval of others
	Tries to comfort everyone

The majority of Italian Canadians have roots in Sicily or southern Italy. Canadian businesspeople may think that all Italians are like the Italian Canadians whom they have had contact with in Canada, but in reality, Italy is a very varied country where you will find all types of physical characteristics—fair, dark, short, tall—with a variety of accents and customs.

■ Italian businesspeople tend to be quite formal in terms of introductions and dress. When you introduce yourself, say your last name only, and then shake hands. Wait until invited to use your first name. Personal and professional titles are used almost all the time in business dealings.

■ Entertaining clients is typically done in restaurants and not in the home.

■ Most Italian businesspeople are not in a hurry, so be patient and do not try to rush the sale.

■ The practice of gift giving will vary. A gift such as a bottle of wine at Christmas is quite common.[c]

BUILDING STRONG RELATIONSHIPS THROUGH STYLE FLEXING

Style flexing IS THE DELIBERATE ATTEMPT TO ADAPT ONE'S COMMUNICATION STYLE TO accommodate the needs of the other person. You are attempting to communicate with the other person on his or her own "channel." Ron Willingham, in his book *Integrity Selling*, reminds us that "people are more apt to buy from you when they perceive you view the world as they view the world."[27] In a selling situation, you should try to determine the customer's most preferred style and flex your own accordingly. If your preferred communication style is Directive and your customer is a Supportive, try to be more personal and warm in your presentation. Once you know the customer's style, flexing your style can make the difference between a presentation that falters and one that exceeds your expectations.[28] Style sensitivity and flexing add value to the sales process.

Throughout the preapproach, you should learn as much as possible about the customer and try to determine his style. Once you are in the customer's presence, do not become preoccupied analyzing the person's style. If you are trying hard to analyze the person's style, you may not listen closely enough to what she is trying to tell you. If you are truly tuned in to the customer, you can absorb many clues that will help you determine her style. After the sales call, analyze the communication and record your findings. Use this information to plan your next contact with the customer.[29] Listen closely to the customer's tone of voice. A Supportive person sounds warm and friendly. The Reflective customer's voice is more likely to be controlled and deliberate. Pay particular attention to gestures. The Emotive individual uses his hands to communicate thoughts and ideas. The Directive also uses gestures to communicate but is more controlled and less spontaneous. The Reflective person appears more relaxed, less intense. The Emotive individual is an open, impulsive communicator, while the Reflective person is quite cautious. The Supportive type is personal and friendly, while the Reflective person may seem difficult to get to know. To avoid relationship tension, consider the following suggestions for each of the four styles.

Building Relationships with Emotive Customers

The Platinum Rule Do Unto Others As They Want Done Unto Them.

If you are attempting to sell products to an Emotive person, keep in mind the need to move at a pace that will hold the attention of the prospect. Be enthusiastic and avoid an approach that is too stiff and formal. Take time to establish goodwill and build relationships. Do not place too much emphasis on the facts and details. To deal effectively

---

Selling in Action

The Platinum Rule®

The Platinum Rule®, created many years ago by Dr. Tony Alessandra, provides each of us with the motivation we need to treat others the way they want to be treated. This rule is a simple, proven method for building strong relationships with our customers.

"Do Unto Others As They Want Done Unto Them."

The Platinum Rule® (www.platinumrule.com) is at the heart of the style-flexing sales strategy. When we take time to determine if the customer is behaving as an Emotive, Directive, Reflective, or Supportive, we can then treat them the way they want to be treated.[d]

with Emotive people, plan actions that will provide support for their opinions, ideas, and dreams.[30] Plan to ask questions concerning their opinions and ideas, but be prepared to help them get "back on track" if they move too far away from the topic. Maintain good eye contact and, above all, be a good listener.

Building Relationships with Directive Customers

The key to relating to Directives is to keep the relationship as businesslike as possible. Developing a strong personal relationship is not a high priority for Directives. In other words, friendship is not usually a condition for a good working relationship. Your goal is to be as efficient, time disciplined, and well organized as possible, and to provide appropriate facts, figures, and success probabilities. Most Directives are goal-oriented people, so try to identify their primary objectives and then determine ways to support and help with these objectives. Early in the sales presentation, ask specific questions and carefully note responses. Look for specific points you can respond to when it is time to present your proposal.

Building Relationships with Reflective Customers

The Reflective person will respond in a positive way to a thoughtful, well-organized approach. Arrive at meetings on time and be well prepared. In most cases it is not necessary to spend a great deal of time building a social relationship. Reflective people appreciate a no-nonsense, businesslike approach to personal selling. Use specific questions that show clear direction. Once you have information concerning the prospect's needs, present your proposal in a slow, deliberate way. Provide as much documentation as possible. Do not be in too big a hurry to close the sale. Never pressure the Reflective person to make quick decisions.

Building Relationships with Supportive Customers

Take time to build a social relationship with the Supportive person. Spend time learning about the things that are important in this individual's life—family, hobbies, and major interests. Listen carefully to personal opinions and feelings. Supportive individuals like to conduct business with sales personnel who are professional but friendly. Therefore, study their feelings and emotional needs as well as their technical and business needs. Throughout the presentation, provide personal assurances and support for their views. If you disagree with a Supportive person, curb the desire to disagree too assertively; Supportive people tend to dislike interpersonal conflict. Give them the time to comprehend your proposal. Patience is important.

As you develop your communication-style identification skills and become more adept at style flexing, you are better able to manage the relationship process. With these skills, you should be able to open more accounts, sell more to established customers, and more effectively meet the pressures of competition. Most important, your customers will view you as a person better able to understand and meet their needs.

Word of Caution

It is tempting to put a label on someone and then assume the label tells you everything you need to know about that person. If you want to build an effective sales partnership with a prospect, you must acquire additional information about that person. Stuart

Atkins, a respected authority on communication styles and author of *The Name of Your Game*, says we should be careful not to use labels that make people feel boxed in, typecast, or judged. He believes we should not classify *people*; we should classify their *strengths* and *preferences* to act one way or another under certain circumstances.[31] You must also be careful not to let the label you place on yourself become the justification for your own inflexible behaviour. Try not to let the label justify or reinforce why you are unable or unwilling to communicate effectively with others.

REVIEWING KEY CONCEPTS

- Discuss how communication style influences the relationship process in sales.

  Many sales are lost because salespeople fail to communicate effectively with the prospect. Communication-style bias contributes to this problem. Every salesperson who is willing to develop style sensitivity and engage in appropriate style flexing can minimize one of the most common barriers to success in selling.

- Identify the two major dimensions of the communication-style model.

  The communication-style model is based on two continuums that assess two major aspects of human behaviour: dominance and sociability. By combining them as horizontal and vertical continuums we create quadrants that define four styles of communication. We have called these the Emotive, Directive, Reflective, and Supportive styles.

- Explain the four communications styles in the communication-style model.

  The Emotive style combines high sociability and high dominance, whereas the Directive style combines high dominance and low sociability. The Reflective style combines low dominance and low sociability, whereas the Supportive style combines low dominance and high sociability.

- Learn how to identify your preferred communication style and that of your customer.

  With practice you can learn to identify your preferred communication style. The starting point is to rate yourself on each scale (dominance and sociability) by placing a check mark at a point along the continuum that represents how you perceive yourself. Completion of the dominance and sociability indicator forms will help you achieve greater awareness of your communication style. This same approach can be used to identify the customer's preferred style.

- Learn to achieve interpersonal versatility and build strong selling relationships with style flexing.

  A third dimension of human behaviour—versatility—is important in dealing with communication styles that are different from your own. You can adjust your own style to meet the needs of others—a process called *style flexing*. Style flexing is an attempt to change or alter your style to meet the needs of the customer.

Key Terms

Review Questions

1. What is the meaning of the term *communication style*?

2. Describe the five major principles that support communication-style theory.

3. What are the benefits to the salesperson who understands communication style?

4. What two dimensions of human behaviour are used to identify communication style?

5. Describe the person who tends to be high in sociability.

6. What are the four communication styles? Develop a brief description of each.

7. What is the reaction of most people who study communication styles for the first time? Why does this reaction surface?

8. Define *style flexing*. How can style flexing improve sales productivity?

9. Explain the statement, "Your greatest strength can become your greatest weakness."

10. What suggestions would you give to a salesperson who is planning to meet a new prospect who displays the Reflective communication style?

Application Exercises

1. Communication, or behaviour, styles are the basis for one of the most popular training programs. Worldwide, 47 million people have participated in Wilson and DiSC programs. An understanding of communication styles assists us in building better personal and business relationships. As indicated in this chapter, the first step in applying what you have learned about communication styles is to identify and understand your own style. Using the Online Communication Style Assessment tool at www.pearsoncanada.ca/manning, assess your communication style.

   a. Do you agree with your assessment of your most preferred style? How about your results on your secondary style?

   b. Referring back to the material presented in this chapter, identify the strengths and weaknesses of your style.

   c. Identify the styles you enjoy working with best. Identify the styles you enjoy working with least.

   d. Referring to the behaviours listed on pages 116–117, can you identify those behaviours you tend to exhibit when you feel stressed?

   e. Explain why you think so many individuals and companies have participated in these programs. From Figure 5.12 on page 112, list the names of other training programs you could use to identify your most preferred style.

2. Self-awareness is important in personal selling. As we get to know ourselves, we can identify barriers to acceptance by others. Once you have identified your most preferred communication style, you have taken a big step in the direction of self-awareness. We have noted that self-ratings can sometimes be misleading because some people lack a high degree of self-awareness. They do not see themselves as others see them. Consider asking four or five people, co-workers for example, to assess and print the profile of your communication style using the online assessment. Then compare these ratings with your self-rating.

3. Many salespeople, after being introduced to communication-style concepts, attempt to categorize each of their customers. They report that their relationships become mutually more enjoyable and productive. Select four people whom you know quite well (e.g., supervisor, subordinate, customer, teacher, friend, or member of your sports team). Using the two behavioural continuums in this chapter, determine these people's communication styles. Using your own descriptive terminology in conjunction with terminology in this chapter, develop a descriptive behavioural profile of each of these people. Explain how this information could improve your relationship with each of these people.

4. To assess your ability to style flex, assume you are going to make four sales calls on customers displaying each of the four communication styles. For purposes of illustration, consider your first call is on an Emotive customer with a communication style like Rick Mercer's. The second call is on a Supportive customer with a communication style like Anne Murray's;

the third is on a Reflective customer with a communication style like Peter Mansbridge, and the last is on a Directive customer like Kevin O'Leary. For each of these customers, refer to the online communication style assessment, and assess the behaviours you would demonstrate as you established your relationship with them. Print each of the profiles and compare them to one another. Did you flex your style of communication to better interact with the customer representing Rick Mercer's style versus the customer representing Anne Murray's style? Did you flex differently for the customers representing Peter Mansbridge and Kevin O'Leary?

5. Myers-Briggs Personality Types and Jungian Personality Types are two very popular descriptions of the material in this chapter. Using your search engine, access the Internet sites that refer to these concepts. Type in "Jungian + personality profiles" to access the Jungian personality types. To access the Myers-Briggs types, type in "Myers-Briggs + personality profiles." Does the number of hits indicate anything about the validity and popularity of these theories? Examine specific queries about both. Do you see the relationship between the theories and the material in this chapter? Each year, about 2.5 million North Americans complete the Myers-Briggs Type Indicator (MBTI). Why is this psychological assessment instrument so popular?

ROLE-PLAY EXERCISE

For the purpose of this role play, assume the role of Ray Ito, who is described in the case problem below. Ray is described as a quiet, amiable person who displays the Supportive communication style. You will meet with Vera Maynard, who is also described in the case problem.

For the purpose of this role play, assume that Vera displays the characteristics of the Directive communication style. Prior to the role play, study the chapter material on style flexing and information on how to sell to persons who have the Directive communication style.

Reality Selling Video Case Problem

Ray Ito has been employed at CanTrust Real Estate for almost two years. Prior to receiving his real estate licence, he was a property manager with a large real estate agency in another community. During his first year with CanTrust, he was assigned to the residential property division and sold properties totalling $3 875 000. He then requested and received a transfer to the commercial division.

Three months ago, Ray obtained a commercial listing that consisted of 10.5 hectares (26 acres) of land near a growing residential neighbourhood. The land is zoned commercial and appears to be ideally suited for a medium-sized shopping centre. Ray prepared a detailed prospectus and sent it to Vera Maynard, president of Consumer Growth Corporation, a firm specializing in development of shopping centres. One week later he received a letter from Ms. Maynard requesting more information. Shortly after receiving Ray's response, Ms. Maynard called to set up an appointment to inspect the property. A time and

date were finalized, and Ray agreed to meet her plane and conduct a tour of the property.

Ray is a quiet, amiable person who displays the Supportive communication style. Friends say that they like to spend time with him because he is a good listener.

Questions

1. If Ms. Maynard displays the characteristics of the Directive communication style, how should Ray Ito conduct himself during the meeting? Be specific as you describe those behaviours that would be admired by Ms. Maynard.

2. If Ms. Maynard wants to build rapport with Ray Ito, what behaviour should she display?

3. It is not a good idea to put a label on someone and then assume the label tells us everything about the person. As Ray attempts to build rapport with Ms. Maynard, what other personal characteristics should he try to identify?

PART II

ROLE-PLAY EXERCISE
Developing a Relationship Strategy

SCENARIO

You are Dana Davis, senior account representative for Specialty Fasteners, Canada's largest and most competitive manufacturer of stainless steel fasteners. Your company is ISO 9002 certified and has earned many accolades, including three consecutive J. D. Power & Associates awards for customer satisfaction. Over the years, your company has continually invested in automation technology as a means of ensuring consistent manufacturing quality and cost leadership. You have recently received a request to quote on a large order for T316 stainless steel fittings and are now making a sales call on the purchasing agent to see if you can secure the order. On the way to the purchasing agent's office, you drop by the customer's receiving area to check on an unrelated issue and you notice a very large shipment of T304 stainless steel fasteners, a much less expensive grade of stainless steel. When you asked the receiving clerk where it came from, you were surprised to hear that it was from a minor competitor, one not normally capable of being price competitive on large orders. And, when you asked whether the material was supposed to be T316 stainless, the clerk told you that the packing slip didn't specify. It simply stated stainless steel. When he showed you the packing list, you immediately recognized the bill of material as identical to what you had recently quoted.

CUSTOMER PROFILE

Tyler Harper is senior purchasing agent at Regina Fabricators, Saskatchewan's largest stainless steel fabricator. He has negotiated over a dozen purchase agreements with you. Tyler takes pride in purchasing quality materials at the best price. He knows that the quality of the materials he buys determines the quality of the finished goods that Regina Fabricators manufactures.

SALESPERSON PROFILE

You have been employed by Specialty Fasteners for about four years. After completion of an extensive sales training program, you were assigned to a territory in Saskatchewan, and were soon promoted to senior account representative. You have approximately 60 accounts, but Regina Fabricators is the largest.

PRODUCT

Specialty Fasteners manufactures and sells the broadest range of stainless steel fasteners available in Canada. It manufactures T304 grade stainless fasteners for general applications, and the more expensive T316 grade stainless fasteners for use in more corrosive atmospheres, such as those found in pulp mills, chemical plants, and salt water environments. Customers always specify the grade of stainless they need depending on their end-use application.

INSTRUCTIONS

During the early stages of the role play, you will want to obtain more information from the customer and resolve any misunderstandings. You want to obtain an order for T316 stainless steel fasteners, and maintain a good relationship with this important customer. Keep in mind that ethical decisions can greatly influence the relationship between a salesperson and the customer. (You might want to reflect on the important information covered in Chapter 3 prior to your meeting with Tyler Harper.)

Chapter 6
Creating Product Solutions

Learning Objectives

After studying this chapter, you should be able to

1   Explain the importance of developing product solutions that add value.

2   Describe the importance of becoming an expert regarding product knowledge.

3   Discuss the importance of becoming an expert regarding company knowledge.

4   Describe how expert knowledge of competition and industry trends improves personal selling.

5   List major sources of product, competitor, and industry information.

6   Explain how to add value with a feature–benefit strategy.

 Reality Selling Video Series—Amy Vandaveer/*Texas Monthly*

For more than 10 years, Amy Vandaveer has had a highly successful sales career. She has a bachelor's degree in marketing and has sold sales technology software, sales training programs, and media services. Currently, Amy is a sales representative for *Texas Monthly* (**www.texasmonthly.com**), a magazine that focuses largely on leisure activities and events in Texas. *Texas Monthly*'s sales staff is responsible for selling the large amount of advertising space available in the magazine. It may sound like a relatively easy job; after all, *Texas Monthly* has a large, loyal reader base and would be an attractive advertising outlet for many businesses. Remember, though, that *Texas Monthly* has many direct and indirect competitors, all of whom are trying to sell their services to the same group of businesses Amy works with.

Because of the many options available to a prospective advertiser, Amy must become an expert on what her customers want, what *Texas Monthly* can offer them, and what *Texas Monthly*'s competitors can offer. By doing so, she can improve her ability to answer customers' questions and emphasize the benefits—in the context of her customers'

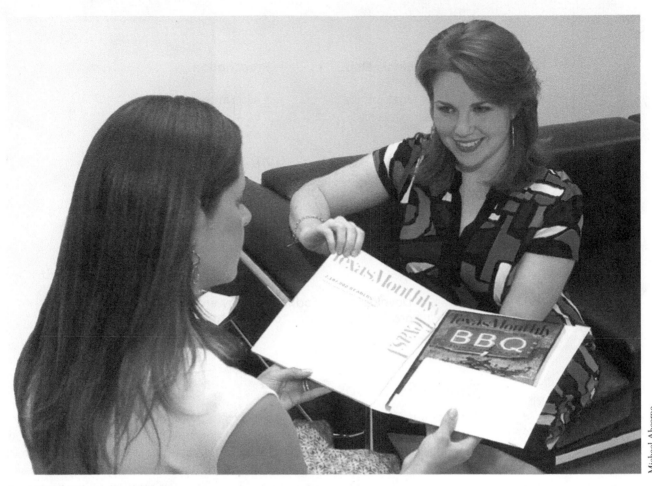

Amy Vandaveer

needs—of choosing *Texas Monthly* over other advertising outlets. She is no longer just selling advertising space; instead, she can offer her customers her own knowledge and experience in creating solutions that address their needs.[1]

DEVELOPING A PRODUCT SOLUTION THAT ADDS VALUE

As noted in Chapter 2, a product strategy helps salespeople make correct decisions concerning the selection and positioning of products to meet identified customer needs. The **product strategy** is a well-conceived plan whereby a sales representative becomes a product expert, selling product benefits and creating value-added solutions (see Fig. 6.1). Configuring value-added solutions is discussed in detail in Chapter 7. A McKinsey survey of more than 1200 business-to-business purchasing decision makers revealed that, among the habits that undermine the sales experience, the second "most destructive" was a lack of salesperson knowledge about either their own products or those of their competitors.[2]

product strategy A well-conceived plan for sales that emphasizes acquiring extensive product knowledge, learning to select and communicate appropriate product benefits that will appeal to the customer, and creating value-added solutions.

Strategic/Consultative Selling Model

Strategic step	Prescription
Develop a personal selling philosophy	☑ Adopt marketing concept ☑ Value personal selling ☑ Become a problem solver/partner
Develop a relationship strategy	☑ Maintain high ethical standards ☑ Project professional image ☑ Manage the relationship process
Develop a product strategy	☐ Become a product expert ☐ Sell benefits ☐ Configure value-added solutions

Figure 6.1 Developing a product strategy enables the salesperson to custom-fit products or services to the customer's needs.

Selling Solutions

solution A mutually shared answer to a recognized customer problem.

A **solution** is a mutually shared answer to a recognized customer problem. In many selling situations, a solution is more encompassing than a specific product. It often provides measurable results such as greater productivity, increased profits, or less employee turnover. Selling a solution, versus selling a specific product, usually requires a greater effort to define and diagnose the customer's problem.[3] Think of **solution selling** as a process by which the salesperson uncovers and clarifies a customer's problem, works with the customer to create a vision of how things could be better, and then develops a plan for implementing the vision.[4]

solution selling A process by which the salesperson uncovers and clarifies a customer's problem, works with the customer to create a vision of how things could be better, and then develops a plan for implementing the vision.

Most salespeople have adopted a broad definition of the term *product* to encompass information, services, ideas, tangible products, or some combination of these that satisfies the customer's needs, with the right solution.[5] Let's look at the sales process at two firms.

> Newmac Manufacturing of Debert, Nova Scotia manufactures a complete line of furnaces, boilers, and stoves, and sells them through its distributor network across Canada and the United States. Beyond its core business, its manufacturing experience has allowed it to sell structural components, pressure vessels, combustion chambers, fume hoods, and many other products. A Newmac salesperson can help configure a range of product solutions to satisfy the needs of customers across a broad range of industries.[6]

> Loki Management Systems, a Richmond, B.C.-based software developer, provides product solutions that help companies create employee work schedules, increase employee satisfaction and retention, reduce staffing and overtime costs, save management time, and reduce payroll errors. The company initially targeted companies in the healthcare industry, but has since expanded into the hospitality, manufacturing, and field service industries.[7]

From the customer's point of view, salespeople employed by Newmac Manufacturing and Loki Management Systems sell information and expertise as well as products and services. Customers view the problem-solving ability these salespeople provide as a very important part of what these salespeople provide. When you sell a complex product or service, or one that can be customized for specific customers, it is knowledge and expertise that create value.

A recent Corporate Executive Board study of more than 1400 business-to-business customers found that they completed much of their decision making—such as researching solutions, ranking options, setting requirements, benchmarking pricing, and so on—before even having a conversation with a supplier.[8] With this information-rich, Internet-driven marketplace, often salespeople will have to be more insightful regarding unrecognized needs the customer may not have considered, and sell solutions to these needs. If they don't, they likely will find themselves in a price war with their competitors. Salespeople in this environment will have to master the use of what are called "implication" or "pain" questions to help customers discover their unrealized needs. These questions will be discussed in detail later in Chapter 11.

Tailoring the Product Strategy A product strategy should be tailored to the customer's buying needs. Transactional buyers are usually well aware of their needs. Most of these customers have conducted their own research and have a good understanding of the product that will meet their needs. The office manager who frequently buys a large amount of copy paper knows that this standard item can be purchased from several vendors, and that the quality of the paper usually does not vary from one vendor to another. The consultative buyer may lack needs awareness and will usually welcome clarification of needs. The customized solution appeals to the customer's desire for choices that are tailored to his or her needs. Developing a product strategy for the strategic alliance customer usually offers the greatest challenge. Study of the proposed alliance partner can be very time-consuming, but the rewards of a successful partnership may be substantial. In some cases, the company that wishes to form an alliance with a new customer must be prepared to make a large investment in capital-intensive technology and additional personnel.[9]

Explosion of Product Options

Domestic and global markets are overflowing with a vast array of goods and services. In some industries the number of new products introduced each year is mind-boggling. Makers of consumer products, for example, churn out as many as 30 000 new products each year. Want to buy a product in the securities and financial services field? In the fastest-growing segment—mutual funds—there are now approximately 4000 licensed financial advisors in Canada selling more than 5000 different mutual funds.[10] For the customer, this much variety creates a "good news–bad news" situation. The good news is that almost all buyers have a choice when it comes to purchasing a product or service; people like to compare various options. The bad news is that having so many choices often complicates the buying process.

One of the most important roles of the salesperson is to simplify the customer's study of the product choices. Later in this chapter we discuss how product features (information) can add value when converted into specific benefits (knowledge) that can help the buyer make an intelligent buying decision.

Creating Solutions with Product Configuration

The challenge facing both customers and salespeople in this era of information overload is deciding which product applications, or combination of applications, can solve the customer's buying problem. If the customer has complex buying needs, then the salesperson may have to bring together many parts of the company's product mix to develop a custom-fitted solution. The product selection process is often referred to as **product configuration**.

product configuration The solution of complex buying needs; for instance, when the salesperson brings together many different parts of the company's product mix or uses specialized software to develop a custom-fitted solution.

Salespeople representing Cisco Systems are often involved in the sale of new products to new and established customers. They use Cybrant Solutions Architect software to quickly identify solutions. The software helps salespeople ask prospects the right questions to discover their needs and then configures a solution that best meets those needs.[11]

Amy Vandaveer takes pride in her ability to create solutions based on product configuration. In fact, every proposal she prepares is customized to fit the needs of a *Texas Monthly* customer.

Many companies use product configuration software to develop customized product solutions quickly and accurately. It incorporates product selection criteria and associates them directly with customer requirements. Members of the sales force can use the sales configurator to identify product options, prices, delivery schedules, and other parts of the product mix, while working interactively with the customer. Most of today's product configuration software can be integrated with contact management software programs such as Salesforce, ACT!, and NetSuite. In addition to improving the quality of the sales proposal, this software reduces the time-consuming process of manually preparing written proposals.

A major element of product configuration is *quotation management*. Quick and accurate pricing is critical in today's fast-paced sales environment. Leading companies are aggressively automating their quotation management process.[12]

Preparing Written Proposals

Written proposals are frequently part of the salesperson's product strategy. It is only natural that some buyers will want the proposed solution put in writing. A **written proposal** can be defined as a specific plan of action based on the facts, assumptions, and supporting documentation about a buying solution that are included in the sales presentation.[13] A well-written proposal adds value to the product solution and can set you apart from the competition. It offers the buyer reassurance that you will deliver what you have promised. Written proposals, which are often accompanied by a sales letter, vary in terms of format and content. Many government agencies, and some large companies, issue a request for proposal (RFP) that specifies the format of the proposal. Most effective proposals include the following parts:

written proposal A specific plan of action based on the facts, assumptions, and supporting documentation about a buying solution that are included in the sales presentation. Written proposals vary in terms of format and content.

Budget and overview. These tell the prospect the cost of the solution you have prescribed. Be specific as you describe the product or service features to be provided, and itemize the price. When you confirm pricing with a proposal, misunderstandings and mistakes can be avoided.

Objective. The objective should be expressed in terms of benefits. A tangible objective might be "to reduce payroll expense by 10 percent." An intangible objective might be stated as "to increase business security offered by a company with a reputation for dependability." Focus on specific benefits that relate directly to the customer's needs.

Strategy. Briefly describe how you will meet your objective. How will you fulfill the obligations you have described in your proposal? In some cases this section of your proposal includes specific language: "Your account will be assigned to Sue Zhou, our senior lease representative."

Schedule. Establish a time frame for meeting your objective. This might involve the confirmation of dates with regard to acquisition, shipping, or installation.

Rationale. With a mixture of logic and emotion, present your rationale for taking action now. Once again, the emphasis should be on benefits, not features.[14]

Some written proposals follow a specific format developed by the company. The length of a proposal can vary from a single page to dozens of pages for a complex product.

The proposal should be printed on quality paper and be free of any errors in spelling, grammar, or punctuation. Before completing the proposal, review the content one more time to be sure you have addressed all of the customer's concerns. Bob Kantin, author of *Sales Proposals Kit for Dummies*, says the proposal is really the first "product" that the customer receives from you, so be sure it is perfect.[15] Neil Rackham, noted author and sales consultant, recommends addressing your proposal to the "invisible" customer. Very often the proposal will be reviewed by individuals the salesperson has never met. And these are often the people who will make or break the deal.[16]

The remainder of this chapter is divided into five major sections. The first two examine the kinds of product information and company information required by the salesperson. The third section describes the type of information about the competition that is helpful to salespeople. Sources of information are covered in the fourth section, and the fifth section describes how product features can be translated into buyer benefits.

BECOME A PRODUCT EXPERT

ONE OF THE MAJOR CHALLENGES FACING SALESPEOPLE IS WINNING THE CUSTOMER'S TRUST. A survey reported in *Sales & Marketing Management* ranked product knowledge as the number one characteristic of salespeople who are able to build trust.[17] Ideally, a salesperson will possess product knowledge that meets and exceeds customer expectations, increasing sales effectiveness and willingness to pay.[18]

Tom Peters says that when it comes to product knowledge, remember: "More, more, more. And, more important: Deeper, deeper, deeper." In summary: "He or she who has the largest appetite for Deep Knowledge wins."[19] This section reviews some of the most common product information categories: (1) product development and quality improvement processes, (2) performance data and specifications, (3) maintenance and service contracts, and (4) price and delivery. Each is important as a potential source of knowledge concerning the product or service.

A quick response to a customer's questions about product configurations or pricing can serve as a product strategy improvement within the sales process. This salesperson is adding value by using his notebook and cell phone to access and quickly communicate information.

Comstock/Stockbyte/Getty Images

Effective Sales Letter Writing Is a Must

Salespeople are increasingly using sales letters to describe features and benefits, to position products, to build relationships, and to provide assurances to customers. Sales letters also are used in conjunction with prospecting plans. Several standard rules apply to all written sales letters. These include:

1. Sales letters should follow the standard visual format of a business letter. They should contain, in the following order, either a letterhead or sender's address, the date, the inside address (the same as on the outside of the envelope), a salutation, the body, a complimentary closing, a typed name and handwritten signature of sender, and a notation of enclosures (if there are any).

2. Placement of the letter on the paper should provide balanced white space bordering the entire letter. Three to five blank lines should separate the date and inside address; a single blank line should separate the inside address and the salutation, the salutation and the opening paragraph of the letter, and each paragraph. A single blank line should separate the last paragraph and the complimentary closing. Single spacing should generally be used within the paragraphs.

3. Proper business punctuation includes a colon after the salutation and a comma after the complimentary close.

4. Most sales letters include at least three paragraphs. The first paragraph should indicate why you are writing the letter, the second paragraph should be a summary of the benefits proposed, and the third paragraph should state what the next action step will be for the salesperson, the customer, or both.

5. Proper grammar and spelling must be used throughout the entire letter. Business letters provide opportunities to build a stronger relationship with the customer and to close the sale. Improper placement, punctuation, spelling errors, or weak content conveys a negative impression to the reader and may result in a lost sale.

6. The use of the personal pronoun "I" should be minimized in the sales letter. To keep the letter focused on the customer's needs, the pronouns "you" and "your" should appear throughout the body of the letter.

Product Development and Quality Improvement Processes

Companies spend large amounts of money in the development of their products. In **product development**, the original idea for a product or service is tested, modified, and retested several times before it is offered to the customer. Each modification is made to improve the product. Salespeople should be familiar with a product's development history. Often this information will set the stage for stronger sales appeals.

Patagonia, a company that makes high-quality sports and outdoor equipment and clothing, uses a unique product development process. Patagonia hires many expert kayakers, skiers, climbers, and fishermen who, under actual conditions, help develop and test the company's products. Patagonia wins high praise for many of its product innovations.[20] Quality improvement continues to be an important long-term business strategy for most successful companies.[21] Salespeople need to identify processes for quality improvement that provide a competitive advantage and be prepared to discuss this information during the sales presentation. Toyota, Ritz-Carlton Hotels, and Xerox are examples of companies that have won awards for implementing important quality controls. **Quality control**, which involves measuring products and services against established standards, is one dimension of the typical quality improvement process.

Laurel Steel of Burlington, Ontario is a supplier of cold-drawn steel and has earned its reputation through a continuous pursuit of quality. Quality assurance manager Sandro DeSordi says, "We were the first North American cold-finisher to receive ISO 9002 registration and among the first to earn QS 9000 registration so it seems fitting that we were first to achieve ISO/TS16949 as well." This latter certification has replaced QS 9000 and includes additional and stricter requirements that satisfy almost all automotive manufacturers around the world and assure them that if they do business with Laurel Steel, they can expect the highest level of quality service.[22]

> **product development** The testing, modifying, and retesting of an idea for a product several times before offering it to the customer.

> **quality control** The evaluation or testing of products against established standards. This has important sales appeal when used by the salesperson to convince a prospect of a product's quality.

Performance Data and Specifications

Most potential buyers are interested in performance data and specifications. Here are some typical questions that might be raised by prospects:

> "What is the frequency response for this stereo loudspeaker?"
> "What is the anticipated rate of return on this mutual fund?"
> "What is the energy consumption rating for this appliance?"
> "Are all of your hotel and conference centre rooms accessible to persons with physical disabilities?"

A salesperson must be prepared to address these types of questions in the written sales proposal and the sales presentation. Performance data are especially critical when the customer is attempting to compare the merits of one product with another.

To become familiar with the performance of Whirlpool appliances, salespeople literally "live" the brand. The company rented and redesigned an eight-bedroom farmhouse near corporate headquarters and outfitted it with Whirlpool dishwashers, refrigerators, washers, dryers, and microwaves. Salespeople, in groups of eight, live at the house for two months and use all of the appliances. Whirlpool engineers visit

Get the Word Out: Writing and Speaking Builds Credibility

There are several thousand consultants in Canada, some who work full time and some part time. If you decide to choose this as a career, you need to be able to differentiate yourself, and build credibility with prospective clients. The solution: writing and speaking; that is, get the word out. That's why you will see many consultants promote themselves as consultant, speaker, and author. Consider these examples:

■ Deborah Reynolds is an author, business consultant, and professional speaker, and president of Vancouver-based About Face Image Consulting. She has authored *Inspired Style* and *Your IMAGE* (ebook).

■ Barry Siskind is a trade show consultant, speaker, and president of Toronto-based International Training and Management Company. He promotes himself as "The Trade and Consumer Show Specialist," and has written *Powerful Exhibit Marketing*, along with several other books.

■ Steven J. Schwartz, president of SJS Productions, bills himself as the sales doctor. He has written three books on selling, including *So Your Foot's In the Door — Now What?*

■ Jim Domanski, president of Ottawa-based Teleconcepts Consulting, has been dubbed by *Financial Post* as "Canada's reigning tele-management guru." His website has a number of articles for prospective clients, and he publishes a regular e-newsletter, freely available to anyone who registers.

■ Rosalie Moscoe is a speaker, health and wellness consultant, and author. She has published many articles in magazines, in newspapers, and on the Internet, and has authored a book and e-book *Frazzled Hurried Woman! Your Stress Relief Guide to Thriving...Not Merely Surviving*.

■ Lynda Goldman is a writer, speaker, and consultant, and president of Montreal-based Lynda Goldman Ink. She provides copywriting services and draws credibility from the 31 business and communication books she has written, including *How to Make a Million Dollar First Impression*.

■ Colette Robicheau is a time management consultant and coach, and president of Halifax-based Organize Anything. She has studied at four universities, and has certificates, diplomas, and degrees, along with many professional memberships and accreditations. Books? No. But, she is currently working on her first one: *The Power of Three Organizing*.

Of course, your image can be damaged and your credibility lost if you have poor writing and speaking skills. Maybe you can find a consultant to help you.

Sources: Company websites, **www.siskindtraining.com**; **www.sjsproductions.com**; **www.teleconceptsconsulting.com**; **www.healthinharmony.com**; **www.lyndagoldmanink.com**; **www.organizeanything.com**; all accessed March 12, 2014.

the home and present information on design, performance data, and specifications. A recent graduate of the training program says, "I have a confidence level that's making a difference in my client contacts."[23]

Maintenance and Service Contracts

Prospects often want information concerning maintenance and care requirements for the products they purchase. The salesperson who can quickly and accurately provide this information will have the edge. Proper maintenance will usually extend the life of the product, so this information should be provided at the time of the sale.

Today, many salespeople are developing customized service agreements that incorporate the customer's special priorities, feelings, and needs. They work hard to acquire a real understanding of the customer's specific service criteria. If call-return expectations are very important to the customer, the frequency and quantity of product-related visits per week or month can be included in the service contract. Customized service agreements add value to the sale and help protect your business from the competition.[24]

Price and Delivery

Potential buyers expect salespeople to be well versed in price and delivery policies and be in a position to set prices and plan deliveries. If a salesperson has pricing authority, buyers perceive the person as someone with whom they can really talk business. The ability to set prices puts the salesperson in a stronger position.[25] Decision-making authority in the area of pricing gives the salesperson *more power and responsibility*. If the salesperson negotiates a price that is too low, the company may lose money on the sale. Price objections represent one of the most common barriers to closing a sale, so salespeople need to be well prepared in this area.

In most situations, the price quotation should be accompanied by information that creates value in the mind of the customer. The process of determining whether or not the proposal adds value is often called **quantifying the solution**. When the purchase represents a major buying decision, such as the purchase of a new computer system, quantifying the solution is important. One way to quantify the solution is to conduct a cost–benefit analysis to determine the actual cost of the purchase and savings the buyer can anticipate from the investment (see Table 6.1).

Another way to quantify the solution is to calculate return on investment (ROI). As products and services become more complex and more expensive, customers are more likely to look at the financial reasons for buying. This is especially true in business-to-business selling. Salespeople who can develop a sales proposal that contains specific information on ROI are more likely to get a favourable response from key decision makers. Chief financial officers, for example, are more inclined to approve an expensive purchase if it results in a good return on investment.[26]

Performing accurate ROI calculations typically requires the collection of detailed financial information. You may need to help the prospect collect information within the company to build a case for the purchase. BAX Global, with offices throughout Canada and the United States, offers customers multi-modal shipping solutions. It has the capability to employ more than one mode of transportation for a customer. In order to develop a customized solution for the customer, the sales representative must collect a great deal of data from the prospect. Transportation modes (e.g., trucks, trains, ships, airplanes) vary in terms of cost, speed, dependability, frequency, and other criteria, so preparation of the sales proposal can be a complicated process.[27]

The use of ROI selling requires more work up front, but it may lead to shorter sales cycles. The salesperson who is not well schooled in financial issues or who cannot compute and supply price information accurately may be at a serious disadvantage. In Chapter 7, we discuss how to position products according to price.

BECOME A COMPANY EXPERT

WE SHOULD NEVER UNDERESTIMATE INFORMATION ABOUT THE COMPANY ITSELF AS A STRONG appeal that can be used during the sales presentation. This is especially true when the customer is considering a strategic alliance. Before teaming up with another company, the

quantifying the solution The process of determining if a sales proposal adds value. Quantifying the solution is especially important in situations where the purchase represents a major buying decision.

Table 6.1 Quantifying the Solution with Cost–Benefit Analysis

Quantifying the solution often involves a carefully prepared cost-benefit analysis. This example compares the higher-priced Phoenix semitruck trailer with the lower-priced FB model, which is a competing product.

Cost Savings of the Phoenix Versus FB Model for a 10-Year Period (All Prices Are Approximate)	Cost Savings
Stainless steel bulkhead (savings on sandblasting and painting)	$ 425.00
Stainless steel rear door frame (savings on painting)	425.00
Air ride suspension (better fuel mileage, longer tire life, longer brake life)	3 750.00
Hardwood or aluminum scuff (savings from freight damages and replacement of scuff)	1 000.00
LED lights (last longer; approximate savings: $50 per year 10 years)	500.00
Light protectors (save $50 per year on replacement 10 years)	500.00
Threshold plate (saves damage to entry of trailer)	200.00
Internal rail reinforcement (saves damage to lower rail and back panels)	500.00
Stainless steel screws for light attachment (savings on replacement cost)	200.00
Domestic oak premium floor 1-3/8 (should last 10 years under normal conditions)	1 000.00
Doors—aluminum inner and outer skin, outside white finish, inside mill finish, fastened by five aluminum hinges (savings over life of trailer)	750.00
Five-year warranty in addition to standard warranty covers bulkhead rust, LED lights, floor, scuff liner, glad hands, rear frame, mud flap assembly, and threshold plate (Phoenix provides a higher trade-in value.)	1 500.00
Total approximate savings of Phoenix over 10-year period (All the preceding is standard equipment on a Phoenix; this trailer will sell for $23 500; an FB standard trailer would sell for $19 500.)	$10 750.00
Less additional initial cost of Phoenix over FB standard	4 000.00
Overall cost savings of Phoenix over FB trailer	$ 6 750.00

strategic alliance buyer will want to learn a great deal about the firm the salesperson represents. In many cases, you are selling your company as much as or more than you are selling a product.[28]

Some companies, such as Bass Pro Shops, Delta Hotels and Resorts, and TD Waterhouse, have what might be called "brand power," because these companies and the products they sell are well known. However, if you are selling colonial or custom furniture made by Rock Wood Casual Furniture of Pickering, Ontario, or wind turbines manufactured by Endurance Wind Power of Surrey, B.C., you may find it necessary to spend time providing information about your company. In this section we examine the types of information needed in most selling situations.

Knowing, understanding, and being able to clarify information in product literature adds value within the sales process. Customers seek out the "product experts" who can assist them in making intelligent buying decisions.

LifePhotoStudio/Shutterstock

Company Culture and Organization

Many salespeople take special pride in the company they work for. Salespeople employed by Xerox Canada feel good that the company was recognized as one of Canada's best employers for 2014. Xerox Canada provides generous tuition subsidies for job-related courses, a paid company-wide Day of Sharing so employees can volunteer time to their favourite charitable organization, maternity leave top-up payments, top-up payments for parental leaves for adoptive parents, and many other benefits.[29]

As noted in Chapter 3, character and integrity are the hallmarks of a successful sales organization. UPS Incorporated chairman and CEO Michael L. Eskew (2005) says, "The strategies change and the purpose changes, but the values never change."[30]

Every organization has its own unique culture. **Organizational culture** is a collection of beliefs, behaviours, and work patterns held in common by people employed by a specific firm. Most organizations over a period of time tend to take on distinct norms and practices. At Home Depot of Canada Inc., a statement of core values communicates what the company holds important and guides everyone in the organization as they serve the company's customers (see Fig. 6.2). Research indicates that the customer orientation of a firm's salespeople will be influenced by the organization's culture. A supportive culture that encourages salespeople to offer tailor-made solutions to buyer problems will set the stage for long-term partnerships.[31]

Many prospects will use the past performance of a company to evaluate the quality of the current product offering. If the company has enjoyed success in the past, there is good reason to believe that the future will be bright.

organizational culture A collection of beliefs, behaviours, and work patterns held in common by people employed by a specific firm.

Company Information Our Company Our Community Our Associates Media Relations

About Us

Awards

Investor Relations

History

Leadership

Values

GREAT CAREERS BUILT HERE

VISIT OUR CAREERS SITE ▶

The Home Depot's values guide the beliefs and actions of all associates on a daily basis. Our values are the fabric of the company's unique culture and are central to our success. In fact, they are our competitive advantage in the marketplace. Associate pride and our "orange blooded" entrepreneurial spirit are distinctive hall marks of our culture.

1. Taking care of our people:
The key to our success is treating people well. We do this by encouraging associates to speak up and take risks, by recognizing and rewarding good performance and by leading and developing people so they may grow.

2. Giving back to our communities:
An important part of the fabric of The Home Depot is giving our time, talents, energy and resources to worthwhile causes in our communities and society.

3. Doing the right thing:
We exercise good judgment by "doing the right thing" instead of just "doing things right". We strive to understand the impact of our decisions, and we accept responsibility for our actions.

4. Excellent customer service:
Along with our quality products, service, price and selection, we must go the extra mile to give customers knowledgeable advice about merchandise and to help them use those products to their maximum benefit.

5. Creating shareholder value:
The investors who provide the capital necessary to allow our company to grow need and expect a return on their investment. We are committed to providing it.

6. Building strong relationships:
Strong relationships are built on trust, honesty and integrity. We listen and respond to the needs of customers, associates, communities and vendors, treating them as partners.

7. Entrepreneurial spirit:
The Home Depot associates are encouraged to initiate creative and innovative ways of serving our customers and improving the business and to spread best practices throughout the company.

8. Respect for all people:
In order to remain successful, our associates must work in an environment of mutual respect, free of discrimination and harassment where each associate is regarded as part of The Home Depot team.

Courtesy Home Depot of Canada Inc.

Figure 6.2 Companies such as Home Depot of Canada Inc. communicate their core values to customers, suppliers, employees, and other stakeholders.

Company Support for Product

Progressive marketers support the products they sell. In some cases, product support takes the form of sales tools that can be used in preparation for a sales call or during a sales call. Salespeople for Hunter Douglas Canada, a manufacturer of window fashions, have a Dealer Merchandising Portfolio. With this aid, salespeople can help dealers select and order sample books, brochures, videos, in-store display material, and many other items.[32]

Company support after the sale is also important. Tool-and-die firm Jagemann Stamping Company often uses a sales team made up of a salesperson, an engineer, and line workers. Line workers can often answer the technical questions raised by a customer.

Canadian and Australian businesspeople have a lot in common. Everyone in Australia speaks English, and business dress is similar in both countries. However, subtle differences do exist.

■ When you greet an Australian businessperson, give your full name and then firmly shake hands.

■ Australians tend to be modest people who often root for the underdog. Keep information about your power and wealth to yourself.

■ Although Australian businesspeople tend to be informal and friendly, they still expect you to be a good listener and be completely familiar with your product.

■ Keep your presentations simple. Australians want you to get to the point.[a]

Whenever there is a problem or defect, a small group of line workers is sent out with either a salesperson or an engineer to investigate. This involvement raises the workers' commitment to the customer.[33]

BECOME THE INDUSTRY EXPERT—KNOW YOUR COMPETITION

ACQUIRING KNOWLEDGE OF YOUR COMPETITION IS ANOTHER IMPORTANT STEP TOWARD developing complete product knowledge. Salespeople who have knowledge of their competitors' strengths and weaknesses are better able to emphasize the benefits they offer and add value. Prospects often raise specific questions concerning competing firms. If you cannot provide answers or if your answers are vague, the sale may be lost.

Salespeople need to become experts in the industry they represent. In many cases, this means moving beyond the role of product specialist and becoming a business analyst. Staying current and developing an understanding of business processes takes time and may require additional education.[34] If your clients work in the banking industry, read the appropriate trade journals and become active in professional associations that serve bankers' needs.

Develop and Communicate a Healthy Attitude toward Your Competition

Regardless of how impressive your product is, the customer will naturally seek information about similar products sold by other companies. Therefore, you must acquire facts about competing products before the sales presentation. It has never been easier to obtain information about competing products. Check the competitor's website, annual reports, press releases, and marketing material. Once armed with this information, you will be more confident in your ability to handle questions about the competition.

The attitude you display toward your competition is of the utmost importance. Every salesperson should develop a set of basic beliefs about the best way of dealing with competing products. Here are a few helpful guidelines:

1. *In most cases, do not refer to the competition during the sales presentation.* This shifts the focus of attention to competing products, which is usually not desirable.

2. *Never discuss the competition unless you have all your facts straight.* Your credibility will suffer if you make inaccurate statements. If you do not know the answer to a specific question, simply say, "I do not know."

3. *Never criticize the competition.* You may be called on to make direct comparisons between your product and competing products. In these situations, stick to the facts and avoid emotional comments about apparent or real weaknesses.

4. *Be prepared to add value.* The competition may come to your prospect with a comparative advantage in price, delivery, or some other area. Be prepared to neutralize the competitor's proposal with a value-added approach. If your competitor has slow delivery, encourage the customer to talk about why prompt delivery is important.[35]

Customers appreciate an accurate, fair, and honest presentation of the facts. They generally resent highly critical remarks about the competition. Avoid mudslinging at all costs. Fairness is a virtue that people greatly admire.

SOURCES OF PRODUCT, COMPANY, AND INDUSTRY INFORMATION

THERE ARE SEVERAL SOURCES OF PRODUCT INFORMATION AVAILABLE TO SALESPEOPLE. SOME of the most common include: (1) Web-based catalogues and other product literature developed by the company, (2) sales training programs, (3) plant tours, (4) internal sales and sales support team members, (5) customers, (6) the product, and (7) publications.

Web-Based Sources, Catalogues, and Marketing-Related Sales Support Information

Most companies prepare materials that provide a detailed description of their product. This information is usually quite informative, and salespeople should review it carefully. If the company markets a number of products, a sales catalogue is usually developed. To save salespeople time, many companies give them computer software that provides a constantly updated, online product catalogue. Advertisements, promotional brochures, and compact discs can also be valuable sources of product information.

Mitsubishi Caterpillar Forklift America presents its basic product information online, so it's available to dealer representatives in the privacy of their homes, hotel rooms, or wherever else they bring their laptops. Each of the seven product information courses takes about an hour. To reinforce basic product knowledge, the company offers advanced instructor-led courses.[36] Some companies are using interactive distance learning (delivered via satellite) to present different types of sales training.

Engage in Plant Tours

Many companies believe that salespeople should visit the manufacturing plant and see the production process firsthand. Such tours not only provide valuable product information but also increase the salesperson's enthusiasm for the product. A new salesperson may spend several days at the plant getting acquainted with the production process. Experienced personnel within the organization can also benefit from plant tours.

Build Strong Relationships with Internal Sales and Sales Support Team Members

Team selling has become popular in part because many complex sales require the expertise of several sales and sales support personnel. Expertise in the areas of product design, finance, or transportation may be needed to develop an effective sales proposal. Pooled commissions are sometimes used to encourage team members to share information and work as a team.

Today's Wired Customers Have a Lot of Product, Competitive, and Industry Knowledge

Persons who actually use the product can be an important source of information toward improved sales performance.[37] They have likely researched your products and those of your competitors on the Web, observed their performance under actual working conditions, and can provide an objective assessment of the products' strengths and weaknesses. Some companies collect testimonials from satisfied customers and make this persuasive information available to sales staff. Patagonia customers include mountain bikers, backcountry skiers, sailors, paddlers, and fly fishermen. The company's success lies in maintaining a close connection to persons who actually use its products.[38]

Salespeople employed by semiconductor manufacturer Intel Corporation are expected to take the company's business customers from the conceptual stage of their purchase all the way to delivery of the finished product. Dialogue with customers begins very early in the sales cycle when customers need help designing the end product.[39] This approach requires the empowerment of the sales force with greater depth and breadth of product information.

Using CRM to Find Product Information

New salespeople can be overwhelmed by the amount of information they need to master. This includes information about the company and its people, processes, products, and customers. A sales organization can now make learning easier with information technology. Stored information can now be made available to new salespeople through a variety of delivery channels. Depending on security levels, an employee can access data from nearly anywhere, at any time. Training software can enable new salespeople to learn at their own pace about company information such as product specifications, features, benefits, uses, and selling points.

New people can find electronic copies of previous sales proposals to help determine appropriate solutions.

Configuration software can enable a new salesperson to select and price components for a proposal while assembling a custom-tailored solution and be assured that all necessary parts will be included and compatible. **Salesforce .com**, as well as most other CRM suppliers, allows approved partners to integrate their product configuration software. One example is BigMachines Express. This software enables users to quickly and easily select and price the best products, and add them to sales quotes and opportunities. Access **www.bigmachines.com** for more information including demos, videos, case studies, and so forth. The speed and functionality of CRM assures that customers obtain information when needed and adds crucial efficiency to performing many sales-related tasks.

Researching and Using Products

The product itself should not be overlooked as a source of valuable information. Salespeople should closely examine and, if possible, use each item they sell to become familiar with its features. Investigation, use, and careful evaluation of the product will provide a salesperson with additional confidence.

Reading and Studying Publications

Trade and technical publications such as *Canadian Grocer* and *Advertising Age* provide valuable product and industry information. Popular magazines such as *Canadian Business* and the business section of the newspaper also offer salespeople considerable information about their products, their competition, and their customers. Publications such as *Consumer Reports* test products extensively and report the findings in nontechnical language for the benefit of consumers. These reports are a valuable source of information.

Word of Caution

Is it possible to be overly prepared? Can salespeople know too much about the products and services they sell? The answer to both questions is generally no. Communication problems can arise, however, if the salesperson does not accurately gauge the prospect's level of understanding.[40] There is always the danger that a knowledgeable salesperson will overwhelm the potential buyer with facts and figures. This problem can be avoided when salespeople adopt the feature–benefit strategy.

E-learning has become popular because it is inexpensive and fast, and it can be geared to the flexible schedules of salespeople. This regional sales team is receiving sales training from the company's home office.

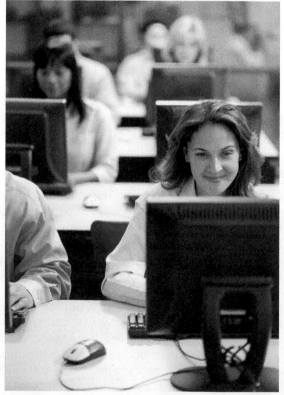

Fuse/Getty Images

CREATING VALUE WITH A FEATURE–BENEFIT STRATEGY

FREDERICK W. SMITH, FOUNDER OF FEDERAL EXPRESS, FIRST PROPOSED THE CONCEPT OF overnight delivery in a paper that he wrote as an undergraduate at Yale University. The now-famous paper was given a "C" by his professor. Many years later, Smith said, "I don't think that we understood our real goal when we first started Federal Express. We thought that we were selling the transportation of goods; in fact, we were selling peace of mind."[41]

Throughout this chapter we emphasize the importance of acquiring information on the features of your product, company, and competition. Now it is important to point out that successful sales presentations translate product features into benefits that meet a specific need expressed by the customer. The "peace of mind" that Frederick W. Smith mentioned is a good example of a buyer benefit. When a product feature is converted to a buyer benefit, "you are talking the customer's talk" with solution-oriented statements that make an impact on the customer.

Distinguish between Features and Benefits

To be sure we understand the difference between a product feature and a buyer benefit, let us define these two terms.

A **feature** is data, facts, or characteristics of your product or service. Features often relate to craftsmanship, design, durability, and economy of operation. They may reveal how the product was developed and manufactured. Product features are often described in the technical section of the written sales proposal and in the literature provided by the manufacturer. Salespeople new to selling and unfamiliar with the importance of benefits have a tendency to throw out information about a product or service without tying that information to the essential needs of the customer. In general, the salesperson might perform a **feature dump,** listing a series of features without enabling the customer to see what benefits these features provide. Ultimately, prospects and existing customers consistently want to know, "What's in it for me?"[42]

A **benefit** is whatever provides the consumer with personal advantage or gain. It answers the question, "How will I benefit from owning or using the product?" If you mention to a prospect "We have one of the most extensive fibre networks in the city with direct connection to your office park," you are talking about a product feature. If you go on to point out, "This means that your wait time is reduced drastically and your employees will be more productive and 60 percent faster than by working with your traditional telecommunications provider," you are pointing out benefits.

General versus Specific Benefits Neil Rackham, author of *The SPIN Selling Fieldbook*, says that a statement can be a benefit only if it meets a specific need expressed by the buyer. When you link a benefit to a buyer's expressed need, you demonstrate that you can help solve a problem that has been described by the customer. A general benefit shows how a feature can be helpful to a buyer, but it does not relate to a specific need expressed by the buyer. Here are two examples of specific benefits:

> "Our water purification system meets the exact specifications you have given us for environmental compliance."

> "Our XP400 model meets the safety criteria you've spelled out."

feature Anything that a customer can feel, see, hear, taste, smell, or measure to answer the question, "What is it?" Features often relate to craftsmanship, durability, design, and economy of operation.

feature dump Listing a series of features without enabling the customer to see what benefits these features provide.

benefit Something that provides the customer with personal advantage or gain to answer, for the customer, the question, "How will I benefit from owning or using the product?"

Rackham says that benefit statements linked to the customer's expressed need are especially effective in large and complex sales.[43]

Incorporating Advantage Statements Some sales training programs suggest that salespeople need to include advantages in the sales presentation. **Advantages** are characteristics (i.e., features) of the product that can be used or will help the buyer. Consider the following statement:

> "Prior to shipping, all of our containers are double wrapped. This means that our product is completely free from contamination when it arrives at your hospital."

Some salespeople develop an advantage statement for each important product feature. Unfortunately, these advantages are often included in the sales presentation even when the buyer has not expressed a need for this information. When this happens, the advantage can be described as a general benefit.

Successful salespeople focus on specific benefits that relate to a need explicitly expressed by the customer. Less successful salespeople take the position that the best way to create value is to present as many benefits as possible. They use a "shotgun" approach to benefits, assuming that more benefits create higher volume. Today's customer measures value by how well your product benefits fit their needs. High-performance salespeople work hard to discover which benefits the customer really cares about.[44]

Use Bridge Statements

We know that people buy benefits, not features. One of the best ways to present benefits is to use a bridge statement. A **bridge statement** is a transitional phrase that connects a statement of features with a statement of benefits. This method permits customers to connect the features of your product to the benefits they will receive. A sales representative for a food wholesaler, for example, might use a bridge statement to introduce a new snack food:

> "This product is nationally advertised, *which means* you will benefit from more presold customers."

Some companies prefer to state the benefit first and the feature second. When this occurs, the bridge statement may be a word such as "because."

> "You will experience faster turnaround and increased profits *because* the first order includes point-of-purchase advertising materials that focus on the Valentine's Day promotion you have planned."

Identify Features and Benefits

A careful analysis of the product will help identify both product features and customer benefits. Once all the important features have been identified, arrange them in logical order. Then write beside each feature the most important benefit the customer will derive from that feature. Finally, prepare a series of bridge statements to connect the appropriate features and benefits. Using this three-step approach, a hotel selling conference and convention services and a manufacturer selling electric motors used to power mining equipment developed

Table 6.2 Convert Product Features to Benefits

Salespeople employed by a hotel can enhance the sales presentation by converting product features to benefits.

Feature	Benefit
Facilities	
Our hotel conference rooms were recently redecorated.	Which means all your meetings will be held in rooms that are attractive and comfortable.
Our rooms were completely redecorated this year and many are now designated non-smoking.	Which means your people will find the rooms clean and attractive. In addition, those who wish can select a non-smoking room.
Food Services	
We offer four different banquet entrées prepared by our executive chef, who was recently selected Chef of the Year by the Canadian Federation of Chefs and Cooks.	Which means your conference will be enhanced by delicious meals served by a well-trained staff.
Our hotel offers 24-hour room service.	Which means your people can order food or beverages at their convenience.

feature–benefit worksheets (see Tables 6.2 and 6.3). Notice how each feature is translated into a benefit that would be important to someone purchasing these products and services. Table 6.3 reminds us that company features can be converted to benefits.

Avoid Information Overload

Knowing your product has always been essential to good selling, but concentrating on product alone can be a serious mistake. Salespeople who love their products and possess

Table 6.3 Convert Company Features to Benefits

Here we see company features translated into customer benefits.

Feature	Benefit
Our company has the largest selection of motors in the area.	Which means you will have an excellent choice of models to meet any specific needs you may have.
We hire only certified service technicians.	Which means your equipment will be kept running in peak condition by well-qualified service personnel.
Our company has an inventory of all major spare parts.	Which means you will have less equipment downtime and will make higher profits.

vast product knowledge about them may overload their customers with product data they neither need nor want. This practice is sometimes described as a "data dump." With the aid of specific types of questions (see Chapter 11), the customer's needs can be identified. Once the customer's needs are known, the salesperson can develop a customized sales presentation that includes selected features that can be converted to specific benefits.

REVIEWING KEY CONCEPTS

- Explain the importance of developing product solutions that add value.

  A product strategy helps salespeople make the right decisions concerning the selection and positioning of products to meet specific customer needs. It is a carefully conceived plan that emphasizes becoming a product expert, selling specific benefits, and configuring value-added solutions.

- Describe the importance of becoming an expert regarding product knowledge.

  Salespeople should become product experts and possess product knowledge that meets or exceeds customer expectations. Some important product information categories include product development and quality improvement processes, performance data and specifications, maintenance and service contracts, and price and delivery.

- Discuss the importance of becoming an expert regarding company knowledge.

  Information about the company can be used to develop strong appeals that can enhance the sales presentation, especially in a situation where there are many look-a-like competing products. This is especially true when the customer is considering a strategic alliance. Important company information includes an understanding of the firm's culture and organization, and company support for products offered.

- Describe how expert knowledge of competition and industry trends improves personal selling.

  Prospects often raise specific questions concerning competing firms. Salespeople who have knowledge of their competitors' strengths and weaknesses are better able to emphasize the benefits they offer and add value. The attitude you display toward your competition is of the utmost importance.

- List major sources of product, competitor, and industry information.

  Salespeople gather information from many sources. Company websites, literature, and sales training programs are among the most important. Other sources include factory tours, customers, competition, industry publications, the Internet, and actual experience with the product itself.

- Explain how to add value with a feature–benefit strategy.

  In the sales presentation and in preparing the written sales proposal, your knowledge of the product's features and your company's strengths must be presented in terms of the resulting benefits to the buyer. We distinguished between general and specific benefits. Specific benefits, linked to a customer's expressed need, are very effective.

Key Terms

advantages **142**

benefit **141**

bridge statement **142**

feature **141**

feature dump **141**

organizational culture **135**

Review Questions

1. Provide a brief description of the term *product strategy*.

2. Distinguish between *product features* and *buyer benefits*.

3. What is *product configuration*? Provide an example of how this practice is used in the sale of commercial stereo equipment.

4. Review the Home Depot of Canada Inc. statement of corporate values on page 136 and then identify the two items that you believe contribute the most to a salesperson's career success.

5. Define *organizational culture*. How might this company information enhance a sales presentation?

6. Basic beliefs underlie the salesperson's method of handling competition. What are four guidelines a salesperson should follow in developing basic beliefs in this area?

7. Explain what the customer's expectations are concerning the salesperson's attitude toward competition.

8. List and briefly describe the five parts included in most written sales proposals.

9. What are the most common sources of product information?

10. Distinguish between a general benefit and a specific benefit. Why do customers respond positively to specific benefits?

Application Exercises

1. Obtain, if possible, a copy of a customer-oriented product sales brochure or news release that has been prepared by a marketer. (Many salespeople receive such selling tools.) Study this information carefully; then develop a feature–benefit analysis sheet.

2. Today many companies are automating their product configuration and proposal-writing activities. Go to the Internet and find these software providers: **www.bigmachines.com/salesforce.php** and **www.results-online.com**. Click on each company's demonstration software and study the design of each product.

3. Select a product you are familiar with and know a great deal about. (This may be an item you have shopped for and purchased, such as a smartphone or an automobile.) Under each of the categories listed, fill in the required information about the product.

    a. Where did you buy the product? Why?

    b. Did product design influence your decision?

    c. How and where was the product manufactured?

    d. What different applications or uses are there for the product?

    e. How does the product perform? Are there any data on the product's performance? What are they?

    f. What kinds of maintenance and care does the product require? How often?

    g. Could you, as a sales representative, sell the product you have written about in categories (a) through (f)? Why or why not?

4. Visit Dell Canada (**www.dell.ca**) and click on a product solution. You have decided that you want a desktop computer, and your primary needs are preparing paper assignments, spreadsheets, PowerPoint presentations, and doing Internet searches. You do not have a lot of extra money to spend, so you are searching for an inexpensive product solution. Notice that Dell quantifies the solution for you as you click on it. Print out your solution and bring it to class, and be prepared to compare your quantified solution with that of other students.

5. With the product solution you created for the previous application exercise, prepare a list of product features and the benefit or benefits associated with each feature. If you were a salesperson selling this product solution to a customer, which benefits would you emphasize? Explain.

ROLE-PLAY EXERCISE

Study the convention centre information included in "Partnership Selling: A Role Play/Simulation" on your companion website **www.pearsoncanada.ca/manning**. Pay particular attention to pricing on the meals and meeting rooms. Click on the sales proposal link and configure a sales proposal for your instructor (using your school name and address), who is responsible for setting up a student awards meeting. The meeting includes a banquet-style meal of chicken Wellington for 26 attendees from 5:30 to 8:00 p.m. on the last Wednesday of next month. The meal will be served at 5:45 p.m., and the awards session is scheduled from 6:45 to 8:00 p.m. in the same room. The seating should be banquet style. Present the completed proposal to another student (acting as your customer) and communicate the features and benefits of your proposal.

Reality Selling Video Case Problem

Texas Monthly is a regional magazine covering politics, business, and culture, but focusing largely on leisure activities and events in Texas. The magazine has a large real estate advertising section, as well as classified sections in which nearly all advertisers are Texas-based businesses appealing to a prospective buyer who is interested in connecting with Texas history and culture. It also has a large, loyal reader base all over Texas, mostly urban, well-educated, and affluent, and the magazine's salespeople pride themselves on their ability to find creative solutions for their customers.

Today, Amy Vandaveer, a sales representative for *Texas Monthly*, is meeting with the marketing director for the Woodlands Town Center, a major community development organization. The Woodlands is a planned community outside of Houston and the recently added Woodlands Town Center includes restaurants, shops, and a hotel and convention centre.

The marketing director's goal is to make the Woodlands Town Center a destination for Houston residents, rather than another area serving people who already live in the Woodlands. Up to this point, the Woodlands Town Center has mostly relied on word of mouth and the positive publicity that it received after winning awards to attract visitors; now, the marketing director is interested in using more print advertising and has scheduled this meeting with Amy to learn more about the possibilities of advertising with *Texas Monthly*.

As a rule, Amy uses relatively informal presentations on her sales calls. The most significant part of her presentation is a copy of *Texas Monthly*; showing potential customers a recent issue gives them the opportunity to see the magazine's overall look and feel and gives them a good look at the context in which their ads would appear. Over the course of the informal presentation, Amy also shows the customer statistics on the reader base of *Texas Monthly* and the ways in which they respond to ads in the magazine, as well as a price sheet for various types of ads.

After listening to what the Woodlands Town Center needs, Amy proposes a four-page colour ad, which can also be printed separately from the magazine for use as a brochure. Although the price depends on the number of stand-alone brochures that are ordered, she estimates that the cost of the ad would be about $50 000. She and the marketing director agree on a timeline for a more formal proposal that can be shared with the rest of the Woodlands Town Center board, and Amy moves on to the rest of her day. (See the chapter opener on page 124 and Reality Selling Today Role Play 3 in Appendix 1 on page 428 on for more information.)

Questions

1. Explain how Amy Vandaveer can use the three prescriptions for a product-selling strategy in preparing and presenting product solutions.

2. What are the major benefits that Amy incorporates into her presentation?

3. What are the most likely objections that the marketing director might raise?

4. In addition to the actual product strategy, how important will information about *Texas Monthly* (its history, mission, past performance, etc.) be in closing the sale?

PARTNERSHIP SELLING: A ROLE PLAY/SIMULATION

Visit the role play simulation materials provided in the Student Resources section of your companion website at **www.pearsoncanada.ca/manning**. *A Contents page lists appropriate page references for the activities.*

Read *Employment Memorandum 1*, which introduces you to your new training position with the Hotel Convention Centre. You should also study the product strategy materials that follow the memo to become familiar with the company, product, and competitive knowledge you will need in your new position.

Read *Customer Service/Sales Memorandum 1* and complete the two-part customer/service assignment provided by your sales manager. In item 1, you are to configure a price–product sales proposal; in item 2, you are to write a sales cover letter for the sales proposal. Note that the information presented in the price–product sales proposal will consist of product facts or features, and the information presented in your sales cover letter should present specific buyer benefit statements. These forms should be custom-fitted to meet your customer's—B. H. Rivera's—specific needs. All the product information you will need is in the product strategy materials provided as enclosures and attachments to *Employment Memorandum 1*.

Chapter 7
Product-Selling Strategies That Add Value

Learning Objectives

After studying this chapter, you should be able to

1 Describe positioning as a product-selling strategy.

2 Explain the 3D Product Solutions Selling Model.

3 Discuss product-positioning options.

4 Explain how to sell your product with a price strategy.

5 Explain how to sell your product with a value-added strategy.

Introduction

You have just finished paying off your college loans and it's time to replace that old rust bucket with a new car. You have looked at the sport-compact cars available, but they all seem so small. Now you are eagerly looking at cars in the sports sedan category. The cars in this niche offer a good blend of comfort, design, and performance. However, there are almost too many choices. *Road & Track* says there are 11 different automobiles in this group. The list price starts at $72 785 for the Cadillac CTS-V. The Audi A4 and Jaguar X-Type offer all-wheel drive; all the rest offer front- or rear-wheel drive. As you learn more about the choices available, it becomes clear that each manufacturer has taken steps to differentiate its product.[1]

Several years ago automobile manufacturers from around the world began to develop and position cars for the sports sedan segment. Research indicated that demand for these cars would increase. The result was the introduction of 11 different marques, each with its own unique characteristics. At the dealer level, the process of product differentiation continues. If you want something more than standard equipment, the salesperson can describe

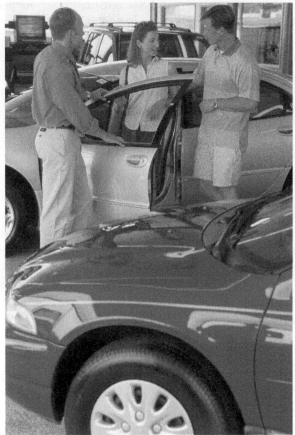

Salespeople at the dealer level in the crowded sports-sedan market play an important role in positioning their brand for competitive advantage. Adding value depends on the salesperson's ability to provide a competitive analysis using knowledge of the manufacturer, the automobile, and the dealership.

Comstock/Stockbyte/Getty Images

a variety of options that can add $10 000 or more to the price. Each car can be accessorized to meet your personal needs. The dealer can also help position this product with modern facilities, customer-friendly service policies, and a reputation for honesty and integrity.

Some automobile manufacturers see the sports sedan category as critical to their success. At BMW, the 3 Series sports sedan accounts for nearly half of the company's sales worldwide. Sports sedans can be very profitable because many buyers purchase expensive options such as special wheel and tire packages, anti-skid electronics, ground-effects trim, and top-of-the line audio systems.

PRODUCT POSITIONING—IN A COMPETITIVE MARKETPLACE

LONG-TERM SUCCESS IN TODAY'S DYNAMIC GLOBAL ECONOMY REQUIRES THE CONTINUOUS positioning and repositioning of products.[2] **Positioning** involves those decisions and activities intended to create and maintain a certain conception of the firm's product in the customer's mind. It requires developing a marketing strategy aimed at influencing how a particular market segment perceives a product in comparison to the competition.[3] In a market that has been flooded with a variety of sport-utility vehicles (SUVs), Land Rover has been positioned as a dependable vehicle that can climb a steep, rock-covered hillside

positioning Decisions and activities intended to create and maintain a certain conception of the firm's product in the customer's mind.

with ease. Every effort has been made to create the perception of safety, durability, and security. To give sales representatives increased confidence in the Land Rover, the company has arranged plant tours and the opportunity to observe actual testing of the Land Rover under extremely demanding conditions. Good positioning means that the product's name, reputation, and niche are well recognized. However, a good positioning strategy does not last forever. The positioning process must be continually modified to match the customer's changing wants and needs.[4]

Essentials of Product Positioning

Most salespeople use a combination of marketing and sales strategies to position their products based on the unique needs of each of their customers. Therefore, every salesperson needs a good understanding of the fundamental practices that contribute to product positioning. This chapter begins with a brief introduction to the concept of product differentiation. This is followed by an explanation of how products have been redefined in the age of information. The remainder of the chapter is devoted to three selling strategies that can be used to position a product. Emphasis is placed on positioning your product with a value-added strategy. In the age of information, salespeople who cannot add value to the products they sell will diminish in number and influence.

Salesperson's Role in Product Differentiation

differentiation Your ability to separate yourself and your product from that of your competitors.

With so much publicly available product and competitive information, one of the basic tenets of sales and marketing is the principle of product differentiation. **Differentiation** refers to your ability to separate yourself and your product from that of your competitors. It is the key to building and maintaining a competitive advantage.[5] The competitors in virtually all industries are moving toward differentiating themselves on the basis of quality, price, convenience, economy, or some other factor. Salespeople, who are on the front line of many marketing efforts, assume an important role in the product differentiation process. Differentiating your product helps you stand out from the crowd. It often allows you to distance yourself from the competition. In many cases, the process of differentiation creates barriers that make it difficult for the buyer to choose a competing product simply on the basis of price.[6]

Custom-Fitting and Communicating the Value Proposition

A well-informed customer will usually choose the product that offers the most value. Therefore, salespeople need to position their product with a value proposition. A **value proposition** is the set of benefits and values the company promises to deliver to customers to satisfy their needs. The value proposition presented by Porsche promises driving performance and excitement.[7] Kinko's, which is now part of FedEx, is attempting to differentiate itself from Sir Speedy, AlphaGraphics, and print shops found at Office Depot, OfficeMax, and Staples. The new value proposition promises that 1200 FedEx Kinko's locations offer a breadth of services unparalleled in the industry. These new centres leverage the traditional strengths and brand awareness of FedEx and Kinko's.[8] Salespeople have an important responsibility to custom-fit and then attractively communicate aspects of the value proposition that meet the specific needs of the customer.

value proposition Set of benefits and values the company promises to deliver to customers to satisfy their needs.

Quantifying the Value Proposition In many situations, salespeople must quantify the value proposition. This is especially true when the customer is a business buyer. (Business buyer behaviour will be discussed in Chapter 8.) The value quantification process raises customer comprehension levels as they discover the merits of buying your product or service.[9] Let's assume you are selling Kenworth trucks and one of your customers is Day & Ross Transport, based in Hartland, New Brunswick. This large company is planning to purchase 200 new trucks. Your Kenworth diesel trucks cost 10 percent more than rivals' trucks. Within your proposal you should try to quantify the benefits of buying Kenworth trucks, which may include greater reliability, higher trade-in value, and plush interiors that will help the buyer attract better drivers.[10] Understanding the Three Dimension (3-D) Product Solutions Selling Model concept discussed next enables a salesperson to position and differentiate the most valuable parts of the value proposition.

THE THREE-DIMENSION (3-D) PRODUCT SOLUTIONS SELLING MODEL

TED LEVITT, FORMER EDITOR OF *Harvard Business Review*, SAYS THAT PRODUCTS ARE PROBLEM-solving tools. People buy products if they fulfill a problem-solving need. Today's better-educated and more demanding customers are seeking a *cluster of satisfactions*. **Satisfactions** arise from the product itself, from the company that makes or distributes the product, and from the salesperson who sells and services the product.[11] As noted in Chapter 6, many companies are attempting to transform themselves from *product selling* to *solution selling*. Figure 7.1 provides a description of **The Three-Dimension (3-D) Product Solutions Selling Model.** The 3-D Product Solutions Selling Model illustrates the product, company, and salesperson features available to satisfy the customer's potential 3-D cluster of satisfactions. To develop and sell solutions with many competitive "look-alike" products, salespeople must be familiar with the unique satisfactions that meet the needs of each customer.

satisfactions The positive benefits that customers seek when making a purchase. Satisfactions arise from the product itself, from the company that makes or distributes the product, and from the salesperson who sells and services the product.

Three-Dimension (3-D) Product Solutions Selling Model Model that illustrates the product, company, and salesperson features available to satisfy the customer's potential 3-D cluster of satisfactions.

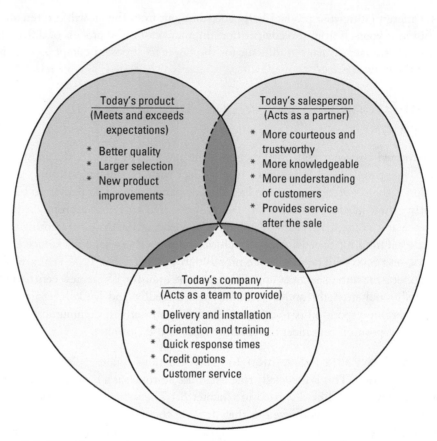

Figure 7.1 The Three-Dimension (3-D) Product Solutions Selling Model
A successful product strategy should include a cluster of satisfactions that meets
the needs of today's better-educated and more demanding customers. Drawing
from this cluster, with the 3-D Product Solutions Selling Model the salesperson can
configure value-added solutions that meet and potentially exceed individual
customer's needs.

To illustrate how the concept of a cluster of satisfactions works in a business setting, let us examine an important buying decision. Elaine Parker, a sales representative
for Elmore Industries Incorporated, sells metals for manufacturing operations. Over
a period of six months, she frequently called on a prospect that had the potential to
become a valued customer. During every call, the buyer's receptionist told her the
company was happy with its present supplier. Elaine refused to give up and finally the
buyer agreed to see her. At first, she was greeted with cool silence, so she decided to
ask him some questions about his business, such as: "How's the slow economy affecting
your sales?" The buyer's answers focused on materials costs. He said his company could
not raise prices nor cut quality. He wanted to lower costs but was unsure how it could
be done. Elaine suggested he consider trying some new alloys that were less expensive
than the standard metals he had been purchasing. As she described the new alloys, the
buyer's interest began to build. She offered to make a full presentation to the buyer and
his engineers at a follow-up meeting. The second meeting was a success. Soon after

that meeting, Elaine received her first order from the customer. Within a year, she had become the customer's most trusted adviser on technological developments in the industry and his exclusive supplier.[12]

Elaine Parker used questions to engage the customer and identify his problem. She also provided answers to questions raised by the customer:

Questions related to the product

What product is best for our type of operation?
Are there new product developments we aren't aware of?
Does the solution meet our quality standards?
Given the cost of this product, will we maintain our competitive position in the marketplace?

Questions related to the company

Does this company provide the most advanced technology?
What is the company's reputation for quality products?
What is the company's reputation for standing behind the products it sells?
Is there a technical support team available?

Questions related to the salesperson

Does the salesperson possess the knowledge and experience needed to recommend the right product?
Can the salesperson clearly communicate specific buyer benefits?
Can the salesperson serve as a trusted adviser?
Will this salesperson provide support services after the sale?

Understanding the 3-D Product Solutions Selling Model—or cluster of satisfactions product-selling model as it is sometimes referred to—enables salespeople to custom-fit solutions that successfully position, yet differentiate, their solutions in today's competitive and often complex situations. Elaine Parker used all three parts of the cluster of satisfactions product-selling model to differentiate and position her selling solution—a product that exceeded the customer's expectations, relationship skills that set her apart as a trusted partner, and technical customer-support personnel. In many of today's selling situations, the products offered by various suppliers are very similar, often referred to as "look-alike" products. In these situations, while being able to meet the product needs of the customer, the competitive advantage may be the knowledge and relationship skills of the salesperson and/or the company's support personnel. For example, salespeople in the competitive automobile-retailing marketplace face this situation. The service departments and the knowledge and relationship-building skills of the salesperson are increasingly becoming the most important parts of successfully meeting customers' needs.

Salespeople who are knowledgeable in all areas of the 3-D Product Solutions Selling Model are better able to position a product. This knowledge also helps to achieve product differentiation, understand the competition, and prepare an effective value proposition. The competitive analysis worksheet (Table 7.1) can help you discover ways to position your product as the superior choice over your competition.

A Word of Caution Because many of today's information-age products are very complex, product differentiation must be handled with care. Salespeople are sometimes

Table 7.1 Competitive Analysis Worksheet

A value-added product-selling strategy is enhanced when salespeople analyze product, company, and salesperson attributes of the competition in relation to benefits they offer. This information helps the salesperson create value within the sales process.

	My Company	Competitor A	Competitor B
Product Attributes			
Quality			
Durability			
Reliability			
Performance			
Packaging flexibility			
Warranty			
Brand			
Company Attributes			
Reputation			
Industry leadership			
Facilities			
Ease of doing business			
Distribution channels			
Ordering convenience			
Returns, credits, etc.			
Salesperson Attributes			
Knowledge/Expertise			
Responsiveness			
Pricing authority			
Customer orientation			
Honesty/integrity			
Follow-through			
Presentation skills			

tempted to use technical lingo—real and invented—to impress the buyer. This problem often surfaces in a situation in which the salesperson is not sure how to describe the value-added features of the product. Robert Notte, technology chief for travel outfitter Backroads, says that during the telecom boom, salespeople representing WorldCom (now MCI) and other firms babbled endlessly, using industry jargon that was often unintelligible. "They wanted you to be impressed," Robert Notte says. Some customers were so intimidated that they were afraid to ask questions—or make a buying decision.[13]

PRODUCT-POSITIONING STRATEGIES TO SELL NEW (VS. MATURE) AND LOW-PRICED (VS. VALUE-ADDED) PRODUCTS

PRODUCT POSITIONING IS A CONCEPT THAT APPLIES TO BOTH NEW AND EXISTING PRODUCTS. Given the dynamics of most markets, it may be necessary to reposition products several times during their lifespan, because even a solid popular product can lose market position quickly. Salespeople have assumed an important and expanding role in positioning products. To succeed in our information-drenched society, marketers must use a more direct and personalized form of communication with customers. Advertising directed toward a mass market will often fail to position a complex product.

Throughout the remainder of this chapter, we discuss specific ways to use various product-positioning strategies. We explain how salespeople can (1) position new and emerging products versus mature and well-established products, (2) position products with price strategies, and (3) position products with value-added strategies.

Selling New Products versus Well-Established Products

Products, like human beings, are born, grow up, mature, and grow old. In marketing, this process is known as the **product life cycle**; it includes the stages a product goes through from the time it is first introduced to the market until it is discontinued. As the product moves through its cycle, the strategies relating to competition, promotion, pricing, and other factors must be evaluated and possibly changed. The nature and extent of each stage in the product life cycle are determined by several factors:

> **product life cycle** Stages of a product from the time it is first introduced to the market until it is taken off the market, including the stages of introduction, growth, maturity, and decline.

1. the product's perceived advantage over available substitutes;
2. the product's benefits and the importance of the needs it fulfills;
3. competitive activity, including pricing, substitute product development and improvement, and effectiveness of competing advertising and promotion; and
4. changes in technology, fashion, or demographics.[14]

As we attempt to develop a product-selling strategy, we must consider where the product is positioned within its life cycle. The sales strategy used to sell a new and emerging product will be much different from the strategy used to sell a mature, well-established product (see Fig. 7.2).

Selling New and Emerging Products Selling strategies used during the new and emerging stage (see Fig. 7.2) are designed to develop a new level of expectation, change habits, and in some cases establish a new standard of quality.[15] The goal is to build desire for the product. Highly talented and resourceful salespeople are needed during the product introduction phase.[16] Salespeople must be resourceful, possess information regarding every aspect of the product, and be able to present a convincing value proposition.[17]

When Brother International Corporation introduced its line of Multi-Function Centre (MFC) machines, the goal was to convince buyers that one machine could replace five separate machines. However, before buyers would give up their copy machine, fax machine, laser printer, and other machines, they asked some hard questions. Is a multi-function machine reliable? Does the quality match that of the current machines? Finding

Figure 7.2 New versus Mature Product-Selling Model

There are different product-selling strategies for positioning new versus mature products. Selling new products requires successfully providing new insights to add value, while selling mature products requires positioning product and company superiority over competition.

the best machine for each customer is challenging because Brother offers more than 10 different MFC models to choose from.

In some cases the new product is not a tangible item. Several years ago, IntraLinks closed its first big sale, a $50 000 contract, with J.P. Morgan. The company got its start providing the financial services industry with the secure transmission of highly confidential information across the Internet. Patrick Wack and his business partners convinced J. P. Morgan and other financial firms that they did not need to rely on an army of foot messengers and FedEx trucks to deliver sensitive documents. They were not only selling a new product, they were selling a vision that included new levels of expectations. The value proposition focused on faster, more secure document transfer, which, in the customer's mind, translated into improved customer service and cost savings. Today Patrick Wack is selling this document transfer concept to customers in a variety of business communities.[18]

Selling Mature and Well-Established Products Mature and well-established products are usually characterized by intense competition as new brands enter the market. Customers who currently buy your product will become aware of competing products. With new and emerging products, salespeople may initially have little or no competition, and their products may dominate the market. However, this condition may not last long.

Sun Life Financial regularly provides its agents with new products. Yet the company finds that competing insurance companies quickly copy them. When competing products enter the market, Sun Life sales agents must adopt new strategies. One positioning strategy Sun Life uses is to emphasize the company's history of superior service to policyholders for over 150 years and its undeniable financial strength. It is a growth-focused company headquartered in Canada but with offices in more than 20 countries. Corporate Knights named Sun Life as one of 13 Canadian companies to make its list of the 2014 Global 100 Most Sustainable Corporations in the World.[19] Agents often describe Sun Life as a supportive company that gives high priority to service after the sale and a stable organization that will be around to service future needs. The objective is to create an awareness in the customer's mind that Sun Life is a solid company with a long history of good service to policyholders.

The relationship strategy is often critical in selling mature and well-established products. To preserve market share and ward off competitors, many salespeople work hard to maintain a strong relationship with the customer. At Sun Life, salespeople have found that good service after the sale is one of the best selling strategies because it builds customer loyalty.

Selling Products with a Price Strategy

Product, promotion, distribution, and price are the four elements that make up the marketing mix. Pricing decisions must be made at each stage of the product life cycle. Therefore, setting the price can be a complex process. The first step in establishing price is to determine the firm's pricing objectives. Some firms set their prices to maximize their profits; they aim for a price as high as possible without causing a disproportionate reduction in unit sales. Other firms set a market share objective; management may decide that the strategic advantage of an increased market share outweighs a temporary reduction in profits. Many of the new companies doing business on the Internet have adopted this approach.

Pricing strategies often reflect the product's position in the product life cycle. When large high-definition flat-screen televisions were in the new and emerging stage, customers who wanted this innovative product were willing to pay $5000 or more for a unit.

Transactional Selling Tactics that Emphasize Low Price Some marketers have established a positioning plan that emphasizes low price and the use of transactional selling tactics. These companies maintain a basic strategy that focuses on meeting competition. If the firm has meeting competition as its pricing goal, it makes every effort to charge prices that are identical or close to those of the competition. Once this positioning strategy has been adopted, the sales force is given several price tactics to use. Salespeople can alter (lower) the base price through the use of discounts and allowances. Discounts and allowances can take a variety of forms. A few of the more common ones follow:

Quantity discount. The quantity discount allows the buyer a lower price for purchasing in multiple units or above a specified dollar amount.

Seasonal discount. With seasonal pricing, the salesperson adjusts the price up or down during specific times to spur or acknowledge changes in demand. Off-season travel and lodging prices provide examples.

Promotional allowance. A promotional allowance is a price reduction given to a customer who participates in an advertising or a sales support program. Many salespeople give supermarkets promotional allowances for advertising or displaying a manufacturer's products.

Trade or functional discount. Channel intermediaries, such as wholesalers, often perform credit, storage, or transportation services. Trade or functional discounts cover the cost of these services.[20]

quantity discount A price reduction made to encourage a larger volume purchase than would otherwise be expected.

seasonal discount Adjusting prices up or down during specific times to spur or acknowledge changes in demand.

promotional allowance A price reduction given to a customer who participates in an advertising or sales support program.

trade or **functional discount** A discount given to channel intermediaries to cover the cost of the services they provide.

Another option available to salespeople facing a buyer with a low-price buying strategy is to "unbundle" product features. Let's assume that a price-conscious customer wants to schedule a conference that will be accompanied by a buffet-style meal. To achieve a lower price, the salesperson might suggest a cafeteria-style meal, thereby eliminating the need for servers. This product configuration involves less cost to the seller and the cost savings can be passed on to the buyer. Timken Company, a century-old bearing maker, has adopted bundling as a way to compete with other manufacturers around the world. The company now surrounds its basic products with additional components in order to provide customers with exactly what they need. These components can take the form of electronic sensors, lubrication systems, castings, or installation and maintenance. Giving customers bundling options has given Timken a big advantage over foreign competitors who often focus on the basic product. Salespeople who represent Timken have flexible pricing options.[21]

These examples represent only a small sample of the many discounts and allowances salespeople use to compete on the basis of price. Price discounting is a competitive tool available to large numbers of salespeople. Excessive focus on low prices and generous discounts, however, can have a negative impact on profits and sales commissions.

Consequences of Using Low-Price Tactics Pricing is a critical factor in the sale of many products and services. In markets where competition is extremely strong, setting a product's price may be a firm's most complicated and important decision. The authors of *The Discipline of Market Leaders* encourage business firms to pick one of three disciplines—best price, best product, or best service—and then do whatever is necessary to outdistance the competition. However, the authors caution us not to ignore the other two disciplines: "You design your business to excel in one direction, but you also have to strive to hit the minimum in the others."[22] Prior to using low-price tactics, everyone involved in sales and marketing should answer these questions:

- *Are you selling to high- or low-involvement buyers?* Some people are emotionally involved with respected brands, such as BMW, Sony, and BlackBerry. A part of their identity depends on buying the product they consider the best. Low-involvement buyers care mostly about price.[23]

- *How important is quality in the minds of buyers?* If buyers do not fully understand the price–quality relationship, they may judge the product by its price. For a growing number of customers, long-term value is more important than short-term savings that result from low prices.

- *How important is service?* For many buyers, service after the sale is a critical factor. Even online customers, thought to be very interested in price, rate quality of service very highly. This is especially true in business-to-business sales. A survey conducted by Accenture reported that 80 percent of nearly 1000 corporate buyers rate a strong brand and reliable customer service ahead of low prices when deciding which companies to do business with online.[24]

Influence of Electronic Business on Pricing Companies large and small are racing to discover new sales and marketing opportunities on the Internet. Products ranging from personal computers to term insurance can now be purchased from various websites. Salespeople who are involved primarily in transactional selling and add little or no value to

How Do Customers Judge Service Quality?

In the growing service industry, there is intense price competition. From a distance, one gets the impression that every buyer decision hinges on price alone. However, a closer examination of service purchases indicates that service quality is an important factor when it comes to developing a long-term relationship with customers.

How do customers judge service quality? Researchers have discovered valuable insights about customer perceptions of service quality. They surveyed hundreds of customers in a variety of service industries and discovered that five service-quality dimensions emerged:

1. *Tangibles:* Details the customers can see, such as the appearance of personnel and equipment.

2. *Reliability:* The ability to perform the desired service dependably, accurately, and consistently.

3. *Responsiveness:* The willingness of sales and customer service personnel to provide prompt service and help customers.

4. *Assurance:* The employees' knowledge, courtesy, and ability to convey trust and confidence.

5. *Empathy:* The provision of caring, individualized attention to customers.

Customers apparently judge the quality of each service transaction in terms of these five quality dimensions. Companies need to review these service-quality dimensions and make sure that each area measures up to customers' expectations. Salespeople should recognize that these dimensions have the potential to add value to the services they sell.[a]

the sales transaction will often not be able to compete with online vendors. To illustrate, consider the purchase of insurance. Many Canadians might visit an online site such as term4sale.ca or termcanada.com to get comparison quotes for term insurance, and then purchase their insurance needs online. A well-informed buyer can make a choice with limited risk. However, when purchasing long-term care insurance, disability insurance, or a whole life insurance policy, most buyers want the help of a well-informed agent. These policies are more complex, and the premiums can be high.

Investors now have more choices than they have had in the past. Persons who need little or no assistance buying stocks can visit Questrade online or the website of another discount vendor. The person who wants help selecting a stock can turn to a full-service broker such as TD Waterhouse Private Client services. Full-service brokers can survive and may prosper as long as they can add value to the sales transaction. The new economy is reshaping the world of commerce and every buyer has greater choice.

Selling Your Product with a Value-Added Strategy

Most high-performing salespeople have adopted sales strategies that emphasize *value-added* selling. Salespeople can add value to their product with one or more intangibles: with improved insights and knowledge of customer needs, product benefits, and competitive offerings; stronger relationship and partnership building; better use of sales technologies, more dependable product deliveries, better service after the sale, and innovations that truly improve the product's value in the eyes of the customer. In today's highly competitive marketplace, these value-added benefits give the company a unique niche and a competitive edge. Salespeople who don't make selling and delivering high-value solutions a high priority will consistently lose sales to competitors.[25]

To understand fully the importance of the value-added concept in selling and how to apply it in a variety of selling situations, it helps to visualize every product as being four-dimensional. The **Value-Added Product-Selling Model** is made up of four "possible" products: the generic product, the expected product, the value-added product, and the potential product (see Fig. 7.3).[26]

Generic Product—The Starting Point

The **generic product** is the basic, substantive product you are selling. Generic product describes only the product category—for example, life insurance, rental cars, clothing, hotels, or personal computers. Every Ritz-Carlton hotel offers guest rooms, food and beverage service (i.e., restaurants, bars, and banquet space), meeting rooms, guest parking, and other basic services. For customers who visit Tilley Endurables, the generic product is the men's and women's travel and adventure clothing and accessories they find there. The generic products at a bank are money that can be loaned to customers and basic chequing account services. The capability of delivering a generic product gives the marketer the right to play in the game, to compete in the marketplace.[27] Generic products, even the lowest-priced ones, often cannot compete with products that are "expected" by the customer.

Expected Product—Understanding the Customer's Perceived Needs

Every customer has minimal purchase expectations that exceed the generic product itself.[28]

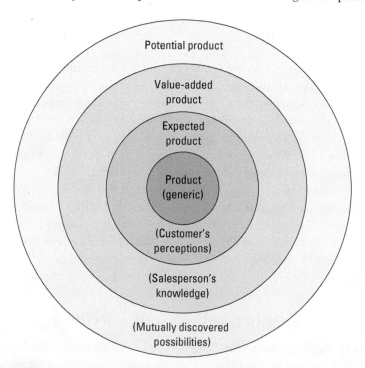

Figure 7.3 The Value-Added Product-Selling Model
An understanding of the Value-Added Product-Selling Model is essential when the salesperson is developing a presentation that first must meet, and then exceed, the customer's expectations. Exceeding a customer's expectations is extremely important in building long-term partnerships.

Source: "The Value-Added Product-Selling Model" from *Marketing Success Through Differentiation of Anything* by Theodore Levitt. Copyright © 1980 by Harvard Business Publishing. Used by the permission of Harvard Business Publishing.

Ritz-Carlton must offer not only a comfortable guest room, but also a clean one. Some customers expect a "super" clean room. The **expected product** is everything that represents the customer's minimal expectations. The customer at Tilley Endurables will expect quality products, a good selection, competitive prices, fashionable accessories, and well-informed salespeople.

expected product Everything that represents the customer's minimal expectations.

The minimal purchase conditions vary among customers, so the salesperson must acquire information concerning the expected product that exists in the customer's mind. When the customer expects more than the generic product, the product can be sold *only* if those expectations are met. Every customer perceives the product in individualized terms, which a salesperson cannot anticipate.

Determining each customer's expectations requires the salesperson to make observations, conduct background checks, ask questions, and listen to what the customer is saying. You are attempting to discover both feelings and facts. Top salespeople encourage the customer to think more deeply about the problems they face and discover for themselves the value of a solution. They *avoid* offering solutions until the needs are clearly spelled out. If the buyer says, "The average gas mileage for our fleet of delivery trucks is only 3.4 km per litre," the salesperson might respond with this question: "How does this low mileage rate affect your profitability?" To move the customer's attention from the expected product to a value-added product, you need to keep the customer focused on solutions.[29]

Research reported in the *Harvard Business Review* indicates that it is very difficult to build customer loyalty if you are selling only the expected product. Customer satisfaction and loyalty do not always move in tandem.[30] The customer who purchases the services of Ernst & Young Consulting may feel satisfied after the project is completed but may never do business with the company again. Customer loyalty is more likely to increase when the purchase involves a value-added product.[31]

Value-Added Product—Maximizing Your Customer's Satisfaction The **value-added product** exists when salespeople offer customers more than they expect. Coupling CRM with a differentiation strategy provides one way for a salesperson to add value.[32] When you make a reservation at one of the Ritz-Carlton hotels and request a special amenity such as a tennis lesson, a record of this request is maintained in the computer system. If you make a reservation at another Ritz-Carlton at some future date, the agent will inform you of the availability of a tennis court. The guest who buys chocolate-chip cookies in the gift shop at one location may find some waiting in the room in Montreal two weeks later. The hotel company uses modern technology to surprise and delight guests.[33] Tilley Endurables provides many things to enhance customers' shopping experiences. At their retail store locations, customers get free cookies, shop in an engaging environment, and can have alterations to clothing done in minutes. Even at its online location, the company adds value for its customers. It provides information on its products, service, and guarantees, and even provides traveller tips, a checklist for packing, advice concerning pickpockets, and more.[34] Among the most important factors that contribute to the value-added product is the overall quality of employees with whom the customer has contact. Sales and sales support staff who display enthusiasm and commitment to the customer add a great deal of value to the product.[35]

value-added product Product that exists when salespeople offer the customer more than they expect.

Potential Product After the value-added product has been developed, the salesperson should begin to conceptualize the **potential product**—what may remain to be done; that is, what is possible.[36] As the level of competition increases, especially in the case of mature products, salespeople must look into the future and explore new possibilities.

potential product What may remain to be done to a product—that is, what is possible.

In the highly competitive food services industry, restaurant owners like to do business with a distribution sales representative (DSR) who wants to help make the business profitable. The DSR who assumes this role becomes a true partner and looks beyond the customer's immediate and basic needs. The potential product might be identified after a careful study of the restaurant's current menu and customer base. To deliver the potential product, a salesperson must discover and satisfy new customer needs, which requires imagination and creativity.

Steelcase Incorporated, a leading manufacturer of office furniture, has developed the "Think" chair, which is 99 percent recyclable and can be disassembled with basic hand tools in about five minutes. This $900 chair meets a growing demand for products made of parts that can be recycled several times and manufactured in ways least harmful to the environment. Steelcase developed this "potential product" after learning that customers are increasingly seeking environmentally safe products and are sometimes willing to pay a premium for them.[37]

The potential product is more likely to be developed by salespeople who are close to their customers. Many high-performing salespeople explore product possibilities with their customers on a regular basis. Potential products are often mutually discovered during these exchanges.

Steelcase's "Think" chair answered its customers' wishes for potential products that are more environmentally safe. It is 99 percent recyclable.

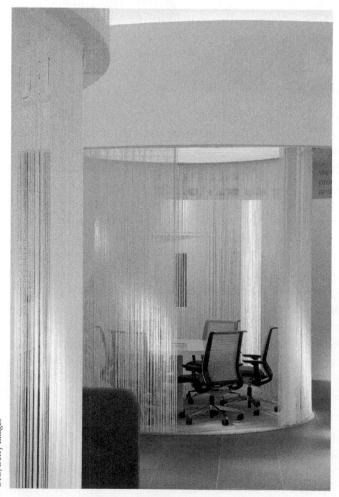

UIG/Getty Images

Distributing Product Information with CRM

Today, salespeople are challenged to manage a steady stream of information about customers (needs) and products (solutions). From this stream of information, the salesperson must select product information that is relevant to a specific customer and deliver the information in a manner that can be understood by the customer. Customer relationship management (CRM) assists the busy salesperson by providing tools that can collect information and rapidly link it to those who need it. Most CRM systems can receive and organize information from many sources, within and outside the organization. For example, Salesforce.com is linked to Google AdWords, an online advertising service. Advertisements placed on search engines, including Google, direct users to pages with forms to complete for more information. The data entered on these forms are downloaded directly into Salesforce.com. The statistics generated by the service permits a quick analysis of online advertising. Once information is received from the various sources, sales professionals can add value to this information by summarizing, combining, and tailoring the information to meet a customer's needs.

When new information about a product is received, the customer database can be quickly searched to find those customers who might have an interest. The new product data can be merged into an email, fax, or letter to those customers, along with other information (benefits) that can help the recipients assess its value. Later, the CRM system can display an alert, reminding the sales professional to follow up on the information that was shared with the customer.

Every indication points toward product-selling strategies that add value becoming more important in the future. New-product life cycles are shrinking, so more companies are searching for ways to add value during the new and emerging stage. Some companies that have experienced low profits selling low-priced products are reinventing those products. They search for product features that provide benefits customers think are worth paying for. Maytag Corporation developed the expensive, environment-friendly Neptune washing machine for customers who will pay more for a washer that uses less water. Tilley Endurables continues to create value for customers by regularly adding new and better products to its product lines.

Value Creation Investments for Transactional, Consultative, and Strategic Alliance Buyers

In most cases, investments in value creation during the transactional sale are minimal. With such sales, salespeople usually place emphasis on finding ways to eliminate any unnecessary costs and on avoiding delays in processing the order. Technology investments can sometimes play a big role in improving efficiencies.[38] For example, customers may be encouraged to order products online.

A considerable amount of value creation takes place in consultative sales. Higher investments in value creation are permitted because companies need to invest in developing a good understanding of the customer's needs and problems. This is especially true in large, complex sales where creating custom-tailored solutions and delivering more real benefits to the customer provide the opportunity for higher margins. If your company is selling mobile autonomous robots, the sales cycle will be quite long and investments will be quite high. Sales representatives may take several weeks to study the applications of this product in a hospital, a manufacturing plant, or a large warehouse facility. The use of these robots may eventually result in significant cost savings for the customer.[39]

The age of information has created many career opportunities for people who want to sell professional services. Strong demand for professional services has surfaced in such diverse fields as business consulting, telecommunications, banking, computer technology, training, and health care. When Laura Ricciuto began her career as a consultant, she did not have to decide how to price her services. As part of an MBA small business consulting group, Laura's clients were charged $250 per day for her time. Upon graduation, Laura decided to start her own consultancy: Kaizen Marketing & Creative Design House. Laura initially focused on market research, business planning, and strategy development. She has since expanded into a number of more tactical marketing-related issues: brand development, graphic design, advertising campaigns, Web development, and more. Laura had to decide how much to charge for her various services. Should she price them on an hourly basis or on a project basis? Here are some things she had to consider when determining her fees:

- *Experience:* In the case of Laura Ricciuto, new clients benefit from what she has learned from her many previous consulting contracts.

- *Exclusivity:* Having her office in a smaller Canadian city, Laura is one of few people with expertise in certain aspects of business consulting, and she can charge more for these. Specialists often charge higher fees than generalists.

- *Target Market:* Some markets are less price sensitive. Laura could probably charge higher prices to larger corporations as they are often accustomed to paying higher fees. Smaller business clients are more price-sensitive and resist higher fees.

- *Value:* Ultimately, Laura had to judge how important her service is to particular clients. She understood that the greater the value she could provide to her clients, the higher the fees she could charge.[b]

Value-creation investments in strategic alliance sales are the highest. As noted in Chapter 2, strategic alliances represent the highest form of partnering. Building an alliance is always preceded by a careful study of the proposed partner. Creating value often requires leveraging the full assets of the company so that investments go well beyond the sales force. Alliances are often developed by a team of specialists from such areas as finance, engineering, and marketing. A proposed alliance may require investments in new technology, manufacturing facilities, and warehouses.[40]

REVIEWING KEY CONCEPTS

- Describe positioning as a product-selling strategy.

  Success in today's dynamic global economy requires the continuous positioning and repositioning of products. Product positioning involves those decisions and activities intended to create and maintain a certain concept of the firm's product in the customer's mind. Salespeople can make an important contribution to the process of product positioning.

- Explain the 3-D Product Solutions Selling Model.

  Today's better educated customers are often seeking a cluster of satisfactions. They seek satisfactions that arise from today's new Three-Dimension (3-D) Product Solutions Selling Model that includes (1) the product itself, (2) the company that makes or distributes the product, and (3) the salesperson who sells and services the product.

- Discuss product-positioning options.

  We described the major product-positioning strategies available to salespeople: positioning new and emerging products versus mature and well-established products, positioning with a price strategy, and positioning with a value-added strategy.

- Explain how to sell your product with a price strategy.

  Pricing decisions must be made at each stage of the product life cycle. Some companies use transactional selling tactics that emphasize low price. Salespeople are often given permission to alter (lower) the base price through the use of discounts and allowances. Consequences of using low-price tactics are discussed in this chapter.

- Explain how to sell your product with a value-added strategy.

  To understand fully the importance of the value-added concept in selling, it helps to visualize every product as being four-dimensional. This range of possibilities includes the generic product, the expected product, the value-added product, and the potential product.

Key Terms

differentiation   **150**

expected product   **161**

generic product   **160**

positioning   **149**

potential product   **161**

product life cycle   **155**

promotional allowance   **157**

quantity discount   **157**

satisfactions   **151**

seasonal discount   **157**

Three-Dimension (3-D) Product Solutions Selling Model   **151**

trade or functional discount   **157**

value proposition   **151**

value-added product   **161**

Value-Added Product-Selling Model   **160**

Review Questions

1. Why has product differentiation become so important in sales and marketing?

2. According to Ted Levitt, what is the definition of a product? What satisfactions do customers want?

3. Explain what is meant by *positioning* as a product-selling strategy. What is a *value proposition* ?

4. Why have salespeople assumed an important role in positioning products?

5. Briefly describe the influence of electronic business on pricing. What types of products are sold on the Internet?

6. Read the Selling Today feature titled "How Do Customers Judge Service Quality?" on page 159. How might this information help a salesperson who wants to adopt the value-added selling strategy?

7. What are some of the common ways salespeople add value to the products they sell?

8. What are the four possible products that make up the *Value-Added Product-Selling Model;* i.e., the *total product?*

9. Describe the differences between a generic product and a value-added product.

10. Is it true that selling products with a low-price strategy largely ignores customer satisfaction? Discuss.

Application Exercises

1. Search the Internet for two competing industrial supply catalogues or two competing direct-mail catalogues. Assume one of the represented businesses is your employer. After studying the catalogues, make a comparative analysis of your company's competitive advantages.

2. Several weeks ago, Joy Hong fell in love with the Scion tC coupe. After reading about the car in a magazine, she decided to visit a local Scion dealer. A test drive convinced her to place an order. What happened next was very frustrating. The salesperson immediately started recommending options she should add to the basic

car: automatic transmission ($1050), remote engine starter ($743), performance exhaust sytem ($725), alloy wheels ($1578), rear spoiler ($653), paint protection film ($520), hood deflector ($190), and special acoustic system ($355). Suddenly the price of $21 490 exceeded $27 300 without taxes—and not including a destination charge and a pre-delivery inspection charge—considerably more than she had planned to spend. Joy returned home without placing an order. Assume the role of sales trainer, and suggest ways that the salesperson can improve his ability to position this product so it meets the customer's needs.

3. The Ritz-Carlton hotel chain illustrates the total product concept discussed in this chapter. Research value-added information on the Ritz-Carlton chain by accessing the **www.ritzcarlton.com** website. Choose a location and click "Meetings." Click "Quick Facts" and print the information presented. Circle at least five features you consider to be value-added features. Examine the room rates by clicking on "Accommodations." On the fact sheet you printed, record the room rate for a single- and double-occupancy room.

4. Call a local financial services representative who specializes in stock, bond, or equity fund transactions. Ask what percentage of clients rely on the information given to make complex decisions on their investments. Also ask this person whether customers believe that advice on customer-fitting investment programs adds value to their decision making. Find out whether financial products are getting more or less complex, and what effect this will have on providing value-added service in the future.

ROLE-PLAY EXERCISE

Study the convention centre information included in "Partnership Selling: A Role Play/Simulation" online in the Student Resources section at **www.pearsoncanada.ca/manning**. Analyze this information and determine the value-added product that would appeal to the customer, a meeting planner. Prepare a value proposition that summarizes the mix of key benefits on which your product is positioned. The proposition might include the free limousine service to and from the airport. Present your value proposition to another class member who will assume the role of the customer. Consider using information sheets, pictures, and other materials that will enhance your presentation.

Reality Selling Video Case Problem

Many of the most profitable companies have discovered that there are "riches in market niches." They have developed products and services that meet the needs of a well-defined or a newly created market. Steelcase Incorporated, a leading source of information and expertise on work effectiveness, has been working hard to develop products that meet the needs of people who do most of their work in an office environment. The company motto is "The Office Environment Company." One of its newest products is the "Think" chair. Steelcase also developed the Personal Harbor Workspaces, self-contained, fully equipped, and totally private pod-like workstations. Steelcase sales literature describes the product as ideal for companies that are tired of waiting for the future: "They were developed to support the individual within a highly collaborative team environment, and they work best when clustered around common work areas equipped with mobile tables, carts, benches, screens, and other Steelcase Activity Products.

These 'commons' are meant to be flexible spaces that enhance communication and facilitate interaction."

Steelcase realized that selling this advanced product would not be easy, so a decision was made to develop an advanced sales team to presell the Personal Harbor before its major introduction. Once the team started making sales calls, it became evident that a traditional product-oriented sales presentation would not work. The Personal Harbor was such a departure from conventional office design that many customers were perplexed. Sue Sacks, a sales team member, said, "People acted as if we had fallen from Mars." Team members soon realized that to explain the features and benefits of the product, they had to begin studying new organizational developments such as team-oriented workforces and corporate re-engineering. The advanced sales team was renamed the "advanced solutions" team. Sales calls put more emphasis on learning about the customers' problems and identification of possible solutions. Members of the team viewed themselves as consultants who were in a position to discuss solutions to complex business problems.

The consultative approach soon began to pay off in sales. One customer, a hospital, was preparing to build a new office building and needed workstations for 400 employees. The hospital had formed a committee to make decisions concerning the purchase of office equipment. After an initial meeting between the Steelcase sales team and the hospital committee, a visit to the Steelcase headquarters was arranged. The hospital committee members were able to tour the plant and meet with selected Steelcase experts. With knowledge of the hospital's goals and directions, Sue Sacks was able to arrange meetings with Steelcase technical personnel who could answer specific questions. As a result, the hospital placed an order worth more than a million dollars.

Questions

1. To fulfill a customer's needs, salespeople must be prepared to communicate effectively with customers who are seeking a cluster of satisfactions (see Fig. 7.1). Is it likely that a customer who is considering the Personal Harbor Workspaces will seek information concerning all three dimensions of the 3-D Product Solutions Selling Model? Explain your answer.

2. What product-selling strategies are most effective when selling a new and emerging product such as Personal Harbor Workspaces?

3. Sue Sacks and other members of her sales team discovered that a traditional product-oriented presentation would not work when selling the Personal Harbor Workspaces. Success came only after the team adopted the consultative style of selling. Why was the product-oriented presentation ineffective?

4. Sue Sacks and other members of the advanced solutions team found that the consultative approach resulted in meetings with people higher in the customer's organization. "We get to call on a higher level of buyer," she said. Also, the team was more likely to position the product with a value-added strategy instead of a price strategy. In what ways did the advanced solutions team members add value to their product? Why was less emphasis placed on price during meetings with the customer?

PART III
ROLE-PLAY EXERCISE
Developing a Product Strategy

SCENARIO

TD Canada Trust is a full-service bank with a reputation for excellent customer service. Personal selling efforts by customer service representatives, financial advisers, and financial planners are considered an integral part of the bank's customer service program.

CUSTOMER PROFILE

At age 45, Angela Cormier is looking forward to early retirement. To supplement her company-sponsored retirement program, she purchased a guaranteed investment certificate (i.e., a term deposit) in the amount of $4000 each year. The annual percentage yield earned on these term deposits is currently in the range of 1.2 to 2.4 percent. Angela is not interested in stocks and bonds because she sees these products as high-risk investments.

SALESPERSON PROFILE

Susan Ray is a financial planner with TD Canada Trust. She can provide a wide range of financial products, such as stock and bond mutual funds, blue chip stocks, diversified mutual funds, fixed annuities, money market funds, and guaranteed investment certificates. Susan feels that Angela Cormier may be a good candidate for investment in fixed annuities. She plans to call Ms. Cormier to request an appointment.

PRODUCT

Susan plans to suggest that instead of purchasing term deposits each year, Angela Cormier purchase a five-year term fixed annuity at an annual yield of 3 percent. The minimum single premium purchase is $5000. This product, offered by General Electric Capital Assurance Company, gives the customer a guaranteed principal and a fixed rate of return. At the contract maturity date, the customer can select several payout options. This is a tax-deferred annuity, which means that the customer won't pay income taxes on earnings until she chooses to withdraw the funds. Angela could add funds to her fixed annuity account throughout the contract period. Also, she need not close the account at the end of the contract period but could allow her money to continue to grow at the same interest rate. If Angela withdraws funds prior to the end of the contract, she would be assessed a withdrawal charge.

INSTRUCTIONS

For this role-play activity, you will assume the role of Susan Ray. You will meet with Angela Cormier, a role played by another student, and determine her current and future financial plans. You will determine if she might benefit by investing in this fixed annuity. Prior to meeting with Angela, review the following material in Chapter 6:

- Adding value with a feature–benefit strategy
- Use of bridge statements
- General versus specific benefits

Also think about the implications of the 3-D Product-Selling Model (Fig. 7.1). At the beginning of the role play, use appropriate questions to acquire information regarding Angela's needs. Be prepared to recommend this product and close the sale if you feel that Angela will benefit from this purchase.

Chapter 8
The Buying Process and Buyer Behaviour

Learning Objectives

After studying this chapter, you should be able to

1   Discuss the meaning of a customer strategy.

2   Explain the difference between consumer and business buyers.

3   Understand the importance of alignment between the selling process and the customer's buying process.

4   Understand the buying process of transactional, consultative, and strategic alliance buyers.

5   Discuss the various influences that shape customer buying decisions.

 Reality Selling Video Series—Ashley Pineda/Pulte Group

Ashley Pineda is a new home sales representative for PulteGroup (**www.pultegroupinc .com**). The company offers different product lines: homes for first-time home buyers, move-up homes, and active adult communities. With three different customer groups, Ashley must have a general understanding of the buying motives of each group. In her work with individual customers in each of these groups, she must develop an in-depth understanding of that customer's buying interests.

Most of Ashley's customers are in the first-time home-buyers group who have lived in an apartment but have developed an interest in purchasing a home. Because she has developed an in-depth understanding of this buying group, a central purpose of Ashley's sales presentations is to educate her prospects on renting versus owning and the benefits of owning a home. She also understands that this customer group often knows little about the logistics of owning a home; therefore, she provides her prospects with information and on-site impressions about the neighbourhood, the area, the amenities of the community, as well as shopping areas and schools around the neighbourhood. All these details help Ashley's customers envision raising their children in one of Pulte's neighbourhoods.

Ashley Pineda

Another very important thing Ashley understands about the buying needs of this first-time buying group is the question of the financing of their new home. Ashley typically needs to address the following questions from her customers: What about our credit scores? What qualifies us to buy a new home? Do we need a down payment? What will our monthly payment be? Will it be comfortable with our budget? PulteGroup supplies Ashley with the knowledge to be able to professionally provide and implement that knowledge and make customers feel comfortable with the financial scenario involved in owning their first home.

Buyers tend to buy from people they like and trust. Considering that many customers buy the largest asset they may ever own from sales professionals like Ashley, trust in the seller becomes especially critical. Therefore, building rapport and trust throughout the whole buying process is essential for Ashley to be successful. Furthermore, Ashley describes having a positive mindset, good time management, and multitasking abilities as the most important skills to be a successful salesperson in her particular business. In essence, sales reps like Ashley have to be able to run their own business in the communities for which they are responsible.

DEVELOPING A CUSTOMER STRATEGY

The greatest challenge to salespeople in the age of information is to understand realized and unrealized needs and improve responsiveness to customers. In fact, a growing number of sales professionals believe that the customer has supplanted the product as

Jerry Acuff, author of *Stop Acting Like a Seller and Start Thinking Like a Buyer,* encourages salespeople to develop a customer strategy that adds value. He says, "In order to think like a buyer, salespeople must understand the buying process and focus on what the customer is looking for."
Source: Jerry Acuff

the driving force in sales today. This is especially true because many of today's customers no longer care where or from whom they buy. They are a new generation of aggressive, Internet-empowered customers. They are "new experts." They are confident and determined because they are equipped with purchasing firepower unavailable to any previous generation. They employ three power tools to get their way:

1. Instant comprehensive information from the Internet about all products and services sold online and offline.

2. Immense choice in every segment of commerce—a wide variety of options and prices in every local community and from every corner of the world.

3. Real-time price comparison at the moment and location of purchase on increasingly advanced technology.[1]

Jerry Acuff, author of *Stop Acting Like a Seller And Start Thinking Like a Buyer,* encourages salespeople to develop a customer strategy that adds value. Acuff says, "In order to think like a buyer, salespeople must understand the buying process and focus on what the customer is looking for."[2]

Adding Value with a Customer Strategy

A **customer strategy** is a carefully conceived plan that will result in maximum customer responsiveness. One major dimension of this strategy is to achieve a better understanding of the customer's buying needs and motives. As noted in Chapter 1, information has become a strategic resource (see Fig. 1.2). When salespeople take time to discover needs and motives, they are in a better position to offer customers a value-added solution to their buying problem.

Every salesperson who wants to develop repeat business should figure out a way to collect and systematize customer information. The authors of *Reengineering the Corporation* discuss the importance of collecting information about the unique and particular needs of each customer:

> Customers—consumers and corporations alike—demand products and services designed for their unique and particular needs. There is no longer any such notion as the customer; there is only this customer, the one with whom a seller is dealing at the moment and who now has the capacity to indulge his or her own personal tastes.[3]

customer strategy A carefully conceived plan that will result in maximum customer responsiveness.

The first prescription for developing a customer strategy focuses on the customer's buying process (see Fig. 8.1). Buying procedures and policies can vary greatly from one buyer to another. This is especially true in business-to-business selling. If a salesperson fails to learn how the buyer plans to make the purchase, then he or she may find the selling process out of alignment with the customer's buying process. Keith Eades, author of *The New Solution Selling*, says:

> If we haven't defined how our buyers buy, then we make assumptions that throw us out of alignment with our buyers. Misalignment with buyers is one of selling's most critical mistakes.[4]

The second prescription focuses on why customers buy. This topic will be discussed in detail later in this chapter. The third prescription for developing a customer strategy emphasizes building a strong prospect base, which is discussed in Chapter 9.

Complex Nature of Customer Behaviour

The forces that motivate customers can be complex. Arch McGill, a former vice-president of IBM, reminds us that "individual customers perceive the product in their own terms, and that these may be unique, idiosyncratic, human, emotional, end-of-the-day, irrational, erratic terms."[5] Different people doing the same thing—such as purchasing a commercial office building—may have different needs that motivate them, and each

Strategic/Consultative Selling Model	
Strategic step	**Prescription**
Develop a personal selling philosophy	☑ Adopt marketing concept ☑ Value personal selling ☑ Become a problem solver/partner
Develop a relationship strategy	☑ Maintain high ethical standards ☑ Project professional image ☑ Manage the relationship process
Develop a product strategy	☑ Become a product expert ☑ Sell benefits ☑ Configure value-added solutions
Develop a customer strategy	☐ Understand the buying process ☐ Understand buyer behaviour ☐ Develop prospect base

Figure 8.1 Strategic/Consultative Selling Model
Today, one of the greatest challenges to salespeople is to improve responsiveness to customers. A well-developed customer strategy is designed to meet this challenge.

buyer may have several motives for a single action. The proliferation of market research studies, public opinion polls, surveys, and reports of "averages" makes it easy to fall into the trap of thinking of the customer as a number. The customer is a person, not a statistic. Companies that fully accept this basic truth are likely to adopt a one-to-one marketing strategy based on a bedrock concept: *Treat different customers differently.*[6]

CONSUMER VERSUS BUSINESS BUYERS

Consumer buyer behaviour REFERS TO THE BUYING BEHAVIOUR OF INDIVIDUALS AND households who buy goods and services for personal consumption. The Canadian consumer market consists of more than 35 million people who purchase many billions of dollars' worth of goods and services each year. **Business buyer behaviour** refers to the buying behaviour of organizations that buy goods and services for use in the production of other products and services that are sold, rented, or supplied to others.[7] In many business buying situations, several people work together to reach a decision. The **buying centre** is a cross-functional team of decision makers who often represent several departments. Each team member is likely to have some expertise needed in a particular purchase decision. Salespeople must continually identify which individuals within a firm will be members of the buying centre.[8]

It is not uncommon for salespeople to sell products and services to both consumer and business buyers. A well-established interior decorating firm will likely work with homeowners as well as commercial clients who own hotels, restaurants, or offices. A salesperson employed by an automobile dealership will often sell to corporate customers who maintain a fleet of cars or trucks as well as to consumers who buy vehicles for personal use.

There are some similarities between consumer markets and business markets. Both involve people who assume the role of buyer and make purchase decisions to satisfy needs. These two markets differ, however, in some important areas. Figure 8.2 provides a brief review of some of these differences. A business purchase is likely to involve more participants, who may be well trained, in the decision-making process. Most purchasing agents spend time learning how to buy better.[9]

Types of Business Buying Situations

There are three major types of business-to-business buying situations. The amount of time and effort organizational buyers spend on a purchase usually depends on the complexity of the product and how often the decision must be made.[10] At one extreme is the *new-task buy*, which may require extensive research. At the other extreme is the *straight rebuy*, which is a fairly routine decision. In the middle is the *modified rebuy*, which will require some research.[11]

New-Task Buy A first-time purchase of a product or service is a **new-task buy**. Depending on the cost and complexity of this purchase, the buying decision may require several weeks for information gathering and the involvement of numerous participants. In some cases, a buying committee is formed to consider the new product's quality, price, and service provided by suppliers. Salespeople who are involved in new-task buying situations must rely heavily on consultative selling skills.

consumer buyer behaviour Buying behaviour of individuals and households who buy goods and services for personal consumption.

business buyer behaviour Buying behaviour of organizations that buy goods and services for use in the production of other products and services that are sold, rented, or supplied to others.

buying centre A cross-functional team of decision makers who often represent several departments.

new-task buy A first-time purchase of a product or service.

Consumer Buyers	Business Buyers
Purchases made for individual or household consumption	Purchases made for some purpose other than personal consumption
Decisions usually made by individuals	Decisions frequently made by several people
Purchases often made based on brand reputation or personal recommendations with little or no product expertise	Purchases often made according to precise technical specification based on product expertise
Purchases based primarily on emotional responses to product or promotions	Purchases based primarily on rational criteria
Individual purchasers may make quick decisions	Purchasers may engage in lengthy decision process
Products are consumer goods and services for individual use	Products are often complex; classified by how organizational customers use them

Figure 8.2 Differences between Consumer and Business Buyers

Source: Solomon Michael R.; Stuart Elnora W., *Marketing: Real People, Real Choices*, © 2003. Printed and Electronically reproduced by permission of Pearson Education, Inc., Upper Saddle River, New Jersey.

straight rebuy A routine purchase of previously purchased goods or services.

Straight Rebuy A **straight rebuy** is a routine purchase of items needed by a business-to-business customer. Let's assume you have decided to open a new restaurant and need a steady supply of high-quality cooking oil. After talking to several restaurant suppliers and testing several oils, you select one that meets your needs. Your goal now is to simplify the buying process with the use of a straight rebuy plan. As long as the supplier continues to meet your criteria for price, quality, service, and delivery, future purchases will be routine. Organizations often use the straight rebuy approach for such items as cleaning supplies, copy paper, and cartridges for computer printers. Salespeople must constantly monitor every straight rebuy situation to be sure the customer is completely satisfied. A competing supplier will be quick to exploit any sign of dissatisfaction by the customer.

Modified Rebuy The tide of change is a powerful force in the world of business. From time to time, your customers may wish to modify product specifications, change delivery schedules, or renegotiate prices. When Canada's second-largest food retailer, Sobeys, purchased the country's fourth-largest food retailer, Safeway, in 2013, Sobeys immediately demanded a 1 percent discount from all of its suppliers, with the added condition that there be no price increases in 2014. This tactic has been increasingly used by large supermarket chains. Loblaw, Canada's largest food retailer, for example, has in the past refused to accept price increases and has even made deductions from suppliers' invoices.[12] Such actions often force suppliers to become involved in a **modified rebuy** or risk loss of the account. A modified rebuy often requires the involvement of several participants. Well-trained professional salespeople work hard to provide outstanding service after the sale and anticipate changes in customer needs. Some salespeople regularly ask their customers what they value most about the existing buying situation and how improvements can be made in this area.

Building Strategic Alliances In Chapter 2, we described strategic alliances as the highest form of partnering. Alliances are often formed by companies that have similar business interests and believe the partnership will help them gain a mutual competitive advantage. Large companies often form several alliances. Some strategic alliances take the form of systems selling. **Systems selling** appeals to buyers who prefer a packaged solution to a problem from a single seller, thereby avoiding all the separate decisions involved in a complex buying situation.[13]

Several years ago, Kinko's reinvented itself as a document solutions provider for business firms of all sizes. Full-service Kinko's stores began offering the buyer networks of computers equipped with popular software, ultra-fast colour printers, high-speed Internet connections, and, of course, a variety of document preparation services. After Kinko's was purchased by FedEx, a network of 1200 digitally connected FedEx Kinko's locations began offering a wider selection of customized, needs-based document solutions. One large financial institution consolidated the services of 13 vendors by forming an alliance with FedEx Kinko's.[14] Systems selling efforts at FedEx Kinko's have become an important strategy for winning and holding accounts.

Types of Consumer Buying Situations

As noted previously, consumer buying behaviour refers to purchases of products for personal or household use. The amount of time consumers devote to a purchasing decision can vary greatly depending on the cost of the product, familiarity with the product, and the importance of the item to the consumer. Few buyers invest much effort in selecting a tube of toothpaste, but most will devote extensive time to decision making over the purchase of a new automobile or a home. Consumer buying can fall into one of three categories depending on the degree of consumer involvement.

Habitual Buying Decisions A **habitual buying decision** usually requires very little consumer involvement, and brand differences are usually insignificant.[15] For frequently purchased, low-cost items such as shampoo or paper towels, consumer involvement in the decision-making process is very low. Supermarket shoppers often display habitual buying behaviour as they select items.

Variety-Seeking Buying Decisions A **variety-seeking buying decision** is also characterized by low customer involvement, but also by important perceived brand differences.[16] Brand switching is not uncommon for such decisions because buyers can be influenced by advertising appeals, coupons, or lower prices to try a new brand. Brand switching is usually motivated by the desire for variety rather than dissatisfaction.[17]

modified rebuy Purchasing when the buyer wants to reconsider product specifications, prices, or suppliers.

systems selling A type of selling that appeals to buyers who prefer a packaged solution to a problem from a single seller, thereby avoiding all the separate decisions involved in a complex buying situation.

habitual buying decision A consumer buying decision that requires very little involvement and in which brand differences are usually insignificant.

variety-seeking buying decision A consumer buying decision motivated by the desire for variety rather than by product dissatisfaction.

complex buying decision An often lengthy consumer buying decision characterized by a high degree of involvement.

Complex Buying Decisions A **complex buying decision** is characterized by a high degree of involvement by the customer. Consumers are likely to be highly involved when the product is expensive, purchased infrequently, and highly self-expressive.[18] The purchase of a vacation home, a long-term care insurance policy, an expensive boat, or a costly piece of art would require a complex buying decision. The learning process for some purchases can be very lengthy.

ACHIEVING ALIGNMENT WITH THE CUSTOMER'S BUYING PROCESS

THE FOUNDATION OF A SUCCESSFUL SALES EFFORT IS KNOWING HOW BUYERS BUY. If salespeople don't know what the customer's decision-making process is and they proceed according to their own agenda, they risk losing the sale. If salespeople have not defined how buyers buy, then they make assumptions that throw their sales process out of alignment with the buyer's buying process.[19] Too often salespeople rely on generalizations about the buyer's decision-making process rather than acquiring specific information.

buying process The stages a buyer goes through when making a buying decision.

The **buying process** is a systematic series of actions, or a series of defined, repeatable steps, intended to achieve a result.[20] Organizational purchasing structures and buying procedures can vary greatly from company to company, so we need to be clear on how decisions are being made within each account. In some cases, the steps in the buying process have been clearly defined by the organization and this information is available to any potential supplier. However, this information may not tell us the whole story. Salespeople need to obtain answers to these types of questions:

How urgent is my proposal to the buyer? When will the buying decision be made?

Will "political" factors within the organization influence how the decision is made?

Has the money needed to purchase my product been allocated?

Which person or persons in the buying organization will actually use or supervise the use of the product I am selling?[21]

Customers make buying decisions in many ways, so understanding each individual buyer's decision-making process is central to success in personal selling. Some buyers will have multiple buying processes. Buying decisions involving a straight rebuy, for example, will likely differ from buying decisions involving a new-task buy.[22]

Steps in the Typical Buying Process

The term "process" brings to mind a set formula that applies to every situation. But buying decisions are made in different ways, so it would be inappropriate to view the buying process as a uniform pattern of decision making. However, there is a model— a form of decision making that buyers usually apply to their unique circumstances. Figure 8.3 shows the typical stages in the buying-decision process: need awareness, evaluation of solutions, resolution of problems, purchase, and implementation. This model is especially helpful in understanding organizational buying decisions and large

Figure 8.3 Typical Buying Process Model
In this figure, for purposes of illustration, the Typical Buying Process Model is aligned with the two most popular Selling Process Models. It is important for salespeople to understand the customer's unique buying process, and where the customer is in that buying process, and then align the sales process to satisfy their customer's needs.

consumer acquisitions. Consumers who make habitual buying decisions often skip or reverse some of these stages.[23]

Need Awareness Need awareness is the first stage in the buying process. The buyer recognizes that something is imperfect or incomplete. The need for energy conservation technology may surface when oil prices rise to higher levels. The need for a customer service training program may become evident when surveys show a decline in customer satisfaction. Salespeople can add value at this stage of the buying process if they can help determine the magnitude of the customer's problem and identify a solution. For example, a sales representative may be able to help the buyer estimate the cost of poor customer service and recommend a way to improve service. Customers often need help in determining whether they have a problem large enough to justify the cost of a proposed solution.[24]

Evaluation of Solutions Buyers who experience need awareness usually begin searching for information that will help them evaluate possible problem solutions. They realize, at this point, that the problem they face is amenable to some type of solution. In some cases, there are several solutions that the customer needs to study. Salespeople can add value at this stage by providing useful information that helps the customer make an informed choice. In some cases, the value justification can be presented in terms of cost reduction or increased revenue. In other cases, the value justification may be intangible, such as customer satisfaction, improved security, or reduced stress. In business-to-business selling situations, value justification that can be measured is usually the most powerful.

To establish a true partnership with customers, you need to be sure that you are offering them information that will help them achieve their objectives. If you possess a good understanding of the customer's buying process, you will know what that customer is trying to accomplish.[25]

Resolution of Problems At this stage of the buying process, the customer is aware of a need and has evaluated one or more solutions. While the customer has decided to do something, he or she is likely to have issues and concerns that must be resolved before moving ahead. This is especially true in the case of complex sales.[26]

Some customers will want the proposed solution in writing. Competitors may be invited to submit written proposals. A well-written proposal is one way to add value, as described in Chapter 6. Customers may request specific information that can only be provided by the supplier's engineers or accountants. Customers may insist on visiting the supplier's manufacturing plant so that they can see the production process firsthand. Buyers often need help to overcome obstacles that prevent them from moving to the purchase stage of the buying process.[27]

Purchase After all of the customer's obstacles and concerns have been overcome, the purchase decision is made. Professional salespeople create value in many ways at this stage of the buying process.[28] First, they can make sure the purchase is "hassle free." This may mean working with the customer to arrange the best financing or to supervise delivery and

There is no longer any such notion as *the* customer—there is only *this* customer, the one whom a seller is dealing with at the moment. Discovering the individual needs of this customer can be challenging.

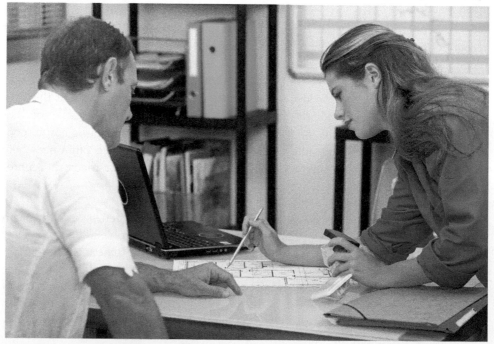

Auremar/Shutterstock

installation of the product. Salespeople can add value by becoming a "customer advocate" within their own organization. This may mean negotiating with various departments to expedite the order. Buyers want to work with salespeople who are able to quickly solve any order fulfillment problems.[29]

Implementation The first sale is only the beginning of the salesperson's relationship with the buyer. Repeat sales occur when your company as supplier has demonstrated the ability to add value in various ways after the sale. Value creation can take the form of timely delivery, superior installation, accurate invoicing, follow-up contacts by the salesperson, or anything else that is important to the customer.

UNDERSTANDING THE BUYING PROCESS OF THE TRANSACTIONAL, CONSULTATIVE, AND STRATEGIC ALLIANCE BUYER

THE NEXT STEP IN UNDERSTANDING THE CUSTOMER'S BUYING PROCESS IS TO DISCUSS THREE value creation selling approaches that appeal to certain types of customers. In Chapter 2, we briefly introduced transactional, consultative, and strategic alliance selling. We will now discuss when to work effectively with each type of buyer.[30]

Transactional Process Buyer

Transactional buyers are well aware of their needs and usually know a great deal about the products or services they intend to purchase. In a truly transactional sale, buyers will become frustrated if the salesperson attempts to use needs assessment, problem solving, or relationship building. They are not looking for new information or advice from the salesperson. Most transactional buyers have conducted their own research and, in most cases, have decided which product best meets their needs. They don't want hand-holding and they don't want the salesperson to waste their time.[31]

How can a salesperson add value to a transactional sale? If the buyer is already aware of his or her needs, has evaluated solutions, and has no issues or concerns that need to be resolved, then the salesperson needs to focus on the purchase stage of the five-part buying process model (see Fig. 8.3). Do whatever is necessary to facilitate a convenient and hassle-free purchase. Eliminate any unnecessary costs or delays in processing the order. The transactional buyer may quickly turn to a competitor if he or she experiences unnecessary costs or delays.

Consultative Process Buyer

Consultative selling, a major theme of this text, was described in Chapter 2. This sales approach appeals to buyers who lack needs awareness or need help evaluating possible solutions. Some buying decisions require assistance from a consultative salesperson because the product is very complex or the cost of the product is very high. The purchase of a new home provides a good example in the consumer arena. Home buyers usually seek the assistance of an experienced realtor. The purchase of Internet phone-calling equipment provides a good example in the business-to-business arena.

Organizations that are considering the purchase of complex Internet telephone equipment—to provide voiceover Internet protocol, or VoIP capability—seek answers to several questions: Can we keep a portion of our traditional phone network or must we adopt an all-Internet phone system? Will the new system provide the same voice quality as our traditional system? Internet phone-calling equipment is available from several suppliers, including Avaya Incorporated and Cisco Systems Incorporated. Blackberry has recently added mobile VoIP capability through its Blackberry Messenger (BBM) service. Some customers will need help comparing the technology available from these and other suppliers.[32]

Successful consultative salespeople focus a great deal of attention on needs awareness, which is step one in the buying process model (see Fig. 8.3). This is where salespeople can create the most value by helping customers gain an understanding of their problems and creating solutions that correct these problems.[33] Many customers seek help defining needs and solutions, but avoid dealing with sales representatives who simply want to sell a product.

Consultative selling encompasses the concept that salespeople should conduct a systematic assessment of the prospect's situation. This usually involves collecting as much information as possible prior to the sales call and using a series of carefully worded questions to obtain the customer's point of view during the sales call. Two-way communication will provide for a mutual exchange of ideas, feelings, and perceptions.

The consultative salesperson will help the customer evaluate solutions and help resolve any problems that surface prior to the purchase stage. Consultative salespeople also work hard to add value at the implementation stage of the sales process. This may involve supervising product delivery and installation, servicing warranties, and providing other services after the sale.

Strategic Alliance Process Buyer

As noted previously, the goal of strategic alliances is to achieve a marketplace advantage by teaming up with another company. Alliances are often formed by companies that have similar business interests and seek to gain a mutual competitive advantage. Dell, for example, formed a partnership with Microsoft and Intel to provide customized e-business solutions. In the highly competitive global market, going it alone is sometimes more difficult.[34]

Step one in building an alliance is a careful study of the proposed partner. This research is often coordinated by senior management and may involve persons working in the areas of sales, marketing, finance, and distribution. At some point, representatives from both companies will meet and explore the mutual benefits of the alliance. Both parties must be prepared to explain how they will add value once the alliance is formed.

The Buyer Resolution Theory

Several theories explain how customers arrive at a buying decision. One traditional point of view is based on the assumption that a final buying decision is possible only after the prospect has answered five logical questions (see Fig. 8.4). This is called the

Buyer resolution theory recognizes that a purchase is made only after the prospect has made five buying decisions that result from specific, affirmative responses to the five key questions.	
Why should I buy?	Realistically, it is difficult to provide prospects with an answer to this question. In many cases, salespeople fail to help customers become aware of a need. Therefore, large numbers of potential customers are not sufficiently persuaded to purchase products that will provide them with genuine buyer benefits.
What should I buy?	If a prospect agrees that a need does exist, then a sales representative is ready to address this buying decision. He or she must convince the prospect that the product being offered will satisfy the need. In most cases, the buyer can choose from among several competing products.
Where should I buy?	As products become more complex, customers are giving more attention to "source" decisions. In a major metropolitan area someone who wants to buy a LaserJet 3160 or a competing product will be able to choose from several sources.
What is a fair price?	Today's better-educated and -informed consumers are searching for the right balance between price and value (i.e., buyer benefits). They are better able to detect prices that are not competitive or that do not correspond in their minds with the product's value.
When should I buy?	A sale cannot be closed until a customer has decided when to buy. In some selling situations, the customer will want to postpone the purchase because of reluctance to part with the money.

Figure 8.4 Buyer Resolution Theory
This theory, sometimes referred to as "The 5 Ws Theory," focuses attention on questions the customer may need answers to before making a purchase decision. The absence of an answer to any of these questions will likely result in a customer objection.

buyer resolution theory. One strength of this buying theory is that it focuses the salesperson's attention on five important factors that the customer is likely to consider before making a purchase: need, product, source, price, and time. Answers to these five questions provide valuable insights about the customer's buying strategy. One important limitation of this theory is that a salesperson cannot always anticipate which of the five buying decisions might be most difficult for the prospect to make. If the selling process does not mesh with the buying process, a sale is less likely. There is no established sequence in which prospects make these five decisions, so a highly inflexible sales presentation would not be effective.

buyer resolution theory A selling theory that a purchase will be made only after the prospect has made five buying decisions about need, product, source, price, and time.

UNDERSTANDING BUYER BEHAVIOUR

ALTHOUGH EVERY CUSTOMER IS UNIQUE, SALESPEOPLE NEED TO UNDERSTAND THE IMPORTANT social and psychological influences that tend to shape customer buying decisions. We will review concepts that come from the fields of psychology, sociology, and anthropology. Figure 8.5 illustrates the many forces that influence buying decisions.

Basic Needs That Influence Buyer Behaviour

Basic human needs have changed little throughout our economic history. However, the ways in which needs are fulfilled have changed greatly in the age of information.[35] The starting point for developing an understanding of the forces influencing buying decisions is a review of the individual needs that shape the customer's behaviour. To gain insights into customer behaviour motivated by both physiological and psychological needs, it is helpful to study the popular hierarchy of needs developed by Abraham Maslow.

Selling in Action
Selling to Couples

There are many situations in which salespeople sell to a couple rather than to an individual: real estate, mutual funds, cars, wedding rings, insurance. These situations can pose additional challenges for salespeople. Each person in a couple may, for example, bring a hidden agenda to the purchase. An unseasoned salesperson risks alienating or offending one partner and perhaps, as a result, losing the sale.

According to Marilyn Powers, a practising therapist, couples exhibit one of three communications stages: a fusion stage, a power struggle stage, or an independent stage. Couples in the fusion stage think and feel alike and try to avoid conflict. As a result, they make hasty decisions, often without providing adequate information to the salesperson. This may result in the sale being cancelled or in after-sale customer dissatisfaction. To prevent this, the salesperson needs to ask sufficient questions during the need discovery stage of the sales process to be sure he or she fully understands the couple's needs.

Couples in the power struggle stage actively seek a win-lose solution, where one partner's "win" over the other partner is more important than the actual purchase decision. Here, the salesperson needs to slow the sales process and craft a "win-win" solution for the couple. The best way to do this is to focus on each person, being sure to establish and understand each individual's needs. Through active listening—paraphrasing and restating each participant's comments—the salesperson may be able to defuse the

emotional situation, keeping the communication lines open and establishing some common ground. Unfortunately, there will be instances where it is apparent that one key decision maker will win the power struggle. Here, some salespeople argue that it is best to align with that person as it will be impossible to keep both participants happy; other salespeople argue that it is best to remain impartial and to avoid getting involved in the power struggle.

Couples in the independent stage often have different opinions about what they should buy, but they are willing to continue their search for a third solution that may be better than either of their independent solutions. A salesperson who encounters this situation may need to give the couple additional time to communicate with each other and should not try to close the sale too quickly.

Judith C. Tingley and Lee E. Robert, authors of *GenderSell: How to Sell to the Opposite Sex*, suggest some tips to use, depending on whether the salesperson is a man or a woman. They suggest that male salespeople must be careful to avoid being patronizing or condescending toward women when trying to sell to a mixed-gender couple. A male salesperson should greet the woman first, keep her involved throughout the sales process, and be careful to use gender-neutral language. Female salespeople need to build credibility quickly, be more rational and less emotional in their selling style, and treat both partners with equal respect.[a]

Figure 8.5 The Buyer Behaviour Model
This model illustrates the many complex psychological and sociological forces that influence buyer behaviour.

Maslow's Hierarchy of Needs According to Abraham Maslow, basic human needs are arranged in a hierarchy according to their strength (Fig. 8.6). His theory rests on the assumption that as each lower-level need is satisfied, the need at the next level demands attention.

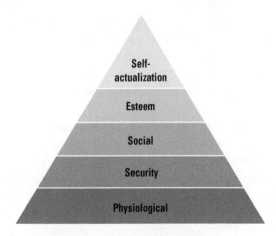

Figure 8.6 Maslow's Hierarchy of Needs Model
The forces that motivate customers to make specific buying decisions are complex. This model illustrates Maslow's hierarchy of needs.

Source: Abraham H. Maslow, Robert D. Frager (editor), and James Fadiman (editor), *Motivation and Personality,* 3rd ed. (Upper Saddle River, NJ: Pearson Education, 1987), p. 193. Reprinted and electronically reproduced by permission of Pearson Education, Inc. Upper Saddler River, New Jersey.

physiological needs Primary or physical needs, including food, water, air, warmth, and sleep.

Physiological Needs   Sometimes called "primary" needs, **physiological needs** include the needs of food, water, and sleep. Maslow placed our physiological needs at the bottom of the pyramid. He believed that these basic needs tend to be strong in the minds of most people.

Security Needs   After physiological needs have been satisfied, the next need level that tends to dominate is safety and security. **Security needs** represent our desire to be free from danger and uncertainty. The desire to satisfy the need for safety and security can be an important buying motive. Buyers want to feel secure that their salesperson is highly ethical and the products they are considering will perform as they expect. If a customer does not feel safe and secure in a transaction, it will almost always destroy any opportunity for a successful relationship and sale to develop.

security needs Our desire for protection from the elements and to be free from danger and uncertainty; buying decisions to support these needs could include clothing, shelter, and insurance.

Social Needs   The need to belong, and other **social needs**, reflects our desire for identification with a group and approval from others. These needs help explain our continuing search for long-term, mutually rewarding business and social relationships. B2B buyers want acceptance and approval from those with whom they work, including their boss and team members. B2C buyers want approval from their friends and family members. Partnering style relationship strategies and value-added product and presentation solutions provide customers and clients an important element of social needs satisfaction.

social needs Needs that reflect a person's desire for affection, identification with a group, and approval from others.

Esteem Needs   At the fourth level of Maslow's needs hierarchy are **esteem needs**, which reflect our desire to feel worthy in the eyes of others. We seek a sense of personal worth and adequacy—a feeling of competence.[36] Salespeople who custom-fit a value-added solution that meets and exceeds their clients' needs provide a feeling of competency to buyers in complex buying situations. Assurances and outstanding service after the sale also make the customer feel worthwhile in making correct buying decisions.

esteem needs The desire to feel worthy in the eyes of others, to develop a sense of personal worth and adequacy or a feeling of competence and importance.

Self-Actualization Needs   Maslow defined the term **self-actualization** as a need for self-fulfillment, a tapping of one's full potential. It is the need to "be all that you can be," to have mastery over things you are doing. Working with customers engaged in the buying decision process to discover the value-added and potential products described in Chapter 7 is an example of them meeting their need for self-fulfillment. Developing a trust-filled, problem-solving role with a buyer concerned about finding a long-term, highly ethical, partnering style salesperson is another example of fulfilling the buyer's need for self-actualization.

self-actualization The need for self-fulfillment; a tapping of one's full potential to meet a goal; the need to be everything one is capable of being.

The five-level needs hierarchy model developed by Maslow is somewhat artificial in certain instances. At times, several of our needs interact during a sale. Consider the business lunch where you are not only conducting business with a client but are also satisfying your need to consume food and beverages, to engage in social activities, and perhaps to seem important in your own eyes and, you hope, the eyes of your customer. The model also provides salespeople with a practical way of understanding which need is most likely to dominate customer behaviour in different buying situations.

Group Influences That Affect Buying Decisions

As noted earlier, the people around us influence our buying decisions. These **group influences** can be classified into four major areas: (1) role influences, (2) reference groups,

group influences Forces that other people exert on customers' buying behaviour.

Selling to the Four Generations

It is important to understand the context in which people from different generational groups live and work. After all, success in personal selling requires the ability to create rapport and develop trust with buyers who may differ from us. Picture yourself as a Millennial (Generation Y) who was born between 1981 and 1994. Chances are you welcome the latest high-tech communications technology and do not resent the never-ending sea of information that demands your immediate attention and response. Some of the customers you call on are members of the Baby Boomer Generation, who were born between 1946 and 1964. These individuals may welcome traditional memos, letters, phone calls, and face-to-face communications, and feel uncomfortable working in today's wireless world. Generation Xers, born between 1965 and 1980, want proof; relationships are less important—be careful with chitchat. Matures, who have an in-built need to conform, prefer a traditional face-to-face sales process. Generational differences shaped by sociological, political, and economic conditions can influence our values. Dave Stein, author of *How Winners Sell*, says "Before you ever meet that prospect, understand that 'different' in terms of cross-generational selling is neither right nor wrong; it's just different."[b]

Dave Stein, Sales Expert, Speaker and Author

(3) social class, and (4) culture and microcultures.[37] (See Fig. 8.7.) Salespeople who understand these roles and influences can develop the type of insight customers view as being valuable.

Role Influence Throughout our lives, we occupy positions within groups, organizations, and institutions. Closely associated with each position is a **role**—a set of characteristics and expected social behaviours based on the expectations of others. All the roles we assume (e.g., student, member of the school board, or position at work) influence not only our general behaviour but also our buying behaviour. In today's society, for example, a woman may assume the role of mother at home and purchasing manager at work. In the manager's role, she may feel the need to purchase a conservative wardrobe, enrol in a leadership training course, or join a professional association. These various roles can play an important part in motivating certain buying decisions.

Reference Group Influence A **reference group** consists of the categories of people to which you see yourself belonging and with which you habitually compare yourself. The popular four-generation model—the matures, baby boomers, generation Xers, and

role A set of characteristics and expected social behaviours based on the expectations of others. All the roles we assume may influence our buying behaviour.

reference group Two or more people who have well-established interpersonal communications and tend to influence the values, attitudes, and buying behaviours of one another. They act as a point of comparison and a source of information for a prospective buyer.

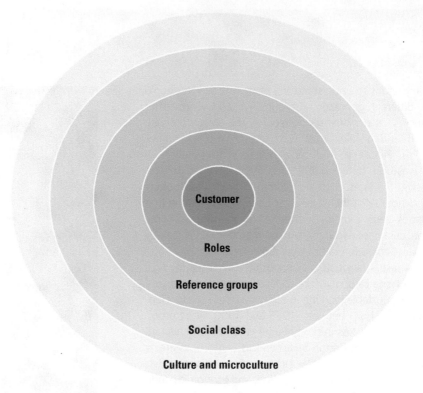

Figure 8.7 Group Influences That Affect Buying Decisions Model
To gain additional insights into customers' motivations, salespeople can study group influences that affect buying decisions.

generation Y's—provides an excellent example representing influences of the members of each of these age categories. Not understanding their influences often destroys some aspect of the sales process leading to a successful sale. Members of a reference group tend to influence the values, attitudes, and behaviours of one another.[38] The reference group may act as a point of comparison and a source of information for the individual member.[39] In the business community, the Canadian Professional Sales Association may be a reference group for its members. As a member of a reference group, each of us may observe other people in the group to establish our own norms, and these norms can strongly affect purchasing decisions.

social class A group of people who share similar values, interests, and behaviours.

Social Class Influence A **social class** is one of society's relatively permanent and ordered divisions whose members share similar values, interests, and behaviours.[40] The criteria used to rank people according to social class vary from one society to another. In some societies, land ownership allows entry into a higher social class. In other societies, education is a major key to achieving upper-class status. Social class, in most cases, is not determined by a single factor. It is determined by a combination of such factors as income, education, occupation, and accumulated wealth.

Social class can have a major influence in B2C purchasing situations. The purchase of consumer products such as homes, cars, vacations, clothing, and entertainment are heavily influenced by social class membership. A home may be purchased as a vacation home or a primary residence depending on the buyer's social class. A glass of red wine will likely be purchased by a different social class member than a glass of Budweiser beer, as will be tickets to live theatre as opposed to tickets to a movie theatre.

Cultural Influence Culture can be defined as the accumulation of values, rules of behaviour, forms of expression, religious beliefs, and transmitted behaviour patterns for a people or society that shares a common language and environment. Culture tends to encourage or discourage particular behaviours and mental processes.[41] We maintain and transmit our culture chiefly through language. Culture has considerable influence on buying behaviour. Today, culture in Canada is getting more attention because of rapid increases in immigration. As cultural diversity increases, companies must re-examine their sales and marketing strategies. Within most cultures are groups whose members share value systems based on common life experiences and situations. We call such a group a **microculture**. Some microcultures, such as generation Y (born between 1981 and 1994), Blacks, Chinese, Southeast Asians, and Aboriginal Canadians, are important market segments.[42] These microcultures need to be understood by salespeople because they can significantly affect customer buying behaviour.

culture The values, rules of behaviour, forms of expression, religious beliefs, and transmitted behaviour patterns for a people or society that share a common language and environment.

microculture Value systems shared by communities based on common life experiences and situations that differ from those of the dominant society's culture.

Perception—How Customer Needs Are Formed

Perception is the process through which sensations received through sight, hearing, touch, taste, and smell are interpreted using our knowledge and experience. Buyer behaviour is often influenced by perception.[43] When Volkswagen announced that it would build an ultra-luxury car that would sell for more than $100 000, many people questioned the merits of this decision. Could the maker of the Beetle and the Golf compete in the market segment dominated by Lexus, Mercedes Benz, Jaguar, and BMW? Selling of the Volkswagen Phaeton has been discontinued in North America, even though most automobile journalists viewed it as a true luxury car.[44] Was perception the barrier to sales growth?

perception A process through which sensations are interpreted using our knowledge and experience.

We tend to screen out or modify stimuli, a process known as *selective attention*, for two reasons. First, we cannot possibly be conscious of all inputs at one time; just the commercial messages we see and hear each day are enough to cause sensory overload. Second, we are conditioned by our social and cultural background, and by our physical and psychological needs, to use selectivity.

Buyers may screen out or modify information presented by a salesperson if it conflicts with their previously learned attitudes or beliefs. The business buyer who feels the new office furniture designs that combine individual work space will only encourage impromptu employee chitchat is apt to use selective attention when the salesperson begins discussing product features. Salespeople who can anticipate this problem of selective attention should acquire as much background information as possible before meeting with the prospect. During the first meeting with the prospect, the salesperson should make every effort to build a strong relationship so that the person opens up and freely discusses personal perceptions. Salespeople who do this have accepted one of the great truisms in sales and marketing: "Facts are negotiable. Perception is rock solid."

Managing Multiple Contacts with CRM

Salespeople often find that groups of their contacts have common interests and buying motives. Customers and prospects may be segmented into groups by buying influences, by the products they purchase, by the industries they are involved in, or by their size. Customer relationship management (CRM) software can enable the salesperson to easily link contacts together as groups and "mass produce" information that appears custom-fitted to the need of each person in the specific group. For example, each owner of a specific product may receive from the salesperson a telephone call, personalized letter, or report that describes the benefits of a new design feature available.

Buying Motives

buying motive An aroused need, drive, or desire that initiates the buying-decision process.

Every buying decision has a motive behind it. A **buying motive** can be thought of as an aroused need, drive, or desire that stimulates purchasing behaviour intended to satisfy the aroused need. Our perceptions influence or shape this behaviour. An understanding of buying motives provides the salesperson with the reasons why customers buy. Unfortunately, some buyers will not or cannot tell you their buying motives. A company may be planning a new product launch and want to keep this initiative a secret. In some cases, revealing important information may make the customer feel vulnerable. And some customers may not be aware of one or more buying motives that will influence the purchase decision.[45]

dominant buying motive The motive that has the greatest influence on a customer's buying decision.

As you might expect, some buying decisions are influenced by more than one buying motive. The buyer of catering services may want food of exceptional quality served quickly so that all the guests can eat together. This customer may also be quite price conscious. In this situation, the caterer should attempt to discover the **dominant buying motive (DBM)**. The DBM will have the greatest influence on the buying decision.[46] If the customer is anxious to make a good impression on guests who have discriminating food tastes, then food quality may be the dominant buying motive. Successful salespeople have adopted a product strategy that involves discovery of the buying motives that influence the purchase decision. In Chapter 10, we describe a need identification process that can be used to discover customers' buying motives.

emotional buying motive A motive that prompts the prospect to act as a result of an appeal to some sentiment or passion.

rational buying motive A motive that prompts the prospect to act because of an appeal to the prospect's reason or better judgment, such as price, quality, and availability of technical assistance. Generally these result from an objective review of available information.

Emotional versus Rational Buying Motives A careful study of buyer behaviour reveals that people make buying decisions based on both emotional and rational buying motives. An **emotional buying motive** is one that prompts the prospect to act because of an appeal to some sentiment or passion. When customers buy expensive Harley-Davidson motorcycles, they are paying for much more than a high-flying "hog"; they are purchasing entry into a community of like-minded enthusiasts who share a passion for all things Harley.[47] Emotions can be powerful and often serve as the foundation of the dominant buying motive.[48] A **rational buying motive** usually appeals to the prospect's reason or judgment based on objective thought processes. Some common rational buying motives include quality, price, and availability of technical assistance.

Emotional Buying Motives A surprising number of purchases are guided by emotional buying motives. Recent research indicates that buying is a lot more emotional than most marketers thought. Many buyers are guided more by feelings than by logic.[49] Even technology firms sometimes rely on emotional appeals as part of their marketing strategy. Doing business in Canada, or anyplace else in the world, is never purely a rational or logical process. Recognize that there is an emotional component to every sale, and tune in to the emotional cues such as body language, tone of voice, and emotive words. With the power of empathy, you can get on the same page, emotionally, as your customer.[50] Consumer buying behaviour may be frequently motivated by emotional buying motives; however, in high-dollar purchasing decisions, rational decision making may be a barrier as the buyer considers the cost/benefit of a purchase.

Rational Buying Motives A purchase based on rational buying motives is generally the result of an objective review of available information. The buyer closely examines product or service information with an attitude that is relatively free of emotion. Business buyers are most likely to be motivated by such rational buying motives as on-time delivery, financial gain, competent installation, saving of time, increased profits, reduced costs, or durability. Business buyers representing large firms, such as BlackBerry, Air Canada, and Canadian National Railways, rely on a buying process that is more formalized than the consumer buying process. Purchases made by these companies usually call for detailed product specifications, formal approval, and written purchase orders. The business buyer and the salesperson work closely during all stages of the buying process, which begins with a precise definition of the customer's problem. Salespeople who sell to business buyers spend a great deal of time gathering, interpreting, and disseminating customer-specific information.[51] It is important to recognize that business buyers also use emotional decision making, deciding in many cases if they like the salesperson with whom they are working. As one B2B buyer stated to one of the authors during his previous sales career, "If I like you, you will have the best quality, price, and service. If I don't like you, you won't." A value-added relationship strategy is important in these situations.

Patronage versus Product Buying Motives Another way to help explain buyer perceptions and behaviour is to distinguish between patronage and product buying motives. Patronage buying motives and product buying motives are learned reasons for buying. These buying motives are important because they can stimulate repeat business and referrals.

Patronage Buying Motives A **patronage buying motive** is one that causes the prospect to buy products from one particular business. The prospect has usually had prior direct or indirect contact with the business and has judged this contact to be beneficial. In those situations where there is little or no appreciable difference between two products, patronage motives can be highly important. At a time when look-alike products are very common, these motives take on extra importance. Some typical patronage buying motives are superior service, complete selection of products, competence of sales representatives, and ability to buy online.

Product Buying Motives A **product buying motive** is one that leads a prospect to purchase one product in preference to another. Interestingly enough, this decision is sometimes made without direct comparison between competing products; the buyer simply believes that one product is superior to another. Numerous buying motives trigger

patronage buying motive A motive that causes the prospect to buy a product from one particular company rather than another. Typical patronage buying motives include superior service, attractive decor, product selection, and competence of the salesperson.

product buying motive A motive that causes the prospect to buy one particular product brand or label over another. Typical product buying motives include brand, quality, price, and design or engineering preference.

Strategic Initiatives Identified	Need Awareness	Evaluation of Solutions	Resolution of Problems	Purchase	Implementation
Present and/or design unique strengths that fit the strategic initiative.	Partner with customers to understand unique needs in new and improved ways.	Configure or adapt superior solutions to unique needs.	Provide assistance and advice to overcome problems and provide solutions.	Adapt and suggest effective methods to purchase and enjoy solutions.	Assist and/or train customers in maximum satisfaction from purchase.

Figure 8.8 Creating Value throughout the Buying Process Model
This is a sample list of methods for creating value throughout each of the steps in the buying process. Specific methods should be created after arriving at a careful understanding of the unique needs of the individual customer.

prospects to select one product over another, including brand, quality, price, and design or engineering preference.

It is hard to imagine how salespeople can create value for customers unless they understand the customer's buying motives. Figure 8.8 provides various examples of how salespeople can put this understanding into creating value at different stages of the buying process.

To fully understand the customer's buying strategy, the salesperson must conduct a careful needs discovery or assessment. This is done by asking appropriate questions, listening to the customer's responses, and making careful observations. Chapter 11 provides in-depth coverage of these important adaptive selling skills.

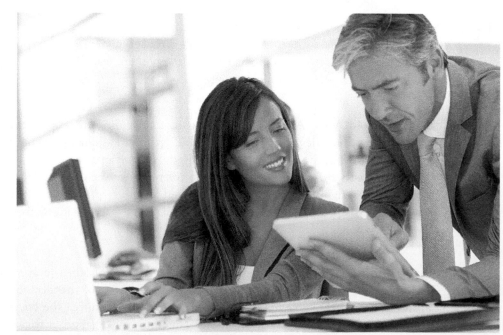

Goodluz/Shutterstock

Different Business Buying Processes in Different Cultures

Going global? If so remember that your business customers might have different ways of getting back to you in their buying process, based on the country they come from.

- The Japanese decision-making process is a total group process, with all levels involved in the final decision.
- A Chinese decision is usually a group process headed by a senior negotiator.
- For Germans, even the most routine decisions are made by top-level management.

Also, remember:

- Discussions with Chinese businesspeople tend to be long and repetitive, and everything should be written down.
- For Latin American business dealings, socialization and relationship-building comes before negotiations.
- Germans are very systematic, with great emphasis on detail.[c]

REVIEWING KEY CONCEPTS

- Discuss the meaning of a customer strategy.

  The importance of developing a *customer strategy* was introduced in this chapter. This type of planning is necessary to ensure maximum customer responsiveness. Buying procedures and policies can vary greatly from one buyer to another. If a salesperson does not learn how the buyer plans to make the purchase, then there is the strong possibility that the selling process will be out of alignment with the customer's buying process.

- Explain the difference between consumer and business buyers.

  Business buyer behaviour was compared to consumer buyer behaviour. Three types of business buying situations were discussed: straight rebuy, new-task buy, and the modified rebuy. Systems selling, a common business buying strategy, was also discussed. Three types of consumer buying situations were defined: habitual buying decisions, variety-seeking buying decisions, and complex buying decisions.

- Understand the importance of alignment between the selling process and the customer's buying process.

  Customers make buying decisions in many ways, so it would be inappropriate to view the buying process as a uniform pattern of decision making. However, there is a common decision-making model that most

buyers apply to their unique circumstances. The typical stages in the buying decision process are needs awareness, evaluation of solutions, resolution of problems, purchase, and implementation.

- Understand the buying process of transactional, consultative, and strategic alliance buyers.

  Three value-creation selling approaches that appeal to certain types of customers were discussed: the transactional process buyer, the consultative process buyer, and the strategic alliance process buyer. The consultative process buyer offers the greatest challenge to most salespeople.

- Discuss the various influences that shape customer buying decisions.

  We noted that buyer behaviour is influenced in part by individual (physical and psychological) needs. Maslow's popular model ranks these needs. There are also a number of group influences that shape our psychological needs to various degrees. Buyer behaviour is influenced by the roles we assume, reference groups, social class, and culture. *Perception* was defined as the process of selecting, organizing, and interpreting information inputs to produce meaning. We discussed *emotional* and *rational buying motives* and compared *patronage* and *product buying motives*.

Key Terms

Review Questions

1. According to the Strategic/Consultative Selling Model, what are the three prescriptions for the development of a successful customer strategy?

2. List and describe the three most common types of business-to-business buying situations.

3. Describe the five major steps in the typical buying process.

4. List and describe three value-creation selling approaches that appeal to various types of customers.

5. According to the buyer resolution theory, a purchase is made only after the prospect has made five buying decisions. What are they?

6. Explain how Maslow's hierarchy of needs affects buyer behaviour.

7. Describe four group influences that affect buyer behaviour.

8. What is meant by the term *perception*?

9. Distinguish between emotional and rational buying motives.

10. J. D. Power, founder of J. D. Power and Associates, says, "We define quality as what the customer wants." Do you agree or disagree with his observations? Explain your answer.

Application Exercises

1. Select several advertisements from a trade magazine. Analyze each one and determine which rational buying motives the advertiser is appealing to. Explain whether these advertisements also appeal to emotional buying motives. Then select a magazine that is aimed at a particular consumer group—for example, *Chatelaine*, *Canadian Business*, or *Better Homes and Gardens*. Study the advertisements and determine what buying motives they appeal to.

2. The $40 000-plus Hyundai Genesis 3.8 GT automatic, which entered the North American market as a 2010 model (in 2009), is a far cry from the popular Elantra. Hyundai's new flagship model was designed to compete with Lexus, Mercedes Benz, Cadillac, and BMW. The Genesis is positioned as another choice in the luxury-car market. Will potential customers accept the Genesis as a true luxury car? Will customer perceptions play a role in acceptance of this new model?

3. J. D. Power and Associates is a global marketing information services firm that helps businesses and consumers make better decisions through credible customer-based information. The company provides an unbiased source of marketing information based on opinions of consumers. Visit **www.jdpower.com/ca** and become familiar with the type of information services offered. View some of the studies done on Canadian consumer satisfaction and be prepared to discuss interesting findings in class.

4. Assume your college or university is considering buying 100 new PCs for student labs throughout the campus. Describe who you think will be involved in the buying centre (by role), and what you think the motives might be for each of them.

5. Assume your college or university is considering replacing its mainframe computer. Its current mainframe computer is now 15 years old and has been creating problems for some time. The cost of a modern replacement is estimated at between $1.5 and $2 million. Will this be a new-task buy, a modified rebuy, or a straight rebuy? If you were a salesperson selling mainframe computers, how would you treat this opportunity? Explain.

ROLE-PLAY EXERCISE

In this role play, you will assume the role of a salesperson working at a clothing store. The inventory includes a wide range of business professional clothing such as suits, sport coats, dress shirts, and accessories; the store also offers a full range of business casual clothing. A member of your class will assume the role of a customer who visits your store for the purpose of buying clothing for work. He or she is about to graduate and will start work at a new job in approximately two weeks. In addition to clothing, your store offers complete alteration services and credit plans. During the role play, you should develop a relationship with the customer using strategies discussed in previous chapters and determine the customer's needs with questions, attentive listening, and observation.

Reality Selling Video Case Problem

Ashley Pineda, featured at the beginning of this chapter, is a new home sales representative for the PulteGroup (see website at www.pultegroupinc.com). The company engages in the homebuilding and financial services businesses. Its homebuilding business includes the acquisition and development of land primarily for residential purposes and the construction of housing on such land targeted for first-time, first and second move-up, and active adult home buyers. As of March 31, 2010, its homebuilding operations offered homes for sale in 842 communities. The company's financial services business consists of mortgage banking and title operations. It arranges financing through the origination of mortgage loans for its homebuyers, sells such loans and the related servicing rights, provides title insurance policies as an agent, and provides examination and closing services to its home buyers. PulteGroup offers a one-stop shopping experience for prospective customers. Sales reps help clients to finance their homes (with Pulte Mortgage) and to close their homes with PGP Title. One of PulteGroup's key strengths is the ability to provide customers with an exceptional home-buying experience and, ultimately, satisfaction with their homes. Being able to offer everything under one roof and walk the customers through each step of the entire home-buying process makes their home-buying experience very comfortable.

Ashley Pineda sells the company's Centex product line, which is primarily geared toward first-time home buyers by delivering quality homes at an affordable price. Ashley describes a typical selling process as follows: When customers walk in the door, she engages with them by welcoming them and building rapport. The company provides its sales reps with a consultative questioning strategy that allows the reps to smoothly walk the customers through the buying process. The questions, for example, may ask customers about their location preferences or what they consider most important when they buy a home. Ashley asks these types of questions to help her guide first-time home buyers through the variety of different homes available, ranging from one- to two-storey homes, from three to five bedrooms, from 1183 to 2600 square feet, and a price range from $95 000 to $150 000. Across various options, the customers are asked how well the different options align with their needs and wants.

The customers are also given the opportunity to touch and feel their future homes. This process typically involves a car tour through the neighbourhood, where they are shown the different homes' features and colours, and walk-throughs of both completed homes and homes under construction. The latter type helps to demonstrate the quality of Pulte's workmanship, the insulation, and the energy efficiency of a home. Altogether this allows potential customers to feel comfortable with the construction of the homes and the home-buying process.

In the next step, Ashley typically talks about financing issues with first-time homebuyers, such as the amounts of their monthly payments and potential down payments. PulteGroup equips Ashley with the knowledge to be able to professionally provide that information and make customers feel comfortable with the financial scenario involved in owning their first home. Once the customer is comfortable with the financial scenario, Ashley and her customer can move forward toward opening the agreement to buy a home. Generally, when you sign a contract, you are opening the agreement to take the next steps These steps include financing, completing

construction, and ultimately closing on the home and moving in. That entire process typically lasts from 45 days to approximately four months. (See the chapter opener on page 169 and Reality Selling Today Role Play 6 in Appendix 1 on page 432 for more information.)

Questions

1. Which of the prescriptions of the Strategic/Consultative Selling Model (see Figure 8.1 on page 172) does Ashley Pineda follow? Please explain.
2. How does Ashley elicit the needs and preferences of the prospective customers? What questions does she ask?
3. Outline a typical buying process that a middle-class couple with two young kids goes through in a first-time home buy. What questions and problems might arise at different stages of the buying process?
4. What might be key influencing factors for the couple's home-buying decisions? To what extent are rational and emotional buying motives important?
5. Put yourself in the position of Ashley Pineda. How can she create value at different stages of the young couple's buying process? Give examples.
6. Ashley sells new homes in the company's Centex product line, which is primarily geared toward first-time home buyers. One of her job responsibilities is to monitor competition. Who might be direct and indirect competitors that Ashley should watch?

Chapter 9
Developing and Qualifying Prospects and Accounts

Learning Objectives

After studying this chapter, you should be able to

1 Discuss the importance of developing a prospect or account base.

2 Identify and assess important sources of prospects and accounts.

3 Describe criteria for qualifying prospects and accounts.

4 Explain common methods of collecting and organizing prospect and account information.

5 Describe the steps in managing the prospect or account list.

Salesforce.com offers hosted applications that manage customer information for sales, marketing, and customer support, providing clients with a rapidly deployable alternative to buying and maintaining enterprise software. The company's applications are used by approximately 80 000 clients for generating sales leads, maintaining customer information, and tracking customer interactions. Dave Levitt (see next page) joined Salesforce .com as a regional sales manager in 2008 and leads a team of six sales representatives.

With prior experience as a direct salesperson in the enterprise software industry, Levitt has profound knowledge about how to approach and qualify prospects in his business. For his sales representatives, there are various ways to get in touch with potential customers: Some prospects will inquire at the company's website, and that will be forwarded directly to the sales representative so that she can follow up. Direct-response advertising, trade shows, or customer referrals can also be important sources of prospects. Besides having the customers reach out to them, salespeople at Salesforce.com also try to utilize knowledge on the company's 80 000 or so customers. For example, if the sales representative has a chemical company as one of his prospects, he will take a look at the CRM

Dave Levitt

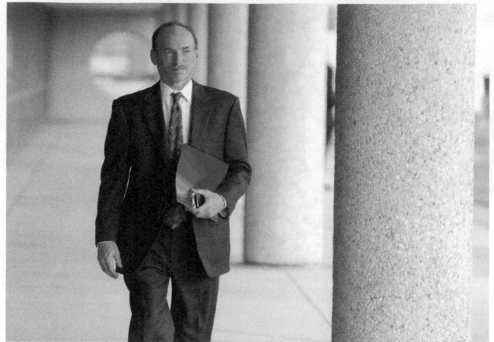

Michael Ahearne

system and ask: What other chemical companies are current customers and how did they benefit from using our services? Then the representative could use reference selling and thus demonstrate credibility to the prospect.

According to Dave Levitt, the key to successful selling is empathy—i.e., the ability to understand the customer's business so that the sales representative can identify areas where he can add value. Levitt points out, "We cannot count on the customer to know what we offer, because our services can be applied in many different ways. The burden is on the sales representative to use his industry and product knowledge to probe and uncover opportunities, and then to qualify and pursue them accordingly." Hence, the salesperson has to be able to look at accounts holistically, understand what the real business drivers are at a company, and then apply Salesforce.com's service solutions in different areas.

Account-based software vendors such as Salesforce.com, NetSuite, and Oracle Siebel are helping companies develop effective customer relationship management (CRM) systems. These systems are at the heart of every successful one-to-one marketing initiative.

PROSPECTING AND ACCOUNT DEVELOPMENT —AN INTRODUCTION

prospecting A systematic process of identifying potential B2C customers.

account or **business development** A systematic process of identifying potential B2B customers.

prospect A potential customer who meets the qualification criteria established by you or your company.

GERHARD GSCHWANDTNER, PUBLISHER OF *Selling Power*, SAYS, "THE MAIN PURPOSE OF A salesperson is not to make sales, but to create customers."[1] Identifying and developing potential customers is an important aspect of the customer strategy. In the terminology of personal selling, this process is often referred to as **prospecting** in Business-to-Consumer (B2C) selling. In Business-to-Business (B2B) selling, this process is often referred to as **account or business development.** Throughout this chapter, we will use these terms interchangeably. A potential **prospect** or account is an individual who, or a business that, meets the qualification criteria established by you or your company.

Some B2B companies employ account or business development representatives (Fig. 9.1) whose primary responsibility is to locate and establish account relationships and then turn them over to a strategic account manager or the field sales organization.[2] The account manager or member of the field sales organization then manages the entire sales process through to a successful conclusion, including closing and servicing the sale.

Finding prospects who can make the decision to purchase is not as easy as it sounds. This is especially true in business-to-business sales. In many situations, the salesperson must make the sales presentation to multiple decision makers. One of these decision makers might be the technical expert who wants an answer to the question: Does the product meet the company's specifications? Another decision maker may be the person who will actually use the product. The employee who will use the forklift truck you are selling may be involved in the purchase decision. Of course, there is often a "purse-string" decision maker who has the ultimate authority to release funds for the purchase. During periods of economic uncertainty, the decision-making process often moves upward. It is sometimes difficult to make connections with upper-level executives. One solution is to plan a joint sales call involving a higher-level executive from your own company.[3]

The goal of prospecting is to build a qualified **prospect base** made up of current customers and potential customers. Building a large prospect base involves the use of CRM software to monitor movement of the customer through the sales process. Many successful companies find that current customers account for a large percentage of their sales. Every effort is made to devise and implement a customer strategy that builds, fosters, nurtures, and extends relationships with established customers. CRM software is critical to building this kind of partnership with a large customer base.[4]

prospect base A list of current and potential customers.

POSITION DESCRIPTION BUSINESS DEVELOPMENT REPRESENTATIVE

The **Business Development Representative** (BDR) engages with accounts, targeting key and influential contacts. The BDR will be responsible for qualifying opportunities and staging initial sales meetings for the field sales organization.

Primary Responsibilities
- Drive sales opportunities by staging introductory sales meetings, product demonstrations, and on-site meetings for the field sales organization.
- Work an assigned enterprise account list; proactively identify revenue-generating customers via email campaigns and outbound phone calls.
- Perform pre-call planning including, but not limited to, researching accounts, identifying key influencers and decision makers, formulating initial sales plan of action, etc.
- Maintain and manage the SFDC database, including comprehensive data entry, precise follow-up planning, lead and opportunity tracking, pipeline reporting, etc.
- Collaborate with marketing, support, sales management, product management and account management to maintain an effective level of prospecting activity and pipeline growth.

Required Skills/Experience
- Degree required
- Minimum two years B2B enterprise account development experience
- Strong communication skills; ability to establish rapport with customers quickly
- Experience meeting/exceeding prospecting goals and account development metrics
- Microsoft Office and Customer Relationship Management (CRM) skills

Figure 9.1 The Account Business Development (ADR) Position Description
Account Development of Business Development Representatives in Business-to-Business (B2B) selling are responsible for engaging with key influential contacts and qualifying sales opportunities.

Importance of Prospecting and Account Development

Every salesperson must cope with customer attrition—that is, the inevitable loss of customers over a period of time, which can be attributed to a variety of causes. Unless new prospects are found to replace lost customers, a salesperson eventually faces a reduction in income and possible loss of employment. Paul Tindall of Toronto-based Coaching Works says, "Top performers prospect consistently. Low performers don't."[5] To better understand the significance of prospecting, let us examine a few common causes of customer attrition.

1. *The account may have a one-time need or there is an extended period of time between purchases.* Because of this, CB Richard Ellis's Susana Rosas realizes new prospects for commercial real estate must be continually added to her prospect base.

2. *The customer may move to a new location outside the salesperson's territory.* The Canadian population is very mobile. This cause of attrition is especially common in the retail and service areas and is a major issue experienced by Tom James Company's Alex Homer with many of his successful upwardly mobile clients.

3. *A firm may go out of business or merge with another company.* In some areas of business, the failure rate is quite high. In recent years we have witnessed a record number of mergers, which has caused massive changes in purchasing plans.

4. *A loyal buyer or purchasing agent may leave the position because of promotion, retirement, resignation, or serious illness.* The replacement may prefer to buy from someone else.

5. *Sales are lost to the competition.* In some cases, the competition offers more value. The added value may take the form of better quality, a better price, a stronger relationship, better service, or some combination of these factors.

Some studies reveal that the average company loses 15 to 20 percent of its customers every year. Depending on the type of selling, this figure might be higher or lower. Clearly, many customers are lost for reasons beyond the salesperson's control. If salespeople want to maintain stable earnings, they will need to develop new customers.

Joe Girard, once recognized by the *Guinness Book of Records* as the world's greatest salesperson, used the "Ferris wheel" concept to illustrate the relationship between prospecting and the loss of customers due to attrition.[6] As people get off the Ferris wheel, the operator fills their seats one at a time, moves the wheel a little, and continues this process until all the original riders have left the wheel and new ones have come aboard (Fig. 9.2). In reality, of course, established customers do not come and go this fast. With the passing of time, however, many customers will be replaced.

PROSPECTING REQUIRES PLANNING

PROSPECTING SHOULD BE VIEWED AS A SYSTEMATIC PROCESS OF LOCATING POTENTIAL CUSTOMERS. Some prospecting efforts can be integrated easily into a regular sales call. Progressive marketers do three things to improve the quality of their prospecting effort:

1. *Increase the number of people who board the Ferris wheel.* You want to see a continuous number of prospects board the Ferris wheel because they are the source of sales opportunities. If the number of potential prospects declines sharply, the number of sales closed will also decline.

2. *Improve the quality of the prospects who board the Ferris wheel.* Companies often establish quality standards that ensure a steady supply of prospects with high profit potential.

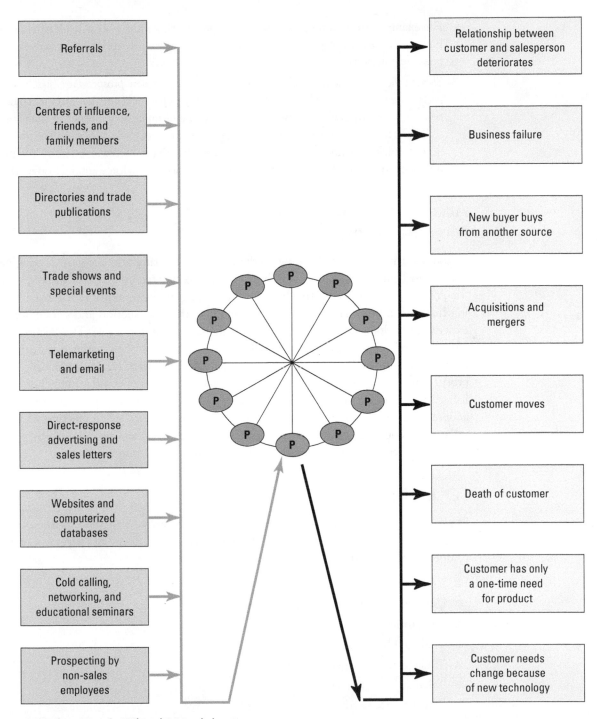

Figure 9.2 The "Ferris Wheel" Model
The "Ferris wheel" model, which is aimed at supplying an ongoing list of prospects, is part of world sales record holder Joe Girard's customer strategy.

For example, some companies focus their prospecting efforts on consultative process buyers. These are prospects who often lack need awareness and need help evaluating possible solutions.

3. *Shorten the sales cycle by quickly determining which of the new prospects are qualified prospects—qualified as to need, authority to buy, ability to pay, and willingness to purchase the product.* Gerhard Gschwandtner says, "Time is the ultimate scorekeeper in the game of selling." He points out that many salespeople do not meet their sales goals because they do not quickly qualify new prospects.[7] Later in this chapter we will examine qualifying practices and discuss how to shorten the sales cycle with sales force automation methods.

Account Development and Prospecting Plans Must Be Assessed Often

In today's dynamic, ever-changing marketplace, prospecting and account development plans must be monitored continuously. Some prospecting techniques that worked well in the past may become ineffective because of changing market conditions. Midwest Training Institute, a firm that helps companies improve their production and sales efficiency, experienced a dramatic sales decline during the first quarter of the year. This decline came after years of steady sales increases. Joel Pecoraro, president of the company, initiated a thorough investigation and discovered that his sales staff were relying primarily on one prospecting approach that was no longer successful: The salespeople were calling established customers. Pecoraro designed an incentive program that rewarded salespeople who adopted new prospecting techniques, such as attending an association meeting where the salesperson could meet potential prospects or speaking at a meeting attended by persons who might need the services offered by Midwest Training Institute.[8]

SOURCES OF PROSPECTS

EVERY SALESPERSON AND COMPANY MUST DEVELOP A PROSPECTING AND ACCOUNT development system suited to a particular selling situation. There are several sources of prospects, and each should be carefully examined.

- Referrals
- Centres of influence, friends, and family members
- Directories
- Trade publications
- Trade shows and special events
- Telemarketing and email
- Direct-response advertising and sales letters
- Websites
- Computerized databases
- Cold calling
- Networking
- Educational seminars
- Prospecting by non-sales employees

Referrals

The use of referrals as an account development approach has been successful in a wide range of selling situations. In most cases, referral leads result in higher close rates, larger sales, and shorter sales cycles. A **referral** is a prospect who has been recommended by a current customer or by someone who is familiar with the product. Satisfied customers, business acquaintances, and even prospects who do not buy can often recommend the names of persons who might benefit from purchasing the product. Liberty Mutual's Marcus Smith realizes that customers are more likely to give a referral if they perceive value in the solution he offers. When you build value into your sales process, you increase the odds that the customer will give you a referral. Jim Domanski, CEO of Teleconcepts Consulting of Kanata, Ontario, says that when you have a referral, there is an explicit or implicit endorsement of you, your company, and your product by the source.[9]

Endless Chain Referrals One approach to obtaining referrals, called the endless chain referral, is easy to use because it fits naturally into most sales presentations. A salesperson selling long-term health care insurance might ask, "Miss Chen, who do you know who might be interested in our insurance plan?" This open-ended question gives the person the freedom to recommend several prospects and is less likely to be answered with no response. Be sure to use your reference's name when you contact the new prospect— "Mary Chen suggested that I call you...."

Referral Letters and Cards The referral letter method is a variation of the endless chain technique. In addition to requesting the names of prospects, the salesperson asks

referral A prospect who has been recommended by a current customer or by someone who is familiar with the product.

Your request for a referral is more likely to receive a positive response if made after you have built a strong, trusting relationship. In most cases, referral leads result in higher close rates, larger sales, and shorter sales cycles.

visi.stock/Shutterstock

the customer to prepare a note or letter of introduction that can be delivered to the potential customer. The correspondence is an actual testimonial prepared by a satisfied customer. Some companies use a referral card to introduce the salesperson. The preprinted card has a place for your customer to sign the new prospect's name and his or her own name, and can be used as part of the sales presentation.

Within the field of personal selling, there is not complete agreement regarding the timing of the referral request. Some sales training programs encourage salespeople to request the referral immediately after closing the sale. Others point out that if you are working with a new customer, it takes time to earn the customer's trust. The customer may feel there is a risk involved in giving you referrals. Once you have built a strong, trusting relationship with the customer, referral requests are more likely to receive a positive response.[10]

Referral Organizations Some salespeople have found that membership in a referral organization is an effective way to obtain good leads. Business Network International (BNI) is one of the largest business networking organizations, with over 3600 chapters worldwide (www.bni.com). BNI offers its members the opportunity to share ideas, contacts, and referrals.[11] In addition, some local organizations, such as breakfast clubs, offer referrals as a member benefit.

Centres of Influence, Friends, and Family Members

The centre-of-influence method involves establishing a relationship with a well-connected, influential person who is willing to provide prospecting information. This person may not make buying decisions but has influence on other people who do. To illustrate, consider the challenge facing Gary Schneider, creator of a powerful software product that would help small farmers optimize their crop selection. After spending several years developing the product, Gary and his wife began selling it one copy at a time. During one cold call on a major crop insurer, Gary met a senior researcher who immediately saw the benefits of the software product. This respected researcher was in a position to influence buying decisions at his company and to provide prospect information for other crop insurers.[12]

A person who is new to the field of selling often uses friends and family members as sources of information about potential customers. It is only natural to contact people we know. In many cases, these people have contacts with a wide range of potential buyers.

Directories

Directories can help salespeople search out new prospects and determine their buying potential. A list of some of the more popular directories is provided here.

ProFile Canada, an Owen Media Partners company, maintains an online database of more than 1 million Canadian businesses. It advertises its database—see **www .profilecanada.com**—as having "the greatest depth of free information on individual companies found on any website in Canada."

Frasers.com provides a comprehensive online directory and search tool for Canadian manufacturers and industrial firms operating in Canada and the United States.

Scott's Directories offers an extensive portfolio of online business and industrial databases that are searchable by key terms so you can identify prospects by segments of interest to you: government, education, manufacturing, medical, industrial, etc. You can access more than 35 Canadian and 350 U.S. directories (www.scottsinfo.com).

ThomasNet.com lists more than 610 000 manufacturers, distributors, and MRO suppliers across Canada and the United States. You can find suppliers or prospective customers through a free search by geographic location, product category, or supplier category.

Polk City Directories provide detailed information on citizens of a specific community. Polk, in business for more than 140 years, publishes about 1100 directories covering 6500 communities in Canada and the United States (www.citydirectory.com).

These are just a few of the better-known directories. There are hundreds of additional directories covering national, regional, and local business and industrial firms. Some directories are free, while others must be purchased for a nominal fee. One of the most useful sources of free information is the telephone directory. Most telephone directories have a classified (yellow pages) section that groups businesses and professions by category. Web Yellow Pages (www.yellowpages.ca) allows you to search businesses by category across Canada.

If you are involved in the sale of products in international markets, International Trade Canada offers several services to assist you, such as the Canadian Trade Commissioner Service, which has a ground presence in more than 150 cities worldwide. This service can provide you with market intelligence and identification of potential customers, suppliers, or distributors and agents. Another valuable resource is the Export Development Corporation, a Crown corporation that helps Canadian exporters compete throughout the world. The corporation provides a wide range of financial and risk management services, and country and market information on most countries where Canadians sell. On its website (www.edc.ca), you can also view Canadian export performance data by country and view country economic and credit summaries.

Trade Publications

Trade publications provide a status report on every major industry. If you are a sales representative employed by GFS Canada, Sysco Canada, Pratts Wholesale, or one of the other food wholesalers that supply supermarkets, convenience stores, and restaurants, then you

From the Field
Account Development with Your Partners

When Megan Michael sees a new office building going up, she stops her car and makes inquiries about who is to occupy the building. As a sales representative for BKM Total Office, an office furniture supplier, she needs to be aware of new office space. However, this approach is not her most important prospecting method. She has found the telephone to be her most effective prospecting tool. Michael speaks regularly with her customers to find out if they know companies that might need BKM's products. Architects, designers, and builders who have previously worked with Michael have proved to be good sources of referrals. The key to her prospecting success is maintaining a strong relationship with her customers. She realizes that you must be an effective partner before you can ask for help.[a]

Research studies indicate that it is much easier to identify good prospects and actually close sales at a trade show.

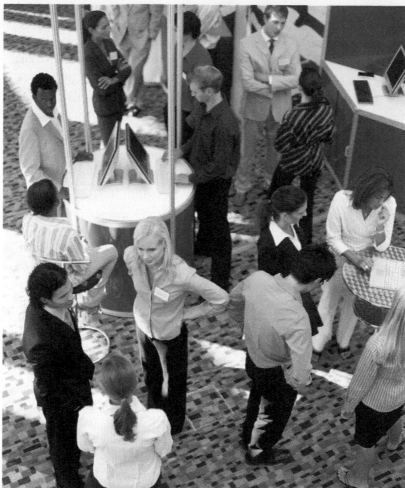

George Doyle/Getty Images

will benefit from a monthly review of *Canadian Grocer* magazine. Each month, this trade publication reports on trends in the retail food industry, as well as new products, problems, innovations, and related information. Trade journals such as *Women's Wear Daily*, *Home Furnishings*, *Pulp & Paper Canada*, *Purchasing b2b*, *Industrial Distribution*, and *Canadian Underwriter* are additional examples of publications that might help salespeople identify prospects.

Trade Shows and Special Events

A trade show is a large exhibit of products that are, in most cases, common to one industry, such as electronics or office equipment. The prospects walk into the booth or exhibit and talk with those who represent the exhibitor. In some cases, sales personnel invite existing customers and prospects to attend trade shows where they will have an opportunity to demonstrate their newest products.

Research studies indicate that it is much easier to identify good prospects and actually close sales at a trade show. In most cases, fewer sales calls are needed to close a sale if the prospect was qualified at a trade show. Once a trade show contact has been identified and

Bentley Motor Cars invited a number of potential clients to the famous Le Mans 24-hour endurance race. This special event helped the company develop its prospect base.

Jasen Vinlove/ZUMA Press/Newscom

judged to be a qualified lead, information regarding the lead should be carefully recorded. When a prospect enters a Xerox Corporation booth, a salesperson uses a few questions to qualify the lead and types the answers into an on-screen form. Xerox uses software developed by NewLeads to record and process data obtained from prospects who have been qualified by a salesperson working in the booth.[13] Special events—such as a hockey game, a golf tournament, a reception for a dignitary, or a charity event—are also great sources for prospects. Bentley Motor Cars invited a number of potential clients to the famous Le Mans 24-hour endurance race. Prospects watched the Bentley race car compete while sipping champagne. In Canada, charity events serve as a venue for cultivating wealthy clientele who can afford a Bentley automobile.[14]

Telemarketing and Email

Telemarketing is the practice of marketing goods and services through telephone contact. It is an integral part of many modern sales and marketing campaigns. One use of telemarketing is to identify prospects. A financial services company used telemarketing to identify prospects for its customized equipment leasing packages. Leads were given to salespeople for consideration. Telemarketing also can be used to quickly and inexpensively qualify prospects for follow-up. Some marketers use the telephone to verify sales leads generated by direct mail, advertisements, or some other method.

telemarketing The practice of marketing goods and services through telephone contact.

Although the response rate for sales emails is quite low, they have proven to be a source of leads for many salespeople. Ideally, sales emails should be sent only to existing customers or others who have "opted in" to receive them. When you use *broadcast* emails, there is a risk that you will be blocked and end up on a spammer blacklist. Online sales specialist Mac MacIntosh says those who use broadcast emails should stay within anti-spam laws by giving recipients the right to opt out of future emails.[15]

Putting your company name in the subject line can help get emails opened by prospects who are familiar with it. Some salespeople send newsletters to current and prospective customers. Lee Levitt, director of sales for software consultant IDC, sends a monthly newsletter to current IDC clients and professionals at large technology companies. He wants to expose them to services his company can provide. Levitt says, "The key is to offer something of value they can quickly digest and use in day-to-day work."[16]

Direct-Response Advertising and Sales Letters

Many advertisements invite the reader to send for a free booklet or brochure that provides detailed information about the product or service. In the category of business-to-business marketing, advertising has strong inquiry-generating power. Some firms distribute postage-free response cards (also known as *bingo cards*) to potential buyers. Recipients are encouraged to complete and mail the cards if they desire additional information. In some cases, the name of the person making the inquiry is given to a local sales representative for further action.

Sales letters, sent by email or by Canada Post, can easily be incorporated into a prospecting plan. The prospecting sales letter is sent to persons who are in a position to make a buying decision. Shortly after the letter has been mailed (i.e., three or four days), the prospect is called and asked for an appointment. The call begins with a reference to the sales letter. To make the letter stand out, some salespeople include product information. As noted in Chapter 6, all sales letters must be written with care. To get results, sales letters must quickly get the reader's attention.

Websites

website A collection of webpages maintained by a single person or organization.

Thousands of companies and businesspeople have established websites. A **website** is a collection of webpages maintained by a single person or organization. Large firms, such as Century 21, maintain websites that feature 20 to 30 webpages. Websites frequently offer prospects the opportunity to acquire product information that can help them make a buying decision. Financial services companies describe home financing and refinancing options. Salesforce.com's website provides detailed descriptions of Salesforce.com products and solutions. When someone clicks on a webpage and requests information, they will likely become a prospect. Some websites offer an incentive to leave contact information.

Computerized Databases

With the aid of electronic data processing, salespeople can match product features with the needs of potential customers quickly and accurately. In many situations, a firm will develop its own computerized database. In other cases, it is more economical to purchase the database from a company that specializes in collection of such information. One example is Salesgenie, offered by *info*Canada. Salesgenie maintains 1.5 million Canadian businesses in its database, and has recently added 13.5 million Canadian consumers as well.[17] With the aid of this software, you can easily obtain lead generation and prospect selection information for different market segments. Gary Hand, president of Alliance Security Systems, needs to keep his sales team supplied with plenty of leads. Salesgenie provides him with a list of prospects by geographical location and by the value of each

Prospecting with Social Media

Social media provide an excellent opportunity for finding prospects and reaching out to them. For example, LinkedIn offers an advanced search tool that you can use to narrow down your search and find people by company, job function, organizational position, etc. In Twitter, you can use tools such as FollowerWonk, TweetDeck, Hoot-Suite, or SproutSocial to identify users based on the words they use in their bios and their tweets. These tools make it easy to find those users who are tweeting about your products or services, or your company. Creating a business page on Facebook is a very straightforward way to get on the radar of your potential customers.

Once you find prospects on social media, it's extremely important to remember the nature of these media: They are personal networks. Sending a cold message such as

"We offer shipping solutions that are tailor-made for your particular needs…" is very likely to end up where all unsolicited emails and cold prospecting efforts end up: in the recycle bin. Instead of spamming people with unwanted messages, focus on building relationships with relevant customers, since relationships are what social media are all about. Joining these circles, groups, and pages that your customers are members of and that are relevant to you and your business is one way of starting new relationships. Also a wise use of social media is monitoring what people are saying about your products and joining those conversations. In all of your social media presence, you should always follow the rules of participation: Your messages should be relevant, targeted, reasonably expected, and timely.[b]

house. Salesgenie handles these two classifications easily and has therefore become a major time saver.[18] Salesgenie can provide salespeople with leads in such diverse market segments as medical services, engineering, architecture, agriculture, and education.

With the aid of a personal computer (PC), salespeople can develop their own detailed customer files. This means that salespeople can accumulate a great deal of information

*info*Canada is just one of several companies that maintain databases of consumers and businesses and provide salespeople with an excellent way to prospect for customers.

InfoCanada

Cisco Systems' Global CRM Software Application

Cisco has committed to deploying the Salesforce.com CRM solution to 25 000 global users. Salesforce.com provides Cisco with effective prospect management tools, such as dashboards, account planning tools, and reports regarding partner relationships.

- Dashboards track metrics such as opportunities, lead conversion rates, number of account plans, and top accounts for sales representatives and managers. Salespeople can create their own reports to chart their progress.

- Account planning, which had previously been difficult to manage on a worldwide basis, is increasingly leveraged with Salesforce.com.

- Partners are part of Cisco's customer "eco system." Overall productivity and effectiveness are improved by extending leads to partners, such as resellers, and tracking their conversion to opportunities and ultimately to sales.

about individual customers and use this information to personalize the selling process. For example, a PC can help an independent insurance agent maintain a comprehensive record for each policyholder. As each client's status changes (marriage, birth of children, etc.), the record can easily be updated. With the aid of an up-to-date database, the agent can quickly identify prospects for various existing and new policy options.

Cold Calling

cold calling Method of prospecting in which the salesperson selects a group of people who may or may not be actual prospects, and then calls—by phone or personal visit—on each one.

With some products, such as Alex Homer's custom clothing line offered by Tom James Company, cold call prospecting is an effective approach to prospect identification. In **cold calling**, the salesperson selects a group of people he anticipates may become actual prospects and then calls—by phone or personal visit—on each one. The sales representative for a wholesale medical supply firm might call on every hospital in a given community, assuming that each one is a potential customer. Many new salespeople must rely on cold calling because they are less likely to get appointments through referrals.

Edward Jones Corporation, a financial services company, is a strong supporter of cold calling. Sales representatives knock on doors and introduce themselves with a friendly, professional message: "Hi, my name is Brad Ledwith. I represent the Edward Jones Corporation, and we sell financial services. We're a unique firm because we try to do all of our business face-to-face. I just wanted to stop by and let you know that I've opened up a Jones office in the area and to find out if it's okay to contact you when I have an investment idea."[19] Sales representatives such as Brad Ledwith connect personally with members of their communities. This kind of cold call opener is often referred to as an **elevator speech.**

elevator speech A 30-second message that summarizes what you want people to know about you, your company, and your product line.

This is a 30-second message that summarizes what you want people to know about you, your company, and your product line. Practising the elevator speech in front of a mirror can significantly improve its effectiveness.

Successful cold calls do not happen spontaneously. Some strategic thinking and planning must precede telephone calls and personal visits. Who do you contact? What do you say during the first few seconds? In order to appear confident and competent, carefully develop your opening remarks. If you appear to be nervous or unprepared, the prospect will assume you lack experience. Many salespeople who make cold-call phone calls prepare a well-polished script. The script helps keep you on message and guarantees you will not leave out important information.[20]

Canadian sales trainer and coach Steven J. Schwartz suggests that cold calls can be turned into hot calls through a telephone contact system that uses good call planning, strategic scripting, and effective script delivery. His book *How to Make Hot Cold Calls* explains his system, and his website offers a number of personal diagnostic tools for salespeople. (Visit www.hotcoldcalls.com and click on "Toolbox.")

Networking

One of the most complete books on networking is *Dig Your Well Before You're Thirsty* by Harvey Mackay. He says, "If I had to name the single characteristic shared by all the truly successful people I've met over a lifetime, I'd say it's the ability to create and nurture a network of contacts."[21] Networking skills are of special importance to new salespeople, who cannot turn to a large group of satisfied customers for referrals and leads. Professionals (accountants, lawyers, consultants, etc.), entrepreneurs, managerial personnel, and customer service representatives must develop networking skills. Networking skills are also of critical importance to job seekers because at any given time about 80 percent of all available jobs are not posted in the classifieds or on Internet job boards.[22]

In simple terms, **networking** is the art of making and using contacts: people meeting people and profiting from the connections. Barry Siskind, an Ontario-based consultant, sees networking as a three-act process. In act one, you must be able to approach someone and

networking The practice of making and using contacts. It involves people meeting people and profiting from the connections.

Most salespeople use CRM software in the development of their prospecting and sales forecasting plan. This software allows the convenient preparation and management of prospect lists.

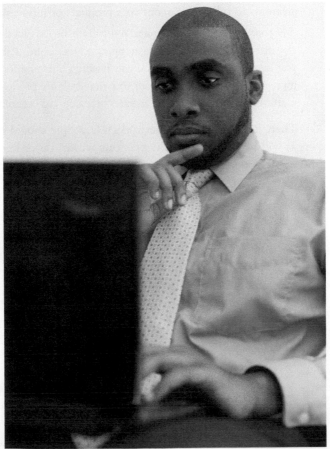

Fancy Collection/Superstock

engage them in conversation. Act two is when you "net-chat," a term Siskind uses to describe the technique of collecting and giving information and finding out as much as you can about the other person in the shortest time possible. Act three is where you disengage. Although networking is one of the premier prospecting methods, some salespeople are reluctant to seek referrals in this manner. In addition, many salespeople do not use effective networking practices. Skilled networkers suggest the following guidelines for identifying good referrals:

1. *Meet as many people as you can.* Networking can take place on an airplane, at a Rotary Club meeting, at a trade show, or at a professional association meeting. Don't make the mistake of limiting your networking activities to business contacts. The term **social network** refers to your set of *direct and indirect contacts.* An indirect contact might be the brother of a close friend. The brother works for a large company and can help you see more clearly into the operation of this firm.[23]

2. *When you meet someone, tell the person what you do.* Give your name and describe your position in a way that explains what you do and invites conversation. Instead of saying, "I am in stocks and bonds," say "I am a financial planner who helps people make investment decisions." Listen more than you talk. Developing and perfecting an elevator speech, mentioned earlier, can be very effective when networking.

3. *Do not do business while networking.* It usually is not practical to conduct business while networking. Make a date to call or meet with the new contact later.

4. *Offer your business card.* The business card is especially useful when the contact attempts to tell others about your products or services.

5. *Edit your contacts and follow-up.* You cannot be involved with all your contacts, so separate the productive from the nonproductive. Send a short email message to contacts you deem productive and include business information or brochures—anything that increases visibility.[24] Make sure your materials are professional. Use inexpensive contact management software, such as Salesforce.com, to organize your contact information.

There are three types of networks salespeople should nurture (Fig. 9.3). Every salesperson will be well served by networking within his or her own organization. You never know when someone in finance or shipping will be needed to help solve a problem or

social network Your set of direct and indirect contacts.

Figure 9.3 Networking Model
Top-performing salespeople recognize that networking can take place in three areas.

provide you with important information. A second form of networking involves establishing contacts inside your industry. Make contact with experts in your field, top performers, leaders, successful company representatives, and even competitors. The third form of networking involves business contacts with people outside your industry, such as bankers, government officials, developers, and other people in your community. The local golf course may be a good place to make these contacts.[25]

Educational Seminars

Many salespeople are using educational seminars as a method of identifying prospects. Seminars provide an opportunity to showcase your product without pressuring prospects to buy. Many banks, accounting firms, wine merchants, and consulting companies use seminars to generate new prospects. Previously we mentioned that Edward Jones's sales representatives often make cold calls on prospects. They also schedule seminars that provide prospects with an opportunity to acquire information regarding the potential benefits of investing in a mutual fund, estate planning, or tax-free investing. A complimentary lunch is usually served before the informative presentation. When inviting prospects, be clear about the seminar's content and always deliver what you promise.

Prospecting and Account Development by Non-Sales Employees

Should service technicians, receptionists, bank tellers, and other non-sales personnel be involved in prospecting? For a growing number of firms, the answer is yes. Prospecting need

---

Selling in Action

Account Development with Seminars

The use of educational seminars has become an important prospecting method. You can educate prospective customers with brochures, news releases, catalogues, or your website, but educational seminars offer the advantage of face-to-face contact. Barbara Siskind, in her book *Seminars to Build Your Business*, identifies 15 objectives for hosting seminars. Here are a few of the most important.

- *Obtain sales leads*. This is one of the most common objectives for seminars. You can obtain the names of attendees and arrange appointments for future sales calls. Seminars may also help identify actual product users, technical support people, or engineers, who, while they may not be the decision makers, may influence the purchase decision.
- *Promote your place of business*. Your place of business can become a destination for people who might otherwise not consider visiting it. You have an

opportunity to create awareness of your company and develop a positive image for your entire operation and its capabilities.

- *Showcase and demonstrate your expertise*. Seminars allow you to show a carefully targeted group of people that you really know your stuff. Salespeople can be supported by technical experts and others in the organization who can address clients' specific concerns.

Polaroid Canada used educational seminars where imaging specialists assisted prospective clients in exploring imaging solutions. Toronto-based Charon Systems, Inc., a systems integrator that deploys networks for organizations, regularly organizes seminars for 80 to 100 technology people from mid-sized firms. President David Fung estimates that 25 percent of prospects become clients.[c]

not be the exclusive responsibility of the sales force. Janet Dixon, a UPS sales representative, needed help making contact with an important prospect. This person wouldn't take her calls. She talked to the UPS service provider (a driver), who called on this account and requested his help. He had serviced this company for years and was like part of the family. He knew the prospect personally and persuaded her to accept a call from Janet.[26]

Combination Approaches

In recent years, we have seen an increase in the number of prospecting and account development approaches used by salespeople. In many cases, success in selling depends on your ability to use a combination of the methods described in this chapter. For example, the large number of prospects identified at a trade show might be used to develop an effective telemarketing program. Prospects are called and an effort is made to set up a personal call. Prospects identified at a trade show or educational seminar might also be sent a sales-oriented newsletter, a sales letter, or an email message inviting them to visit your webpage.

QUALIFYING PROSPECTS AND ACCOUNTS

ONE OF THE MOST IMPORTANT KEYS TO SUCCESS IN PERSONAL SELLING IS THE ABILITY TO qualify prospects. **Qualifying** is the process of identifying prospects who appear to have a need for your product and should be contacted. Top salespeople use good research and analysis skills to qualify leads effectively.[27]

The qualifying process is also the first opportunity to consider what the needs of the buyer might be and how those needs are matched by the characteristics of the product being sold.[28] Some sales organizations link the qualifying process with the need discovery step in the consultative sales process. In most cases, this linkage will depend on the nature and complexity of the prospect's buying process. The more complex the buying process, the more likely these two sales functions will be separate steps in the sales process. We will fully explore the need discovery step in Chapter 11.

Every salesperson needs to establish qualifying criteria. This process involves finding answers to several basic questions.

1. *Does the prospect or account have a need for my product?* If you sell copy machines, it might appear that every business firm is a prospect. However, a firm that is outsourcing its copy work to FedEx Kinko's may not be a legitimate prospect. Qualifying involves probing for real needs. Let's assume you sell real estate for a large agency. You receive a call from someone who believes that owning a home is a good investment. At this point, it's important to find out what else makes owning a home important for that person. Get permission to ask questions and then determine the person's real needs. In the final analysis, you may decide it would be a waste of your time and the prospect's time to visit several homes that are on the market.[29]

2. *Does the prospect or account have the authority to buy my product?* Ideally, you should talk to a person who has authority to buy or who can influence the buying decision. Talking to the right person within a large organization may involve collecting information from several sources. Some buying decisions are made by individuals and others are made by a committee. In B2B selling, high-cost products often require the approval of a decision maker higher up in the organization.

3. *Does the prospect or account have the financial resources to buy my product?* It is usually not difficult to obtain credit information for consumers and business buyers. If you are selling products to a business, the *Dun & Bradstreet Reference Book* is an excellent source of credit information. A local credit bureau can provide credit information for a consumer buyer. While the collection of credit information is not difficult, detecting financial instability can be much more complicated. In recent years, we have seen a steady stream of corporate scandals involving accounting irregularities, inflated balance sheets, and outright fraud.[30] Salespeople must be aware of the possibility that a customer may provide incorrect or misleading information.

4. *Does the prospect or account have the willingness to buy my product?* Rick Page, author of *Hope Is Not a Strategy*, reminds us that many prospects evaluate products but do not buy. When an evaluation stalls, the prospect may have determined that the need is not of great enough magnitude or urgency to make the purchase. Also, in some cases there is not enough support within the company to reach closure. Rather than walk away from this situation, some salespeople move higher in the organization to determine the level of support for the purchase.[31]

A large number of senior executives say they get involved in the sale early in the decision process, yet salespeople have difficulty meeting with high-level decision makers. Most senior executives will not meet with salespeople who are making cold calls. When appointments are granted, the time allocated may be very short; five to ten minutes is not uncommon. How do you establish credibility for yourself and your company in a short time period? Be sure you know a great deal about the company before the appointment and be prepared to demonstrate your knowledge of the company and the industry it serves. Do not propose solutions until you fully understand the buyer's problems. Be sure to communicate value.[32]

This list of questions can be revised to meet the needs of many different types of salespeople. A sales representative for an industrial equipment dealer will see the qualifying process differently from the person who sells commercial real estate. The main consideration is providing accurate answers to each question.

COLLECTING AND ORGANIZING PROSPECT INFORMATION

THE INTERNET AND THE INFORMATION REVOLUTION CONTINUE TO MAKE ACQUIRING AND managing sales leads much easier.[33] When it comes to collecting and organizing prospect information, salespeople have a large assortment of computer-based systems available. Companies such as Salesforce.com, Oracle, NetSuite, Sage, and Microsoft all offer software applications designed to collect and organize prospect information. Most of these Sales Force Automation (SFA) Systems or Customer Relationship Management (CRM) Systems, as they are now known, have preset categories or fields that contain sales data on the prospect. This **sales data** is the information seen in most CRM systems, including the contact name, title, address, phone number, email address, etc. It may also include information about what products have been purchased, what sales opportunities exist in the future, who the various members or influencers are in the buying centre, their preferred communication styles (refer to Chapter 5), past sales and forecasted sales volume, and percentage change and date of closing the sale. All of the sales data information about the prospect or account in a CRM system is presented in the account screen report.

sales data Information available from a company's CRM system.

Figure 9.4 shows an account screen report for Able Profit Machines. The information in this report, including any notes about previous sales calls, is accessed and studied before the salesperson makes a sales call.

When bringing new prospects into the database, it is expected that the salesperson will acquire this sales data and enter it into the records kept on the prospect. In most CRM systems, this information goes into the shared database that allows other members of the sales team to access information and make additions as they work with prospects. In the event a new salesperson takes over an existing prospect or account database, all of this information can be accessed quickly and used to plan sales strategies to work effectively with prospects.

Sales Intelligence

sales intelligence Information that goes beyond data, giving salespeople access to insights into the prospect's marketplace, their firm, their competitors, and even the prospects themselves.

In addition to collecting sales data, the collection of **sales intelligence** is necessary when the sale is complex and requires a long closing cycle. Sales intelligence goes beyond data, giving salespeople access to insights into the prospect's marketplace, their firm, their

---

Contact Screen

Account 2: Aeroflot Airlines
Contact: Mr. John Poltava
Phone: 214-555-6113
Fax: 214-555-2856
Title: V.P. Purchasing
Dear: John

Last Results: Qualified
ID/Status: Prospect
Firm Size: 3,500 People
Network Now: 10 Novell Systems
Workstations: 2,750
Account Code: Airline

Address: 499 Park Avenue
Suite 213
Email: jpolt21@aeroflot.com
City: Saskatoon
State: SK
ZIP Code: S7K 0J5

Network Need: WAN
Likelihood: 0.80
Dollar Amount: $75,000
Date Close: 1/31

Notes Screen

11/09:   John wants to meet soon. Will have his key people at meeting, including their CFO and CEO. John said new network expenditures should cut costs and enhance their bottom line by 4%. Need Joe to do a needs analysis. Maybe need Charlene also as she is best at the numbers when she does the configuration.

11/02:   John is an emotive. Very interested in new network to improve productivity and bottom line. They have a very ambitious company-wide 5-year projection of 12% bottom line after taxes. They need a WAN system that connects their offices in 20 airports and 12 warehouses. Lots of problems including a lack of centralized file sharing and document control, inability for their remote employees to efficiently access and share files with the corporate office and a number of website issues that were causing security concerns. John has been with Aeroflot since '97. He will decide on vendor after his management information systems director chooses a system. John said to call a Mr. Ortega at Southern Motors in Regina. Ortega, it seems, is in the market now. Sent him a thank you for the Ortega information.

Figure 9.4 The CRM Account Report
This account report shows sales data for Aeroflot Airlines. Information in both the Contact Screen and Notes Screen, from previous sales calls, was entered by Account Manager Lee Bizon, of NewNet Systems.
Copyright © salesforce.com, inc. Used with permission of Salesforce.

competitors, and even about the prospects themselves. Sales intelligence is needed today over and above sales data because prospects are looking for insights and knowledge from salespeople above and beyond the product features and benefits. In many buying situations today, prospects using advanced search engines have already learned about features and benefits. In terms of sales intelligence, prospects and accounts expect salespeople to know answers to many of the following questions. Answers to these questions create much of the value that results in successfully turning prospects and accounts into long-term customers.

Do you know me? You need to know more than my name and title. Do you know my role, my goals, how I am evaluated, and how long I have been with the organization? Do you know about the projects I am working on, my style of doing business, and what the requirements are for me to meet my objectives? Do you know about previous dealings I have had with your company? Do I have a favourable opinion of your company and do you know my role and the role of other influencers in the decision-making process?

Do you know my company and my marketplace? Do you know my company mission statement, culture, and vision for the future? Do you know clearly what we are doing, how we are performing in the marketplace, what issues keep us up all night, who our competitors are, and what they are doing? Do you know where we fit into the existing competitive landscape? Are we the leader or are we in the position of having to play catch-up to survive? Can you relate what you sell directly to what we need to accomplish our goals? Do you know who our partners are or what effect the current economy has on our business?

Do you have any special value-add? You have a product or service you think we need, but what else can you bring to the table? Are there additional resources you can bring to bear to solve my problems or improve my internal business processes? Can you educate me on how you are truly different from the other players in your area of expertise so I can support my recommendation to work with you? Can you help me build a case for return on investment (ROI)?[34]

Answers to these questions come from many sources. CRM suppliers like Salesforce. com, infogroup.ca, Sales-i.com, and Vecta.net have programs that supply this kind of sales intelligence to companies and salespeople. Salesforce's recently acquired Radian6, used by more than one-half of the Fortune 500 companies, tracks social media for pertinent information on prospects.[35] Their Data.com product tracks B2B account information and supplies prospect and account information to their subscribers.[36] OneSource is one example of a supplier of sales intelligence. OneSource supplies sales intelligence to Cardinal Logistics Management, a major provider of logistics, transportation, and supply-chain solutions to large retailers, manufacturers, and distribution companies. Cardinal's salespeople must know each account inside and out in order to sell logistics solutions effectively to their 5000 customers. OneSource supplies 24/7, anywhere access to detailed customer profiles, executive contact data and biographies, financial statements, news trade articles, and analyst reports. A special feature keeps salespeople up to date on any and all developments within their customer's company and their industry, including both their customer's customers and their competitors.[37]

Most importantly, this information must be entered into the company's CRM system to get a 360-degree view of the prospect. The information will also be used to move the prospect through the steps in the sales process.

MANAGING THE PROSPECT BASE

HIGH-PERFORMING SALESPEOPLE TODAY ARE FOCUSED ON EFFECTIVELY MANAGING SALES activities for all prospects in their database (Fig. 9.5). This means that the size and number of prospects are more carefully considered. Too few prospects in various stages of the sales cycle can quickly signal problems. Alternatively, too many customers can drain a salesperson's resources so that too little effort is focused on prospects with the best opportunities. This is a particular problem when salespeople spend too much effort

NewNet Systems, Edmonton Market Prospect/Account/Contact List

Lee Bizon, Account Executive   Casey Arnold, Sales Manager

Account	Contact	Phone	Email
Able Technologies, Inc.	Mr. Bradley J. Able	254-555-1000	bja@able.com
Aeroflot Airlines	Mr. John Poltava	214-555-6113	jpolt21@aeroflot
Southern Motors	Mr. Dwayne Ortega	972-555-4094	d_ortega@btas.com
Bryan Enterprises	Mr. Bill Bryan	214-555-4567	bbryan@bryan.com
Computer Products	Ms. Joanna Barkley	713-555-2345	j_b@yahoo.com
Computerized Labs	Mr. Sam Pearlman	713-555-5454	spman@complabs.com
Designers Associates	Dr. Simon Sayers	972-555-6866	sisa@designers.net
Ellis Enterprises	Mr. Timothy P. Ellis	214-555-1234	tpellis75@mchsi.com
Engineering Software Inc.	Mr. Ian Cortez	214-555-8979	ian@exso.com
General Contractors	Mr. Brian Allan	214-555-2947	brian@gentors.com
International Studios	Mr. Robert G. Kelly	214-555-3456	rgk@internstudio.com
Johnson and Associates	Mr. Ralph Johnson	817-555-3212	rjohnson13@mchsi.com
Lakeside Clinic	Dr. Jeff Gray	214-555-6600	jgray@lakeside.com
Landers Engineering	Ms. Colleen Landers	817-555-6121	clanders@aol.com
Media Conglomerate	Mr. Joe Romera	214-555-9090	Joro@media.com
Mercy Hospital	Ms. Kerri Mathers	214-555-1880	kmathers@mercy.com
Modern Designs	Ms. Cheryl Castro	214-555-1098	ccastro@modes.com
Murray D'Zines	Ms. Karen Murray	817-555-1111	kmuray@dzines.com
Piccadilly Studio	Ms. Judith Albright	214-555-3084	jalbright@Pic.com
Quality Builders	Ms. Sherry Britton	817-555-6886	sherry@qbuild.com

Figure 9.5 The Account Base
This CRM record presents a complete list of accounts for NewNet Systems Account Manager Lee Bizon. Note this list includes the Account Name, Contact Person, Phone Number, and Email Address.

on prospects that have limited potential. CRM software can help organize customer data into meaningful and easy-to-interpret information.

To effectively and efficiently manage the prospect base, sales managers and salespeople often conduct an **account analysis** to estimate the sales potential for each prospect. It is a necessary step before deciding how to allocate sales calls across accounts. The portfolio model and the sales process model are two popular conceptual tools for performing account analyses and deciding how much time and effort, and what sales strategies, to use with the contacts in the database.

account analysis An estimate of the sales potential for each account.

Portfolio Models

Portfolio models involve the use of multiple factors when classifying accounts. Figure 9.6 illustrates a typical four-cell model based on two factors: overall account opportunity for

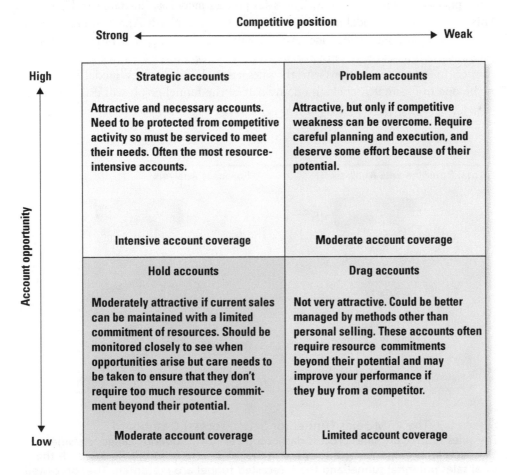

Figure 9.6 The Portfolio Model
This portfolio model uses account opportunity (forecasted sales) and competitive position (the ability to capitalize on opportunity) to classify how much sales effort should be made on individual accounts in the prospect database. Those prospects listed in the strategic accounts cell (high sales forecast and strong position for closing the sale) will receive the largest amount of sales effort, while those in the drag accounts cell will receive little, if any, attention.

the seller and the seller's competitive position—that is, the ability to capitalize on these opportunities.[38]

The portfolio model provides an excellent framework to facilitate communication between salespeople and the various sales support personnel. Teamwork at this stage in the sales cycle can develop improved strategies for working successfully with different accounts and contacts in the account base. Portfolio models are most effective where salespeople must understand individual customer needs and where relationship strength is important to sales success.

Sales Process Models

Sales process models, also referred to as "sales funnel models," classify prospects based on where they are in the sales process. The **sales process model** is the total set of prospects being pursued at any given time. The sales process model is illustrated in Figure 9.7. This six-step process model includes Prospect, Qualified, Needs Analysis, Presentation, Negotiations, and Closed/Service. An account might be simply a prospect who has potential but has not been contacted, a qualified prospect ready for a needs analysis, or a prospect in serious negotiations with the salesperson. In sales process model reports such as the one in Figure 9.7, clicking on any part of the funnel graph will drill down into

Figure 9.7 The CRM Sales Funnel (or Sales Process) Dashboard
The sales funnel, or "sales process dashboard" as it is frequently called, classifies prospects according to where they are in the sales process. In this figure, both the total sales potential funnel and the forecasted funnel are presented. The forecasted funnel amounts are arrived at by multiplying the total sale by the forecast amount or likelihood the salesperson projected for successfully closing the sale. The sales forecast needs to be accurate because it is the amount most firms use to project future operating results for the company. You can click any stage on these two charts and drill down to find the underlying data.
Copyright © salesforce.com, inc. Used with permission of Salesforce.

and report all the supporting data on prospects in each stage of the sales process. Where an account is in the sales process has implications for if and when the salesperson will be able to close the sale.

The sales cycle for complex technical sales, such as computer networking installations, might be several months in duration. The number of prospects in the funnel for selling such installations may be small compared to the number for an insurance or real estate salesperson. Insurance salespeople know they need to contact a larger number of people to gain permission to make a smaller number of presentations to make an even smaller number of sales. In any selling situation, it is important that salespeople balance their portfolio of prospects that are at various stages of the selling process.[39] A **balanced funnel** enables salespeople to know how many prospects and how much revenue are needed at each stage in the sales process to meet sales projections and quotas.[40] As indicated earlier with Joe Girard's "Ferris wheel" concept, this means that salespeople must ensure that sufficient prospects are regularly added to the funnel to ensure that it does not become empty. In addition to the number of prospects, the quality of the prospects added to the funnel and the ability of the salesperson to manage the sales process will affect the number of sales opportunities that are successfully closed.

Salespeople need to ensure that they "work" the whole funnel so that it is always in balance. They should work on sales opportunities near the bottom of the funnel first; that is, close those that are near the end of the sales process. Then they should work on adding new prospects and those that are in the earlier stages of the sales process. Prospecting is an activity that some salespeople dislike, but if it is not given sufficient attention there is a real danger that the funnel or pipeline will empty. Finally, salespeople should work on those opportunities that are in the sales process, moving them along through the funnel and ensuring there are regular, predictable sales over time.[41]

Pipeline Management, Pipeline Analytics, and Pipeline Dashboards

This process of managing all the prospects in the salesperson's sales funnel to ensure that sales objectives are met is called **pipeline management**. CRM software provides an efficient and effective tool for forecasting and managing pipelines. Using sales data entered into the account detail, contact screens, notes applications, etc., sales forecasts can be updated continually as prospects move through the stages in the sales process. Prospects in the database who are no longer qualified, for whatever reason, can be quickly dropped from the sales funnel.

Pipeline analytics, defined as the ability to conduct sophisticated data analysis and modelling, are found in most CRM systems. Using pipeline analytics, new reports can be generated regarding the movement of prospects through the sales pipeline. These reports can be more clearly presented with the use of dashboards. **Pipeline dashboards** (Fig. 9.8) are at-a-glance visualizations that define, monitor, and analyze the relationships existing in the pipeline. Sales team members, including the sales manager, working together from a shared CRM database, can collaborate to create value and enhance the sales strategies to help the salesperson move prospects through the pipeline to a successful sale. CRM

balanced funnel A portfolio of prospects where there is a sufficiently large number of prospects at each stage in the sales process.

pipeline management Process of managing all the prospects in the salesperson's sales funnel to ensure that sales objectives are met.

pipeline analytics Ability to conduct sophisticated data analysis and modelling, allowing salespeople to generate new reports regarding the movement of prospects through the sales funnel.

pipeline dashboards At-a-glance visualizations that define, monitor, and analyze the relationships existing in the pipeline or sales funnel.

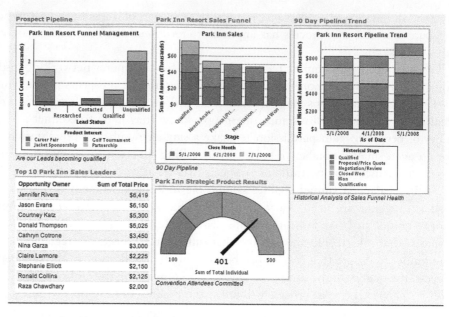

Figure 9.8 Pipeline Dashboards
These additional pipeline dashboards are at-a-glance visualizations that define, monitor, and analyze the relationships existing in the pipeline or funnel. Pipeline analytics exist in most modern CRM systems and are used to produce these important prospect movement reports. The salesperson can quickly and easily access detailed information on specific prospects, and then use this information to plan strategies for moving the prospect to the next stage of the sales process.
Copyright © salesforce.com, inc. Used with permission of Salesforce.

pipeline dashboards allow the user to quickly and easily drill down into the reports and records supporting them. This provides for quick updates as prospects move through the sales funnel. Dashboards can also provide insight into the need to add new prospects as existing ones are moved through the stages of the sales process.

Doing Business in Germany

Germany represents the world's third-largest economy and is an important Canadian trading partner. If you are a salesperson planning a business trip to Germany, keep in mind that there is greater formality in the German business community.

■ Germany has been described as a "low-context" culture in which words carry most of the information. Messages tend to be explicit and direct. In this culture, negotiations (verbal or written) tend to be explicit in defining terms of the agreement. In comparison, China is a high-context culture in which exact phrasing and the verbal part of the messages tend to be less significant than your relationship with the other person.

■ There is a strong emphasis on punctuality, so avoid being late for appointments. Germans tend to make appointments far in advance.

■ Lunch is the most common meal for business meetings. Dining etiquette in Germany involves eating continental style—holding the fork in the left hand continually and the knife in the right hand.

■ The sales presentation should include data and empirical evidence that support your proposal. Brochures and other printed information should be serious and detailed, not flashy.[d]

REVIEWING KEY CONCEPTS

- Discuss the importance of developing a prospect or account base.

  Prospect identification has been called the lifeblood of selling. A continuous supply of new customers must be found to replace those lost for various reasons. *Prospecting* and *account development* are systematic processes for locating potential customers. Both require careful planning.

- Identify and assess important sources of prospects and accounts.

  Analysis of both your product and your existing customers can help to identify, locate, and profile your prospects. Important sources of new customers include referrals (endless chain referrals and referral letters and cards), centres of influence, friends and family members, directories, trade publications, trade shows and special events, telemarketing and email, direct-response advertising and sales letters, websites, computer databases, cold calling, educational seminars, networking, and prospecting by non-sales employees. Social media can also be used to secure new prospects.

- Describe criteria for qualifying prospects and accounts.

  Prospecting techniques produce a list of names that must be evaluated using criteria developed by each salesperson. The process of prospect evaluation is called *qualifying*. The qualifying process involves finding answers to several basic questions: Does the prospect have a need for my product? Can the prospect make the buying decision? Can the prospect pay for the purchase? Does the prospect have the willingness to buy my product? An estimate of the volume of sales that could be generated from this prospect and the prospect's credit rating also should be determined.

- Explain common methods of collecting and organizing prospect and account information.

  Most companies rely on customer relationship management (CRM) systems to keep track of sales data. The collection of sales intelligence beyond sales data enables salespeople to impress their knowledgeable customers with insights that are above and beyond the product and/or service features and benefits.

- Describe the steps in managing a prospect or account list.

  Salespeople need to allocate their resources wisely to make the most of the prospect base. They do so by conducting account analyses, using either the portfolio model or the sales funnel model.

Key Terms

account analysis **217**

account development **196**

balanced funnel **219**

business development **196**

cold calling **208**

elevator speech **208**

networking **209**

pipeline analytics **219**

pipeline dashboards **219**

pipeline management **219**

prospect **196**

prospect base **197**

prospecting **196**

qualifying **212**

referral **201**

sales data **213**

sales intelligence **214**

sales process model **218**

social network **210**

telemarketing **205**

website **206**

Review Questions

1. List and briefly explain the common causes of customer attrition.

2. Describe three steps progressive marketers take to improve the quality of their prospecting effort.

3. List the major sources of prospects.

4. Explain how the endless chain referral prospecting and account development method works.

5. Discuss how direct-response advertising and sales letters

can be used to identify prospects.

6. What is *networking* ? How might a real estate salesperson use networking to identify prospects?

7. What does the term *qualifying* mean? What are the four basic questions that should be answered during the qualifying process?

8. What are the most common methods of organizing prospect information?

9. When is sales intelligence important? What are the three most important pieces of sales intelligence a salesperson needs to know?

10. Describe two popular models for performing an account analysis.

Application Exercises

1. Prior to getting involved in networking, it's a good idea to prepare an *elevator speech*. This is a 30-second pitch that summarizes what you want people to know about you. You might think of yourself as a "product" to be sold to an employer who has a job opening. Make your presentation upbeat and brief. Who are you? What are you currently doing? What type of work are you looking for? Practise the presentation alone in front of a mirror and then present it to one or two class members.

2. You are a sales representative for Xerox Canada, which has just designed a new, less expensive, and better quality copying machine. From the material in this chapter, identify the sources you would use in developing your prospect list. Make a list of 15 prospects you would plan to contact.

3. You are in the process of interviewing for a sales position with Sun Life Financial in Toronto. In addition to filling out an application form and taking an aptitude test, one of the tasks the agency manager requests of you is to develop a list of prospects with whom you are acquainted. He informs you that this list will represent the prospects you will be working with during the first few weeks of employment. The agency manager recommends that you list at least 50 names. Prepare a list of 10 acquaintances you have who would qualify as prospects.

4. Sales automation software is most commonly used in the prospecting phase of selling. New-product releases are continually being developed that provide additional features and benefits to salespeople. The software used in this book is marketed by a leader in the field. Access **www.salesforce.com** and research the latest additions to Salesforce, such as Radian6 and Data.com. View the introductory videos on their new products.

5. Locating companies to work for is a form of prospecting. Assuming you are interested in changing careers, develop a list of 10 companies for which you would like to work. Assign each company a priority according to your interest, from the most desirable (1) to the least (10). Organize your list into six columns showing the company name, telephone number, address, person in charge of hiring, prospect information, and priority. What sources did you use to get this information?

↻ ROLE-PLAY EXERCISE

For this role play, you will assume a sales position at a Lexus dealership. You have just completed a successful sale by signing the papers for the second new Lexus this customer has purchased in the past four years. Because you know your customer has had a very successful experience with his first Lexus, you have decided to use the referral methods described in this chapter. Review the material on referrals and plan what you will say to your customer to build your prospect base. Pair off with another student who will assume the role of your customer. Explain that satisfied customers often know other people who would consider purchasing a Lexus. You might say, "Considering the positive experience you have had as a Lexus owner, you probably know others who appreciate fine automobiles. Is there anyone who comes to mind?" If, after probing, your customer doesn't recall someone immediately, ask permission to call him later to see if anyone has come to mind. Ask this person for actual names, addresses, and other qualifying information about prospective customers he knows. Also ask the customer if he would write a referral note or letter that you could use.

Reality Selling Video Case Problem

Dave Levitt, featured at the beginning of this chapter, is a regional sales manager for Salesforce.com. The CRM solution provider is exclusively a cloud-computing vendor offering hosted applications. This model sets the company apart from competitors such as SAP, Oracle, or Microsoft, who are predominantly on-premise providers. Cloud-computing systems have a high degree of flexibility as they can be customized for each individual account and implemented within a very short time frame. Salesforce.com's unique selling proposition is therefore closely linked to the speed with which a client can gain the benefit: Cloud-computing implementation times are typically weeks or months, whereas competitive on-premise solutions can take years to be implemented. Therefore, the total cost of ownership is much lower, and the ROI is much higher and comes in faster.

Before getting in touch with a prospect, Levitt's sales representatives typically spend a substantial amount of time preparing for a sales call and keeping up with news releases. Such upfront investigative work is necessary to uncover such things as changes in top management or factors that are driving a company to change a business model. Working for a CRM company, Salesforce.com's salespeople have comprehensive access to additional news and information about each of their customers and prospects. Hence, by the time representatives have decided to pick up the phone to prospect, they already have a sense for why they are calling and what the value proposition is going to be specifically for that account.

For providers of enterprise software solutions, it is important to have contacts and relationships with three different types of individuals within the prospective customer company: (1) executive financial influencers who have ultimate responsibility for the budget and the project itself, (2) a coach who can give guidance on a day-to-day basis, and (3) IT specialists who can facilitate the process and who would be the custodians after the implementation of the solution. Therefore, the sales representative has to be an orchestrator of resources within Salesforce.com for different buying influencers in the prospect's organization at different points in the sales cycle. For example, the salesperson would include a technical employee from Salesforce.com as part of the sales team who could apply the customer's needs to the product itself and perform demonstrations of software. One would also need to incorporate an internal sales executive that aligns with the customer's executive. Furthermore, the internal services organization or a third-party implementation partner is needed to explain and execute the implementation of the product. There could also be a wide variety of other specialists, depending on which specific tasks have to be accomplished.

Typically, the sales representative would start to qualify the opportunity through conversations with the coach. Using various questioning techniques during the initial discovery process, the sales representative has to understand the following: What is the prospect's business model? Why might the prospect be interested in our offerings? What is their problem and how big is it? What is the complexity of the problem the prospect is trying to address? Will there be a good fit? Is it worth investing the time and money it takes to win the account? What is their time frame? How are they going to measure success?

If the initial discovery shows that the problem can be addressed, the sales representative would then ask for access to the ultimate decision maker and all the other key stakeholders. Then she would perform a similar discovery as was done with the first person (i.e., the coach), constantly trying to qualify the value of the service solution offering and making sure that it is worth pursuing the opportunity (as, for large opportunities, it could be a one-year investment to win it). So the sales representative has to make sure and qualify that (1) it is a legitimate opportunity, (2) it can be won, and (3) it is worth winning. As Levitt emphasizes, it has to be a win-win perspective: "We do not sell a commodity, but a specialty. We do not compete on price alone, but on quality and value." (See the chapter opener on page 195 and Reality Selling Today Role Play 7 in Appendix 1 on page 434 for more information.)

Questions

1. Imagine you are in the position of Dave Levitt, selling CRM services to different business clients. What would be the most promising sources of prospects for you?
2. What criteria does Dave Levitt use for qualifying the prospect?

3. What questions does Dave Levitt ask to understand the needs of the customer?

4. What product features does Dave Levitt highlight that will help a user of Salesforce.com improve his business?

5. Does it appear that Dave Levitt is utilizing previously collected sales intelligence to impress the potential buyer with insights that are above and beyond the product features and benefits? Please specify.

PART IV

ROLE-PLAY EXERCISE
Developing a Customer Strategy

SCENARIO

You are a sales representative employed by Park Shores Resort and Convention Centre. One of your primary responsibilities is to identify prospects and make sales calls that result in the development of new accounts. During each of these calls, you plan to build a relationship with the customer and describe selected value-added guest services and amenities offered by the Park Shores. You also try to learn as much as possible about the customer's buying process.

CUSTOMER PROFILE

Mohammed Ansari is the founder and Chief Executive Officer of Dynamic Security Inc., a growing high-tech firm with more than 300 employees. The company manufactures and sells security systems for use in residential homes, retail stores, and commercial buildings. According to a recent article in *The Globe and Mail*, Dynamic Security is poised to grow very rapidly in the next year. The article described Mohammed Ansari as a workaholic who usually works 80 hours each week. Delegation does not come easily to this personable, hard-charging entrepreneur.

SALESPERSON PROFILE

You have just completed the Park Shores sales training program and now want to develop some new accounts. In addition to taking care of established customers, you plan to call on at least four new prospects every week.

PRODUCT

Park Shores International is a full-service hotel and convention centre located in Toronto, Ontario. The hotel recently completed a $4.8 million renovation of its meeting and banquet rooms.

INSTRUCTIONS

For this role-play activity, you will meet with Mohammed Ansari, role-played by another student, who appears to be a good prospect. During the first sales call, plan to learn more about Mohammed as an individual and acquire more information about Dynamic Security. This meeting will provide you with the opportunity to begin building a long-term partnership. During the first meeting with a prospect, you like to present a limited amount of important product information. In this case, the length of the appointment is 15 minutes, so you should not try to cover too much information. To prepare for the first sales call, read *Employment Memorandum Number 1* in "Partnership Selling: A Role Play/Simulation" online in the Student Resources section at **www.pearsoncanada.ca/manning**. This memo describes the value-added guest services and amenities offered by Park Shores. For the purpose of this role play, Mohammed Ansari should be considered a consultative process buyer. You can assume that he will need help identifying and evaluating possible solutions. As you prepare for the first call, think about what may take place during future calls. Review the steps in the typical buying process (see Fig. 8.3). Keep in mind that today's more demanding customers are seeking a cluster of satisfactions. Study the Three-Dimension Product Solutions Selling Model (Fig. 7.1) prior to meeting with Mohammed Ansari.

Chapter 10
Approaching the Customer with Adaptive Selling

Learning Objectives

After studying this chapter, you should be able to

1   Describe the three prescriptions that are included in the presentation strategy.

2   Discuss the two-part preapproach process.

3   Describe team presentation strategies.

4   Explain how adaptive selling builds on four broad strategic areas of personal selling.

5   Describe the six main parts of the presentation plan.

6   Explain how to effectively approach the customer.

7   Describe seven ways to convert the prospect's attention and arouse interest.

 Reality Selling Video Series—Alim Hirani/ Hilti Corporation

The worldwide Hilti Group (**www.hilti.com**) specializes in providing leading-edge technology to the global construction industry. With some 20 000 employees in more than 120 countries around the world, Hilti actively pursues a value-added orientation in all of its activities.

As part of this orientation, Hilti puts its new salespeople through a rigorous training curriculum that includes one month of pre-training on Hilti products and services, three weeks of intensive training in product and services sales, and two weeks on software applications. In addition, these salespeople also ride along with experienced sales managers to get hands-on experience. Furthermore, the company offers refresher courses to keep its salespeople updated on Hilti's products and services, the construction market, and corporate strategy. Equipped with this in-depth knowledge and the value orientation that is deeply rooted in the corporate culture, salespeople like Alim Hirani (on the right in the photo at the top of the next page) are always well prepared to approach customers to make sales presentations, demonstrate and explain Hilti's products and services, and show the customers both the tangible and intangible benefits that Hilti can offer.

Alim Hirani

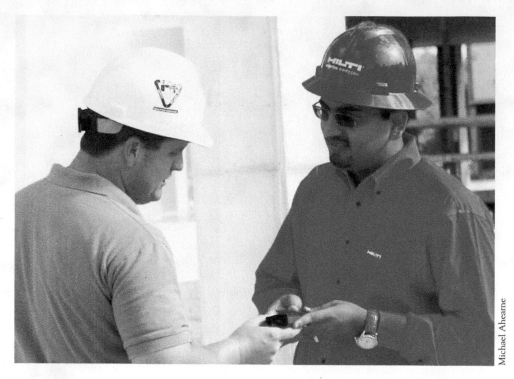

Michael Ahearne

With a direct sales model, Hilti relies heavily on its salespeople to make the connection and deliver its values to its global customers. Alim is a strong believer that he and his sales team are the face of the company. His credibility is embedded in Hilti's credibility and vice versa. He always makes sure that his sales presentations are well prepared in advance. More importantly, he builds and maintains rapport with his customers from the very beginning of the business relationship because such partnership mentality motivates the customers to disclose their actual concerns. In the end, customers value only solutions that address their actual needs, and Alim—as a Hilti salesperson—knows that very well.

DEVELOPING THE PRESENTATION STRATEGY

THE PRESENTATION STRATEGY COMBINES ELEMENTS OF THE RELATIONSHIP, PRODUCT, AND customer strategies. Each of the other three strategies must be developed before a salesperson can develop an effective presentation strategy.

The **presentation strategy** is a well-conceived plan that consists of three prescriptions: (1) establishing objectives for the sales presentation, (2) developing the presale presentation plan needed to meet these objectives, and (3) renewing one's commitment to provide outstanding customer service (Fig. 10.1).

The first prescription reminds us that we need to establish one or more objectives for each sales call. High-performance salespeople like Alim Hirani understand that it is often possible to accomplish several things during a single call. A common objective of sales calls is to collect information about the prospect's needs. Another common objective is to develop, build, or sustain a relationship with those who will make the buying decision.

A carefully prepared presentation plan ensures that salespeople will be well organized during the sales presentation and prepared to achieve their objectives. A six-step

presentation strategy A well-conceived plan that consists of three prescriptions: establishing objectives for the sales presentation, preparing the presale presentation plan needed to meet these objectives, and renewing one's commitment to provide outstanding customer service.

Strategic/Consultative Selling Model*	
Strategic step	**Prescription**
Develop a personal selling philosophy	☑ Adopt marketing concept ☑ Value personal selling ☑ Become a problem solver/partner
Develop a relationship strategy	☑ Maintain high ethical standards ☑ Project professional image ☑ Manage the relationship process
Develop a product strategy	☑ Become a product expert ☑ Sell benefits ☑ Configure value-added solutions
Develop a customer strategy	☑ Understand the buying process ☑ Understand buyer behaviour ☑ Develop prospect base
Develop a presentation strategy	☐ Prepare objectives ☐ Develop presentation plan ☐ Provide outstanding service

* Strategic/consualtive selling evolved in response to increased competition, more complex products, increased emphasis on customer needs, and the growing importance of long-term relationships.

Figure 10.1 The Strategic/Consultative Selling Model
This model provides the foundation for a value-added consultative presentation strategy.

presentation plan is introduced later in this chapter. Establishment of objectives for the sales presentation and preparation of the presale presentation plan must be guided by a strong desire to offer outstanding customer service. Achieving excellence is the result of careful needs analysis, correct product selection, clear presentations, informative demonstrations, win-win negotiations, and flawless service after the sale. Salespeople who are committed to doing their best in each of these areas will be richly rewarded.

Presentation Strategy Adds Value

How does precall planning add value? Value is added when you position yourself as a resource—not just a vendor. You must prove that you have important ideas and advice to offer.[1] A well-planned presentation adds value when it is based on carefully developed sales call objectives and on a presentation plan created to meet those objectives. Good planning ensures that the presentation is customized and adapted to meet the needs and time constraints of the prospect. Increasingly, customers' time is very limited and they want a concise and thoughtful presentation. Careful planning is the key to delivering more value and increasing your sales productivity.[2]

Salespeople need to be aware of the changing needs of their customers or risk losing out to their competition. Some salespeople do not pay enough attention to how they conduct business with their established customers. Without a precall plan, it's easy to miss opportunities to increase your knowledge of the customer's business, sell new products, or discover ways to improve service.[3]

PLANNING THE PREAPPROACH

PREPARATION FOR THE ACTUAL SALES PRESENTATION IS A TWO-PART PROCESS. PART ONE IS referred to as the **preapproach**. The preapproach involves preparing presale objectives and developing a presale presentation plan. Part two is called the **approach** and involves making a favourable first impression, securing the prospect's attention, and transitioning to need identification (Fig. 10.2). The preapproach and approach, when handled correctly, establish a foundation for an effective sales presentation.

The preapproach should be viewed as a key step in preparing for each sales presentation. Professional salespeople complete the preapproach for every presentation whether it involves a new account or an established customer. Top salespeople often spend two or

preapproach Activities that precede the actual sales call and set the stage for a personalized sales approach, tailored to the specific needs of the prospect. This involves the planning necessary for the actual meeting with a prospect.

approach The first contact with the prospect, either face-to-face or by telephone. The approach has three objectives: to build rapport with the prospect, to capture the person's full attention, and to generate interest in the product you are selling.

Figure 10.2 Preparing for the Presentation
Preparing for the presentation involves planning for the activities that occur before meeting the prospect and for the first few minutes of actual contact with the prospect.

three hours planning for a 25-minute sales call. The preapproach includes the first two prescriptions for developing a presentation strategy: establishing objectives and creating a presale presentation plan.

Establishing Presentation Objectives

Preparation for a sales call is part research, part planning, and part critical thinking. Sales representatives employed by Nalco Chemical Company prepare for each sales call by filling out a 13-point precall planner. One section of this form requires the salesperson to identify the objectives of the call. Nalco is a company that emphasizes professionalism, long-term partnerships, and staying focused on customer needs.[4]

In Chapter 8, we introduced the five stages of the typical buying process (see Fig. 8.3). When you are calling on a *consultative* or *strategic alliance* buyer, you will usually not cover all of these stages during a single sales call. Multi-call sales presentations are especially common in complex sales. Therefore, it's best to develop presentation objectives suitable for each stage of the buying process. During the first stage—need awareness—prospects may or may not be aware of their needs or problems. The need awareness stage is the "investigation" stage. Uncovering and clarifying needs will require the use of appropriate questions (covered in detail in Chapter 11). The following presentation objectives would be appropriate during the first call on a new prospect:

- Establish rapport and begin building a relationship with the prospect.
- Obtain permission to ask need identification questions.
- Obtain personal and business information to establish the customer's profile.

During stage two of the buying process—evaluation of solutions—the customer is ready to consider possible solutions. In some cases, there may be several solutions that must be evaluated. Presentation objectives for stage two might include the following:

- Involve the customer in a product demonstration.
- Provide value justification in terms of cost reduction and increased revenues.
- Compare and contrast the features of, for example, a truck fleet lease plan with a fleet purchase plan.

Every sales call should have an **action objective**. An action objective is something that you want the customer to do during the sales presentation: provide specific financial information; schedule a visit to your manufacturing plant; agree to a trial use of your product; agree to a follow-up meeting; or place an order. An action objective brings a sharp focus to the sales presentation.[5]

action objective Something that you want the customer to do during the sales presentation.

Once you have an appointment with the prospect and the presentation objectives have been established, consider sending a fax or email message that outlines the agenda for the meeting. This will confirm the appointment and clarify the topics to be discussed.[6]

Multi-call sales presentations are common in many areas, including the retail field. The sale of recreational vehicles, leased automobiles, boats, and quality sound systems for home or business typically require more than one sales call. High-end clothing companies, retail stores, and independent tailors make office calls to sell tailored clothing. One example is Tom James Clothing introduced in Chapter 1. This progressive retailer, with a reputation for superior customer service, makes office calls upon request. Working with a customer at his office usually requires more than one sales call.[7]

Approaching Prospects in Relationship-Focused Countries

In most countries of the world, business is conducted through established relationships and social networks. People in relationship-focused countries—including most of Africa, Central and South America, Arab countries, and the Asia/Pacific region—prefer to do business after personal relationships and trust have been established. It is often difficult to approach prospects directly in these countries, so, if you are trying to make new contacts, you may need a third-party introduction to help bridge the relationship gap. You may use trade associations, chambers of commerce, banks, or even consultants who specialize in arranging introductions in some countries. Attending international trade shows is one of the best ways to make foreign contacts—people attend these shows expressly to make business connections. Another increasingly popular method is to participate in a trade mission. The Department of Foreign Affairs and International Trade (DFAIT) plans, coordinates, and executes trade missions—sometimes led by the prime minister of Canada—to promote Canadian businesses abroad. In recent years, trade missions have been supported by governments at all levels: federal, provincial or territorial, and municipal.[a]

Team Presentation Strategies

In today's ever-changing business environment, team selling has surfaced as a major development. Team selling is ideally suited to organizations that sell complex or customized products and services that require direct communication between customers and technical experts. Sales teams can often uncover problems, solutions, and sales opportunities

Team Selling, Buying Committees, and "Chatter"

Sales of complex or customized products and services invariably involve two teams of people—the selling team and the buying committee or team. Important communications occur between and among members of the two teams. Information about technical and financial matters, information technology, facilities management, and other sales-related issues is exchanged throughout the sales process. Salesforce.com has introduced a system called "Chatter" to facilitate collaborative communication throughout the sales process.

Chatter is linked to the Salesforce.com CRM system and incorporates the benefits of social media. Chatter is a secure, cloud-based online service similar to most social media systems. Members of both teams may create personal profiles. Those creating profiles may introduce themselves in a manner similar to, for example, introductions on Facebook. This personalizes the people working together and makes it easy for anyone with access in both companies to get acquainted with everyone involved in the sales transaction. Users can follow selected personnel in either company, sort the profiles by expertise, and form networks of specialists. Messages are easily transmitted among all participants and recorded for reviewing later. Although it appears to be social media, wise users should retain a "casual business" writing style and avoid too much informality.

Chatter conversations can pertain to specific subjects so users receive real-time news feeds and participate in the development of each part of the solution. This creates value for the total transaction in that anyone in the buying company not involved in the solution development, such as a board of directors, can review the exchanges to understand the results achieved. Sections of the Chatter system are for people within the selling company to confidentially comment and exchange ideas on how to best solve problems and move the sale ahead. When it is time for the sales presentation, everyone following Chatter's continuous collaboration will be well prepared to confirm that the proposed solution is a good fit. The presentation contributions by sales team members can be better organized and coordinated. For more information, go to **salesforce.com/chatter**.

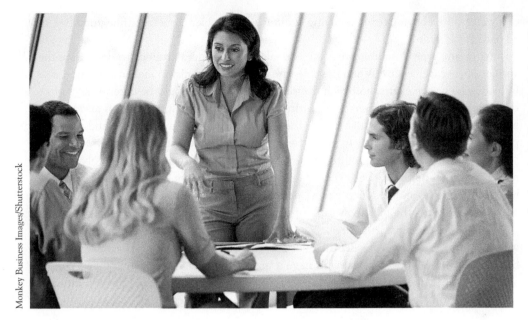

Monkey Business Images/Shutterstock

that an individual salesperson working alone might not discover.[8] In some situations, the involvement of technical experts can shorten the selling cycle. The team approach often results in more precise need identification, improved selection of the product, and more informative sales presentations.

Team sales presentations require a more detailed precall plan than individual sales calls. Each team member must have a clear understanding of the role he or she will play during the sales call. Sales presentation objectives should be clearly stated. Team members should share detailed information about the customer, understand the basics of a consultative sales presentation, and be prepared to add value.[9]

Companies that have moved to team sales have discovered that this approach is not easily executed. At Hickok Cole Architects, team selling is the primary approach used to obtain new accounts. However, the team selling process was not easily mastered by staff members. Determining who would communicate when, and determining how presentations would fall into place seamlessly, took months of practice among the company's teams, which often consisted of six or more people. Without sufficient practice, the staff at Hickok Cole discovered that team presentations were sometimes disorganized.[10]

A variation of the team approach to selling is used by some marketers. Salespeople are trained to seek the assistance of another salesperson or to actually turn the customer over to another salesperson when problems surface. The other salesperson may bring to the selling situation a greater ability to identify the customer's needs or to select the appropriate product. Salespeople who have well-prepared presale objectives know when to seek assistance from another professional.

Strategies for Selling to a Buying Committee

In some cases, salespeople must address and satisfy both the individual and collective concerns of each participant in a multi-buyer situation. The decision makers may be members of a well-trained buying team, a buying committee assembled for a one-time purchase, or a board of directors.

As in any type of selling situation, the salesperson should attempt to determine the various buying influences. When possible, the role of each decision maker, the amount of influence he or she exerts, and each decision maker's needs should be determined before the presentation. Careful observation during the presentation can reveal who may use the product (user influencer), who controls the finances (financial influencer), and who can provide the expertise necessary to make the correct buying decision (technical influencer).

When you make a group selling presentation, make sure all parties feel involved. Any member of the group who feels ignored could prevent you from closing the sale. Be sure to direct questions and comments to all potential decision makers in the group. As early as possible, identify the most powerful influences.

Find out if there are any silent team or committee members. A *silent member* is one who will influence the buying decision but does not attend the presentation. Silent members are usually senior managers who have a major influence on the buying decision. If a silent member does exist, you must find a way to communicate, directly or indirectly, with this person.[11]

Adaptive Selling: Builds on Four Strategic Areas of Personal Selling

At the very heart of *adaptive selling* is the belief that every sales call must be tailored to the unique needs, wants, and concerns of the customer. As noted in Chapter 5, adaptive selling involves altering sales behaviours in order to improve communication with the customer. Better identifying and responding to the customer's needs frequently requires complex behavioural adjustments before and during the sales call. These adjustments are based on the relationship needs and product needs of the customer. Salespeople today must develop a broader repertoire of selling strategies and apply more effective information-acquisition skills.[12]

The strategic planning that takes place during the preapproach can greatly enhance the adaptive selling process. This plan includes *strategies* that you use to position yourself with the customers and *tactics* you will use when you are face-to-face with a customer. Planning the approach involves consideration of how the *relationship, product,* and *customer* strategies can enhance the sales presentation.

Review the Relationship Strategy As noted in Chapter 5, salespeople need to think of everything they say or do in the context of their relationship with the customer. Customers want a quality product and a quality relationship. Building and nourishing a long-term partnership with the customer often begins with attention to many small details. Confirming an appointment with a brief email message and arriving for the appointment a few minutes early sends a positive message to the customer before the first face-to-face meeting.

The first contact between a salesperson and a prospect is very important. A positive or negative first impression can be formed in a matter of seconds. The customer is receiving a variety of verbal and nonverbal messages that can either facilitate or detract from the sales call. Your behaviours and appearance create an image that others observe and remember. Identification of the customer's preferred communication style should be given a high priority during the initial contact. Once you are in the presence of the customer,

Michael Ahearne

The strategic planning and preparation that takes place during the preapproach can greatly enhance the adaptive selling process. This planning includes a clear understanding of the relationship, product, and customer strategies. This planning and preparation enabled Lana and her sales team to create a presentation strategy that met the relationship and product needs of Ron, one of her largest customers.

absorb the many clues that will help you with style identification. Then use *style flexing* to accommodate the needs of that person.

Review the Product Strategy During the preapproach, you will learn some new things about the potential customer. You will no doubt acquire information that did not surface during the prospecting stage. If this is the case, it pays to take another look at your product. Now it will be easier to identify features with special appeal to the person you are calling on. In addition, you can more accurately identify questions that the prospect might raise.

Product knowledge, combined with knowledge of the customer, builds confidence. Salespeople who are confident in their ability to alter the sales approach as needed are much better prepared to engage in adaptive selling.[13] Customers today are anxious to do business with salespeople who have developed "expert power."

Review the Customer Strategy Personal selling provides us with the opportunity to apply the marketing concept during every contact with the customer. All energies can be directed toward an individual who is likely to think and act differently from anyone else. Customers today have become increasingly sophisticated in their buying strategies. They have higher expectations for value-added products and long-term commitments. A customer strategy focuses on understanding the customer's needs, wants, and buying conditions. A careful review of the information contained in the prospect database is an essential part of reviewing the customer strategy. With this understanding, adaptive selling strategies are formulated to meet both the relationship and product needs of the customer.

DEVELOPING THE SIX-STEP PRESENTATION PLAN

Once you have established objectives for the sales presentation, the next step (prescription) involves developing the presentation plan. This plan helps you achieve your objectives. Today, with increased time constraints, fierce competition, and rising travel costs, the opportunity for a face-to-face meeting with customers may occur less frequently. The few minutes you have with your customers may be your only opportunity to win their business, so careful planning is more critical than ever.

Planning the Presentation

Once you have sufficient background information, you are ready to develop a "customized" presale presentation plan. Preparing a customized sales presentation can take a great deal of time and energy. Nevertheless, this attention to detail gives you added confidence and helps you avoid delivering unconvincing hit-or-miss sales talks. The plan is developed after a careful review of the **six-step presentation plan** (Fig. 10.3). In most cases, the sales process includes the following activities:

1. *Approach.* Preparation for the approach involves making decisions concerning effective ways to make a favourable first impression during the initial contact, to secure the prospect's attention, and to develop the prospect's interest in the product. The approach should set the stage for an effective sales presentation.

The Six-Step Presentation Plan	
Step One: Approach	☐ Review Strategic/Consultative Selling Model ☐ Initiate customer contact
Step Two: Need Discovery	☐ Ask strategic questions ☐ Determine customer needs ☐ Select product solution
Step Three: Presentation	☐ Select presentation strategy ☐ Create presentation plan ☐ Initiate presentation
Step Four: Negotiation	☐ Anticipate buyer concerns ☐ Plan negotiating methods ☐ Initiate win-win negotiations
Step Five: Close	☐ Plan appropriate closing methods ☐ Recognize closing clues ☐ Initiate closing methods
Step Six: Servicing the Sale	☐ Follow through ☐ Follow-up calls ☐ Expansion selling

Service, retail, wholesale, and manufacturer selling

Figure 10.3 The Six-Step Presentation Plan
A presale plan is a logical and orderly outline that features a salesperson's thoughts from one step to the next in the presentation. Each step in this plan is explained in Chapters 10 to 15.

2. *Need discovery*. The need discovery process is one of the most critical parts of the selling process. If the salesperson is unable to discover the prospect's buying needs and select a product solution that meets those needs, the sale may be lost. Chapter 11 covers all aspects of the need discovery process and selecting products that meet individual needs.

3. *Presentation*. Three types of need-satisfaction presentation strategies are available to adapt the sales presentation to the needs of the prospect. After deciding which strategy to use, the salesperson carefully prepares the presentations following the guidelines presented. Selling tools or proof devices are used to demonstrate and document the benefits presented. Chapter 12 is devoted exclusively to adapting presentations to meet customer needs.

4. *Negotiation*. Buyer resistance is a natural part of the selling–buying process. An objection, however, does present a barrier to closing the sale. For this reason, all salespeople should become skilful at negotiating resistance. Chapter 13 covers this topic.

5. *Close*. As the sales presentation progresses, there may be several opportunities to close the sale. Salespeople must learn to spot closing clues. Chapter 14 provides suggestions on how to close sales.

6. *Servicing the sale*. The importance of developing a long-term relationship with the prospect was noted in previous chapters. This rapport is often the outgrowth of post-sale service. Learning to service the sale is an important aspect of selling. Chapter 15 deals with activities that build value-adding partnerships.

Adapting the Presentation Plan to the Customer's Buying Process

A truly valuable idea or concept is timeless. The six parts of the presale presentation plan checklist have been discussed in sales training literature for many years; therefore, they might be described as fundamentals of personal selling. These steps are basic elements of most sales and frequently occur in the same sequence. However, the activities included in the six-step presentation plan must be selected with care. Prior to developing the sales call plan, the salesperson must answer one very important question: Do these activities relate to the customer's buying process? As noted in Chapter 8, purchasing structures and buying procedures can vary greatly from company to company. In some cases, the steps in the buying process have been clearly defined by the organization and this information is available to vendors. Selling steps are of little value *unless* they are firmly rooted in your customer's buying process.[14]

THE APPROACH

After a great deal of preparation, it is time to communicate with the prospect, either by face-to-face contact, by telephone, or by some other appropriate method of communication. We refer to the initial contact with the customer as the *approach*. A high-quality and professional approach is a powerful way to add value and differentiate yourself from your competitors.[15] All the effort you have put into developing relationship, product, and customer strategies can now be applied to the presentation strategy. If the approach is effective, you will be given the opportunity to make the sales presentation. If, however, the approach is not effective, the chance to present your sales story may be lost. You can be the best-prepared salesperson in the business but without a good approach, there may be little chance for a sale.

The approach has three important objectives. First, you want to build rapport with the prospect. This will be accomplished with your *telephone and/or social contact*. Second, you want to capture the person's full attention with your *business contact*. These first two steps are extremely important in establishing how much *influence* you will have throughout the rest of the sales process. Never begin your sales story if the prospect seems preoccupied and is not paying attention. Third, you want to *transition to the next stage of the sales process*. In the early part of the sales process, this will likely be the need discovery; in multi-call presentations it may be one of the other stages in the sales process such as the presentation, negotiations, or closing the sale. In some selling situations, the first contact with the customer is a telephone call. The call is made to schedule a meeting or, in some cases, to conduct the sales presentation. The face-to-face sales call starts with the social contact and continues with the business contact. The telephone contact, social contact, and business contact are discussed in this section.

Establish Your Credibility Early During your approach, everything you do affects the amount of credibility and influence you will have throughout the sales process. Your actions will either increase your perceived value or detract from it.[16] Thomas A. Freese (**www.qbsresearch.com**), author of *Secrets of Question Based Selling*, says credibility is critical to your success in sales. Credibility is an impression that people form of you very early in the sales process.[17] Sometimes little things can erode your credibility before you have a chance to prove yourself. Strategic communications consultant and executive coach Mark Jeffries (**www.markjeffries.com**), in a new training video called *The Art of Networking*, provides examples regarding how misspelled words or grammatical errors in an email, arriving late for an appointment, answering a cell phone or reading an email while with a customer, failing to maintain good eye contact, acknowledging only certain members of a buying group, or failing to send the prospect information that was promised can quickly weaken the amount of influence you have in a relationship. Failure to be well prepared for the sales call will also undermine your credibility. Credibility grows when the customer realizes you are a competent sales representative who can add value throughout the sales process.

The Telephone Contact

A telephone call provides a quick and inexpensive method of scheduling an appointment. Appointments are important because many busy prospects will not meet with a salesperson who drops in unannounced. When you schedule an appointment, the prospect knows about the sales call in advance and can therefore make the necessary preparations.

Some salespeople use the telephone exclusively to establish and maintain contact with the customer. As noted in Chapter 1, inside salespeople rely almost totally on the telephone for sales. **Telesales**—not to be confused with *telemarketing*—includes many of the same elements as traditional sales: gathering customer information, determining needs, prescribing solutions, negotiating buyer concerns, and closing sales. Telesales calls are usually unscripted, as opposed to the scripted calls widely used in

telesales Using the telephone to acquire information about the customer, determine needs, suggest solutions, negotiate buyer concerns, and close the sale.

telemarketing. In some situations, telesales calls are as dynamic and unpredictable as face-to-face sales calls.

In Chapter 4 we examined some of the factors that influence the meaning we attach to an oral message from another person. With the aid of this information, we can see that communication via telephone is challenging. Since the person who receives the call cannot see our facial expressions, gestures, or posture, he or she must rely wholly on the sound of our voice and the words used. The telephone caller has a definite handicap.

The telephone has some additional limitations. A salesperson accustomed to meeting prospects in person may find telephone contact impersonal. Some salespeople try to avoid using the telephone because they believe it is too easy for the prospect to say no. It should be noted that these drawbacks are more imagined than real. With proper training, a salesperson can use the telephone effectively to schedule appointments. When you make an appointment by telephone, use the following practices:

1. *Plan in advance what you will say.* It helps to use a written presentation plan as a guide during the first few seconds of the conversation. What you will say is determined by the objectives of the sales call. Have a calendar available to suggest and confirm a date, time, and place for the appointment. Be sure to write it down.

2. *Politely identify yourself and the company you represent.* Set yourself apart from other callers by using a friendly tone and impeccable phone manners. This approach helps you avoid being shut out by a wary gatekeeper (secretary or receptionist).

3. *State the purpose of your call and explain how the prospect can benefit from a meeting.* In some cases, it is helpful to use a powerful benefits statement that gets the prospect's attention and whets the person's appetite for more information. Present only enough information to stimulate interest.

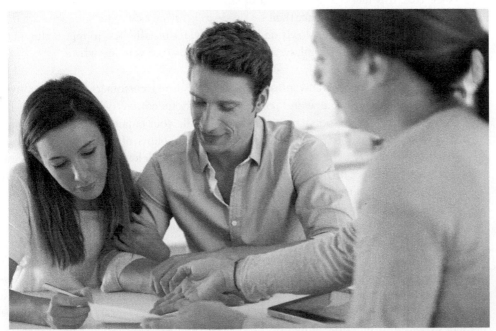

Capturing the customer's full attention is a major objective of the approach. Attention has become a very scarce resource in today's fast-paced world.

Goodluz/Shutterstock

4. *Show respect for the prospect's time by telling the person how long the appointment will take.* Once the prospect agrees to meet with you, say, "Do you have your appointment calendar handy?" Be prepared to suggest a specific time: "Is Monday at 9:00 a.m. okay?"

5. *Confirm the appointment with a brief note, email message, or letter with the date, time, and place of your appointment.* Enclose your business card and any printed information that may be of interest to the prospect.[18]

You should anticipate resistance from some prospects. After all, most decision makers are very busy. Be persistent and persuasive if you genuinely believe a meeting with the prospect can be mutually beneficial.

Effective Use of Voice Mail The growing popularity of voice mail presents a challenge to salespeople. What type of message sets the stage for a second call or stimulates a return call? It's important to anticipate voice mail and know exactly what to say if you reach a recording. The prospect's perception of you is based on what you say and on voice quality. The following message almost guarantees that it will be ignored:

> Ms. Simpson, I am Paul Watson and I am with Elliott Property Management Services. I would like to visit with you about our services. Please call me at 555-1500.[19]

Note that this message provides no compelling reason for the prospect to call back. It offers no valid information that would stimulate interest. The voice-mail message should be similar to the opening statement you would make if you had face-to-face contact with the prospect:

> Ms. Simpson, my name is Paul Watson and I represent Elliott Property Management Services. We specialize in working with property managers. We can help you reduce the paperwork associated with maintenance jobs and provide an easy way to track the progress of each job. I would like the opportunity to visit with you and will call back in the morning.[20]

Note that this message is brief and describes benefits that customers can receive. If Paul Watson wants a call back, then he needs to give the best time to reach him. He should give his phone number slowly and completely. It's usually best to repeat the number. If you are acting on a referral, be sure to say who referred you and why.

Effective Use of Email Many prospects and established customers like the convenience of email correspondence and prefer it to telephone contact. Your challenge is to make it easy for your correspondents to read and handle your email. Always use a meaningful, specific subject line. People who receive large amounts of email may selectively choose which ones to read by scanning the subject lines and deleting those of no interest. An email with a subject line titled "Action Steps from Our 9/28 Meeting" is more likely to be read than a subject line like "Meeting Notes."[21]

The email message should tell the reader what you want and then encourage a response. Identify the main point of your email within the first or second paragraph. Format the email so it's easy to read. This may require the use of headings (with capitals or boldface print) to identify the main elements of the memo. Proofread all emails for proper grammar, punctuation, and spelling.[22] Always use the grammar and spell check tools. Messages that contain errors may misrepresent your competence. Finally, use a signature file—a small block of text that automatically follows each email you send. A typical signature file includes your full name, title, affiliation, and phone number, and in some cases a slogan.

The goal of good social contact is to build rapport. Building rapport leads to credibility, which leads to trust. Once trust is established, the customer is likely to open up and share information.

StockLite/Shutterstock

The Social Contact—Building Rapport

According to many image consultants, "First impressions are lasting impressions." This statement is essentially true, and some profitable business relationships never crystallize because some trait or characteristic of the salesperson repels the prospective customer. Sales personnel have only a few minutes to create a positive first impression. Susan Bixler, author of *The New Professional Image*, describes the importance of the first impression this way:

> Books are judged by their covers, houses are appraised by their curb appeal, and people are initially evaluated on how they choose to dress and behave. In a perfect world this is not fair, moral, or just. What's inside should count a great deal more. And eventually it usually does, but not right away. In the meantime, a lot of opportunities can be lost.[23]

Planning Personal Visits Using CRM

Personally visiting prospects and customers helps build strong relationships, yet travelling is expensive and time consuming. A salesperson is challenged to plan visits that optimize the investment represented by each trip. Access to customer relationship management (CRM) contact records helps salespeople quickly identify all the accounts in a given geographic area that can be visited during one trip.

CRM empowers salespeople to rapidly review and compare an area's contacts on the basis of their stage in the sales process, the potential size of the account or purchase, the likelihood of a sale, and the contribution the visit could make to information gathering and relationship building. A well-managed CRM database provides salespeople with appropriate business and social topics to discuss when calling selected prospects for an appointment.

Building rapport should lead to credibility, which leads to trust. Once trust is established, the prospect is likely to open up and share information. This information will provide clues regarding ways to create value. To be certain that your first impression is appropriate, review the material in Chapters 3, 4, and 5. The information in those chapters is timeless and will serve you well today and in the future.

The brief, general conversation during the social contact should hold the prospect's attention and establish a relaxed and friendly atmosphere for the business contact that is to follow. As mentioned in Chapter 4, there are three areas of conversation that should be considered in developing a social contact:

1. *Comments on here-and-now observations*. These comments may include general observations about the victory of a local athletic team, an article in *The Globe and Mail*, or specific comments about awards on display in the prospect's office. Janis Taylor, sales representative with Trugreen Chemlawn, likes to start each new appointment by seeking "common ground" with her prospects. She looks for such items as a picture of the prospect's children or a trophy.[24]

2. *Compliments*. Most customers will react positively to sincere compliments. Personal items in the prospect's office, achievements, or efficient operation of the prospect's business provide examples of things that can be praised. A salesperson might say, "I learned recently that your company is ranked number one in customer satisfaction by J. D. Power and Associates."

3. *Search for mutual acquaintances or interests*. Discovering that you have mutual friends or interests can serve as the foundation for a strong social contact. Most people enjoy talking about themselves, their hobbies, and their achievements. Debra Fine, author of *The Fine Art of Small Talk*, says, "Small talk isn't stupid. It's the appetizer for all relationships."[25]

Guidelines for Good Social Contact The social contact should be viewed as rapport-building communication on a personal basis. This brief conversation establishes the foundation for the business contact, so it should never be viewed as an insignificant part of the presentation strategy. The following guidelines can help you develop the skills needed to make a good social contact.

1. *Prepare for the social contact*. Conduct a background check on topics of interest to the person you are contacting. This includes reviewing information in the prospect database, reading industry reports, and searching the Internet. Once you arrive at the customer's office, you will discover additional information about the person's interests. Most people communicate what is important to them in the way they personalize their work environment.

2. *Initiate social contact*. The most effective opening comments should be expressed in the form of an open-ended question, such as, "I understand you have just been elected president of the United Way?" You can improve the possibility of a good response to your verbal question by applying nonverbal communication skills. Appropriate eye contact, voice inflections that communicate enthusiasm, and a warm smile will increase the customer's receptivity to your opening comments.

3. *Respond to the customer's conversations*. When the customer responds, it is imperative that you acknowledge the message both verbally and nonverbally. The verbal

response might be "That is really interesting" or any other appropriate comment. Nonverbally, let the customer know you are listening by taking notes, maintaining good eye contact, and occasionally nodding your head. These gestures communicate that you want her to continue talking.

4. *Keep the social contact focused on the customer.* Because you cannot control where a conversation might go, you may be tempted to focus the conversation on topics with which you are familiar. A response such as, "Several years ago I was in charge of our company's United Way campaign and we had a difficult time meeting our goal" shifts the focus of the conversation back to you. While an occasional short personal reference may be appropriate, it is best to keep the conversation focused on topics that are of interest to the customer. Dale Carnegie said that one of the best ways to build a relationship is to encourage others to talk about themselves.

Communication on a personal basis is often the first step in establishing a common language that can improve communication between the salesperson and the prospect. How much time should be devoted to the social contact? There is no easy answer to this question. The length of the conversation will depend on the type of product or service sold, how busy the prospect appears to be, and your awareness of topics of mutual interest.

In many cases, the rapport-building conversation will take place over lunch or dinner. Some sales professionals contend that social conversation should occur before the meal is served, reserving business conversation until later. In some cases, it may be during a sporting event, such as a golf outing. It may also occur during a social event, such as a live theatre play that is offered in appreciation of prior or future business. Many successful sales have been closed during or after a social event. This explains why some companies enrol their sales staff and other customer contact personnel in dining etiquette classes.

The Business Contact

Converting the prospect's attention from the social contact to the business proposal is an important part of the approach. When you convert and hold your prospect's attention, you have fulfilled an important step in the selling process. Furthermore, without this step, the door has been closed on completing the remaining steps of the sale.

Some salespeople use a carefully planned opening statement or a question to attract the customer's attention to the sales presentation. A statement or question that focuses on the prospect's dominant buying motive is, of course, more likely to achieve the desired results. Buyers must like what they see and hear, and must be made to feel that it will be worthwhile to hear more.

CONVERTING THE BUYER'S ATTENTION AND AROUSING INTEREST

THROUGHOUT THE YEARS, SALESPEOPLE HAVE IDENTIFIED AND USED A NUMBER OF EFFECTIVE ways to capture the prospect's attention and arouse interest in the presentation. Seven of the most common will be explained in the following material:

■ Agenda approach
■ Product demonstration approach

- Referral approach
- Customer benefit approach
- Question approach
- Survey approach
- Premium approach

We also discuss combining two or more of these approaches.

Agenda Approach One of the most effective ways to move from the social contact to the business contact is to thank the customer for taking time to meet with you and then review your goals for the meeting. You might say, "Thank you for meeting with me this morning. I would like to accomplish three things during the time you have given me." This statement shows that you value the person's time and have preplanned a specific agenda. Always be open to changing the agenda based on suggestions from the customer.[26] This approach is welcomed by buyers in multi-call situations.

Product Demonstration Approach This straightforward method of getting the prospect's attention can be achieved by showing the actual product, a sample, a mock-up, a video, or a well-prepared brochure either in print form or on a computer screen. It is a popular approach used by sales representatives who sell convention services, technical products, pharmaceuticals, photographic equipment, automobiles, construction equipment, office furniture, and many other products. In many multi-call situations, salespeople leave samples for the customer to examine and try at a later date. Trish Ormsby, a sales representative who sells security systems, uses her portable computer to create a visual image of systems that meet the customer's security needs.[27]

Referral Approach Research indicates that another person will be far more impressed with your good points if these points are presented by a third party rather than by you. The referral approach is quite effective because a third party—a satisfied customer—believes the prospect will benefit from your product. This type of opening statement has universal appeal among salespeople from nearly every field. When you use the referral approach, your opening statement should include a direct reference to the third party. Here is an example: "Mrs. Follett, my name is Kurt Wheeler, and I represent the Cross Printing Company. We specialize in printing all types of business forms. Mr. Ameno—buyer for Raybale Products, Incorporated—is a regular customer of ours, and he suggested I mention his name to you."

Customer Benefit Approach One of the most effective ways to gain a prospect's attention is to immediately point out benefits of purchasing your solution or value proposition. As noted in Chapter 7, the benefit could focus on either the product, company, or salesperson. Begin with the most important issue (or problem) facing the client. When using this approach, the most important buyer benefit is included in the initial statement. For example, the salesperson selling a portable Sony projector might open with this statement:

> The Sony VPL-CS4 lightweight projector strikes a balance among cost, size, brightness, and convenience. It's a good choice for a quick business trip or for a work-at-home presentation.

Effective Design and Use of the Business Card

The business card continues to be a powerful tool for salespeople. It provides a personal touch in our high-tech world. The business card is a convenient way to communicate important information to customers and others involved in the sales process. When you develop your business card, keep these tips in mind.

- Use eye-catching items such as your company logo, raised letters, and textured paper. The card should be tasteful and pleasing to the eye. Do use a white background.

- The card should feature all current contact information such as your email address, telephone numbers, and mailing address. List a home phone number only if there's a second line for business calls.

- Consider using both sides of the card. You might print your customer service philosophy on the back of the card or list the products you sell.

Give your cards generously to anyone who might need to contact you later. Always offer your business card when networking. The card is useful when the contact tells others about your products or services. How you respond to someone else's business card is important also. According to communications trainer Mark Jeffries, mentioned earlier, when someone hands you their business card, find something about it you can comment on before putting it away. You can comment on things such as the design, the company, or the individual's title. He contends that people will have a favourable memory of you, if done successfully.[b]

A *company benefit* example taken from the financial services field:

> When you meet with a Scotia McLeod investment specialist, you can obtain advice on a family of 48 professionally managed no-load mutual funds.

The customer benefit approach is also used with what is sometimes referred to as the *elevator speech*. The elevator speech focuses on the benefit of working with the salesperson and is used to open the door and establish credibility to meet a need. It is about offering to take excellent care of the prospect. The elevator speech should be short, prepared well in advance, and extensively rehearsed before it is used. It is used most appropriately in the initial call on a prospect where the prequalifying research indicates that the buyer is more interested in the benefits of working with a highly qualified salesperson than finding a new product solution or supplier. Here is an employment services example of a salesperson benefit statement using the elevator speech approach:

> Hello, I'm Kevin Zhang. I partner with companies like yours that need to find talented people to help their business grow and become more profitable.

As noted, the key to achieving success with the customer benefit approach is preparation. Prospects are annoyed when a salesperson cannot quickly communicate the benefits of meeting with them. Bruce Klassen, sales manager for Do All Industrial Supply, says, "Our salespeople begin the sales process by researching the prospect and the company. We need to be sure that our product line is going to benefit that prospect before we make even an initial sales approach."[28]

Question Approach The question approach has two positive features. First, a question almost always triggers prospect involvement. Very few people will avoid answering a direct question. Second, a question gets the prospect thinking about a problem that the salesperson is prepared to solve.

Molly Hoover, a sales training consultant, conducts training classes for sales managers and car dealers who want to better understand the subtleties of selling to the female car buyer. She suggests an approach that includes a few basic questions such as:

Is the vehicle for business or pleasure?
Will you be buying within the next week or so?[29]

These opening need-related questions will be discussed in detail in the next chapter and are generally not difficult to answer, yet they get the customer mentally involved. Some of the best opening questions are carefully phrased to capture attention. The authors of *The Sales Question Book* offer some good examples:

Are you aware that we just added three new services to our payroll and accounting package? Could I tell you about them?
We are now offering all our customers a special service that used to be reserved for our largest accounts. Would you be interested in hearing about it?[30]

Once you ask the question, listen carefully to the response. If the answer is yes, proceed with an enthusiastic presentation of your product. If the answer is no, then you may have to gracefully try another approach or thank the prospect for their time and depart. The use of questions will be discussed in detail in the next chapter and will provide information on the specific types of questions to use to approach your customer.

Survey Approach Astrid Goodman is a Certified Financial Planner (CFP) and a Fellow of the Canadian Securities Institute (FCSI), this latter designation being the highest honour in Canadian financial services. She is also a Chartered Life Underwriter (CLU). Astrid Goodman wears three hats and provides advice in three areas: financial management, investment management, and risk management. When she meets with potential clients, she follows closely the process prescribed by the Financial Planning Standards Council of Canada. Early in the process, she must gather client data to understand the client's goals and expectations. She must also ask a series of questions, perform a number of calculations, and compile reports to determine the client's financial status: where he or she stands currently, including any problems or opportunities that might exist.[31] Data collection through the survey approach is an important part of the problem-solving philosophy of selling. It is often also used in selling office machines, business security systems, and other products where need cannot be established without careful study.

The survey approach offers many advantages. It is generally a nonthreatening way to open a sales call. You are simply asking permission to acquire information that can be used to determine the buyer's need for your product or service. Because the survey is tailor-made for a specific business, the buyer is given individual treatment. Finally, the survey approach helps avoid a premature discussion of price. Price cannot be discussed until the survey is completed and the client's needs are completely understood. We will discuss the survey and needs discovery in detail in Chapter 11.

Premium Approach The premium approach involves giving the customer a free sample or an inexpensive item. A financial services representative might give the customer a booklet that can be used to record expenses. Product samples are frequently used by persons who sell cosmetics. Creative use of premiums is an effective way to get the customer's attention.

The agenda, product demonstration, referral, customer benefit, question, survey, and premium approaches offer the salesperson a variety of ways to set the stage for the

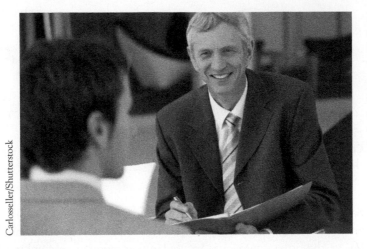

The survey approach offers many advantages. It is generally a non-threatening way to open a sales call. You simply ask permission to acquire information that can be used to determine the buyer's need for the product.

presentation strategy. With experience, salespeople learn to select the most effective approach for each selling situation. Table 10.1 provides examples of how these approaches can be applied in real-world situations.

Combination Approaches A hallmark of consultative selling is flexibility. Therefore, a combination of approaches sometimes provides the best avenue to need identification.

Table 10.1 Business Contact Worksheet

This worksheet illustrates how to prepare effective real-world approaches that capture the customer's attention.

Method of Approach	What will you say?
1. Agenda	1. (Office supply) "Thank you for meeting with me, Ms. Zhou. During the next 45 minutes, I plan to accomplish three things."
2. Product demonstration	2a. (Retail clothing) "We have just received a shipment of new fall sweaters from Braemar International."
	2b. (Business forms manufacturer) "Our plant has just purchased a $300 000 Harris Graphics composer, Mr. Reichart. I would like to show you a copy of your sales invoice with your logo printed on it."
3. Referral	3. (Food wholesaler) "Paula Doeman, procurement manager for St. Joseph's Hospital, suggested that I provide you with information about our computerized 'Order It' system."
4. Customer benefit	4. (Real estate) "Mr. and Mrs. Stuart, my company lists and sells more homes than any other company in the area where your home is located. Our past performance would lead me to believe we can sell your home within two weeks."
5. Question	5. (Hotel convention services) "Mrs. McClaughin, will your 2011 Annual Franchisee Meeting be held in April?"
6. Survey	6a. (Custom-designed computer software) "Mr. Pham, I would like the opportunity to learn about your accounts receivable and accounts payable procedures. We may be able to develop a customized program that will significantly improve your cash flow."
	6b. (Retail menswear) "May I ask you a few questions about your wardrobe? The information will help me better understand your clothing needs."
7. Premium	7. (Financial services) "I would like to give you a publication entitled *Guaranteed Growth Annuity*."

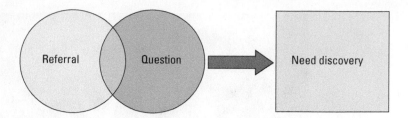

Figure 10.4 Combination Approach
Combination approaches provide a smooth transition to the need discovery part of the consultative-style presentation.

Sales personnel who have adopted the consultative style will, of course, use the question and survey approaches most frequently. Some selling situations, however, require that one of the other approaches be used, either alone or in combination with the question and survey approaches (see Fig. 10.4). An example of how a salesperson might combine referral and question approaches follows:

Salesperson: Carl Hamilton at Simmons Modern Furniture suggested that I visit with you about our new line of compact furniture designed for today's smaller homes. He believes this line might complement the furniture you currently feature.

Customer: Yes, Carl called me yesterday and mentioned your name and company.

Salesperson: Before showing you our product lines, I would like to ask you some questions about your current product mix. First, what do you currently carry in the area of bedroom furniture?

Suggesting the use of a combination approach, noted sales authority Linda Richardson of Richardson Learning Systems advises to "go in armed to the gills with a full portfolio of knowledge, insights, data, and ideas. Use that portfolio to engage customers by sharing insights and asking business challenge questions that show that you know what you are talking about and that lead into your value. Intelligent questions provide as much insight as answers. They give you insights into the customer's thinking and jumpstart the collaborative process. They also help you validate that your insight is relevant."[32]

Coping with Sales Call Reluctance

The transition from the preapproach to the approach is sometimes blocked by sales call reluctance. Fear of making the initial contact with the prospect is one of the biggest obstacles to sales success. For new salespeople, the problem can be career-threatening. **Sales call reluctance** includes thoughts, feelings, and behavioural patterns that conspire to limit what a salesperson is able to accomplish. It is an internal, often emotional, barrier to sales success. Sales call reluctance can be caused by several different thought patterns:[33]

- Fear of taking risks
- Fear of group presentations
- Lack of self-confidence
- Fear of rejection

sales call reluctance Fear of making the initial contact with the prospect.

Regardless of the reasons for sales call reluctance, you can learn to deal with it. Here are some suggestions:

- *Be optimistic about the outcome of the initial contact.* It is better to anticipate success than to anticipate failure. Martin Seligman, professor of psychology at the University of Pennsylvania and author of the bestselling book *Learned Optimism,* says that success in selling requires a healthy dose of optimism.[34] It is important to frequently recommit yourself to the double-win, value-adding approach to working with customers discussed earlier. The anticipation of failure is a major barrier to making the initial contact.

- *Practise your approach before making the initial contact.* A well-rehearsed effort to make the initial contact increases your self-confidence and reduces the possibility that you may handle the situation badly.

- *Recognize that it is normal to feel anxious about the initial contact.* Even the most experienced salespeople experience some degree of sales call reluctance, and this reluctance can surface anywhere in the sales process.

- *Develop a deeper commitment to your goals.* Abraham Zaleznik, professor emeritus at Harvard Business School, says, "If your commitment is only in your mind, then you'll lose it when you encounter a big obstacle. If your commitment is in your heart *and* your mind, you'll create the power to break through the toughest obstacles."[35]

Selling to the Gatekeeper

Many decision makers have an assistant or secretary who manages their daily schedule. This person is commonly referred to as the "gatekeeper." If you want to reach the decision maker, work hard to align yourself with the person who schedules this person's appointments. Rule number one is to treat the gatekeeper with respect. Learn his or her name and what he or she does. Keep in mind that this person can be an important source of information. For example, the gatekeeper can tell you how the buying process works and provide information regarding new developments in the company. This person may be able to help you make a preliminary qualification before you reach the decision maker. When you treat this person as an expert by soliciting his or her views, you establish a relationship that can pay big dividends today and in the future.[36] When possible, use personal referrals from someone the prospect knows. If you have met the prospect previously, describe the meeting and tell the gatekeeper why you feel a second meeting would be beneficial.

REVIEWING KEY CONCEPTS

- Describe the three prescriptions that are included in the presentation strategy.

Developing a presentation strategy involves preparing presale objectives, developing a presale presentation plan, and providing outstanding customer service.

The presentation strategy combines elements of the relationship, product, and customer strategies.

- Discuss the two-part preapproach process.

Preparation for the sales presentation is a two-part process. Part one is referred to as the *preapproach* and involves preparing presale objectives and developing a presale presentation plan. It's best to develop presentation objectives for each stage of the buying process. Part two is called the *approach* and involves making a good first impression, securing the prospect's attention, and transitioning to need identification.

- Describe team presentation strategies.

  In recent years, team selling has surfaced as a major development. Sales teams can often uncover problems, solutions, and sales opportunities that no individual salesperson could discover working alone. Team sales presentations require a more detailed precall plan than individual sales calls. Without careful planning and extensive practice (rehearsal), team presentations are likely to be delivered in a disorganized manner.

- Explain how adaptive selling builds on four broad strategic areas of personal selling.

  Adaptive selling involves altering sales behaviours in order to improve communication with the customer. Salespeople today are challenged to develop a broader repertoire of selling strategies. Salespeople skilled in adaptive selling consider how the relationship, product, and customer strategies can enhance the sales presentation.

- Describe the six main parts of the presentation plan.

  After collecting background information, salespeople need to create a customized presale presentation plan. The plan is developed after careful study of the six-step presentation plan that includes approach, need discovery, presentation, negotiation, close, and servicing the sale.

- Explain how to effectively approach the customer.

  The approach may involve face-to-face contact, telephone contact, or some other appropriate method of communication. If the approach is effective, the salesperson will be given an opportunity to make the sales presentation. A major goal of the *social contact* is to make a good first impression, build rapport, and establish credibility. The *business contact* involves converting the prospect's attention from the social contact to the sales presentation.

- Describe seven ways to convert the prospect's attention and arouse interest.

  Over the years, salespeople have identified several ways to convert the prospect's attention and arouse interest in the presentation. Some of the most common ways include the agenda approach, product demonstration approach, referral approach, customer benefit approach, question approach, survey approach, and premium approach.

Key Terms

action objective **229**
approach **228**
preapproach **228**
presentation strategy **226**

sales call reluctance **246**
six-step presentation plan **234**
telesales **236**

Review Questions

1. What is the purpose of the preapproach? What are the two prescriptions included in the preapproach?
2. Explain the role of objectives in developing the presale presentation plan.

3. Why should salespeople establish multiple-objective sales presentations? List four possible objectives that would be appropriate for stage one and stage two of the buying process.

4. Compare and contrast team sales presentations and individual sales calls.

5. Describe the major steps in the presentation plan. Briefly discuss the role of adaptive selling in implementing the presentation plan.

6. What are the major objectives of the approach?

7. Briefly describe the four guidelines that can help you make a good social contact.

8. What are some rules to follow when leaving a message on voice mail? On email?

9. What methods can the salesperson use to convert the prospect's attention to the sales presentation?

10. Discuss why combination approaches are considered an important consultative-selling practice. Provide one example of a combination approach.

Application Exercises

1. Assume that you are a salesperson who calls on retailers. For some time, you have been attempting to get an appointment with the head buyer for one of the best retailers in the city to persuade her to carry your line. You have an appointment to see her in 90 minutes. You are sitting in your office now and it will take you about 30 minutes to drive to your appointment. Outline what you should be doing between now and the time you leave to meet your prospect.

2. Tom Nelson has just graduated from Red River College with a major in marketing. He has three years of experience in the retail grocery business and has decided he would like to work as a salesperson for the district office of Procter & Gamble. Tom has decided to telephone and set up an appointment for an interview. Write out exactly what Tom should *plan* to say during his telephone call.

3. Concepts from Dale Carnegie's *How to Win Friends and Influence People* can help you prepare for the social contact. Access the Dale Carnegie Training website (**www.dalecarnegie.com**) and examine the courses offered. Search for the Sales Advantage Course. Read the course description and review the two main things you will learn in this program. View the online sales action plan demo video to learn how Dale Carnegie's Web-based coaching program enhances what is learned in the course.

4. Canadian author and sales trainer Steven J. Schwartz is internationally known for his expertise in helping salespeople get appointments. Visit his website at **www.hotcoldcalls.com** and hit "Toolbox." One of the items here is a 24-question self-assessment tool that can help you identify mistakes you might make when initially contacting prospects by telephone. Complete the survey and assess how well you did. Continue until you get all answers correct.

5. You are being interviewed for a sales position with a national electronics retailer. The job is very important to you as it will help pay your living expenses while you complete your studies. During the interview, the manager says, "We are known for honesty and outstanding service, and we expect any salesperson we hire to sell only products that meet customer needs. Please take 10 minutes and write five questions that you would ask a customer who approaches you in our store and wants to buy a digital camera. I will also want to know why you have chosen the questions you have chosen." What questions will you ask? Defend your choices.

↻ROLE-PLAY EXERCISE

Research a new computer that you would like to purchase in the future or that you have just purchased. Strategically, prepare to meet a prospect who has been referred to you by a friend and who would like to purchase a similar computer. Using Table 10.1, prepare four different business contact statements or questions you could use to approach your prospect. Review the material in this chapter and then pair off with another student, who will assume the role of your prospect. First, role-play the telephone contact and set up an appointment to get your prospect into your store to meet with you and look at the computer. Second, role-play the approach you will use when the prospect actually comes into the store. Review how well you made the approach.

Reality Selling Video Case Problem

The global construction industry is a lucrative market, with customer needs ranging from measuring products to sophisticated construction solutions. Hilti, the company featured in the vignette at the start of this chapter, provides its customers around the world with leading-edge construction products and services with outstanding added value. Hilti prides itself on its direct sales model, which allows its salespeople and service teams to work directly *with* and *for* the customer.

Alim Hirani, an account manager for Hilti, adopts the relationship marketing approach in his selling strategy. He often starts his sales calls, which have been carefully planned, with ice breakers such as asking about the customer's family rather than making the sale immediately. His sales presentations may take place in clients' offices or even at construction sites. Consequently, he must always plan well in advance the best way to make his sales presentations for specific sales calls. At all times, he must attempt to establish his own and his company's credibility by demonstrating the premium value that Hilti's products and services can offer his clients. Whenever possible, Alim tries to get the customer involved in product demonstration "because, after all, 'seeing is believing.'" Once the customers see for themselves the benefits of Hilti's product features, moving the customers from the investigation and evaluation stages to the action stage is just a formality.

Alim sells not only individually but also as part of a team. For major clients who require a complete package

of building/construction, mechanical/electrical, telecom, and interior finishing products and services, Alim works closely with his team members to make sure the information he acquires from the customer during initial contacts is made available to other salespeople and technical personnel on the team. In the construction industry, closing the sale is—most of the time—just the beginning. Well-trained product application specialists join Alim to offer customers after-sale services, technical support, and training. (See the chapter opener on page 225 and Reality Selling Today Role Play 8 in Appendix 1 on page 435 for more information.)

Questions

1. Why should Alim Hirani adopt the three prescriptions for the presentation strategy?

2. Salespeople are encouraged to establish multiple-objective sales presentations. What are some objectives Alim Hirani should consider when he calls on construction managers at the construction site?

3. What are some special challenges Alim Hirani faces when he makes his sales presentations in a non-office setting?

4. Put yourself in the position of a construction salesperson. Can you envision a situation in which you might combine different ways to convert the prospect's attention and interests into action? Explain.

PARTNERSHIP SELLING: A ROLE PLAY/SIMULATION

Developing a Relationship Strategy

Visit the role play/simulation materials provided in the Student Resources section of your companion website at **www.pearsoncanada.ca/manning**. *A Contents page lists appropriate page references for the activities.*

Read *Employment Memorandum 2*, which announces your promotion to account executive. In your new position, you will be assigned by your instructor to one of the two

major account categories in the convention centre market, either the *association accounts market* or the *corporate accounts market*. The association accounts market includes customers who are responsible for planning meetings for their association or group. The corporate accounts market includes customers who are responsible for planning meetings for the company they represent. You will remain in the account category for the rest of the role plays.

Note the challenges you will have in your new position. Each of these challenges will be represented in the future *sales memoranda* you will be receiving from your sales manager. Read *Sales Memorandum 1* for the account category you are assigned. (Note that "A" means association and your customer is Erin Adkins, and "B" means corporate and your customer is Leigh Combs.) Follow the instructions in the sales memorandum and strategically prepare to approach your new customer. Your call objectives will be to establish a relationship (social contact), share an appealing benefit, and find out if your customer is planning any future conventions (business contact).

You may be asked to assume the role of a customer in the account category that you are not assigned as a salesperson. Your instructor will provide you with detailed instructions for correctly assuming this role.

Chapter 11
Determining Customer Needs with a Consultative Questioning Strategy

Learning Objectives

After studying this chapter, you should be able to

1 Outline the benefits of the consultative sales process.

2 Describe the four parts of the need-satisfaction model.

3 Discuss the use of questions to discover customer needs.

4 Describe the importance of active listening and the use of confirmation questions.

5 Select solutions that match customer needs.

 Adaptive Selling Training Video Series—*Questions, Questions, Questions*

The effective use of questions is the starting point of the consultative sales process. Questions are used to build adaptive-style selling relationships, discover customer needs, and adapt and present product solutions that meet those needs. Questions span the entire sales process and are also used to successfully negotiate, close, and service a sale.

Questions, Questions, Questions, the second video in our Adaptive Selling Today Training Video Series, introduces and shows how to use the four adaptive selling questions described in this chapter. An Internet telephone systems sales representative featured in the video learns that one of his largest accounts may be going with another supplier. The salesperson's company brought in a new sales training program on how to use questions effectively, and the salesperson is the first to learn the system. With his newly acquired knowledge and skills, the salesperson schedules another call to see if he can, with the use of questions, re-establish his relationship and salvage the sale.

In this follow-up call, we find out how well he has learned to adapt and use questions to discover and better understand the customer's needs, create value, solve the customer's

The effective use of questions is the starting point of the consultative sales process.

Michael Ahearne

buying problem, and retain the account. Throughout the three-part video, the salesperson learns about the following four-part multiple questioning strategy and what these questions will reveal during the consultative sales presentation.

SURVEY questions	Reveal	Problems and situation
PROBING questions	Reveal	Pain and implications
NEED-SATISFACTION questions	Reveal	Pleasure and need satisfaction
CONFIRMATION questions	Reveal	Mutual understanding

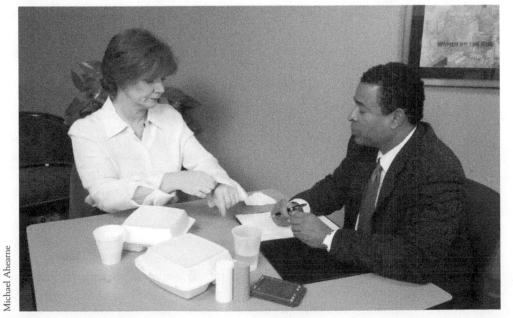

Michael Ahearne

Extensive research regarding the use of questions in the sales process reveals the importance of developing and perfecting a multiple questioning strategy to understand and solve customer needs. The adaptive questions video dramatically presents how these questions are used in the process.

The Six-Step Presentation Plan	
Step One: Approach	☑ Review Strategic/Consultative Selling Model ☑ Initiate customer contact
Step Two: Need Discovery	☐ Ask strategic questions ☐ Determine customer needs ☐ Select product solution
Step Three: Presentation	☐ Select presentation strategy ☐ Create presentation plan ☐ Initiate presentation
Step Four: Negotiation	☐ Anticipate buyer concerns ☐ Plan negotiating methods ☐ Initiate win-win negotiations
Step Five: Close	☐ Plan appropriate closing methods ☐ Recognize closing clues ☐ Initiate closing methods
Step Six: Servicing the Sale	☐ Follow through ☐ Follow-up calls ☐ Expansion selling

Service, retail, wholesale, and manufacturer selling

Figure 11.1 Creating the Sales Presentation
The consultative sales process involves adding value by accurately determining the prospect's needs and selecting an appropriate product or service.

The use of an effective questioning strategy, so important to the consultative sales process, is one of the greatest challenges facing salespeople. Need discovery and questioning will be explored in this chapter (Fig. 11.1), and the sales presentation will be presented in the next chapter.

THE CONSULTATIVE SALES PROCESS ADDS VALUE

A GROWING NUMBER OF SALESPEOPLE, LIKE THE INTERNET TELEPHONE SYSTEM SALESPERSON pictured on the previous page, have adopted the consultative sales process. New competitive structures and customer demands have forced companies to continuously adapt and redefine their value-adding processes.[1] Consultative selling, as introduced in Chapter 2, is a value-adding process. Consultative selling involves meeting customer needs by asking strategic questions, listening to customers, understanding—and caring about—their problems, selecting the appropriate solution, creating the sales presentation, and following through after the sale. Consultative selling is a very customer-centric form of selling that creates value for the customer and, in the process, creates value for the firm.[2] This approach is very different from product-oriented selling. As one author noted, "Product-oriented selling can easily lapse into product evangelism." Product-oriented selling is usually inefficient and ineffective.[3,4]

New entrants in the field of personal selling sometimes wonder why some people excel in selling products or services, while others, who seem to work just as hard, fall short of meeting company or personal selling goals. The answer can be found by reviewing the behaviours displayed by top sales performers from Fortune 500 and smaller entrepreneurial-based companies. High-performance sales personnel have learned how to skilfully diagnose and solve problems better than their competitors.[5] This consultative problem-solving capability translates into the following:

Increased Customer Satisfaction Customers prefer to purchase solutions that truly meet their needs. The solution that is "just right" for the customer adds value, maximizes satisfaction, and sets the stage for a partnership relationship and repeat business. In some cases, the right solution will cost more than the customer planned to pay, but the added value will usually compensate for the higher price.

Jeff Thull, author of *Mastering the Complex Sale* and *The Prime Solution*, states, "In too many buyer–seller relationships, there is a value gap where the customer is not getting the satisfaction they believe was promised."[6] Consultative salespeople with the ability to diagnose and solve customer problems are able to close this value gap.

More Sales Closed The extra time taken to carefully solve the customer's buying problem will set the stage for closing more sales. A certain amount of buyer resistance surfaces in nearly every selling situation. Understanding your customer's needs and configuring the most suitable solution from available options adds value to both your customer and your company. It will help you avoid unnecessary objections from the customer.

Fewer Order Cancellations and Fewer Returns It is always disappointing to have a customer cancel an order a few days after the sale was closed. The frequency of order cancellations can be reduced with consultative-style selling. Returned merchandise is another serious problem. Whether the product is returned or needs to be reconfigured, the expense will often wipe out the profit earned on several sales.

Increased Business and Referrals Many business firms do not make a profit on the first sale. In fact, some firms do not earn a profit until the customer has placed the third or fourth order. The same is true for the salesperson. Without repeat business and a steady list of referrals, the salesperson will generally not experience the financial and psychic rewards described in Chapter 1. If at any point the customer does not feel the treatment was fair, the time and cost invested in partnership building and obtaining the initial order, as well as future sales, may be lost. Repeat business also builds a sense of pride within everyone associated with the business.

Satisfied customers represent a potent form of sales promotion. A group of satisfied customers forms what might be called an "auxiliary" sales force. Through word-of-mouth advertising, especially with the availability of social media and blogging, these people are referring potential customers and building new business for both the salesperson and the firm. Most of us can't resist sharing positive experiences with friends and business acquaintances.

The sales environment is changing. In competitive markets, success increasingly hinges on developing and maintaining mutually rewarding customer relationships.[7] Salespeople using the consultative sales presentation model are able to create more value and gain competitive advantage in their markets.

THE FOUR-PART NEED-SATISFACTION MODEL

To be most effective, the salesperson should think of the sales process as a four-part model. The Consultative Sales Process Guide features these four parts (Fig. 11.2).

Part One—Need Discovery

Since the emergence of the marketing concept discussed in Chapter 2, where the activities of a firm revolve around the needs of the customer, need discovery forms the essence of salespeople being able to create value, meet the needs of their customers, and execute the firm's commitment to the marketing concept. A review of the behaviours displayed by high-performance salespeople helps in understanding the importance of precise need discovery. They have learned how to skilfully diagnose and solve the prospect's problems better than their competitors can. This problem-solving capability translates into more repeat business and referrals, and fewer order cancellations and returns.[8]

Unless the selling situation requires mere order taking (customers know exactly what they want), need discovery in the information economy is a critically important part of the sales presentation. It may begin during the qualifying stage of building the prospect database or during the approach if the salesperson uses questions or a survey during the initial contact with the customer. Need discovery generally begins after you transition from the approach. In multi-call situations, need discovery may be the primary call objective during the first or second call. In most multi-call settings, it is wise to reconfirm the needs discovered in earlier calls.

The pace, scope, depth, and time allocated to inquiry depend on a variety of factors, including the sophistication of the product, the selling price, the customer's knowledge of the product, the product applications, and, of course, the time available for dialogue between the salesperson and the prospect. Each selling situation is different, so a standard set of guidelines for need discovery is not practical. Additional information on need discovery is presented later in the chapter.

Part Two—Selection of the Solution

The emphasis in sales and marketing today is on determining buyer needs and then selecting or configuring custom-fitted solutions to satisfy these needs. Therefore, an important function of the salesperson is product selection, also often referred to as *product configuration*. Product recommendations in complex sales generally involve writing a detailed product proposal. The salesperson must choose the product or service that will provide

Figure 11.2 The Consultative Sales Process Guide
To be most successful, the salesperson should think of the sales presentation as a four-part process.

Asking Questions—Not Telling—at CARQUEST

CARQUEST Auto Parts (www.carquest.ca) promises to deliver what customers need. To achieve this lofty goal, the company enrolled its 1200 outside sales force members in *Action Selling*. A major objective of this sales training program is to help salespeople become trusted business consultants. They learned that asking—not telling—is the key to sales success. Emphasis throughout the course is placed on asking more and better questions. Duane Sparks, who developed *Action Selling*, says, "The success rate of sales calls rises significantly when more than two specific customer needs are uncovered by questioning."[a]

maximum satisfaction. When making this decision, the salesperson must be aware of all product options, including those offered by the competition.

Salespeople who have the ability to conduct an effective, value-added needs analysis can achieve the status of trusted adviser. Mary Langston is a personal shopper who works in a large department store and helps customers update their wardrobes. When asked what her days are like, she says, "It starts and ends with being a good listener." She promises her customers that she will never let them walk out of the store with clothing that does not look right.[9]

Part Three—Need Satisfaction through Informing, Persuading, and/or Reminding

The third part of the consultative sales process consists of creating a need-satisfaction sales presentation and communicating to the customer, both verbally and nonverbally,

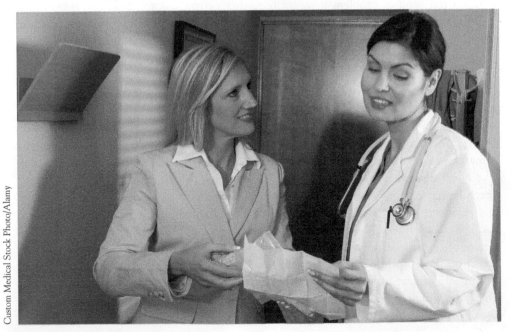

Custom Medical Stock Photo/Alamy

Pharmaceutical salespeople generally have only a short time to present their product. In some situations, the doctor may immediately indicate a willingness to prescribe. However, in other situations the salesperson may be asked to make an informative need-satisfaction presentation to several members of the practice.

the satisfaction that the product or service can provide. The salesperson places less emphasis on the use of questions and begins making value-adding statements. These value-adding statements are organized into a presentation that informs, persuades, or reminds the customer of the most suitable product or service. In several of the remaining chapters, we discuss specific strategies used in conjunction with the sales presentation/ demonstration, negotiating buyer resistance, and closing and servicing the sale.

Part Four—Servicing the Sale

Servicing the sale is a major way to create value. These activities, which occur after closing the sale, ensure maximum customer satisfaction and set the stage for a long-term relationship. Service activities include expansion selling, making credit arrangements, following through on assurances and promises, and dealing effectively with complaints. This topic is covered in detail in Chapter 15.

In those cases where a sale is normally closed during a single sales call, the salesperson should be prepared to go through all four parts of the Consultative Sales Process Guide. However, when a salesperson uses a multi-call approach, preparation for all the parts is usually not practical. The person selling networking systems or investments, for example, almost always use a multi-call sales process. Need discovery (part one) is the focus of the first call.

CREATING VALUE WITH NEED DISCOVERY

A LAWYER DOES NOT GIVE THE CLIENT ADVICE UNTIL THE LEGAL PROBLEM HAS BEEN CAREfully studied and confirmed. A doctor does not prescribe medication until the patient's symptoms have been identified. In like manner, the salesperson should not recommend purchase of a product without thorough need identification. You start with the assumption that the prospect's need or problem is not known. The only way to determine and confirm the need or problem is to get the other person talking. Effective relationship builders are willing to listen to better understand customer challenges. They ask questions that lead to consultative conversations, which open doors to greater opportunities.[10] You must obtain information to properly clarify the need, propose a single solution, or offer a range of solutions.

Customers may not realize that they actually have a problem. Even when they are aware of their need, as noted earlier by Salesforce.com's Dave Levitt, given the wide range of solutions and new products available today they may not realize that an actual solution to their problem exists. Bringing new insights regarding both their buying problem and enhanced solutions creates value for your customer.

need discovery A process in which the salesperson establishes two-way communication by asking appropriate questions and listening carefully to the customer's responses.

Need discovery (sometimes called *need analysis* or *needs assessment*) begins with precall preparation, when the salesperson is acquiring background information on the prospect. As noted in Chapter 9, this part of need discovery is also referred to as *qualifying the prospect*. Need discovery, and in some cases the qualification process, continues once the salesperson and the customer are engaged in a real dialogue. Through the process of need discovery, the salesperson establishes two-way communication by asking appropriate questions and listening carefully to the prospect's responses. These responses will usually provide clues concerning the customer's dominant buying motive (see Fig. 11.3).

Figure 11.3 Three Dimensions of Need Discovery

Need Discovery—Asking Questions

The effective use of questions to achieve need identification and need satisfaction is one of the greatest challenges facing most professional salespeople. The types of questions you ask, the timing of those questions, and how you pose them will greatly affect your ability to create customer value. In many situations, asking high-value-added questions that enlighten your prospects both about their needs and possible solutions results in an immediate sale.

From the Field
The Question Not Asked

Having an effective questioning strategy is critical to the success of today's consultative salesperson. This requires asking the right questions at the right time. But failing to ask important questions can also lead to serious consequences.

Since its premium-quality beer first rolled off the bottling line in 2000, Toronto-based Steam Whistle Brewing has been focused on one thing: making one beer, and making it "really, really well." The company has a passion for quality. Its world-class Pilsner has only four all-natural ingredients: spring water, malted barley, hops, and yeast.

Shortly after it began production, the company experimented with "oxygen scavenger" bottle caps. Oxygen causes premature quality deterioration of many food products, including beer. The salesperson who sold the caps was excited about the quality improvement his caps would provide. Shortly after Steam Whistle Brewing began using the new caps, however, customer complaints began to surface concerning "flakes" in their beer. After investigating a number of possible causes, the company determined the flakes were caused by the oxygen scavenger caps. The salesperson failed to ask one important question: "Is your beer pasteurized?" These caps work only when activated by the heat of pasteurization, as with the beer produced at Canada's larger commercial breweries. Craft breweries tend to avoid pasteurization as, although it increases shelf life, it negatively affects taste.

Steam Whistle Brewing took quick action to win back dissatisfied customers it could identify, and it immediately improved its filling/capping procedures to ensure its quality was restored. Since then, the "Good Beer Folks" at Steam Whistle have won many awards for their beer.[b]

The strategic approach to asking questions has been the focus of two major studies. These studies were conducted in response to the emergence of the marketing concept and the evolution of the consultative and strategic selling eras discussed in Chapter 2. The research was conducted by Neil Rackham for his book *SPIN Selling* and SPIN Selling Sales Training programs, and Xerox Learning Systems for their successful Personal Selling Skills (PSS) course.

The SPIN Selling Model According to research conducted by Neil Rackham during the strategic selling era (see Chapter 2, Table 2.1: Evolution of Personal Selling) on more than 35 000 salespeople, mastering the use of questions can increase one's success in sales by 17 percent.[11] Questions help clarify the exact dimensions of the problem, help the customer evaluate a range of solutions, and assist the customer in evaluating the potential outcome of the solution that is implemented.[12] Rackham's research focused on strategies for making large-ticket sales and is based on a close examination of successful salespeople. Rackham found that the investigative or need discovery stage of the sales process has the most impact on the buyer's decision to purchase a product. He recommends a multiple-question approach that involves using four types of questions in a specific sequence (see Selling in Action on p. 267). SPIN sales training programs are presented by Huthwaite, Inc. (**www.huthwaite.com**).

Personal Selling Skills Model The importance of questioning to establishing two-way communication was revealed in another study conducted during the consultative selling era. Research conducted by Xerox Learning Systems was used to develop the original Xerox Personal Selling Skills training program. Sales personnel were interviewed to identify the characteristics of a successful sales call. The results were quite surprising. A successful sales call lasts an average of 30 minutes. During this period, the salesperson asks an average of 13.6 questions, discusses an average of 7.7 product features, and describes approximately six product benefits. During the successful sales call, the customer asks approximately eight questions.[13] This 18-month study of behavioural differences among high-, average-, and low-performance salespeople illustrates that a successful sales call is a model of good two-way communication. Regarding the specific use of questions, the results revealed that high performers:

- Use effective questions to gather information and build a clear, complete, mutual understanding of customer needs.

- Guide the direction of a sales call by striking an appropriate balance between open and closed questions.

- Use their questioning strategy to facilitate an open exchange of information.[14]

This study has been used to create and update the very successful Personal Selling Skills training program, now presented by AchieveGlobal (**www.achieveglobal.com**).

The art and science of using questions was also discussed by Socrates more than 2500 years ago. He noted, among other things, that questions tend to make people think. It's nearly impossible to remain passive when confronted with a direct question. Today there are sales training programs, such as Michael Hargrove's "Using the Socratic Selling Methods" and books such as Kevin Daley's *Socratic Selling: How to Ask the Questions That Get the Sale,* that include many of the observations made by Socrates.[15]

Doing Business in Belgium

Belgium is a country in northwestern Europe on the North Sea. It has long been a strategic crossroads of Europe. The country is culturally divided into Dutch-speaking Flanders to the north of Brussels and French-speaking Wallonia to the south. A small population of German speakers is in the south. Avoid confusing the different languages and cultures. This mistake could come across as insulting. Be sure your business cards are printed in the appropriate language for the area you are visiting. Do not expect one selling strategy to work within its borders given the cultural differences.[c]

In every selling situation, you want the prospect to be actively thinking, sharing thoughts, and asking questions. Appropriate questions reduce tension and build trust in a selling situation because they communicate interest in the other person's welfare. Until the person begins to talk freely, the salesperson will have difficulty diagnosing and solving the customer's problems.

The Four-Part Consultative Questioning Strategy

Table 11.1 illustrates the use of a multiple questioning strategy to discover customer needs. This strategy is based upon the research studies discussed earlier, as well as that conducted for the *Questions, Questions, Questions* sales training video described in the

Table 11.1 Types of Questions Used in Conjunction with Consultative Selling

Type of Question	Definition	When Used	Example
Survey	*Discovers basic facts* about the buyer's *problem* and existing situation	Usually at the beginning of a sale	"Can you describe the problems you experience travelling to each of the pro golf tournaments?"
Probing	*Designed to uncover pain and clarify the circumstances and implications* surrounding the customer's problem	When you feel the need to obtain more specific information to fully understand the problem	"Are the travel problems affecting your concentration when you are preparing for the event?"
Confirmation	*Used throughout the sales process to verify* the accuracy and assure a mutual understanding of information exchanged by the salesperson and the buyer	After important information has been exchanged	"So, you think the uncertainty associated with commercial air travel is having some effect on your game?"
Need-Satisfaction	*Designed to move the sales process toward commitment and action;* focuses on the pleasure or payoff achieved from the proposed solution	When you change the focus from the problem to a discussion of the solution	"With fractional ownership of your own jet, what personal benefits would this bring to your performance in the 30 tournaments you play each year?"

(*Note:* Salesperson selling fractional ownership of a jet aircraft to a well-known golf professional on the Professional Golf Association (PGA) Tour who is currently using commercial air travel)

opening material for this chapter. The four types of questions are situation questions, probing questions, confirmation questions, and need-satisfaction questions. Developing skill in the use of these questions will work best if the consultative salesperson develops the mindset that it is more important to understand the customer than it is to persuade the customer. You will note similarity to the SPIN Selling and Personal Selling Skills questioning strategies, as well as to those found in other popular selling books.

Survey Questions Reveal Customer's Problems At the beginning of most sales presentations, there is a need to collect basic facts about the buyer's existing situation and problem. **Survey questions** —or *information-gathering questions*, as they are sometimes called—are designed to obtain this knowledge. To accomplish this, there are two types of survey questions.

survey questions Questions used to help the salesperson collect information about the buyer's existing situation and problem.

General survey questions help the salesperson discover facts about the buyer's problem and existing situation and are often the first step in the partnership-building process. Rackham refers to these as *situation questions*. Here is a sampling of general survey questions that can be used in selected selling fields:

general survey questions Questions used early in the sales presentation to help the salesperson discover facts about the buyer's existing situation.

I understand that your regional facilities don't necessarily use the same delivery carriers. Is that correct? (*Shipping service*)

Tell me about the challenges you are facing in the area of data storage. (*File server*)

What is your current rate of employee turnover? (*Customer service training*)

Can you provide me with information on the kinds of meetings and conventions you plan for your clients and employees? (*Hotel convention services*)

Can you describe the style of home furnishings you prefer? (*Retail home furnishings*)

In most selling situations, general survey questions are followed by specific survey questions.

specific survey questions Questions designed to give prospects a chance to describe in more detail a problem, issue, or dissatisfaction from their point of view.

Specific survey questions are designed to give prospects a chance to describe in more detail a problem, issue, or dissatisfaction they are experiencing from their point of view. These specific survey questions (see Selling in Action on p. 267), or *problem questions* as they are referred to in the SPIN selling sequence, are designed to delve more deeply into the customer's buying situation. Here are five examples of specific survey questions:

Has it occurred to you that by not consolidating your shipping with one carrier, you're likely spending more than is really necessary? (*Shipping service*)

How do you feel about installing another server to your system? (*File server*)

To what extent is employee turnover affecting your customer service? (*Customer service training*)

What meal function features are most important to your guests? (*Hotel convention services*)

Are you looking for an entertainment centre that blends in with your existing furniture? (*Retail home furnishings*)

Survey questions, general or specific, should not be used to collect factual information that can be acquired from other sources, such as your CRM prospect database, prior to the sales call. The preapproach prospect qualification effort is especially important when the salesperson is involved in a large or complex sale. These buyers expect the salesperson to do his or her homework and to not waste the buyer's time asking general survey questions and discussing basic factual information that is available from other sources. Rackham's research revealed that more experienced salespeople tended to ask more specific survey or problem questions, and ask them sooner.

Although survey questions are most often used at the beginning of the sales presentation, they can also be used at other times. Gaining a better understanding of the customer's situation or buying problem may be necessary at any time during the sales presentation. We present the four types of questions in a sequence that has proven to be effective in most selling situations. However, it would be a mistake to view this sequence as a *rigid* plan for every sales presentation. High-performing salespeople spend time strategically preparing tentative questions before they make the sales call. Table 11.2 provides some examples. Note that both open and closed questions are listed. **Open questions** require the prospect to go beyond a simple yes/no response. **Closed questions** can be answered with a yes or no, or a brief response.

Open questions are very effective in certain selling situations because they provoke thoughtful and insightful answers. The specific survey question "What are the biggest challenges you face in the area of plant security?" focuses the prospect's attention on problems that need solutions. Closed questions, however, can be equally effective when the sales conversation needs to be narrowed or focused on a specific issue.

open questions Questions that require the prospect to respond with more than just a yes or no response.

closed questions Questions that can be answered yes or no or with a brief response.

Probing Questions Reveal Customer's Pain Early in the sales process, the salesperson should make every effort to fully understand the buying problem and the pain, implications, or consequences surrounding the problem. This is especially important when the problem is difficult to describe, the solution is complex, and the potential impact of a wrong decision is enormous.[16]

Table 11.2 Need Discovery Worksheet

Preplanned questions—sometimes used in conjunction with company-supplied forms—are often used in service, retail, wholesale, and manufacturer selling. Salespeople who use the consultative approach, such as Johnny in the *Questions, Questions, Questions* video, frequently record answers to their questions and use this information to correctly select and recommend solutions in subsequent calls in their multi-call sales situations. Open and closed questions used in the area of financial services appear in the following list.

Preplanned Questions to Discover Buying Motives	Customer Response
1. "Now, as I understand it, you're currently pursuing an Internet phone system to offset your high cellular costs?" *(Closed/General Survey/Situational)*	
2. "Are you aware that with the system you are currently using, your brokers may have to keep their laptops on in order to make and receive Internet calls?" *(Closed/Specific Survey/Problem)*	
3. "So what happens if, say, your broker is waiting for an important return call and then inadvertently logs off his or her laptop without a way to roll over the client's return call into a centralized system?" *(Open/Probing/Pain/Implication)*	
4. "Let's see if we understand this—the brokers won't support the system you're considering because it doesn't include instant messaging. And since the brokers would be the primary users of the new system, you're concerned that the system will fail without their support. Is that correct?" *(Closed/Summary-Confirmation)*	
5. "What if we could develop a communications system for you that included IM and met the SEC requirements? What positive impact could that have on your situation?" *(Open/Need-Satisfaction/Pleasure)*	

Probing questions help you uncover and clarify the pain, implications, and circumstances surrounding the customer's buying problem. They are used more frequently in large, complex sales. These questions often uncover the current level of customer concern, fear, or frustration related to the problem. The following probing questions, also referred to as *implication* questions in Rackham's *SPIN Selling*, are more focused than the survey questions presented earlier:

> But doesn't every incorrect label cost you to ship to an incorrect address, then cost you again to have it shipped back to you? (*Shipping service*)
>
> What would the consequences be if you choose to do nothing about your current server situation? (*File server*)
>
> How does senior management feel about employee turnover and the related customer service problem? (*Customer service training*)
>
> Is poor service at the meal function negatively affecting the number of people who will return to your seminar? (*Hotel convention services*)
>
> Is it important that you have easy access for connecting your DVD, TIVO, and wireless LAN network? (*Retail home furnishings*)

Probing or implication questions help the salesperson and customer gain a mutual understanding of *why* a problem is important. Asking effective probing questions requires extensive knowledge of your company's capabilities, much insight into your customer's buying problem, and a great deal of practice.

The best sales presentations are characterized by active dialogue. As the sales process progresses, the customer becomes more open and shares perceptions, ideas, and feelings freely. A series of appropriate probing questions stimulates the prospect to discover things not considered before.

Confirmation Questions Reveal *Mutual Understanding*

Confirmation questions are used throughout the sales process to verify the accuracy and assure a mutual understanding of information exchanged by the salesperson and the buyer (see Table 11.1). They are used to gain commitment, a critically important part of achieving success in larger complex sales. Without commitment throughout the sales process, the chances of a successful sale evaporate rapidly.

These questions, which are an important update to the research on the use of questioning strategies, help determine whether there is mutual understanding of the problems and circumstances the customer is experiencing, as well as the possibilities for a solution. Throughout the sales process, there is always the potential for a breakdown in communication. Perhaps the language used by the salesperson is too technical. Information and initial needs discovered during the qualifying stage of the need discovery may have changed. Maybe the prospect is preoccupied and has not listened closely to what has been said. Many confirmation questions are simple and to the point.

> If I understand you correctly, the monitoring system must be set up at both your corporate headquarters and at the manufacturing operation. Is that correct? (*File server*)
>
> I want to be sure I am clear that you feel there is a direct relationship between employee turnover and the problem that exists in customer service. (*Customer service training*)
>
> Did you say your seminar attendance dropped 12 percent last year? (*Hotel convention services*)
>
> So you want a new entertainment centre that blends with your current light-coloured oak furniture? (*Retail home furnishings*)

The length of the sales process can vary from a few minutes during a single-call presentation to weeks or even months in a complex multi-call sales presentation. As the sales process progresses, the amount of information available to the salesperson and the customer increases. As the need discovery progresses, the customer's buying criteria or buying conditions surface. **Buying conditions** are those qualifications that must be available or fulfilled before the sale can be closed. The customer may buy only if the product is available in a certain configuration or can be delivered by a certain date. In some selling situations, product installation or service after the sale is considered an important buying condition by the customer. In a large, complex sale, several buying conditions may surface. The salesperson has the responsibility of clarifying, confirming, and gaining commitment on each condition. The same is true for gaining commitment on each of the specific benefits presented to the customer.

One of the best ways to clarify, confirm, and gain commitment on several buying conditions is with **summary confirmation questions.** To illustrate, let us consider a situation in which Laura Feng, sales manager at a major hotel, has interviewed a prospect who wants to schedule a large awards banquet. After a series of survey, probing, and confirmation questions, Laura feels confident that the information she collected is sufficient for her to prepare a proposal. However, to be sure all the facts have been collected, Laura asks the following summary confirmation question to gain commitment on the important buying conditions:

> Let me summarize the major items you have mentioned. You want all banquet attendees served within an eight-minute time frame after the opening speaker has finished his speech? And you need a room that will comfortably seat 60 persons banquet-style, and 10 of these persons will be seated at the head table. Is this correct?

Once all the buying conditions are confirmed, Laura can prepare a proposal that reflects the specific needs of her customer. The result is a win-win situation for the customer and the salesperson. The chances of closing the sale greatly improve. In multi-call sales processes, it is wise to begin subsequent calls with summary confirmation questions that re-establish what was discussed during the previous call(s):

> (*Re-qualifying the new prospect*) I would like to revisit the information we have in our database about your company's purchasing procedures. You prefer limiting your suppliers and developing long-term partnerships where they are as committed as you are to your profitability and your customers' total customer satisfaction. You also require e-commerce linkages that allow your people to review the status of their order, delivery dates, and the projected costs, including transportation and financing. Is that correct?

> (*The second call in a multi-call sale situation*) Let me begin by going over what we discussed in our last visit. Your current shipper gives you a 50 percent discount and provides a custom-label printer? *If the customer responds in the affirmative, the salesperson continues with another summary-confirmation question.* You also have to buy fairly expensive custom labels and, at around $90 a pack, you're spending over $20 000 just on labels. Is that still correct?

This enables the salesperson to verify that the previously discovered buying conditions have remained the same and not changed since the last meeting. Summary-confirmation questions are also used to effectively clarify, confirm, and gain commitment to several product benefits after they have been presented, generally one at a time.

buying conditions Qualifications that must be available or fulfilled before the sale can be closed.

summary confirmation questions Questions used to clarify and confirm buying conditions.

Commitment to the value of the benefits usually results in transitioning the presentation to the closing and servicing of the sale.

Need-Satisfaction Questions Reveal Pleasure The fourth type of question used in the sales process is fundamentally different from the other three. **Need-satisfaction questions** are designed to focus on the solution and the benefits of the solution. These are helpful questions that move the sales process toward commitment and action. The chances of closing the sale greatly improve because need-satisfaction questions—or, as they are sometimes called, *solution* or *pleasure* questions—focus on specific benefits and build desire for a solution.

need-satisfaction questions Questions designed to move the sales process toward commitment and action by helping to clarify the problem in the prospect's mind and by building a desire for your solution.

Survey, probing, and confirmation questions focus on understanding and clarifying the customer's problem. Need-satisfaction questions help the prospect see how your product or service provides a solution to the problem you have uncovered. The opportunity to close the sale greatly improves because you have cast the solution in a pleasurable light.

In most cases, need-satisfaction questions are used after the salesperson has created awareness of the seriousness of the buyer's problem. The questions you ask will replace his or her current levels of concern, pain, or frustration with pleasurable thoughts about a solution. The following examples provide insight into the use of need-satisfaction—or, as *SPIN Selling* refers to them, *need-payoff*—questions:

> And if I told you that I can offer you cost savings of at least 5 percent over your current shipping expenses, would that be meaningful? (*Shipping service*)
>
> Tests on similar applications show that a new file server can increase data storage by 30 to 40 percent. How much do you feel you would achieve? (*File server*)

In many selling situations, a product demonstration is an essential stage in the sales process. In this case, the salesperson might use the following need-satisfaction question:

> What benefits would you see if we provided a demonstration of one of our training modules to senior management so they can understand what you and I have discovered about reducing employee turnover? (*Customer service training*)

Once the prospect's needs are clearly identified, need-satisfaction questions can be valuable closing tools. Consider this example:

> Considering the benefits we have summarized and agreed on, and noting the fact that our staff will deliver an outstanding meal function, would you like to sign this confirmation so we can reserve the rooms and schedule the meals that you need? (*Hotel convention services*)

Need-satisfaction questions such as these are very powerful because they build desire for the solution and give ownership of the solution to the customer. When the prospect understands which parts of the problem(s) your solution can solve, you are less likely to invite objections. In some cases, you may identify problems that still need to be clarified. When this happens, you can use survey, probing, or confirmation questions to obtain more information.

At this point, you have received only a basic introduction to the four most common types of questions used during the selling process. (For more insight into the application of questions to the sales process, view the three videos in the *Questions, Questions, Questions* series referred to in this chapter's opening vignette. Also refer to the Role-Play Application Exercises on pages 276–277.) We will revisit these important sales tools later in this chapter and in Chapters 12, 13, 14, and 15.

Questions, Questions, Everywhere

The use of questions to discover needs and present solutions is discussed in several popular personal selling books. For comparison purposes, the approximate equivalents to the four types of questions described in this chapter are listed.

Selling Today by Manning, Ahearne, Reece, and MacKenzie	*The Spin Selling Fieldbook* by Rackham	*The New Solution Selling* by Eades	*The New Conceptual Selling* by Heiman, Sanchez, with Tuleja	*Secrets of Question Based Selling* by Freese
Survey	Situation	Open	Confirmation	Status
Probing	Problem	Control	New Information	Issue
Confirmation	Implication	Confirming	Attitude	Implication
Need-Satisfaction	Need-Payoff		Commitment	Solution
			Basic Issue	

The questions above are listed in the sequence presented by the authors. To determine the exact definition of each type of question, check the source.

Qualifying to Eliminate Unnecessary Questions

It is important to avoid the use of unnecessary questions during a sales call. Pre-qualifying the prospect, as described in Chapter 9, is especially important when the prospect is a business buyer. Successful salespeople acquire as much information as possible about the prospect before the first meeting. They use sources such as the prospect's website, LinkedIn, previous phone calls or emails, and information recorded in the salesperson's CRM system. This prior understanding of the prospect allows the salesperson to direct the qualifying conversation using effective confirmation questions such as "Your website mentions your company has recently expanded into a new product market. Can you tell me more about that?" Buyers expect the salesperson to be well informed about their operation and not waste time asking a large number of basic survey questions. Confirmation questions communicate this prior knowledge and allow the salesperson and customer to move ahead in the consultative sales process with more important probing and need-satisfaction questions.

Robert Jolles, author of *Customer-Centered Selling*,[17] suggests that salespeople be careful when determining whether the person they are meeting with has the authority to make the purchase decision. According to Jolles, asking a survey question such as "Are you the one who will be making the decision on this purchase?" encourages prospects without decision-making authority to lie in order to maintain their pride in the situation. Instead, Jolles recommends the question, "Who, besides yourself, will be responsible for this purchase decision?" This subtle yet strategic rephrasing to a confirmation/survey question allows the prospect to tell the truth and maintain his or her dignity.

NEED DISCOVERY—LISTENING TO AND ACKNOWLEDGING THE CUSTOMER'S RESPONSE

To FULLY UNDERSTAND THE CUSTOMER, WE MUST LISTEN CLOSELY AND ACKNOWLEDGE EVERY response. The authors of *First Impressions* offer these words of advice to salespeople who use questions as part of the need discovery process: "What you do after you ask a question can reveal even more about you than the questions you ask. You reveal your true level of interest in the way you listen."[18] Most of us are born with the ability to hear, but we have to learn how to listen. The starting point is developing a listening attitude. Always regard the customer as worthy of your respect and full attention.[19] Salespeople with high levels of customer orientation truly care about customers, and thus engage in actions that customers value such as listening to customer feedback and solving customer problems. Once you have made a commitment to becoming a good listener, develop active listening skills.

active listening The process of feeding back to the prospect what you as a listener think the person meant, in terms of both content and feelings. It involves taking into consideration and exhibiting both verbal and nonverbal messages.

Developing Active Listening Skills **Active listening** is the process of sending back to the prospect what you as a listener think the person meant, in terms of both content and feelings. Active listening requires intense involvement as you concentrate on what you are hearing, exhibit your listening attitude through your nonverbal messages (see Chapter 4), and feed back to the prospect what you think he or she meant.[20] Developing active listening skills involves three practices that can be learned by any salesperson willing to make the commitment:

- *Focus your full attention.* This is not easy because the delivery of the messages we hear is often much slower than our capacity to listen. Thus, we have plenty of time to let our minds roam, to think ahead, and to plan what we are going to say next. Our senses are constantly feeding us new information while someone is trying to tell us something. Staying focused is often difficult and involves use of both verbal and nonverbal messages.[21] To show that you are paying attention, lean toward the prospect while murmuring "uh-huh," "okay," or "I understand," and nod in agreement when appropriate. Avoid nodding rapidly or saying "uh-huh" loudly or frequently because this will communicate impatience or a desire to turn the conversation back to yourself.[22]

CRM—Reviewing Account Status

Salespeople regularly review the status of their prospect's records in their customer relationship management (CRM) databases. In some cases, this is done on the computer screen. In other situations, a printed copy of the records can enhance the process.

Salespeople review their files to ascertain at what phase in the Consultative Sales Process Guide (see Fig. 11.2) each prospect is currently in. Then they decide what action to take to help move the prospect to the next phase. Sales managers can be helpful with this process, especially for new salespeople. Managers can help salespeople evaluate the available information and suggest strategies designed to move to the next phase.

Even experienced salespeople count on their sales managers to help plan presentations. Managers can help salespeople evaluate their contacts' needs, select the best solution, and plan a presentation most likely to succeed.

It is important to listen to the emotion involved in your customer's comments. A poor listener listens to facts; a good listener listens to emotions. Theoretically, 20 percent of communications is strictly facts and 80 percent is emotion—the emotion we all have and put into every thought. Listening for the emotions in your client's conversation enables you to receive the entire message.[23] Emotional buying motives were discussed in detail in Chapter 8.

Within every sales presentation there will be times when silence should be welcomed. Use silence to control the flow of information and draw out the customer. Customers are often inclined to fill silence by talking. Throughout an effective sales presentation, the customer should be talking more than the salesperson.[24]

- *Paraphrase the customer's meaning.* After the customer stops talking, pause for two or three seconds and then state in your own words, with a confirmation question, what you think the person meant. This technique not only helps ensure understanding but also is an effective customer relations strategy. The customer feels good knowing that not only are you listening to what has been said, you are also making an effort to ensure accuracy. In addition to paraphrasing the content, use questions to dig for full understanding of the customer's perceptions.[25] The use of survey or probing questions is appropriate any time you need to clarify what is being said by the prospect.

- *Take notes.* Although note-taking is not necessary in every sales presentation, it is important in complex sales where the information obtained from the customer is critical to the development of a buying solution. Taking accurate notes is a good way to demonstrate to the customer that you are actively listening. When you take notes, you increase your memory of what you heard. Your notes should be brief and to the point.[26] If the information you receive from the customer is too technical or unfamiliar, do not hesitate to ask for clarification of information you don't understand.

Need Discovery—Establishing Buying Motives

The primary goal of questioning, listening, and acknowledging is to uncover prospect needs and establish buying motives. Our efforts to discover prospect needs can be more effective if we focus our questioning on determining the prospect's primary reasons for buying. When a customer has a definite need, it is usually supported by specific buying motives.

The greatest time investment in personal selling is on the front end of the sales process. First you must plan the sales call and then, once you are face-to-face with the customer, you can begin the need discovery stage. It is during the early stage of the sales process that you can create the greatest value for the customer.[27]

SELECTING SOLUTIONS THAT CREATE VALUE

SALESPEOPLE ARE NO LONGER SELLING JUST A "PRODUCT"; INSTEAD THEY ARE PROVIDING a valuable "solution" to customer problems.[28] Consultative salespeople act as product experts and generally provide a customized solution. The second part of the consultative sales process consists of selecting or configuring a solution that satisfies the prospect's buying motives.

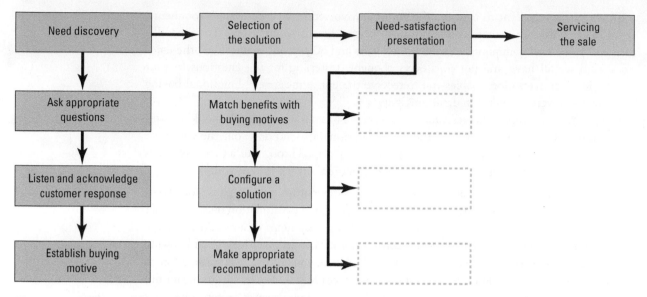

Figure 11.4 Three Dimensions of Product Selection

As we have noted, most salespeople bring to the selling situation a variety of products and/or services. In today's information economy, salespeople are increasingly selling related services as a part of their product solution. This is especially true in the Western industrialized countries where profit margins on B2B goods-related solutions are declining. In Germany, for example, six of the 30 largest firms have established specific organization units to offer services.[29] The challenge to select the correct solution is growing. Digesting relevant information, perceiving patterns, and determining the unique solution that will work in each unique selling situation requires a considerable amount of time and effort.[30] This process done correctly can create significant value for the customer and build a long-term partnership of repeats and/or referrals.

After identifying the buying motives, the salesperson carefully reviews the available product options. At this point, the salesperson is searching for a specific solution to satisfy the prospect's buying motives. Once the solution has been selected, the salesperson makes a recommendation to the prospect (see Fig. 11.4). The following customer response to this process illustrates the value created when this process is done correctly: "She listened to and worked with the ideas that I had concerning my desires and preferences, as well as made recommendations that complemented and enhanced the vision that I had for my home."[31]

Selecting Solutions—Match Specific Benefits with Buying Motives

As we noted in Chapter 7, products and services represent problem-solving tools. People buy products when they perceive that they fulfill a need. We also noted that today's more demanding customers seek a cluster of satisfactions that arise from the product itself, from the company that makes or distributes the product, and from the salesperson who sells and services the product. Tom Reilly, author of *Value-Added Selling*, says, "Value-added sales-people sell three things: the product, the company, and themselves."[32] This is the Three-Dimensional (3-D) Product Solutions Selling Model discussed in Chapter 7 (see Fig. 7.1). When possible, the salesperson should focus on benefits related to each dimension of value. Of course, it is a mistake to make benefit statements that do not relate to the specific needs of the customer. High-performance salespeople present benefits that are precisely tailored to the customer's needs. Benefits that are not relevant to the customer's needs waste time and may invite objections.[33]

Selecting Solutions—Product Configuration

Most salespeople bring to the sale a variety of products or services. Salespeople who represent food distributors can offer customers a mix of several hundred items. Most pharmaceutical sales representatives can offer the medical community a wide range of products. Best Buy, a large retailer of electronics, offers customers a wide range of audio and visual entertainment options. The customer who wants to purchase a sound system, for example, can choose from many combinations of receivers, speakers, and so on. Selecting the right solution is referred to by many sales organizations as *product configuration*.

If the sale involves several needs and the satisfaction of multiple buying motives, selection of the solution may take several days or even weeks and may involve the preparation of a detailed sales proposal. In addition, research conducted by Neil Rackham revealed that top-performing salespeople tend to introduce their solutions later in the sale—after several problems were uncovered.

A company considering the purchase of automated production equipment would likely present this type of challenge to the salesperson. The problem needs careful analysis before a solution can be identified.

Configuration Solutions (**www.configsc.com**) is one of many providers of product configuration solutions. Its software applications help configure-to-order organizations quote, market, and sell highly customized and complex products and service offerings. Its advanced technology and industry-focused solutions help salespeople automate a wide range of customer product solutions—regardless of the complexity or variability of their products, processes, or services.[34]

Electronic catalogues also play an increasingly important role in the product selection or product configuration process. Software programs such as Configure One's (**www.configureone.com**) Web-based *Concept E-Catalog* enable salespeople to rapidly implement and easily maintain electronic catalogue solutions for business-to-business and business-to-consumer applications. *Concept E-Catalog* software enables salespeople to find product solutions faster. Its electronic catalogue fully integrates with its other products (e-commerce and configurator software) or can stand alone. With its e-commerce software, salespeople and customers can have access to product solutions 24/7.

Salesforce.com, with its AppExchange integration program, also provides product selection and electronic catalogue capability. BigMachines, recently voted Best Quote App, provides on-demand product configuration, pricing, and proposal capabilities that can be easily added to Salesforce.com's on-demand CRM solution. BigMachines enables salespeople to streamline the entire opportunity-to-quote-to-order process, all within the familiar Salesforce.com CRM interface. Capabilities include guided selling, product configuration, complex pricing and discounting, approval workflow, and proposal generation.[35] Electronic product configurators, product catalogues, and e-commerce enable salespeople to create value for the customer by providing time sensitive, professionally prepared, information-rich alternatives in selecting solutions that meet the unique needs established during the need discovery. For many salespeople, the use of sales force technology has changed their methods of selling.[36]

In some selling situations, the salesperson will solely create the solution based on the needs analysis. In more complex selling situations, however,[37] both the salesperson and the customer often play an active role and together co-create the solution. This co-creation process takes place through conversations between the customer and the salesperson. Research reveals this process often helps customers better understand their own needs and conceive of possible solutions that fit those needs. This application of the value-added 3-D Product Solutions Selling Model discussed in Chapter 7 (see Fig. 7.1) creates value and, as a consequence, customers make smarter buying choices that conform to the salesperson's solutions and sales propositions.

Selecting Solutions—Make Appropriate Recommendations

The recommendation strategies available to salespeople are similar to those used by a doctor who must recommend a solution to a patient's medical problem. In the medical field, three possibilities for providing patient satisfaction exist. In situations in which the patient easily understands the medical problem and the appropriate treatment, the doctor can make a recommendation and the patient can proceed immediately toward a cure. If the patient does not easily understand the medical problem or solution, the doctor may need to discuss thoroughly with the patient the benefits of the recommended treatment. If the medical problem is not within his or her medical specialty area, the doctor may recommend a specialist to provide the treatment. In consultative selling, the salesperson has these same three counselling alternatives.

Recommend Solution—Customer Buys Immediately The selection and recommendation of products to meet the customer's needs may occur at the beginning of the sales call, such as in the product approach; during the presentation, just after the need discovery; or near the end, when minor resistance has been negotiated. At any of these three times, the presentation products that are well matched to the prospect's needs may result in an immediate purchase.

Recommend Solution—Salesperson Makes Need-Satisfaction Presentation This alternative requires a presentation of product benefits, including demonstrations and negotiating buyer concerns, before the sale is closed. In this situation, the prospect may not be totally aware of a buying problem and the solution may not be easily understood or apparent. Because of this, the salesperson needs to carefully define the problem and communicate a solution to the customer. The need-satisfaction presentation will be discussed in Chapter 12.

Recommend Another Source Earlier, we indicated that professional salespeople may recommend that a prospect buy a product or service from another source, maybe even a competitor. If, after a careful needs assessment, the salesperson concludes that the products represented do not satisfy the customer's needs, the consultative salesperson should recommend another source.

Paul Roos, a sales representative for Hewlett-Packard, once met with a customer who wanted to buy a newly introduced HP product for an application where it would not work. Paul explained why the product would not work and then took time to configure a competing product to meet the customer's needs. He lost that sale to a competitor, but the assistance provided confirmed his integrity and made a lasting impression on the customer. That customer later became a high-value account.[38] In situations like Paul Roos's, where the unique needs of a customer cannot be solved and an alternative recommendation is made to buy from another supplier, long-term partnerships are often created that result in future sales and/or referred business. This creates value for the customer who is looking for a unique solution.

Need Discovery and the Transactional Buyer

Throughout this chapter, you have been given a comprehensive introduction to the consultative sales process. It is important to keep in mind that the fundamentals of consultative selling must be customized to meet the individual needs of the customer. For example, some of the guidelines for developing an effective consultative presentation must be abandoned or greatly altered when you are working with a transactional buyer. In most cases, transactional buyers understand what product they need and when they need it. The Internet has armed many transactional buyers with a great deal of information, so the salesperson who spends time asking survey questions or making a detailed informative presentation may be wasting the customer's time. Most of these buyers want the salesperson to configure a product solution that focuses on pricing and delivery issues.[39]

When working with the transactional buyer, it is important to understand the difference between a transaction and a consultative relationship. Transactions create one-time value; consultative relationships create long-term value and a stable business foundation.[40]

Involving the Prospect in the Need Discovery

In most selling situations, there is a certain amount of time pressure. Rarely does a salesperson have an unlimited amount of time to spend with the customer. As noted earlier, the salesperson is often allotted only 30 minutes for the sales call. Some buyers limit all their appointments to 30 minutes or less.

Figure 11.5 illustrates an ideal breakdown of time allocation between the salesperson and the prospect during three parts of the sales process. In terms of involvement, the prospect assumes a greater role during the need discovery stage. As the salesperson begins the product selection process, the prospect's involvement decreases. During the need-satisfaction stage, the salesperson is doing more of the talking, but note that the prospect is never excluded totally.

Transitioning to the Presentation

As we note in Chapter 10, there is a need to make an effective transition from the approach to the need discovery stage. There is the same need to transition from the need

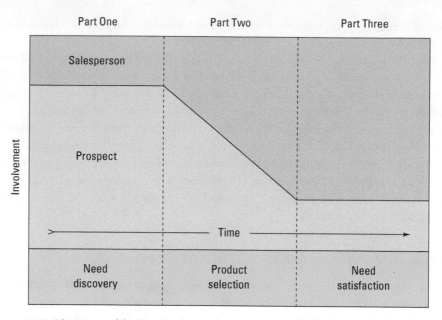

Figure 11.5 Time Used by Both the Salesperson and the Prospect During Each Part of the Consultative Sales Presentation

discovery/product selection stage to the need-satisfaction presentation stage. As noted earlier, if your customer buys immediately, you will transition to the close and conduct those activities associated with servicing the sale. Those activities will be discussed in Chapters 14 and 15. If you and your customer decide another supplier might better meet his or her needs, you might transition directly to servicing the sale to achieve a future sale or a referral.

If it is decided that a need-satisfaction presentation is needed to communicate specific features and benefits, make a statement such as "I would like to point out some of the specific benefits of the solution we have agreed upon." If the need-satisfaction presentation is made during a separate call of a multi-call presentation, the transition should include a summary-confirmation question covering the buying conditions discussed. The summary-confirmation question would be used in closing the existing call and opening the next call. Creating and involving the prospect in the need-satisfaction presentation stage will be discussed in detail in Chapter 12.

PLANNING AND EXECUTION—FINAL THOUGHTS

THE IMPORTANCE OF STRATEGIC PLANNING AND EXECUTION OF THE NEED DISCOVERY AND product selection parts of the consultative sales presentation model is explained in this chapter. Figure 11.6 summarizes the key concepts that must be addressed during the planning and execution process. These planning and execution activities will impact your ability to create customer value and build a partnering relationship. This approach can be used in the three major employment settings: service, B2B, and B2C.

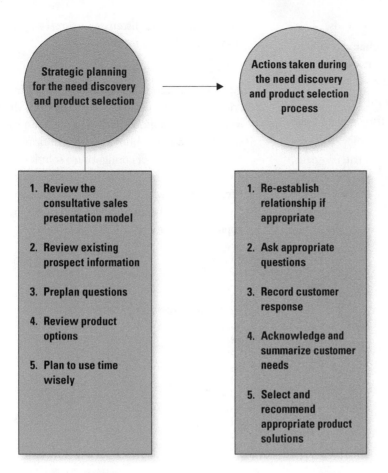

Figure 11.6 Strategic Planning for the Need Discovery and Product Selection
Need discovery and product selection activities are the first steps in creating value
and building a partnering relationship with your customer.

REVIEWING KEY CONCEPTS

- Outline the benefits of the consultative sales process.

  Salespeople use the consultative sales presentation because this customer-focused selling model results in increased customer satisfaction, more closed sales, and more repeat and referred business. Research indicates that high-performance salespeople have learned how to skilfully use the consultative model to diagnose and solve their customers' buying problems better than their competitors.

- Describe the four parts of the need-satisfaction model.

  A well-planned and well-executed consultative sales process is an important key to success in personal selling. To be most effective, the presentation should be viewed as a four-part process: need discovery; selection of the solution; need satisfaction through informing, persuading, or reminding; and servicing the sale.

- Discuss the use of questions to discover needs.

  The most effective sales process is characterized by two-way communication. It should be encouraged with survey, probing, confirmation, summary-confirmation, and need-satisfaction questions.

- Describe the importance of active listening and the use of confirmation questions.

  Beware of assuming information about the prospect, and be sure the language of your presentation is clearly understood. Listen attentively as the prospect responds to your questions or volunteers information. The effective use of confirmation questions to enhance active listening assures a mutual understanding of buying motives.

- Select solutions that match customer needs.

  After making a good first impression during the approach and getting the customer's full attention, the salesperson begins asking questions. During the process of, or shortly after, determining and/or confirming customer needs, the process of configuring a solution begins. The salesperson's ability is tested during this part of the sale because this is where the prospect's buying motives are matched with benefits, a solution is configured, and appropriate solutions are recommended.

Key Terms

active listening **268**

buying conditions **265**

closed questions **263**

confirmation questions **264**

general survey questions **262**

need discovery **258**

need-satisfaction questions **266**

open questions **263**

probing questions **264**

specific survey questions **262**

summary confirmation questions **265**

survey questions **262**

Review Questions

1. List and describe the four parts of the Consultative Sales Process Guide.

2. Describe the findings of the two major research projects on the strategic use of questions in selling.

3. List and describe the four types of questions commonly used in the selling field.

4. Define the term *buying conditions*. What are some common buying conditions?

5. Describe the process of active listening, and explain how it can improve the listening efficiency rate.

6. Discuss the three dimensions of need discovery.

7. Describe the three dimensions of selecting a product solution.

8. Describe the ideal time allocation for each part of the consultative sales presentation between the salesperson and the prospect.

9. Describe the nature of the need discovery process when working with a transactional buyer.

10. Describe how to transition to the presentation part of the consultative sales presentation model.

ROLE-PLAY APPLICATION EXERCISES FOR THE *QUESTIONS, QUESTIONS, QUESTIONS* VIDEO SERIES

Most sales skill development exercises used in the classroom are product-oriented. As noted on page 254, "Product-oriented selling can easily lapse into product evangelism." This three-part video series on questioning focuses on the customer's buying process, consultative selling, and building high-quality partnerships.

The goal of this series is the identification and clarification of the customer's problem and finding a solution.

The first video focuses on the appropriate use of survey and confirmation questions to identify the customer's problem. The second video introduces the use of probing and need-satisfaction questions. Probing questions examine and clarify the potential issues surrounding the customer's problem, while need-satisfaction questions focus the sales process on the appropriate solution. The third video demonstrates the use of these questions in a challenging, yet typical, contemporary sales setting.

The role-play exercises presented below challenge the participant to understand, apply, and integrate questioning skills presented in this chapter and in the video series. Product information for these exercises is found in "Partnership Selling: A Role Play/Simulation" online in the Student Resources section at **www.pearsoncanada. ca/manning**. See pages 5 to 26. Customer information will be found in the B. H. Rivera Contact Report presented on page 26. (Disregard any other information on this page.) You will assume the role of a newly hired salesperson as described in the Position Description on page 8. Refer to the questioning material and examples presented on pages 261–266. Use a need discovery worksheet like the one on page 263 for developing your questions.

After viewing the video *Questions—Discovering and Confirming Customer Problems*, study the online role play/simulation material (pages 5 to 26). Refer to the Contact Report on page 26. (As noted, disregard any other information on this page.) Assume you were assigned to this account and you are meeting B. H. Rivera to inquire about additional information regarding when the meeting will be held and what audiovisual equipment might be needed.

Prepare a list of general survey and specific survey questions that reveal when, during the next month, the meeting will be held and what, if any, audiovisual equipment (see pages 21–22) might be needed. Plan to use a summary-confirmation question to verify the existing four items on the Contact Sheet. Using the questions you have created, role-play this part of the need discovery process.

After viewing the video *Questions—Discovering Pain and Pleasure* and reviewing the information you prepared in the role play above, prepare three probing questions. These questions should clarify and reveal a mutual understanding of issues and consequences regarding food service, facility design, and audiovisual equipment. Also, using the information on pages 5 to 24, prepare five need-satisfaction questions that reveal how the features of your convention centre provide a solution to the buying situation. Select appropriate proof devices to demonstrate these specific benefits. Using these questions, meet again with B. H. Rivera and role-play this part of the questioning process. Prepare and use confirmation questions as the need arises.

After viewing the video *Questions—Getting it Right* and using the information in the first two role plays, prepare a need-satisfaction presentation to Cameron Rivera, a new meeting planner just hired at Graphic Forms. Cameron, a cousin of B. H., was previously employed as a training coordinator at West College. Due to extensive growth in the company, B. H. has turned all meeting planning over to Cameron. Cameron will make the final selection of a facility for the meeting described on page 26, plus 11 more identical meetings to be scheduled in the next 12 months. You have also been informed that the Marriott and Sheraton hotels will be making presentations (note the comparative room, parking, and transportation rates). You will travel to Graphic Forms to make your presentation. Prepare appropriate survey, probing, confirmation, and need-satisfaction questions and presentation strategies that will help secure this important account—then role-play this presentation.

Reality Selling Video Case Problem

When Deborah Karish wakes up in the morning, she does not have to worry about a long commute to work. Her office is in her home. As an Amgen (**www.amgen.com**) pharmaceutical sales representative, Deborah spends most of her day visiting hospitals, medical clinics, and doctors' offices. She spends a large part of each day serving as a consultant to doctors, head nurses, pharmacists, and others who need information and advice about the complex medical products available from her company. As might be expected, she also spends a considerable amount of time conducting informative presentations designed to achieve a variety of objectives. In some situations, she is introducing a new product, and in other cases she is providing up-to-date information on an existing product. Some of her presentations are given to individual health care professionals, and others are given to a group. Each of these presentations must be carefully planned.

Deborah uses informative and reminder presentations almost daily in her work. Informative presentations are given to doctors who are in a position to prescribe her products. The verbal presentation often is supplemented with audiovisual aids and printed materials. Reprints of articles from leading medical journals are often used to illustrate the success of her products in treating patients. These articles give added credibility to her presentations. Some of her informative presentations are designed to give customers updates on the prescription drugs she sells. Reminder presentations are frequently given to pharmacists who must maintain an inventory of her products. She has found it necessary to periodically remind pharmacists of product delivery procedures and policies, and of special services available from Amgen. She knows that without an occasional reminder, a customer can forget information that may be beneficial.

In some cases, a careful needs analysis is required to determine if her products can solve a specific medical problem. Each patient is different, so generalizations concerning the use of her products can be dangerous. When doctors talk about their patients, Deborah must listen carefully and take good notes. In some cases, she must get additional information from company support staff. If a customer needs immediate help with a problem, she gives the person a toll-free 1-800 number to call for expert advice. This line is an important part of the Amgen customer service program.

Deborah's career in pharmaceutical sales has required continuous learning. In the beginning she had to learn the meaning of dozens of medical terms and become familiar with a large number of medical problems. If a doctor asks, "What is the bioavailability of Neupogen?" she must know the meaning of the medical term and be knowledgeable about this Amgen product.

Deborah also spends time learning about the people with whom she works. She recently said, "If I get along with the people I work with, it makes my job a lot easier." When meeting someone for the first time, she takes time to assess his or her communication style and then adapts her own style to meet his or her needs. She points out that in some cases the competition offers a similar product at a similar price. In these situations, a good relationship with the customer can influence the purchase decision.

Questions

1. Would need discovery be an important part of Deborah Karish's sales process with a new medical practice? Explain.
2. Would Deborah use the same questioning strategy with medical personnel such as the office manager or receptionist that she would with medical professionals such as nurses or doctors?
3. Describe the nature of the multi-call sales process that Deborah might use.
4. Describe what Deborah might plan to do in the first call, in the second call, and in a third call on the same medical practice.

PARTNERSHIP SELLING: A ROLE PLAY/SIMULATION

Visit the role play/simulation materials provided in the Student Resources section of your companion website at **www.pearsoncanada.ca/manning.** A *contents page lists appropriate page references for the activities.*

UNDERSTANDING YOUR CUSTOMER'S BUYING STRATEGY

Read *Sales Memorandum 2* ("A" or "B" depending on the account category you were assigned in Chapter 10). Your customer has called you back because you made such a good approach in call 1, and wants to visit with you about a convention recently assigned. In this call, you are to use the information gathered in sales call 1 to re-establish a good relationship, discover your customer's convention needs, and set an appointment to return and make a presentation.

Follow the instructions carefully and prepare survey questions prior to your appointment. Keep your survey questions general and attempt to get your customer to share information openly. Use specific survey questions later during the appointment to gain more insight. Be careful about doing too much of the talking. In the need discovery, your customer should do most of the talking, with you taking notes and using them to ask confirmation and summary confirmation questions in order to check the accuracy of your perceptions concerning what the customer wants. After this meeting, you will be asked to prepare a sales proposal using the information you have gathered.

Your instructor may again ask you to assume the role of a customer in the account category that you are not assigned as a salesperson. If so, you will receive detailed customer instructions, which you should follow closely. This will provide you with an opportunity to experience the strategic/consultative/partnering style of selling from a customer's perspective.

Extensive research regarding the use of questions in the sales process reveals the importance of developing and perfecting a multiple questioning strategy to understand and solve customer needs. The adaptive questions video dramatically presents how these questions are used in the sales process.

Chapter 12
Creating Value with the Consultative Presentation

Learning Objectives

After studying this chapter, you should be able to

1   List and describe three types of need-satisfaction presentation strategies.

2   Present guidelines for creating consultative presentations that add value.

3   Describe the elements of a persuasive presentation strategy.

4   Describe the elements of an effective group presentation.

5   Develop selling tools that add value to your sales demonstrations.

Chris Wylie (see page 281) is a sales representative for Ecolab. With more than $6 billion in global sales, Ecolab is the global leader in cleaning, sanitizing, food safety, and infection control products and services. The company has more than 26 000 employees worldwide. Ecolab serves customers in more than 160 countries across North America, Europe, Asia, Latin America, the Middle East, and Africa. The company delivers comprehensive programs and services to various industries, including food service, food and beverage processing, hospitality, health care, government and education, retail, and others.

Chris Wylie is a territory manager in Ecolab's Institutional Business unit, which is the core of Ecolab. In his territory, Chris serves approximately 80 customers throughout the month. Most of his customers are restaurants, but he also calls on some hotels and a few hospitals. When visiting a customer, he first meets with his contact, which would typically be the general manager, procurement manager, or executive chef. He asks them a series of questions about their business and operations (e.g., how busy they have recently been, whether they had any problems or repairs, or whether a big

Chris Wylie

event like a banquet is coming up). Through these questions, Chris gains insight into his customer's operations, which will later help him create his solutions and sales presentation.

As a part of his call, Chris also has to take care of servicing Ecolab's products by making sure that the dispensers for the products and the dishwashers are working properly, that the calibrations are set correctly, and so forth. Throughout his presentation, Chris constantly tries to discover different needs such as determining needed repairs, identifying up-selling or cross-selling opportunities, and expanding the business with that customer by showing him or her new products.

Besides serving his existing customer base, Chris also engages in new business selling. In a typical prospecting type of sales call, Chris would meet with the general manager or the executive chef, introduce himself and Ecolab, and eventually ask them whether he can conduct a need discovery survey of their kitchen to see what their operation looks like and assess whether he can provide any additional value with some of Ecolab's products and services. Then Chris would typically do a series of tests on the current chemicals and equipment that the prospect is using to see if they are functioning effectively and efficiently. Based on these tests, Chris creates a value proposition in terms of cost savings or results improvements (e.g., improved glassware or dishware results). Since Ecolab products are not sold on price, Chris then presents those improved results to demonstrate to the prospect the Ecolab value of excellent service and quality products.

NEED SATISFACTION—SELECTING A PRESENTATION STRATEGY

CONDUCTING BUSINESS IN THE TWENTY-FIRST CENTURY INFORMATION ECONOMY, WHICH IS based on the assets of knowledge and information, requires that we think about ways to improve the sales presentation. Here is how one author described this challenge:

> As we move from the rutted byways of the Industrial Age to the electronic thoroughfares of the Information Age, business presentations become a measure of our ability to adapt to new surroundings. The most successful and forward-thinking companies already have assigned presentations a new, fundamental and strategic importance.[1]

After you have configured a solution that matches the customer's needs, you must select which presentation strategy to emphasize (see Fig. 12.1). Need satisfaction can be achieved through selecting an informative, persuasive, or reminder presentation strategy;

The Six-Step Presentation Plan	
Step One: Approach	☑ Review Strategic/Consultative Selling Model ☑ Initiate customer contact
Step Two: Need Discovery	☑ Ask strategic questions ☑ Determine customer needs ☑ Select product solution
Step Three: Presentation	☐ Select presentation strategy ☐ Create presentation plan ☐ Initiate presentation
Step Four: Negotiation	☐ Anticipate buyer concerns ☐ Plan negotiating methods ☐ Initiate win-win negotiations
Step Five: Close	☐ Plan appropriate closing methods ☐ Recognize closing clues ☐ Initiate closing methods
Step Six: Servicing the Sale	☐ Follow through ☐ Follow-up calls ☐ Expansion selling

Service, retail, wholesale, and manufacturer selling

Figure 12.1 Creating value with the presentation.

creating the presentation plan; and initiating the presentation. Salespeople, such as Ecolab's Chris Wylie, often will use a combination of the three presentation strategies.

Need Satisfaction—The Informative Presentation Strategy

To be informative, a message must be clearly understood by the customer. Of course, clarity is important in any presentation, but it needs special attention in a presentation in which the primary purpose is to inform. The **informative presentation** emphasizes factual information typically taken from technical reports, company-prepared sales literature, or written testimonials from persons who have used the product.

This type of presentation is commonly used to introduce new products, highly complex products, and services of a technical nature. Salespeople such as Ecolab's Chris Wylie and Hilti's Alim Hirani play a key role in the ultimate success of a firm's new product innovations.[2] Pharmaceutical sales representatives frequently use the informative presentation strategy to describe the details of their products to a physician who may be engaged in an educated search for a prescription drug best suited to meet their patient's medical need.[3] This strategy emphasizes clarity, simplicity, and directness, and in many cases is welcomed by the reflective and directive communication-style customers presented in Chapter 5. Salespeople need to keep in mind the "less is more" concept. Too often the prospect is given far too much information and detail.[4]

It is important to keep in mind the partner/problem-solver role of the salesperson when making an informative presentation. Today information is not just plentiful but available directly to customers in overwhelming amounts. As a result, customers no longer value sales professionals as just information providers. To use the informative presentation strategy effectively, the salesperson must transition from an information conveyer to the role of a trusted business advisor.[5]

Need Satisfaction—The Persuasive Presentation Strategy

Many salespeople believe that when a real need for their product exists, the stage is set for a persuasive presentation. **Persuasion** is a communication process by which you motivate someone else to voluntarily do something you'd like them to. The key word is "voluntarily." Persuasion is not compelling or manipulating others to do what you want. You must present your audience with a legitimate choice of options. True persuasion occurs when someone not only chooses your preferred option but also feels good about it afterward.[6] The major goals of the **persuasive presentation** are to influence the prospect's beliefs, attitudes, or behaviour, and to encourage buyer action. Persuasive sales presentations include a subtle transition stage where the dialogue shifts from an intellectual emphasis to an emotional appeal. This situation may occur when Ecolab's Chris Wylie discovers a safety issue that needs immediate attention. Every buying decision is influenced by both reason and emotion, but the amount of weight given to each of these elements during the decision-making process can vary greatly depending on the prospect.[7]

In the field of personal selling, persuasion is an acceptable strategy once a need has been identified and a suitable product has been selected. When it is clear that the buyer will benefit from ownership of the product or service, an enthusiastic and persuasive sales presentation is usually appropriate. The persuasive presentation strategy requires a high level of training and experience to be effective, because a poorly planned and delivered persuasive presentation may raise the prospect's anxiety level. The persuasive presentation, when handled improperly, can trigger fear or distrust.

Need Satisfaction—The Reminder Presentation Strategy

Studies show that awareness of a company's products and services declines as promotion is stopped. This problem represents one of the reasons many companies employ *missionary* salespeople to maintain an ongoing awareness of and familiarity with their product lines. Other types of salespeople also use this presentation strategy. Route salespeople rely heavily on a **reminder presentation** (sometimes called *reinforcement presentation*) to maintain their market share. Salespeople such as Tom James Company's Alex Homer, introduced in Chapter 1, know that if they do not make frequent calls and remind customers of their products, customers may turn to the competition (see Fig. 12.2).

The reminder presentation is sometimes a dimension of service after the sale (see Chapter 15). Sales personnel, such as the B2B detail salesperson described in Chapter 1, who work with repeat customers are in a good position to remind them of products or services they offer. In a B2C selling situation, retail sales personnel can remind their regular customers of additional products in their own department or another department located in some other area of the business. Some products require special care and maintenance. Busy customers may need to be reminded of the maintenance services offered by your company. In some cases, the service department is a major profit generator, so reminder calls need to be given a high priority.

reminder presentation
Sometimes called the *reinforcement presentation,* this strategy assumes that the prospect has already been involved in an informative or persuasive presentation and understands at least the basic product features and buyer benefits.

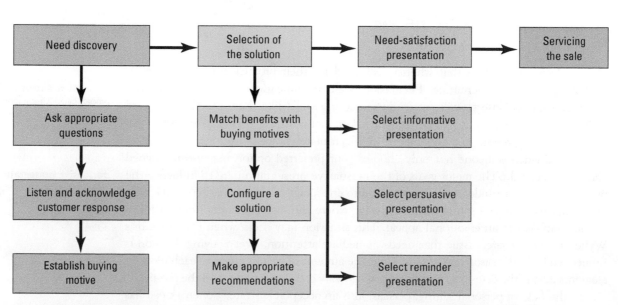

Figure 12.2 The three strategies to use in developing an effective need-satisfaction presentation.

Reminder presentations are often used by salespeople who may have been unsuccessful in a previous call. Sometimes when the buyer has a strong relationship with a competing supplier, the best you can hope is that the current relationship weakens. You want to be top of mind when that happens, and a reminder presentation can often achieve that result. There are also some customers who, after they understand that you are truly committed to getting their business, will eventually give you a trial order.

Some customers get used to the great quality and service you provide and begin to view your product as a commodity. Once this happens, the customer may ask for a price reduction. To keep customers focused on value rather than price, remind them (from time to time) of the value-added services you provide.[8]

GUIDELINES FOR CREATING A PRESENTATION THAT ADDS VALUE

It is important to distinguish between a planned consultative presentation and a **canned presentation.** In most cases, the canned presentation, also referred to as the *memorized* or *scripted presentation*,[9] is built around a standard set of steps, ignores the unique needs of each customer, and is presented in the form of a repetitive speech given to all customers interested in a particular item. Although an effective planned presentation will generally add value from the customer's perspective, a canned presentation today will likely be discounted by the customer and may take away from the value a product has to offer. With the planned consultative presentation, the salesperson is considered a strategic resource and partner for the customer, rather than just a provider of a product or service.[10]

In some group selling situations, a variation of the canned presentation has to be presented because the audience has such a wide variety of needs. In any case, every effort should be made to understand those needs and adapt the group presentation as much as possible to meet the needs of the audience. More will be presented later in this chapter on group presentations.

Strategic planning, of course, sets the stage for an effective consultative presentation that adds value to the sale (see Fig. 12.3). Some of the most important ways to create value with the presentation are discussed next.

canned presentation Or *memorized* or *scripted presentation*, is built around a standard set of steps, ignores the unique needs of each customer, and is presented in the form of a repetitive speech given to all customers interested in a particular item.

Adapt the Presentation to Meet the Unique Needs of the Customer

Salespeople who have mastered adaptive selling skills adjust their sales strategies in ways that better fit customer needs and preferences.[11] In consultative selling, each presentation is custom tailored because, as we found in Chapter 11 on need discovery, individual client problems and priorities are unique. In other words, every aspect of the sales presentation should be adapted to the needs or problems mutually identified by the prospect and the salesperson.

It is possible to develop a sales demonstration so structured and so mechanical that the prospect feels like a number. We must try to avoid what some veteran marketing people refer to as the *depersonalization* of the selling–buying process. If the demonstration is overly structured, it cannot be personalized to meet specific customer wants and needs.

Figure 12.3 Strategic Planning for the Presentation
Salespeople who truly represent value to their customers plan ahead strategically for the actions taken during the consultative sales presentation.

Bell Helicopter (**www.bellhelicopter.com**) manufactures helicopters in Canada and the United States. It sells a product with countless custom options, and each option changes its price and performance. One customer may want a helicopter for emergency medical care and another may want one for electronic news gathering. Bell's sales force, all of whom are licensed helicopter pilots, can introduce the Bell product line with a video presentation and then follow up with a demonstration flight if requested. Sales representatives also have access to a sales configuration system that supports the customization process. Price and performance data can be quickly determined for each accessory needed by the customer. The software automatically provides answers to the numerous questions that can surface during the sales presentation.[12]

In most business-to-business selling situations, it would be a mistake to present all of the product benefits. Some benefits may be of no interest to the target customer. Effective precall preparation and well-executed need discovery activities minimize the possibility that you will spend time discussing features that provide no benefit to the customer.

Cover One Idea at a Time and Use an Appropriate Amount of Detail

Pace the demonstration so that the customer does not become confused. In response to what was learned in the need discovery, offer one idea at a time, and be sure the customer understands each point before moving on. When you neglect this practice, there is the danger that the customer's concentration will remain fixed on a previous point. Some presentations are ruined by a salesperson who moves too rapidly from one point to another.

There are at least two types of presentations that are doomed to failure. One is a sales presentation that is too basic and leaves the prospect with the feeling of being "patronized." It is important to avoid "talking down" to a customer. The other provides the prospect with too much detail. It is overly technical and leaves the buyer in a confused and frustrated state of mind. Salespeople who sell the same product every day sometimes lose sight of the fact that some customers cannot understand a highly technical presentation.

It is a good idea to assume that no one has time to waste. Make your presentation as concise and to the point as possible. The prospect will be greatly annoyed if you use 10 minutes to make a point that could have been covered in two or three minutes. Several years ago, the "KISS" principle was introduced to the field of selling. This popular acronym stands for "Keep It Simple and Straightforward." Put another way, never make your presentation more complex than it needs to be. Make sure the terms you use and ideas you present are familiar to your customers.

Use Proof Devices to Demonstrate Buyer Benefits

A well-planned and well-executed sales demonstration is one of the most convincing forms of proof. This is especially true if your product has dramatic points of superiority.

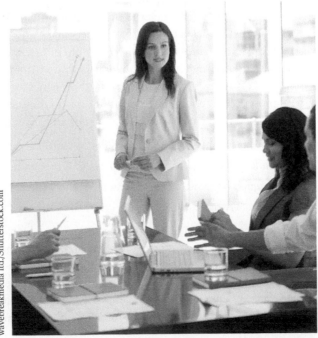

wavebreakmedia ltd./Shutterstock.com

When salespeople use effective visual proof devices in their presentations, research indicates that retention increases from 14 to 38 percent and the time needed to present a concept is reduced by up to 40 percent.

Business-to-business salespeople representing Epson, Canon, Hewlett-Packard, and other manufacturers can offer the customer a wide range of printers. What is the real difference between a $2000 printer and an $8000 printer? The most effective way to provide proof of this buyer benefit is to show the customer material that has been printed on both printers. By letting the prospect compare the samples, the salesperson is converting product features to a buyer benefit. Be prepared to prove every claim you make with tests, findings, and performance records.

Proof Devices We have noted that when trust is present, customers are more open to the sales presentation. One way to build trust is to use a proof device that enhances your credibility. A **proof device** can take the form of a statement, a report, a testimonial, customer data, or a photograph. A salesperson selling conference services for a large hotel/conference centre might use the following proof statement: "We were selected by *Training* magazine as one of Canada's top 10 conference centres." Later, the salesperson shows the customer photographs of the conference facilities and guest rooms. Then the customer is given a copy of a testimonial letter from a satisfied customer. The statement, photos, and letter help build the customer's confidence in the product. Later in this chapter, in the Selling Tools section, we will examine proof devices in more detail.

proof device A device such as a statement, report, testimonial, customer data, or photograph that is used to enhance the salesperson's credibility during a sales presentation.

Appeal to As Many Senses as Appropriate

In conducting a sales demonstration, it is a good idea to appeal to all appropriate senses. Each of the five senses—sight, hearing, smell, touch, and taste—represents an avenue by which the salesperson can attract the prospect's attention and build desire. Although sight is considered the most powerful attention-attracting sense, it may not be the most important motivating force in every selling situation. When presenting a food product, taste and aroma may be critical. Designers and decorators tell us that most furniture buyers still want to touch and feel the product before they buy it.

Paul Speck understands the importance of reaching the prospect through as many senses as possible. He and his two brothers make and sell red, white, rosé, sparkling, ice, and late-harvest wines from their Henry of Pelham winery in St. Catharines, Ontario to bars, restaurants, and even to individuals who visit and tour their winery. They, and the staff at the winery, are proud to discuss their wines and the history of their wine making with prospective customers. Depending on who they are speaking with, the sales presentation for a quality wine can highlight any or all of four areas:

- *Consumer demand.* The wine's sales potential is described in realistic terms.
- *Marketing strategies.* Suggested ways to merchandise the wine are discussed.
- *Bouquet.* The distinctive fragrance of the wine is introduced.
- *Taste.* A sample of the wine is given to the prospect in a good-quality wineglass.

Note that a sales presentation featuring these appeals will reach the prospect through four of the five senses. Collectively, these appeals add value. When you involve more than one sense, the sales presentation is more informative and persuasive. Of course, even with wine, referrals help. It certainly doesn't hurt that Natalie MacLean—author of *Red, White, and Drunk All Over* and *Unquenchable: A Tipsy Quest for the World's Best Bargain Wines*—has recommended the winery's Baco Noir among the 12 wines she recommended for 2014.[13]

Balance Telling, Showing, and Involvement

A Chinese proverb says, "Tell me, I'll forget; show me, I may remember; but involve me and I'll understand."[14] Some of the most effective sales demonstrations combine telling, showing, and involvement of the prospect. To plan an effective demonstration, consider developing a demonstration. Simply divide a sheet of paper into four columns. Head the first column "Feature to Be Demonstrated." Head the second column "Proof Device to Be Used." Head the third column "What I Will Say," and head the fourth column "What I or the Customer Will Do." List the major features you plan to demonstrate in proper sequence in the first column. In the second column, describe the proof devices you will use. In the third column, describe what you will say about the feature, converting the feature to a customer benefit. In the fourth column, describe what you (or the customer) will do at the time this benefit is discussed. A sample demonstration worksheet appears in Figure 12.4.

When appropriate and possible, try to involve the customer in the sales presentation. The best way to highlight the aesthetics, technology, and ergonomics of Teknion's AL3 executive swivel chair is to have the customer sit in it. Toronto-based Teknion is a leading international designer, manufacturer, and marketer of quality office systems and related furniture. To fully appreciate its products, customers really need to see and try them.

If it is not possible for the prospect to participate in demonstrations or handle the products, sales literature, pictures, or brochures placed in the person's hands may help. After the sales call, these items remind the prospect of not only who called but also why.

Demonstration Worksheet			
Feature to Be Demonstrated	**Proof Device to Be Used**	**What I Will Say (Include Benefit)**	**What I or the Customer Will Do**
Special computer circuit board to accelerate drawing graphics on a colour monitor screen	Monitor and software	"This monitor is large enough to display multiple windows. You can easily compare several graphics."	Have the customer bring up several windows using the computer keyboard.
Meeting room setup at a hotel and conference centre	Floor plan	"This setup will provide a metre of elbow space for each participant. For long meetings, the added space provides more comfort."	Give the customer a tour of the room and invite her to sit in a chair at one of the conference tables.

Figure 12.4 The demonstration worksheet.
The demonstration worksheet enables the salesperson to strategically plan and then rehearse demonstrations that strengthen the presentation.

Develop Creative Presentations

Presenting product features and buyer benefits in an interesting and appealing way requires some amount of creativity. Creativity is needed to adapt a sales presentation that can gain attention, increase desire, and add value. The ability to come up with problem-solving answers or different ways of looking at situations is greatly valued in today's fast-changing business environment. Creativity is enhanced by expertise in the field of endeavour. For salespeople, this means knowledge of the sales process, of the product, and of human behaviour. Creativity is also enhanced by the capacity for divergent thinking and a willingness to take risks.[15]

Consider the Use of Humour—in Moderation

According to Burt Teplitzky, author of *Sell It with Humor,* humour, if used in moderation and used appropriately, can work wonders to break down barriers, build rapport, and foster long-term and mutually beneficial customer relationships. If used improperly, it can distance you from your customer. Teplitzky suggests that one should never tell jokes off the cuff when speaking to customers. He suggests that your use of humour should be preplanned and communicate that you don't take yourself too seriously.

One part of the sales process in which he likes to use humour is the transition to the presentation. He might open his presentation with a line such as, "Before we get started, I promise not to bore you with a long presentation…. I'm sure I can do it with a short one." As he says, this would never go over in a comedy club, but in an environment where people are glad for any release, they appreciate the humour. Humour should never be used to attack anybody, nor should it be used during your transition to the close.[16]

Choose the Right Setting

The location of the sales demonstration can make a difference. Some companies routinely rent space at a hotel, motel, or conference centre so that the demonstration can be conducted in a controlled environment free of noise and other interruptions. However, in these busy times, prospects are often unwilling or unable to participate in a presentation held off premises. In these situations, many organizations do have conference rooms that can be reserved with advance notice.

Document the Value Proposition

In Chapter 7, we defined *value proposition* as a set of key benefits and values the salesperson promises to deliver to satisfy the customer's needs. Salespeople must be prepared to substantiate the points presented during the sales presentation. Recent research indicates that salespeople often make claims of savings and benefits to the customer but fail to back them up. Failure to demonstrate and document claims is a common barrier to closing the sale.[17]

In many cases, the most effective value proposition is one that focuses on favourable points of difference between your product and *the next best alternative.* The salesperson recognizes that the customer can purchase the product from one or more competitors. Once the customer's requirements and preferences are clearly understood, and knowledge of the competitor's product is acquired, the salesperson can focus on key points of difference.

The most effective value proposition describes the few elements that matter most to your customer. This approach recognizes that today's buyers are extremely busy and want to do business with salespeople who fully grasp the critical issues in their business and are able to deliver a value proposition that is simple yet powerfully captivating. Focus on favourable points of difference between your product and the *next best alternative*.[18]

Quantifying the Solution

In Chapter 6, we explained that the process of determining whether a sales proposal adds value is called *quantifying the solution*. If the cost of the proposal is offset by added value, closing the sale will be much easier. In business-to-business selling, quantifying the solution is very common. Let's assume you represent a manufacturing company that sells robots—programmable machines capable of performing a variety of tasks. The two primary benefits are (1) payroll cost savings and (2) vastly improved quality. One way to quantify the solution in this case is to use simple **cost–benefit analysis** (see Table 6.1). This involves listing the costs to the buyer and the savings to be achieved from the purchase of the robots.

Another way to quantify the solution is to calculate the net profits or savings—or **return on investment (ROI)**—expressed as a percentage of the original investment. Using the following formula, you can determine the return on a given investment:

$$\text{ROI} = \text{Net Profits (or Savings)} \div \text{Investment} \times 100$$

If the robotic system costs $16 000 but saves the firm $4000, the ROI is 25 percent ($4000 ÷ $16 000 × 100 = 25%). Some companies set a minimum ROI for new products or cost-saving programs. Salespeople typically acquire this information at the need assessment stage, then include it in the written proposal.

Space does not permit an in-depth review of the many methods of quantifying the solution, such as payback period, opportunity cost, net present value, after-tax cash flow, turnover, and contribution margin.

cost–benefit analysis An analysis of the costs versus the benefits to the customer as a result of making a particular purchase.

return on investment (ROI) The net profits or savings that the customer will see from investing in a particular purchase.

Check Sales Tools

Be sure to check every item to be used in conjunction with the sales demonstration. If you are using audiovisual equipment, be certain that it is in good working condition. Always carry an extension cord and a spare bulb. If you are making a laptop presentation, be sure you can go online in front of the customer. If you plan to demonstrate a website, save it on a hard disk instead of going online. Be prepared for technological snags by having multiple backups. Always carry extra batteries for your laptop.[19]

Summarize Major Points

The allotted time for a presentation usually provides the opportunity to present a significant amount of information. Most people talk at a speed of about 125 words per minute. In a short time span of just 15 minutes, the customer may be bombarded with approximately 1900 words. For this reason, the salesperson should occasionally use a summary-confirmation question to summarize and confirm major points. The customer needs this form of value-added assistance.

GUIDELINES FOR A PERSUASIVE PRESENTATION STRATEGY THAT ADDS VALUE

EARLIER IN THIS CHAPTER, WE INTRODUCED YOU TO THE PERSUASIVE PRESENTATION STRATEGY as one of the three strategies you could choose in creating a need-satisfaction presentation. A study on persuasion in the *Journal for Management in Engineering* reported that effective communicators recognize that conviction (emotion) is more vital to persuasion than position (logic). People make decisions based primarily on what they feel and then test or rationalize their choice with logic. Table 12.1 illustrates the contrast between traditional technical communication and persuasive communication.[20]

Technical communication, illustrated in the first column of Table 12.1, would be more appropriate for the *informative presentation strategy* introduced in Chapter 11. Persuasive communication, appropriately used, will enhance the success of the *persuasive presentation strategy*.

There are many ways to incorporate persuasion into a presentation strategy and most, if used appropriately, will create value for the customer. In this section, we review a series of guidelines that should be followed during preparation of a persuasive presentation.

Place Special Emphasis on the Relationship

Relationships are enhanced by the salesperson's ability to communicate in compelling and creative ways.[21] Throughout this book, we emphasize the importance of the relationship strategy in selling. Good rapport between the salesperson and the prospect establishes a foundation for an open exchange of information. Robert Cialdini, writing in the *Harvard Business Review*, says the science of persuasion is built on the principle of liking: *People like those who like them.*

Salespeople, acting as relationship managers, play a key role in the development and management of partnering relationships.[22] Establish a bond with the prospect early by uncovering areas of common interest, using praise when it's appropriate, and being completely trustworthy.[23] Don't forget to adapt your communication style to accommodate the needs of the customer (see Chapter 5). Also remember that good salespeople today use smart social-media strategies to enhance customer relationships. They make it their business to stay connected to their customers through Twitter, Facebook, and LinkedIn.[24] When building important partnering relationships, remember that most people don't care how much you know until they know how much you care.

Table 12.1 Technical vs. Persuasive Communication	
Technical Communication	**Persuasive Communication**
Impersonal, objective	Personal, subjective
Intellectual response	Emotional response
Emphasizes features	Emphasizes benefits
Information-driven	Influence-driven

Target Emotional Links and Use a Persuasive Vocabulary

Emotional links are the connectors between your messages and the internal emotions of your prospect.[25] Some common emotional links in the business community are quality improvement, on-time delivery, increased market share, innovation, customer service, and reduction of operating expenses. Targeting just a few emotional links can increase your chances of closing the sale. When you target emotional links, use persuasive words. Research conducted on persuasion suggests the following list of words to use in persuasive communication. Consider the appropriate use of these words when planning a persuasive presentation strategy:

emotional links The connectors that link a salesperson's message to the customer's emotions and increase the chances of closing a sale—for example, quality improvement, on-time delivery, service, innovation.

*you	*advantage
save	guarantee
money	security
health	discovery
easy	*new
now	*benefits
safety	positive
results	proven

Note: *Many marketing people agree that the words with asterisks are probably the most important in selling and advertising.

Sell Specific Benefits and Obtain Customer Reactions

People do not buy things; they buy what the things will do for them. At Mattress Firm, Edith Botello realizes her customers do not buy a mattress; they buy a relaxing, comfortable, uninterrupted, physically healthy night of rest. Chief information officers do not buy computers or programming services; they buy timely, easy to access, easy to understand, economically priced information. Every product or service offers the customer certain benefits. The benefit might be ease of operation, greater comfort, security, feelings of confidence, or economy.

Global Business Insight

Patience and Sensitivity Help Clinch the Deal

Going global? If so, pack plenty of patience and sensitivity. And be prepared to emphasize value-added selling. Too often Canadians rely on the "time is money" belief and they take shortcuts in some key areas. For example, they do not spend enough time learning about the culture of the country they are visiting. Also, they often fail to take the time needed to build a relationship with the client.

Assaf Kedem, a representative of Intercomp, recalls having lunch with two prospects in Germany. For three hours, the German executives asked questions about where Assef was from and talked about their favourite foods and interests. Business was never discussed. Kedem viewed that long lunch as an important first step in building a relationship that will last for years.[a]

If you are selling Allstate insurance, for example, you should become familiar with the service features. One feature is well-trained employees, and another is the convenient location of Allstate offices throughout Canada. The benefit to customers is greater peace of mind in knowing that they will receive good service at a nearby location. Allstate salespeople understand the importance of selling the company, the product, and themselves.

After you state the feature and convert it into a buyer benefit, obtain a reaction from the customer by using confirmation or need-satisfaction questions (refer to Table 11.1). You should always check to see if you are on the right track and if your prospect is following the logic of your presentation. Here are some examples:

Feature	Benefit	Question
Seven-hour battery life*	Fewer work interruptions when travelling	"Battery life is important to you, isn't it?" (*Confirmation question*)
Automatic climate control system for automobile	Temperature in car not varying after initial setting	"Would you like the luxury of setting the temperature and then not worrying about it?" (*Need-satisfaction question*)
*Feature of Fujitsu Lifebook laptop		

The feature–benefit–reaction or, as IBM salespeople call it, the *FBR approach*, is used by many high-performance salespeople. Involving the customer with appropriate questions helps you maintain two-way communication.

Use of Showmanship

Showmanship is defined as an interesting and attractive way of communicating an idea to others. If done tastefully and appropriately, it can do a lot to improve the persuasiveness and effectiveness of a sales presentation. Showmanship in selling need not be equated with sensational or bizarre events. It may be a very subtle act such as the furnishing and accessorizing, or "staging" as it is sometimes called, of a home being shown by PulteGroup's Ashley Pineda, introduced in Chapter 8. Another example of showmanship would be carefully placing a fine diamond on a piece of black velvet before showing the jewel to the customer.

Some good examples of showmanship can be seen at trade shows, where new products are displayed. One company demonstrated the fireproof quality of their insulation by holding a piece of it in front of a blowtorch. In simplest terms, showmanship is the act of presenting product features and benefits in a manner that will gain attention and increase desire. It is never a substitute for thorough preparation and knowledge of your customer, company, and product. And effective showmanship is never based on deceit or trickery. It should not be gaudy or insincere. When showmanship detracts from the image, the product, or the salesperson, it is counterproductive.

Minimize the Negative Impact of Change

As we noted earlier, salespeople are constantly threatening the status quo. They sell people the new, the different, and the untried. In nearly all selling situations, the customer is being asked to consider change of some sort and, in some cases, it is only natural for the person to resist change. Whenever possible, salespeople should try to help the prospect view change in a positive and realistic way. Change is more acceptable to people who understand the benefits of it and do not see it as a threat. Always anticipate the one question (spoken or unspoken) that every buyer asks: "How will this product benefit me?" To minimize the impact of change, be sure to personalize the benefit with a specific reference to the customer's need.

Place the Strongest Appeal at the Beginning or End

Research indicates that appeals made at the beginning or end of a presentation are more effective than those given in the middle. A strong appeal at the beginning of a presentation gets the prospect's attention and possibly develops interest. Made near the end of the presentation, the appeal sets the stage for closing the sale.

Use the Power of Association with Metaphors, Stories, and Testimonials

Research reveals that salespeople who use the power of association through sharing information they previously experienced with other clients help their customers better understand their own needs and make smarter buying choices.[26] Metaphors, sometimes referred to as *figurative language*, are highly persuasive sales tools. Metaphors are words or phrases that suggest pictorial relationships between objects or ideas. With the aid of metaphors, you can paint vivid pictures for prospects that will command their attention and keep their interest. The success of the metaphor rests on finding common ground (shared or well-known experiences) so that your message gets a boost from a fact already

Preparing a sales presentation for a group is more demanding than one-on-one sales calls. Too much reliance on technical devices during a demonstration can affect the relationship, which is important to partnering effectively with prospects.

Andresr/Shutterstock

known or believed to be true. A salesperson presenting Cobalt boats, a line of high-quality runabouts selling for $30 000 to $300 000, might refer to his products as "the Steinways of the runabout class."[27] Stories not only help you sell more products but also help you enrich relationships with your customers. Salespeople, such as Liberty Mutual's Marcus Smith introduced in Chapter 2, often use stories about a timely settlement for a large loss to explain the benefits of adequate insurance protection. A good story focuses the customer's attention and can effectively communicate the value of a product or service. The story should be appropriate to the customer's situation, short, and told with enthusiasm.[28]

Many salespeople find it beneficial to quote a specific third party. Third-party testimonials from satisfied customers can help a prospect feel confident about using your product.

GUIDELINES FOR A GROUP SALES PRESENTATION

PREPARING A SALES PRESENTATION FOR A GROUP IS MORE DEMANDING THAN ONE-ON-ONE sales calls. Meeting the diverse needs of the audience can be very challenging. Therefore, *Rule One* is to identify the titles and roles of the people who will attend. Among those attending, who is most likely to influence the buying decision? If you learn that the audience will include the prospect's CEO, your CEO should be there. Anticipate that the audience will include demanding, high-level decision makers who will likely ask some difficult questions. Be prepared![29]

Rule Two is to check out the meeting room in advance. Take note of the room configuration, audiovisual capabilities, seating options, available lighting, and the adequacy of heating or air conditioning. Always arrive at the meeting room about 60 minutes before the meeting begins. Use the first 40 minutes to check and double-check presentation tools, seating arrangements, lighting, etc. Use the other 20 minutes for building rapport with attendees as they arrive.

Rule Three is to be sure your presentation is characterized by clarity and simplicity. Minimize the number of features and benefits you present. Focus on the few benefits that appeal to your prospect. Don't use jargon or technical terms that might confuse persons in attendance. If you are part of a team sales presentation (see Chapter 10), then be sure every team member understands their responsibility and the amount of time they will be given for their presentation. Give the team time for rehearsal before the group presentation.

Rule Four is to anticipate the diversity of questions such as finance, delivery, competition, and service, in addition to traditional product issues you are likely to be asked. You must be prepared with answers that are concise and persuasive. Questions should be welcomed because they help you understand what is truly important to the customer.

Enhancing the Group Presentation with Mental Imagery

mental imagery The ability to visualize an object, concept, or action not actually present.

Mental imagery is the ability to visualize an object, concept, or action not actually present. A sales demonstration can be greatly enhanced with the use of auditory and visual imagery. Today there is no shortage of compact, lightweight portable presentation devices. Sony Electronics, Hitachi Software, and NEC offer sales professionals projectors that weigh only a few pounds and project a clear, bright image. These presentation tools also offer quick and easy setup.[30]

Impatica, a company that specializes in the delivery and viewing of PowerPoint presentations over the Internet and wireless networks, has developed a small, lightweight device that enables salespeople to project presentations wirelessly from a BlackBerry handheld device. Users need only hook the ShowMate to the VGA port projector, LCD, or plasma screen and the BlackBerry will deliver the PowerPoint presentation using Bluetooth technology.[31] Of course, salespeople should never rely solely on presentation tools to sell products. Dianne Durkin, president of the consulting firm Loyalty Factor, offers this advice:

> When a salesperson is tied to the technical device and the presentation, they miss the opportunity to build the personal relationship by asking questions and listening to the customer. A questioning and listening strategy is the secret weapon for the salesperson.[32]

Audiovisual Presentation Fundamentals

Many companies provide their salespeople with such audiovisual aids as videotapes or computer-based presentations. Unfortunately, they sometimes fail to explain how to use these tools in the most effective way. Here are some suggestions on how to use audiovisual presentations to achieve maximum impact:

1. As noted earlier, do not rely too heavily on "bells and whistles" to sell your products. Audiovisual technology provides support for the major points in your presentation, but it does not replace an interactive sales demonstration.

2. Be sure the prospect knows the purpose of the presentation. Preview the material and describe a few highlights. Always try to build interest in advance of the audiovisual presentation.

3. Be prepared to stop the presentation to clarify a point or to allow the prospect to ask questions. Do not permit the audiovisual presentation to become a barrier to good two-way communication.

4. At the conclusion of the audiovisual presentation, review key points and allow the prospect an opportunity to ask questions.

Many firms have learned that one of the keys to closing a large, complex sale is to conduct a plant tour.

Tyler Olson/Shutterstock

Gina Gallo is a third-generation family winemaker who not only knows how to make wines offered by E. & J. Gallo Winery, but also knows how to sell them. The year she spent as a member of the sales force helped her learn about consumers' buying habits and the needs of customers that resell Gallo wines. Gina Gallo sees some similarities between winemaking and sales. The better you understand your vineyards, the soil, and the grapes, the greater the chance you have of creating an excellent wine. The better you understand your customer's needs, the better you can relate to and fulfill those needs.[b]

SELLING TOOLS FOR EFFECTIVE DEMONSTRATIONS

NEARLY EVERY SALES ORGANIZATION PROVIDES ITS STAFF WITH PROOF DEVICES OR SALES tools of one kind or another to use in the demonstration part of the consultative presentation. Some companies refer to these as *marketing tools*. Many proof devices and sales tools, when used correctly, add value to the sales effort. If the company does not provide these items, the creative salesperson secures or develops sales tools independently. In addition to technology-based presentations, sales personnel can utilize a wide range of other selling tools. Creative salespeople are continually developing new types of sales tools. The following section summarizes some of the most common proof devices and selling tools used today.

Product and Plant Tours

Without a doubt, the best selling aid is usually the product itself. As noted previously, Bell Helicopter uses an effective video to describe various products—although some customers still will not buy without a demonstration ride. In the growing market for ergonomic office chairs, ranging in price from $700 to $1500, furniture makers know the best way to close the sale is to provide an opportunity for the customer to sit in the chair. With growing awareness of the hazards of poor sitting posture and bad ergonomics, more people are searching for a comfortable work chair.[33]

Doug Adams was the first salesperson hired by a major manufacturer of high-quality optical equipment. Although he was not a technician or an engineer, he quickly realized that the equipment had product superiority that physicians would recognize if they saw it demonstrated. During the first year, he sold 28 machines, far surpassing the expectations of his employer.[34]

As noted in a previous chapter, plant tours provide an excellent source of product information. Engineered Machine Products (EMP) makes high-efficiency thermal management systems for cooling engines. Products are made at its state-of-the-art manufacturing facility, and the company has learned that the key to closing many large, complex sales is a facility tour.[35]

Models

Sometimes, it is not practical to demonstrate the product itself because it is too big or immobile. It is easier to demonstrate a small-scale model or cross-section of the original equipment. A working model, like the actual product, can give the prospect a clear picture of how a piece of equipment operates.

With the aid of modern technology, it is possible to create a model in picture form. ClosetMaid (**www.closetmaid.com**), a manufacturer of ventilated wire for commercial closets and other storage products, uses desktop visualization software to create a three-dimensional presentation that allows customers to see exactly what the finished facility will look like. Sales representatives can print out a hard copy so the customer has a picture of the custom-designed model for future reference. With the aid of this visualization technology, ClosetMaid salespeople can modify closet layouts on screen and produce a detailed bill of materials for each project.[36]

Photos, Illustrations, and Brochures

The old proverb "One picture is worth a thousand words" can be put into practical application by a creative salesperson. A great deal of information can be given to the prospect with the aid of photos and illustrations. Chris Roberts, area manager for Downing Displays (**www.downingretail.com**), a manufacturer of trade-show displays, says that the photo presentation book is the most important item he takes on a first sales call. He says, "Because what we sell is very visual, it's important for the client to *see* the displays."[37]

Many companies develop brochures that visually reinforce specific need or benefit areas. Brochures can be effective during the initial discussion of needs when the salesperson wants to provide a brief overview of possible solutions. Someone planning to remodel a kitchen might be given a number of brochures that feature colour photos of numerous countertop materials and kitchen design examples.[38]

Portfolios

A **portfolio** is a portable case or loose-leaf binder containing a wide variety of sales-supporting materials. The portfolio is used to add visual life to the sales message and to prove claims. Advertising salespeople such as *Texas Monthly*'s Amy Vandaveer, introduced in Chapter 6, customize portfolios to appeal to the unique interests and needs of individual clients. She carefully selects sales tools to include, such as the following items:

- Sample advertisements used in conjunction with other successful campaigns
- Selected illustrations that can be incorporated into advertisements
- A selection of testimonial letters
- Rate cards
- Market research studies and results on readership and buying habits
- Case histories of specific clients who have used the media with success

The portfolio has been used as a sales aid by people who sell interior design services, insurance, real estate, securities, and convention services. It is a very adaptable proof device that can be revised at any time to meet the needs of each customer.

portfolio A portable case or loose-leaf binder containing a wide variety of sales-supporting materials. It is used to add visual life to the sales message and to prove claims.

Reprints

Leading magazines and journals sometimes feature articles that directly or indirectly support the salesperson's product. A reprint of the article can be a forceful selling tool. It is also an inexpensive selling tool. Pharmaceutical and medical sales representatives often use reprints from journals that report on research in the field of medicine. A few years ago, Closure Medical Corporation received approval to sell Dermabond (**www.dermabond.com**), a surgical glue used to close cuts. This innovative product received national attention when the prestigious *Journal of the American Medical Association* concluded that gluing a wound could be just as effective as sewing it shut. Salespeople representing Dermabond used the article to help educate doctors on the product's merits and applications.[39] In many cases, prospects are far more impressed with the good points of your product if a third party presents them than if you do. A reprint from a respected journal can be very persuasive.

Catalogues

A well-designed catalogue shows the range and comprehensiveness of your product line. It may include specifications needed for installation and current price information. If you plan to give customers a copy of your catalogue, review the important features, such as a comprehensive index or important appendix material.[40]

Graphs, Charts, and Test Results

Graphs and charts can be used to illustrate changes in variables such as payroll expense, fuel consumption, or return on investment. For example, a bar graph might be used to illustrate the increase in fuel costs over a 10-year period. While graphs are usually quite descriptive, the layperson may misunderstand them. It is best to interpret the graph for the prospect. Do not move too fast, because the full impact of the message may be lost.

Test results from a reliable agency can be convincing. This is especially true when the test results are published by a respected independent agency, such as J. D. Power and Associates.

Bound Paper Presentations

While many salespeople use some type of presentation technology in conjunction with the sales demonstration, bound paper presentations are still a popular medium for many sales and marketing organizations.[41] With the aid of computer-generated graphics, sales-people find it easy to print attractive graphs, charts, and other proof information. Product guarantees and warranties are sometimes included in a bound paper presentation. Some marketers use guarantees and warranties to differentiate their products from competing products. Customer testimonials represent another common element of bound paper presentations. A testimonial letter from a prominent satisfied customer provides persuasive evidence that the product has support in the industry. Prospects also like bound paper presentations because the document is readily available for future reference.

Laptop Computers and Demonstration Software

A survey conducted by *Selling Power* magazine found that 87 percent of salespeople use laptops during their sales presentations.[42] Many salespeople report that the laptop computer is the single most powerful sales tool they use. Many of the things needed during the demonstration can be stored in the computer. If the customer is interested in a specific product, pull up the appropriate brochure on your laptop screen. If the client wants a copy of printed material or a videotape, you can either print the pages or send them via email. If the customer raises a question regarding product availability, use your laptop to access the information. You can place an order and, in some cases, print an invoice.[43] Thanks to modern computer technology, it's possible to conduct impressive multiple, simultaneous product demonstrations without leaving your office. Let's assume you are presenting a new employee disability insurance plan to members of the 3M Canada human resources staff. One key decision maker is based in London, Ontario, and the other is in the United States. With the aid of Pixion PictureTalk software or a similar product, you can use the Internet to conduct the demonstration for both persons in real time. Sales managers might use this same approach to train members of their sales team in remote offices.

Personal computers (PCs), with the support of online presentation technologies and presentation software, have played an important role in increasing sales force productivity. Salespeople have instant access to customer data, so they can easily customize the sales presentation. Many salespeople report that PC–based presentations, using graphics software, are very effective. Today's PC can produce striking visuals and attractive printed material that can be given to the customer for future reference.

Enhancing Demonstrations with PowerPoint The PowerPoint software program from Microsoft has been available to salespeople for 20 years. PowerPoint is so common that many prospects will find the standard presentation graphics very familiar, even dull. Salespeople who want their demonstration to look unique and different can create their own corporate template, animate their logo, or put video clips of their company information into the PowerPoint presentation. When developing a PowerPoint presentation, use bold, simple, and large fonts (such as Arial and Verdana) and put graphics on several slides. Limit the number of words to 15 or fewer per slide. Keep in mind two quality alternatives to PowerPoint: Apple's Keynote and Corel's Presentations.[44]

Creating Electronic Spreadsheets For many years, salespeople have been using electronic spreadsheets to prepare sales proposals. The electronic spreadsheet is an excellent tool for organizing the numbers involved in preparing quotes, such as quantities, costs, and prices. CB Richard Ellis's Susana Rosas, introduced in Chapter 4, frequently uses electronic spreadsheets to justify the purchase or rental of commercial properties. The electronic spreadsheet allows the user to answer "What if ..." questions about the effects of lowering costs or raising prices. Once the preparation work is finished, the electronic spreadsheet itself can be printed and used as the proposal or to accompany the proposal.[45] The spreadsheet data can also be converted to a chart or graph that can enhance the proposal. When presenting the spreadsheet on a laptop computer, with minor adjustments, client questions regarding alternative proposals can be quickly generated. Many computers sold today include an electronic spreadsheet program. The leading electronic spreadsheet, Excel, is part of Microsoft's Office suite of products. If you have access to Excel or any other electronic spreadsheet software, you can explore the power of this tool for preparing proposals.

Web-Based Demonstrations Salespeople who want to avoid long airport security lines, lengthy terminal wait times, high-priced hotels, and expensive rental car rates are turning to Web-conferencing solutions. Popular alternatives to in-person sales presentations include GoToMeeting, WebEx Communications Sales Center, Raindance Meeting Edition, Adobe's Macromedia Breeze 5, and Microsoft Office Live Meeting. Some salespeople create computerized demonstrations that are stored in a central library and accessed on demand. With a few clicks of a mouse, presenters can call up the information they wish to showcase using a Web browser. The salesperson can show PowerPoint presentations, present product features, and conduct question-and-answer sessions in real time. Prior to scheduling an online meeting, be sure to find out if the customer's firewall restricts the usage of your Web-conferencing software.[46]

Rehearse the Presentation

While you are actually putting on the presentation, you will need to be concentrating on a variety of details. The movements you make and what you say and do should be so familiar to you that each response is nearly automatic. To achieve this level of skill, you need to rehearse the presentation.

Rehearse both what you are going to say and what you are going to do. Say the words aloud exactly as if the prospect were present. It is surprising how often a concept that seems quite clear as you think it over becomes hopelessly mixed up when you try to discuss it with a customer. Rehearsal is the best way to avoid this embarrassing situation. Whenever possible, have your presentation/demonstration videotaped before you give it. Play it back and watch for these things:[47]

- Do you frequently use words that take away from your professional image? Examples include "you know" and "like."
- Check your pace—are you talking too rapidly or too slowly?
- Do you present information with clarity? Are you convincing?

Plan for the Dynamic Nature of Selling

The sales presentation is a dynamic activity. From the moment the salesperson and the customer meet, the sales presentation is being altered and fine-tuned to reflect the new information available. The salesperson must be able to execute strategy instantaneously. In the movie *Top Gun*, Kelly McGillis asks Tom Cruise, "What were you thinking up there?" He replies, "You don't have time to think. You take time to think up there, you're dead." By this he means that one's response must be habit and reflex.[48]

During a typical presentation, the salesperson asks numerous questions, discusses several product features, and demonstrates the appropriate product benefits. The customer is asking questions and, in many cases, voicing concerns. The successful sales presentation is a good model of two-way communication. Because of the dynamic nature of the sales presentation, the salesperson must be prepared to apply several different selling skills to meet the variety of buyer responses. Figure 12.5 illustrates how the various selling skills

Consultative Selling Skills	Parts of the Sales Presentation			
	Need Discovery	Selecting Solution	Need-Satisfaction Presentation	Servicing the Sale
Questioning Skills	As a question approach To find needs and buying motives To probe for buying motives To confirm needs and buying motives	To confirm selection	To confirm benefits To confirm mutual understanding To increase desire for a solution	To make suggestions To confirm delivery and installation To resolve complaints To build goodwill To secure credit arrangements
Presenting Benefits	As a benefit approach To discover specific benefits	To match buying motives	To build support for the solution	To make suggestions To use credit as a close
Demonstrating Skills	As a product approach To clarify need	To clarify selection	To strengthen product claims	When making effective suggestions
Negotiating Skills	To overcome initial resistance to sales interviews To overcome buyer's need concerns	To overcome buyer's product concerns	To overcome buyer's source, price, and time concerns	In handling complaints To overcome buyer's financing concerns
Closing Skills	When customer has made a buying decision	When buyer immediately recognizes solutions	Whenever buyer presents closing signals	After suggestion To secure repeats and referrals

Figure 12.5 The Selling Dynamics Matrix
In creating effective presentations, the salesperson should be prepared to meet a wide range of buyer responses with effective questions, benefit statements, demonstrations, negotiating methods, and closing methods.

can be applied during all parts of the sales presentation. In creating effective presentations, the salesperson should be prepared to meet a wide range of buyer responses with effective questions, benefit statements, demonstrations, negotiating methods, and closing methods. Methods for negotiating, closing and confirming, and servicing the sale will be described in the next three chapters.

REVIEWING KEY CONCEPTS

- List and describe three types of need-satisfaction presentation strategies.

  Once you have selected a solution that matches the customer's needs, you must decide which presentation strategy to emphasize. Need satisfaction can be achieved through informing, persuading, or reminding. The salesperson can, in some cases, use a combination of these presentation strategies.

- Present guidelines for creating consultative presentations that add value.

  The perception of value is enhanced with a well-developed consultative presentation, whether it be the informative, persuasive, or reminder need-satisfaction presentation strategy. A sales presentation that adds value is the result of both planning and practice with the guidelines described in this chapter. An effective, well-organized demonstration helps to make the buying process less complicated.

- Describe the elements of a persuasive presentation strategy.

There are many ways to incorporate persuasion into a sales presentation and most will—if used appropriately—create value for the customer. Seven specific methods are presented.

- Describe the elements of an effective group presentation.

  Group presentations are almost always more challenging than one-on-one sales calls. Be sure you identify the titles and roles of the persons who will attend. Check out the meeting room in advance to assess audiovisual capabilities and seating options. As you prepare your presentation, take into consideration the needs of the audience. In many cases, audiovisual tools can be used to enhance the group presentation.

- Develop selling tools that add value to your sales demonstrations.

  Selling tools, also called *proof devices*, used to demonstrate the benefits of your solution will add value to the sale presentation. Be prepared to use one or more of the 10 tools discussed in this chapter.

Key Terms

canned presentation **285**

cost–benefit analysis **291**

emotional links **293**

informative presentation **283**

mental imagery **296**

persuasion **283**

persuasive presentation **283**

portfolio **299**

proof device **288**

reminder presentation **284**

return on investment (ROI) **291**

showmanship **294**

Review Questions

1. Distinguish among the three types of need-satisfaction presentations: informative, persuasive, and reminder.

2. List the guidelines to follow in planning an effective consultative presentation.

3. Discuss the advantages of using a presentation worksheet.

4. Explain why a salesperson should organize the sales presentation so that it appeals to as many of the five senses as possible.

5. What are the guidelines to be followed when developing a persuasive sales presentation?

6. Develop a list of the sales tools that the salesperson should consider when planning a sales demonstration.

7. Describe the merits of a bound paper presentation. What can be done to strengthen the persuasive power of a bound paper presentation?

8. Explain how magazine and trade journal reprints can be used to assist the salesperson in a persuasive sales presentation.

9. Describe the audiovisual presentation fundamentals.

10. What are some of the common sales functions performed by laptop computers and demonstration software?

Application Exercises

1. In many selling situations, it is difficult, if not impossible, to demonstrate the product itself. List other means that can be used to demonstrate product features and benefits.

2. Develop a list of sales tools you could use in a job interview. What tools could you use to demonstrate your skills and capabilities?

3. As noted in this chapter, demonstration software is becoming increasingly popular. Real estate salespeople are using this software to showcase homes to prospective buyers. Assume you are a salesperson for Coldwell Banker Real Estate Canada, and you have a customer who wants a $300 000 to $400 000 detached home in the area near your college or university. The home should have three or more bedrooms and two or more bathrooms. Visit the **www.realtor.ca** website and click on "Residential Properties."

Enter your region or city and then complete the information requested. Request a search for homes that meet your criteria. How many homes meet your criteria? From your search, select two homes and click on "More Information." What information can you use as part of your sales demonstration to the customer?

4. You have decided to try tutoring as a means of earning some extra money. Which sales tools would be appropriate for you to use? Which sales tools should you consider developing as you prepare presentations for prospective clients? Explain how you might use them in the future.

5. Bring a product of your choice to class and be prepared to give a presentation that will include a product demonstration. Consider how you can use telling, showing, and, most importantly, involvement.

ROLE-PLAY EXERCISE

Study the product selling strategy memo and proof devices found on pages 40–44 in "Partnership Selling: A Role Play/ Simulation" online in the Student Resources section at **www.pearsoncanada.ca/manning**. In this role play, you will be selling to a human resources manager who is interested in controlling costs for a regional meeting of company employees. All 75 of the attendees will be staying at the hotel—50 of them will be driving to the hotel and the other 25 will be flying. Prepare a comparative cost–benefit graph to show the total amount this meeting planner can expect to save by selecting your hotel. Use the proof devices you have prepared to demonstrate the cost savings to the meeting planner. Plan also to use the map on page 12 to demonstrate the ease of finding the hotel.

Reality Selling Video Case Problem

Ecolab (www.ecolab.com) is the global leader in cleaning, sanitizing, food safety, and infection prevention products and services. With more than 14 000 sales and service experts, Ecolab employs the industry's largest and best-trained direct sales and service force, which advises and assists customers in meeting a full range of cleaning, sanitation, and service needs. Chris Wylie, the Ecolab sales representative featured at the beginning of this chapter, is continually prospecting for new accounts, servicing existing accounts, and introducing new products and services. He primarily calls on restaurants and hotels to sell and service a wide array of cleaning and sanitizing products such as bathroom air fresheners, bathroom cleaners, dispensers, floor cleaners, glass cleaners, dish machines, detergents, dish racks, and safety equipment.

In his sales demonstrations, Chris follows certain guidelines and tries to add value in various ways. Sales reps at Ecolab utilize the HELP sales process and move toward a survey solution they can sell their customers. The sales rep's goal is to determine the decision-making team, uncover the relevant facts, identify the problem/opportunity, and present the implications of the problem such that the customer decides to accept the solution that is presented by Ecolab. One central element of the HELP sales process is a so-called three-minute demo in which Chris can show the prospect deficiencies in his or her kitchen that he or she might not be aware of. To that end, he possesses a series of measurement tools to test the chemicals and certain concentration ratios. After conducting the whole series of tests and analyzing the results, Chris goes back to his customer and asks for a few minutes of his or her time to show that same survey on his piece of restaurant equipment (e.g., a dish machine). Through specific guidelines, Chris can show the prospect certain machine deficiencies that he or she has with the current provider. Chris can then demonstrate the features and benefits that Ecolab can offer to overcome these deficiencies.

In his sales demonstrations, Chris tries to interact with his customers to get them involved and to fully capture their attention. He even engages customers in the survey process by asking them to execute parts of the tests with him. In addition, Chris involves his customers by asking questions such as, "What do you think this result means? Let's think about this together for a second." Then he leads the customer into developing a good solution for the result they got. In this way, Chris helps customers paint their own picture of the problem. Chris knows that this kind of customer engagement is much more effective and eye-opening than just telling the customer about the deficiencies.

In some situations, it might be difficult or even impossible for Chris to demonstrate a product itself. An example could be a dishwasher that is too large and heavy to be taken to the customer's or prospect's location. If Chris makes claims about how efficient Ecolab's machine is compared to others, it appears that his customers would have to take his word on that. Another way to demonstrate the effectiveness and efficiency of a dishwasher that he is trying to pitch would be to bring the prospect into an existing account that already uses the dishwasher. This would enable Chris to show how the dishwasher operates while somebody is actually using it. (See the chapter opener on page 280 and Reality Selling Today Role Play 9 in Appendix 1 on page 436 for more information.)

Questions

1. If you were in the position of Chris Wylie and found a potential serious health problem in one of your customer's kitchens, which presentation strategy or combination described in this chapter would you use? List and describe five guidelines you would use in creating your presentation. What demonstration tools would you use?

2. Make a list of buyer concerns that a salesperson like Chris Wylie would typically expect from new prospects. How could different elements of a sales demonstration be used to overcome these concerns? Think about it as a two-step sales call: In the first step, Chris would ask for permission to conduct a survey of the kitchen and/or bathroom. In the second step, he would ask the prospect to buy from him.

3. In the video case, which of the six actions (as listed on the right-hand side of Figure 12.3) does Chris Wylie take during his presentation/demonstration?

4. In some situations, it might be difficult or even impossible for Chris Wylie to specifically demonstrate a product or service. What other means can Chris use to demonstrate the features and benefits of, for example, large products or intangible services?

PARTNERSHIP SELLING: A ROLE PLAY/SIMULATION

Visit the role play/simulation materials provided in the Student Resources section of your companion website at **www.pearsoncanada.ca/manning**. *A contents page lists appropriate page references for the activities.*

Developing a Sales Presentation Strategy—The Demonstration

Read *Sales Memorandum 3* ("A" or "B" depending on the category you were assigned in sales call 1). In this role play, your call objectives are to make a persuasive presentation, negotiate any customer concerns, and close and service the sale.

At this time you should complete item 1 of the presentation plan, and prepare and price a product solution. This will include completing the sales proposal form. You should also obtain a three-ring binder with pockets in the front and back for the development of a portfolio presentation. In this binder, you should prepare your presentation and demonstration, following the instructions in items 2a, 2b, 2c, and 2d under the presentation plan. The presentation and demonstration materials should be placed in the three-ring binder as a part of your portfolio presentation. (Use the product strategy materials—i.e., photos, price lists, menus, awards, etc.—provided to you with *Employment Memorandum 1*.)

Using PowerPoint and Excel software, you may want to produce computer-generated presentation graphics to enhance your demonstrations. You should also consider using presentation paper and sheet protectors. You may want to select a person as your customer and rehearse the use of these materials.

Chapter 13
Negotiating Buyer Concerns

Learning Objectives

After studying this chapter, you should be able to

1 Describe the principles of formal negotiations as part of the win-win strategy.

2 Describe common types of buyer concerns.

3 Discuss specific methods of negotiating buyer concerns.

4 Outline methods for creating value in formal negotiations.

5 Describe how to work with buyers who are trained in negotiation.

Marriott International Inc. (**www.marriott.com**) is a world-renowned company with approximately 8500 salespeople and 3000 lodging properties around the world—more than 50 of them in Canada. One of its properties is the Marriott Houston Hobby, which is located within a mile of the Hobby Airport in Houston, Texas. Apart from accommodation, the hotel offers comprehensive meeting facilities complemented by expert catering and audiovisual resources. Corporate catering manager Heather Ramsey, in the photo at the top of the next page, is in charge of convention and meeting sales at the Marriott Houston Hobby. She always has a ready response when customers raise concerns about prices and the tranquility of an airport hotel. She emphasizes the value to the customers by describing the state-of-the-art meeting and conference facilities offered by the hotel, its convenience to travellers, as well as other unique features not offered by the competition. Sometimes customers do not communicate openly about their needs and concerns to Heather. She often must work hard to identify their actual needs to offer them the best value and bring benefits to the hotel as well. Her negotiation process

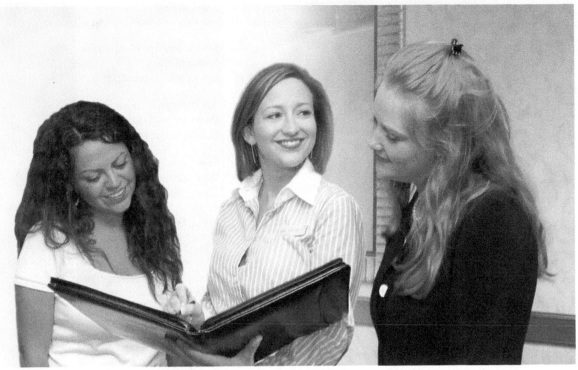

Heather Ramsey

with new customers will normally involve identifying their actual needs and then listening to, clarifying, and negotiating concerns that the customers express.

NEGOTIATING BUYER CONCERNS AND PROBLEMS

MANY SALES PROFESSIONALS ARE VERY PROFICIENT IN NEED DISCOVERY AND SELECTING THE right solution, but are weak in the area of negotiating an agreement that is favourable both to the customer and to the salesperson's firm. Many buyers with responsibility for purchasing have formal training in how to negotiate favourable terms. Most customers are studying competitive offers and increasingly attempting to secure the best deal possible. These market conditions require salespeople to anticipate buyer concerns and plan collaborative win-win negotiated solutions prior to meeting with their customers (see Fig. 13.1). A recent poll reports that as many as 83 percent of sales executives from 25 industries generally enter negotiations with no formal strategy![1] Another common mistake is making last-minute concessions in order to close the sale.[2] In this chapter, we describe effective strategies for anticipating and negotiating buyer concerns.

We have noted previously that the heaviest time investment in value-added selling is on the front end of the sale. This is especially true for large, complex sales that require a long sales cycle. Identifying the customer's needs and developing the best solution can be very time-consuming. However, when you do these things effectively, you are creating value in the eyes of the customer. When you build value on the front end of the sale, price becomes less of an issue on the back end.[3]

The Six-Step Presentation Plan	
Step One: Approach	☑ Review Strategic/Consultative Selling Model ☑ Initiate customer contact
Step Two: Need Discovery	☑ Ask strategic questions ☑ Determine customer needs ☑ Select product solution
Step Three: Presentation	☑ Select presentation strategy ☑ Create presentation plan ☑ Initiate presentation
Step Four: Negotiation	☐ Anticipate buyer concerns ☐ Plan negotiating methods ☐ Initiate win-win negotiations
Step Five: Close	☐ Plan appropriate closing methods ☐ Recognize closing clues ☐ Initiate closing methods
Step Six: Servicing the Sale	☐ Follow through ☐ Follow-up calls ☐ Expansion selling

Service, retail, wholesale, and manufacturer selling

Figure 13.1 Negotiating customer concerns and problems

FORMAL INTEGRATIVE NEGOTIATION—PART OF THE WIN-WIN RELATIONSHIP STRATEGY

FRANK ACUFF, NEGOTIATIONS TRAINER AND AUTHOR OF *How to Negotiate Anything with Anyone, Anywhere Around the Globe*, says, "Life is a negotiation."[4] Negotiating skills have application almost daily in our personal and professional lives. Some of the more traditional personal selling books discuss how salespeople should "handle" buyer objections. The message communicated to the reader was that personal selling was a "we versus they" process resulting from distributive negotiations: Somebody wins and somebody loses. The win-win solution, where both sides win, was not offered as an option. In this chapter, we focus on integrative negotiations, which are built on joint problem-solving, trust, and rapport to achieve win-win situations.[5]

Ron Willingham, author of two books on integrity selling, says, "When trust and rapport are strong, negotiation becomes a partnership to work through customer concerns. But when trust and rapport are weak, almost any negotiation becomes too combative."[6] Trust and rapport must be established on the front end of the sale and maintained throughout the sales process. High-performance salespeople, like Heather Ramsey, take time to discover the customer's needs and try to recommend the best

Negotiations—Solving the Tough Problems

One of the biggest challenges to the adaptive selling and partnering strategy is evident as one deals with the tough problems that often come up during the negotiation stage of the sales process. In this new Adaptive Selling Today Negotiations Video, Lana, a medical equipment representative, is faced with the following tough problems: dealing with an angry customer about pricing issues, dealing with skepticism about sourcing and timing issues, dealing with how to be understood about product issues, and dealing with how to walk away yet keep the door open to salvage the order. The customer, Dr. Arroyo, director of a hospital radiology department, has a huge responsibility to make the right selection at the right price, and he therefore has concerns that require an adaptive negotiations strategy. Hopefully, Lana's negotiation skills result in a win-win solution. Refer to the Application Exercises at the end of the chapter on p. 331 for more information.

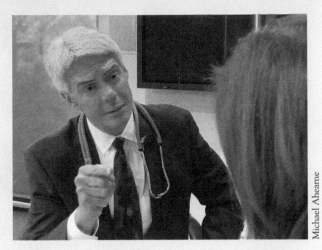

Michael Ahearne

Dr. Arroyo is a tough negotiator who uses all he knows to get the right solution.

possible solution. Always keep in mind that any agreement that leaves one party dissatisfied will come back to hurt the other party later, sometimes in ways that cannot be predicted.[7]

What is **negotiation** ? One definition is "working to reach an agreement that is mutually satisfactory to both buyer and seller." It involves resolving the problems or concerns that prevent people from buying.[8] As we noted in Chapter 1, the salesperson increasingly serves as a consultant or resource and provides solutions to buyers' problems. The consultant seeks to establish and maintain long-term relationships with customers. The ability to negotiate problems or concerns is one of the most effective ways to create value for the customer. Figure 13.2 outlines the steps a salesperson can take to anticipate and negotiate problems.

negotiation Working to reach an agreement that is mutually satisfactory to buyer and seller.

Negotiation Is a Process

By definition, negotiations seek to move polarized parties into the realm of common interests.[9] Negotiations can take place before the sales call or at any time during the sales presentation. Early negotiations may involve the meeting location, who will attend the sales presentation, or the amount of time available for the first meeting. Salespeople sometimes make early concessions to improve the relationship. This approach, however, may set a costly precedent for later in the sale.[10] Some concessions can have a negative influence on the sales presentation.

In most cases, you can anticipate that the most important negotiations will take place during stage three of the buying process (see Fig. 8.3). Resolution of problems can

Figure 13.2 Negotiating Buyer Concerns
Salespeople today must be prepared to anticipate and negotiate buyer concerns and problems.

Strategic planning for negotiation of buyer concerns

1. Anticipate buyer concerns.
2. Review common types of buyer concerns.
3. Review methods of negotiating buyer concerns.
4. Prepare a negotiation worksheet.

Activities during negotiations

1. Recognize and understand verbal and nonverbal clues.
2. Validate the problem.
3. Find some point of agreement.
4. Do not allow anger to surface.
5. Answer buyer concerns.
6. Be alert for closing clues.

sometimes be time-consuming. Establishing a strategic alliance, described in Chapter 1 as the highest form of partnering, requires lengthy negotiations that may extend over weeks, months, or even years. Once the alliance is finalized, negotiations continue when concerns voiced by one party or the other surface.

Negotiation is defined as "working to reach an agreement that is mutually satisfactory to both buyer and seller." It involves building relationships instead of making one-time deals.

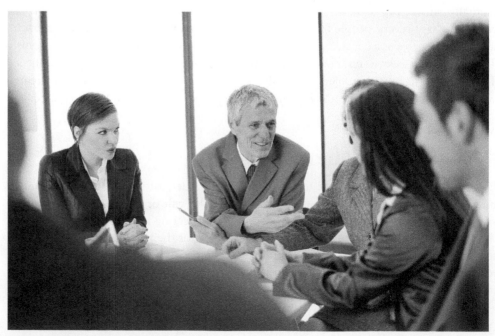

Zurijeta/Shutterstock

Planning for Formal Negotiations

Professional buyers are well-trained negotiators. To negotiate with them effectively, salespeople first need to engage in detailed planning. Ironically, one of the most common mistakes negotiators make is not doing their homework in advance.[11]

Gather Information before the Negotiation "Exhaustive preparation is more important than aggressive argument."[12] Robert H. Schuller offers invaluable advice about this crucial step.[13] First, a salesperson should prepare from both counterparts' points of view by identifying the similarities and differences of the goals and objectives of both sides. Then information sources are tapped. The information might be from business associates, buyers' websites, or even previous vendors for the same buyers. The salesperson should bear in mind that negotiation is an information game: the more, the better.[14]

Decide Team versus Individual Negotiations for Both Seller and Buyer The next logical step in this preparatory process is to decide who will be in the negotiations. For Susanna Rosas, who works in a business-to-business selling context at CB Richard Ellis, it is not unusual to create a cross-functional team consisting of individuals from finance, construction, and zoning to bring to a meeting with the buying centre at the buyer's premises. Other situations might call for her to bring senior managers from her firm. If teams are involved, make sure there is a leader and establish guidelines for information exchange among the team members. Creating a cohesive negotiation team can pay off with higher profits after the conclusion of negotiations.[15]

Understand the Value of What You Are Offering It is important for Salesforce.com's Dave Levitt to know what is of real value to the customer and not consider value only in terms of purchase price. The real value of what you are offering may be a value-added intangible such as expert product knowledge, superior configuration programming, seamless integration with other vendors, short set-up times, effective training, product support, or a reputation for honest dealings. An important aspect of the negotiation process is discovering what is of utmost importance to the buyer (see Table 13.1). The focus of personal selling today should be the mutual search for value. Some salespeople make the mistake of offering a lower price the moment buyer concerns surface. In the customer's mind, price may be of secondary importance compared with the quality of service after the sale. Detailed tactics for creating values in formal negotiations appear at the end of the chapter.

Determine Your Goals and Financial Objectives Two important concepts warrant mentioning. First is **BATNA** (Best Alternative to Negotiated Agreement), defined as "what alternative(s) will be acceptable to you if your negotiation does not succeed."[16] You will likely make concessions in formal negotiations; therefore, you must assess both your own and your customer's BATNA. The second important planning tool is **ZOPA** (Zone of Possible Agreement), defined as the space between the seller's walk-away point and the buyer's highest willingness to pay.[17] The walk-away point represents the lowest offer a party would be willing to accept and is also called the *reservation value*. For example, if your walk-away point is $42.65M and the highest price the buyer is willing to pay is $48M, your ZOPA is any offer that falls within this range, or a zone of $5.35M ($=$48M - $42.65M$).[18]

BATNA Best Alternative to Negotiated Agreement.

ZOPA Zone of Possible Agreement.

Table 13.1 Negotiating Buyer Concerns

Objections are often requests for more information to justify the buying decision. Objections can tell us a lot about the real source of hesitation and what type of information the customer is seeking.

Buyer's Concern	Source of Hesitation	Request for
"Price too high"	Perceived cost vs. benefit	Value articulation
"Think about it"	Afraid to make a bad decision	Create comfort, provide proof
"Talk to boss"	Unable to justify decision	Risk reduction, benefit review
"Need more quotes"	Unsure you're the best option	Targeted solutions, value
"Set with current supplier"	Doesn't see benefit of change	Differentiation
"Bad history"	Past experience is affecting current review	Offer proof of change ·

Negotiating Buyer Concerns from Hide-and-Seek by Nancy J. Martini. Copyright © 1998. Used by permission of Nancy J. Martini.

Ed Brodow (**www.brodow.com**), popular speaker, international consultant, and author of *Negotiating Bootcamp*, contends it is best to *aim high* when configuring your solution. In his new training video *Six Principles of Negotiation*, he suggests *doing your homework* and preparing a range of terms that include the maximum you could expect to receive, what you would hope to receive, and your bottom line, or the minimum you could accept before having to walk away from the sale. In many buying situations today, buyers expect there to be alternative solutions with alternative pricing.

Prepare an Agenda An agenda outlines what will and will not be discussed and in what sequence. As the seller, you want to achieve "small wins" to create goodwill before dealing with tough issues. Therefore, you want to prioritize these items on your proposed agenda. Sometimes items should be discussed simultaneously rather than sequentially.[19] Experienced buyers, however, also come to the meeting table with a detailed agenda. Negotiations might start with a discussion about the agenda itself.

Review Adaptive Selling Styles The successful negotiation of buyer concerns is based in large part on understanding human behaviour. This knowledge, coupled with a good measure of common sense, helps us overcome most buyer concerns. In one-on-one negotiations, adaptive selling styles are useful (see Chapter 5). The Platinum Rule of negotiating is, "Do unto others as they want done unto them."[20] When negotiations are conducted in teams, the situation gets more complicated. The role of the negotiation leader is to maintain smooth information exchange and foster strong relationships despite various communication styles.[21]

Prepare a Negotiations Worksheet Your planning must be systematically organized. It helps to predict and classify possible resistance with the aid of a negotiations worksheet. To illustrate how this form works, let us review an example from the food industry. Mary Turner is a salesperson for Durkee Famous Foods. She represents more than 350 products. Mary calls on supermarkets daily and offers assistance in the areas of ordering and merchandising. Recently, her company decided to offer retail food stores an allowance of $1 per case of olives if the store purchased 15 or more cases. Prior to talking with her customers about this offer, Mary sat down and developed a negotiations worksheet, shown in Figure 13.3. We cannot anticipate every possible problem, but it is

Negotiations Worksheet		
Customer's concern	Type of concern	Possible response
"Fifteen cases of olives will take up valuable space in my receiving room. It is already crowded."	Need	Combination direct denial/superior benefit "You will not have to face that problem. With the aid of our merchandising plan you can display 10 cases immediately on the sales floor. Only 5 cases will become reserve stock. You should move all 15 cases in about two weeks."
"This is a poor time of the year to buy a large order of olives. People are not buying olives at this time."	Time	Combination indirect denial/third-party testimony "I agree that it has been a problem in the past, but consumer attitudes seem to be changing. We have found that olives sell well all year long if displayed properly. More people are using olives in the preparation of omelettes, pizza, and other dishes. Of course, most relish trays feature olives. We will supply you with point-of-purchase material that provides kitchen-tested ways to use this high-profit item."
"I have to stay within my budget."	Price	Superior benefit "As you know, olives represent a high-profit item. The average margin is 26 percent. With the addition of our $1.00 per case allowance, the margin will rise to about 30 percent. This order will give you a good return on your investment."
"I am very satisfied with my present supplier."	Source	Combination question/trial order "What can I do to get you to take just a trial order?"

Figure 13.3 Negotiations Worksheet
Before the presentation, it is important to prepare a negotiations worksheet. Note how combination methods are frequently used to effectively respond to customer concerns.

possible to identify the most common problems that are likely to arise. The negotiations worksheet can be a useful tool.

Conducting the Negotiation Session

During the formal negotiation session, it is beneficial to master the skills presented throughout this book—i.e., good social contact, asking good questions, listening actively, using proof devices, and applying methods of negotiating objections. There are a number of golden rules that a salesperson should internalize to be successful in formal negotiations. These include understanding the problem, creating alternative solutions, periodically recapitulating what has been agreed, and making wise concessions in a timely manner.

Understand the Problem David Stiebel, author of *When Talking Makes Things Worse!*, says we need to understand the difference between a misunderstanding and a true disagreement. A *misunderstanding* is a failure to accurately understand the other person's point. For example, the salesperson believes the customer is primarily interested in price, but the customer's primary need is on-time delivery. A *disagreement*, in contrast, is a failure to agree that would persist despite the most accurate understanding.[22] Be certain that both you and the prospect are clear on the true nature of what each party's needs are regarding the issues to be negotiated (see Table 13.1). When the prospect begins talking, listen carefully and then listen some more. With *probing questions*, you can fine-tune your understanding of the problem.

Create Alternative Solutions That Can Add Value When the prospect finishes talking, it is a good practice to validate the problem using a *confirmation question*. This helps to isolate the true problem and reduce the chance of misunderstanding. The confirmation question might sound like this: "I think I understand your concern. You feel the warranty does not provide you with sufficient protection. Is this correct?" By taking time to ask this question, you accomplish two important objectives. First, you are giving personal attention to the problem, which pleases the customer. Second, you gain time to think about the best possible response.

The best possible response is very often an alternative solution. In formal negotiations, this is often referred to as **"logrolling."**[23] Many of today's customers do not want to hear that there is only one way to do things, or a single solution. In the age of information, people have less time to manage their work and their personal lives, so they expect new levels of flexibility. For Marriott's Heather Ramsey, there are many issues such as group pricing, alternative menus, complimentary rooms, etc. that can be introduced into the negotiations for convention services. In many cases, these additional issues take the focus off price and can actually create value for the customer and possibly for the seller. Here are additional issues that can be introduced into negotiations when a buyer is focused on price: delivery dates, financing, contract length, quality, exclusivity clauses, levels of service support, and warranties.

logrolling Offering an alternative solution.

Periodically Review Acknowledged Points of Agreement Negotiating buying problems is a little like the art of diplomacy: It helps to know what points of agreement exist. This saves time and helps establish a closer bond between you and the prospect. At some point during the presentation, you might summarize by using a *summary-confirmation question*: "Let us see if I fully understand your position. You think our product is well constructed and will provide the reliability you are looking for. You also believe our price is fair. Am I correct on these two points?"

Once all the areas of agreement have been identified, there may be surprisingly few points of disagreement. The prospect suddenly sees that the advantages of ownership far outweigh the disadvantages. Now that the air is cleared, both the salesperson and the customer can give their full attention to any remaining points of disagreement.

The business environment is sometimes turbulent. Hence, it might be advisable in negotiations to "pack a reserve parachute." To avoid buyers' frustration when things do not go as agreed upon, lay the groundwork for the unexpected and be open about backup plans with the buyers.[24]

Do Not Make Concessions Too Quickly Give away concessions methodically and reluctantly, and always try to get something in return. Negotiations consultant Ed Brodow suggests that when preparing to make a concession, we should prepare to get something in return by asking, "If we do this for you, will you do this for us?" A concession given too freely can diminish the value of your product.[25] Giving a concession too easily may also send the signal that you are negotiating from a position of weakness. Neil Rackham, author of several books on spin selling, says, "Negotiate late, negotiate little, and never let negotiation become a substitute for good selling."[26]

Timing and the Pareto Law Time plays a critical role in negotiations. In negotiations, experience with the Pareto Law reveals that 80 percent of your results are generally agreed upon in the last 20 percent of your time. Since influence tactics are more likely to exert an effect when their target is under time pressure, negotiators should use time as a strategic weapon by buying more time to fully consider concessions or by giving a deadline to speed up agreement.[27]

Know When to Walk Away

For many reasons, salespeople must sometimes walk away from a potential sale. If the customer's budget doesn't allow the purchase of your product, don't press the issue. If the customer's best offer is not favourable for your company, don't continue to waste your time. If the buyer is only interested in the lowest possible price and you represent a marketer committed to a value-added sales strategy, consider withdrawing from negotiations. If you discover that the prospect is dishonest or fails to keep his word, discontinue negotiations. Be aware of how much flexibility (your BATNA and ZOPA) you have in terms of price, specifications, delivery schedules, and so forth, and know when you have reached your walk-away point.[28] A popular country and western song reminded us that "you got to know when to hold them, know when to fold them, know when to walk away, and know when to run." This is good advice when you are involved in negotiations.

Finally, when appropriate, document negotiated settlements in writing. These will be helpful when formal contracts are drawn up. Negotiation minutes will also serve as a control tool for follow-up actions.

COMMON TYPES OF BUYER CONCERNS

Salespeople learn that patterns of buyer resistance exist and, therefore, they can anticipate that certain concerns may arise during the sales call. With this information, it is possible to be better prepared for each meeting with a customer. The great majority of buyer concerns fall into five categories: need, product, source, time, and price.

Concerns Related to Need for the Product

If you have carefully completed your precall planning, then the prospect will likely have a need for your product. You can still expect, however, that the initial response may be, "I do not need your product." This might be a conditioned response that arises nearly every time the prospect meets with a sales representative. It may also mask the real reason for not buying, which might be lack of funds, lack of time to examine your proposal carefully, or some other reason. Sincere need resistance is one of the greatest challenges that a salesperson faces during the early part of the sales process. Think about it for a moment. Why would any customer want to purchase a product that does not seem to provide any real benefits? Unless we can create need awareness in the prospect's mind, there is no possible way to close the sale.

If you are calling on business prospects, the best way to overcome need resistance is to prove that your product is a good investment. Every business hopes to make a profit. Therefore you must demonstrate how your product or service can contribute to that goal. Can your product increase sales volume? Can it reduce operating expenses? If the owner of a hardware store says, "I already carry a line of high-quality tools," point out how a second line of less expensive tools will appeal to another large segment of buyers. With the addition of the new line, the store will be in a better position to compete with other stores (discount merchandise stores and supermarkets) that sell inexpensive tools.

Concerns about the Product or Service

You will recall from Chapter 8 that consultative process buyers may lack needs awareness or need help evaluating possible solutions. As such, the product (solution) often becomes the focal point of buyer resistance. When this happens, try to discover specific reasons why the prospect has doubts about your product or service. Often you may find that one of the following factors has influenced the buyer's attitude:

1. *The product or service is not well established.* This is a common form of buyer resistance if you are selling a new or relatively new product. People do not like to take risks. They need plenty of assurance that the product is dependable. Use laboratory test results, third-party testimonials from satisfied users, or an effective demonstration to create value.

2. *The present product or service is satisfactory.* Change does not come easily to many people. Purchasing a new product may mean adopting new procedures or retraining employees. In the prospect's mind, the advantages do not outweigh the disadvantages, so buyer resistance surfaces. To overcome this resistance, you must build a greater amount of desire in the prospect's mind. Concentrate on a value proposition that gives your product or service a major advantage over the existing one, or reconfigure the product and offer customized services to better meet the customer's needs.

Concerns Related to Source

Concerns related to source can be especially challenging when the prospect is a relationship buyer. The buyer may already have well-established partnerships with other companies. If the prospect feels genuine loyalty to his or her present supplier, you will have to work harder to establish a relationship and begin the need discovery process.

When dealing with the loyalty problem, it is usually best to avoid direct criticism of the competing firm. Negative comments are apt to backfire because they damage your professional image. It is best to keep the sales presentation focused on the customer's problems and your solutions.

There are positive ways to cope with the loyalty concern. Here are some suggestions:

1. *Work harder to identify problems your company can solve with its products or services.* With the help of good questions, you may be able to understand the prospect's problems better than your competitors do.

2. *Point out the superior benefits of your product or company.* The logic of your presentation may override the emotional ties that may exist between the prospect and the present supplier.

3. *Work on recruiting internal champions to build more support for your message.* Use referrals whenever possible.[29]

4. *Try to stay visible and connected.* Take every opportunity to connect with prospects and to meet new ones. Patricia McCallum is a sales representative at Century 21 B.J. Roth Realty in Barrie, Ontario. She has been a member of BNI Canada, an international marketing organization specializing in word-of-mouth referrals, for nearly ten years. There are 287 BNI chapters in Canada, with 5830 members. Patricia relates how a referral she received when she first joined has resulted in a series of sales. She received a referral from one of the original members of her BNI chapter and says, "That first client was so happy with my services, they referred me to someone they knew, who referred me to someone they knew, eventually resulting in four new clients."[30] Salespeople can benefit from memberships in networking groups, breakfast clubs, or community and charity involvement. These all help increase visibility and make connections.

Concerns Related to Time

stall Resistance related to time.

If a prospect says, "I want time to think it over," you may be encountering concerns related to time. Resistance related to time is often referred to as the **stall.** A stall usually means the customer does not yet perceive the benefits of buying now. In most cases, the stall indicates that the prospect has both positive and negative feelings about your product. Consider using *probing questions* to determine the negative feelings: "Is it my company that concerns you?" "Do you have any concerns about our warranty program?"

It is all right to be persuasive if the prospect can truly benefit from buying now. If the price may soon rise, or if the item may not be available in the future, then you should provide this information. You must, however, present this information sincerely and accurately. It is never proper to distort the truth in the hope of getting the order.

Renewing a contract also calls for renegotiations. In these cases, be up front and explain the benefits in precise terms as to what additional values the new price will bring to the client. Sometimes it is advisable to offer a break in the payment schedule to overcome the client's adverse feelings about the price hike.[31] To enhance the relationship with long-term business partners, the seller sometimes has to look at the market to re-evaluate what is really fair pricing and voluntarily renegotiate with the buyer to lower the price before the buyer asks for it.[32]

Concerns Related to Price

Price objections are one of the biggest obstacles salespeople have to conquer.[33] There are two important points to keep in mind concerning price resistance. First, it is one of the most common forms of buyer resistance in the field of selling. Therefore, you must learn to negotiate skilfully in this area. Second, it may be nothing more than an excuse. If you are selling a product or service to a transactional buyer, price may be the primary barrier to closing the sale. When people say, "Your price is too high," they probably mean, "You have not sold me yet." In the eyes of most customers, value is more important than price. Always try to position your product with a convincing value proposition. Customers who perceive added value are less likely to choose a competing product simply on the basis of price. We will present specific tactics to deal with this issue shortly.

SPECIFIC METHODS OF NEGOTIATING BUYER CONCERNS

THERE ARE EIGHT SPECIFIC METHODS OF NEGOTIATING BUYER CONCERNS. IN ANALYZING EACH buyer concern, we should try to determine which method can be most effective. In most cases, we can use a combination of the following methods to negotiate buyer concerns.

Direct Denial

direct denial Involves refuting the prospect's opinion or belief. The direct denial of a problem is considered a high-risk method of negotiating buyer concerns.

Direct denial involves refuting the opinion or belief of a prospect. The direct denial of a problem is considered a high-risk method of negotiating buyer concerns. Therefore, you should use it with care. People do not like to be told they are wrong. Even when the facts prove the prospect is wrong, resentment can build if we fail to handle the situation properly.

When a prospect offers buyer resistance that is not valid, we sometimes have no option other than to openly disagree. If the person is misinformed, we must provide accurate information. For example, if the customer questions the product's quality, meet the concern head-on with whatever proof seems appropriate. It is almost never proper to ignore misinformation. High-performance salespeople counter inaccurate responses from the prospect promptly and directly.

The manner in which you state the denial is of major importance. Use a win-win approach. Be firm and sincere in stating your beliefs, but do not be offensive. Above all, do not patronize the prospect. A "know-it-all" attitude can be irritating.

Indirect Denial

Sometimes the prospect's concern is completely valid or at least accurate to a large degree. The best approach is to bend a little and acknowledge that the prospect is at least partially correct. This method is referred to as the **indirect denial.** After all, if you offered a product that were objection-proof, you would likely have no competitors. Every product has a shortcoming or limitation.[34] The success of this method is based in part on the need most people have to feel that their views are worthwhile. For this reason, the indirect denial method is widely used. An exchange that features the use of this approach follows. The salesperson is a key account sales representative for Tele-Direct Atlantic.[35]

indirect denial Often used when the prospect's concern is completely valid, or at least accurate to a large degree. The salesperson bends a little and acknowledges that the prospect is at least partly correct.

SALESPERSON: The total cost of placing your one-quarter-column ad in the Yellow Pages of the five different directories you have chosen is $32 000.

PROSPECT: As a builder, I want to reach people who are planning to build a home. I am afraid my ad will be lost among the hundreds of ads featured in your directories.

SALESPERSON: Yes, I agree that the Yellow Pages in our directories do feature hundreds of ads, but the section for general contractors features less than 30 ads. Our design staff can prepare an ad that can be highly visible and can set your company apart from ads placed by other contractors. In addition, we will do the same with your website.

Note that the salesperson used the words, "Yes, I agree" to reduce the impact of denial. The prospect is less likely to feel that her point of view has been totally disproved. One note of caution: Avoid the "Yes… but" response. When you use the word *but*, it invalidates anything preceding it. A more effective response would be, "I understand your concerns, Ms. Thomas; however, there is another way to view this issue."[36]

Feel–Felt–Found Successful salespeople are sensitive to clues that indicate that the client feels something is wrong. One way to empathize with the client's concerns is to use the "feel–felt–found" strategy. Here is how it works. George Hutchison, when he was chairman and CEO of North Bay, Ontario–based Equisure Financial Network Inc., was an ace negotiator who regularly used this method. When someone raised a major concern, he would often say to the person, "I know how you *feel*. Others have *felt* the same way. However, we've *found* that…"[37] Besides offering empathy, this method reassures the person that others have successfully overcome the same concerns.

Questions

Throughout this chapter, we have described several situations where probing or confirmation questions can enhance the negotiation process. We must also keep in mind the important role of need-satisfaction questions. In Chapter 11, we noted that *need-satisfaction questions* are designed to move the sales process forward toward commitment and action. These questions focus on the solution.[38] Consider the following exchange that involves a price concern:

> BUYER: It would be difficult for our human resources department to absorb the cost of your psychological tests.
>
> SELLER: What would a 10 percent reduction in employee turnover save your company?

In these examples, the questions are designed to get the customer's attention focused on the solution. These questions also give ownership of the solution to the prospect. See Chapter 11 for more examples of the need-satisfaction question.

Superior Benefit

superior benefit A benefit that will, in most cases, outweigh the customer's specific concern.

Sometimes the customer raises a problem that cannot be answered with a denial. For example: "Your television commercial proposal does not include payroll costs for actors who will be used during the shoot. This means we must cover this expense." You should acknowledge the valid objection and then discuss one or more superior benefits: "Yes, you are correct. We do conduct the talent search and coach the actors throughout the development of the commercial. In addition, if you are not happy with the performance of the actors, we will conduct a second search for new actors and remake the commercial at no additional cost to you." A **superior benefit** is a benefit that in most cases outweighs the customer's specific concern.

Demonstration

If you are familiar with your product as well as that of your competition, this method of negotiating buyer resistance is easy to use. You know the competitive advantages of your product and can discuss these features with confidence.

At Mattress Firm, Edith Botello realizes product demonstration is one of the most convincing ways to overcome buyer skepticism her customers might have. With the aid of an effective demonstration, you can overcome specific concerns. Sometimes a second demonstration is needed to overcome buyer skepticism. This demonstration can provide additional proof. High-achieving sales personnel know when and how to use proof devices to overcome buyer resistance.

Trial Offer

trial offer Involves giving the prospect an opportunity to try the product without making a purchase commitment.

A **trial offer** involves giving the prospect an opportunity to try the product without making a purchase commitment. The trial offer (especially with new products) is popular with customers because they can get fully acquainted with your product without making a major commitment. Assume that a buyer for a large restaurant chain says, "I am

The product demonstration is one of the most convincing ways to overcome buyer skepticism.

Deklofenak/Shutterstock

sure you have good cooking oil, but we are happy with our present brand. We have had no complaints from our managers." In response to this comment, you might say, "I can understand your reluctance to try our product. However, I do believe our oil is the finest on the market. With your permission, I would like to ship you 20 litres of our oil at no cost. You can use our product at selected restaurants and evaluate the results. If our oil does not provide you with superior results, you are under no obligation to place an order."

Third-Party Testimony

Studies indicate that the favourable testimony of a neutral third party can be an effective method of responding to buyer resistance. Let us assume that the owner of a small business states that he can get along without the services of a professional landscaper. The salesperson might respond in this manner: "Some business owners feel the way you do. However, once they contract for our service, they do not regret the decision. Mark Williams, owner of Williams Hardware, says our service completely changed the image his business projects to the public." Third-party testimony provides a positive way to solve certain types of buying problems. The positive experiences of a neutral third party almost never trigger an argument with the prospect.

Postpone Method

Today's customers are well informed and may want to engage in negotiations early in the sales process. The customer may raise concerns that you would prefer to respond to later in the presentation. Let's assume you are calling on an office manager who is interested in well-equipped cubicles for eight employees. Soon after you present some product

postpone method A method salespeople use to delay a response when a customer raises a concern that would be better handled later in a sales presentation.

information, the customer says, "How much will eight well-equipped cubicles cost us?" Using the **postpone method,** your response might be, "I would prefer to answer that question in a few minutes. Once I learn what features you prefer, I can calculate a cost estimate." Every customer concern should be taken seriously. Always try to explain why you want to postpone the response.

Combination Methods   As noted previously, consultative selling is characterized by flexibility. A combination of methods sometimes proves to be the best way to deal with buyer resistance. For example, an indirect denial might be followed by a question: "The cost of our business security system is a little higher than that of the competition. The price I have quoted reflects the high-quality materials used to develop our system. Wouldn't you feel better entrusting your security needs to a firm with more than 25 years of experience in the business security field?" In this situation, the salesperson also might consider combining the indirect denial with an offer to arrange a demonstration of the security system.

A salesperson might attempt to turn the objection into a *trial close* by concluding the sale without prejudicing the opportunity to continue the selling process with the buyer should they refuse to commit themselves. This might take the form of, "If I can address this final concern of yours, will you buy it?[39] See Figure 13.3 on p. 315 for more examples of combination methods.

CREATING VALUE DURING FORMAL NEGOTIATIONS

THE CHALLENGE A SALESPERSON FACES IN ALMOST EVERY NEGOTIATION IS TO SELL PRODUCTS and services based on fair and unique value propositions, not simply on the basis of price.[40] When salespeople reduce whatever they are selling to a simple commodity by relying on price to close sales, there is no customer loyalty.[41] In this section, we focus on how a salesperson can tactfully create value for buyers during formal negotiations without compromising profits.

THE PITFALLS OF PAYING TOO LITTLE

It's unwise to pay too much. But it's worse to pay too little.

When you pay too much, you lose a little money, that is all.

When you pay too little you sometimes lose everything, because the thing you bought was incapable of doing the thing it was bought to do.

The common law of business balances prohibits paying a little and getting a lot. It can't be done.

If you deal with the lowest bidder, it is well to add something for the risk you run.

–John Ruskin, British Writer

How to Deal with Price Concerns

As we have noted, price resistance is common, so we must prepare for it. There are some important "dos and don'ts" to keep in mind when price concern surfaces.

Do Clarify Price Concerns with Questions When you are confronted with price resistance, determine what the customer is really saying. You will recall from Chapter 11 that *specific survey questions* encourage the customer to give you more details. The following questions might be used when price concerns surface:

> When you say our prices are higher, could you be more specific, please?
> What did you anticipate the price to be?

When the customer says budget is the primary reason for delaying the purchase, you might ask, "If you had the budget, would you buy?" Questions can help you determine what the customer is really thinking.[42]

Do Add Value with a Cluster of Satisfactions As noted in Chapter 7, a growing number of customers seek a cluster of satisfactions that includes a good product, a salesperson who is truly a partner, and a company that stands behind its products (see Fig. 7.1). Many business firms are at a competitive disadvantage when the price alone is considered. When you look beyond price, however, it may become obvious that your company offers more value for the dollar.

Stephen Smith, senior account manager for Bell Atlantic, says that price is like the tip of the iceberg—it is often the only feature the customer sees. Salespeople need to direct the customer's attention to the value-added features that make up the bulk of the iceberg that is below the surface (Fig. 13.4).[43] Do not forget to sell yourself as a high-value element of the sales proposal. Emphasize your commitment to customer service after the sale. Listen carefully to identify and reconfirm what intangibles in addition to the product or service the customers *actually* value.[44]

Do Not Make Price the Focal Point of Your Sales Presentation You may need to discuss price, but do not bring it up too early. The best time to deal with price is after you have reviewed product features and discussed buyer benefits. You increase the chances for a win-win outcome by increasing the number of issues you can resolve. If you negotiate price along with delivery date, support services, or volume purchases, you increase the opportunities for a trade-off so you and the customer both win something of value.[45]

Do Not Apologize for the Price When you do mention price, do so in a confident and straightforward manner. Do not have even a hint of apology in your voice. Convey to the prospect that you believe your price is fair and make every effort to relate price to value. Many people fear paying too much for a product or service. If your company has adopted a value-added strategy, point out this fact to the prospect. Then discuss how you and your company add value.

Do Point Out the Relationship between Price and Quality In our highly competitive, free-enterprise economy, there are forces at work that tend to promote fair pricing. The highest quality can never be obtained at the lowest price. Quality comes from the Latin word *qualitas*, meaning, "What is the worth?" When you sell quality, price is more likely to be secondary in the prospect's mind. Always point out the value-added features that create the difference in price. Keep in mind that cheap products are built down to a price rather than up to a standard.[46]

Do Explain and Demonstrate the Difference between Price and Cost Price represents the initial amount the buyer pays for the product. Cost represents the amount the buyer pays for a product as it is used over a period of time. The price–cost comparison is particularly relevant with a product or service that lasts a long time or is particularly

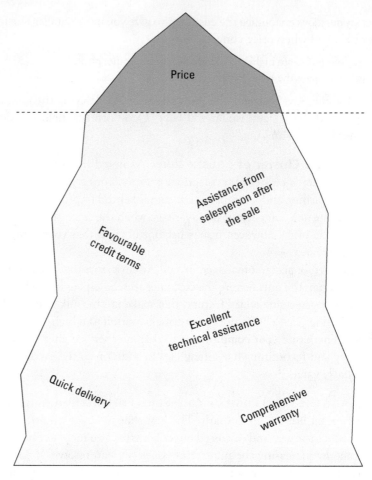

Price

Assistance from salesperson after the sale

Favourable credit terms

Excellent technical assistance

Quick delivery

Comprehensive warranty

Figure 13.4 The Price Iceberg
A sales proposal is sometimes like an iceberg. The customer sees the tip of the iceberg—the price—but does not see the value-added features below the surface.

reliable. Today, airlines are comparing the price and cost of small regional jets manufactured by Bombardier of Canada with large jets sold by Boeing and Airbus. Sales representatives at Bombardier compare their smaller $21 million cost of the 50 passenger CRJ200 with the larger $150 million cost of the 150 passenger A320 offered by Airbus, and point out the fast speed (534 MPH) and low fuel consumption of the CRJ200.

Negotiating Price with a Low-Price Strategy

As noted in Chapter 7, some marketers have positioned their products with a price strategy. The goal is to earn a small profit margin on a large sales volume. Many of these companies have empowered their salespeople to use various low-price strategies such as quantity discounts, trade discounts, seasonal discounts, and promotional discounts. Some salespeople are given permission to match the price of any competitor. Many *transactional buyers* are primarily interested in price and convenience during negotiations, so consider eliminating features that contribute to a higher selling price.

The Canadian Professional Sales Association helps salespeople master the negotiation process.

WORKING WITH BUYERS WHO ARE TRAINED IN NEGOTIATION

IN RECENT YEARS, WE HAVE SEEN AN INCREASE IN THE NUMBER OF TRAINING PROGRAMS developed for professional buyers. Some salespeople are also returning to the classroom to learn negotiation skills. Learning how to negotiate is one of the linchpins of effective selling.[47] The Canadian Professional Sales Association offers a popular course, "Effective Negotiating Strategies," which is designed to provide salespeople with the keys to successful negotiation.

Professional buyers often learn to use specific tactics in dealing with salespeople. Homer Smith, author of *Selling through Negotiation*, provides the following examples.

Budget Limitation Tactic[48]

The buyer may say, "We like your proposal, but our budget for the convention is only $8500." Is the buyer telling the truth, or is the person testing your price? The best approach in this instance is to take the budget limitation seriously and use appropriate negotiation strategies. One strategy is to reduce the price by eliminating features or items, sometimes described as **unbundling.** In the case of a truck fleet sale, the salesperson might say, "We can deliver the trucks with a less powerful engine and thus meet your budget figure. Would you be willing to purchase trucks with less powerful engines?"

Take-It-or-Leave-It Tactic[49]

How do you respond to a buyer who says, "My final offer is $3300. Take it or leave it"? A price concession is, of course, one option. However, this is likely to reduce profits for the company and lower your commission. An alternative strategy is to confidently review the superior benefits of your product and make another closing attempt. Appealing to the other person's sense of fairness also may move the discussion forward. If the final offer is totally without merit, consider calling a halt to the negotiation to allow the other party to back down from his or her position without losing face.[50]

Let-Us-Split-the-Difference Tactic[51]

In some cases, the salesperson may find this price concession acceptable. If the buyer's suggestion is not acceptable, then the salesperson might make a counteroffer.

"If ... Then" Tactic

This approach involves the buyer saying something like, "Unless you agree immediately to a price reduction of 20 percent, we'll have to look elsewhere for a supplier." In this situation, the consequence could be serious. The correct response depends upon the outcome of the assessment of the balance of power conducted during the preparation. If the buyer does have a number of options, all of which offer the same kind of benefits as yours, then you may have to concede. If your product offers clear advantages over the competition, then you may be able to resist the challenge.

Selling in Action

You Don't Get What You Deserve, You Get What You Negotiate

Chester L. Karrass, creator of the Effective Negotiating seminar, says, "In business, you don't get what you deserve; you get what you negotiate." This is good advice for the job seeker. Most employers will not propose the highest wage possible at the beginning of the offer. If you want a higher starting wage, you must ask for it. Employers often have a predetermined range for each position and the highest salary is reserved for the applicant who brings something extra to the job. To prepare for a productive negotiation, you must know your own needs and you must know something about the worth of the position. Many employers will tell you the salary range prior to the interview. The Internet can be a good source of salary information for certain types of jobs. In terms of your needs, try to determine what you care about the most: Interesting work? Future promotion? A flexible work schedule? If you are willing to negotiate, you can increase your pay by hundreds or even thousands of dollars. Be prepared to sell yourself, negotiate the salary you feel is appropriate, and achieve a win-win solution in the process.[b]

Ron Barbaro, chairman of The Brick Group Income Fund and former chairman and CEO of the Ontario Lottery and Gaming Corporation, says that when he first started in sales, he was not a good salesperson but he had determination and was a good worker. It was this determination and hard work that enabled him to sell more than $1 million worth of insurance in his first year. He went on to become president of Prudential Insurance Company of America's Canadian and worldwide operations. His determination—and undoubtedly the negotiating and problem-solving skills he learned while selling—helped him close what he refers to as his toughest, but most rewarding, sale.

When Ron Barbaro was chairman of the board for the Metro Toronto Zoo, he was instrumental in bringing the first giant panda exhibit to Canada from Asia. "They wouldn't give the pandas to us, nor would they sell them to us," says Ron. He eventually succeeded in negotiating a panda exhibit rental.[c]

"Sell Low Now, Make Profits Later" Tactic

In this situation, also referred to as the "Reward in Heaven" tactic, the buyer may say something like, "If you can reduce the price another $500 on this job, I will give you all my future work." This may be a genuine statement, and in fact may meet your own objective of gaining a foothold in your buyer's business. You might respond with "Because of the price I have quoted, I am unable to discount this job. However, if you do give me this job and your future jobs, I will discount your future work." This negotiation approach can actually create value for both you and your customer.

These tactics represent only a sample of those used by professional buyers. To prepare for these and other tactics, salespeople need to plan their negotiating strategies in advance and have clear goals. Decide in advance on the terms you can and cannot accept. It is important that you have the authority to set prices. Buyers want to do business with someone who has decision-making authority. Daniel Skarlicki, a specialist in organizational behaviour at the University of British Columbia, says, "Simply put, negotiations are won or lost in the planning and preparation, not at the negotiating table. Don't wing it."[52]

REVIEWING KEY CONCEPTS

- Describe the principles of formal negotiations as part of the win-win strategy.

  Negotiations play a central role in the selling profession. Generic principles of formal integrative negotiations include preparing for negotiations, knowing the value of what you are offering, understanding the problem, creating alternate solutions, finding some point of agreement, and knowing when to walk away. If a salesperson uses a negotiations worksheet, then it can be much easier to plan systematically.

- Describe common types of buyer concerns.

  Sales resistance is natural and should be welcomed as an opportunity to learn more about how to satisfy the prospect's needs. Buyers' concerns often provide salespeople with precisely the information they need to close a sale. These concerns fall into five broad categories: need, product or service, source, time, and price. Whatever the reasons, the salesperson should *negotiate* sales resistance with the proper attitude, never making too much or too little of the prospect's concerns.

- Discuss specific methods of negotiating buyer concerns.

  We describe seven specific methods of negotiating buyer concerns: the direct denial, indirect denial, need-satisfaction questions, superior benefits, demonstration, trial offer, testimony, and postpone methods. The use of these methods and combinations thereof varies depending on the particular combination of salesperson, product, services, and prospect.

- Outline methods for creating value in formal negotiations.

We have described several specific methods for creating value in formal negotiations, but you should remember that practice in applying them is essential and that there is room for a great deal of creative imagination in developing variations or additional methods. With careful preparation and practice, negotiating buyer concerns about price should become a stimulating challenge to each salesperson's professional growth.

- Describe how to work with buyers who are trained in negotiation.

  Buyers who are trained in negotiation resort to a number of tactics that a salesperson should be prepared for. In any case, the ultimate goal of formal integrative negotiations is to achieve win-win solutions by offering buyers the value they appreciate without compromising the sellers' benefits.

Key Terms

BATNA **313**

direct denial **320**

indirect denial **321**

logrolling **317**

negotiation **311**

postpone method **324**

stall **320**

superior benefit **322**

trial offer **322**

unbundling **328**

ZOPA **313**

Review Questions

1. Explain why a salesperson should welcome buyer concerns.

2. List the common types of buyer concerns that might surface in a presentation.

3. How does the negotiations worksheet help the salesperson prepare to negotiate buyer concerns?

4. Explain the value of using *probing* and *confirmation* questions when negotiating buyer concerns.

5. List eight specific strategies for negotiating buyer resistance.

6. John Ruskin says that it is unwise to pay too much when making a purchase, but it is worse to pay too little. Do you agree or disagree with this statement? Explain.

7. What is the most common reason prospects give for not buying? How can salespeople deal effectively with this type of concern?

8. Professional buyers may have learned to use specific negotiation tactics in dealing with salespeople. List and describe two tactics that are commonly used today.

9. When a customer says, "I want time to think it over," what type of resistance is the salesperson encountering? Suggest ways to overcome this type of buyer concern.

10. Discuss the merits of using need-satisfaction questions to negotiate buyer concerns.

Application Exercises

1. Research for this chapter's Adaptive Selling Today Training Video revealed that anger does surface during the sales presentation and can be very challenging to negotiate. Anger can be something the other party experiences outside of the sale itself, or it can be caused by some aspect of the sale. Lana, the medical equipment salesperson, received an angry call from the doctor she was working with and had to prepare for solving both the anger problem and the reason for it. What three actions did she learn to use in negotiating with an angry customer? Describe how she adapted these actions during the sale to move the doctor's apparent position of "I am going to win; I don't care if you win" to "I want to win and I want you to win also."

2. As was shared by the doctor, it is not unusual for a customer to experience skepticism and doubt about the pricing, timing, supplier, need, and/or product solution during the sales process. Skepticism creates an "I may not win" customer reaction and can prevent the other party from making a good and correct decision, resulting in a "no sale." What three actions did Lana use to help her customer overcome the skepticism he was experiencing?

3. Research also reveals that the most common problem in negotiations is the price problem. Customers often want to be sure they are getting the best price possible, as well as the best product solution. What three actions did Lana use to attempt to achieve a win-win solution with the doctor's concern about staying within a budget? Describe them in detail.

4. The action of "walking away" from a potential sale is often considered a high-risk negotiations strategy. What three actions did Lana employ before she walked away from the sale?

ROLE-PLAY EXERCISE

You work for the sales department of an apparel manufacturing company. Montreal Fashions, a company you met with during a recent trade show, is going to visit your facilities next week. You understand that this company wants to "buy low" but normally places large orders. However, you want to "sell high." Your company might not be able to deliver very large orders unless you invest in new facilities. Montreal Fashions says it will send over a team of three people: the vice president of marketing, the purchasing manager, and a designer. They are interested in developing a collection for the next season and going over a "price exercise" with you. In addition, they are interested in placing a trial order at the price of a bulk order (i.e., large order). Delivery of the order is to be made in two weeks. Unfortunately, this trial order is well below the minimum quantity you're willing to accept, and your company normally needs one month to fill a new order.

1. How do you convey this information to the other departments within your company to prepare for this meeting? Will you invite your boss to the meeting? Why?

2. Using a negotiations worksheet, plan your response to the following statements made by the purchasing manager: (a) We are concerned that you will not be able to meet our quality requirements. (b) Your price is too high. (c) Either take this trial order or we will look for another vendor. Decide at what point in the negotiations on price and delivery date you will turn down or accept the offer. Role-play your response to each of these statements.

Reality Selling Video Case Problem

Each year, public and private organizations send thousands of employees to meetings held at hotels, motels, convention centres, conference centres, and resorts. These meetings represent a multimillion-dollar business in Canada and the United States. Airport hotels such as the Marriott Houston Hobby, introduced at the beginning of this chapter, are a good example of the venues typically selected for these meetings The Marriott Houston Hobby is conveniently located only one mile from the Hobby Airport in Houston, Texas. It has a competitive edge over its competition because it lies outside of the flight path. In addition to convenience and tranquility, the goal of the hotel is to provide guests with outstanding meeting and conference services. The hotel offers 235 deluxe guest rooms, 52 suites, 13 soundproof meeting rooms with state-of-the-art audiovisual technology, and continuous break service that can accommodate any agenda. Lavish customized meal events from a wide variety of international cuisines are a specialty of the Marriott Houston Hobby.

In an ideal situation, Heather Ramsey, corporate catering manager at the hotel, tries to get prospects out for an inspection of the property. Prospects might also sample hors d'oeuvres or lunch during a site tour. This tour, in some ways, fulfills the function of a sales demonstration. Throughout the tour, Heather describes special amenities and services offered by the hotel. She also uses this time to get better acquainted with the needs of the prospect. Once the tour is complete, she escorts the prospect back to her office and completes the needs assessment. Next, she prepares a detailed sales proposal or, in some cases, a contract. The proposal needs to contain accurate and complete facts because when signed, it becomes a legally enforceable sales contract.

For big events, the sales proposal is rarely accepted without modification. Professional meeting planners are experienced negotiators and press hard for concessions. Some have completed training programs developed for professional buyers. The concessions requested may include a lower guest room rate, lower meal costs, complimentary suites, or a complimentary event such as a wine and cheese reception. It might take as long as two months to reach an agreement with sophisticated buyers.

Of course, some buyer resistance is not easily identified. Heather Ramsey says that she follows four steps in dealing with buyer concerns:

1. *Identify the actual needs of the prospects.* To achieve win-win deals, Heather spends time asking specific questions about the customer's needs, such as the audience for the event, the size and timing of the event, and the customer's budget. The prospects normally focus on negotiating details of the food menu, group rates for room rental, and audiovisual facilities.

2. *Locate the resistance.* Some prospects are reluctant to accept the offer, but the reason may be unclear. Heather has discovered that asking open-ended

questions goes a long way in understanding the actual resistance. Once the reason for resistance is uncovered, Heather knows how to deal with it.

3. *Clarify the resistance.* If a prospect says, "I like your facilities, but your prices are a little high," then the salesperson must clarify the meaning of this objection. Is the prospect seeking a major price concession or a small price concession?

4. *Overcome the objection.* Heather says, "You must be prepared for negotiations by understanding both your flexibility and the customer's needs." The hotel must earn a profit or publicity, so concessions can be made only after careful consideration of the bottom line and other intangible benefits.

Heather has discovered that the best way to negotiate buyer concerns is to make sure both the prospect and the resort feel like winners once the negotiations are finalized. If either party feels like a loser, a long-term relationship will not be possible. During peak seasons, Heather might also need to negotiate the schedule of events with prospects to minimize opportunity costs for the hotel while keeping the customers happy by offering off-season concessions. Refer to the opening vignette on page 308 and Reality Selling Today Role Play 10 in Appendix 1 on page 438 for more information.

Questions

1. If you were selling convention services for a hotel located in a large city, what types of buyer concerns would you expect from a new prospect?

2. Let us assume that you are representing the Marriott Houston Hobby and you are meeting with a new prospect at the hotel for a site tour. This prospect is planning to host an important event for 200 guests at your hotel. List the questions that you might ask the prospect to identify her actual needs. In doing so, be specific about the alternatives (e.g., high-end, medium, or regular packages) you can offer and the order you present them.

3. If you meet with a professional buyer who is trained in negotiation, what tactics can you expect the person to use? How would you respond to each of these tactics?

4. What subtle questions will you ask to ascertain that the negotiator is the decision maker without hurting her feelings? What actions will you take if you find out she is not the decision maker?

PARTNERSHIP SELLING: A ROLE PLAY/SIMULATION

Visit the role play/simulation materials provided in the Student Resources section of your companion website at **www.pearsoncanada.ca/manning**. *A Contents page lists appropriate page references for the activities.*

Developing a Presentation Strategy—Negotiating

Refer to *Sales Memorandum 3* and strategically plan to anticipate and negotiate any buyer concerns that may arise during your presentation. You should prepare a negotiations worksheet to organize this part of your presentation.

The instructions for item 2e direct you to prepare negotiations for time, price, source, and product concerns. You will note that your price is approximately $200 more than your customer budgeted for this meeting. You will have to be very effective in negotiating a value-added strategy because your convention centre is not a low-price supplier. (See Chapter 6 on value-added product strategies.)

During the presentation, you should use proof devices from the product strategy materials provided in *Employment Memorandum 1* to negotiate concerns you anticipate. You may also want to use a calculator to negotiate any financial arrangements, such as savings on parking or airport transportation, etc. Using spreadsheet software, you may want to prepare graphs to illustrate competitive pricing. Place these materials in the front pocket of your three-ring binder (portfolio) so that you can easily access them during your presentation. You may want to secure another person to be your customer, instructing him or her to voice the concerns you have anticipated, and then respond with your negotiation strategies. This experience will provide you with the opportunity to rehearse your negotiation strategies.

Chapter 14
Adapting the Close and Confirming the Partnership

Learning Objectives

After studying this chapter, you should be able to

1   Describe the proper attitude to display toward closing the sale.

2   List and discuss selected guidelines for closing the sale.

3   Explain how to recognize closing clues.

4   Discuss specific methods of closing the sale.

5   Explain what to do when the buyer says yes and what to do when the buyer says no.

 Adaptive Selling Training Video Series

Ask For the Order—or **AFTO**, as it is also called—is the third training video in the Adaptive Selling Training Video Series. The video begins with a salesperson who has a fear of closing the sale. Research shows that many sales are lost because salespeople fear asking for the order, and that even when they do, it is not unusual to have to ask three or four times. Along with many successful examples of how to ask for the order, AFTO presents a three-dimensional approach to overcoming any fear one may have of asking for the order.

AFTO presents many closing methods, described in this chapter, that illustrate the importance of adapting your closing questions to the customer's particular buying situation. Specific methods of asking for the order are clearly presented in dramatic sequences, representing a wide variety of selling situations.

AFTO presents a system to use throughout the sales process to gain a better understanding of your customer's needs and ultimately help your customers make sound buying decisions.

Closing should be viewed as part of the selling process—the logical outcome of a well-planned presentation strategy.

Michael Ahearne

ADAPTING THE CLOSE—AN ATTITUDE THAT ADDS VALUE

Victoria Davis, conference services manager at Holiday Inn & Suites in St. Catharines, Ontario looks at closing from the prospect's point of view. Although the special event plan she envisions may seem perfect, she realizes that the customer may have a different point of view. A special event for her hotel may involve a wedding or anniversary, a convention, a national sales conference, a corporate executive retreat, or even a client appreciation event for large or small companies that want to recognize and thank their important customers. She must try to see the actual event through the eyes of her customer and, from this insight, use adaptive closing questions to confirm the sale and begin to build a long-term partnership. Victoria believes that relationship-building skills must be applied at every step of the sales process. If she is continuously adding value throughout the sales presentation, closing a sale and getting a contract will be much easier. This is especially true in those cases in which price might be a barrier to closing.[1]

Throughout the evolution of personal selling, we have seen major changes in the way closing is perceived. Prior to the introduction of consultative selling and the partnering era, closing was typically presented as the most important aspect of the sales process. The early sales training literature also presented closing methods that encouraged manipulation of the customer. Use of any closing method that is perceived by the customer as pushy or manipulative will damage your chances of building a long-term partnership, even if you do get the sale.[2]

Closing should not be viewed as a strategy to win at the expense of the customer. The proper attitude should be "If this is the best solution for the customer, I should help her make the correct decision."[3] Once the best solution is determined, *asking for the order* is the next logical step.

We take the position that in many selling situations, the salesperson needs to assume responsibility for obtaining commitment from the customer. Some closing methods can move the customer from indecision to commitment. When these methods are used effectively, the prospect will not feel pressured. In some cases, we need to simply replace defence-arousing language—such as "This is the lowest price available anywhere"—with a positive *need-satisfaction question,* such as "Wouldn't this new software help you achieve more efficient inventory control?"

Asking for the order is less difficult if the salesperson is strategically prepared for the close. Preparation for the close involves understanding customer needs, custom-fitting solutions, and planning appropriate closing methods. Throughout the sales presentation, the salesperson should recognize closing clues and be prepared to use effective closing methods (Fig. 14.1).[4]

The Six-Step Presentation Plan

Step One:
Approach

☑ Review Strategic/Consultative Selling Model
☑ Initiate customer contact

Step Two:
Need Discovery

☑ Ask strategic questions
☑ Determine customer needs
☑ Select product solution

Step Three:
Presentation

☑ Select presentation strategy
☑ Create presentation plan
☑ Initiate presentation

Step Four:
Negotiation

☑ Anticipate buyer concerns
☑ Plan negotiating methods
☑ Initiate win-win negotiations

Step Five:
Close

☐ Plan appropriate closing methods
☐ Recognize closing clues
☐ Initiate closing methods

Step Six:
Servicing the Sale

☐ Follow through
☐ Follow-up calls
☐ Expansion selling

Service, retail, wholesale, and manufacturer selling

Figure 14.1 Effective closing methods require careful planning.

Review the Value Proposition from the Prospect's Point of View

Closing the sale is usually easier if you look at the *value proposition* from the prospect's point of view. Have you effectively summarized the mix of key benefits? Will your proposal provide a solution that solves the customer's problem? Is your proposal strong enough to win over a customer who is experiencing buying anxieties?

Gene Bedell, author of *3 Steps to Yes*, reminds us that buying often causes emotional stress, sometimes referred to as "buyer's remorse." The following buying anxieties help explain why some customers are reluctant to make a commitment to your proposal.[5]

Loss of options. If the customer agrees to purchase a $5000 design proposal, then that money will not be available for other purchases or investments. Agreeing to purchase a product or service often means that some other purchase must be postponed. Anxiety and stress build as the customer thinks about allocating limited resources.

Fear of making a mistake. If the customer believes that agreeing with a closing request may be the wrong thing to do, he or she may back away just when the decision seems imminent. Fear of making a mistake can be caused by lack of trust in the salesperson.

Social or peer pressures. Some customers make buying decisions with an eye on the opinions and reactions of others. A business buyer may have to justify a purchase to her boss or to employees who will actually use the product. Be prepared to deal with these anxieties as you get closer to closing the sale. Sometimes a little gentle persuasion will help the anxious customer make a decision.

Closing the Sale—The Beginning of the Partnership

Tom Reilly, in his book *Value-Added Selling*, says, "... you don't close sales; you build commitment to a course of action that brings value to the customer and profit to the seller."[6] There is a process that begins with an interesting approach and need discovery. It continues with effective product selection and presentation of benefits, which build desire for the product. After a well-planned demonstration and after negotiating sales resistance, it is time to obtain commitment. Closing should be thought of as the beginning of a long-term partnership.

GUIDELINES FOR CLOSING THE SALE

A NUMBER OF FACTORS INCREASE THE ODDS THAT YOU WILL CLOSE THE SALE (SEE FIG. 14.2). These guidelines for closing the sale have universal application in the field of selling.

Focus on Dominant Buying Motives

Most salespeople incorporate the outstanding benefits of their product into the sales presentation. This is only natural. However, be alert to the *one* specific benefit that generates the most excitement. The buying motive that is of greatest interest deserves special attention. Vince Peters, director of sales training and development for Wyeth-Ayerst International, tells his 8000 pharmaceutical salespeople that the key to closing "is to find out exactly what a prospect is looking for."[7]

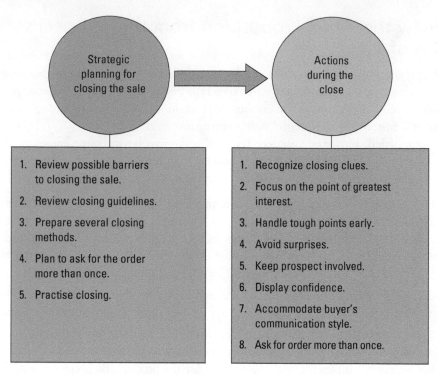

Figure 14.2 The presentation strategy should include reviewing these guidelines for closing and confirming the sale.

Throughout the need discovery stage, pay close attention to the buyer's interests. Focus your closing efforts on the point of greatest interest, and give the prospect a reason for buying.

Longer Selling Cycles and Incremental Commitments

Longer selling cycles have become a fact of life in many industries. One reason for this change is that more decision makers are involved in purchasing some products. A survey of 1300 companies by sales analysis firm CSO Insights indicates that increased competition, more complex buying processes, and higher buyer workloads are also adding time to the sales cycle. The buying cycle for many products can be measured in months and some buying cycles can be measured in years.[8]

incremental commitment
Gradually moving the customer to total commitment (i.e., closing on a purchase) by gaining cumulative commitment with each sales call.

When you are working on a large, complex sale, you should try to achieve **incremental commitment** throughout the sales process. Some form of incremental commitment should be obtained during each step in a multi-call sales presentation. At the conclusion of the first sales call, for example, you may obtain commitment to an agenda for the second call. At the second call, you might obtain commitment for the prospect to tour your company facilities. Each commitment should move the sale forward toward a signed order.

In some cases, the best way to shorten a sales cycle is to create an entirely new way to locate and approach customers. The customer base for Telegraph Hill Robes is upscale hotels and spas. When Maria Spurlock assumed the duties of CEO, the typical sales cycle was six months to two years. Most Telegraph Hill Robes clients were large, established hotels, and decisions regarding the purchase of robes often involved the general manager and the head of housekeeping. Spurlock decided to focus more sales efforts on hotels still under construction. The key decision maker for a hotel under construction is often just one person, the interior designer. By working with designers, she reduced the sales cycle to three months or less.[9]

Negotiate the Tough Points before Attempting the Close

Many products have what might be thought of as an Achilles heel—in other words, the product is vulnerable or appears to be vulnerable in one or more areas. Negotiate a win-win solution to the tough points before you attempt to close the sale. Such factors can lose the sale if you ignore them. The close should be a positive phase of the sales presentation. This is not the time to deal with a controversial issue or problem.

In the case of Rolex watches, BMW automobiles, or Banff Springs Hotel conference facilities, for example, the Achilles heel may be price. Each of these products may seem expensive in comparison with competing ones. People who sell them find ways to establish the value of their product before attempting the close.

Avoid Surprises at the Close

Some salespeople make the mistake of waiting until the close to reveal information that may come as a surprise to the prospect. For example, the salesperson quotes a price but is not specific concerning what the price includes. Let us assume that the price of a central air-conditioning unit is $4000. The prospect believes that the price is competitive

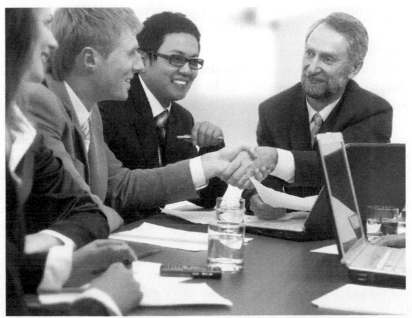

Closing should be viewed as part of the selling process—the logical outcome of a well-planned presentation strategy.

EDHAR/Shutterstock

in relation to similar units on the market and is ready to sign the order form. Then the salesperson mentions casually that the installation charge is an extra $975. The prospect had assumed that the $4000 price included installation. Suddenly the extra fee looms as a major obstacle to closing the sale.

The surprise might come in the form of an accessory that costs extra, terms of the warranty, customer service limitations, or some other issue. Do not let a last-minute surprise damage the relationship with the buyer and threaten the completion of a sale.

"Tough-Mindedness"—Display a High Degree of Self-Confidence at the Close

Do you believe in your product? Do you believe in your company? Do you believe in yourself? Have you identified a solution to the customer's problem? If you can answer yes to each of these questions, then there is no need to display timidity. Look the prospect in the eye and ask for the order. Do not be apologetic at this important point in the sales presentation. The salesperson who confidently asks for the sale is displaying the boldness that is so effective in personal selling.

Ask for the Order More Than Once

Too often, salespeople make the mistake of not asking for the order or asking just once. If the prospect says no, they give up. Michael LeBoeuf, author of *How to Win Customers and Keep Them for Life*, reports that almost two-thirds of all sales calls conclude without the salesperson asking for the order. He also says that a majority of customers say no several times before saying yes.[10] Some of the most productive salespeople ask for the order three, four, or even five times. A surprising number of yes responses come on the fourth or fifth attempt. Of course, not all these closing attempts necessarily come during one call. Determination is a virtue if your product solution solves the customer's problem.

RECOGNIZE CLOSING CLUES

As the sales presentation progresses, you need to be alert to closing clues (sometimes called *buying signals*). A **closing clue** is an indication, either verbal or nonverbal, that the prospect is preparing to make a buying decision. It is a form of feedback, which is so important in selling. When you detect a closing clue, it may be time to attempt a close.

Many closing clues are quite subtle and may be missed if you are not alert. This is especially true in the case of nonverbal buying signals. If you pay careful attention— with your eyes and ears—many prospects will signal their degree of commitment.[11] As we noted earlier in this text, one of the most important personality traits salespeople need is empathy—the ability to sense what the other person is feeling. Recognizing situational clues allows you to modify your self-behaviour to use the appropriate strategy for the close.[12] In this section, we will review some of the most common verbal and nonverbal clues.

Verbal Clues Closing clues come in many forms. Spoken words, or verbal clues, are usually the easiest to perceive. These clues can be divided into three categories: (1) questions, (2) recognitions, and (3) requirements.

closing clue An indication, either verbal or nonverbal, that the prospect is preparing to make a buying decision.

Questions. One of the least subtle buying signals is the question. You might attempt a trial close after responding to one of the following questions:

> Do you have a credit plan to cover this purchase?
> What type of warranty do you provide?
> How soon can our company get delivery?

Recognitions. A recognition is any positive statement concerning your product or some factor related to the sale, such as credit terms or delivery date. Some examples follow:

> We like the quality control system you have recommended.
> I have always wanted to own a boat like this.
> Your delivery schedule fits our plans.

Requirements. Sometimes customers outline a condition that must be met before they will buy. If you are able to meet this requirement, it may be a good time to try a trial close. Here are some requirements that the prospect might voice:

> We will need shipment within two weeks.
> Our staff will need to be trained in how to use this equipment.
> All our equipment must be certified by the plant safety officer.

In some cases, verbal buying clues will not jump out at you. Important buying signals may be interwoven into normal conversation. Listen closely whenever the prospect is talking.

Nonverbal Clues Nonverbal buying clues will be even more difficult to detect. Once detected, this type of signal is not easy to interpret. Nevertheless, you should be alert to body movement, facial expression, and tone of voice. Here are some actions that suggest that the prospect may be prepared to purchase the product.[13]

- The prospect's facial expression changes. Suddenly the person's eyes widen and genuine interest is clear in the facial expression.
- The prospect begins showing agreement by nodding.
- The prospect leans forward and appears to be intent on hearing your message.
- The prospect begins to examine the product or study the sales literature intently.

From the Field
Brand Development Starts with Personal Selling

Building a brand name for a line of "unmentionables" (bras, underwear, and camisoles) can be a challenge. Alka and Mona Srivastava, sisters and business partners, readily agree that they didn't know what they were getting themselves into when they started Florentyna Intima, a lingerie company. The two economics majors knew very little about design, manufacturing, and marketing. Once they had a business plan and some money borrowed from their parents, Alka and Mona began the search for a designer and manufacturer. They needed prototypes to show to customers. Once the prototypes were completed by a firm in Bangkok, they tried to hire a sales representative to present the new line. Unfortunately, no one was willing to represent a line sold by an inexperienced manufacturer. That's when they decided to become salespeople. They hit the road, calling on owners of lingerie boutiques coast to coast and visiting trade shows. Soon buyers were calling with orders. Sales have grown about 30 percent each year.[a]

When you observe or sense one of these nonverbal buying clues, do not hesitate to ask for commitment. There may be several opportunities to close throughout the sales presentation. Important buying signals may surface at any time. Do not miss them.

SPECIFIC METHODS FOR CLOSING THE SALE

THE SALES PRESENTATION IS A PROCESS, NOT A SINGLE ACTION. EACH STEP DURING THE process should create another layer of trust and move the customer closer to making the purchase. Throughout the sales process, you are moving closer to the close by positioning yourself as a valued resource.[14]

There is no *best* closing method. Your best bet is to preplan several closing methods and adapt the ones that seem appropriate to each customer (see Fig. 14.3). Given the complex nature of many sales, it is often a good idea to be prepared to use a combination

Closing Worksheet		
Closing clue (prospect)	Closing method	Closing statement (salesperson)
"That sounds fine."	Direct appeal close	"Good. May I get your signature on this order?"
"What kind of financing do you offer?"	Multiple options close	"We have two financing methods available: 90-day open credit or two-year long-term financing. Which of these do you prefer?"
"Well, we don't have large amounts of cash available at this time."	Assumptive close	"Based on your cash position, I would recommend you consider our lease–purchase plan. This plan allows you to pay a very small initial amount at this time and keep the cash you now have for your everyday business expenses. I will be happy to write up your order on the lease–purchase plan."
The prospect completes a careful reading of the proposal, then looks satisfied (a nonverbal clue).	Combination summary-of-benefits/direct appeal close	"That solution surpasses your quality requirements, meets your time deadlines, and provides your accounting department with the details it requested. Can you get your chief financial officer's signature on the order?"

Figure 14.3 Closing Worksheet
Preparing for the close requires the preplanning of several closing methods. Research indicates that in many selling situations, several closing attempts will be necessary.

of closing methods that fit the customer.[15] Do keep in mind that your goal is not only to close the sale but also to develop a long-term partnership.

Trial Close

A **trial close,** also known as a *minor point close*, is a closing attempt made at an opportune time during the sales presentation to encourage the customer to reveal either readiness or unwillingness to buy. When you are reasonably sure that the prospect is about to make a decision but is being held back by natural caution, the trial close may be appropriate. It is a good way to test the buyer's attitude toward the actual purchase. The trial close can also be effectively adapted to achieving incremental commitment in more complex multi-call sales. A trial close is often presented in the form of a probing or confirmation question. Here are some examples:

> We can arrange an August 1 shipment. Would this date be satisfactory?
> Would you rather begin this plan on July 1 or July 15?
> Is the timing right to do a presentation to the executive committee?
> Will a $2000 down payment be possible at this time?

Some salespeople use the trial close more than once during the sales presentation. After the salesperson presents a feature, converts that feature to a buyer benefit, and confirms the prospect's agreement that the benefit is important, it is appropriate to use a trial close.

In broader terms, it would be appropriate to attempt a trial close after steps two, three, or four of the six-step presentation plan (see Fig. 14.4).

trial close A closing attempt made at an opportune time during the sales presentation to encourage the customer to reveal either readiness or unwillingness to buy.

Direct Appeal Close

The **direct appeal close** has the advantages of clarity and simplicity. This close involves simply asking for the order in a straightforward manner. It is the most direct closing approach, and many buyers find it attractive. Realistically, most customers expect salespeople to ask for the sale.

The direct appeal should not, of course, come too early. It should not be used until the prospect has displayed a definite interest in the product or service. The salesperson must also gain the prospect's respect before initiating this appeal. Once you make the direct appeal, stop talking. John Livesay, a magazine ad director, says being patient at the close is his "secret weapon." He remains silent after asking the customer to buy. He avoids asking more questions or making additional statements. This approach gives the customer time to think about the proposal.[16]

A variation of the direct appeal close involves using a question to determine how close the customer is to making a buying decision. The question might be "How close are we to closing the sale?" This direct question calls for a direct answer. The customer is encouraged to reflect on the progress of the sale.[17]

direct appeal close Involves simply asking for the order in a straightforward manner.

Assumptive Close

The **assumptive close**—sometimes called *take-it-for-granted* close—asks for a minor decision, assuming that the customer has already decided to buy.[18] This closing approach comes near the end of the planned presentation. If you have identified a genuine need, presented your solutions in terms of buyer benefits, presented an effective sales demonstration, and negotiated buyer concerns satisfactorily, it may be natural to assume that the

assumptive close The salesperson asks for a minor decision, assuming that the customer has already decided to buy.

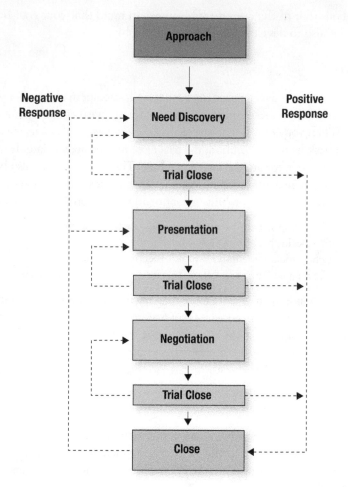

Figure 14.4 The Trial Close
The trial close should be attempted at an opportune time during the sales presentation. It is appropriate to initiate a trial close after steps two, three, or four of the six-step presentation plan.

person is ready to buy. Noted sales consultant Jeffrey Gitomer (**www.gitomer.com**) says the assumptive close is appropriate when the salesperson has removed perceived risks and the prospect has confidence in the salesperson.[19] The assumptive close usually takes the form of a question that focuses on a minor point. Here are some examples:

> "If you feel that Model 211 gives you the major benefits you are looking for, let's schedule delivery for next Tuesday."
> "Since our production systems provide you with the order fulfillment flexibility you require, let's go ahead and place your order."

Most customers will view either of these statements as the natural conclusion of the events that preceded it. Assumptive closes often include a benefit with your request for action.[20]

This closing method provides a subtle way to ask for a decision when you are quite certain the customer has already decided to buy. You are only bringing the selling/buying process to a close.

The assumptive close asks for a minor decision, assuming that the customer has decided to buy.

Pressmaster/Shutterstock

Summary-of-Benefits Close

Let us assume that you have discussed and demonstrated the major benefits of your product and you detect considerable buyer interest. However, you have covered a great deal of material. There is a chance that the prospect will not be able to put the entire picture together without your help. At this point, you should provide a concise summary of the most important buyer benefits. Your goal in the **summary-of-benefits close**—also referred to as the *step-by-step close*—is to re-emphasize the value-added benefits that will help bring about a favourable decision. This closing statement gives you the opportunity to restate how the benefits will outweigh the costs.[21]

Let us see how this closing method works in the management education industry. Foster Zanuto, a representative for Brock University's Management Development Centre, recently called on Ray Busch, director of marketing for a large corporation. Near the end of the sales presentation, Foster summarized the major benefits in this manner:

> Mr. Busch, we can provide you with a state-of-the-art seminar room that will seat 30 people comfortably and four smaller rooms for the workshops you have planned. Our staff will serve a noon lunch. The cost will be $295 per person, including the instructor's fees. Finally, we will see that each of your employees receives a pad of paper, a pen, and a copy of the workshop program. Today I can reserve these facilities for November 24, which is your first preference for a meeting date. Can I go ahead and enter your reservation into our computer?

Notice that Foster has reviewed all the important elements of the value proposition and then asked a *need-satisfaction question*. This question is designed to move the sales process toward commitment and action.

summary-of-benefits close Involves summarizing the most important buyer benefits, re-emphasizing the benefits that will help bring about a favourable decision.

Special Concession Close

special concession close Offers the buyer something extra for acting immediately.

The **special concession close** offers the buyer something extra for acting immediately. A special inducement is offered if the prospect will agree to sign the order. The concession may be part of a low-price strategy such as a sale price, a quantity discount, a more liberal credit plan, or an added feature that the prospect did not anticipate.

You should use this closing approach with care, because some customers are skeptical of concessions. This is especially true when the concession comes after the salesperson has made what appears to be the final offer.

Nicholas Graham, founder and chairman of Joe Boxer Corporation, spends considerable time presenting his novelty underwear line to retailers. Graham recalls that one of his most difficult sales involved Saks Fifth Avenue, the prestigious department store company. He wanted the company to carry Joe Boxer underwear and suggested a Daniel Boone–inspired boxer with a detachable raccoon tail. Graham says, "They had never seen anything so absurd in their life." To close the sale, he let the store take 24 pairs on consignment. "They sold out in one hour," Graham says. Saks has been a committed customer ever since.[22]

Multiple Options Close

multiple options close When the salesperson gives the prospect several options to consider and tries to assess the prospect's degree of interest in each.

In many selling situations, it is a good idea to provide the prospect with options regarding product configuration, delivery, and price. This is especially true when you are dealing with the price-conscious *transactional buyer*. As noted in the previous chapter, today's customer expects new levels of flexibility. In the **multiple options close,** allow the person to examine several different options and try to assess the degree of interest in each one. As you near the point where a close seems appropriate, remove some of the options. This will reduce confusion and indecision.

The multiple options technique is often used in office equipment sales. If a small business owner wants to purchase a copy machine, most vendors will offer several models for consideration. Let us assume that the prospect has examined four models and seems to be uncertain about which one would be the best choice. The salesperson might determine which copier is least appealing and eliminate it as an option. Now the prospect can choose among three copiers. If the prospect seems to favour one copier, it would be appropriate to ask for the order.

When using the multiple options close, follow these simple steps:

1. Configure more than one product solution.
2. Cease showing product options when it appears that the prospect has been given ample selection. Too many choices can result in confusion and indecision.
3. Remove products (or features) that the prospect does not seem genuinely interested in and concentrate on the options the prospect does seem to be interested in.

Balance Sheet Close

balance sheet close A visual way of showing the customer the reasons for making a decision now versus not making a decision now.

The **balance sheet close** appeals to customers who are having difficulty making a decision even though they have been given plenty of information. Let's assume that the customer feels he or she has a choice: Buy now or buy later. The salesperson draws a T on a sheet of paper and writes the captions below on each side of the crossbar.

Reasons for buying now	Reasons for not buying now
1.	1.
2.	2.
3.	3.
4.	4.

To get the process rolling, the salesperson might say, "Let's see how many reasons we can list for buying now." On the left side of the T, the salesperson lists some reasons for buying now. These should be benefits in which the customer has already expressed an interest. On the right side, reasons for not buying now are listed. Throughout the listing process, the salesperson should engage the customer in a dialogue. This closing method will not be effective if the salesperson is doing all the talking.

Management Close

In previous chapters, we have discussed the merits of involving the sales manager or senior executives in sales calls. To close a major account, salespeople sometimes call on top management for help. This is the **management close.** Ryan Hegman, who works for Hegman Machine Tool Inc., recalls a sale that involved a $1.5 million automated manufacturing system. During the sales process, he brought in the president of the company, the vice president of sales, and the lead engineer. "Each added value in a separate way," Ryan explains. One important reason to involve management is to make prospects feel that your whole company's resources will be available to support the customer.[23]

management close A close that involves bringing the sales manager or senior management to the sales presentation as a way to help close a sale.

Impending Event Close

The **impending event close**—also known as the *positive/negative technique*—involves making positive use of a negative point. This technique of closing requires that you know the

impending event close Involves making positive use of a negative point.

needs of the prospects well enough to turn their objections into your selling points. More often than not, you will need to have a good relationship with your prospects to make the method work.

For example, the salesperson might say, "As you have agreed, our product does have several advantages over the competing offerings. I also want to share with you that we cannot make delivery before the middle of next month (the negative point) due to high demand (the positive point). However, I believe you're not looking for delivery until the end of next month (make sure you know this as a fact), so if you place this order today, delivery will not be a problem."

Combination Closes

In some cases, the most effective close is one that combines two or more of the closing methods we have discussed. To illustrate, let us observe Colleen White as she attempts to close a sale in the office of a buyer for a large department store. Colleen represents a firm that manufactures a wide range of leather clothing and accessories. Near the end of her planned presentation, she senses that the prospect is quite interested in her products but seems reluctant to make a decision. This is how Colleen handles the close:

> Ms. Taylor, I have described several benefits that seem especially important to you. First, you agree that this line will be popular with the fashion-conscious shoppers your store caters to. Second, you indicated that the prices I quoted will allow you excellent profit margins, and third, if we process your order now, you will have the merchandise in time for the pre-holiday buying period. With this in mind, let's go ahead and process your order today.

Notice that this close starts with a summary of benefits and ends with an assumptive close.

Adapting to the Customer's Communication Style

In Chapter 5, we examined the concept of communication styles and achieving versatility through style flexing. We noted that people with different behaviour styles will make their decisions in very distinct ways. We need to take the prospect's style into consideration when deciding how to approach the close.[24]

Directive Most Directives are goal-oriented individuals who are ready to make quick decisions once they believe your solution meets their needs. They like doing business with salespeople who display confidence that they can give customers the benefits they want. The Directive may reject your trial close just to test your confidence level. The highly assertive Directive will respect persistence and determination.

Emotive The Emotive needs social acceptance, so provide support for their opinions and ideas. Maintain good eye contact and be a good listener. Don't let this buyer's emotional statements throw you off balance. Spontaneous statements, spoken dramatically and impulsively, should be expected.

Supportive You can expect the Supportive customer to be slow in making the buying decision. This buyer is more apt to worry about change or taking risks. It's important to understand his or her perceived risks so that you can provide reassurance before asking for a buying decision. Curb the desire to put pressure on the Supportive customer—it may make this buyer more indecisive. Patience is important.

Reflective Before you ask the Reflective customer for a buying decision, make sure you review important factual information. These buyers are less likely to be influenced by emotion. Ask Reflectives, "Is there any other information I can provide before you make a decision?" Never pressure the Reflective customer to make a quick decision.

Practise Closing

Your success in selling will depend in large part on learning how to make these eight closing methods work for you. Gaining experience using adaptive selling techniques can result in increased recognition of opportunities and greater effectiveness.[25] You will not master these approaches in a few days or a few weeks, but you can speed up the learning process with preparation and practice. Role playing is the best-known way to experience the feelings that accompany closing and to practise the skills needed to close sales. To prepare the role play, anticipate various closing scenarios and then prepare a written script of the drama.[26] Find someone (your sales manager, friend, or spouse) to play the role of the customer and give that person a script to act out. Practise the role play in front of a video recorder, and then sit back and observe your performance. The video monitor provides excellent feedback. Use the closing worksheet (see Fig. 14.3) to prepare for practice sessions.

Michael Ahearne

Applying the Platinum Rule. People with different behaviour styles will make their buying decisions in very distinct ways. Therefore, the prospect's communication style must be taken into consideration when deciding how to adapt the close.

CONFIRMING THE PARTNERSHIP WHEN THE BUYER SAYS YES

CONGRATULATIONS! YOU HAVE CLOSED THE SALE AND HAVE ESTABLISHED THE BEGINNING of what you hope will be a long and satisfying partnership with the customer. Before preparing to leave, be sure that all details related to the purchase agreement are completed. Check everything with the buyer, and then ask for a signature if necessary.

Once the sale has been closed, it is important to take time to reassure the customer. This is the **confirmation step** in closing the sale. Before you leave, reassure the customer by pointing out that he or she has made the correct decision, and describe the satisfaction that will come with ownership of the product. The reason for doing this is to resell the buyer and to prevent buyer's remorse. **Buyer's remorse** (sometimes called *cognitive dissonance*) is an emotional response that can take various forms such as feelings of regret, fear, or anxiety.[27] It is common to wonder whether we have made the right decision. Compliment the customer for making a wise choice. Once the sale is closed, the customer may be required to justify the purchase to others. Your words of reassurance will be helpful.

Before leaving, thank the customer for the order. This is very important. Everyone likes to think that a purchase is appreciated. No one should believe that a purchase is taken for granted. Even a small order deserves words of appreciation. In many cases, a follow-up thank-you letter is appropriate.

In several previous chapters we said that a satisfied customer is one of the best sources of new prospects. Never hesitate to ask, "Do you know anyone else who might benefit from owning this product?" or a similar question. Some customers may even agree to write an introductory letter on your behalf.

confirmation step Reassuring the customer after the sale has been closed, pointing out that he or she has made the correct decision. This may involve describing the satisfaction of owning the product.

buyer's remorse Feelings of regret, fear, or anxiety that a buyer may feel after placing an order.

What to Do When the Buyer Says No

High-performance salespeople learn to manage disappointment. A strong display of disappointment or resentment is likely to close the door to future sales. Losing a sale may be painful, but it can also be a valuable learning opportunity. Doing some analysis of what went wrong can help you change the outcome of future sales. Here are some things you should do after a lost sale.[28]

1. *Make sure the deal is really dead.* There is always a chance that the prospect's decision can be changed. You might want to mount a last-ditch effort and reopen the presentation.

2. *Review the chain of events.* When you experience a no-sale call, try to benefit from the experience. If you were part of a sales team, get each member's reaction. Soon after the prospect has said no, schedule a debriefing session. If you worked alone, engage in honest self-analysis. If you carefully look at your performance during every aspect of the sales process, you may be able to identify weaknesses that can be corrected.

3. *Interview the customer.* Obtaining feedback requires a delicate approach. If you probe too aggressively, you may appear argumentative. If your approach is too passive, and the client's comments are general, you will not know how to improve. The key is to

Before leaving, thank the customer for the order. This is very important. Everyone likes to know that a purchase is appreciated.

Kurhan/Fotolia

couch your questions in neutral terms. Rather than asking, "Why didn't we get the order?" try this approach: "Thank you for considering our company. We hope to do business with you at some time in the future. Would you mind helping me understand any shortcomings in our sales proposal?"

Always keep the door open for future sales. Tell the prospect you would love to work with him or her at some time in the future. Then put this person back on your prospect list, record any new information you have learned about the prospect, and continue to keep in touch. Marvin Gottlieb, president of The Communication Project, recalls the loss of a very large piece of business from a large IT firm. This company decided to begin doing its own training rather than outsource it to Gottlieb's company. Rather then give up hope, Gottlieb continued to maintain relationships with key people at the IT firm. After four years, he was invited to present information on a needed service. He closed a $50 000 sale in less than a month.[29]

Prepare the Prospect for Contact with the Competition Some prospects refuse to buy because they want to take a close look at competing products. This response is not unusual in the field of selling. You should do everything possible to help the customer make an intelligent comparison. It is always a good practice to review your product's strong points one more time. Give special emphasis to areas in which your product has a strong competitive advantage. Make it easy for the person to buy your product at some future date.

Chris Van Wiechen, a sales consultant at Collins Nissan in St. Catharines, Ontario, uses social media to remind prospective customers of their visit to the dealership. He knows that after visiting several car dealerships and test driving a number of vehicles, customers may have difficulty differentiating one vehicle from another. Chris prepares a video where he does a walk-around, carefully describing all of the things he wishes the customer to remember and consider when making his or her decision. Then he uploads the video to Youtube and sends a link to the video by email to his customer.[30]

REVIEWING KEY CONCEPTS

- Describe the proper attitude to display toward closing the sale.

  Some of the early closing methods encouraged manipulation of the customer. Use of any closing method that is perceived by the customer as pushy or manipulative will damage your chances of building a long-term partnership. Closing should not be viewed as a strategy to win at the expense of the customer. Once the customer's need has been confirmed, salespeople should determine the most ethical and effective method of moving the buyer from indecision to commitment.

- List and discuss selected guidelines for closing the sale.

  Long sales cycles require multiple commitments. These commitments need to be obtained from the prospect throughout a multi-call sales presentation. The buying motive that is of greatest interest deserves special attention at the close. Always negotiate tough points before attempting the close, display a high degree of confidence, and ask for the order more than once.

- Explain how to recognize closing clues.

  The salesperson must be alert to *closing clues* from the prospect. These clues fall into two categories:

verbal and nonverbal. Verbal clues are the easiest to recognize, but they may be subtle as well. Again, it is important to be an attentive listener. The recognition of nonverbal clues is more difficult, but careful observation helps in detecting them.

- Discuss specific methods of closing the sale.

  Several closing methods may be necessary to get the prospect to make a buying decision; therefore, it is wise for the salesperson to preplan several closes. These closing methods should be chosen from the list provided in this chapter and then customized to fit the product and the type of buyer with whom the salesperson is dealing. In some selling situations, the use of *combination closes* is very effective. Flexing to the customer's communication style is important.

- Explain what to do when the buyer says yes and what to do when the buyer says no.

  The professional salesperson is not discouraged or offended if the sale is not closed. Every effort should be made to be of further assistance to the prospect—the sale might be closed on another call. Continue to keep in touch. Even if the sale is lost, the experience may be valuable if it is analyzed in order to learn from it.

Key Terms

assumptive close (take-it-for-granted close) **343**
balance sheet close **346**

buyer's remorse **350**
closing clue **340**

Review Questions

1. List some aspects of the sales presentation that can make closing and confirming the sale difficult to achieve.

2. Describe three buying anxieties that sometimes serve as barriers to closing the sale.

3. What guidelines should a salesperson follow for closing the sale?

4. Why is it important to review the value proposition from the prospect's point of view?

5. Define the term *incremental commitment*. Why is it important to achieve incremental commitments throughout the sale?

6. Explain how the multiple options close might be used in the sale of men's and women's suits.

7. Is there a best method to use in closing the sale? Explain.

8. What is meant by a trial close (the minor point close)? When should a salesperson attempt a trial close?

9. Explain the summary-of-benefits close (step-by-step close).

10. What confirming steps should a salesperson follow when the customer says yes? What should be done when the customer says no?

Application Exercises

1. Which of the following statements, often made by prospects, would you interpret as buying signals?

   a. "How much would the payments be?"

   b. "Tell me about your service department."

   c. "Our company already has an older model that seems good enough."

   d. "We do not have enough cash flow right now."

   e. "How much would you allow me for my old model?"

   f. "I do not need one."

   g. "How does that switch work?"

   h. "When would I have to pay for it?"

2. You are an accountant who owns and operates an accounting service. You have been contacted by the president of an advertising agency about the possibility of having you audit her business on a regular basis. The president has indicated that she has investigated other accounting firms and thinks that they price their services too high. With the knowledge you have about the other firms, you know you are in a strong competitive position. You also realize her account would be profitable for your firm. You would really like to capture this account. How will you close the deal? List and describe two closing methods you might use in this situation.

3. Zig Ziglar (d. 2012), Brian Tracy, and Tom Reilly are well-known authors and speakers on the subject of closing the sale. Access each of their websites—**www.ziglar.com, www.briantracy.com, www.tomreillytraining.com**—and research the books, courses, and videos they have available for companies and individuals to purchase and learn more about closing the sale. Prepare a summary of what you find available. Does the material in this chapter parallel the kind of information these individuals present?

4. If the prospect is ready to buy before you have presented all of your selling points, should you make an effort to complete your sales presentation? Explain your answer.

5. Books have been written explaining hundreds of different closes that salespeople can use. One close

that some salespeople commonly use is called the impending doom close. This is one of many closing techniques we would never recommend in our book. Using your search engine, find out how this particular close works. (Search for impending doom technique as well as impending doom close.) Explain why you would never expect to see this close recommended in our book.

ROLE-PLAY EXERCISE

Examine the superior benefits of the convention centre identified in "Partnership Selling: A Role Play/Simulation" online in the Student Resource section at **www.pearsoncanada.ca/manning**. Specifically, research the qualities of the "five-star" executive chef, the award-winning renovation of the facility, the cost of parking and transportation to and from the airport, and the easy highway access to and from the facility. You should assume the role of director of sales and, with this information, prepare a closing worksheet on the combination of summary-of-benefits and direct appeal closes for a prospective customer. Using the information from the audiovisual presentation guide, prepare a special concession close, allowing free use of the laser pointer and wireless microphone (a $107.50 value) for a group presentation to the 23 people who will be staying in single rooms at the hotel. Role-play the close of a sale using these closing methods to a prospect who is seriously considering using one of your competitors.

Reality Selling Video Case Problem

The team at Heart of Niagara can help make your dreams come true. The team can help you plan a special event—large or small—in one of several venues. If you want to show appreciation to your retiring chief executive officer, the Heart of Niagara team will make sure the party is truly special. They can help organize wedding parties, employee reward and recognition nights, strategy planning retreats for businesses, or even corporate team-building events. One large corporate client holds an annual gathering at Holiday Inn & Suites—the largest of the three hotel properties owned by Heart of Niagara—for approximately 300 current and retired employees to recognize and celebrate their achievements.

Victoria Davis, conference services manager at Holiday Inn & Suites, is an important part of the sales team. She enjoys working with customers to ensure that their needs are completely understood and can be accommodated. Her customers vary greatly in terms of age, education, income, and social class. The key to working effectively with all of these people is relationship building. Once she builds rapport with clients and establishes a foundation built on trust, they are more likely to open up and discuss their needs. Conference services managers have at their disposal a wide range of planning tools, including facilities and event production expertise, but customer needs guide the use of these resources.

Victoria finds that if the sales presentation is well planned and delivered, and if thoughtful questions are asked throughout the process, closing a sale or confirming a contract is easier. She believes that good listening skills and careful probing can help uncover dominant buying motives. For example, the client who wants an event with a special theme may have difficulty expressing her thoughts. Victoria must probe and listen closely in order to understand the customer's desires. She must also create value throughout the presentation in order to set the stage for the close, or to confirm the contract. A special event can cost anywhere from a few thousand dollars to $100 000 or more, so price can sometimes be a barrier to closing.[31]

Questions

1. What closing clues should Victoria look for?
2. What trial closes would be appropriate?
3. What tough points should be negotiated before attempting to close or confirm a contract?
4. Can you visualize a situation in which Victoria might use a multiple options close? Explain.
5. Assume that a large corporation wants to schedule a recognition event for 40 people. This event will begin with cocktails and appetizers and end with a served meal. Special entertainment will precede the meal. What items might be included in a summary-of-benefits close?

PARTNERSHIP SELLING: A ROLE PLAY/SIMULATION

Visit the role play/simulation materials provided in the Student Resources section of your companion website at **www.pearsoncanada.ca/manning.** *A Contents page lists appropriate page references for the activities.*

Developing a Sales Presentation Strategy—Closing the Sale

Refer to *Sales Memorandum 3* and strategically plan to close the sale with your customer. To consider the sale closed, you will need to secure the signature of your customer on the sales proposal form. This will guarantee your customer the accommodations listed on the form. These accommodations may change depending on the final number of people attending your customer's convention. This is an important point to keep in mind when closing the sale; however, you still must get the signature to guarantee the accommodations.

Follow the instructions carefully and prepare a closing worksheet (see *Strategic Planning Form C*) listing at least four closes using the methods outlined in this chapter. Two of these methods should be the summary-of-benefits and the direct appeal. Remember that it is not the policy of your convention centre to cut prices, so your methods should include value-added strategies.

Use proof devices to make your closes more convincing and place them in the front pocket of your three-ring binder/portfolio for easy access during your presentation. You may want to ask another person to be your customer and practise the closing strategies you have developed.

Chapter 15
Servicing the Sale and Building the Partnership

Learning Objectives

After studying this chapter, you should be able to

1 Explain how to build long-term partnerships with customer service.

2 Describe current developments in customer service.

3 List and describe the major customer service methods that strengthen the partnership.

4 Explain how to add value with expansion selling.

5 Explain how to deal effectively with complaints.

 Introduction

WFS Ltd.—formerly Windsor Factory Supply—is one of Canada's largest general-line industrial distributors. The company started as a two-man operation in Windsor, Ontario, in 1955. Jerry Slavik and Cliff Cretney, both 22 years old, decided to leave another distributor and begin their own company. They had $500 between them and raised an equal amount from relatives. Joe Sobocan joined the company a few months later, and Cliff soon left for personal reasons. Jerry and Joe began an employee profit-sharing plan as the company grew, with the intention that it would someday become 100 percent employee-owned. This occurred in 1995, shortly after Jerry and Joe retired. WFS now has 10 Canadian branches, one branch in South Carolina, and a warehouse near Detroit, Michigan. There are 247 WFS employees. Sales are approaching $100 million, far beyond the first-year sales of approximately $50 000. WFS currently has more than 3500 suppliers and more than 4500 customers. How has it achieved its tremendous growth? The company has a strong internal culture and a healthy business philosophy. The company's foundation is built on *quality, satisfaction,*

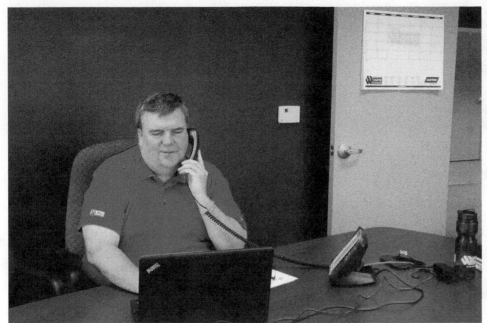

Rick Thurston, president of WFS Ltd., says, "Our business is built on relationships. Of course, we are always looking for opportunities, but we know that sometimes it is important to curb growth so that quality service to existing customers is not compromised."

H.F. (Herb) MacKenzie

and *dependability*, and it is known for outstanding **customer service**. President Rick Thurston describes the company philosophy as one based on the belief that being able to service existing customers is more important than gaining new customers, since a large amount of incremental business comes from the current customer base. He says, "Our business is built on relationships. Of course, we are always looking for opportunities, but we know that sometimes it is important to curb growth so that quality service to existing customers is not compromised. A great example is our most recent expansion into the United States. We had been asked on many occasions to open up more facilities to support customer growth there, but we recognized that our successful Canadian approach would not necessarily be a fit for all U.S. markets. After many years of fine-tuning our relationship with one key customer, we finally decided to open a South Carolina branch."[1]

Servicing the sale encompasses a variety of activities that take place during and after the implementation stage of the buying process (Fig. 8.3). In this chapter, we present servicing the sale as a three-part process: follow-through on assurances and promises; follow-up with ongoing communication after the sale; and expansion selling, which involves the identification of additional needs and providing solutions (Fig. 15.1). Each of these strategies can add value and build the partnership.

customer service All the activities that enhance or facilitate the sale and use of a product.

BUILDING LONG-TERM PARTNERSHIPS WITH CUSTOMER SERVICE

IN A WORLD OF INCREASED GLOBAL COMPETITION AND NARROWING PROFIT MARGINS, customer retention through value-based initiatives can mean the difference between increasing or eroding market share. Progressive marketers are searching for ways to differentiate their service from that of competitors and build emotional loyalty through value.[2]

The Six-Step Presentation Plan

Step One: Approach	☑ Review Strategic/Consultative 　Selling Model ☑ Initiate customer contact
Step Two: Need Discovery	☑ Ask strategic questions ☑ Determine customer needs ☑ Select product solution
Step Three: Presentation	☑ Select presentation strategy ☑ Create presentation plan ☑ Initiate presentation
Step Four: Negotiation	☑ Anticipate buyer concerns ☑ Plan negotiating methods ☑ Initiate win-win negotiations
Step Five: Close	☑ Plan appropriate closing methods ☑ Recognize closing clues ☑ Initiate closing methods
Step Six: Servicing the Sale	☐ Follow through ☐ Follow-up calls ☐ Expansion selling

Service, retail, wholesale, and manufacturer selling

Figure 15.1 Servicing the Sale
Servicing the sale involves three steps: follow-through, follow-up calls, and expansion selling.

A sales organization that can develop a reputation for servicing each sale is sought out by customers who want a long-term partner to help them with their buying needs. Satisfied customers represent an "auxiliary" sales force—a group of people who will recommend customer-driven organizations to others. If customers are pleased with the service they receive after the sale, be assured that they will tell other people. Research shows that when someone has a good customer service experience, he or she tells an average of six people; when someone experiences outstanding customer service, he or she tells twice as many.[3]

Achieving Successive Sales

In Chapter 2, we defined *partnering* as a strategically developed, long-term relationship that solves the customer's problem. A successful partnering effort results in successive sales and referrals.

Many of today's large companies want to partner with suppliers who sell and deliver quality products and services that continually improve their processes and profits. The first sale is only the beginning of the relationship—an opportunity to earn a repeat sale. Repeat sales come after the supplier demonstrates the ability to add value in various ways.[4] This value may take the form of timely delivery, superior installation, accurate invoicing, technical know-how, social contacts, or something else that is important to the customer. In business-to-business sales, the relationship should intensify as the supplier delivers extensive postsale support. Taking the customer's point of view and acting in the customer's interest, often described as *customer advocacy*, is a major factor underlying repeat business.[5]

Responding to Increased Postsale Customer Expectations

According to Ted Levitt, author of *The Marketing Imagination*, people buy expectations, not products. They buy the expectation of benefits you promised. Once the customer buys your product, expectations increase. Levitt points out that after the sale is closed, the buyer's attitude changes. The buyer expects the salesperson to remember the purchase as a favour bestowed on him or her by the buyer. Nitin Nohria, business professor and co-author of *What Really Works: The 4-2 Formula for Sustained Business Success*, says, "Customers are enormously punishing when companies don't meet their expectations."[6]

This salesperson is preparing a thank-you note that will strengthen the relationship with the customer.

Micro10x/Shutterstock

Increased customer expectations after the sale is closed require a strategic plan for servicing the sale. Certain aspects of the relationship, product, and customer strategies can have a positive influence on the customer's heightened expectations.[7] In most business-to-business sales, the salesperson cannot service the sale alone. To manage the account properly, the salesperson will need assistance from shipping, technical support, engineering, and other departments. Customer service is increasingly a team effort.[8]

How do you respond to a customer who has increased expectations?

- *First, you should be certain your customer strategy is on target.* You must fully understand the needs and wants of the customer. What is the customer trying to accomplish, and how can you help him or her do it better?

- *Second, you should focus like a laser beam on follow-through and follow-up activities.* Throughout every sales presentation, the salesperson will offer assurances and make some promises. The salesperson's credibility will be tarnished if any of these commitments is ignored.

- *Third, you should re-examine your product strategy.* In some cases, you can enhance customer satisfaction by suggesting related products or services. If the product is expensive, you can follow through and offer assistance in making credit arrangements. If the product is complex, you can make suggestions concerning use and maintenance. Each of these forms of assistance may add value to the sale.

High Cost of Customer Attrition

Financial institutions, public utilities, airlines, retail stores, restaurants, manufacturers, and wholesalers face the problem of gaining and retaining the patronage of clients and customers. These companies realize that keeping a customer happy is a good strategy. To regain a lost customer can be four to five times more expensive than keeping a current customer satisfied.[9]

There is no longer any doubt that poor service is the primary cause of customer attrition. Surprisingly few customers (12 to 15 percent) are lost because of product dissatisfaction. No more than 10 to 15 percent of lost customers leave because of price considerations. Some studies have found that from 50 to 70 percent of customer attrition is because of poor service.[10] A carefully developed strategic plan to reduce customer defection will pay big dividends.

Larry Rosen, chairman and CEO of Harry Rosen Inc., fully embraces the customer-for-life philosophy. He says, "We don't look at a person who walks into our store as an immediate sale. We look at him with a potential lifetime value. If we can provide enlightened service and advice and earn a man's trust, chances are he will be loyal to our organization for life. This relationship-based aspect of our selling is perfectly captured in our brand promise—'Harry Rosen is in the business of assisting men develop a personal, confident image, in all aspects of their life—any day, any time and any occasion.' To help us develop these quality relationships with our clients we spend over a million dollars annually training our selling associates about providing ongoing service and expertise."[11]

CURRENT DEVELOPMENTS IN CUSTOMER SERVICE

IN HIS BOOK *Business @ the Speed of Thought*, BILL GATES PREDICTS THAT IN THIS millennium, customer service will become the primary value-added function.[12] He recognizes that customer service is the primary method of building and extending the partnership. Customer service, in its many forms, nourishes the partnership and keeps it alive. Salespeople are in a unique position to enhance *customer satisfaction* and *trust*, the two major contributors to relationship quality.[13] With adequate orientation and training, members of the sales force can build long-term, profitable customer relationships. Recent research indicates that the building process involves five important service behaviours that are especially important in the context of business-to-business selling.[14]

- **Diligence.** Diligence combines two types of service behaviours: responsiveness and reliability. In today's highly competitive, time-starved business environment, salespeople must provide service in a timely manner. Service behaviours that demonstrate both reliability and responsiveness include following up on commitments, returning phone calls, fulfilling customer requests, and being available when needed. There is a growing trend in which companies rely on their customers' needs, concerns, and future plans.

- **Information communication.** This service behaviour involves regularly relaying product information to the customer in a clear and concise manner. Communicating information must encompass the entire sales process. Early on, this may involve drawing objective comparisons between your product and competitive offerings, and continually reiterating a clear case for your product. After the sale is closed, information communication often involves providing updated information on product usage.

- **Inducements.** This service behaviour is aimed at personalizing the relationship with the customer. In Chapter 4, we noted that the manner in which salespeople establish, build, and maintain relationships is not an incidental aspect of personal selling. Some service behaviours provide the customer with an incentive, or an inducement, for maintaining the relationship with the salesperson. Becoming genuinely interested in the customer, talking in terms of the customer's interests, or doing special favours can strengthen the relationship with the customer.

- **Empathy.** As the information age unfolded and the global economy heated up, we learned that it takes more than quick and accurate information communicated through advanced technology to retain customers. Empathy is one of those high-touch abilities that mark the fault line between salespeople who are highly productive and those who are average or below average in terms of productivity.[15] Salespeople who display a strong willingness to help customers and make an effort to understand them are demonstrating empathetic behaviour.

■ **Sportsmanship.** This service behaviour can be defined as a salesperson's willingness to tolerate setbacks and disappointments without displaying negativism. It means demonstrating good social judgment and professionalism during all customer interactions. If you have a 10:00 a.m. appointment with a customer but are required to wait until 10:30 a.m. for the meeting to begin, how will you handle this disappointment?

Computer-Based Systems

Customer-friendly computer-based systems are frequently used to enhance customer service, loyalty, and sales growth.[16] Computers give both the salesperson and the customer ready access to information and problem-solving alternatives. Nantucket Nectars provides a good example of a company that has enhanced customer service with computer-based systems. The 150 distributors can log on to the company's website to place and check orders. Nantucket Nectars's 85 field salespeople can log on to NectarNet, a dedicated company website, from their homes to check on the status of customer orders and determine inventory levels.[17]

The sales staff at Harry Rosen Gentlemen's Apparel, the highly successful clothing retailer mentioned earlier in this chapter, use technology to establish a more personal relationship with the customer. In a matter of seconds, salespeople can review a customer's complete buying history, his or her birthday and anniversary, clothing sizes, favourite colours, children's names, or any other information that the customer has willingly provided. With this information, salespeople are better able to bond with their customers. Maggie Chung, a sales manager in the Vancouver store, says, "At Harry Rosen, I've really learned the value of customer relationships. I have some customers who visit me almost monthly."[18]

CUSTOMER SERVICE METHODS THAT STRENGTHEN THE PARTNERSHIP

CUSTOMER SERVICE ENCOMPASSES ALL ACTIVITIES THAT ENHANCE OR FACILITATE THE SALE and use of one's product or service. The skills required to service a sale are different from those required prior to the sale (Fig. 15.2). High-performance sales personnel do not abdicate responsibility for delivery, installation, and warranty interpretation or other customer service responsibilities. They continue to strengthen the partnership with follow-through, follow-up, and expansion selling.

Adding Value with Follow-Through

A major key to an effective customer service strategy is follow-through on assurances and promises that were part of the sales presentation. Properly managing customer relationships enhances the value creation during and after the selling process.[19] Did your sales presentation include claims for superior performance; promises of speedy delivery;

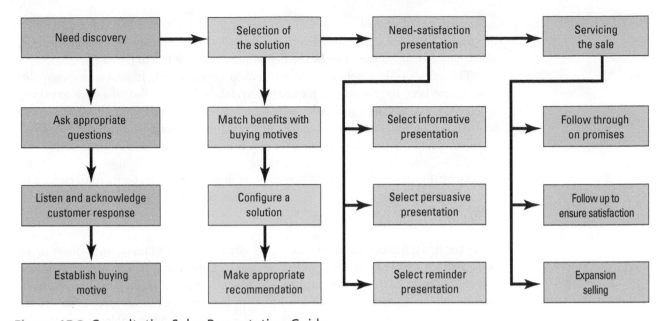

Figure 15.2 Consultative Sales Presentation Guide
The completed Consultative Sales Presentation Guide illustrates the ways in which high-performance salespeople use value-added strategies to service the sale and build repeat business and referrals. Customer service provides many opportunities to strengthen the partnership.

assistance with credit arrangements; or guaranteed factory assistance with installation, training, and service?

Most sales presentations are made up of claims and promises that the company can fulfill. However, fulfillment of these claims will depend to a large degree on after-sale action. Postsale follow-through is the key to holding that customer you worked so hard to develop. The first sale can be the beginning of a long-term partnership, or it can be the last sale. The following services can help ensure a second sale and successive sales.

Make Credit Arrangements Credit has become a common way to finance purchases. This is true of industrial products, real estate, automobiles, home appliances, and many other products. Closing the sale will often depend on your ability to develop and present attractive credit plans to the customer. Even if you do not get directly involved in the firm's credit and collection activities, you must be familiar with how the company handles these matters. Salespeople need to establish a relationship with the credit department and learn how credit analysts make their decisions.[20]

Making credit decisions gets a lot tougher when you are conducting business in foreign countries. Overseas transactions can be complex, and in some cases there is little recourse if a customer does not pay. Doron Weissman, president of Overseas Brokers, a freight forwarder and export brokerage firm, says, "When I sell my services, I automatically qualify the account to make sure they're financially able to meet my demands. If not, I move on."[21]

Schedule Deliveries Many organizations are adding value with on-time deliveries. A late delivery can be a problem for both the supplier and the customer. To illustrate, let us assume that the supplier is a manufacturer of small appliances and the customer is a department store chain. A late delivery may mean lost sales because of out-of-stock conditions, cancellation of the order by the department store, or loss of future sales.

The causes of late delivery may be beyond your control. It is your responsibility, however, to keep the customer informed of any delays. You can also take steps to prevent a delay. Check to be sure your order was processed correctly. Follow up to see if the order was shipped on time. Always remember: "Every time an order is handled, the customer is handled. Every time an order sits unattended, the customer sits unattended."[22]

Be Present During Delivery When the first delivery is made, be there to be sure the customer is comfortable with the purchase. Check to determine if the order is complete and be available to offer assistance.[23]

Monitor Installation Buyer satisfaction is often related to proper installation of the product. This is true of consumer products such as security systems, central air-conditioning, solar heating systems, and carpeting. It is also true of industrial products such as electronic data processing equipment and air-quality control systems. Some salespeople believe it is to their advantage to supervise product installation; they are then able to spot installation problems. Others make it a practice to follow up on the installation to be sure no problems exist.

Offer Training in the Use or Care of the Product For certain industries, it is essential that users be trained in how to use the new product. This is true of factory equipment, electronic cash registers, farm implements, and a host of other products. Technology has become so complex that many suppliers must provide training as part of the follow-up to ensure customer satisfaction. Most organizations that sell computers and other types of electronic equipment for office use now schedule training classes to ensure that customers can properly use and care for the products. These companies believe that users must be skilled in handling their equipment.

Provide Price Change Information Price changes need not be a serious problem if they are handled correctly. The salesperson is responsible for maintaining an up-to-date price list. As your company issues price changes, record them accurately. Customers expect you to quote the correct price the first time.

Preventing Postsale Problems

There are ways to prevent postsale problems. The key is conscientious follow-up to be sure everything has been handled properly. Get to know the people who operate your shipping department. They are responsible for getting the right products shipped on time, and it is important that they understand your customers' needs.

Become acquainted with people in the credit department. Be sure that they maintain a good, businesslike relationship with your customers. This is a delicate area; even small mistakes—a "pay now" notice sent too early, for example—can cause hurt feelings. If your company uses customer support staff to resolve postsale problems, be sure to get acquainted with the people who provide this service.

Schedule regular account reviews to determine the level of customer satisfaction. The focus of these reviews should be key decision makers. Are there lingering service-type issues that make you vulnerable to the competition? You want to be certain there are no open doors for your competitors. If you discover a problem, act quickly to resolve it. In some cases, these formal account reviews will uncover opportunities to improve customer service. You will also become more of a consultant in the eyes of the customer.[24]

Adding Value with Customer Follow-Up

Customer follow-up methods usually have two major objectives. One is to express appreciation for the purchase and thus to enhance the relationship established during the

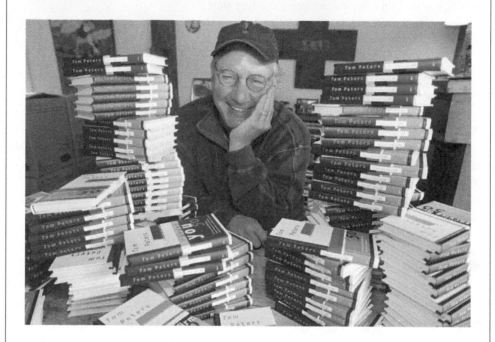

CREATING THE LIFETIME CUSTOMER

When we build a plant or purchase a computer—when we acquire just about any new asset—by accounting conventions, it begins to depreciate on day one. But there is one asset that can appreciate over the years. That asset is the well-served customer, who becomes the most significant sustainer of the business, the lifetime customer.

Tom Peters believes there is one asset that can appreciate over the years. That asset is the well-served customer, who becomes the most significant sustainer of the business, the lifetime customer.

Source: Toby Talbot/AP Images

sales presentation. You no doubt thanked the customer at the time the sale was closed, but appreciation should be expressed again a few days later. The second purpose of the follow-up is to determine whether the customer is satisfied with the purchase. Both of these methods will strengthen the buyer–seller relationship and build a partnership that results in additional sales.[25]

In survey after survey, poor service and lack of follow-up after the sale are given as primary reasons people stop buying from a particular supplier. Most customers are sensitive to indifferent treatment by the sales representative. With this fact in mind, you should approach follow-up in a systematic and businesslike way. There are five follow-up methods.

Personal Visit This is usually the most costly follow-up method, but it may produce the best results. It is the only strategy that allows face-to-face, two-way communication. When you take time to make a personal visit, the customer knows that you really care.

Use the personal follow-up to keep the customer informed of new developments, new products, or new applications. This information may pave the way for additional sales.

Use the personal visit to reassess where you stand with the account. The reassessment process should involve something more than a "How's it going?" question. If you want the customer to see you as a partner, ask the tough questions: "Are there any problems that I need to address?" "Can you suggest any ways we can better serve your business?" Tom Reilly, author and sales trainer, says, "Your perceptions of your performance are meaningless. It's the customer's perceptions that count."[26]

Personal visits provide a wonderful opportunity to engage in **value reinforcement**. Value reinforcement means getting credit for the value you create for the customer. You might review all of your follow-through activities so the customer realizes the many ways you have added value. Whenever possible, document your value-added services and point out any benefits that the customer has received. In some cases, positive bragging is an effective value reinforcement technique.[27]

value reinforcement Reinforcing to the customer the value they are getting from their purchase.

Telephone Call The telephone provides a quick and efficient way to follow up a sale. A salesperson can easily make 10 or 12 phone calls in a single hour, and the cost will be minimal. If you plan to send a thank-you card or letter, follow it up with a thank-you call. The personal appeal of the phone call will increase the effectiveness of the written correspondence. The telephone call has one major advantage over written correspondence: It allows for a two-way exchange of information. Once an account is well established, you may be able to obtain repeat sales by telephone.

Email Message In many cases, it is a lot quicker to send an email message than to make a phone call. Salespeople report that they waste a lot of time playing "phone tag." Some customers prefer email messages and may become irritated if you do not adhere to their wishes. If you know that a customer is not in the habit of checking email all that often, use the telephone as a back-up method. When in doubt, use parallel channels of communication.

Follow-up calls allow for a two-way exchange of information. In many cases, once an account is well established, you may be able to obtain repeat sales by telephone.

Nathan Michaels/Superstock

Confirming Immediately with CRM

Close-up and personal information sharing creates a core on which successful relationships may be built and sustained. Friends have long supplemented their personal visits with notes, letters, emails, telephone calls, and, now, Facebook posts.

CRM technology offers new ways to save time in addition to enhancing and extending relationship-rich communications. Enlightened salespeople use Chatter, instant messaging, and email in addition to faxes and phone calls as fast, and thus effective, methods to give information to their customers. Email (texting and Twitter) can be particularly useful to quickly convey temporary messages such as those that confirm, affirm, or verify.

Letter or Card Written correspondence is an inexpensive and convenient form of customer follow-up. Letters and cards can be used to thank customers for their business and to promise continued service. Erin Sammy, a sales representative at Henley Honda in St. Catharines, Ontario, places a personalized thank-you card, along with his business card, in each vehicle he sells.[28] Some companies encourage their salespeople to use a formal letter typed on company stationery. Other companies have designed special thank-you cards, which are signed and sent routinely after a sale is closed. The salesperson may enclose a business card. These thank-you cards do have one major limitation: They are

Salesperson Erin Sammy of Henley Honda always places a personalized thank-you card in each vehicle he sells, along with his business card.

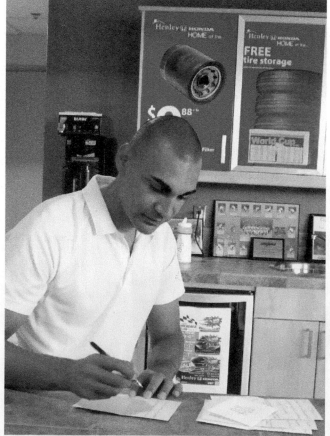

H.F. (Herb) MacKenzie

mass produced and therefore lack the personal touch of handwritten cards and envelopes. Personalized notes, birthday cards, and anniversary cards can make a positive impression.

Call Report The **call report** is a form that serves as a communications link with persons who can assist with customer service. The format varies, but generally it is a simple form with only four or five spaces. Salesforce's Chatter, mentioned earlier, is an excellent example of a call report. With Chatter, all stakeholders in a sale are copied with the latest information and action regarding the sale. A call report is an important solution to the problem of communication between the company personnel and the customer. It is a method of follow-through that triggers the desired action. It is simple, yet business-like.

call report A written summary that provides information on a sales call to people in the sales organization so that follow-up action can be taken as necessary.

Follow-up programs can be as creative or ingenious as you wish. Every sales organization competes on value, so you must continually think of new ways to add value. Creative use of your interpersonal communication skills can keep your messages fresh and personalized. Keep in mind that people buy both from the head and from the heart. Let customers know how much you care about their business.[29] You can use these five methods independently or in combination. Your main consideration should be some type of appropriate follow-up that (1) tells customers you appreciate their business, and (2) determines whether they are satisfied with the purchase.

Adding Value with Expansion Selling

Personal selling is the process of identifying and filling the customer's needs. As the salesperson learns more about the customer and establishes a relationship based on trust and mutual respect, opportunities for expansion selling will arise. Expansion selling can take three forms: full-line selling, cross-selling, and upselling.

Full-Line Selling Sometimes called *suggestion selling*, **full-line selling** is the process of recommending products or services that are related to the main item sold to the customer. The recommendation is made when, in the salesperson's judgment, the product or service can provide additional satisfaction. To illustrate, let's look at the sale of new houses. Many contractors offer customers who want to differentiate their home a variety of options, including marble in the entryway, granite countertops, gourmet kitchen appliances, or Jacuzzi-like tubs for the bathroom. Customization is an important value-added service for many customers.[30]

full-line selling The process of suggesting products or services that are related to the main item being sold to the customer.

Full-line selling is no less important when selling services. For example, a travel agent has many opportunities to suggest related products. Let us assume that a customer purchases a two-week vacation in Ireland. The agent can offer to book hotel reservations or schedule a guided tour. Another related product would be a rental car. Sometimes, a new product is simply not "right" without related merchandise. A new business suit may not look right without a new shirt and tie. An executive training program held at a fine hotel can be enhanced with a refreshment break featuring a variety of soft drinks, fresh coffee, and freshly baked pastries.

Customers will view full-line selling as a form of value-added service when it is presented correctly. There is a right way and a wrong way to make recommendations. Here are some guidelines to follow:

1. *Plan for full-line selling during the preapproach step.* Before meeting with the customer, develop a general plan that includes your objectives for this important dimension of selling. Full-line selling is easier when you are prepared.

2. *Make recommendations after you have satisfied the customer's primary need.* While there are some exceptions to this rule, it's usually best to meet the primary need first. In the case of a new home purchase, for example, the customer should first select the model home and then make decisions regarding the upgrades.

3. *Make your suggestions thoughtful and positive.* "We will deliver your new copy machine on Monday. Would you like us to deliver some quality copy paper?" Avoid questions such as, "Can we ship anything else?" This question invites a negative response.

4. *When appropriate, demonstrate the suggested item or use sales tools to build interest.* If you have suggested a shirt to go with a new suit, allow the customer to see it next to the suit. If you are calling on a business or commercial account, show the customer a sample or at least a picture if the actual product is not available.

Full-line selling is a means of providing value-added service. When you use it correctly, customers will thank you for your thoughtfulness and extra service. It is also a proven sales-building strategy.

Cross-Selling We have seen an increase in the use of cross-selling to grow sales volume. **Cross-selling** involves selling products that are not directly associated with products that you have sold to an established customer. A bank customer who has a home equity loan might be contacted and asked to consider the purchase of a mutual fund. The customer who has purchased a townhouse might be a candidate for a security service. One financial services company, Quick & Reilly, has trained its 600 customer service representatives to use cross-selling when customers call regarding their current investments. By completing the cross-selling training program, the representatives learned how to assess the caller's financial goals and develop a tailored proposal of products and services. Quick & Reilly achieved a 35 percent sales increase after developing the cross-selling program.[31]

> **cross-selling** Selling to an established customer products that are not directly related to products the customer has already bought.

A growing number of companies use cross-selling to discover additional sources of business within established accounts. Buyers generally welcome cross-selling efforts because they are searching for ways to consolidate purchases. They like the convenience of buying several items from the same source.[32] Cross-selling is most effective in those situations in which the salesperson and the customer enjoy a true partnership.

Salespeople who have a good understanding of the customer's needs and have earned the customer's respect will face less resistance when recommending a product or service. To achieve success with cross-selling, you need to use *survey questions* and *probing questions* (see Chapter 11). A general survey question such as "Can you tell me more about your expansion plans?" may uncover information needed to position your cross-selling sales strategy. However, you will likely need to use probing questions to uncover and clarify a buying problem that may open the door to a cross-selling opportunity. Keep in mind that cross-selling has to be a well-thought-out part of your strategy and process.[33]

> **upselling** The effort to sell better-quality products.

Upselling The effort to sell better-quality products is known as **upselling**. It is an important selling method that often adds customer value. Mike Weber, sales manager at Young Electric Sign Company, offers us two important tips on upselling. First, you need a well-established relationship with the customer—a relationship built on trust. Second, you need to continually qualify the prospect throughout the buying process. As you hear customers tell you more about their needs, you may see an opportunity to upsell. Weber says his salespeople usually engage in upselling at the design stage. The customer is shown a rough sketch of the desired sign and another rendition of something better. The added value of the more expensive option will become obvious to the customer.[34] In many selling situations, such factors as durability, comfort, or operating economy help justify the higher-priced product. A professional salesperson explains to the customer why it is in his or her best interest to spend "just a little more" and get the best value for their dollar. Most customers are more concerned with making the right purchase than they are with making the least expensive purchase.[35]

Preplan Your Service Strategy

Servicing the sale is a very important dimension of personal selling, so a certain amount of preplanning is essential. It helps to preplan your service strategy for each of the three areas we have discussed: follow-through, follow-up, and expansion selling. You cannot anticipate every aspect of the service, but you can preplan important ways to add value once the sale is implemented. Develop a servicing-the-sale worksheet, like the one shown in Figure 15.3, prior to each sales presentation.

Servicing-the-Sale Worksheet	
Method of Adding Value	**What You Will Say or Do**
Follow-Through	
Set up a secure website or Extranet so the client can track the production and delivery of custom-engineered seed research equipment.	Set up the secure website in a timely manner and then contact the customer when it is operational. Explain how to access the website and review the benefits of using this source of assistance.
Schedule training for persons who will be using the new technology.	Send the training schedule to the customer and confirm the dates with a follow-up call.
Follow-Up	
Send a thank-you letter to each member of the team who made the purchase decision.	Express sincere appreciation for the purchase and explain the steps you will take to ensure a long-term partnership.
Check to be certain that the training was effective.	Visit the customer's research facility and talk with the employees who completed the training. Answer questions and provide additional assistance as needed.
Expansion Selling	
Suggest the purchase of global positioning (GPS) technology to enhance use of seed research equipment.	"GPS technology will enable you to track all your research and plot the findings on your computer."

Figure 15.3 Servicing-the-Sale Worksheet
Follow-through on assurances and promises, customer follow-up, and expansion selling must be carefully planned. Use of this worksheet will help you preplan ways to add value.

Partnership-Building Strategies Should Encompass All Key People

Some salespeople do a great job of communicating with the prospect but ignore other key people involved in the sale. To illustrate how serious this problem can be, let us look at the approach used by Jill Bisignano, a sales representative for a major restaurant supply firm. Jill had called on Bellino's Italian Restaurant for several years. Although she was always very friendly to Nick Bellino, she treated the other employees with nearly total indifference. One day she called on Nick and was surprised to learn that he was retiring and had decided to sell his restaurant to two long-time employees. As you might expect, it did not take the new owners long to find another supplier. Jill lost a large account because she had failed to develop a good personal relationship with other key employees. It pays to be nice to everyone.

Here is a partial list of people in your company and in the prospect's company who can influence both initial and repeat sales:

1. *Receptionist.* Some salespeople simply do not use common sense when dealing with the receptionist. This person has daily contact with your customer and may schedule most or all calls. To repeatedly forget this individual's name or display indifference in other ways may cost you dearly.

2. *Technical personnel.* Some products must be cleaned, lubricated, or adjusted on a regular basis. Take time to get acquainted with the people who perform these duties. Answer their questions, share technical information with them if necessary, and show appreciation for the work they are doing.

3. *Stock clerks or receiving clerks.* People who work in the receiving room are often responsible for pricing incoming merchandise and making sure that these items are stored properly. They may also be responsible for stock rotation and processing damage claims.

4. *Management personnel.* Although you may be working closely with someone at the departmental or division level, do not forget the person who has the final authority and responsibility for this area. Spend time with management personnel occasionally and be alert to any concerns they may have.

This is not a complete list of the people you may need to depend on for support. There may be other key people who influence sales. Always look beyond the customer to see who else might influence the sale as partnerships can be built upon different levels of the organization.[36]

PARTNERING WITH AN UNHAPPY CUSTOMER

We have learned that unhappy customers generally do not initiate a verbal or written complaint. This means that postsale problems may not come to the attention of salespeople or other personnel within the organization. We also know that unhappy customers do share their negative experiences with other people. A dissatisfied customer will typically tell eight to ten people about their problem.[37] A double loss occurs when the customer stops buying your products and takes steps to discourage other people from buying them. When complaints surface, salespeople should view the problem as an opportunity to strengthen the business relationship. Conflict resolution is another aspect of problem solving important to the customer–salesperson relationship.[38] To achieve this goal, follow these suggestions:

1. *Give customers every opportunity to disclose their feelings.* Companies noted for outstanding customer service rely heavily on telephone systems, such as toll-free hotlines, to ensure easy access. At Federal Express, Cadillac Division of General Motors, and IBM—to name a few companies—specially trained advisers answer the calls and offer assistance. When a customer purchases a Ford vehicle, the salesperson introduces the customer to service staff who provide a key role in providing postsale service. The goal is to personalize the relationship with another member of the service team. Ford has discovered that after-sale contact builds a perception of value.[39] When customers do complain, by telephone or in person, encourage them to express all their anger and frustration. Do not interrupt. Do not become defensive. Do not make any judgments until you have heard all the facts as the customers see them. If they stop talking, try to get them to talk some more. How you deal with anger is very important. Encourage the angry customer to vent his or her feelings. By asking questions and listening carefully to the response, you can encourage the person to discuss the cause of the anger openly. After venting feelings and discussing specific details, the angry customer will expect a response. Briefly paraphrase what seems to be the major concern and express a sincere desire to find ways to solve the problem.[40]

2. *Keep in mind that it does not really matter whether a complaint is real or perceived.* If the customer is upset, you should be polite and sympathetic. Do not yield to the temptation to say, "You do not really have a problem." Remember, problems exist when customers perceive they exist.[41]

From the Field

Sometimes No Is the Best Response

Today, salespeople need to recognize when they have too many customers, the wrong customers, or customers who are too demanding. Too many customers drain precious sales resources and endanger a salesperson's ability to serve his or her most important accounts. Jeff Multz, director of sales and marketing at FirstWave Technologies, found he was serving too many customers. He relates an example that occurred when he owned his own consulting business. He realized that 80 percent of his customers were a drain on his business, so he called 3000 of them to explain that he could no longer serve them. Partly as a result, his sales increased by 50 percent the next year, but his profit increased by 50 percent in just five months.

David Sutcliffe, CEO of Richmond, B.C.–based Sierra Wireless, found he was serving the wrong customers—price-sensitive ones who were buying small quantities, but demanding special attention. He gave them a competitor's name and contact information. He says, "I know they're

thinking I'm out of my mind. But if your competitors are so busy choking on those small orders, you can focus on and win the more profitable opportunities."

Linda Collier, CEO of Mississauga-based Tri-Ad International Freight Forwarding, relates how she made a major investment in a new distribution centre to satisfy an important client. After the five-year contract was signed, the customer made demands for changes that cost considerable further investment. She agreed to the demands as she was also doing approximately $6 million dollars of freight business with the customer at the time. The deal was ultimately not profitable, but Linda hoped to renew the contract on more favourable terms. Unfortunately, the customer walked away from the relationship. Within two months, the customer even took its freight business away and gave it to a U.S. firm. The lesson: When a customer demands too much, don't be afraid to say no. Reflecting on her experience, she says, "This won't happen to us again."[d]

3. *Do not alibi.* Avoid the temptation to blame the shipping department, the installation crew, or anyone else associated with your company. Never tear down the company you work for. The problem has been placed in your hands, and you must accept responsibility for handling it. "Passing the buck" will only leave the customer with a feeling of helplessness.

4. *Politely share with the customer your point of view concerning the problem's cause.* At least explain what you think happened. The customer deserves an explanation. At this point, a sincere apology is usually appropriate.

5. *Decide what action must be taken to remedy the problem.* Take action quickly and offer a value-added atonement. Don't just do what is expected; delight customers by exceeding their expectations. Winning customer loyalty today means going beyond making it right.[42]

The value of customer complaints can emerge in two forms. First, complaints can be a source of important information that may be difficult to obtain by other means. Second, customer complaints provide unique opportunities for companies to *prove* their commitment to service. Loyalty builds in the customer's mind if you do a good job of solving his or her problem.[43]

A Word of Caution When you are dealing with major or minor customer service problems and an apology is necessary, do not use email. When a minor problem surfaces, call the customer personally. Do not delegate this task to someone else in your organization. If you need to apologize for a major problem that has occurred, meet with the customer in person. Schedule the meeting as soon as possible.[44]

REVIEWING KEY CONCEPTS

- Explain how to build long-term partnerships with customer service.

  Servicing the sale is a major dimension of the selling process, with the objectives of providing maximum customer satisfaction and establishing a long-term partnership. Servicing the sale encompasses a variety of activities that take place during and after the buying process. In this chapter, we present servicing the sale as a three-part process: follow-through on assurances and promises, follow-up with ongoing communication after the sale, and expansion selling.

- Describe current developments in customer service.

  In the new millennium, customer service has become a primary value-added function. Salespeople are in a unique position to enhance customer satisfaction and trust by displaying five important service behaviours: diligence, information communication, inducements, empathy, and sportsmanship.

- List and describe the major customer service methods that strengthen the partnership.

  A major key to an effective customer service strategy is follow through on assurances and promises that were part of the sales presentation. Follow-through services may involve making credit arrangements, scheduling deliveries, monitoring installation, training in the use or care of the product, providing product updates, and similar services. Salespeople can also add value with a sincere expression of appreciation. Follow-up methods include personal visits, telephone calls, email messages, letters, or call reports.

A salesperson depends on the support of many other people in servicing a sale. Maintaining good relationships with support staff members who help service your accounts is well worth the time and energy required.

- Explain how to add value with expansion selling.

As the salesperson learns more about the customer, opportunities for expansion selling will arise. Expansion selling can take three forms: full-line selling, cross-selling, and upselling.

- Explain how to deal effectively with complaints.

Dealing effectively with an unhappy customer should be thought of as an opportunity to strengthen the business relationship. Always give the customer every opportunity to disclose feelings. Encourage the angry customer to vent his or her feelings and listen closely to what is said. Briefly summarize what seems to be the major concern and express a sincere desire to find ways to solve the problem.

Key Terms

call report **369**
cross-selling **370**
customer service **357**

full-line selling (or suggestion selling) **369**
upselling **370**
value reinforcement **367**

Review Questions

1. You are currently a sales manager employed by a company that sells long-term care insurance. Tomorrow you will meet with five new sales trainees. Your major goal is to explain why it is important to service the sale. What important points will you cover?

2. Define *customer service*. List the three major activities associated with this phase of personal selling.

3. Explain how full-line selling fits into the definition of customer service. How does *full-line selling* differ from *cross-selling*?

4. List and describe three current developments in customer service.

5. Adding value with follow-through can involve several postsale services. List five possible services.

6. How does credit become part of servicing the sale?

7. This chapter describes the value of the lifetime customer. Is it realistic to believe that people will become lifetime customers in our very competitive marketplace?

8. Define *upselling* and explain how it can add value.

9. What types of customer service problems might be prevented with the use of a call report?

10. Describe the steps for partnering with an unhappy customer.

Application Exercises

1. You are a salesperson working in the paint department at a Canadian Tire store. A customer has just purchased 75 litres of house paint. Assume that your store carries everything in the painting line and list as many items as you can think of that could be used for expansion selling. Explain how your suggestions of these items could be a service to the customer.

2. You work as a wholesale salesperson for a plumbing supply company. One of your customers, a contractor,

has an open line of credit with your company for $10 000 worth of products. He is currently at his limit; however, he is not overdue. He just received word that he has been awarded a $40 000 plumbing contract at the local airport. The contract requires that he supply $9000 worth of plumbing products. Your customer does not have the cash to pay for the additional products. He informs you that unless you can provide him with some type of financing, he may lose the contract.

He says he can pay you when he finishes his next job in 60 days. Explain what you will do.

3. You have just interviewed for a job that you would really like to have. You have heard that it is a good idea to follow up an interview with a thank-you note or letter and an indication of your enthusiasm for the position. Select the strategy you will use for your follow-up and explain why you chose it.

4. Using your search engine, examine the Internet for information on customer satisfaction. Type in "customer satisfaction + selling." Are you surprised by the number of queries on this subject? Examine some of the queries related to what customers have said about specific company customer service programs. Be prepared to discuss some of what you find in class.

5. *Buyer's remorse* was explained in Chapter 14. It is a common response customers have after making an important purchase. You are a salesperson who has been very successful selling cars to young families. Knowing that buyer's remorse is a common response, how can you use this to help service a sale and build a partnership? Explain.

↻ ROLE-PLAY EXERCISE

Visit the role play/simulation materials provided in the Student Resources section of your companion website at **www.pearsoncanada.ca/manning**. A *Contents page lists appropriate page references for the activities.*

An important aspect of personal selling is the need to add value with follow-through and follow-up. Both of these account management activities can be time-consuming, especially if the salesperson is not skilled at setting up appointments that fit into a busy schedule. In this role play, you are to set up three follow-through meetings with a customer who has just purchased conference services from the convention centre you represent. First, you must contact your client three days from today to confirm the availability of the Revolving Platform Room (see *Partnership Selling*, p. 47) for the meeting of 300 people. Second, you must contact this same client a week from today to get approval on the number of chicken Wellington banquet-style dinners needed (see *Partnership Selling*, p. 15, and *Guarantees* on p. 25). And, third, because your client isn't sure about the need for a microphone (see *Partnership Selling*, pp. 21—22), you need to call your client the day before the meeting, which is scheduled four weeks from today, to verify whether you or your client will supply a microphone.

Equipped with a calendar, you should establish dates and times when your client will be available to talk or meet with you. Before you meet with your client, plan to recommend at least two times of the day that fit into your schedule for each of your meetings. If your client cannot meet at either of these times, ask your client to recommend a time. Do not start out by asking when your client is available because this could conflict with your busy schedule. Write the agreed-on times and dates in your calendar, suggesting your client do the same, so there will be no misunderstandings. Because these dates are deadlines, suggest that your client call you back if, for some reason, the schedule changes. Inform your client that you will plan to be at the hotel when the client's meeting starts and that you will be available to make sure everything is properly scheduled. Give your client your phone number and email address and ask him or her to contact you if there are any questions between now and the meeting date. Have another student role-play the customer and, after the role play, assess your customer service.

🎥 Reality Selling Video Case Problem

WFS Ltd., introduced in the opening vignette, is one of Canada's most respected industrial distributors. Many customers remain loyal to WFS because they value outstanding service; a broad range of industrial, automotive, and construction products; and a supplier that will work closely with them to solve their buying problems. The success of WFS can be traced to a number of factors:

- A *desire to build as many relationships and the strongest relationships possible with all customers.* WFS frequently moves employees to new positions within the company: A warehouse person may become an outside salesperson and later be transferred to inside sales; an outside salesperson may be transferred to purchasing or back to inside sales. (Rick Thurston, now president, began as a driver/delivery person at the Leamington branch in 1984.) This creates maximum flexibility within the company but, more importantly, means that inside salespeople know the difficulties that outside salespeople face, and they often have personal contacts within customer firms. It also means that outside salespeople have had the benefit of training and learning while in the warehouse and on the inside sales desk. As a result, customers frequently have strong relationships with and trust in several WFS employees who they know can help them.

- A *strong belief that work should be rewarding for all employees.* "Employee happiness is very important to us. Happy employees help build positive relationships with customers," says Rick Thurston. Employees share many experiences, from going to major sporting events to having company parties and picnics. Twice, for example, all of the employees shared an expense-paid trip to Las Vegas. The company also sponsors many community events and encourages volunteerism among its employees. There is an excellent employee benefits package, which includes education and recreation allowances. This employee investment has been rewarded many times over. At one point, the company had gone four years without a single absentee day. Employees even provide important input on management. In fact, a management committee, including the president, is elected each year.

- An *investment in customer service and a strong service culture.* The company has invested in computer equipment and programming and is able to tell customers immediately how much inventory it has and where that inventory is located. Purchasing, payables, invoicing, receivables, account profiles, sales and other financial reports, and vehicle maintenance schedules are all computerized. Employees are empowered to make decisions whenever customer service is an issue. On one occasion, two employees took a company van and left Windsor to get some material in Pittsburgh, Pennsylvania, for a customer who urgently needed it, and they returned immediately with the material. If a customer calls to order something that is urgently needed but the delivery truck has left for the day, the customer is never told to wait for the next delivery. Someone else within the company will see that the order gets delivered.

- A *willingness to experiment and grow to meet changing customer needs.* In 2008, WFS acquired Keep Industrial Supply, which provided three new locations, and its customer relationships and business solutions complemented those of WFS. With the addition of the South Carolina operation, the company now has 10 branches and numerous on-site customer integrated-supply agreements. Many WFS customers now check inventory, place orders, or check order status online. The company has also established commodity management programs with its best customers, whereby it manages all of the general supply items for these companies. WFS is always willing to add items to its inventory for customers who will buy them, and an increasing number of customers are taking advantage of this service.[45]

Questions

1. How might a WFS salesperson add value with full-line selling? Cross-selling?
2. What types of follow-through activities and follow-up calls should WFS salespeople be prepared to initiate? How can inside salespeople be used to help maintain value-added customer relationships?
3. How can commodity management programs and other special inventory management programs be used to add value for WFS? How can such programs contribute to the company's long-term success?
4. Assume that you have just received a phone call from an important customer who says, "We just received a shipment that is needed urgently, but there are some problems with it. We need you to take some action fast." What will you do? Be specific. How might you partner with this unhappy customer?

PARTNERSHIP SELLING: A ROLE PLAY/SIMULATION

Visit the role play/simulation materials provided in the Student Resources section of your companion website at **www.pearsoncanada.ca/manning**. *A contents page lists the appropriate page references for the activities.*

Developing a Sales Presentation Strategy—Servicing the Sale

Refer to *Sales Memorandum 3* and strategically plan to service the sale with your customer. After closing the sale—getting the customer's signature—there are several steps to take in order to add value and build customer confidence and satisfaction. These steps are important to providing total quality customer service and should provide for repeat sales and a list of referred customers.

Following the instructions in item 2g of your presentation plan, you need to schedule a future appointment to telephone or personally call and confirm the number of people attending the convention, as well as the final room and menu needs (see the convention centre policies). Also during this conversation you might suggest beverages for breaks, audiovisual needs, and any other items that will make this an outstanding convention for your customer.

You should have your calendar available to suggest and write down dates and times for this future contact. Any special materials, such as a calendar, can be placed in the back pocket of your portfolio. You may want to ask another person to be your customer and practise the customer service strategies you have prepared.

At this point, you should be strategically prepared to make the presentation to your customer as outlined in *Sales Memorandum 3*. Your instructor will provide you with further instructions.

PART V

ROLE-PLAY EXERCISE
Developing a Presentation Strategy

SCENARIO

This role play is a continuation of the Part IV role-play exercise. You recently met with Mohammed Ansari, founder and chief executive officer of Dynamic Security Inc. The purpose of the first sales call was to begin the relationship-building process and present selected value-added guest services and amenities offered by the Park Shores Resort and Convention Centre. You also obtained some information regarding the customer's buying process.

CUSTOMER PROFILE

Prior to starting Dynamic Security, Mohammed Ansari spent 12 years working in sales and sales management at General Electric Corporation (GE), described by *Fortune* magazine as America's most admired company. Working for GE was a great learning experience for Mohammed, who is trying to apply the GE success formula to Dynamic Security. He is the classic extrovert, a person who combines high sociability and high dominance.

SALESPERSON PROFILE

You are new to the field of selling, but you are a quick learner. The first visit with Mohammed Ansari went well, and now you are preparing for the second sales call. Mohammed is planning a large banquet to recognize his employees but has not yet selected a location for this event. While working for GE, Mohammed attended more than 25 business conferences and was disappointed by many of them. Too often, they were held at look-alike hotels that served bland food typically served by poorly trained waiters who displayed little enthusiasm. You took notes throughout the meeting and will address these concerns during the second sales call.

PRODUCT

The Park Shores Resort is a full-service hotel and convention centre. After completion of a recent $4.8 million renovation, the Park Shores Resort received the

Excellence in Renovation Design Award from the Ontario Architectural Association.

INSTRUCTIONS

The first sales call was basically an informative presentation. Near the end of the visit, Mohammed Ansari did disclose his plans for a large recognition banquet to be held on October 25, the company's second anniversary. No other information was provided, but Mohammed agreed to a second meeting to be held the following week.

Based on the information collected during the first call, you are now planning a persuasive presentation that will involve the first three steps of the six-step presentation plan (see Fig. 15.1). At the office of Mohammed Ansari—to be role-played by another student—you will need to re-establish the relationship and then initiate the agenda approach (see Chapter 10). Begin the presentation with appropriate survey, probing, and confirmation questions. These questions should be preplanned using information found in Chapter 11.

As the need discovery phase of the presentation progresses, the customer's buying criteria or buying conditions should surface. Prior to the second sales call, you should also select and be prepared to demonstrate appropriate selling tools (proof devices). A variety of selling tools suitable for reproduction can be found in "Partnership Selling: A Role Play/Simulation" online in the Student Resource section at **www.pearsoncanada.ca/manning**. Ensure that you preplan feature/benefit selling statements that appeal to Mohammed Ansari's needs. The importance of selling specific benefits and obtaining customer reactions cannot be overemphasized (see Chapter 11).

A major objective of the second sales call is to move the sale forward by convincing Mohammed Ansari that the Park Shores Resort offers an outstanding combination of value-added guest services and amenities and is prepared to meet his needs. The sale will not be closed during the second call, but you will try to obtain a commitment to prepare a formal sales proposal to be presented to Mohammed Ansari within 48 hours. (See *Partnership Selling*, p. 45, on your companion website for a sample sales proposal form.)

Chapter 16
Opportunity Management: The Key to Greater Sales Productivity

Learning Objectives

After studying this chapter, you should be able to

1 Discuss the four dimensions of opportunity management.

2 List and describe time management strategies.

3 Explain factors that contribute to improved territory management.

4 Identify and discuss common elements of a records management system.

5 Discuss stress management practices.

Introduction

Many of the best salespeople we know had no intention of pursuing a career in sales, but had experiences early in their lives that helped them develop personality traits and abilities that have certainly contributed to their success. During her school years, Paula Shannon acted in plays, practised public speaking, and participated in a number of competitive sports, most notably gymnastics. She spent a year studying in Belgium, where she learned to adapt to another culture and social setting and learned a third language. Paula now speaks six languages.

Paula credits managing a large paper route at a young age with helping to teach her about responsibility. Later, she worked as a waitress, did some interpretation on a tour bus, sold clothing and other retail items, and spent a summer in customer service for a large commercial waste management firm. In Europe, Paula worked as a management trainee for Berlitz International. This program helped give her a solid grounding in general business: operations, finance, accounting, human resources, and sales. Following her management training, Paula Shannon began to handle sales for several Berlitz language

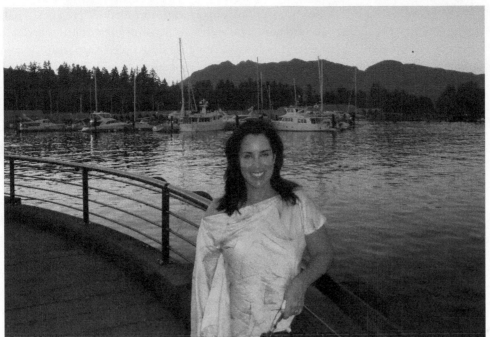

Most people who achieve success in selling, such as Paula Shannon of Lionbridge Technologies, have a strong work ethic. They are "self-starters" who are committed to managing opportunities that will help them achieve their personal and professional goals.

centres. Paula says her belief and confidence in the product she was selling was evident. She credits her boss at the time, Anita Komlos, whom she describes as "one of the most natural and effective salespeople I have ever known," with helping her learn how to probe effectively and how to know when to "shut up."

Paula Shannon has managed to learn something of value from everything she has done. She is clearly focused on managing herself and her career. Today, Paula Shannon is senior vice president and chief sales officer for Boston-based Lionbridge Technologies, Inc. She manages its global sales force of 70 from her home office in Montreal.[1]

OPPORTUNITY MANAGEMENT— A FOUR-DIMENSIONAL PROCESS

WHAT MAKES A SALESPERSON SUCCESSFUL? SOME PEOPLE BELIEVE THE MOST IMPORTANT factor is hard work. This is only partly true. Some people work hard but do not accomplish much. They lack purpose and direction. This lack of organization results in wasted time and energy. Hard work must be preceded by careful planning. Every moment spent planning, according to some experts in self-management, saves three or four moments in execution.[2]

Wasting time and energy is the slippery slope to failure in the age of information. Many salespeople are drowning in information, and the flood of messages each day leaves little time to think and reflect. Sales and sales support personnel, like most other knowledge workers, are working under tighter deadlines. The response time to customer inquiries has been shortened, and customers are less tolerant of delays. Thus, prioritizing different sales force decisions becomes important to managing productivity.[3]

opportunity management A four-dimensional process consisting of time, territory, records, and stress management.

As pressures build, it's easy to overlook opportunities to identify prospects, make sales, and improve service to customers. The ability to perceive opportunities and seize them is an important characteristic of high-achieving salespeople.[4] **Opportunity management** should be viewed as a four-dimensional process consisting of the following components:

1. *Time management.* There are only about 250 business days per year. Within each day, there is only so much time to devote to selling. Selling hours are extremely valuable. When salespeople are asked to evaluate the major challenges they face in their work, "Not enough time" is often rated number one. Dealing with information overload and achieving balance in life are also major challenges.

2. *Territory management.* A **sales territory** is a group of customers and prospective customers assigned to a single salesperson. Every territory is unique. Some territories consist of one or two cities or counties, while others encompass several provinces, all of Canada, or several countries. The number of accounts within each territory also varies. Today, territory management is becoming less of an art and more of a science.

sales territory A group of customers and prospective customers assigned to a single salesperson.

3. *Records management.* Every salesperson must maintain a certain number of records. These records help to "systematize" data collection and storage. A wise salesperson never relies on memory. Some of the most common records include planning calendars, prospect forms, call reports, summary reports, and expense reports.

4. *Stress management.* A certain amount of stress comes with any selling position. Some salespeople have learned how to take stressful situations in stride. Others allow stress to trigger anger and frustration. Learning to cope with various stressors that surface in the daily life of a salesperson is an important part of the self-management process.

TIME MANAGEMENT

A salesperson can increase sales volume in two major ways. One is by improving selling effectiveness, and the other is by spending more time in face-to-face selling situations. The latter objective can best be achieved through improved time and territory management.

Improving the management of both time and territory is a high priority in the field of selling. These two closely related functions represent major challenges for salespeople.

Let us first look closely at time management. There is definitely a close relationship between sales volume and number of customer contacts made by the salesperson. You have to make calls to get results.

Time-Consuming Activities

Some salespeople who have kept careful records of how they spend their time each day are surprised to learn how little they spend in face-to-face selling situations. A national survey of 1500 salespeople from 13 industries found that on average, salespeople spend 60 percent of their time on administrative duties or travel.[5] Administrative duties can include such things as completion of sales records and time spent on customer follow-through and follow-up. Salespeople need to examine carefully each

Managing His Time to Manage His Personal Self-Development

Alex Pettes believes in the power of personal goals and self-development. As a 35-year-old vice president of sales and marketing, he set a personal goal to become company president by age 40. Four months before his fortieth birthday, he achieved his goal. Many who know Alex were not surprised. Alex has his own personal mission statement that he repeats to himself three times each day. He is a strong believer in and continually practises self-development: physically, spiritually, socially, and academically. He believes that education does not end with a degree, and he has two of them.

Early in his career, Alex decided he didn't have a lifetime to get a lifetime of experience, but he found a solution: read books by people who have spent their time and effort to present their experiences and philosophies to others. Alex says, "By reading books, you bypass all the tons of earth that was required to be mined to get at the ounce of gold, the few nuggets of wisdom that it took others years to learn."

Alex's advice: Get out of bed twenty minutes earlier than usual and spend that time reading books related to your job, your industry, or your personal self-development. Early in the morning, your mind is fresh, and you will find that the routine quickly becomes an important part of your life. People who do this will, over a year, read 15 to 20 books. Chances are good that your peers and competitors are not doing this, so you will quickly out-distance them with knowledge and new ideas.

Alex says, "I consider myself Alex Pettes Inc., a personal services corporation dedicated to maximizing the income and potential of Alex Pettes. I am committed to investing in my own business (myself and my personal development) regardless of whether my employer or someone else is doing it." After all, he adds, "Who cares more about you than you?"[a]

Alex Pettes, president of TFI Food Equipment Solutions, has his own personal mission statement that he repeats to himself three times each day. He is a strong believer in and continually practises self-development: physically, spiritually, socially, and academically.

Courtesy of Alex Pettes

of these activities and determine whether too much or too little time is spent in any area. One way to assess time use is to keep a time log. This involves recording, at the end of every hour, the activities in which you were engaged during that time.[6] At the end of the week, add up the number of minutes spent on the various activities and ask yourself, "Is this the best use of my time?" Once you have tabulated the results of your time log, it should be easy to identify the "time wasters." Pick one or two of the most wasteful areas, and then make plans to correct the problem. Set realistic goals that can be achieved. Keep in mind that wasting time is usually a habit. To manage your time more effectively, you need to form new habits. Changing habits is hard work, but it can be done.[7]

Time Management Methods

Sound time-management methods can pave the way to greater sales productivity. The starting point is forming a new attitude toward time conservation. You must view time as a scarce resource not to be wasted.[8] The time-saving strategies presented here are not new, nor are they unique. Time-conscious people in all walks of life are using them.

Develop a Series of Personal Goals According to Alan Lakein, author of *How to Get Control of Your Time and Your Life*, the most important aspect of time management is knowing what your goals are. He is referring to all goals—career goals, family goals, and life goals. People who cannot or do not sit down and write out exactly what they want from life lack direction. Brian Tracy, who developed the "Law of Direction" says, "Your ability to set clear, specific goals will do more to guarantee you higher levels of success and achievement than any other single skill or quality."[9]

The goal-setting process requires that you be clear about what you want to accomplish. If your goal is too general or vague, progress toward achieving that goal is difficult to observe. Goals such as "I want to be a success" or "I desire good health" are much too general. The major principles that encompass goal setting are outlined in Table 16.1.

Goals have a great deal of psychological value to people in selling. Sales goals, for example, can serve as a strong motivational force. To illustrate, let us assume that Maria Paulson, sales representative for a cosmetic manufacturer, decides to increase her sales by 15 percent over the previous year. She now has a clear goal to aim for and can begin identifying specific steps to achieve the new goal.

Maria Paulson has established a long-term goal as part of a yearly plan. Some goals require considerable time and should be part of a one-year plan. Next, Maria should set aside an hour or so at the end of each month to decide what she wants to accomplish during the coming month. Weekly planning is also important. Once a week—Friday is

---

Table 16.1 Goal-Setting Principles

The following goal-setting principles give you the power to take control of the present and the future.

1. *Reflect on the things you want to change in your life.* Then prepare written goals that are specific, measurable, and realistic.

2. *Develop a written goal-setting plan that includes the steps necessary to achieve the goal.* Review your plan daily—repetition increases the probability of success.

3. *Modify your environment by changing the stimuli around you.* This may involve finding a mentor or spending less time with persons who are negative.

4. *Monitor your behaviour, and reward your progress.* Reinforcement from yourself and/or others is necessary for change.

Source: Barry L. Reece and Rhonda Brandt, *Effective Human Relations: Personal and Organizational Applications*, Boston: Houghton Mifflin Company, 2005. Reprinted by permission of the publisher.

Gerald L. Manning

a good time—set goals for the next week and develop a plan for reaching them. Finally, Maria should develop a daily plan.[10]

Prepare a Daily To-Do List Sales professionals who complete the time management course offered by FranklinCovey are encouraged to engage in event control. This involves planning and prioritizing events every day.[11] Start each day by thinking about what you want to accomplish. Then write down the activities (Fig. 16.1). Putting your thoughts on paper (or in your computer) forces you to clarify your thinking. Investment firm regional director Heather Gardner records her daily planned activities in her BlackBerry and Microsoft Outlook calendar. On a typical day, the BlackBerry will show entries for every half hour. Gardner works through her detailed to-do list by adhering to one unshakable rule: Avoid nonpaying activities during working hours.[12]

Now you should prioritize your "to-do" list; do not let outside distractions interfere with your plan. Begin each day with the highest-priority task.

Date _____

DAILY TO DO LIST

Priority	Items to do
3 ←	— Call Halifax Motors to check on installation of copy machine.
2 ←	— Call Price Optical to make an appointment for product demonstration.
4 ←	— Attend Chamber of Commerce at 3:00 PM
1 ←	— Call Simmons Furniture and deal with customer complaint.

Notes for tomorrow:

Figure 16.1 Daily To-Do List
A daily list of activities can help us set priorities and save time. Today, this list is often recorded electronically in most CRM systems. The list is one of the first things salespeople see when they access the software each day.

Maintain a Planning Calendar Ideally, a salesperson needs a single place to record daily personal and business appointments, deadlines, and tasks. Unfortunately, many salespeople write daily tasks and appointments on any slip of paper they can find: backs of envelopes, business cards, napkins, or Post-it notes. Hyrum W. Smith, author of *The 10 Natural Laws of Successful Time and Life Management,* calls these pieces of paper "floaters." They just float around until you either follow through on them or lose them. It's a terribly disorganized method for someone who wants to gain greater control of his or her life.[13] The use of floaters often leads to the loss of critical information, missed appointments, and lack of focus. Select a planning calendar design (the FranklinCovey Day Planner is one option) that can bring efficiency to your daily planning efforts. You should be able to determine at a glance what is coming up in the days and weeks ahead (Fig. 16.2).

personal digital assistant A small, personal device that stores information and provides many of the features common to laptop computers.

Many salespeople use a **personal digital assistant** (PDA) to organize information. Small, pocket-size PDAs, such as those available from Apple or BlackBerry, offer many of the features common to laptop computers. The salesperson can send and receive emails or text messages and download important customer information. Salespeople can also input their customer notes immediately after a sales call. The PDA also serves as an electronic memo pad, calendar, expense log, address book, and more. These organizers can be used to keep track of appointments and serve as a perpetual calendar.

Organize Your Selling Tools You can save valuable time by finding ways to organize sales literature, business cards, order blanks, samples, and other items needed during a sales call. You may waste time on a callback because some item was not available during your first call. You may even lose a sale because you forgot or misplaced a key selling tool.

If you have a great deal of paperwork, invest in one or more file cabinets. Some salespeople purchase small, lightweight cardboard file boxes to keep their materials organized. These boxes can easily be placed in your car trunk and moved from one sales call to another. The orderly arrangement of selling tools is just one more method of time conservation.

The key to regular use of the four time-saving techniques already described is *commitment.* Unless you are convinced that efficient time management is important, you will probably find it difficult to adopt these new habits. A salesperson who fully accepts the "time is money" philosophy will use these techniques routinely.

Saving Time with Meetings in Cyberspace and Other Methods of Communication

As the cost of travel increases, more and more salespeople are asking the question, "Is this trip necessary?" Instead of travelling to a customer's office, some salespeople schedule a telephone conference call. A modern alternative to this type of conference call is a meeting in cyberspace. The voice of each meeting participant travels over an audio connection and attendees view visuals—e.g., PowerPoint presentations—on their desktop computers. Nerac Inc., an information-services company, often schedules Web conferences for potential customers. The sales representative can bring online a Nerac researcher who presents an introduction to the company's closely guarded databases. Clients get to watch the researcher at work over the Internet.[14]

June 201_

SUNDAY	MONDAY	TUESDAY	WEDNESDAY	THURSDAY	FRIDAY	SATURDAY
	1	**2** 10:30 Wheat First Securities; 12:00 Lunch with Ray Williams; 3:00 Farrell's Service Centre	**3** 9:00 Demonstration at Ryerson University; 11:00 Demo at Mills Inc.; 3:30 Meet with Helen Sisson	**4** 9:00 Austin & Son Storage; 10:30 Demo at CMP Sporting Goods; 1:00 Attend Computer Trade Show	**5** 9:00 Sales Meeting at Holiday Inn; 1:30 Demo at Omega Homes	**6** 10:00 Take Dana to soccer game
7	**8** 8:00 to 12:00 Sales Training; 1:30 Meet with M.I.S. staff at Mohawk College	**9** 9:30 Park Realty; 11:00 White Tire Service; 2:00 Demo at Ritter Seafood	**10** 9:00 Demonstration at Ross accounting services; 11:00 Prospecting; 2:30 Meet with technical support staff	**11** 8:30 Meet with Helen Hart; 12:00 Lunch with Tim; 1:00 Demo at Collins Wholesale; 4:00 Parent-Teacher conference	**12** 9:00 Demo at Seneca College; 1:00 to 5:00 Update sales records	**13** 9:00 10-K run (starts at YMCA building)
14	**15**	**16**	**17**	**18**	**19**	**20**

MAY 201_

S	M	T	W	T	F	S
31					1	2
3	4	5	6	7	8	9
10	11	12	13	14	15	16
17	18	19	20	21	22	23
24	25	26	27	28	29	30

JULY 201_

S	M	T	W	T	F	S
				1	2	3	4
5	6	7	8	9	10	11
12	13	14	15	16	17	18
19	20	21	22	23	24	25
26	27	28	29	30	31	

NOTES

Figure 16.2 Monthly Planning Calendar Sample
Shown are 11 days of a monthly planning calendar for a computer service sales representative. Monthly planning calendars such as this one are now a key function of most CRM systems.

Some customers actually prefer telephone contact for certain types of business trans-actions. Here are some situations in which the phone call is appropriate.

- Call the customer in advance to make an appointment. You will save time, and the customer will know when to expect you.
- Use the telephone to keep the customer informed. A phone call provides instant communication with customers at a low cost.
- Build customer goodwill with a follow-up phone call. Make it a practice to call customers to thank them for buying your product and to determine whether the customer is satisfied with the purchase.

Some customers prefer to be contacted by email, and it would be a mistake to ignore their preference. Busy people often discourage telephone calls to minimize interruptions.

Voice-mail telephone systems are used by companies of all sizes. These systems not only answer the phone and take messages but also provide information-retrieval systems that are accessible by telephone. This technology is especially useful for salespeople who

With the aid of fax machines and computer scanning equipment, salespeople can send and receive documents in seconds. Hard-copy documents are often needed to move the sales process to a successful outcome.

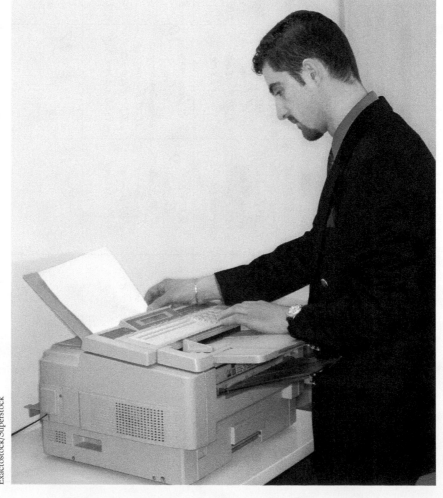

Exactostock/Superstock

need to exchange information with others. For many salespeople, the cell phone has become a convenient and time-saving sales tool that can be used to facilitate communication with customers and the main office.

Fax machines and computer scanning equipment take telecommunication a step further. With this equipment, salespeople can send and receive documents in seconds, using standard cable or telephone lines. Detailed designs, charts, and graphs can be transmitted across the country or around the world.

TERRITORY MANAGEMENT

MANY MARKETING ORGANIZATIONS HAVE FOUND IT HELPFUL TO BREAK DOWN THE TOTAL market into manageable units called sales territories. As noted earlier in this chapter, a *sales territory* is the geographic area where prospects and customers reside. While some firms have developed territories solely on the basis of geographic considerations, a fairly common approach is to sub-divide a geographic territory on the basis of customer or product considerations. For example, publisher Pearson Canada used to have several salespeople call on a single customer: one specialized on Business and Economics; one on Science, Engineering, and Mathematics; and one on Social Sciences and Humanities. In 2014, the sales force was reorganized so that each salesperson managed a smaller number of customers, but sold the entire catalogue of textbooks to them.[15] Some marketers assign sales representatives to key industries. For example, a firm might have one salesperson focus on educational institutions, another on financial institutions, and a third on small business accounts. Regardless of how the sales territory is established, it is essentially a specific number of present and potential accounts that can be called on conveniently and economically. Although uncontrollable by the salesperson, it is acknowledged by managers and researchers as an important factor in enabling salespeople to perform well.[16]

What Does Territory Management Involve?

To appreciate fully the many facets of territory management, it will be helpful to examine a typical selling situation. Put yourself in the shoes of a salesperson who has just accepted a position with a firm that manufactures a line of high-quality tools. You are responsible for a territory that covers Manitoba and Saskatchewan, which includes 88 auto supply firms that carry your line of tools. It also includes 38 stores that do not carry your tools. On the basis of this limited information, how would you carry out your selling duties? To answer this question, it will be necessary to follow these steps:

Step 1: Classify All Customers. Salespeople often divide their territory by area code, by industry, by product, or by projected sales volume. Always divide your territory in a way that makes sense.[17] If you classify customers according to potential sales volume, then you must answer two questions: What is the dollar amount of the firm's current purchases? What amount of additional sales might be developed with greater selling effort? Store A may be purchasing $3000 worth of tools each year, but potential sales for this firm amount to $5000. Store B currently purchases $2000 worth of tools a year, and potential sales amount to $2500. In this example, store A clearly deserves more time than store B.

It is important to realize that a small number of accounts may provide a majority of the sales volume.[18] Many companies get 75 to 80 percent of their sales volume from 20 to 25 percent of their total number of customers. The problem lies in accurately identifying which accounts and prospects fall into the top 20 to 25 percent category. Once this information is available, you can develop customer classification data that can be used to establish the frequency of calls and the level of resources to be allocated to these customers.[19] Jennifer Kline, a pharmaceutical salesperson employed by Schering-Plough's animal care division, gives a high priority to loyal customers. Kline says, "The people who are writing for you will continue to write for you if you serve them well."[20]

The typical sales territory is constantly changing, so the realignment of territories from time to time is necessary. One division of AT&T uses MapInfo ProAlign software to realign its sales territories. Accounts are segmented based on industry, size, dollar volume, and complexity. The sales manager enters a variety of account information and then produces maps that show accounts in different configurations.[21]

Step 2: Develop a Routing and Scheduling Plan. Many salespeople have found that travel is one of their most time-consuming nonselling activities. A great deal of time can also be wasted just waiting to see a customer. The primary objective of a sales routing and scheduling plan is to increase actual selling by reducing time spent travelling between accounts and waiting to see customers.

If a salesperson called on only established accounts and spent the same amount of time with each customer, routing and scheduling would not be difficult. In most cases, however, you need to consider other variables. For example, you may be expected to develop new accounts on a regular basis. In this case, you must adjust your schedule to accommodate calls on prospects. Another variable involves customer service. Some

Selling in Action

Balancing Career and Family

Women today know that they will probably be working for pay for part or all of their adult lives. Most will also perform multiple roles that can be stressful and tiring. Many women who work full-time in sales also assume the responsibilities of wife and mother. Ellyn Foltz, vice president of sales and marketing for Dataline Incorporated, maintains a fully equipped personal computer (PC) and Internet hookup at her home. She gets up early and usually spends about 90 minutes on her work while family members are eating breakfast. In the evening, she logs on and completes two or three hours of work after her son is in bed. Foltz has structured her life so that she does not have to make "impossible choices" between work and family. She turned down a high-profile job that would have required constant travel.

Jill Doran, director of national accounts for National Car Rental, says that her employer gives her the tools and support she needs to maintain balance in her life. She took maternity leave for each of her children and now has the freedom to work from her home part of each week. When she is at home, Doran checks her voice mail and email frequently to be sure she is responsive to each of her national accounts. She records everything in her daytimer to avoid work–family conflicts.

As women struggle to balance career and family choices, many employers are doing more to help. Women, as well as men, who work in sales, often have the option of spending part of every week working from home.[b]

salespeople devote considerable time to adjusting warranty claims, solving customer problems, and paying goodwill visits.

There are no precise rules to observe in establishing a sales routing and scheduling plan, but the following guiding principles apply to nearly all selling situations:

1. Obtain or create a map of your territory and mark the location of present accounts with pins or a marking pen. Each account might be colour-coded according to sales potential. This will give you a picture of the entire territory. Many companies are using mapping software to create a territory picture that can be viewed on the computer screen. With the aid of TerrAlign (www.terralign.com) mapping software, salespeople can align sales territories by account size or geography, analyze sales information, generate maps and reports, and produce territory recommendations.[22]

2. If your territory is geographically quite large, consider dividing it into smaller areas. Postal codes provide one option. You can then plan work in terms of several trading areas that make up the entire territory.

3. Develop a routing plan for a specific period of time. This might be a one- or two-week period. Once the plan is firm, notify customers of your anticipated arrival time by phone, letter, or email.

4. Develop a schedule that accommodates your customers' needs. Some customers appreciate getting calls on a certain day of the week or at a certain hour of the day. Try to schedule your calls in accordance with their wishes.

5. Think ahead and establish one or more tentative calls in case you have some extra time. If your sales calls take less time than expected or if there is an unexpected cancellation, you need optional calls to fill the void.

6. Decide how frequently to call on the basis of sales potential. Give the greatest attention to the most profitable customers. Many salespeople use the 80/20 rule. They spend 80 percent of their time calling on the most productive customers and 20 percent calling on smaller accounts and prospects.[23]

Sales Call Plans

You can use information from the routing and scheduling plan to develop a **sales call plan.** This proposal is a weekly action plan, usually initiated by the sales manager. Its primary purpose is to ensure efficient and effective account coverage.

The form most sales managers use is similar to the one shown in Figure 16.3. One section of the form is used to record planned calls. A parallel section is for completed calls. Additional space is provided for the names of firms called on.

The sales manager usually presents the sales call plan to individual members of the sales staff. The plan's success depends on how realistic the goals are in the eyes of the sales staff, how persuasive the sales manager is, and what type of training accompanies the plan's introduction. It is not unusual for members of the sales force to respond with comments such as, "My territory is different," "Do not put me in a procedural straitjacket," or "My territory cannot be organized." The sales manager must not only present the plan in a convincing manner but also provide training that helps each salesperson implement the plan successfully.

sales call plan A plan developed with information taken from the routing and scheduling plan. The primary purpose of the plan is to ensure efficient and effective account coverage.

Sales Call Plan

Salesperson _____   For week ending _____

Territory _____   Days worked _____

_____

| **Planned Calls** | **Total Completed Calls** |

Number of planned calls _____   Number of calls only _____

Number of planned
presentations_____   Number of presentations _____

Number of planned
telephone calls_____   Number of telephone calls _____

Account Category Planning   Number of orders _____

A. Account calls _____   Total km travelled _____

B. Account calls _____   A. Account calls _____

C. Account calls _____   B. Account calls _____

C. Account calls _____

Companies called on	Address	Date	Customer rating	Comments about call

Figure 16.3 Sales Call Plan
The sales call plan is part of most CRM systems and is sent electronically.

RECORDS MANAGEMENT

ALTHOUGH SOME SALESPEOPLE COMPLAIN THAT PAPERWORK IS TOO TIME-CONSUMING AND reduces the amount of time available for actual selling, others recognize that accurate, up-to-date records actually save time. Their work is better organized and quick accessibility of information often makes it possible to close more sales and improve customer service.[24]

A good record-keeping system gives salespeople useful information with which to check their own progress. For instance, an examination of the sales call plan at the end of the day provides a review of who was called on and what was accomplished. The company also benefits from complete and accurate records. Reports from the field help management make important decisions. A company with a large sales force operating throughout a wide geographic area relies heavily on information sent to the main office.

Common Records Kept by Salespeople

A good policy is never to require a record that is not absolutely necessary. The only records worth keeping are those that provide positive benefits to the customer, the salesperson, or the personnel who work in sales-supporting areas of the company. Each record should be brief, easy to complete, and free of requests for useless detail. Where possible, the format should provide for the use of check marks as a substitute for written responses. Completing sales record forms should not be a major burden.

What records should you keep? The answer to this question will vary depending on the type of selling position. Some of the records most commonly kept by salespeople are described in this section.

Customer and Prospect Files Most salespeople find it helpful to keep records of customers and prospects. Each of these files has space for name, address, telephone and fax numbers, and email address. Other information recorded might be the buyer's personal characteristics, the names of people who might influence the purchase, or appropriate times to make calls. Most salespeople have replaced their card files with computerized record systems.

Call Reports The call report (also called an *activity report*) is a variation of the sales call plan described earlier in this chapter. It is used to record information about the people on whom you have called and what took place. The call report is one of the most basic records used in the field of selling. It provides a summary of what happened during the call and an indication of what future action is required. The call reports (daily and weekly) featured in Figure 16.4 are typical of those used in the field.

We are seeing less emphasis on call reports that require only numbers (e.g., calls made each day, number of proposals written). Companies that emphasize consultative selling are requesting more personal information on the customer (information that expands the customer profile) and more information on the customer's short- and long-range buying plans.

Expense Records Both your company and the government agencies that monitor business expenses will require a record of selling expenses. These usually include such items as meals, lodging, travel, and, in some cases, entertainment expenses. Several expense-reporting software packages are now available to streamline the expense-reporting process. Automated expense reports save the salesperson a great deal of time and allow expenses to be reimbursed while the salesperson is still on the road.

Sales Records The records used to report sales vary greatly in design. Some companies require daily reports, others weekly ones. As you would expect, one primary use of the sales report is to analyze salespeople's performance.

You can take certain steps to improve a reporting system. Charley Cohon, president of Prime Devices, wanted his salespeople to turn in sales call reports each Monday. However, sales representatives often delayed writing these reports until well after the calls were made. His salespeople were anxious to call on prospects but not eager to write reports. To

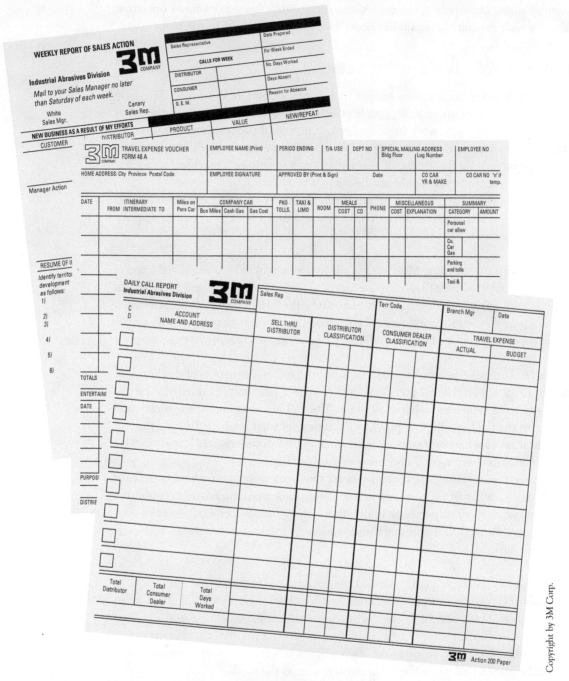

Figure 16.4 Call Report, Expense Voucher, and Weekly Sales Report
These are three of the records most commonly kept by 3M salespeople. Many salespeople process these forms electronically.

improve his reporting system, Cohon offered his salespeople a dedicated phone number just to receive and retrieve voice mail. Sales reps could call in their reports, which would be transcribed by a clerk in the office.[25]

Some records should be completed right away, while you can easily recall the information. Accuracy is always important. It can be embarrassing to have an order sent to

Salespeople often use CRM systems to record handwritten notes taken during meetings with the customer.

PhotoAlto/Superstock

the wrong address simply because you transposed a figure. Take time to proofread forms and use a spell checker.

You should re-examine your territory management plan continually. Update it often so it reflects the current status of your various accounts. When possible, use a laptop computer or PDA and appropriate software to improve your records management system. Computers can help you achieve increased selling time and enhance customer service.

Maintaining Perspective

Personal selling is often characterized by emotional highs and lows. It's easy to lose perspective and drift into an emotional low during what seems like a sales slump. Carefully prepared records can serve as a reality check. For example, you may be upset by low first-quarter sales. A check of your records, however, could indicate that first-quarter sales were low during the previous year.[26]

STRESS MANAGEMENT

PERSONAL SELLING PRODUCES A CERTAIN AMOUNT OF STRESS, IN PART FROM THE NON-routine nature of sales work. Each day brings a variety of new experiences, some of which may cause stress. Prospecting, for example, can be threatening to some salespeople. Long hours on the job, the loss of leisure time, and too little time for family members can also be stressful and cause burnout if not coped with properly.[27] While "variety is the spice of life," there is a limit to how much diversity one can cope with. One of the keys to success in selling is learning how to bring order to the many facets of the job. We also must be physically and mentally prepared to handle work-related stress.

Stress refers to two simultaneous events: an external stimulus called a stressor, and the physical and emotional responses to that stimulus (anxiety, fear, muscle tension, surging heart rate, and so on). Negative, threatening, or worrisome situations accumulated over time can cause depression and burnout and make you sick.[28] In personal selling, too much negative stress hurts relationships and productivity. Some stress is beneficial because it helps keep us motivated, but too much stress can be unhealthy if left unchecked.

Stress might be caused by trying to figure out ways to meet a sales quota or schedule travel throughout a sales territory. Missed appointments, presentations before large groups, and lack of feedback concerning your performance also can create stress. Ironically, some of the time-saving tools used by salespeople (e.g., cell phones and email) make it difficult for them to escape the pressures of their job. Many salespeople feel they are "on call" 24 hours a day.

As noted in Chapter 1, information surplus has replaced information scarcity as an important new problem in the age of information. Increasingly, knowledge workers report tension with colleagues, loss of job satisfaction, and strained personal relationships as a result of information overload. Too much information also crowds out quiet moments needed for reflection and to restore balance in our lives.[29] It is not possible to eliminate stress from your life, but you can adopt stress management strategies that can help you cope with it. Four stress management strategies are discussed next.

Develop a Stress-Free Home Office

Many salespeople maintain a home office. With a little effort, it's possible to create a less stressful home office environment. Install a business line for phone, email, and fax that rings only in the office. It's not professional to have other family members answering business calls. If your office is not an appropriate meeting space, meet with clients at their office or at a restaurant. Establish set hours. Try not to let work hours extend into evenings and weekends. Let your neighbours and friends know you keep office hours and cannot be disturbed during "working" hours.[30]

Global Business Insight

Doing Business in England

Linda Phillips, co-director of Executive Etiquette Company, says, "First and foremost is the British attention to detail." English businesspeople also tend to be more formal in terms of dress and person-to-person communication. It's helpful to study English business customs before visiting that country.

■ Introductions in England tend to be very formal. The British look for whose name is spoken first. If you are calling on a client named Robert Timmons, the introduction of your sales manager would be, "Mr. Timmons, I would like you to meet Raymond Hill, my sales manager." In this case the client's name is

first because he is the more important person. Never address someone by his or her first name unless you are invited to do so.

■ Making decisions is often a time-consuming process, so don't expect a quick close.

■ Do not use aggressive sales techniques, such as the hard sell, and avoid criticism of competing products. Focus on objective facts and evidence during the presentation.

■ It would be poor manners to discuss business after the business day in England. This is true even when you have drinks or a meal with a businessperson.[c]

Maintain an Optimistic Outlook

Optimistic thoughts give rise to positive attitudes and effective relationships with customers. According to Martin Seligman, professor of psychology and author of *Learned Optimism*, optimists are more likely to view problems merely as temporary setbacks. They focus on their potential success rather than on their failures. Pessimists, in contrast, tend to believe bad events will last a long time and tend to give up more easily when faced with a challenge.[31]

Seligman reminds us that optimism is a learned behaviour. For example, you can spend more time visualizing yourself succeeding. If you want to succeed at something, picture yourself doing it successfully. The visualization process needs to be repeated over and over again.[32]

Practise Healthy Emotional Expression

When stress occurs, you may undergo physiological and psychological changes. Your heartbeat quickens, your blood pressure rises, and tension builds. To relieve the pressure, you may choose a *fight* or a *flight* response. With a fight response, you might unleash an avalanche of harsh words or ignore a person with whom you are dealing. These reactions, of course, are not recommended. This behaviour may damage relationships with team members, customers, or customer support personnel.

A flight response is running away from the problem. Rather than facing the issue squarely, you decide to turn your back on it. Flight is usually not satisfactory, as the problem will seldom go away by itself. If you feel stress from an impractical quota, for example, talk to your sales manager and try to get the quota reduced. Don't just give in to the feeling of being overwhelmed. Diminished personal accomplishment can add to further burnout and stress.[33] If you are spending too much time away from family and friends, take a close look at your territory management plan and try to develop a more efficient way to make sales calls. It is not possible to eliminate those elements that cause us stress, but we can find ways to cope with daily stressors. There are stress management activities that can be used during brief pauses in your day (see Table 16.2).

Table 16.2 Five-Minute Stress Busters

- Take five minutes to identify and challenge unreasonable or distorted ideas that precipitated your stress. Replace them with ideas that are more realistic and positive.
- Take a five-minute stress-release walk outdoors. Contact with nature is especially beneficial.
- Enjoy stress relief with a gentle five-minute neck and shoulder massage.
- Spend five minutes visualizing yourself relaxing at your favourite vacation spot.
- Take a five-minute nap after lunch.
- Spend five minutes listening to a recording featuring your favourite comedian.

Source: "Five-Minute Stress Busters" by Barry L. Reece and Rhonda Brandt from *Effective Human Relations: Personal and Organizational Applications*. Copyright © 2008. Used by the permission of Cengage Learning/Global Rights and Permissions Administration.

Increasingly, in the age of information, physical exercise is a very important part of a stress management program. Exercise also helps us maintain peak mental performance.

Monkey Business Images/Shutterstock

Maintain a Healthy Lifestyle

An effective exercise program—jogging, tennis, golf, racquetball, walking, or some other favourite exercise—can counter the harmful chemicals that build up in your bloodstream after a prolonged period of stress. Salespeople at Owens Corning formed a sales wellness advisory team (SWAT). The team organized a health screening for Owens's 600 salespeople and instituted an incentive program that rewarded those who reached exercise goals.[34]

The food you eat can also play a critical role in helping you manage stress. Health experts agree that the typical Canadian diet—high in saturated fats, refined sugars, additives, caffeine, and too much sodium—is the wrong menu for coping with stress. Employees of Husky Injection Molding Systems Ltd. in Bolton, Ontario, enjoy fresh, healthy food in an attractive cafeteria environment. The company's wellness centre provides exercise equipment and fitness classes to motivate an active, healthy lifestyle.[35]

An additional way to handle stress is to come to work rested and relaxed. You need to get enough quality sleep. The number of hours of sleep required for good health varies from person to person, but seven or eight hours seems to be about right for most people. The critical factor is whether you feel rested in the morning and prepared to deal with the day's activities. In many respects, salespeople must possess the same self-discipline as professional athletes. Sales work can be physically demanding. Lack of proper rest, poor eating habits, excessive drinking, and failure to exercise properly can reduce one's ability to deal with stress and strain.

REVIEWING KEY CONCEPTS

- Discuss the four dimensions of opportunity management.

  All salespeople can learn more about their products and improve their selling skills. However, there is no way to expand time. Our only option is to find ways to improve in the four dimensions of opportunity management discussed in this chapter: time management, territory management, records management, and stress management.

- List and describe time management strategies.

  Effective time management methods can pave the way to greater sales productivity. To achieve greater time conservation, salespeople should adopt the following time-saving strategies: Develop a series of personal goals; prepare a daily "to-do" list; maintain a planning calendar; organize your selling tools; and save time with meetings in cyberspace and other methods of communication.

- Explain factors that contribute to improved territory management.

  The first step in territory management is the classification of all customers according to sales volume or some other appropriate criteria. You should normally spend the most time with accounts that have the greatest sales potential. The second step requires developing a routing and scheduling plan. This plan should reduce time spent travelling between accounts. Salespeople are often guided by a *sales call plan*.

- Identify and discuss common elements of a records management system.

  A good record-keeping system provides many advantages. Accurate, up-to-date records can actually save time because work is better organized. The company also benefits because sales reports provide an important communication link with members of the sales force. Today, computers are used to develop more efficient record-keeping systems. Common records kept by salespeople include customer and prospect files, call reports, expense records, and sales records.

- Discuss stress management practices.

  There is a certain amount of stress associated with sales work. This is due in part to the non-routine nature of personal selling. Salespeople must learn to cope with factors that upset their equilibrium. Stress management strategies include developing a stress-free home office, maintaining an optimistic outlook, practising healthy emotional expression, and maintaining a healthy lifestyle.

Key Terms

opportunity management **382**
personal digital assistant **386**
sales call plan **391**

sales territory **382**
stress **396**

Review Questions

1. The From the Field boxed feature (p. 383) describes how Alex Pettes manages his time for self–improvement. Why is it important for salespeople to have a self-improvement plan?

2. Opportunity management has been described as a four-dimensional process. Describe each dimension.

3. List and briefly describe the four goal-setting principles.

4. How can a salesperson use a time log to improve time management?

5. List four techniques the salesperson should use to make better use of valuable selling time.

6. Effective territory management involves two major steps. What are they?

7. What is a *sales call plan*? Explain how it is used.

8. Describe the records most commonly kept by salespeople.

9. What is *stress*? What are some indicators of stress?

10. Table 16.2 describes six "five-minute stress busters." Which of these do you think are most important for persons employed in the sales field? Explain.

Application Exercises

1. The key to successful time management lies in thinking and planning ahead. You must become conscious of yourself and decide what you want from your time. You can manage your time only when you have a clear picture of what is going on within and around you. To assess the quality of your working time, it is helpful to keep a careful record for a certain amount of time, showing exactly how you have used your day. Over this period of time, write down everything you have done and how long it took. Next you can appraise your use of time and decide whether or not it was put to good use. Some pertinent questions you might ask yourself in appraising your use of time are suggested by the following "time analysis" questions:

   a. What items am I spending too much time on?

   b. What items am I spending too little time on?

   c. What items offer the most important opportunities for saving time?

   d. What am I doing that does not need to be done at all?

   e. How can I avoid overusing the time of others?

   f. What are some other suggestions?

2. Deciding on a goal can be the most crucial decision of your life. It is more damaging not to have a goal than it is not to reach a goal. It is generally agreed that the major cause of failure is the lack of a well-defined direction. A successful life results not from chance, but from a succession of successful days. List three goals for yourself in these four categories: career, family, education, interpersonal relations.

3. Interview someone you know who uses a planning calendar. What kind is it: pocket, desk, or some other type? How long has the person been using it? How important is the calendar to daily, weekly, monthly, and yearly planning? Has the person ever considered discontinuing its use? What are the person's suggestions for someone who does not use one? Write down your answers.

3. Time management is an important part of a successful salesperson's job. Using your search engine, examine the Internet for information on time management. Type "time management + selling." Examine the training products and services available on this topic. Be prepared to discuss some of what you find in class.

4. Territory management involves classifying customers and developing a routing and scheduling plan. You have just been hired to demonstrate—not sell—a new inventory management product to stores that sell grocery products. As your first task, the manager has asked you to prepare a list of up to 20 stores in your territory—try looking within a one-mile radius of your college or university or home. Classify these customers. Prepare a scheduling plan and be prepared to defend the plan you have made.

ROLE-PLAY EXERCISE

Using the information in the Chapter 15 role-play exercise, develop a contact plan regarding the future contacts you set up (see p. 376). Your sales manager has scheduled a status report meeting to go over your activities with this account. With this information and with the information written in your calendar, plan to meet with your sales manager to talk about the account management meetings you have scheduled. Plan to cover how this schedule enhances both your time and territory management and adds value to the sale.

Reality Selling Video Case Problem

Paula Shannon, introduced at the beginning of this chapter, spends part of most weeks away from her Montreal home-based office, managing a global team of 70 sales professionals for Boston-based Lionbridge Technologies, Inc. Some indicators of her success: 1) Under her direction, Lionbridge placed second for Best Sales Team in the American Business Awards; 2) Paula was recognized with the inaugural International Stevie Award as Best Sales

Executive; and 3) Among more than 600 entrants, Paula received a second Stevie Award as Best Canadian Executive. Some qualities recognized by the Stevie awards include leadership, innovation, perseverance, creativity, teamwork, and integrity. There are many things that must come together to create success at this level. Paula Shannon is a person who has managed herself and her career with meticulous detail; her success is not an accident. Paula Shannon notes six principles that she believes have contributed to her success:

1. *Be self-confident, but be humble and respectful.* Customers buy from salespeople who are confident and professional, not from those who are arrogant or self-centred. Paula says, "Some of the best people I have worked with have been able to combine self-confidence with a genuine interest in and respect for our customers' business issues and needs."

2. *Communicate clear, simple customer solutions in a language they understand.* Some salespeople have a tendency toward bafflegab—sprinkling their discussion with technical jargon without explaining it—mistakenly believing that this will impress their customers. Yet most customers want a clear, simple solution to their buying problems. Paula says, "The art of making complex issues simple seems to be one of the most important things a salesperson can do. When done well, this results in a 'call to action' and a sense of mission or purpose to see the job through."

3. *Be a prolific reader.* Paula Shannon reads both fiction and nonfiction for pleasure. She also reads *The Wall Street Journal* daily, *Fortune*, *CIO Insight*, *Selling Power*, *The Economist*, *Harvard Business Review*, and numerous reports, industry newsletters, and specialized publications. Paula says, "I know that the ability to digest large volumes of information has always been a key to my success. Whether I am getting up to speed on a project, a new deal, or an opportunity, or staying current on business trends or technology shifts, my reading is something that has helped me at every level of my secondary education and my career."

4. *Have fun and love what you do.* Salespeople who work too hard are often subject to burnout. You need time for yourself and to relax. Paula logs more than 240 000 kilometres by air a year. There is no doubt she works hard, but she also plays hard. Paula says, "I rarely schedule work for myself over the weekends and save time for my family, sports, friends, and fun. As a result, I remain energetic, positive, and upbeat. These are all things that are important when interacting with both colleagues and customers."

5. *Develop competence with technology.* At one point in her career, Paula purchased her own laptop. She recognized that she could improve her own efficiency if she could work on correspondence and client proposals while away from her office. Paula says, "Sales requires extraordinary time management, immediacy, customer focus, and access to and the exchange of information. Technology is an essential tool in the equation." Speaking of the impact of technology on herself and her sales team, she adds, "Our ability to respond to customers, solve problems, and deliver information has improved five-fold. Remote access to a shared store of centralized information has helped us, as service providers, to manage global projects, report on status, improve quality, and coordinate worldwide teams."

6. *Develop both depth and breadth of knowledge.* Paula credits some of her success to the fact that she has taken several "career meanderings" during her career—lateral moves and an occasional step downward. Speaking of this, Paula says, "In sales—deep technical or product and service—offering expertise is crucial to your success and credibility with customers. However, those skills alone, without broader business or cultural context, result in someone whose options become increasingly limited as their career progresses."

Questions

1. Which of Paula Shannon's "six principles for success" will make the most important contribution to a career in personal selling? Explain.

2. Reflect on your own approach to accomplishing things. Then select two of Paula's principles that you would find easy to adopt. Also select two principles you would find difficult to adopt. Explain your choices.

3. What things, among the many that Paula does, do you think help her manage stress most effectively? Explain.

4. How important do you think time management is to Paula? Records management? Territory management?

Chapter 17
Management of the Sales Force

Learning Objectives

After studying this chapter, you should be able to

1 Describe how leadership skills can be applied to sales management.

2 List and discuss the qualities of an effective sales manager.

3 Discuss recruitment and selection of salespeople.

4 Describe effective orientation and training practices.

5 Explain effective sales force motivation practices.

6 Develop an understanding of selected compensation plans.

7 List and discuss criteria for evaluating sales performance.

 Reality Selling Video Series

Jaime Barauh, pictured at the top of the next page, district sales manager for McKesson Pharmaceutical (**www.mckesson.com**), started her career at this largest North American pharmaceutical distributor company as a salesperson calling on retail independent pharmacies. She attributes her success to the training she received from the company and from her previous managers. In a highly competitive and ever-changing pharmaceutical industry, continuing training about new products and services is critical. McKesson adopts a multi-layer training program. This includes a comprehensive online curriculum covering all products and services the company is offering, hands-on training with current managers, and frequent updates. The company also runs regional and national sales conferences where managers can network with peers and receive updated information. All new recruits also spend two weeks in the corporate distribution centre working as actual distribution staff to familiarize themselves with an extensive line of products.

An avid learner, Jaime Barauh was soon promoted to district sales manager of McKesson's distribution hub. Working under her supervision are five account managers

Jaime Barauh

Michael Ahearne

who are responsible for approximately $750 million in sales. As a sales manager, she makes sure that her subordinates are empowered to fulfill their responsibilities. At the same time, she sets a good example for her subordinates with her strong work ethic. She subscribes to the principle that a good leader should keep regular and open communication with followers without micro-managing, which is the enemy of creativity and motivation. She is also actively involved in recruiting and training new staff because she believes that such early involvement in the process will help build a strong sales team.

APPLYING LEADERSHIP SKILLS
TO SALES MANAGEMENT

IF YOU ENTER THE FIELD OF PERSONAL SELLING AND EXPERIENCE SUCCESS, YOU MAY BE GIVEN the opportunity to manage a sales force. Some salespeople are asked to accept the promotion but decline the offer. They do not want to give up a job they thoroughly enjoy. Many of the salespeople who do move into management positions, however, become exemplary leaders and advance to positions that offer even greater challenges.

Thanks to the efforts of James Kouzes and Barry Posner and their many years of research on this topic—summarized and reported in their best-selling book, *The Leadership Challenge*—we know a great deal about leadership. Their book is based on countless interviews and observations conducted around the world.

Lindsay Levin, managing director of Whites Limited, was one of many exceptional leaders cited by the authors of *The Leadership Challenge*. Whites Limited, based in London, England, is an auto dealership built around three departments—sales, service, and parts. Soon after assuming her new management position, Lindsay began searching for answers to one important question: "What do our customers really think of us?" She visualized Whites as a company where every customer would say, "My experience at Whites was amazing." With input from customer focus groups, she was able to identify some areas that needed improvement. She then asked employees to talk about changes they would like to implement and to form small, voluntary teams to work on them.

· Lindsay Levin also visualized a company where everyone is treated with respect and feels involved and valued. She took the position that leaders can never have enough communication with their people. She never hesitated to let the employees know what she was thinking and what she believed. She talked about her values often and listened attentively when employees expressed their views. Levin also recognized employee accomplishments with personal thanks and formal awards.

People who rise to the position of sales manager must understand the difference between leadership and management. Managers who lack certain leadership skills can actually deteriorate salesperson performance.[1] Leadership is the process of inspiring, influencing, and guiding employees to participate in a common effort.[2] Stephen Covey, author of *The 8th Habit*, says, "Leadership is communicating people's worth and potential so clearly that they come to see it in themselves."[3] Leaders are made, not born. Leadership is a series of skills that can be acquired through study and practice.

sales management The process of planning, implementing, and controlling the personal selling function.

Sales management is the process of planning, implementing, and controlling the personal selling function.[4] The sales manager typically performs such management functions as planning, recruiting, training, budgeting, development of compensation plans, and assessing sales force productivity. Managing the sales force is an external management function focused on bringing in orders and revenue from outside the company. However, it also requires coordination and cooperation with almost every internal department, including marketing, finance, and distribution.[5]

The true essence of sales management has been captured by Lisa Gschwandtner, editor-in-chief of *Selling Power* magazine. She describes the sales manager as a leader, coach, mentor, facilitator, goal setter, motivator, number cruncher, and communicator.[6] Figure 17.1 describes the most popular topics covered in training programs

Planning and Organizing Activities (total = 13 topics)

Goal setting for salespeople	76%
Developing sales strategies	58%
Strategic sales planning	56%
Recruiting new salespeople	52%
Organizing salespeople	52%
Sales forecasting	50%

Management and Development Activities (total = 19 topics)

Motivating salespeople	82%
Leading salespeople	66%
Training salespeople	64%
Territory management	62%
Time management	60%

Evaluation and Control Activities (total = 10 topics)

Evaluating salespeople	64%

Figure 17.1 Most popular topics covered in training programs for sales managers
Source: "Most Popular Topics Covered in Training Programs for Sales Managers from An Empirical Investigation of Sales Management Training Programs for Sales Managers" from *Journal of Personal Selling & Sales Management* by Rolph Anderson; Rajiv Mehta; James Strong. Copyright © 1997 by M.E. Sharpe, Inc., Publisher. Used by permission of M.E. Sharpe, Inc. Publisher.

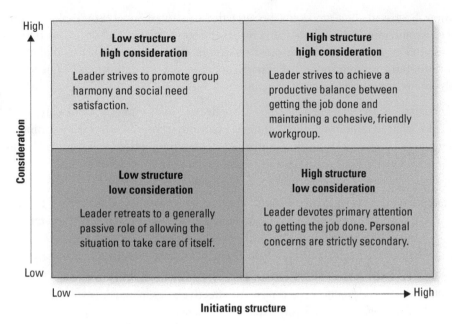

High

Low structure high consideration	High structure high consideration
Leader strives to promote group harmony and social need satisfaction.	Leader strives to achieve a productive balance between getting the job done and maintaining a cohesive, friendly workgroup.
Low structure low consideration	High structure low consideration
Leader retreats to a generally passive role of allowing the situation to take care of itself.	Leader devotes primary attention to getting the job done. Personal concerns are strictly secondary.

Consideration

Low

Low ──────────────────────────► High

Initiating structure

Figure 17.2 Basic Leadership Styles
This matrix is similar to the Leadership Grid (formerly called the Managerial Grid) developed by Robert Blake and Jane Mouton. The Leadership Grid is based on two leadership style dimensions: concern for people and concern for production.
Source: "Basic Leadership Styles" from *Management* by Robert Kreitner. Copyright © 2007 by Houghton Mifflin Harcourt Publishing Company. Used by permission of Houghton Mifflin Harcourt Publishing Company.

designed for sales managers. Needless to say, it's a job that requires many qualities and skills. Today's sales manager is more likely to function in a virtual office environment. Sales force automation permits salespeople to receive data on their laptops or home computers. The use of other technology—videoconferencing, teleconferencing, email, and voice mail—reduces the need for frequent face-to-face contact with members of the sales team.[7]

Sales managers can have a dramatic influence on the salespeople they supervise. Depending on the leadership qualities adopted, sales managers can have an advantageous, neutral, or even detrimental effect on the performance of sales subordinates.[8] Effective leadership has been discussed in hundreds of books and articles. A careful review of this material indicates that most successful supervisory-management personnel have certain behaviours in common. Two of the most important dimensions of leadership—consideration and structure—have been identified in research studies conducted by Ohio State University researchers.[9] By making a matrix out of these two independent dimensions of leadership, researchers have identified four styles of leadership (see Fig. 17.2).

Structure

Sales managers who display **structure** clearly define their own duties and those of the sales staff. They assume an active role in directing their subordinates' work. Policies and procedures are clearly defined, and subordinates know what is expected of them. Salespeople

structure A leadership characteristic displayed by sales managers who clearly define their own duties and those of the sales staff, and who assume an active role in directing their subordinates.

also know how well they are doing because the structured supervisor evaluates their productivity and provides feedback. Structure is the set of written and unspoken policies, practices, and expectations that surround the job of the salesperson. It can include job descriptions, territory definitions, call reports, and sales process definitions.[10] The following behaviours provide evidence of structure:

1. *Planning takes place on a regular basis.* The effective sales manager thinks ahead and decides what to do in the future. Strategic planning is the process of determining the company's current position in the market, determining where you want to be and when, and making decisions on how to secure the position you want. Strategic planning gives meaning and direction to the sales force.

2. *Expectations are clearly communicated.* The law of expectations, according to Brian Tracy, states, "Whatever you expect, with confidence, becomes your own self-fulfilling prophecy."[11] There is a strong connection between what you expect to accomplish and what you actually achieve. Sales managers must effectively formulate their expectations and then communicate them with conviction to the sales force.

3. *Decisions are made promptly and firmly.* An effective sales manager is willing and able to make decisions in a timely way. An ineffective manager often postpones important decisions, hoping the problem will go away. Of course most decisions cannot be made until all the facts are available. A good sales manager keeps the lines of communication open and involves subordinates in making the truly important decisions.

4. *Performance of salespeople is appraised regularly.* All employees want to know "where they stand" with the manager. An effective sales manager provides regular feedback. When a salesperson is not performing up to established standards, the sales manager takes immediate action.

Although structure is an important aspect of sales management, too much structure can sometimes create problems. In an effort to become better organized and more systematized, some sales organizations have developed detailed policies and procedures that rob salespeople of time, energy, and creativity. Filling out endless reports and forms, for example, can cause unnecessary frustration and may reduce productivity. Overcontrolling sales managers aren't just annoying, they are also inefficient.[12]

Consideration

consideration A leadership dimension displayed by sales managers who have relationships with salespeople that are characterized by mutual trust, respect for salespeople's ideas, and consideration for their feelings.

A sales manager who displays the leadership dimension of **consideration** is more likely to have relationships with salespeople that are characterized by mutual trust, respect for salespeople's ideas, and consideration for their feelings. A climate of good two-way communication usually exists between the manager and the employee. The following behaviours provide evidence of consideration:

1. *Regular and effective communication receives a high priority.* Whenever possible, the effective manager engages in face-to-face communication with salespeople. Sales managers do not rely entirely on email, letters, or sales reports for information sharing but arrange for face-to-face meetings. John Morrone, vice president of sales for Pitney Bowes Management Services, frequently travels with his salespeople. He says, "My claim to fame is reaching out and touching people."[13] The effective sales manager is a good listener and creates an atmosphere of cooperation and understanding.

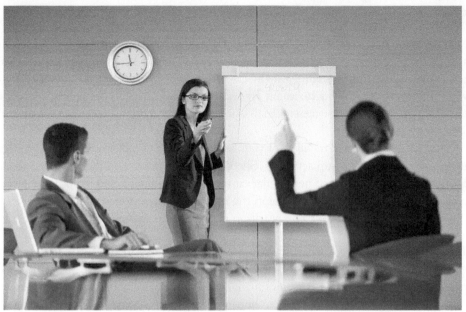

Besides supervising the sales force, sales managers often are involved in establishing sales quotas, developing long- and short-term forecasts, and seeing that goals are achieved.

Olive/Superstock

2. *Each salesperson is treated as an individual.* The sales manager takes a personal interest in each member of the sales force. No one is treated "like a number." The interest is genuine, not artificial. The effective sales manager does not endanger effectiveness by showing favouritism to anyone.

3. *Good performance is rewarded often.* Positive reinforcement is one of the strongest morale-building factors in the work environment. Ken Blanchard, co-author of *The One-Minute Manager*, says, "The key to developing people will always be to concentrate on catching them doing something right instead of blaming them for doing something wrong."[14] Recognition for a job well done is always appreciated.

The recognized standard of sales excellence

CSP - When these three letters follow your name, they pack a powerful message

- 86% gained a competitive advantage in the marketplace
- 72% rank in the top 25% of sales within their respective organizations
- More than half earn personal annual incomes over $75,000 per year
- 9 out of 10 CSPs recommend becoming a Certified Sales Professional (CSP) to others

Courtesy of CPSA Canada

The CPSA Sales Institute has been committed to excellence in the sales profession by maintaining progressive competency standards for sales professionals since 1994. It is the only organization in Canada that offers the Certified Sales Professional (CSP) designation.

Situational Leadership

Mastery of consideration and structure skills is an important first step toward achieving success in sales management. The next step is to match your leadership style to the various situations that surface among members of your sales force. Paul Hershey is credited with the development of **situational leadership**. This leadership approach is based on the theory that the most successful leadership occurs when the leader's style matches the situation.[15]

Let us assume that a member of your sales team has almost totally abandoned customer service and follow-up activities. She is devoting nearly all of her attention to calls on new customers. Many of her regular customers have complained about poor service, and a crisis is developing. At this point, the leadership dimension of *structure* will require the most time and attention. This situation must be corrected immediately.

The Character Test Sales managers who develop consideration and structure skills and the flexibility required to be a situational leader must pass one additional test. If you fail the character test, you fail as a sales manager. Character is composed of your personal standards of behaviour, including your honesty and integrity. If you are seen as an honest broker of advice and assistance, as someone who always tells the truth, trust and respect will build. But building trust is a slow process and it can be irreparably destroyed by a single lie or deception.[16]

Coaching for Peak Performance

"When you die there is an express line at the Pearly Gates for coaches," jokes Canadian consultant, international speaker, and award-winning retailer Donald Cooper (**www.donaldcooper.com**). He recognizes that the ability to be a good coach—to improve the attitudes and skills of others—is both rare and important.[17] A sales manager who develops a leadership style that combines structure and consideration behaviours possesses the skills needed to be an effective coach. **Coaching** is an interpersonal process between the sales manager and the salesperson in which the manager helps the salesperson improve performance in a specific area. The coaching process has two primary areas of focus: helping the salesperson recognize the need to improve his or her performance, and developing the salesperson's commitment to improving performance.[18]

Coaching is often used to correct a specific performance problem such as ineffective prospecting, poorly developed sales presentations, or failure to create value for the customer. We will outline a four-step coaching strategy:

Step one in the coaching process involves documentation of performance problems. In some cases the best approach is to observe and assess performance during actual sales calls. Make note of things the salesperson is neglecting to do.

Step two involves getting the salesperson to recognize and agree that there is a need to improve performance in a specific area. Sales managers should never assume that the salesperson sees the problem in the same way they do.

Step three involves exploring solutions. At this point it's often best to let the salesperson suggest ways to improve performance.

Valuable Advice for Those Who Would Be Leaders

Tom Gunter has spent most of his life in sales: Scott Paper, Frito-Lay Canada, Molson Canada, and now as vice president of sales for ConAgra Foods in Toronto. Tom has eight directors of sales who report to him, and each of them is responsible for four to six account managers. Tom has lots of good advice for aspiring sales leaders. The following are some of Tom's comments:

- *Managing change.* When you must change a culture, you have to create stability and put the appropriate structures and processes in place to succeed. The biggest challenge is getting some people to understand the importance of change, and then training them so they can make the change. The ones who can't get to where you want them may have to go elsewhere.

- *Plateaued salespeople.* Every company has a number of people who don't want to move up in the organization, and you need those steady performers as long as they are open to new concepts and ideas. But if they have lost their motivation, you must have an open and honest talk with them about where they fit and let them decide whether they want to stay. Some may become re-motivated and get excited about helping someone else develop into the company's next senior executive.

- *Sales meetings.* Attendees must be aware of the preparation required and the decisions to be made at the meeting. In addition, the facilitator, timekeeper, and note-taker should be briefed on their roles and responsibilities. If a meeting room is unfamiliar or if there are materials to set up, the manager should arrive early to prepare. This ensures that the meeting starts on time, as starting late shows disrespect to the participants.

- *Coaching.* You should involve the salesperson when delivering feedback. You must offer praise where due, but rather than spout criticism, you are better off asking questions that create a dialogue about possible ways to improve results.

- *Alcohol and drug abuse.* If a salesperson has identified the problem and is seeking help to deal with it, you are required to provide employee assistance to help them overcome the problem. If they fail to acknowledge the problem and continue with the abuse, in spite of your efforts to offer assistance, you should move to termination. It is always advisable to seek legal counsel and involve human resource professionals in these situations as they are delicate and can put your organization in jeopardy if handled poorly.

- *Harassment.* Personalities and outcomes of harassment are very diverse, and each situation requires a different course of action. If a salesperson reports harassment, a sales manager must reserve judgment, listen actively, take many notes, and begin an investigative process. The outcome could include third-party counselling, a meeting with the two individuals, a written apology, suspension of duties, or termination.

- *Termination.* Termination should be the last step after all other options are exhausted, but sometimes it is inevitable. If the employee leaves and feels as though he was treated fairly and respectfully, even if he does not agree with the assessment, it reflects well on the company and manager. It will be recognized internally by other staff and externally by potential hires. Your organization will be known for its good practices.

- *Final thoughts.* A great employee is focused on his or her own development, whereas a great leader is focused on the development of others. Some final words of wisdom: Be clear and consistent, be honest, maintain a sense of humour, and, most important, never ask someone to do something that you wouldn't do yourself.[a]

Step four involves getting a commitment from the salesperson to take action. This step may involve development of a contract—written or verbal—that clarifies the coaching goals, approaches, and outcomes.

A major goal of coaching meetings is to improve performance while enabling sales managers and salespeople to maintain a relationship based on mutual respect and trust. Most salespeople welcome coaching, even when it involves constructive criticism.[19]

RECRUITMENT AND SELECTION OF SALESPEOPLE

CAREFUL RECRUITMENT AND SELECTION OF SALESPEOPLE IS VERY IMPORTANT. THIS IS ONE of the most significant tasks sales managers perform because sales organizations have been forced to become more sophisticated. The authors of *How to Hire and Develop Your Next Top Performer: The Five Qualities That Make Salespeople Great* say that about half of the people working in sales should be doing something else. In addition, they say that about 20 to 25 percent of the salespeople currently employed are selling products or services not suited to their personality.[20] If the research reported by these authors is accurate, then it appears that sales managers are frequently hiring the wrong people.

Successful salespeople are often difficult to identify. The selection of sales personnel today is more of a science and less of an art. Sales managers no longer need to rely on "gut feelings." The ability to identify sales aptitude accurately can be acquired. Many progressive sales organizations recognize the need to help sales managers develop the interviewing skills necessary to make profitable hiring decisions. It is impossible to avoid occasionally hiring a poor performer, but sales managers can improve their average by using some established recruitment and selection guidelines.

Determine Actual Job Requirements

To decide what type of applicant is needed, the manager should first outline the duties the person will perform. The sales manager must have a clear picture of the job requirements before beginning the recruitment process.

Some sales managers make every effort to discover the success factors that contribute to the achievements of their high-performance salespeople. Success factors are the

Ken Blanchard, co-author of *The One-Minute Manager,* says the key to developing people is to concentrate on catching them doing something right. Here we see a salesperson receiving recognition.

Digital Vision/Getty Images

skills, knowledge, abilities, and behaviours considered critical for successful performance. This information may be collected through interviews with salespeople or customers, by observing the salesperson during sales calls, or by some other method.

After a careful study of the duties the salesperson will perform and identification of the success factors, the sales manager should prepare, or have human resources prepare, a job description. A *job description* is an explanation of what the salesperson will do and under what conditions the work will be performed. It is a good idea to spell out in as much detail as possible the abilities and qualities that the applicant needs to be successful. This can be accomplished by answering a few basic questions about the position.

1. Will the person be developing a new sales territory or assuming responsibility for an established territory?

2. Is the product or service well established, or is it new to the marketplace?

3. Will the salesperson work under the sales manager's close supervision or independently?

4. What amount of travel is required? What is the likelihood of eventual transfer? Promotion?

Once the job description has been prepared, the foundation has been established to determine the type of person to be hired. There is no substitute for knowing what the job requires.

Search Out Applicants from Several Sources

To identify the best possible person for the job, sales managers usually seek applicants from more than one source. As a rule of thumb, they try to interview three or more applicants for each opening. Some suggested sources of new employees follow.

1. *Candidates within the company and employee referrals.* One of the first places to look is within your own company. Is there someone in accounting, engineering, customer service, or some other area who aspires to a sales position? These people have the advantage of being familiar with the company's products, policies, operations, and what it takes to please the customer. Companies are also increasingly using referral programs because employees often know of people with similar skills in other organizations. Synnex Canada pays a $500 bonus to employees who refer a friend or family member who is successfully recruited, if the new recruit remains with the company for more than three months.[21]

2. *College and university students.* Many business firms are turning to college and university campuses to recruit salespeople. As noted in Chapter 1, several colleges and universities have developed personal selling certificate and degree programs. Placement offices are usually cooperative about publicizing openings.

3. *Trade and newspaper advertisements.* A carefully prepared newspaper advertisement will often attract well-qualified job applicants. A well-written ad should accurately describe the job requirements and spell out the opportunities. The ad should "sell" the position, but it should not exaggerate its benefits.

4. *Employment agencies and listings.* Canada Human Resources Centre helps companies across Canada assess job applicants and select the best among them, helping to reduce employee turnover, increase productivity, and improve job satisfaction. There

are also many private employment agencies across Canada. These firms specialize in matching applicants to the job and usually do some initial screening for employers. A fee is assessed for the services these agencies provide.

5. *Internet.* Many companies are using the Internet to recruit for sales positions: Monster.ca, Workopolis, and Job Search Canada are popular websites for those seeking sales positions. The Government of Canada job bank, **www.jobbank.gc.ca,** lists thousands of sales jobs across Canada. Job boards can reach candidates in distant places and can locate talented salespeople who are not actively searching for jobs. Vancouver human resources executive Shirley Quinn finds job boards convenient and cost-effective when hiring the best sales and management people.[22]

Select the Best-Qualified Applicant

Once you have identified qualified applicants, the next step is to select the best person. This is becoming more difficult as products become more complex, customers become more sophisticated, and competitors become more aggressive. Selecting the best-qualified applicant will never be easy, but there are some qualifications and characteristics that all sales managers should look for. One of the most important qualities is a high level of interest in and enthusiasm for the job and a high degree of self-motivation.[23] Salespeople have to be self-starters.

Another very important quality is integrity. Dana Telford and Adrian Gostick, authors of *Integrity Works,* say that managers spend about 90 percent of their time on capability-related questions and almost no time on character-based questions. They suggest checking backgrounds and interviewing for character by asking ethics-based questions. Here are a few examples.[24]

What are your three core values?

What does integrity mean to you?

Who are your role models and why?

What would your past manager say about you?

Tell me about a time when you were asked to compromise your integrity.

Bruce Diamond, vice president of sales for a large office equipment company, says, "Our salespeople now need to be much more professional, much more educated about the market, customers, products, and business in general."[25] His strategy for finding good salespeople includes discussions of business trends and developments. During the interview, he poses business situations and asks the candidate to come up with solutions. Diamond says he is impressed when a candidate displays an understanding of profitable revenues and finding the right customers to do business with.

Personality and Skills Testing

To increase the quality of new hires, many companies are placing more emphasis on personality and skills testing. The HR Chally Group developed the Chally Talent Audit, an instrument that can be used to predict performance in a variety of sales positions. The audit provides a skills profile that helps determine strengths and weaknesses in several roles. For example, a candidate may possess the skills needed to develop new accounts, but lack the skills needed for strategic account management. Chally assessment instruments are fully compliant with equal opportunity regulations and are non-discriminatory.[26]

Western Psychological Services developed the Sales Achievement Predictor. This instrument assesses self-confidence, personal diplomacy, competitiveness, and other qualities equally important in sales.[27] Caliper Corporation, a testing service with more than 40 years of experience, developed Caliper Profile, an instrument for personality assessment. Caliper's basic personality profile can be taken online.[28] Online testing has become more popular in recent years. John Wood, vice president of business development at HR Chally Group, recommends that firms rely 30 percent on predictive assessment instruments, 30 percent on a structured interview, 30 percent on references and background checks, and 10 percent on personal reactions to the applicant.[29] Test results should always be used *in conjunction* with information obtained from the interview with the candidate and the findings of reference checks.

ORIENTATION AND TRAINING

ONCE YOU HAVE SELECTED THE BEST-QUALIFIED SALESPERSON, TWO STEPS SHOULD BE TAKEN to ensure that this person becomes a productive member of your staff. First, give the new employee a thorough orientation to your business operation. Provide the orientation *before* the person begins working. This should include a review of your company's history, philosophy of doing business, mission statement, business policies, compensation plan, and other important information.

Selling in Action

Are You Ready for Today's Sales Interview?

The personal interview is an important part of the selection process when filling sales positions. When companies use a series of interviews, the first one often is used to eliminate unacceptable candidates—those who lack maturity, lack enthusiasm, or display poor appearance. Subsequent interviews are used to match people to job qualifications. At Hewlett-Packard, candidates may have as many as six interviews with various people. At Smith Kline, a team approach is used so that candidates do not learn the "right" answers from one interview to the next.

Although interviews vary from one company or interviewer to another, there are some popular questions and requests that you should be prepared to handle:

- Tell me about yourself.
- Describe the sales process as you understand it.

- What books have you read recently on selling or for personal development?
- What is your greatest weakness? Strength?
- What was the most boring job you ever had, and how did you handle it?
- How do you feel about your present (or previous) employer?
- What was the biggest contribution you made to your last employer?
- Sell me this pen (ashtray, laptop computer, lamp).
- Why should we hire you?

Some employers also ask you to complete a test to demonstrate your written communication skills or your ability to handle "the numbers." These are both important skills sales professionals require for success.[b]

Second, initiate a training program that will help the person achieve success. Sales training that is carefully planned and executed can make a major contribution to the performance of every salesperson.[30] Nabisco Corporation developed a two-day Professional Selling Program that helps sales reps plan for and deliver professional presentations. The cost of the training is about $1000 per enrollee. A careful evaluation of the program indicates that the training has resulted in additional sales of more than $122 000 per salesperson and yielded almost $21 000 of additional profit per rep.[31] Study results indicate that salespeople have a more positive view of their job, greater commitment, and improved performance when their sales managers clarify their job role, how to execute their tasks, and how their needs will be satisfied with successful job performance.[32] Figure 17.3 provides a framework for developing an effective sales training program.

Even salespeople with great potential are handicapped when the company fails to provide adequate training. Keep in mind that in the absence of formal training, employees will develop their own approaches to performing tasks.

The size of the firm should not dictate the scope of the training program. Even the smallest marketing organization should have a formal sales training program. Online training often reduces training costs. A program should have three dimensions:

- Knowledge of the product line, company marketing strategies, territory information, and business trends

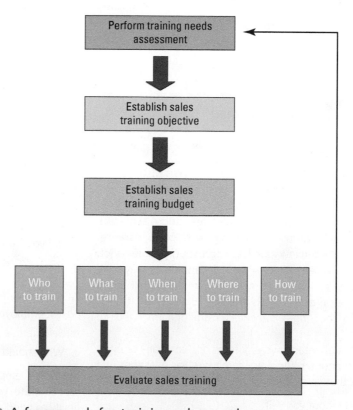

Figure 17.3 A framework for training salespeople
Source: H. F. (Herb) MacKenzie, *Sales Management in Canada* (Toronto, ON: Pearson Prentice Hall, 2008), p. 229.

- Attitude toward the company, the company's products and services, and the customers to be served
- Skill in applying personal selling principles and practices—the "doing" part of the sales training program[33]

An important part of the sales training program is foundation-level instruction. This aspect of sales training focuses on the *basics*. If salespeople are to plan and execute a sales call successfully, they must first master certain fundamental selling skills—the skills that form the foundation for everything salespeople do in their careers. The steps that make up the Six-Step Presentation Plan (i.e., approach, need discovery, presentation, negotiation, close, and servicing the sale) represent fundamental selling skills (see Figure 15.1).

SALES FORCE MOTIVATION

IT IS HELPFUL TO NOTE THE DIFFERENCE BETWEEN INTERNAL AND EXTERNAL MOTIVATION. An **internal motivation** is an intrinsic reward that occurs when a duty or task is performed. If a salesperson enjoys calling on customers and solving their problems, this activity is in itself rewarding, and the salesperson is likely to be self-motivated.[34] Internal motivation is likely to be triggered when sales positions provide an opportunity for achievement and individual growth. **External motivation** is an action taken by another person involving rewards or other forms of reinforcement that cause the worker to behave in ways that ensure receipt of the award.[35] A cash bonus given to salespeople who achieve a sales goal is one example of external motivation. Experts on motivation agree that organizations should attempt to provide a mix of external rewards and internal satisfaction.

A basic contention among too many sales managers has been that sales productivity can be improved by staging more elaborate sales contests, giving more expensive recognition awards, having the right number of prize winners, or picking truly exotic meeting locations.[36] This point of view ignores two things we know for sure about the characteristics of motives. First, motives are individualistic. The desire for social standing (status) may be very strong for one salesperson, but not very important to another salesperson. What satisfies one person's needs may not be important to someone else. Second, motives change throughout our lives. What motivates us early in our career may not motivate us later in life.

Because people bring different interests, drives, and values to the workplace, they react differently to attempts at motivation. The owner of an incentive consulting company rewarded one of his highly productive employees with an attractive mink coat. She thanked him sincerely, took the coat home, but never wore it. When he asked her why, she explained that she didn't wear fur.[37]

Frequently, intrinsic motivators—achievement, challenge, responsibility, advancement, growth, enjoyment of work itself, and involvement—have a longer-term effect on employee attitudes than extrinsic motivators—contests, prizes, quotas, and money. In many cases, sales performance is linked directly to the appreciation the sales manager shows for a job well done. The importance of one-on-one communication cannot be overstated. Everyone likes to be treated as an individual. Taking a personal interest means learning the names of spouses and children, finding out what employees do during their leisure time, and acknowledging birthdays.[38]

internal motivation An intrinsic reward that occurs when a duty or task is performed.

external motivation Action taken by another person that involves rewards or other forms of reinforcement that cause the worker to behave in ways that ensure receipt of the reward.

Sales training that is carefully planned and executed can make a major contribution to the performance of salespeople.

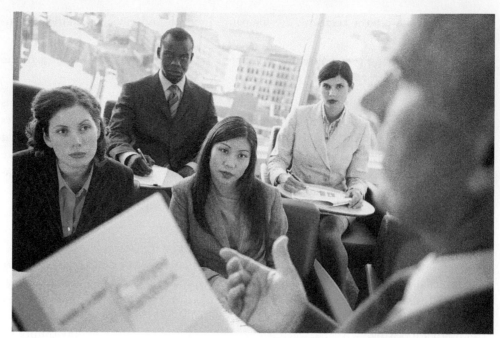

Digital Vision/Getty Images

Effective Use of External Rewards

While criticisms of external rewards have a great deal of merit, the fact remains that large numbers of organizations continue to achieve positive results with carefully developed incentive programs. It is possible to design programs that have long-range benefits for both the organization and the individual employee if you follow these guidelines:

1. Design reward programs that focus on several important aspects of the salesperson's job, such as developing new accounts, expanding sales of existing accounts, and improving customer service after the sale. Keep contest time frames short so more salespeople have an opportunity to win. However, don't use short-term motivation contests too often and don't use the same incentive plan over and over again.

2. Evaluate your incentive program often to determine which plan has the most impact.[39] Is it cash bonuses? Travel? Merchandise? Bill Grassie, manager of compensation and business planning for Sprint, likes to use non-cash incentives because he believes Sprint salespeople have a solid compensation package. He feels non-cash incentives provide a lasting memory, whereas a cash bonus is just one more way to earn money.[40] Of course, a salesperson who is not earning a lot of money in salary and commission might favour a cash incentive.

3. Avoid setting goals that are unrealistic. Some companies are under enormous pressure to meet sales and profit targets. In many cases, sales targets increase while resources decline. One salesperson made President's Club for being 220 percent above quota, and her whole team did well and was recognized as tops in the company. Her boss, the vice president for sales, immediately raised their overall quota by 65 percent for the next year. This was an impossible target and team morale plummeted.

Pressure to reach unrealistic sales goals can produce negative results. Employee loyalty and teamwork erode quickly, and in some cases so do business ethics. Salespeople who fear loss of their job if they do not meet established targets are more inclined to engage in unethical behaviour.[41]

Should sales managers encourage their salespeople to *compete* or encourage them to *cooperate*? This is one of the dilemmas facing managers who want highly motivated salespeople but also want members of the sales team to share important information and become resources to each other. One answer is to develop a plan that rewards sales collaboration and the achievement of specific sales goals, whether individual goals, team goals, or both.[42]

COMPENSATION PLANS

A **compensation plan** FOR SALESPEOPLE COMBINES DIRECT MONETARY PAYMENTS (I.E., SALARY and commissions) and indirect monetary payments (such as paid vacations, pensions, and insurance plans). Compensation practices vary greatly throughout the field of selling. Furthermore, sales managers are constantly searching for the "perfect" sales force compensation plan.[43] Of course, the perfect plan does not exist. Each plan must be chosen to suit the specific type of selling job, the objectives of the firm's marketing program, and the type of customer served.

As noted in Chapter 1, the highest amount of total compensation is earned by salespeople involved in value-added selling. Salespeople who use this approach realize that the solution to the customer's buying problem is more important than price. They are frequently involved in team selling, and in some cases they are rewarded with a team compensation plan.

Increasingly, companies are abandoning compensation plans that are linked to a single target such as a sales quota. At Siebel Systems, an e-business software provider, 40 percent of each salesperson's incentive compensation is based on the customer's reported satisfaction with service and implementation of the products they have purchased. This plan encourages continual customer follow-up, which generates repeat business.[44]

compensation plan A pay plan for salespeople that combines direct monetary pay with indirect monetary payments such as paid vacations, pensions, and insurance plans.

Compensating Your Sales Force in China

There has much been written about the importance of *guanxi*, or networks of personal connections and relationships, in business transactions in China and countries with Chinese influence. In *guanxi* systems, strong social relationships are necessary for building close business relationships, and everyday business takes on solid social elements. In *guanxi* systems it is necessary to recognize mutual social obligations. People with this type of culture assume that all social or work-related favours they make will ultimately be repaid.

A famous study of more than 100 companies operating in foreign countries (either through joint ventures or subsidiaries) has shown that firms operating in Chinese cultures are more likely to include *guanxi* considerations into their sales force management policies than those operating in non-Chinese cultures. In particular, findings show that those firms that recognize the importance of *guanxi* in their business environment are less eager to compensate their sales force merely by commissions. These firms apply systems that rely on salespeople's daily activities and efforts rather than systems that emphasize the amount sold or the number of deals closed as the basis of paying salespeople.[c]

In the field of selling, there are five basic compensation plans. Here is a description of each:

1. *Straight commission plan.* The only direct monetary compensation comes from sales. No sales, no income. Salespeople under this plan are very conscious of their sales. Lack of job security can be a strong inducement to produce results. However, these people may also concentrate more on immediate sales than on long-term customer development.

2. *Commission plan with a draw provision or guaranteed salary.* This plan has about the same impact on salespeople as the straight commission plan. However, it gives them more financial security.

3. *Commission with a draw or guaranteed salary plus a bonus.* This plan offers more direct financial security than the first two plans. As such, salespeople may adhere more to the company's objectives. The bonus may be based on sales or profits.

4. *Fixed salary plus bonus.* Salespeople functioning under this compensation plan tend to be more company-centred and to have a fairly high degree of financial security if their salary is competitive. The bonus incentive helps motivate people under this plan.

5. *Straight salary.* Salespeople who work under this compensation plan are usually more company-centred and have financial security.

According to a *Sales & Marketing Management* research study, most companies participating in the survey used some form of compensation plan that combined base salary and incentive.[45] The salary plus bonus and salary plus commission plans are both quite popular, while determining the right proportion of salary versus incentive depends on many factors.[46]

Strategic Compensation Planning

Many sales managers admit that their current compensation plan does not drive behaviours needed to achieve specific sales objectives. The purpose of strategic compensation planning is to guide salespeople in the right direction. Compensation plans can be designed to achieve a variety of sales objectives:

- *Specific product movement.* Bonus points can be given for the sale of selected items during a specified "push" period.
- *Percentage sales increase.* Sales levels can be established with points that are given only when those levels are reached.
- *Establish new accounts.* A block of points can be awarded for opening a new account, or for expansion selling to existing accounts.
- *Increase sales activity.* For each salesperson, points can be awarded based on the number of calls.[47]

There is no easy way to develop an effective compensation plan. There are, however, some important guidelines for your efforts to develop a good plan.

1. Be sure that your sales and marketing objectives are defined in detail. The plan should complement these goals. If sales and marketing objectives are in conflict with the compensation plan, problems will surely arise.

2. The compensation plan should be field tested before full implementation. Several questions should be answered: Will the new plan be easy to administer? How does the proposed plan differ in terms of payout compared with the existing plan?

3. Explain the compensation plan carefully to the sales force. Misunderstanding may generate distrust of the plan. Keep in mind that some salespeople may see change as a threat.

4. Change the compensation plan when conditions in the marketplace warrant change. One reason for the poor showing of many plans is that firms fail to revise their plans as the business grows and market conditions change. Review the compensation plan at least annually to ensure that it's aligned with conditions in the marketplace and the company's overall marketing strategy.

ASSESSING SALES FORCE PRODUCTIVITY

As the cost of maintaining a sales force increases, sales managers must give more attention to measuring productivity. The goal is to analyze the profitability of each salesperson's sales volume. This task is complicated because sales territories, customers, and business conditions vary.

The problem of measuring sales force productivity is more complicated than it might appear at first glance. In most cases, sales volume alone will not tell you how much profit or loss you are making on the sales of each member of the sales force. A small manufacturer was losing money until he analyzed the profitability of sales generated by each person. He found that one salesperson created a loss on almost every order. This salesperson was concentrating on a market that had become so competitive that she had to reduce the markup to make sales.

Some sales managers view the frequency of calls as an indicator of success. This information is only helpful when compared with the profit earned on each account. The number of calls made on an account should bear some relationship to the sales and profit potential of that account. In some cases, it is possible to maintain small accounts without frequent personal calls.

To compare a salesperson's current productivity with the past can also be misleading. Changes in products, prices, competition, and assignments make comparisons with the past unfair—sometimes to the salesperson, sometimes to the company. It is better to measure cumulative quarterly, semi-annual, or annual results in relation to established goals.

Some sales managers use performance evaluation criteria that communicate to the sales force which elements of their jobs are most important and how they are doing in each area. Evaluating salespeople involves defining the bases on which they will be evaluated, developing performance standards to determine the acceptable level of performance desired on each base, monitoring actual performance, and giving salespeople feedback on their performance.[48] Some of the most common criteria for assessing the productivity of salespeople are:

Quantitative Criteria

Sales volume in dollars or units

Sales volume compared with previous year's sales

Sales volume by product or product line

Number of new accounts opened or accounts lost

Amount of new account sales

Net profit dollars in total, per account, or per product line

Number of customer calls

Qualitative Criteria

Attitude

Product knowledge

Communication skills

Personal appearance

Customer goodwill generated

Selling skills

Initiative

Team collaboration

In most cases, it is best to emphasize assessment criteria that can be expressed in numbers (i.e., quantitative). The preceding quantitative items are especially significant when accompanied by target dates. For example, you might assess the number of new accounts opened during a six-month period. Of course a sales manager should not ignore the other criteria listed here. The other items can affect a salesperson's productivity, and you have to make judgments in these areas.

Some sales managers ask their salespeople to complete a self-evaluation as part of the overall evaluation process. Many salespeople believe that self-evaluation contributes to their personal development.[49]

REVIEWING KEY CONCEPTS

- Describe how leadership skills can be applied to sales management.

  Many capable salespeople have advanced to the position of *sales manager*. This job involves such diverse duties as recruiting, selecting, training, and supervising salespeople. The sales manager is part of the management team and therefore must be a strong leader. Those who rise to the position of sales manager must understand the difference between leadership and management.

- List and discuss the qualities of an effective sales manager.

Effective sales managers help members of their sales force feel confident, strong, and capable of fulfilling their duties. Although the qualities of effective leaders are subject to debate, most research tells us that such people display two dimensions: *structure* and *consideration*. Sales managers who develop a leadership style that combines structure and consideration possess the skills needed to be effective *coaches*.

- Discuss recruitment and selection of salespeople.

  Most sales managers are involved directly or indirectly in recruiting and selecting salespeople. This is an important responsibility because mistakes can be costly. A company's profit and its image can be influenced positively or negatively by each member of the sales force. To increase the quality of new hires, many companies are placing more emphasis on personality and skills testing.

- Describe effective orientation and training practices.

Orientation and training for salespeople are almost daily concerns of the sales manager. These duties should always be viewed as an investment in human resources. They help members of the sales force reach their fullest potential. Figure 17.3 provides a comprehensive framework for training salespeople.

- Explain effective sales force motivation practices.

We discussed the difference between *internal* and *external motivation*. In many cases, intrinsic motivators (achievement, challenge, responsibility, involvement, and enjoyment of work itself) have a longer-term effect on employee attitudes and behaviour than extrinsic motivators (contests, prizes, and money). Sales managers need to discover the individual differences between salespeople to select the most effective motivation strategies.

- Develop an understanding of selected compensation plans.

Compensation plans for salespeople combine direct monetary payments (salary and commissions) and indirect monetary payments, such as paid vacations, pensions, and insurance plans. Compensation practices vary greatly throughout the field of selling. Strategic compensation planning can be used to guide salespeople in the right direction.

- List and discuss criteria for evaluating sales performance.

Assessing sales force productivity is a major responsibility of the sales manager. Sales managers use both quantitative and qualitative criteria. In most cases, it is best to emphasize assessment criteria that can be expressed in numbers (quantitative).

Key Terms

coaching **408**

compensation plan **417**

consideration **406**

external motivation **415**

internal motivation **415**

sales management **404**

situational leadership **408**

structure **405**

Review Questions

1. What is the difference between leadership and management?
2. Are all sales managers' duties the same? Explain.
3. What are the two main leadership qualities displayed by most successful sales managers? Define and explain each of these qualities.
4. List and describe the four basic steps involved in coaching.
5. What is a job description? Explain the importance of job descriptions when selecting salespeople.
6. What are four sources for recruiting new salespeople?

7. What should sales managers look for when selecting new salespeople? Describe at least three important qualities.
8. List and describe three guidelines that should be followed when you design a sales motivation program based on external rewards.
9. List and describe the five basic compensation plans for salespeople.
10. What are the *best* criteria for measuring a salesperson's performance? List additional criteria that should be considered in evaluating individual performance.

Application Exercises

1. Assume that you are a manager of a wholesale electrical supply business. Sales have increased to a level where you need to hire another salesperson. What sources can you use to recruit a good professional salesperson? What criteria can you use in selecting the person you hire?

2. Carefully analyze the following types of selling positions:

   a. A territory selling position for a national manufacturer that requires the salesperson to provide customer service to a large number of accounts plus open up several new accounts each month

   b. A retail sales position in the cosmetics department of a department store

   c. An automobile salesperson who sells and leases new and used cars

   d. A real estate salesperson who sells residential real estate

   Assuming that each of the preceding positions is full-time, identify the type of compensation plan you think is best for each. Supply an explanation for each of your answers.

3. Schedule an appointment with two sales managers. Interview each of them, using the following questions as a guide:

   a. What are your functions as a sales manager?

   b. How do the functions of a sales manager differ from those of a salesperson?

   c. What criteria do you use when selecting salespeople?

   d. What kinds of training programs do you have for new salespeople?

   e. What method of compensation do you use for your salespeople?

   f. How do you evaluate the performance of your salespeople?

   g. What personal qualities are important for becoming a sales manager?

   Write down the answers. Summarize the similarities and differences of the sales managers' responses.

4. You have just been hired as sales manager for the Calgary branch office of a national industrial distributor. It has been five years since you finished your education, and since that time you have had a very successful career selling to mines and manufacturing plants in Ontario and Quebec. As you take over your new position, you notice that if you are not the youngest person in the branch, you are very close to it. At least two salespeople are 20 years older than you. Will *structure* or *consideration* be most important in determining your success as a sales manager? (Note: Do not be a fence-sitter. Make a choice and be prepared to defend it.)

ROLE-PLAY EXERCISE

For the purpose of this role play, assume the role of a sales manager who is currently supervising a sales team made up of 22 salespeople. Your employer manufactures and sells radio equipment for private aircraft. You plan to open a new sales territory in western Canada and need a self-motivated salesperson to assume the position. You have identified a person who seems to be a qualified applicant and you have scheduled a meeting to discuss the position. Using information in this chapter, prepare a list of questions you will ask during the role play. Use these questions to interview another class member who will assume the role of the applicant. After the role play, review the interview process.

Reality Selling Video Case Problem

One of the more interesting developments in sales force management is the use of customer feedback to improve the performance of salespeople. Most of these programs are relatively new and go by a variety of names, such as *360-degree feedback*, *customer-conscious compensation*, and *customer satisfaction rewards*. Organizations that have adopted this assessment strategy believe salespeople can benefit from feedback collected from the customers they serve. Information collected can also be used by the company to improve customer service.

The use of customer-driven evaluation programs is on the increase because of the rising regard for the role of sales at many companies. Tom Mott, a consultant with Hewitt Associates, says, "Salespeople who were volume pushers are now becoming the manager of their company's relationship with the customer." Tom points out that customer feedback is likely to reflect on the performance of the salesperson and the performance of the company. If problems surface in either area, customer dissatisfaction may need attention.

Data collection methodology is not uniform at this point. Some companies use telephone surveys while others use mailed questionnaires. IBM has experimented with a series of in-person meetings that bring together corporate customers, their IBM sales representatives, and the salesperson's boss.

Some salespeople have not welcomed the use of customer evaluations. Maryann Cirenza, senior account executive at Teleport Communications Group (TCG) of New York, said that she felt betrayed when she saw the questionnaire the company was sending to her customers. One of the questions asked, "Does your sales rep know your industry?" Maryann said, "I thought the company was checking up on me." Later, her anger subsided when she learned the survey was not simply a monitoring system but a trial run for a new compensation plan. After field testing the surveys, TCG used customer feedback to set bonuses. MaryAnn Cirenza was actually rewarded for good customer service by earning a bonus of about 20 percent of her base pay.

Greg Buseman, an IBM salesperson, believes the shift to compensation through customer feedback has improved personal selling at his company. He now spends more time understanding the customer's business and learning to be a problem solver for his clients.[50]

Questions

1. Should the customer be given a major voice in determining how salespeople are performing? Explain.
2. Should sales force compensation be linked to customer feedback? What are the advantages and disadvantages of this approach?
3. Assume you are a sales manager preparing to develop and implement a customer feedback system. How might you gain support for this system from members of your sales force? What data collection method would you use?
4. Research indicates that customers rank "understanding of our business" as an important criterion used to evaluate salespeople. Why is this criterion ranked so high?

Appendix 1

Reality Selling Today Role-Play Scenarios

 The 11 role-play scenarios in this appendix are all extensions of the Reality Selling Videos presented throughout the text. Using the information presented in the chapter opening vignettes, case problems, and videos, and the information presented in this section, you will have available the most detailed and realistic setting for selecting, preparing, and presenting a role play.

As you discovered in the videos and related material, these are real salespeople in real selling situations, enjoying successful and rewarding careers in the profession of selling. In these Reality Selling role-play scenarios, you assume these same responsibilities by selecting a similar position in the same office as the sales professionals presented in the videos. Just as they do in the evolution of their careers, you will need to learn about your new company, its products, and, specifically, the customer you will be calling on.

Detailed information is presented in each of the scenarios. Websites are presented to provide more information about the company, its products, and the industry. Reference is made to reviewing the chapter opening vignettes and corresponding case problems for learning more about your new company and selling responsibility.

The role plays presented in this appendix are also specifically designed to prepare for professional selling role-play competitions at the annual college and university competitive event conventions (refer to **http://coles.kennesaw.edu/ncsc** and **www.deca.org/_docs/conferences-competitions/COL_Sales_Rep_Guidelines.pdf/** for more information).

The following companies, sales positions, and customer types are presented:

- The Tom James Company, Alex Homer, **www.tomjames.com**, Custom Clothing—See Chapter 1.

- Liberty Mutual, Marcus Smith, **www.libertymutual.com**, Financial Services—See Chapter 2.

- Mattress Firm, Edith Botello, **www.mattressfirm.com**, Mattress Retailing—See Chapter 3.

- CB Richard Ellis, Susana Rosas, **www.cbre.com**, Commercial Real Estate Services—See Chapter 4.

- *Texas Monthly*, Amy Vandaveer, **www.texasmonthly.com**, Advertising and Sales Promotion—See Chapter 6.

- PulteGroup, Ashley Pineda, **www.pultegroupinc.com**, Home Building—See Chapter 8.

- **Salesforce.com**, Dave Levitt, **www.salesforce.com**, CRM Software—See Chapter 9.

- Hilti Corporation, Alim Hirani, **www.hilti.com**, Construction Products and Services—See Chapter 10.

- Ecolab, Chris Wylie, **www.ecolab.com**, Cleaning and Sanitizing Products and Services—See Chapter 12.

- Marriott International, Heather Ramsey, **www.marriott.com**, Meeting and Convention Services—See Chapter 13.

■ McKesson Pharmaceutical, Jaime Barouh, **www.mckesson.com**, Pharmaceutical Sales—See Chapter 17.

Using the sales information you have learned throughout the book and the sales worksheets presented, prepare to make your sales call.

Reality Selling Role Play 1: Tom James Company

Tom James

Alex Homer

(This mock sales call role-play scenario was created exclusively for use with the *Selling Today: Partnering to Create Value* textbook.)

Your Role at Tom James

You will be a sales representative (professional clothier) for Tom James Company(**www.tomjames.com**), working out of the same office as Alex Homer, featured in the Chapter 1 opening and Reality Selling Video. Tom James specializes in offering complete lines of custom, made-to-measure, and ready-made executive apparel. Clients have the opportunity to create a personality for their wardrobe by selecting from the company's more than 500 suit and 250 shirt fabric options. In addition, the company carries an assortment of accessories such as ties, scarves, belts, and shoes to assist in the completion of the client's wardrobe. In business since 1965, Tom James serves more than 300 000 clients through its 107 offices. Each Tom James client purchases directly from one of the company's professional clothiers, who always come to their clients, as appointments are conducted at the client's location of choice. Refer to the Chapter 1 opening vignette and case problem, and review the Chapter 1 Reality Selling Video for more information.

Your Customer: John Leonard

You are calling on John Leonard, a partner at Leonard & Franklin, a small marketing consulting company. John, who has been in the consulting business for the past 10 years, has built a reputable name for himself and his company after several years of experience with McKinsey & Company. He is a graduate of a prestigious business school, where he graduated with honours. John has a wife and two kids, ages six and eight. John enjoys outdoor activities near Lake Michigan with his family and is a huge fan of the Toronto Blue Jays.

You were referred to John by Mike Kerbanian, who is one of John's former coworkers at McKinsey and one of your repeat customers. Mike had mentioned John's hobbies, his current professional success, and that he runs a very busy consulting firm.

When you called John on the phone, he was extremely busy but mildly receptive. He said that because you came well-referred, he'd be glad to give you 15 minutes as he does not have a lot of time to sacrifice. John expresses that he is very protective of his personal time with his family and, though interested in refreshing his wardrobe, is reluctant to spend time clothes shopping at local boutiques or department stores. You agree to honour his time, and he agrees to the appointment.

Quick Facts about John Leonard's Needs

- In the short phone conversation, John said he is not sure what he might need, but that it has been a while since he last freshened up a suit.

- He wears primarily dark grey, black, and navy—both in solids and stripes. His black solid suit is still in workable condition, though his grey and navy suits have become a little threadbare. He was not sure about the condition of his black and navy pinstripe suits.

- He had mentioned in passing that for the time being, his off-work attire is in good shape, although he has some older shirts and sweaters that could need replacing.

- John typically wears a combination of shirts and either jeans or slacks to the office on casual Fridays, when he is not with a client. When he is with a client, he prefers to wear dark-coloured suits.

Your Call Objectives

You hope to turn John Leonard from a prospect into a first-time customer. This is not an easy job, as John will raise two major objections during the sales call:

- He perceives your price as too expensive and asks you for a 20 percent discount for this first-time purchase of the whole bundle that you offered him.

- He mentions that he once had a suit tailored when he was in Bangkok. When he received it in the mail a few weeks later, he was disappointed. The suit just did not fit him properly, and the cloth did not feel as comfortable as the swatches. So he wonders what his options are if he does not get the quality that he expects.

If his questions are sufficiently answered, he will agree to a sale to try things out.

Reality Selling Role Play 2: Liberty Mutual

Liberty Mutual

Marcus Smith

(This mock sales call role-play scenario was created exclusively for use with the *Selling Today: Partnering to Create Value* textbook.)

Your Role at Liberty

You will be an independent insurance broker for Liberty International Underwriters (**www.libertyiu.com**), working out of the same office as Marcus Smith, featured in the Chapter 2 Reality Selling Video. Liberty International Underwriters is a division of Liberty Mutual Group, a company that operates in both personal and commercial insurance markets. Liberty Mutual's personal insurance products include auto, home, life, and personal liability. In addition, it also offers a wide range of products and services for business. Property insurance, including ocean cargo insurance, represents one of its important lines of business. Liberty International Underwriters was formed in 1999 as a global specialty business with an emphasis on niche insurance products distributed through the independent broker network. (Refer to the Chapter 2 opening vignette and case problem, and review the Chapter 2 Reality Selling Video for more information.)

Your Customer: Farris Footwear Inc.

You will meet with Pat Stanley, the import director at Farris Footwear Inc. Founded in 1980 in Los Angeles, California, this large import–export company serves as a one-stop shop for its customers for a wide variety of footwear, from beach slippers, indoor slippers, sports sandals, sports shoes, and ladies' shoes to cowboy boots. Although its customer base includes retail shoe stores, department stores, and discount stores, the company is shifting its focus to the premium market, where profit margins are higher. Farris Footwear Inc. imports footwear from a number of countries in Asia, Europe, and Latin America. Imports are generally bought under FOB (free on board) shipping point terms of trade, according to which Farris Footwear, rather than the seller, arranges insurance of the goods. Most shipments are made by sea. Monthly imports might reach $1 million during peak seasons. Every two years, Farris Footwear reviews its relationship with its insurance and forwarding agents.

Ocean Cargo Insurance As globalization sweeps across nations, U.S. imports have risen some 40 percent over the past five years. So has the U.S. ocean cargo insurance market.

The basic ocean cargo policy covers perils of the sea (e.g., stranding, sinking, fire, and collision) and perils on the sea (e.g., heavy weather and theft). Other risks such as war and civil commotion might be added to the policy. For shipments that involve multiple modes of transportation, such as a combination of marine transportation and inland transit, additional insurance coverage is required. The client normally signs a contract (called a policy) with an insurance broker, who will then work with insurance company underwriters. Big players in the market are members of the American Institutes of Marine Underwriters (**www.aimu.org**).

The insurance premium (i.e., price) is a function of the sums insured, market conditions, loss experience, and other factors such as risks idiosyncratic to the country of departure. Under an open cargo policy, all goods shipped during the year will be covered, with a maximum amount per shipment.

Quick Facts about Farris Footwear Inc.'s Needs

- Farris Footwear Inc. currently uses two insurance companies: Mandarin Insurance Company for all its imports from Asian countries, and Sasser Insurance Company for its imports from the other countries. Mandarin has been working with Farris for six years, while Sasser signed its contract with Farris two years ago.
- Farris Footwear Inc. receives shipments year round, although peak season is from October to February. The main warehouse is located in its headquarters in California due to its proximity to the port of Long Beach, but it also owns two other transit warehouses in Houston, Texas, and New Jersey.
- Footwear is normally packed in carton boxes, with small sachets of anti-mould chemical, especially for leather shoes.

- Because of the competitive nature of the ocean cargo insurance market, insurance premiums tend to be similar across companies. Farris Footwear Inc. is more interested in value-added services such as shipment tracking, claim resolution, risk management resources, and training.
- Most Farris Footwear Inc. imports are from China, Indonesia, Vietnam, Italy, and Brazil.

Your Call Objectives

In your meeting with Pat Stanley, you hope to identify the decision maker of the insurance agent review process, which will start in a month. You also want to know more about Farris's insurance needs. In addition, you hope to convince Pat that your company can offer outstanding services that go beyond basic ocean cargo insurance.

Reality Selling Role Play 3: Mattress Firm

Mattress Firm
Edith Botello

(This mock sales call role-play scenario was created exclusively for use with the *Selling Today: Partnering to Create Value* textbook.)

Your Role at Mattress Firm

You will be a sales representative for Mattress Firm (**www.mattressfirm.com**), working in the same store as Edith Botello, featured in the Chapter 3 opener and Reality Selling Video. Your company offers sleep solutions, including conventional and specialty mattresses, as well as bedding-related products. Mattress Firm carries the top mattress brands such as Sealy, Stearns & Foster, Tempur-Pedic, Simmons, Serta, Sleep to Live, and more. From the very beginning, the company set out to be a different kind of mattress retailer, focused on creating a unique shopping experience.

One aspect that sets Mattress Firm apart from competition is the buying process. Customers are invited to get fitted for a mattress, just as they do with suits, shoes, and gowns. This is accomplished through the company's so-called Sleep Diagnostic System, which asks the customer a series of questions about their sleep quality and then measures their weight distribution and postural alignment. After this is done, it recommends a type of support and eliminates 80 percent of the beds in the showroom, thus making it simpler for customers to find the right mattress without trying out every single bed. Taking the risk out of buying a mattress by letting the customer know what mattresses are best for them is something that only Mattress Firm offers. (Refer to the Chapter 3 opening vignette, and review the end-of-chapter Reality Selling Video Case for more information.)

Your Customer: Mark Boomershine

Mark and Kelly Boomershine have been married for eight years. They have two kids, Lisa and Marcus, ages three and five. The Boomershines are a typical middle-class family, living in a residential area on the outskirts of a large city. They have an Airedale terrier that Kelly loves and that occupies their bed quite frequently. Mark works as a motor mechanic and Kelly is a hospital nurse who works primarily on night duty. Mark is into sports, but he has had some severe problems with his back recently due to a slipped disk. He went to hospital just a week ago and is now recovering from the surgery at home. For the past couple of days, he has been waking up stiff and hurting. Mark and Kelly have had a relatively inexpensive queen size mattress for six years. They were not planning to replace that mattress, but Mark's back problems have forced them to find a supportive mattress for his recovery as soon as possible. Kelly dislikes sleeping on a firm mattress, which is why their current mattress is fairly soft. However, the couple has doubts that another soft mattress would be the ideal solution for Mark, as friends have been telling them that Mark would need a very firm mattress to support his recovery. Today, Mark enters your store to try out some mattresses that would fit his needs. He needs a supportive mattress quite urgently, but wonders whether he and Kelly might actually need two separate mattresses to fit both of their needs.

Your Call Objectives

In your sales call with Mark Boomershine, you hope to build rapport with him, identify his sleeping needs, and sell him a sleeping solution based on these needs. You have to overcome two major objections raised by Mark: (1) What if his back pain persists over a longer time—even on the new mattress that you recommend? Can he simply exchange the mattress at your store for a new one? (2) Since the mattresses you offer him as a possible solution would mean a fairly high expenditure for the couple, he asks you for a substantial rebate of about 20 percent in case of a purchase. However, the particular mattresses that come into consideration are price regulated (i.e., the contract with the manufacturer dictates that price negotiation is not allowed). If you manage to overcome these objections and present a good solution, Mark would be ready to buy. Since he needs a supportive mattress urgently, Mark would bring Kelly into your store tomorrow to get her blessing and make the final choice among the options under consideration.

Reality Selling Role Play 4: CB Richard Ellis

CB Richard Ellis

Susana Rosas

(This mock sales call role-play scenario was created exclusively for use with the *Selling Today: Partnering to Create Value* textbook.)

Your Role at CB Richard Ellis

You will be a sales representative for CB Richard Ellis (**www.cbre.com**), working out of the same office as Susana Rosas, featured in the Chapter 4 Reality Selling Video. The company offers a variety of premium real estate services, both commercial and industrial. Headquartered in Los Angeles, California, the company has a network of more than 400 branch offices worldwide, with some 30,000 well-trained employees. (Refer to the Chapter 4 opening vignette and case problem and review the Chapter 4 Reality Selling Video for more information.)

Your Customer: Norman Flooring Company

You will meet with Kerry Nelson, the owner of Norman Flooring Company. The company was established in 1996 and specializes in flooring solutions for both residential and industrial markets in Texas. Despite the slowdown of the U.S. economy, Norman Flooring has been enjoying a healthy annual growth rate in revenue of 10 percent in the past few years. In its headquarters in Houston, Texas, the company has two warehouses that are rented on a short term of six months to a year. Each warehouse also has an office where administrative staff control inventory, deliver flooring materials to subcontractors, and handle other clerical issues. The company realizes that with the current growth rate, it will soon see itself constrained by its somewhat limited warehousing facilities. As a result, it is actively looking for larger industrial properties at locations that are not only easily accessible from highways and ports but also close to major developing residential areas.

The Industrial Property Market

Surprisingly, the U.S. industrial property market has not been strongly influenced by the recent U.S. economic slowdown. The three major industrial property markets include distribution hubs, port facilities, and high-tech centres. Last year, rent growth was greatest in the latter two markets, standing at roughly 3 percent, and the lowest in the former market, at about 0.5 percent. The industrial property market is no exception to the supply and demand rule. Net absorption, defined as the balance between increasing demand and new supply, has been very healthy in markets such as Houston, where availability has been falling. Warehousing represents the largest segment of the industrial property sector. About 25 percent of this warehousing segment was new supply. The industrial market outlook is optimistic, with rent growth expected to remain positive over the next few years.

Quick Facts about Norman Flooring Company's Needs

- The company is looking for industrial warehousing facilities that are in very good condition, with little to no deferred maintenance. The area should be at least 16 000 square feet.
- The location should be easily accessible from the Houston port, in an area that is known to be free from flooding risks.
- The initial lease term will be one year, with the possibility of rent-to-own.
- Preferably, the property site should offer available space for expansion.
- The office building is preferably attached to the warehouse.
- The property should have digital surveillance and perimeter fencing with computer-controlled keypad entry access.

Your Call Objectives

In your meeting with Kerry Nelson, you hope to identify the company's warehousing needs. In addition, you hope to convince Kerry that your company can offer outstanding value-added services, such as nationwide property maintenance consulting.

Reality Selling Role Play 5:
Texas Monthly

Amy Vandaveer

(This mock sales call role-play scenario was created exclusively for use with the *Selling Today: Partnering to Create Value* textbook.)

Your Role at *Texas Monthly*

You are a sales representative for *Texas Monthly* magazine (**www.texasmonthly.com**), working out of the same office as Amy Vandaveer, featured in the Chapter 6 Reality Selling Video. Your magazine covers politics, business, and culture, but focuses largely on leisure activities and events in Texas. It has a large real estate advertising section, as well as classified sections in which nearly all advertisers are Texas-based businesses appealing to a prospective buyer who is interested in connecting with Texas history and culture. Through you, your potential customers have access to a large, loyal reader base all over Texas—mostly urban, well educated, and affluent. (Refer to the Chapter 6 opening vignette and case problem and review the Chapter 6 Reality Selling Video for more information.)

Your Customer: Roger Linville Properties

You will meet with Kim Pratt, the marketing director at Roger Linville Properties, a property management company. Kim was referred to you by a family friend, who told you that although Roger Linville Properties has reached most of its residents through simple word-of-mouth publicity, it is now considering increasing its magazine advertising. According to your friend, who met Kim through their daughters' Girl Scout troop, Kim's career began at an advertising agency specializing in real estate, then moved to the client side. In all, Kim has 15 years of experience in the marketing of high-end real estate.

Roger Linville Properties started selling units in its first condo building in 1987 and now has 12 upscale high-rise condo buildings in Houston and Galveston. Each property has a sales manager and a marketing manager, and the individual properties do some advertising controlled by those managers, but Kim is ultimately in control of the company's marketing and advertising strategy.

Your supervisor at *Texas Monthly* has some connections to Roger Linville Properties, and he has been able to tell you more about its current advertising situation. According to him, Roger Linville Properties does the majority of its advertising in magazines available for free in the Houston area. You've seen these glossy magazines in the waiting areas of restaurants and hotels; they cater to an affluent readership with society pages, event news, and ads for upscale products and services. The company also uses some billboards, and individual properties use direct mail and well-publicized open houses to attract prospective residents.

The majority of the Roger Linville buildings are within the city of Houston. You've learned from their website that there are several buildings in the Galleria area, surrounded by luxury shopping and restaurants, and one near the Rice Village shopping arcade in West University. They also have buildings in the downtown theatre district, which has recently become an increasingly popular location for luxury lofts and condos. In Galveston, they have one building in the historic Strand area and several resort-like condos on the beachfront. Judging by the prices and the amenities they offer, such as concierge service and in-building spas, you can tell that their prime market is affluent people looking for a low-maintenance home that they will rarely have to leave. Most of the properties are advertised as second homes, particularly the Galveston condos, which are promoted as the perfect local vacation home.

While on the website, you noticed that the company is currently in the process of building two new properties: one in the River Oaks area, Houston's most exclusive residential neighbourhood, and one in the Woodlands, an affluent master-planned community north of Houston. They will begin preselling units in these two properties in the next few months. In addition, your supervisor has recently heard rumours that Roger Linville has been negotiating to acquire land in the Dallas area, suggesting that the company may be planning expansion there as well.

Your Call Objectives

In your meeting, you hope to convince Kim Pratt that magazine advertising can be more successful than it has been so far, and that *Texas Monthly* is the magazine to use. Hopefully, you will close a deal by the end of the meeting.

Reality Selling Role Play 6: PulteGroup

PulteGroup

Ashley Pineda

(This mock sales call role-play scenario was created exclusively for use with the *Selling Today: Partnering to Create Value* textbook.)

Your Role at PulteGroup

You will be a sales representative for PulteGroup (**www .pultegroup.com**), working in a similar community as Ashley Pineda, featured in the Chapter 8 Reality Selling Video. PulteGroup offers a one-stop shopping experience for prospective customers. Sales reps help clients to finance their homes (with Pulte Mortgage) and to close their homes with PGP Title. Being able to offer everything under one roof and walk the customers through each step of the entire home-buying process makes their home-buying experience very comfortable. PulteGroup offers different product lines: homes for first-time homebuyers, move-up homes, and active adult communities. Just like Ashley Pineda, you will sell the company's Centex product line (see **www.centex.com**), which is primarily geared toward first-time homebuyers. One central purpose of your sales presentations is to educate your prospects on renting versus owning and the benefits of owning a home. You also give prospects information about the neighbourhood, the area, the schools zoned to the neighbourhood, and the amenities of the community, describing the pools and shopping areas in and around the neighbourhood in order to help your customers envision raising their children in one of Pulte's communities. Refer to the Chapter 8 opening vignette and case problem, and review the Chapter 8 Reality Selling Video for more information.

Your Customer: Mary Bartone

Mary Bartone is 37 years old. She is a single mother and has two little kids, Laura and Fred, ages four and two. Mary had been married to Tom Bartone for almost seven years. The first years of their marriage were happy. The Bartones lived in a nice, large apartment in an uptown neighbourhood. They really enjoyed living in this trendy and vibrant part of their city. Both Mary and Tom liked going out to restaurants, cafés, and bars together with their friends, many of whom also lived in or close to the uptown area. In their leisure time, Mary and Tom frequently enjoyed horse riding and going to all kinds of cultural events. Money was never a big issue, since Tom made good money as a design engineer for Honeywell Building Solutions and Mary earned a decent salary as a senior contact representative for the government benefits office. After some years, however, things started to become worse in their relationship, and about one year ago Tom and Mary decided to split up. They went through a painful divorce. After a tedious court battle, custody of the two children was awarded to Mary, with Tom seeing them every other weekend.

For almost a year, Mary and her two kids have been living in a 790-square foot, two-bedroom apartment close to the uptown area, just about three kilometres away from their old apartment, where Tom still lives. Mary feels that the apartment is too small and that the area is not really suited to raising children. Knowing that the apartment would be only an interim solution, Mary has been dreaming about a new home for quite a while.

Quick Facts about Mary Bartone's Needs

- Mary is looking for a house with at least 1200 square feet and three bedrooms.
- Like most parents with young children, Mary is very concerned about her children growing up in a safe and sheltered environment with decent daycare facilities and schools.
- As a single mother who wants to raise her children in the new home, Mary is very much interested in the warranties that PulteGroup can offer as a builder.
- Mary pays great attention to the warmth and feel of a home and having a large backyard for the children to play.
- Mary has bank savings of approximately $60 000. Her annual income (including some alimony) is currently around $55 000. A solid financing solution that is comfortable within her budget is needed.
- Mary is a true family person. Her parents and her younger sister, Susan, who live about 400 kilometres away, come to visit her quite frequently. Before signing a contract for a new home, she will make sure she has her father's blessing.
- Mary is of two minds concerning the location of the house. On the one hand, she knows that having more square footage and a large backyard would require her to move farther out of the city. On the other hand, she does not want to move too far away from the uptown area where her office is located and where Tom and many of her friends live.

Your Call Objectives

In your meeting with Mary, you hope to build rapport with her and identify her needs and requirements for owning a home. You also hope to convince Mary that you can offer her an excellent home in which to raise her children.

Reality Selling Role Play 7: Salesforce.Com

Salesforce.com

Dave Levitt

(This mock sales call role-play scenario was created exclusively for use with the *Selling Today: Partnering to Create Value* textbook.)

Your Role at Salesforce.com

You are a sales representative for **Salesforce.com** (**www.salesforce.com**), just like Dave Levitt in the Chapter 9 Case Problem. Your company is the world leader in on-demand customer relationship management (CRM) services. Unlike most CRM applications, companies that use your services store customer and sales data on **Salesforce.com**. One of the benefits of on-demand CRM services is that customers incur neither up-front capital investment nor on-site administration costs. Your company also offers solutions that are customized to specific customer needs, such as creating different interfaces for different departments and work groups, and providing limited access to data for specific authorized work groups.

Your Customer: Rename Clothing Company

You will meet with Jesse Golden, the marketing director at Rename Clothing Company. A family-owned business in Garden Grove, California, the company is expanding at a fast pace not only in the United States, but also in Latin American markets that the company entered into two years ago. The company currently has a sales force of 20 people and outsources its selling activities for overseas operations to local firms. Each salesperson is responsible for three to four customers. While outsourcing has the advantages of capitalizing on market knowledge of local partners, the company realized it does not have full control over its selling efforts. Domestically, the company has strong relationships with its buyers, but there have been signs of work overload among the sales force. While Rename has three in-house brands that it distributes using its own channel, it does provide sourcing solutions to mid-range and high-end department stores under their private labels. Rename works closely with its suppliers in more than five countries, mainly in Europe and Asia. It also has a small manufacturing facility in California for sample development and small-batch order production.

Quick Facts about Rename Clothing Company's Needs The apparel industry is a sophisticated, fast-moving industry with several designs launched every season, and repeat orders must be met as fast as possible before end-users change their tastes. As a company that operates in mid-range to high end markets, Rename positions itself as a sourcing company with a fast turnaround for its customers. The nature of the industry requires salespeople to be highly diligent in market information gathering, processing, and dissemination across geographic areas and departments.

At present, the in-house salespeople use spreadsheets for almost all of their selling activities, such as recording sales calls, reporting to sales managers, and tracking delivery of orders, to name just a few. Jesse joined the company two months ago and realized that the current system showed clear signs of overload. Mistakes have started to occur more often, and the company has received quite a few complaints about shipment delays, wrong labelling on products, and wrong packaging. As marketing director, Jesse spent several days making sense of disparate information about Rename's domestic sales and has heard mixed reports about its overseas operation. Jesse's secretary lamented that the spreadsheets provided by the sales force are not in a uniform format, making it difficult to consolidate the database. Meanwhile, salespeople claim that their customers are not all the same and they need to customize their spreadsheets so that they can keep track of things more easily.

With high pressure for growth, Rename is looking for an efficient way to consolidate and manage its customer database. Jesse is also in the process of establishing a branch office in Mexico and will staff three local salespeople to manage Rename's business in this growing market. In overseas markets, the focus is more on customer acquisition and lead management, while in domestic markets, Jesse is more concerned with keeping Rename's existing customers happy.

Your Call Objectives

In your meeting with Jesse Golden, you hope to convince him that **Salesforce.com** is the right CRM solution for Rename. You can do this by providing him with interesting facts and benefits **Salesforce.com** can offer (see more information at **www.salesforce.com**). Hopefully, you will close a deal by the end of the meeting.

Reality Selling Role Play 8: Hilti Corporation

Hilti Corporation

Alim Hirani

(This mock sales call role-play scenario was created exclusively for use with the *Selling Today: Partnering to Create Value* textbook.)

You will be a sales representative for Hilti (**www.hilti. com**), working out of the same office as Alim Hirani, featured in the Chapter 10 Reality Selling Video. The company provides the global construction industry with innovative products and services. In addition to a wide variety of high-end products such as measuring systems, drilling and demolition, installation systems, foam systems, and screw fastening systems, the company also offers its customers customized training programs and consulting services. Hilti sales representatives work directly with customers rather than through intermediary parties. (Refer to the Chapter 10 opening vignette and case problem, and review the Chapter 10 Reality Selling Video for more information.)

Your Customer: Ellis Exhibition Inc.

You will meet with Casey Smith, procurement manager for Ellis Exhibition Inc. The company owns a 100 000-square-foot exhibition centre that hosts several local and regional events in Atlanta, Georgia. Some of these events have become a must-see for the local business community. Depending on the theme and the products being showcased, Ellis Exhibition offers exhibitors outstanding display services that include floor plans, display solutions, display installation, and booth dismantlement. After an event, the installation systems are reused, while installation accessories are generally discarded. Casey Smith believes that by buying the right type of installation accessories, Ellis can save a lot of money and therefore offer its exhibitor customers more competitive prices.

Quick Facts about Ellis Exhibition Inc.'s Needs

- Ellis Exhibition Inc. spends about $500 000 a year on installation accessories. These accessories are galvanized, but they can also be painted to match the colour theme stipulated by exhibitors.
- Ellis uses a wide variety of installation accessories, from hexagon nuts and head screws to distance holders.
- Ellis does not want to stock these accessories. Exhibitors who want to use Ellis display services are required to place their order three months in advance. Then, an Ellis accountant will calculate the necessary accessories needed for each event.
- Ellis is extremely concerned with the quality of all of its installation systems and accessories.

Your Call Objectives

In your meeting with Casey Smith, you hope to identify the specific types and the expected quantity of installation accessories. You also want to know about delivery requirements. In addition, you might be able to cross-sell other Hilti products and services, such as sprinkler systems.

Reality Selling Role Play 9: Ecolab

Ecolab
Chris Wylie

(This mock sales call role-play scenario was created exclusively for use with the *Selling Today: Partnering to Create Value* textbook.)

Your Role at Ecolab

You are a sales representative for Ecolab (**www.ecolab. com**), working in a similar territory as Chris Wylie, featured in the Chapter 12 Case Problem. With sales of $6 billion and more than 26 000 associates, your company is the global leader in cleaning, sanitizing, food safety, and infection prevention products and services. Ecolab delivers comprehensive programs and services to foodservice, food and beverage processing, healthcare, and hospitality markets in more than 160 countries. You work in the Institutional Business Unit, which is the core of Ecolab—and the world leader in providing cleaning and sanitation products, programs, and services to customers in a variety of industries. Specifically, you serve the foodservice market, calling on restaurants, cafeterias, etc. Today, you will try to get access to the kitchen facilities of one of the largest prospects in your territory, Angelo's Restaurant.

Your Customer: Francesco Manchini, Owner of Angelo's Restaurant

The owner of the restaurant is Francesco Manchini (known as Frankie by his restaurant friends and patrons). Angelo's is located south of downtown Vancouver in a trendy neighbourhood. Manchini had a great deal of insight into the potential of this area and now has three restaurants located within a three-block radius. His other two restaurants are Pasta e Basta and LaTorre. Based on some initial inspection and speculation, you can assume that each of these restaurants is probably worth $10 000. Angelo's currently uses Swisher, a North American competitor. Swisher was started back in 1986 with the conviction that business people would welcome the opportunity to have their facilities maintained by a true hygiene specialist. You are familiar with the competition and are aware of Swisher's strategy. Typically, they gain the bathroom hygiene business and then look for opportunities in the back of the house. This is exactly what happened at Angelo's. Francesco Manchini has three primary concerns that reflect his problems with Swisher. First, product performance is not to his standards. The Swisher Program is not getting the dishes clean, and spotty dishes are unacceptable for fine dining. Second, the people at Swisher know a lot about bathroom care and maintenance, but they lack a great deal of experience and knowledge about back-of-the-house operations. Third, product service is lacking. Swisher was always front-and-centre when they were trying to get the business, but now they never show up and seldom return service calls in a timely manner.

Francesco has an expressive personality style. He is talkative and very low on self-monitoring. He is a very emotional person and quick to get red-faced when someone angers him or slap them on the back when they please him. He never leaves a conversation without getting in the last word and saying whatever he feels. He is quick to tell someone that they are wrong, particularly salespeople, if he thinks they are giving him a load of garbage. Francesco acknowledges that Swisher's bathroom hygiene services are good, but the decision to move them in the back of the house may not have been such a great idea. He is quick to tell everyone within earshot why he is unhappy with Swisher. Even though there are some problems, he is not sure what the solution is.

You have a 9:30 a.m. meeting scheduled and realize that you probably have about 20 minutes before the lunch push begins to happen.

Quick Facts about Francesco Manchini's Needs Thanks to the approval by Francesco's executive chef, Nino Trappatoni, you have already completed a survey of the kitchen prior to your initial meeting with Francesco Manchini. You uncovered several areas of concern and issues that can be leveraged as opportunities. These may be latent, and the prospect may not realize that there are problems or potential problems.

- Floors are covered in grease by the fryer. Floors are slippery and there are no mats or protective coverings in place.
- Limited drying racks. Dishes stacked on top of each other, including glasses.
- Poor results. Food soil left on dishes was found by doing a Mikroklene test.
- Some dishes on the racks are spotty and covered with soap residue.

- There are no safety devices or equipment, such as eye wash stations, first-aid, etc.
- No product dispensers are in place. It looks as if everything is being poured or sprayed from a bottle.

Your Call Objectives

Since this is your first meeting with Francesco Manchini, you have to introduce yourself and Ecolab to him and try to build rapport. Based on the survey of the kitchen, you then try to convince Francesco to buy from you. To that end, you will have to overcome his objections:

- "We used Ecolab at one of our other properties a few years back. The service was terrible."
- "I am sure that if I sign up with Ecolab, you will forget about me once I commit to the change. What guarantees do I have that you will be there when I need you?"
- "I heard that Ecolab uses more soap than necessary to inflate their sales and rip off the customer."
- "We cannot afford downtime. I am sure that switching over to Ecolab would put the kitchen out of commission for too long. We can't afford to shut our kitchen down to make the change to Ecolab."

Reality Selling Role Play 10: Marriott International, Inc.

Marriott International Inc.

Heather Ramsey

(This mock sales call role-play scenario was created exclusively for use with the *Selling Today: Partnering to Create Value* textbook.)

Your Role at Marriott

You will be a sales representative for Marriott International Inc. (**www.marriott.com**), working out of the same hotel as Heather Ramsey, featured in the Chapter 13 Reality Selling Video. Founded in 1927 by J. Willard and Alice S. Marriott, Marriott has grown from a root beer stand to a multinational company with more than 3000 lodging properties located in some 70 countries around the world. Apart from luxurious hotel accommodation under several well-managed brands, the company also offers outstanding services for meetings and events. From weddings to corporate meetings, Marriott's clients know that they are always in good hands. (Refer to the Chapter 13 opening vignette and case problem, and review the Chapter 13 Reality Selling Video for more information.)

Your Customer: Hiroshi Watanabe/Chris Scott

You will meet with Chris Scott, personal secretary to Mr. Hiroshi Watanabe, owner of a chain of high-end tailor stores in California. Mr. Watanabe and his wife were married 25 years ago in a simple wedding ceremony. The couple immigrated to the United States with only five dollars between them. They worked very hard to make ends meet, and their fate took a turn when both were hired full-time for the first time by a small tailor shop—Mr. Watanabe as a deliveryman and his wife as a helper.

With strong entrepreneurial spirit and incessant learning, they soon opened their own business using their meagre savings. Initial clients were mainly friends, but they soon found a niche in the market by combining traditional Japanese garment making with American contemporary fashion. Before they knew it, celebrities started knocking on their door, asking for custom-made evening gowns and suits. A couple of years later, they opened their first concept store under the name Watanabe and positioned it as a high-end custom-made tailor house. They also provided customers with a full range of custom-designed accessories.

Their two sons soon joined the team, managing stores and franchisees in prime locations in Los Angeles and San Francisco, California. As their silver wedding anniversary is approaching, Mr. Watanabe asks Chris to organize something very special for his wife to make up for the years of hard work the couple has been through.

Event Planning

More information on event planning is available at **www.marriott.com**. You should also be able to get more information on anniversary party ideas from the Internet.

Quick Facts about the Clients' Needs

- The anniversary has to be formal as many celebrities will be invited.
- The menu has to be as bountiful and sumptuous as possible.
- Costs are not a major concern. However, Chris should be shopping for the best offer.
- Chris is in charge of information gathering and screens offers from three major hotels. Chris already has an offer from a Marriott competitor.
- The goal is not only to impress the guests but also Mrs. Watanabe.
- The highlight of the anniversary is a recount of the couple's happy marriage.

Your Call Objectives

In your meeting with Chris Scott, you hope to identify Mr. Watanabe's needs. In addition, you hope to convince him that you provide the best event planning services, which your competitor cannot offer. In doing so, you should be prepared to offer Chris a number of creative ideas to make the event both formal and memorable.

Reality Selling Role Play 11: Pharma Supply

McKesson Pharmaceutical

Jaime Barouh

(This mock sales call role-play scenario was created exclusively for use with the *Selling Today: Partnering to Create Value* textbook.)

Your Role at Pharma Supply

You will be a pharmaceutical sales representative for Pharma Supply, a respected pharmaceutical wholesaler that sells medical supplies and drugs to medical clinics, hospitals, and other health care institutions, and to retail pharmacies, including many small independent retail pharmacies, large pharmacy chains, and pharmacies that are part of large retail operations such as Walmart, Costco, and various supermarket chains. Your company has recently signed an agreement to represent a generic drug manufacturer. You will be introducing a new generic antidepressant drug, fluoxetine (see websites at **www.drugs.com/fluoxetine** and **www.fluoxetine.com**), for Pharma Supply. Competing branded drugs include Eli Lilly's Prozac (see **www.lilly.ca**).

You will start by contacting walk-in clinics and multi-doctor family health practices to get acceptance of your generic drug so that doctors will be comfortable writing prescriptions for a generic alternative. (Refer to the Chapter 17 opening vignette and review the Chapter 17 Reality Selling Video for more information on the nature of a respected pharmaceutical wholesaler. McKesson Pharmaceutical (**www.mckesson.com**), the featured company in the Chapter 17 Reality Selling Video, is a wholesale pharmaceutical distribution business similar to Pharma Supply.)

Your Customer: Family Health Services Clinic

Family Health Services is a downtown clinic. Many of its regular patients live in the immediate area and would be described as lower- to lower-middle income patients. You will meet with Payton Diaz, the clinic manager. Payton has been recently hired at this clinic, but you have met him a number of times previously at another clinic. You would describe Payton as a Supportive (see Chapter 5). Payton always seems quiet and polite, and although you have a friendly relationship, you believe Payton would have a friendly relationship with all salespeople.

Family Health Services has four doctors and two registered nurses:

- Dr. Tom Brown is 36 years old and has been at the clinic for less than a year. He is one of two doctors and begins work at 8:00 a.m. He works each day until 5:00 p.m., but stays on Monday nights until the clinic closes at 8:00 p.m.

- Dr. Lu Bingyu is a bit younger than Tom. She works the same hours as Tom but works late on Friday rather than Monday evenings.

- Dr. Tony Bander is the senior doctor at the clinic and is likely to retire within the next five years. He visits hospital patients each morning and seldom gets to the clinic before noon. He works until 8:00 p.m. Tuesday through Thursday.

- Dr. Jane Blenko works each day from noon until 8:00 p.m. Jane's husband is a doctor at one of the local hospitals.

- Nurse Connie Small comes to the clinic each morning when it opens and works until 5:00 p.m. Ben Brothers, the second nurse, comes to work at noon and works each night until 8:00 p.m.

Quick Facts about Selling to Health Clinics and Medical Practices

- Doctors usually resist seeing salespeople and, when they do, the average duration of a sales call is limited to just one or two minutes.

- Doctors will sometimes meet with salespeople in a group situation, but only when there are very important reasons to do so. Even then, it is common to arrange somewhat of a social meeting as well—perhaps lunch or a small catered meal.

- A typical sales call by a pharmaceutical wholesaler salesperson to a health clinic would normally involve talking to the clinic manager to check inventory, take orders, and ensure that there are no service issues or other problems. Rarely would a wholesaler salesperson have to see the medical practitioners.

- When drugs are involved, the amount of product knowledge required is usually beyond what a wholesaler salesperson would be expected to have, so a product specialist would also be involved in the sales call. When such calls are made, it is important to get to see as many members of the medical staff as possible during a single sales call. This requires working with the clinic manager to coordinate a meeting when everyone can attend.

- Doctors are sometimes reluctant to prescribe generic drugs unless they are certain the drug will be as effective as its branded competitor, even though the cost for a generic alternative can be half the cost of a known brand. However, for patients who must pay for their own prescriptions, doctors will often consider prescribing generic drugs.

Your Call Objectives

During your initial contact, you have developed three call objectives. The first is to re-establish your relationship with Payton. The second is to establish who would be the important people at the clinic who should attend a meeting. Your third objective is to arrange a meeting with the clinic staff, within approximately two weeks, so that the product expert who will accompany you on the subsequent sales call can make a presentation and answer questions for attendees. Your product expert is a well known medical researcher and is widely published in medical journals on the efficacy of the generic anti-depressant you distribute.

You are concerned that Payton has been employed with this clinic for only a short time. Payton may not be comfortable trying to arrange a meeting on your behalf unless you can be convincing that the meeting will be worth everyone's time.

Endnotes

Chapter 1

1. www.salesleadershipalliance.co.uk/sla-community-blog/ interviewneil-rackham-the-original-spin-doctor/ (accessed February 14, 2013).

2. Adapted from Daniel H. Pink, *To Sell Is Human: The Surprising Truth about Moving Others*, (New York, NY: Penguin Group, 2012), pp. 16–19.

3. Michael R. Solomon, Greg W. Marshall, and Elnora W. Stuart, *Marketing: Real People, Real Choices*, 7th ed. (Upper Saddle River, NJ: Prentice Hall, 2012), p. 427.

4. Christian Homburg, Jan Wieseke, and Torsten Bornemann, "Implementing the Marketing Concept at the Employee-Customer Interface: The Role of Customer Need Knowledge," *Journal of Marketing*, July 2009, pp. 64–81.

5. Lucy McCauley, "Voices: The State of the New Economy," *Fast Company*, September 1999, p. 124.

6. Robert H. Bloom, "Looking around the Corner," *Salesforceexp*, November/December 2010, p. 21.

7. Stan Davis and Christopher Meyer, *Blur: The Speed of Change in the Connected Economy* (New York: Addison-Wesley, 1998), p. 9.

8. David Shenk, *Data Smog: Surviving the Information Glut* (New York, NY: HarperEdge, 1997), pp. 27–29.

9. Michael R. Solomon, Greg W. Marshall, and Elnora W. Stuart, *Marketing: Real People, Real Choices*, 7th ed. (Upper Saddle River, NJ: Prentice Hall, 2012), p. 429.

10. Liz C. Wang, Julie Baker, Judy A. Wagner, and Kirk Wakefield (2007), "Can a Retail Web Site Be Social?" *Journal of Marketing*, Vol. 71, pp. 143–157.

11. Gary L. Frankwick, Stephen S. Porter, and Lawrence A. Crosby, "Dynamics of Relationship Selling: A Longitudinal Examination of Changes in Salesperson–Customer Relationship Status," *Journal of Personal Selling and Sales Management*, Spring 2001, p. 135.

12. Greg Ip, "Why High-Fliers, Built on Big Ideas, Are Such Fast Fallers," *Wall Street Journal*, April 4, 2002, p. A–1.

13. Würth Canada, www.wurthcanada.com; BlueSky Personnel Solution, www.blueskypersonnel.com (both accessed March 17, 2014).

14. "The 500 Largest Sales Forces in America," *Selling Power*, October 2009, pp. 58–60.

15. Allison Linn, "Sales Reps, Teachers among Most in Demand," www.msnbc.msn.com/id/17858379 (accessed March 17, 2014).

16. Gabrielle Birkner, "Who Says Titles Don't Matter?" *Sales & Marketing Management*, July 2001, p. 14.

17. "America's Best-Paying Jobs," www.forbes.com/2009/05/04/ america-best-paying-leadership-careersjobs-slide.html (accessed June 23, 2013).

18. "Top-Paying Jobs," http://jobs.aol.com/articles/2009/12/10/ top-paying-jobs (accessed March 17, 2014).

19. Thomas Steenburgh and Michael Ahearne, "Motivating Salespeople: What Really Works," *Harvard Business Review*, July–August 2012, p. 71.

20. Christine Galea, "The 2004 Compensation Survey," *Sales & Marketing Management*, May 2004, pp. 28–34.

21. Michele Marchetti, "What a Sales Call Costs," *Sales & Marketing Management*, September 2000, pp. 80–81.

22. Theodore B. Kinni, "Fast Track to the Top: How to Start Out in Sales and End Up as CEO," *Selling Power*, July/ August, 2007, pp. 56–61.

23. "Women in the Labor Force: A Databook (2009 Edition)," www.bls.gov/cps/wlftable10.htm (accessed June 23, 2013).

24. "Top 20 Best-Paying Jobs for Women In 2012," www.forbes .com/pictures/lmj45jmhi/no-19-marketing-and-sales-manag-ers (accessed March 17, 2014).

25. Carol Hymowitz, "Women Put Noses to the Grindstone, and Miss Opportunities," *Wall Street Journal*, February 3, 2004, p. B1.

26. Bonnie Harris, "Wanted: Women in Finance, Why: Client Base Changing," *The Des Moines Register*, Monday, January 29, 2007, p. 4D.

27. Brett A. Boyle, "The Importance of the Industrial Inside Sales Force: A Case Study," *Industrial Marketing Management*, September 1996, p. 339.

28. David L. Kurtz, H. F. (Herb) MacKenzie, and Kim Snow, *Contemporary Marketing*, 3rd Canadian edition. (Scarborough, ON: Nelson Education, 2013).

29. Personal interview with Nadia Gelmo, Heart of Niagara, March 7, 2014.

30. Canadian Bankers Association, "Your Guide to Financial Services," www.cba.ca/eng/Tools/Brochures/tools_finan-cialservices2.htm (accessed April 18, 2002).

31. The Canadian Real Estate Association, http://creastats .crea.ca/natl/index.htm, January 15, 2014.

32. Pearl Paul, personal interview and correspondence, July 29, 2008.

33. Megan Harman, "Survey Finds Canadians Prefer to Buy Life Insurance Face-to-Face," www.investment executive .com, October 2, 2013 (accessed March 17, 2014).

34. Gerald L. Manning and Barry L. Reece, Intelecom Video Library, *Selling Today*, 9th ed.

35. Ibid.

36. Chris Mckee, personal interview, July 28, 2008; The Hitch house, www.thehitchhouse.com (accessed March 17, 2014).

37. Stoney Creek Furniture, "Home Furnishings Industry To Salute Stoney Creek Furniture National Home Furnishings Association North American Retailer of the Year 2010", www.stoneycreekfurniture.com/current/retailer_of_the_ year.aspx (accessed May 9, 2011).

38. www.igniteyourvision.net/files/DSN_USA_TOP_10.pdf (accessed March 13, 2013).

39. Direct Sellers Association of Canada, www.dsa.ca (accessed March 17, 2014).

40. John R. Sparks and Joseph A. Schenk, "Socialization Communication, Organizational Citizenship Behaviors, and Sales in a Multilevel Marketing Organization," *Journal of Personal Selling and Sales Management*, Spring 2006, pp. 161–80.

41. John Naisbitt, *Megatrends* (New York, NY: Warner Books, 1982), p. 18.

42. Adapted from Daniel H. Pink, *To Sell Is Human: The Surprising Truth about Moving Others* (New York, NY: Penguin Group, 2012), p. 21.

43. Stanley Marcus, "Sales School," *Fast Company*, November 1998, p. 105.

44. Thomas A. Stewart, "Knowledge, the Appreciating Commodity," *Fortune*, October 12, 1998, p. 18.

45. Martin Gargiulo, Gokhan Ertug, and Charles Galunic (2009), "The Two Faces of Control: Network Closure and Individual Performance Among Knowledge Workers," *Administrative Science Quarterly*, Vol. 54, pp. 299–333.

46. Sudheer Gupta (2008), "Channel Structure with Knowledge Spillover," *Marketing Science*, Vol. 27(2), pp. 247–61.

47. Dennis Jenkins, "Entrepreneurial Endeavors for Sales & Marketing Professionals," *American Salesman*, August 2007.

48. Beth Belton, "Technology Is Changing Face of U.S. Sales Force," *USA Today*, February 9, 1999, p. A2.

49. Brian Tracy, *The 100 Absolutely Unbreakable Laws of Business Success* (San Francisco: Berrett-Koehler Publishers, Inc., 2000), p. 192.

50. Linda Corman, "Look Who's Selling Now," *Selling*, July–August 1996, pp. 46–53; "Everyone's a Seller," *Sales & Marketing Management*, March 2003, p. 12.

51. Gerry Khermouch, "Keeping the Froth on Sam Adams," *BusinessWeek*, September 1, 2003, pp. 54–56.

52. Simon J. Bell, Seigyoung Auh, and Karen Smalley (2005), "Customer Relationship Dynamics: Service Quality and Customer Loyalty in the Context of Varying Levels of Customer Expertise and Switching Costs," *Journal of the Academy of Marketing Science*, Vol. 33(2), pp. 169–83.

53. Harry Beckwith, *Selling the Invisible* (New York, NY: Warner Books, 1997), p. 38; see Norm Brodsky, "Street Smarts," *Inc.*, June 2004, pp. 53–54.

54. Alfred M. Pelham and Pamela Kravitz (2008), "An Exploratory Study of the Influence of Sales Training Content and Salesperson Evaluation on Salesperson Adaptive Selling, Customer Orientation, Listening, and Consulting Behaviors," *Journal of Strategic Marketing*, Vol. 16(5), pp. 413–35.

55. Heather Johnson, "Field of Sales," *Training*, July 2004, p. 34.

56. Gerhard Gschwandtner, "Rendezvous with a Rainmaker," *Selling Power*, May 2001, pp. 98–100.

57. Kristine Ellis, "Deal Maker or Breaker?" *Training*, April 2002, pp. 34–7; Michele Marchetti, "Sales Training Even a Rep Could Love," *Sales & Marketing Management*, June 1998, p. 70.

58. Henry Canaday, "In the Trenches," *Selling Power*, March 2007, pp. 25–7.

Sources for Boxed Features

a. Michael Hammer, *The Agenda* (New York, NY: Random House, 2001), p. 6.

b. CBC News, "A Criminal Mind: The Life and Times of Eddie Greenspan," aired January 20, 2005, www.cbc.ca/lifeandtimes/greenspan.html (accessed June 13, 2005); "My Greatest Sale," Eddie Greenspan, interviewed by Laura Pratt, *Profit*, May 2005, p. 36.

c. Gene Koretz, "Women Swell the Workforce," *BusinessWeek*, November 4, 1996, p. 32; Naomi Freundlich, "Maybe Working Women Can't Have It All," *BusinessWeek*, September 15, 1997, pp. 19–22; Keith H. Hammonds, "She Works Hard for the Money," *BusinessWeek*, May 22, 1995, p. 54; Anne Fisher, "Overseas, U.S. Businesswomen May Have the Edge," *Fortune*, September 28, 1998, p. 304; Carol Hymowitz, "Women Put Noses to the Grindstone, and Miss Opportunities," *Wall Street Journal*, February 3, 2004, p. B1.

d. Based on John F. Tanner and George Dudley, "How U.S. Salespeople Differ from Their Peers Overseas," *Value-Added Selling*, February 14, 2005, p. 4.

e. The Jim Pattison Group, www.jimpattison.com (accessed January 4, 2011); Government of British Columbia, Protocol and Events Branch, "Jim Pattison—Vancouver," www.protocol.gov.bc.ca/protocol/prgs/obc/1990/1990_JPattison.htm (accessed February 7, 2010); Diane Francis, "What Makes Jim Pattison Run—and Whistle," *Financial Post*, March 5–7, 1994, p. S3.

Chapter 2

1. For a comprehensive description of the distinct stages in the evolution of personal selling, see Thomas R. Wotruba, "The Evolutionary Process of Personal Selling," *Journal of Personal Selling and Sales Management*, Summer 1991, p. 4.

2. Phillip Kotler and Gary Armstrong, *Principles of Marketing*, 15th ed., (Upper Saddle River, NJ: Prentice Hall, 2013), p. 10.

3. Louis E. Boone and David L. Kurtz, *Contemporary Marketing*, 15th ed. (Mason, OH: Southwestern Publishing, 2012), p. 11.

4. Norihiko Shirouzu, Gregory L. White, and Joseph B. White, "Beyond Explorer Woes, Ford Misses Key Turns in Buyers, Technology," *Wall Street Journal*, January 14, 2002, p. A–1.

5. Jeff Bennett, "Ford Expects Auto Industry Sales Pace to Continue," *Wall Street Journal Online*, May 2010, online.wsj.com (accessed March 7, 2013).

6. Malcolm Fleschner, "World Wide Winner—The UPS Story," *Selling Power*, November/December 2001, p. 58; "50 Best Companies to Sell For," *Selling Power*, November/December 2004, pp. 94–5.

7. "America's 25 Best Sales Forces," *Sales & Marketing Management*, July 2000, p. 59; "The 25 Best Service Companies to Sell For," *Selling Power*, November/December 2004, p. 95.

8. Philip Kotler and Kevin Lane Keller, *Marketing Management*, 14th ed. (Upper Saddle River, NJ: Prentice Hall, 2012), pp. 25–26.

9. Andris A. Zoltners and Prabhakant Sinha, "Sales Territory Design: Thirty Years of Modeling and Implementation," *Marketing Science*, vol. 24, no. 3 (Summer, 2005), pp. 313–31.

10. Robert M. Peterson, George H. Lucas, and Patrick L. Schul, "Forming Consultative Trade Alliances: Walking the Walk in the New Selling Environment," *NAMA Journal*, Spring 1998, p. 11; Beth Belton, "Technology Is Changing Face of U.S. Sales Force," *USA Today*, February 9, 1999, p. 2A.

11. Charles Gottenkieny, "Proper Training Can Result in Positive ROI," *Selling*, August 2003, p. 9.

12. Tim Smith, "Between Solution and Transactional Selling," www.wiglafjournal/selling (accessed March 7, 2013).

13. Thomas R. Wotruba, "The Evolutionary Process in Personal Selling," *Journal of Personal Selling & Sales Management*, Summer 1991, p. 4.

14. Christian Homburg, Nicole Koschate, and Wayne D. Hoyer, "Do Satisfied Customers Really Pay More? A Study of he Relationship between Customer Satisfaction and Willingness to Pay More," *Journal of Marketing*, April 2005, pp. 84–96.

15. Michael R. Solomon, Greg W. Marshall, Elnora W. Stuart, *Marketing—Real People, Real Choices*, 7th ed. (Upper Saddle River: New Jersey, Prentice Hall, 2012), p. 35.

16. Robert E. Miller and Stephen E. Heiman, *Strategic Selling* (New York, NY: Warren Books, 1985), p. 26.

17. Jack Snader, "Is It Consultative Selling or Detailing?" *Newspost*, Fall 1999, pp. 21–32; Patricia Seybold, *The Customer Revolution* (New York, NY: Random House, 2001), p. 1.

18. Fernando Jaramillo, William B. Locander, Paul E. Spector, and Eric G. Harris, "Getting the Job Done: The Moderating Role of Initiative on the Relationship between Intrinsic Motivation and Adaptive Selling," *Journal of Personal Selling & Sales Management*, Winter 2007, pp. 59–74.

19. Keith M. Eades, *The New Solutions Selling* (New York, NY: McGraw-Hill, 2004), pp. 9–10.

20. Marvin A. Jolson, "Broadening the Scope of Relationship Selling," *Journal of Personal Selling & Sales Management*, Fall 1997, p. 77.

21. Keith M. Eades, *The New Solutions Selling*, ibid., pp. 102–04.

22. Excerpt from *The Customer Revolution* by Patricia B. Seybold. Published by Crown Business, © 2001.

23. Christian Homberg, Jan Wieseke, and Torsten Bornemann, "Implementing the Marketing Concept at the Employee-Customer Interface: The Role of Customer Need-Knowledge," *Journal of Marketing*, July 2009, pp. 64–81.

24. Jagdish Sheth and Reshma H. Shah, "Till Death Do us Part. .. But Not Always: Six Antecedents to a Customer's Relational Preference in Buyer–Seller Exchanges," *Industrial Marketing Management*, June 2003, pp. 627–31.

25. Erin Strout, "Fast Forward," *Sales & Marketing Management*, December 2001, pp. 37–38.

26. Geoffrey Brewer, "The Customer Stops Here," *Sales & Marketing Management*, March 1998, pp. 31–32.

27. Gary Armstrong and Philip Kotler, *Marketing—An Introduction*, 11th ed. (Upper Saddle River, NJ: Prentice Hall, 2012), p. 23.

28. Personal Interview, Alex Pettes, president of TFI Food Equipment Solutions, February 22, 2014.

29. Lorrie Grant, "Radio Shack Uses Strategic Alliances to Spark Recovery," *USA Today*, January 26, 2001, p. 3–B.

30. See Cy Charney, "Choose Your Partners," *Value-Added Selling 21*, December 16, 2003, p. 3.

31. For a discussion of strategic selling alliances that involves the sales representatives from two or more organizations, see J. Brock Smith and Donald W. Barclay, "Selling Partner Relationships: The Role of Interdependence and Relative Influences," *Journal of Personal Selling & Sales Management*, Fall 1999, pp. 21–40.

32. www.strategicaccounts.org/ (accessed March 7, 2013).

33. Gary Armstrong and Philip Kotler, *Marketing: An Introduction*, 11th ed., ibid., p. 16.

34. Michael Hammer, *The Agenda* (New York, NY: Random House, 2001), pp. 38–39.

Sources for Boxed Features

a. Erin Anderson and Leonard Lodish (2006), "Leading the effective sales force: the Asian sales force management environment," working paper, pp. 7–8.

b. Tim Smith, "Sales vs. Marketing: Vive la difference," April 2008, www.wiglafjournal/selling (accessed March 7, 2013); Philip Kotler, Neil Rackham, and Suj Krishnaswamy, "Ending the War Between Sales & Marketing," *Harvard Business Review*, July/August 2006, pp. 68–78.; Dave Stein, "Sales and Marketing Alignment, Take 2," *Sales & Marketing Management*, January/February 2007, p. 9; Ken Le Meunier-FitzHugh and Nigel F. Piercy, "Does Collaboration between Sales and Marketing Affect Business Performance?" *Journal of Personal Selling and Sales Management*, 27(3), pp. 207–220.

c. Based on Robert Kreitner, *Management*, 8th ed. (Boston, MA: Houghton Mifflin, 2001), pp. 3–4.

d. Daniel H. Pink, "A Radical Prescription for Sales", *Harvard Business Review*, July-August 2012, p. 77; Brent Adamson, Mathew E. Dixon, and Nicholas Toman, "The End of Solution Sales," *Harvard Business Review*, July August 2012, p. 67.

Chapter 3

1. Daniel Goleman, *Working with Emotional Intelligence* (New York, NY: Bantam Books, 1998), pp. 24–28, 317; Geoffrey James, "Use Emotional Intelligence to Improve Sales," *Selling Power*, January/February 2005, pp. 43–45.

2. Daniel Goleman, *Emotional Intelligence* (New York, NY: Bantam Books, 1995), p. 34; Cary Cherniss and Daniel Goleman (eds.), *The Emotionally Intelligent Workplace*, (San Francisco, CA: Jossey-Bass, 2001), pp. 22–24. For more information on social *competence*, see Daniel Goleman, *Working With Emotional Intelligence* (New York, NY: Bantam Dell, 2006), pp. 22–28.

3. L. B. Gschwandtner and Gerhard Gschwandtner, "Balancing Act," *Selling Power*, June 1996, p. 24.

4. "The World Is Flat: A Brief History of the Twenty-First Century," www.thomaslfriedman.com (accessed July 10, 2010).

5. Matthew McKay, Martha Davis, and Patrick Fanning, *Messages: The Communication Skills Book* (Oakland, CA: New Harbinger, 1995), p. 108.

6. O. C. Ferrell, John Fraedrich, and Linda Ferrell, *Business Ethics: Ethical Decision Making and Cases*, 5th ed. (Boston, MA: Houghton Mifflin Company, 2002), p. 208.

7. Barry L. Reece and Rhonda Brandt, *Effective Human Relations: Personal and Organizational Applications*, 10th ed. (Boston, MA: Houghton Mifflin Company, 2008), pp. 125–126.

8. William M. Pride, Robert J. Hughes, and Jack R. Kapoor, *Business*, 7th ed. (Boston, MA: Houghton Mifflin Company, 2002), p. 40.

9. Patricia Gray, "Business Class," *Fortune*, April 17, 2006, p. 336; Philip Kotler and Gary Armstrong, *Principles of Marketing*, 12th ed. (Upper Saddle River, NJ: Prentice Hall, 2008), p. 568.

10. Alan M. Webber, "Are All Consultants Corrupt?" *Fast Company*, May 2002, pp. 130–134.

11. Brenda Bouw, "In praise of an ethical education," *Globe and Mail*, March 18, 2002, p. C1.

12. Philip Kotler and Kevin Lane Keller, *Marketing Management*, 14th ed. (Upper Saddle River, NJ: Prentice Hall, 2012), p. 630.

13. Betsy Cummings, "Ethical Breach," *Sales & Marketing Management*, July 2004, p. 10.

14. Sun Life Financial, www.sunlife.com, "Who We Are," (accessed March 17, 2014).

15. Michele Krebs, "All the Marketing Men," *Autoweek*, February 16, 1998, p. 11.

16. Joseph A. McKinney and Carlos W. Moore (2008), "International Bribery: Does a Written Code of Ethics Make a Difference in Perceptions of Business?" *Journal of Business Ethics*, 79 (1–2), pp. 103–111.

17. Ken Brown and Gee L. Lee, "Lucent Fires Top China Executives," *Wall Street Journal*, April 7, 2004, p. A8; Carl F. Fey, "How to Do Business in Russia," *Wall Street Journal*, October 27, 2007, p. R4.

18. Steve Sack, "Watch the Words," *Sales & Marketing Management*, July 1, 1985, p. 56.

19. Patricia S. Eyres, "Steps for Staying Out of Court and Trouble," *Selling*, April 2002, p. 10.

20. Michael Schrage, "Internet: Internal Threat?" *Fortune*, July 9, 2001, p. 184.

21. Mary C. Gentile, "Managing Yourself: Keeping Your Colleagues Honest," *Harvard Business Review*, March 2010, www.hbr.org/2010/03/managing-yourself-keeping-your-colleagues-honest/ar/1 (accessed June 1, 2014).

22. Rob Zeiger, "Sex, Sales & Stereotypes," *Sales & Marketing Management*, July 1995, pp. 52–53.

23. Barry L. Reece and Rhonda Brandt, *Effective Human Relations: Personal and Organizational Applications*, 10th ed. (Boston, MA: Houghton Mifflin Company, 2008), p. 110.

24. Betsy Cummings, "Do Customers Hate Salespeople?" *Sales & Marketing Management*, June 2001, pp. 50–51.

25. Ron Willingham, *Integrity Selling for the 21st Century* (New York, NY: Currency Doubleday, 2009), p. 1.

26. Nina Mazar, On Amir, and Dan Ariely (2008), "The Dishonesty of Honest People: A Theory of Self-Concept Maintenance," *Journal of Marketing Research*, 45(4), pp. 633–644.

27. Ron Willingham, "Four Traits All Highly Successful Salespeople Have in Common" (audiotape presentation), Phoenix, AZ, 1998.

28. Price Pritchett, *The Ethics of Excellence* (Dallas, TX: Pritchett & Associates, Inc., n.d.), p. 14.

29. Research on how cheaters justify their actions is cited in Romy Drucker, "The Devil Made Me Do It," *BusinessWeek*, July 24, 2006, p. 10.

30. Robert Kreitner, Barry Reece, and James P. O'Grady, *Business*, 2nd ed. (Boston, MA: Houghton Mifflin Company, 1990), pp. 647–648.

31. Karin Schill Rives, "Workers Find Clause Has Teeth," *News & Observer*, July 29, 2001, p. E-1.

32. John D. Hansen and Robert J. Riggle (2009), "Ethical Salesperson Behavior in Sales Relationships," *Journal of Personal Selling and Sales Management*, 29(2), pp. 151–166.

33. Neil Rackham and John R. DeVincentis, *Rethinking the Sales Force* (New York, NY: McGraw-Hill, 1999), pp. 83–84. A discussion of the trust factor is included in Jacqueline Durett, "A Matter of Trust," *Sales & Marketing Management*, January/February 2007, pp. 36–37.

34. Geoffrey Colvin, "The Verdict on Business: Presumed Guilty," *Fortune*, November 15, 2004, p. 78.

35. O. C. Ferrell, John Fraedrich, and Linda Ferrell, *Business Ethics*, 9th ed. (Mason, OH: South-Western Cengage Learning, 2013), p. 7. The importance of character at the leadership level is described in Noel M. Tichy and Warren G. Bennis, "Making the Tough Call," *Inc.*, November 2007, pp. 36–38.

36. Shankar Ganesan, Steven P. Brown, Babu John Mariadoss, and Hillbun (Dixon) Ho (2010), "Buffering and Amplifying Effects of Relationship Commitment in Business-to-Business Relationships," *Journal of Marketing Research*, 47(2), pp. 361–373.

37. Nathaniel Branden, *Self-Esteem at Work* (San Francisco: Jossey-Bass, 1998), p. 35.

38. Barbara Killinger, *Integrity: Doing the Right Thing for the Right Reason* (Montreal & Kingston: McGill-Queen's University Press, 2007), p. 13.

39. Stephen R. Covey, *The Seven Habits of Highly Effective People*, 2nd ed. (New York, NY: Simon & Schuster, 2004), pp. 18, 92. See Adam Hanft, "The New Lust for Integrity," *Inc.*, February 2004, p. 104.

40. Sharon Begley, "A World of Their Own," *Newsweek*, May 8, 2000, pp. 53–56; Jaren Sandberg, "Office Sticky Fingers Can Turn the Rest of Us into Joe Fridays," *Wall Street Journal*, November 19, 2005, p. Bl.

41. John A. Byrne, "How to Fix Corporate Governance," *BusinessWeek*, May 6, 2002, pp. 69–78.

42. Josh Freed, "Investigators: Drug Salesman Foiled Pharmacist," *The News & Observer*, August 26, 2001, p. 12A.

43. Robert Simons, Henry Mintzburg, and Kunal Basu, "Memo to: CEOs," *Fast Company*, June 2002, pp. 117–121.

44. Marjorie Kelly, "Waving Goodbye to the Invisible Hand," *Business Ethics*, March/April 2002, p. 4. For a somewhat different point of view, see George Stalk, "Warm and Fuzzy Doesn't Cut It," *Wall Street Journal*, February 15, 2005, p. B2.

45. Yochi J. Dreazen, "Pressure for Sales Fostered Abuses at WorldCom," *Wall Street Journal*, May 16, 2002, p. B1. See Norm Kamikow, "Ethics & Performance," *Workforce Performance Solutions*, March 2006, p. 4.

46. Beth Schultz, "Ethics under Investigation," *Network World Framingham*, April 26, 2004, pp. 72–74.

47. Shoshana Zuboff, "A Starter Kit for Business Ethics," *Fast Company*, January 2005, p. 91.

48. Carol Hymowitz, "Management Missteps in '04 Hurt Companies, Endangered Customers," *Wall Street Journal*, December 21, 2004, p. B1; "Edward Jones Agrees to Settle Host of Charges," *Wall Street Journal*, December 21, 2004, p. C1; John Hechinger, "Putman May Owe $100 Million," *Wall Street Journal*, February 2, 2005, p. C1; Erin McClam, "Witness Tells of Coverup," *News & Observer*, January 29, 2005, p. 3D.

49. Robert Simons, Henry Mintzburg, and Kunal Basu, "Memo to: CEOs," *Fast Company*, June 2002 pp. 120–121.

50. Patrick Smith, "You Have a Job, But How About a Life?" *BusinessWeek*, November 16, 1998, p. 30.

51. Mitchell Pacelle, "Citigroup Works on Reputation," *Wall Street Journal*, February 17, 2005, p. C3.

52. Patricia B. Gray, "Business Class," *Fortune*, April 17, 2006, p. 336; Margery Weinstein, "Survey Says: Ethics Training Works," *Training*, November 2005, p. 15; "ERC Survey & Benchmarking," www.ethics.org (accessed July 6, 2010).

53. Dawn Marie Driscoll, "Don't Confuse Legal and Ethical Standards," *BusinessWeek*, July–August 1996, p. 44.
54. Nancy Henderson Wurst, "Who's Afraid of Ethics?" *Hemisphere Magazine*, November 2006, pp. 120–123.
55. Carol Wheeler, "Getting the Edge on Ethics," *Executive Female*, May–June 1996, p. 47.
56. Sharon Drew Morgan, *Selling with Integrity* (San Francisco: Berrett-Koehler, 1997), pp. 25–27.
57. Ibid., pp. 27–28.
58. Tom Peters, *Thriving on Chaos* (New York, NY: Alfred A. Knopf, 1988), p. 521.
59. Gerhard Gschwandtner, "Lies and Deception in Selling," *Personal Selling Power*, 15th Anniversary Issue, 1995, p. 62.
60. Price Pritchett, *The Ethics of Excellence* (Dallas, TX: Pritchett & Associates, Inc., n.d.), p. 18.
61. Ron Willingham, *Integrity Selling for the 21st Century* (New York, NY: Currency Doubleday, 2003), p. 11.

Sources for Boxed Features

a. "Ethics and Social Media: Where Should You Draw the Line?" http://mashable.com/2012/03/17/social-media-ethics/ (accessed July 5, 2013).
b. Michael T. Kenny, "Research, Observe Chinese Protocol to Land Sale," *Selling*, May 2001, p. 10; Jan Yager, *Business Protocol*, 2nd ed. (Stamford, CT: Hannacroix Creek Books, 2001), p. 113.
c. Based on Renee Houston Zemanski, "When the Competition Gets Tough," *Selling Power*, April 2006, pp. 17–19.
d. Sonia Verma, "I Don't Have So Much Faith in Law," *Globe and Mail*, January 15, 2011, p. F3.

Chapter 4

1. Ron Willingham, *Integrity Selling for the 21st Century* (New York, NY: Currency Doubleday, 2003), p. 11.
2. Daniel H. Pink, *A Whole New Mind* (New York, NY: Riverhead Books, 2005), pp. 48–63.
3. Ilan Mochari, "In a Former Life," *Inc.*, April 2001, p. 100.
4. J.D. Power Consumer Center, September 22, 2010, www.jdpower.com.
5. *Partnering: The Heart of Selling Today* (Des Moines, IA: American Media Incorporated, 1990).
6. Paul S. Goldner, "How to Set the Playing Field," *Selling*, April 1998, p. 9.
7. Larry Wilson, *Selling in the 90s* (Chicago: Nightingale Conant, 1988), p. 35.
8. William Keenan, Jr., "Customer Satisfaction Builds Business," *Selling*, March 1998, p. 12.
9. Tim Sanders, *Love Is the Killer App* (New York, NY: Crown Business, 2002), p. 23.
10. Malcolm Fleschner, "Worldwide Winner—The UPS Story," *Selling Power*, November/December 2001, p. 58.
11. Neil Rackham and John R. DeVincentis, *Rethinking the Sales Force* (New York, NY: McGraw-Hill, 1999), pp. 79–83.
12. Phillip C. McGraw, *Self Matters* (New York, NY: Simon & Schuster, 2001), pp. 69–70.
13. Sharon Begley, "Follow Your Intuition: The Unconscious You May Be the Wiser Half," *Wall Street Journal*, August 30, 2002, p. B1; Sharon Begley, "How Do I Love Thee? Let Me Count the Ways—and Other Bad Ideas," *Wall Street Journal*, September 6, 2002, p. B1.
14. Phillip C. McGraw, "Dr. Phil: Know Your Goal, Make a Plan, and Pull the Trigger," *The Oprah Magazine*, September 2001, pp. 60–61; see Barry L. Reece and Rhonda Brandt, *Effective Human Relations: Personal and Organizational Applications*, 9th ed. (Boston, MA: Houghton Mifflin Company, 2005), pp. 95–102.
15. McGraw, *Self Matters*, p. 73.
16. Excerpt from *The New Conceptual Selling: The Most Effective and Proven Method For Face-to-Face Sales Planning* by Stephen E. Heiman, Diane Sanchez. Published by Warner Books, © 1999.
17. David Mayer and Herbert M. Greenberg, "What Makes a Good Salesman," *Harvard Business Review*, July–August 2006, p. 166. For information on how empathy training helps sales representatives improve, see Cliff Edwards, "Death of a Pushy Salesman," *BusinessWeek*, July 3, 2006.
18. Ibid.
19. Eli Jones, Jesse N. Moore, Andrea J. S. Stanaland, and Rosalind A. J. Wyatt, "Salesperson Race and Gender and the Access and Legitimacy Paradigm: Does Difference Make a Difference?" *Journal of Personal Selling and Sales Management*, Fall 1998, p. 74; "Danielle Sacks, the Accidental Guru," *Fast Company*, January 2005, pp. 65–71.
20. Barry L. Reece, *Effective Human Relations: Interpersonal and Organizational Application*, 12th ed. (Mason, OH: South-Western Cengage Learning, 2013), p. 29.
21. Roy M. Berko, Andrew D. Wolvin, and Darlyn R. Wolvin, *Communicating*, 8th ed. (Boston, MA: Houghton Mifflin Company, 2001), p. 45.
22. Ibid., p. 50.
23. Excerpt from *The Professional Image* by Susan Bixler. Published by Penguin Group USA, © 1984.
24. Barbara Pachter and Marjorie Brody, *Complete Business Etiquette Handbook* (New York, NY: Prentice Hall, 1995), p. 14.
25. Adapted from Leonard Zunin, *Contact: The First Four Minutes* (New York, NY: Ballantine Books, [1972]1992), p. 109; Jerry LaMartina, "Shake It, Don't Crush It," *San Jose Mercury News*, June 25, 2000, p. 4PC.
26. Deborah Blum, "Face It!" *Psychology Today*, September/October 1998, pp. 32–69; see Julia Chang, "Selling in Acting," *Sales & Marketing Management*, May 2004, p. 22.
27. Barbara Pachter and Mary Brody, *Complete Business Etiquette Handbook* (Englewood Cliffs, NJ: Prentice Hall, 1995), p. 27; "The Eyes Have It," *Sales & Marketing Management*, January 2002, p. 20.
28. Appropriate clothing for work is discussed in Christina Binkley, "Case Study: Dressing for the Naked CEO," *Wall Street Journal*, August 23, 2007, p. D8.
29. Melinda Ligos, "Does Image Matter?" *Sales & Marketing Management*, March 2001, pp. 52–55.
30. Margaret Webb Pressler, "Camouflage for the Cubicles," *News & Observer*, April 25, 2004, p. 4-E.
31. Susan Bixler and Nancy Nix-Rice, *The New Professional Image* (Adams Media Corporation, 1997), pp. 11–15; Barbara Pachter and Marjorie Brody, *Complete Business Etiquette Handbook* (New York, NY: Prentice Hall, 1995), p. 72.

32. Paul Galanti, "Talking Motivates—Communication Makes Things Happen," *Personal Selling Power*, November–December 1995, p. 88.

33. Susan Berkley, "Hone Your Sharpest Sales Weapon," *Sales & Field Force Automation*, July 1997, p. 24.

34. Joann S. Lublin, "To Win Advancement, You Need to Clean Up Any Bad Speech Habits," *Wall Street Journal*, October 5, 2004, p. B1.

35. David E. Weliver, "My Fair CEO," *Inc.*, October 30, 2001, p. 112.

36. "Is Etiquette a Core Value?" *Inc.*, May 2004, p. 22.

37. Tim Sanders, *Love Is the Killer App* (New York, NY: Crown Business, 2002), p. 18.

38. Stephen Covey, *The Seven Habits of Highly Effective People*, 2nd ed. (New York, NY: Simon & Schuster, 2004), pp. 240–241.

39. Jack Canfield, *The Success Principles* (New York, NY: HarperCollins, 2005), pp. 342–343.

40. Colleen DeBaise, "Offbeat Hobbies May Help Build Relationships with Some Clients," *Wall Street Journal*, February 9, 2005, p. B2.

41. Anne Murphy Paul, "Self-Help: Shattering the Myths," *Psychology Today*, March/April 2001, p. 64; Arnold A. Lazarus and Clifford N. Lazarus, *The 60-Second Shrink* (San Luis Obispo, CA: Impact Publishers), 1997, pp. 3–4.

42. McGraw, *Self Matters*, pp. 69–76.

43. Rick Saulle, "Honor Diversity," *Selling Power*, May 2004, p. 54.

Sources for Boxed Features

a. Dean Keating and Brian Rogers, Janssen Inc., March–June, 2011.

b. "International Snapshot," *Sales & Marketing Management*, November 2001, p. 63; Jan Yager, *Business Protocol*, 2nd ed. (Stamford, CT: Hannacroix Books, 2001), pp. 120–121.

c. Reprinted with permission of the publisher from "Secrets of Power Persuasion for Salespeople" ©2003. Published by Career Press, Pompton Plains, NJ. All rights reserved. See Roger Dawson, "And Your Name Was Again?" *Value-Added Selling 21*, July 16, 2007, p. 2. Used with permission.

d. Based on Andrew S. Gallan, "Bringing CARE to Your Customers," *Sales & Marketing Management*, May 2004, p. 72.

Chapter 5

1. Mike McNamee and Christopher Schmitt, "The Chainsaw Al Massacre," *BusinessWeek*, May 28, 2001, p. 48; Dennis K. Berman and Joann S. Lublin, "Restructuring, Personality Clashes Led to Lucent Executive's Exit," *Wall Street Journal*, May 17, 2001, p. B1; Charles Fishmann, "Jeff Bezos," *Fast Company*, February 2001, pp. 80–82.

2. Douglas A. Bernstein, Louis A. Penner, Alison Clarke-Stewart, and Edward J. Roy, *Psychology*, 9th ed. (Boston, MA: Houghton Mifflin, 2011), p. 518.

3. Robert Bolton and Dorothy Grover Bolton, *People Styles at Work and Beyond*, 2nd ed. (New York, NY: AMACOM, 2009), p. 12–14.

4. Fernando Jaramillo, William B. Locander, Paul E. Spector, and Eric G. Harris, "Getting the Job Done: The Moderating Role of Initiative on the Relationship between Intrinsic Motivation and Adaptive Selling," *Journal of Personal Selling and Sales Management*, Winter 2007, pp. 59–74.

5. David W. Merrill and Roger H. Reid, *Personal Styles and Effective Performance* (Radnor, PA: Chilton Books, 1981), p. 1.

6. For a more complete description of *The Versatile Salesperson* training program, visit the Wilson Learning, www.wilsonlearning.com (accessed January 20, 2013).

7. Robert J. Sternberg, *Thinking Styles* (New York, NY: Cambridge University Press, 1997), p. 8.

8. Robert Bolton and Dorothy Grover Bolton, *People Styles at Work and Beyond*, 2nd ed. (New York, NY: AMACOM, 2009)

9. Geoff James, "Inside the Psychology of Selling," *Selling Power*, January/February 2004, pp. 25–28.

10. The dominance factor was described in an early book by William M. Marston, *The Emotions of Normal People* (New York, NY: Harcourt, 1928). Research conducted by Rolfe LaForge and Robert F. Suczek resulted in the development of the Interpersonal Checklist (ICL), which features a dominant–submissive scale. A person who receives a high score on the ICL tends to lead, persuade, and control others. The Interpersonal Identity Profile, developed by David W. Merrill and James W. Taylor, features a factor called "assertiveness." Persons classified as being high in assertiveness tend to have strong opinions, make quick decisions, and be directive when dealing with people. Persons classified as being low in assertiveness tend to voice moderate opinions, make thoughtful decisions, and be supportive when dealing with others.

11. David W. Johnson, *Reaching Out—Interpersonal Effectiveness and Self-Actualization*, 8th ed. (Boston, MA: Allyn & Bacon, 2003), p. 83.

12. The research conducted by LaForge and Suczek resulted in identification of the hostile–loving continuum, which is similar to the sociability continuum. Their Interpersonal Checklist features this scale. L. L. Thurstone and T. G. Thurstone developed the Thurstone Temperament Schedule, which provides an assessment of a "sociable" factor. Persons with high scores in this area enjoy the company of others and make friends easily. The Interpersonal Identity Profile developed by Merrill and Taylor contains an objectivity continuum. A person with low objectivity is seen as attention seeking, involved with the feelings of others, informal, and casual in social relationships. A person who is high in objectivity appears to be somewhat indifferent toward the feelings of others. This person is formal in social relationships.

13. Pierce J. Howard and Jane M. Howard, "Buddy, Can You Paradigm?" *Training & Development*, September 1995, p. 31.

14. Sam Deep and Lyle Sussman, *Close the Deal* (Reading, MA: Perseus Books, 1999), p. 157.

15. Len D'Innocenzo and Jack Cullen, "Chameleon Management," *Personal Selling Power*, January/February 1995, p. 61.

16. "A Global Profiling Tool," Wilson Learning, Eden Prairie, MN, 1999.

17. Tom Ritchey, *I'm Stuck, You're Stuck* (San Francisco, CA: Berrett-Koehler, Publishers, Inc., 2002), p. 5.

18. Ron Willingham, *Integrity Selling for the 21st Century* (New York, NY: Currency Doubleday, 2003), pp. 20–21.

19. Stuart Atkins, *How to Get the Most from Styles-Based Training* (Beverly Hills, CA: Stuart Atkins, 1996), p. 1.

20. Gary A. Williams and Robert B. Miller, "Change the Way You Persuade," *Harvard Business Review*, May 2002, p. 65.

21. Robert Bolton and Dorothy Grover Bolton, *People Styles at Work and Beyond*, 2nd ed. (New York, NY: AMACOM, 2009), p. 8.

22. David W. Merrill and Roger H. Reid, *Personal Styles and Effective Performance* (Radnor, PA: Chilton Books, 1981), p. 2.

23. Roger Wenschlag, *The Versatile Salesperson* (New York, NY: John Wiley & Sons, 1989), pp. 165–171.

24. Nina Munk, "How Levi's Trashed a Great American Brand," *Fortune,* April 12, 1999, p. 85.

25. "The Top 25 Managers of the Year," *BusinessWeek,* January 14, 2002, p. 65.

26. Stuart Atkins, *How to Get the Most from Styles-Based Training* (Beverly Hills, CA: Stuart Atkins, 1996), p. 3.

27. Ron Willingham, *Integrity Selling* (New York, NY: Doubleday, 1987), pp. 21–23.

28. Eric F. Douglas, *Straight Talk* (Palo Alto, CA: Davies-Black Publishing, 1998), p. 92.

29. Ron Willingham, *Integrity Selling for the 21st Century* (New York, NY: Currency Doubleday, 2003), p. 37.

30. David W. Merrill and Roger H. Reid, *Personal Styles and Effective Performance,* ibid., pp. 134, 135.

31. Stuart Atkins, *The Name of the Game* (Beverly Hills, CA: Ellis & Stewart, 1981), pp. 49–50.

Sources for Boxed Features

a. Personal interview with Ruth Todd, February 9, 2011.

b. Based on Christopher Caggiano, "Psychopath," *Inc.,* July 1998, p. 83.

c. Based on "International Snapshot," *Sales & Marketing Management,* April 2000, p. 70; Jan Yager, *Business Protocol,* 2nd ed. (Stamford, CT: Hannacroix Books, 2001), p. 120.

d. The Platinum Rule by Dr. Tony Alessandra. Copyright © 1974-2014. Used by permission of Dr. Tony Alessandra.

Chapter 6

1. Interview with Amy Vandaveer on April 13, 2013. For additional information regarding *Texas Monthly* magazine, visit www.texasmonthly.com.

2. Paul Nolan, "Are You Committing These B2B Sales Sins?" *Salesforceexp,* November/December 2010, p. 6.

3. Keith M. Eades, *The New Solution Selling* (New York, NY: McGraw-Hill, 2004), pp. 4–5.

4. Geoffrey James, "Solution Selling," *Selling Power,* May 2006, pp. 45–48. This article is based on an interview with Keith Eades, author of *The New Solution Selling.*

5. Michael R. Solomon, Greg W. Marshall, and Elnora W. Stuart, *Marketing: Real People, Real Choices,* 7th ed. (Upper Saddle River, NJ: Prentice Hall, 2012), p. 219.

6. Newmac Furnaces & Boilers, www.newmacfurnaces.com (accessed March 18, 2014).

7. Loki Systems, www.lokisys.com (accessed March 18, 2014).

8. Brent Adamson, Mathew Dixon, and Nicholas Toman, "The End of Solution Sales," *Harvard Business Review,* July/August 2012, p. 62.

9. Neil Rackham and John R. DeVincentis, *Rethinking the Sales Force* (New York, NY: McGraw-Hill, 1999), p. 79.

10. Desjardins Group, www.desjardins.com, "What You Need to Know about Mutual Funds," accessed March 18, 2014; Nancy Allan, Executive Director, Independent Financial Brokers of Canada, letter to Ontario Ministry of Finance, February 4, 2014, available http://www.fin.gov.on.ca/en/consultations/rfp-submissions/independent-financial-brokers-of-canada.pdf (accessed March 18, 2014).

11. Karen E. Starr, "Simple Solutions," *Selling Power,* July/August 2001, p. 22.

12. Christopher Whittier, "Quotation Management: The Revolution is Here to Stay," www.crmresultsonline.com (accessed July 6, 2010).

13. Based on John Fellows, "A Decent Proposal," *Personal Selling Power,* November/December 1995, p. 56.

14. Adapted from John Fellows, "A Decent Proposal," *Personal Selling Power,* November–December 1995, p. 56. See Neil Rackham, "Seven Rules for Creating Winning Sales Proposal's," *Value-Added Selling 21,* December 16, 2003, p. 20.

15. "Feeling under the Gun? Check Your Proposal," *Selling,* October 2001, p. 3.

16. Neil Rackam, "Seven Rules for Creating Winning Sales Proposals," *Value-Added Selling 21,* December 16, 2003, p. 20.

17. "What Kind of Rep Is Most Trustworthy?" *Sales & Marketing Management,* February 2001, p. 90.

18. Robert W. Palmatier, Lisa K. Scheer, and Jan-Benedict E.M. Steenkamp (2007), "Customer Loyalty to Whom? Managing the Benefits and Risks of Salesperson-Owned Loyalty," *Journal of Marketing Research, 44*(2), pp. 158–99.

19. Tom Peters, *Re-Imagine! Business Excellence in a Disruptive Age* (London, UK: Dording Kindersley Limited, 2003), p. 224.

20. "Company Ambassadors," www.patagonia.com/web/us/patagonia.go?assetid=2897&ln=81 (accessed June 26, 2013).

21. Roland T. Rust, Christine Moorman, and Peter R. Dickson (2002), "Getting Return on Quality: Revenue Expansion, Cost Reduction, or Both?" *Journal of Marketing, 66*(3), pp. 7–24.

22. Laurel Steel, www.laurelsteel.com (accessed March 18, 2014).

23. Betsy Cummings, "Welcome to the Real Whirled," *Sales & Marketing Management,* February 2001, pp. 87–88.

24. Ian Gelenter, "Build Satisfaction with a Service Contract," *Selling,* May 1998, p. 7.

25. Tom Reilly, "Should You Set Prices?" *Selling,* August 2000, pp. 1, 14.

26. Gerhard Gschwandtner, "ROI Selling," *Selling Power,* November/December 2004, p. 10.

27. William M. Pride, Robert J. Hughes, and Jack R. Kapoor, *Business,* Eighth Edition (Boston, MA: Houghton Mifflin, 2005), pp. 456–457.

28. Michael Aherne, C. B. Bhattacharya, and Thomas Gruen (2005), "Antecedents and Consequences of Customer-Company Identification: Expanding the Role of Relationship Marketing," *Journal of Applied Psychology, 90*(3), pp. 574–85.

29. eluta.ca, http://www.eluta.ca/jobs-at-xerox#winner:winnermore (accessed March 18, 2014).

30. Michael L. Askew, "What I Know Now," *Fast Company,* November 2005, p. 108.

31. Michael R. Williams and Jill S. Attaway, "Exploring Salespersons' Customer Orientation as a Mediator of Organizational Culture's Influence on Buyer-Seller Relationships," *Journal of Personal Selling & Sales Management,* Fall 1996, pp. 33–52.

32. "Dealer Merchandising Portfolio," *Views: The Inner Circle News,* Winter 2000, p. 10.

33. "Grassroots Problem Solving," *Inc., March 1996*, p. 92.

34. See Brian Tracy, "Analyzing the Competition," *Value Added Selling 21*, September 16, 2003, p. 2.

35. Jim Dickie, "Lowest Price Isn't the Answer," *Selling*, August 2000, p. 14.

36. Bob Mundson, "A Personal Blend," *Training*, February 2004, p. 11.

37. Ashwin W. Joshi (2010), "Salesperson Influence on Product Development: Insights from a Study of Small Manufacturing Organizations, *Journal of Marketing, 74*(1), pp. 94–107.

38. www.patagonia.com (accessed June 29, 2013).

39. Margery Weinstein, "Selling Points," *Training*, June 2007, p. 51.

40. Raj Agnihotri, Adam Rapp, and Kevin Trainor (2009), "Understanding the Role of Information Communication in the Buyer-Seller Exchange Process: Antecedents and Outcomes," *Journal of Business & Industrial Marketing, 24*(7), pp. 474–86.

41. Jill Rosenfeld, "Unit of One," *Fast Company*, April 2000, p. 98.

42. www.consultingsales.com/tips/Using_Features_Advantages_Benefits.html, (accessed March 18, 2014).

43. Neil Rackham, *The SPIN Selling Fieldbook* (New York, NY: McGraw-Hill, 1996), pp. 149–52; *Value-Added Selling 21*, December 26, 2006, p. 4.

44. Gary Hamil, Leading the Revolution (Boston, MA: Harvard Business School Press, 2000), p. 87; Neil Rackham, "Improve This Skill and Boost Sales Up to 27 Percent," *Value-Added Selling 21*, March 2, 2004, p. 1; *Value-Added Selling 21*, December 26, 2006, p. 4.

Sources for Boxed Features

a. "International Snapshot," *Sales & Marketing Management*, March 2000, p. 72; Jan Yager, *Business Protocol*, 2nd ed. (Stamford, CT: Hannacroix Creek Books, 2001), p. 111.

Chapter 7

1. General Motors Canada, http://www.gm.ca/gm/english/vehicles/cadillac/cts/model-detail01-key-features#CTS-VCoupe (accessed February 15, 2014); Peter Egan, "The Best of All Worlds Bunch," *Road & Track*, July 2002, pp. 52–78; "2005 Geneva: Lexus Finesses Next IS Sport Sedan," www.autoweek.com (accessed June 29, 2010); Greg Kable, "Audi A4 Debuts at Frankfurt," *Autoweek*, September 3, 2007, p. 10; Joe Rusz, "Saab 9-3 & XWD" *Road & Track*, October 2007, p. 60.

2. Wayne S. Desarbo, Rajdeep Grewal, and Crystal J. Scott (2008), "A Clusterwise Bilinear Multidimensional Scaling Methodology for Simultaneous Segmentation and Positioning Analyses," *Journal of Marketing Research, 45*(2), pp. 280–92.

3. Michael R. Solomon, Grey W, Marshall, and Elnora W. Stuart, *Marketing: Real People, Real Choices*, 7th ed. (Upper Saddle River, NJ: Pearson Education, 2012), p. 201.

4. D. Lee Carpenter, "Return on Innovation—the Power of Being Different," *Retailing Issues Letter*, May 1998, p. 3.

5. Brian Tracy, "Keeping the Customers You Make," *Selling*, November 2003, pp. 1, 4.

6. Tom Reilly, "You Must Differentiate to Win," *Selling*, April 2001, pp. 1, 10.

7. Gary Armstrong and Philip Kotler, *Marketing: An Introduction*, 14th ed. (Upper Saddle River, NJ: Prentice Hall, 2012), p. 212.

8. Tom Leverton, "Five Questions," *Sales & Marketing Management*, July 2004, p. 13.

9. Theodore Kinni, "The Value Proposition," *Selling Power*, July/August 2005, p. 75.

10. Michael Arndt, "Built for the Long Haul" *Business Week*, January 30, 2006, p. 66.

11. Carl K. Clayton, "Sell Quality, Service, Your Company, Yourself," *Personal Selling Power*, January/February 1990, p. 47.

12. Elaine Parker, "How I Made the Sale," *Value-Added Selling 21*, June 17, 2003, pp. 1–2.

13. Suein L Hwang, "It Was a WOMBAT for the Meatware, But It Was a Good Sell," *Wall Street Journal*, May 15, 2002, p. B1.

14. J. Thomas Russell and W. Ronald Lane, *Kleppner's Advertising Procedure* 18th ed. (Englewood Cliffs, NJ: Prentice-Hall, 2011), p. 93–109.

15. Kevin Zheng Zhou and Kent Nakamoto (2007), "How Do Enhanced and Unique Features Affect New Product Preference? The Moderating Role of Product Familiarity," *Journal of the Academy of Marketing Science*, 35, pp. 53–62.

16. Lawrence B. Chonko and Eli Jones (2005), "The Need for Speed: Agility Selling," *Journal of Personal Selling and Sales Management, 25*(4), pp. 371–382.

17. Mark Leslie and Charles A. Holloway, "The Sales Learning Curve," *Harvard Business Review*, July/August 2006, p. 121.

18. Jess McCuan, "Reeling In the Big One" *Inc* ., August 2004, pp. 43–44; "What Is IntraLinks?" www.Intralinks.com (accessed June 30, 2013).

19. Sun Life Financial, www.sunlife.com, "About Us," (accessed March 18, 2014).

20. Michael R. Solomon, Greg W. Marshall, and Elnora W. Stuart, *Marketing: Real People, Real Choices* 7th ed. ibid., p. 322.

21. Carlos Tejada, "The Allure of Bundling," *Wall Street Journal*, October 7, 2003, p. B 1.

22. Michael Treacy, "You Need a Value Discipline—But Which One?" *Fortune*, April 17, 1995, p. 195.

23. Robert Shulman and Richard Miniter, "Discounting Is No Bargain," *Wall Street Journal*, December 7, 1998, p. A30.

24. Andy Cohen, "Survey Says: Service Beats Price Online," *Sales & Marketing Management*, July 2002, p. 18.

25. Geoffrey James, "Solution Selling," *Selling Power*, May 2006, p. 46.

26. Adapted from a model described in "Marketing Success through Differentiation—of Anything," *Harvard Business Review*, January/February 1980.

27. Joanna Johnson, "A New Perspective on Marketing," *Construction Dimensions*, April 1990, p. 14.

28. Ted Levitt, *Marketing Imagination* (New York, NY: Free Press, 1983), p. 80.

29. Neil Rackham, "Boost Your Sales 20% by Improving This Skill," *Value-Added Selling 21*, June 17, 2003, pp. 1–2.

30. Beth Davis-Sramek, Cornelia Droge, John T. Mentzer, and Matthew B. Myers (2009), "Creating Commitment and Loyalty Behavior among Retailers: What Are the Roles of Service Quality and Satisfaction?" *Journal of the Academy of Marketing Science*, 37, pp. 440–54.

31. Thomas A. Stewart, "A Satisfied Customer Isn't Enough," *Fortune*, July 21, 1997, pp. 112–13.

32. Martin Reimann, Oliver Schilke, and Jacquelyn S. Thomas (2010), "Customer Relationship Management and Firm

Performance: The Mediating Role of Business Strategy," *Journal of the Academy of Marketing Science*, 38, pp. 326–46.

33. "Business Bulletin," *Wall Street Journal*, September 24, 1998, p. A1.

34. Tilley Endurables, www.tilley.com (accessed March 18, 2014).

35. "Study: What Really Matters to Your Customers," *Value-Added Selling 21*, February 14, 2005, p. 4.

36. Ted Levitt, *Marketing Imagination*, ibid. p. 84.

37. Rebecca Smith, "Beyond Recycling: Manufacturers Embrace 'C2C' Design," *Wall Street Journal*, March 3, 2005, p. B1.

38. Neil Rackham and John R. DeVincentis, *Rethinking the Sales Force* (New York, NY: McGraw-Hill, 1999), p. 89.

39. Ibid., pp. 89–90.

40. Ibid., p. 90.

Sources for Boxed Features

a. Adapted from discussion in Leonard L. Berry, A. Parasuraman, and Valerie A. Zeithaml, "The Service-Quality Puzzle," *Business Horizons*, September–October 1988, pp. 35–43; Robert Kreitner, *Management*, 5th ed. (Boston, MA: Houghton Mifflin Company, 1992), pp. 613–14.

b. Personal interview with and correspondence from Laura Ricciuto, April 2011.

Chapter 8

1. Robert H. Bloom, "Sales Management in 2011 and Beyond," *Salesforceexp*, November/December, p. 22.

2. "Nighttime Reading for Daytime Success," *Sales & Marketing Management*, May 2007, p. 44.

3. Excerpt from *Reengineering The Corporation: A Manifesto For Business Revolution* by Michael Hammer and James Champy. Published by Harper Collins, © 1993.

4. Excerpt from *The New Solution Selling* by Keith M. Eades. Published by McGraw-Hill Publishing, © 2004.

5. Tom Peters and Nancy Austin, *A Passion for Excellence* (New York, NY: Random House, 1985), p. 71.

6. "How Well Do You Know Your Customers?" *Sales & Field Force Automation*, January 1999, p. 141.

7. Gary Armstrong and Philip Kotler, *Marketing: An Introduction*, 14th ed. (Upper Saddle River, NJ: Prentice Hall, 2012), pp. 170–71.

8. Michael R. Solomon, Greg W. Marshall, and Elnora W. Stuart, *Marketing: Real People, Real Choices*, 7th ed. (Upper Saddle River, NJ: Prentice Hall, 2012), p. 170.

9. Gary Armstrong and Philip Kotler, *Marketing: An Introduction*, 7th ed. (Upper Saddle River, NJ: Prentice Hall, 2005), p. 169.

10. Michael R. Solomon, Greg W. Marshall, and Elnora W. Stuart, *Marketing: Real People, Real Choices*, 7th ed. ibid., p. 168.

11. Ibid., pp. 168–69.

12. Marina Strauss, "Suppliers Brace for More Price Cuts as Grocery Fight Heats Up," *Globe and Mail*, January 10, 2014, p. B1.

13. Philip Kotler and Gary Armstrong, *Principles of Marketing*, 14th ed. (Upper Saddle River, NJ: Prentice Hall, 2012), p. 171.

14. FedEx, www.fedex.com (accessed June 30, 2013).

15. Philip Kotler and Gary Armstrong, *Principles of Marketing*, 14th ibid., ed., pp. 151–52.

16. Ibid., p. 152.

17. S. Sajeesh and Jagmohan S. Raju (2010), "Positioning and Pricing in a Variety Seeking Market," *Management Science*, 56(6), pp. 949–61.

18. Ibid., pp. 145–46.

19. Keith M. Eades, *The New Solution Selling*, ibid., pp. 32–33. Betsy Cummings, "Proving the Sale Process," *Sales & Marketing Management*, June 2006, p. 12.

20. Keith M. Eades, *The New Solution Selling*, ibid., p. 31.

21. Stephen E. Heiman and Diane Sanchez, *The New Conceptual Selling* (New York, NY: Warner Books, 1999), pp. 190–91.

22. Research reported in Tom Atkinson and Ron Koprowski, "Sales Reps' Biggest Mistakes," *Harvard Business Review*, July–August 2006, p. 1, indicates that 26 percent of the business-to-business buyers say salespeople "don't follow my company's buying process."

23. Philip Kotler and Gary Armstrong, *Principles of Marketing*, 14th ed., ibid., p. 152.

24. Neil Rackham and John R. DeVincentis, *Rethinking the Sales Force* (New York, NY: McGraw-Hill, 1999), p. 66.

25. Bill Stinnett, "Reverse-Engineer the Buying Process," *Selling*, December 2004, p. 16.

26. Neil Rackham and John DeVincentis, *Rethinking the Sales Force*, ibid., p. 68.

27. Monika Kukar-Kinney and Angeline G. Close (2010), "The Determinants of Consumers' Online Shopping Cart Abandonment," *Journal of the Academy of Marketing Science*, 38, pp. 240–50.

28. Hean Tat Keh and Jun Pang (2010), "Customer Reactions to Service Separation," *Journal of Marketing*, 74(2), pp. 55–70.

29. Ibid., p. 69.

30. Neil Rackham and John DeVincentis provide extensive coverage of these three selling modes in *Rethinking the Sales Force*. See also Neil Rackham and John R. DeVincentis, "Let the Customer Define Value—and Sales Will Rise," *Value-Added Selling 21*, January 13, 2004, pp. 1–2.

31. Neil Rackham and John R. DeVincentis, "Let the Customer Define Value—and Sales Will Rise," ibid., pp. 1–2.

32. Ken Brown, "Little-Known Avaya Tackles Cisco in Internet Calling Gear," *Wall Street Journal*, October 26, 2004, p. B1.

33. Neil Rackham and John DeVincentis, *Rethinking the Sales Force*, ibid., p. 74.

34. Philip Kotler and Gary Armstrong, *Principles of Marketing*, 10th ed. (Upper Saddle River, NJ: Prentice Hall, 2004), p. 28.

35. Stan Davis and Christopher Meyer, *Blur: The Speed of Change in the Connected Economy* (New York, NY: Addison-Wesley Publishers, 1998), p. 16.

36. Leilei Gao, S. Christian Wheeler, and Baba Shiv (2009), "The 'Shaken Self': Product Choices as a Means of Restoring Self-View Confidence," *Journal of Consumer Research*, 36(1), pp. 29–38.

37. William M. Pride and O.C. Ferrell, *Marketing*, 10th ed. (Boston, MA: Houghton Mifflin, 1997), pp. 143–48.

38. Douglas A. Bernstein, Alison Clark-Stewart, Edward J. Roy, and Christopher D. Wickens, *Psychology*, 6th ed. (Boston, MA: Houghton Mifflin, 2003), p. 648.

39. C. Page Moreau and Kelly B. Herd (2010), "To Each His Own? How Comparisons with Others Influence Consumers' Evaluations of Their Self-Designed Products," *Journal of Consumer Research*, 36(5), pp. 806–19.

40. Philip Kotler and Gary Armstrong, *Principles of Marketing*, 14th ed., ibid., p. 139–40.

41. Douglas A. Bernstein, et al., *Psychology*, 6th ed., ibid., p. 21.

42. Philip Kotler and Gary Armstrong, Principles of Marketing, 14th ed., ibid., p. 137–38. Gary Armstrong and Philip Kotler, *Marketing: An Introduction*, 7th ed., ibid., p. 145.

43. Louis E. Boone and David L. Kurtz, *Contemporary Marketing*, 16th ed. (Mason, OH: Southwestern Publishing, 2013), p. 150.

44. Roger Hart, "Luxury, VW's Way," *AutoWeek*, December 27, 2004, pp. 18–19; Tom Reilly, "All Sales Decisions are Emotional for the Buyer," *Selling*, July 2003, p. 13.

45. Roy Chitwood, "Hidden Buyer Motives: Handle Them With Care," *Value-Added Selling 21*, April 2, 2007, p. 4.

46. Phil Kline, "Dominant Buying Motive Is the Result of Strong Emotions," *Marketing News*, May 24, 1993, p. 4.

47. Stan Davis and Christopher Meyer, *Blur*, ibid., p. 52.

48. Hakkyun Kim, Kiwan Park, and Norbert Schwarz (2010), "Will This Trip Really Be Exciting? The Role of Incidental Emotions in Product Evaluation," *Journal of Consumer Research*, 36(6), pp. 983–91.

49. Robert McGarvey, "The Buyer's Emotional Side," *Selling Power*, April 2006, p. 35.

50. Ibid., p. 36.

51. Gary Armstrong and Philip Kotler, *Marketing: An Introduction*, 6th ed. (Upper Saddle River, NJ: Prentice Hall, 2003), p. 216; Sid Chadwick, "New Twists in Price vs. Perceived Value," *Sales and Marketing Advisory Magazine*, July/August 2001, p. 6.

Sources for Boxed Features

a. Judith C. Tingley and Lee E. Robert, *GenderSell: How to Sell to the Opposite Sex* (New York, NY: Simon & Schuster, 1999).

b. Douglas A. Bernstein, Alison Clark-Stewart, Edward J. Roy, and Christopher D. Wickens, *Psychology*, 6th ed. (Boston, MA: Houghton Mifflin, 2003), p. 648; Dave Stein, "Selling Across Generation Gaps," *Sales & Marketing Management*, October 2007, p. 9.

c. Erin Anderson and Leonard Lodish (2006), "Leading the effective sales force: the Asian sales force management environment," working paper, pp. 7–8.

Chapter 9

1. Gerhard Gschwandtner, "Thoughts to Sell By," *Personal Selling Power*, Fifteenth Anniversary Issue, 1995, p. 122.

2. Personal Interview, Duane Manning, former director of business development, Parker Aerospace, March 12, 2013.

3. Dorothy Leeds, "Where Are the Real Decision Makers?" *Personal Selling Power*, March 1993, p. 62; Gerhard Gschwandtner, "Getting Squeezed," *Selling Power*, May 2002, p. 10.

4. Terry Hill, "How Do You Sustain and Grow Your Customer Relationships?" *American Salesman*, October 2007, p. 26.

5. Paul Tindall, "Prospecting: It Separates the Best from the Rest," *Sales Exchange*, November 17–23, 2003.

6. For additional information on Joe Girard see "Joe Girard on Becoming The World's Greatest Salesperson," *Harvard Business Review*, July–August 2006, p. 25.

7. Gerhard Gschwandtner, "The Funnel Concept," *Personal Selling Power*, May/June 1993, p. 23.

8. Joel R. Pecoraro, "Panning for Gold," *Sales & Marketing Management*, November 2004, p. 56.

9. Jim Domanski, "Referrals: The Easy Way to Prospect," in *Top Dog Sales Secrets*, Michael Dalton Johnson, ed. (Carlsbad, CA: Penny Union, 2007), pp. 13–15.

10. Geoffrey James, "How to Earn Customer Referrals," *Selling Power*, July/August 2004, pp. 25–28.

11. BNI-International, www.bni.com (accessed March 18, 2014).

12. Thomas Petzinger, Jr., "Selling a 'Killer App' Is a Far Tougher Job Than Dreaming It Up," *Wall Street Journal*, April 3, 1998, p. B1.

13. Daniel Tynan, "Tricks of the Trade Show," *Sales & Marketing Management*, January 2004, p. 27.

14. Ron Donoho, "Steering New Sales," *Sales & Marketing Management*, November 2001, pp. 31–35.

15. Henry Canaday, "Carefully Composed," *Selling Power*, May 2007, pp. 44–46.

16. Ibid., pp. 45–46.

17. Infogroup, www.infogroup.com, "Salesgenie Enhances Lead Generation with Canadian Consumer Data," *News Release*, September 24, 2013 (accessed March 18, 2014).

18. Henry Canaday, "Zeroing In On Prospects," *Selling Power*, March 2006, p. 82.

19. Andy Cohen, "Man About Town," *Sales & Marketing Management*, June 2000, p. 29.

20. John Boe, "Selling is a Contact Sport: Keys to Effective Phone Calling." *American Salesman*, January 2008, p. 26. For more information on cold calls see Scott Stears, "Cold Calls Have Yet to Breathe Their Last Gasp," *Wall Street Journal*, December 14, 2006, p. D2.

21. Maxwell Maltz, Dan S. Kennedy, William T. Brooks, Matt Oechsli, Jeff Paul, and Pamela Yellen, *Zero-Resistance Selling* (Paramus, NJ: Prentice-Hall, 1998), p. 167.

22. Stacy L. Bradford, "Ten Job-Networking Tips," *The News & Observer*, January 30, 2005, p. E7.

23. Tuba Üstüner and David Godes, "Better Sales Networks," *Harvard Business Review*, July–August 2006, pp. 102–12.

24. Michele Marchetti, "Do You Have the Knack for Networking?" *Sales & Marketing Management*, January 1996, p. 30; Deb Haggerty, "Successful Networking Begins as a State of Mind," *Selling*, December 2004, p. 13.

25. Maxwell Maltz, et al., *Zero-Resistance Selling*, ibid., pp. 179–80.

26. Steve Atlas, "Trouble Connecting?" *Selling Power*, September 2001, p. 27.

27. "Are You Generating and Using Quality Leads?" *Value-Added Selling 21*, September 16, 2003, p. 4.

28. Thomas R. Watruba, "The Evolution of Selling," *Journal of Personal Selling and Sales Management*, Summer 1991, p. 7.

29. This example was adapted from "Skills Workshop" by William F. Kendy, *Selling Power*, January/February 2000, p. 26.

30. Mitchell Pacelle, "Former SEC Chairman Levitt Decries Business Ethics in the U.S.," *Wall Street Journal*, June 17, 2002, p. C7; Shoshana Zuboff, "A Starter Kit for Business Ethics," *Fast Company*, January 2005, p. 91.

31. Rick Page, *Hope Is Not a Strategy* (Atlanta, GA: Nautilus Press, 2002), pp. 69–71.

32. "Senior Execs Share Insider Tips," *Selling*, March 2000, pp. 1, 14; Tom Reilly, "Selling to Mr. Big Is Tough, But. . . ," *Selling*, February 2001, pp. 1, 12.

33. Henry Canaday, "Fishing for Big Ones", *Personal Selling Power, Source Book 2008*, p. 46.

34. Jim Dickie and Barry Trailer, "Proactive Sales Intelligence: The New Requirement for Getting Into the Game," Salesforce .com 2007.

35. www.salesforce.com/company/news-press/pressreleas-es/2011/03/110330.jsp (accessed March 12, 2013).

36. www.salesforce.com/data/overview/ (accessed March 12, 2013).

37. Henry Canaday, "Fishing for Big Ones," ibid., pp. 46–47.

38. H. F. (Herb) MacKenzie, *Sales Management in Canada* (Toronto, ON: Pearson Education Canada, 2008), p. 140.

39. Tony Parinello, "Keeping Track of Prospects," www.entrepre-neur.com/article/0,4621,306013,00.html (January 13, 2003, accessed February 14, 2008).

40. Don Thomson, *Keeping the Funnel Full* (French Creek, BC, Mardon Publishing, 2004), p. 7.

41. H. F. (Herb) MacKenzie, *Sales Management in Canada*, ibid., p. 141.

Sources for Boxed Features

a. Based on Sarah Lorge, "The Best Way to Prospect," *Sales & Marketing Management*, January 1998, p. 80.

b. "Prospecting with social media," http://www.examiner.com/article/prospecting-with-social-media (accessed July 5, 2013); "Social Media Prospecting: Every Sale Starts with a Conversation," http://www.krusecontrolinc.com/automotive-social-media-prospecting-every-sale-startsconversation/ (accessed July 5, 2013); "Sales Prospecting Using Social Media," https://social123.com/salestipsguide/sales-prospecting-using-social-media/ (accessed July 5, 2013); "The 5 Dos and Don'ts of Social Media Prospecting," http://marketmesuite.com/blog/the-5-dos-and-donts-of-social-mediaprospecting/ (accessed July 5, 2013); "3 Things to Warm Up Your LinkedIn Prospecting," http://socialmediatoday.com/kendralee/1462981/3-tips-warm-your-linkedin-prospecting (accessed July 5, 2013).

c. Interview with Gene Chahley, Polaroid Canada Inc., May 19, 1997; Barbara Siskind, *Seminars to Build Your Business* (North Vancouver, BC: Self-Counsel Press, 1998), pp. 9–12; Sheldon Gordon, "Punch Up Your Profits," *Profit*, May 1999, pp. 17–22.

d. Barbara Pachter and Marjorie Brody, *Complete Business Etiquette Handbook* (Upper Saddle River, NJ: Prentice Hall, 1995), p. 278; "International Snapshot," *Sales & Marketing Management*, August 2001, p. 64; Jan Yager, *Business Protocol*, 2nd ed. (Stamford, CT: Hannacroix Books, Inc., 2001), pp. 116–17.

Chapter 10

1. Malcolm Fleschner, "Too Busy to Buy," *Selling Power*, March 1999, p. 36.

2. Gina Rollins, "Prepped to Sell," *Selling Power*, September 2006, pp. 74–77.

3. Bradford Agry, "Every Client Meeting Provides a Dynamic New Opportunity," *Selling*, April 2002, pp. 1, 4.

4. Malcolm Fleschner, "Anatomy of a Sale," *Selling Power*, April 1998, p. 76; Gina Rollins, "Prepare for the Unknown," *Selling Power*, July/August 2003, pp. 26–30.

5. Tom Reilly, "Prepare Like a Pro," www.TomReillyTraining.com (accessed April 8, 2007).

6. "Set the Agenda," *Personal Selling Power*, May/June 1995, p. 79.

7. Donna Fenn, "Because His Family Business Makes an Art of Customer Service," *Inc.*, April 2005, p. 94; telephone interview with Pamela Miles, staff member at Mitchells/Richards, March 22, 2005.

8. Philip Kotler and Gary Armstrong, *Principles of Marketing*, 14th ed. (Upper Saddle River, NJ: Prentice Hall, 2012), p. 471–72.

9. Rick Page, *Hope Is Not a Strategy*, (Atlanta, GA: Nautilus Press, 2002), p. 25.

10. Betsy Cummings, "Group Dynamics," *Sales & Marketing Management*, January/February 2007, p. 8.

11. James F. O'Hara, "Successful Selling to Buying Committees," *Selling*, February 1998, p. 8.

12. George R. Franke and Jeong-Eun Park, "Salesperson Adaptive Selling Behavior and Customer Orientation: A Meta-Analysis" *Journal of Marketing Research*, November 2006, pp. 639–702; Leroy Robinson, Jr., Greg W. Marshall, William C. Moncrief, and Felicia G. Lassk, "Toward a Shortened Measure of Adaptive Selling," *Journal of Personal Selling & Sales Management*, Spring 2002, pp. 111–19.

13. The role of confidence in adaptive selling is discussed in Leroy Robinson, Jr., Greg W. Marshall, William C. Moncrief, and Felicia G. Lassak, "Toward a Shortened Measure of Adaptive Selling," *Journal of Personal Selling & Sales Management*, Spring 2002, pp. 111–19.

14. Neil Rackham and John R. Vincentis, *Rethinking the Sales Force* (New York, NY: McGraw-Hill, 1999), p. 217.

15. Graham Roberts-Phelps, "How to Add Value to Every Sales Call," *Selling Power*, March–April 2010, p. 19.

16. Ibid.

17. Thomas A. Freese, *Secrets of Question Based Selling* (Naperville, IL: Sourcebooks, 2003), p. 114.

18. Based on John Fellows, "Your Foot in the Door," *Selling Power*, March 1996, pp. 64–65.

19. Excerpt from "Please, Call Me Back!" *Selling* by Art Sobczak. Copyright © 1999. Used by permission of Art Sobczak.

20. Ibid.

21. Deborah Dumaine, "Managing Customers with E-Mail," *Selling Power*, March 2004, p. 94.

22. Rachel Zupek, "Reply all and Other Email Gaffes," Business.com, September 2007, p. 26.

23. Excerpt from *The New Professional Image* by Susan Bixler and Nancy Nix-Rice. Published by Adams Media Corporation, © 1997.

24. Steve Atlas, "How to Cultivate New Turf," *Selling Power*, January/February 2003, p. 26.

25. Maxine Clayton, "60 Seconds on Small Talk," *Fast Company*, November 2004, p. 43.

26. Dean A. Goettsch, "Make Your First Meeting Count," *Selling*, July 2004, pp. 1, 4.

27. Melissa Campanelli, "Sound the Alarm," *Sales & Marketing Management*, December 1994, pp. 20–25.

28. Carolee Boyles, "Prewarm Cold Calls," *Selling Power*, July/August 2001, p. 30.

29. Abner Little, "Selling to Women Revs Up Car Sales," *Personal Selling Power*, July/August 1990, p. 50.

30. "Six Great Upselling Questions," *Personal Selling Power*, April 1993, p. 44.

31. Interview with Astrid Goodman, Goodman Brown Financial, March 12, 2014.

32. Linda Richardson, "The Richardson Sales Excellence Review"", www.blogs.richardson.com/2012/09/05/challenger_ sale_missing_link/ (accessed April 1, 2013).

33. Theodore Kinni, "How to Identify and Remove the Problems Underlying Call Reluctance," *Selling Power*, November/ December 2004, pp. 69–71; "Types of Call Reluctance," *Value-Added Selling 21*, February 14, 2005, p. 4.

34. Alan Farnham, "Are You Smart Enough to Keep Your Job?" *Fortune*, January 15, 1996, pp. 34–42.

35. "The Disappointment Trap," *Selling Power*, January/February 1999, p. 14.

36. Roy Chitwood, "Still Trying to Slip Past Gatekeepers? Forget It!" *Value-Added Selling 21*, December 16, 2003, pp. 1–2.

Sources for Boxed Features

a. Foreign Affairs and International Trade Canada, www.international.gc.ca (accessed May 1, 2011); Richard R. Gesteland, *Cross-Cultural Business Behavior* (Copenhagen: Handelshøjskolens Forlag, Copenhagen Business School Press, 1999), pp. 19–23.

b. Bryan Ziegler, "Your Business Card Can Be a Powerful Tool," *Des Moines Register*, August 2, 1999, p. 17–B; Kemba J. Dunham, "Here's My Card," *Wall Street Journal*, May 14, 2002, p. B12.

Chapter 11

1. Olaf Ploetner, "The Development of Consulting in Goods-Based Companies," *Industrial Marketing Management, 37*, February 6, 2008, p. 329.

2. V. Kuman, Rajkuman Venkatesan, and Werner Reinartz, "Performance Implications of Adopting a Customer-Focused Sales Campaign," *Journal of Marketing, 72*, September 2008, p. 50.

3. *Going the Distance: The Consultative Sales Presentation* (Pasadena, CA: Intelecom); "The Amgen Difference," www .amgen.com (accessed July 30, 2013).

4. Louis E. Boone and David L. Kurtz, Contemporary Marketing, 11th ed. (Mason, Ohio: Southwestern Publishing, 2004), p. 576; Geoffrey James, "Consultative Selling Strategies," *Selling Power*, April 2004, pp. 17–20.

5. Jack R. Snader, "Developing Consultative Sales Skills," *Pace*, October 1985, p. 49.

6. Jeff Thull, *The Prime Solution*, (Chicago, IL: Dearborn Publishing, 2005), p. 35.

7. Othman Boujena, Wesley J. Johnston, and Dwight R. Merunka, "The Benefits of Sales Force Automation: A Customer's Perspective, *Journal of Personal Selling and Sales Management, 24*, Spring 2009, p. 137.

8. Duane Sparks, *Questions—The Answer to Sales*, The Sales Board: Minneapolis, MN 2005, p. vii.

9. Rose A. Spinelli, "Listening: A Priority in Shopping for Others," *Chicago Tribune*, November 30, 2003, p. 55.

10. Gerhard Gschwandtner, "What Makes Sales Relationships Work?" *Selling Power*, May–June 2010, p. 9.

11. Research for the SPIN model was conducted in the late 1970s and early 1980. Neil Rackham, *SPIN Selling* (New York, NY: McGraw-Hill, 1988); www.huthwaite.com.au/research-ip.html (accessed June 8, 2010).

12. Geoffrey James, "Driving the High-Stakes Sales," *Selling Power*, May 2007, p. 51.

13. "What Do Good Salespeople Have in Common?" *Training*, December 1984, p. 21.

14. Research for the Professional Selling Skills model was conducted in the late 1960s and early 1970s. "Professional Selling Skills," www.achieveglobal.co.nz/_literature/Professional_Selling_Skills (accessed July 29, 2013).

15. Michael D. Hargrove, "Using the Socratic Selling Method," www.bluinc.com/news/socraticselling.html (accessed July 1, 2013).

16. Geoffrey James, "Driving the High-Stakes Sales," p. 52.

17. Robert Jolles, *Customer-Centered Selling: Mastering the Art of Urgency*, 2nd ed. (New York, NY: The Free Press, 2009), pp. 105–106.

18. Ann Demarais and Valerie White, *First Impressions—What You Don't Know About How Others See You* (New York, NY: Bantam Books, 2004), pp. 68–69.

19. Fernando Jaramillo and Douglas B. Grisaffe (Spring 2009), "Does Customer Orientation Impact Objective Sales Performance?" *Journal of Personal Selling and Sales Management, 24*(1), p. 167.

20. Barry L. Reece and Rhonda Brandt, *Effective Human Relations: Personal and Organizational Applications*, 12th ed. (OH: South-Western Cengage Learning, 2013), p. 33.

21. Ibid., p. 34.

22. Demarais and White, *First Impressions*, ibid., p. 70.

23. Abner Little, "Are You Listening," *Selling Power*, May–June 2010, p. 34.

24. William F. Kendy, "The Silence Play," *Selling Power*, July/ August 2007, pp. 29–30.

25. Matthew McKay, Martha Davis, and Patrick Fanning, *Message: The Communication Skills Book* (Oakland, CA: New Harbinger, 1995), p. 15; Susan Scott, *Fierce Conversations* (New York, NY: Viking Penguin, 2002), p. 157.

26. William F. Kendy, "How to Be a Good Listener," *Selling Power*, April 2004, p. 43.

27. Tom Reilly, *Value-Added Selling* (New York, NY: McGraw-Hill, 2003), p. 130.

28. Adam Rapp, Raj Agnihotri, and Lukas P. Forbes (Fall 2008), "The Sales Force Technology–Performance Chain: The Role of Adaptive Selling and Effort," *Journal of Personal Selling and Sales Management, 28*(4), p. 335.

29. Olaf Ploetner, "The Development of Consulting in Goods-Based Companies," p. 329.

30. Geoffrey James, "How to Use the Intuitive Model to Sell," *Selling Power*, May–June 2010, p. 40.

31. Decorating Den Interiors, www.decoratingden.com/meet-our-decorators.html (accessed July 1, 2013).

32. Tom Riley, *Value-Added Selling*, ibid., pp. 17, 167.

33. Kerry L. Johnson, "The Things Dales Masters Do," *Value-Added Selling 21*, April 16, 2007, p. 3.

34. Consona Corporation, www.configsc.com (accessed July 1, 2013).

35. Big Machines, www.bigmachines.com/salesforce.php (accessed March 20, 2014).

36. Adam Rapp, Raj Agnihotri, and Lukas P. Forbes, "The Sales Force Technology–Performance Chain: The Role of Adaptive Selling and Effort," ibid., p. 335.

37. Willem J. Verbeke, Frank D. Belschak, Arnold B. Bakker, and Bart Dietz (July 2008), "When Intelligence Is (Dys)Functional for Achieving Sales Performance," *Journal of Marketing, 72*, p. 44.

38. Paul F. Roos, "Just Say No," *Selling Power*, October 2003, p. 50.

39. Neil Rackham and John DeVincentis, *Rethinking the Sales Force* (New York, NY: McGraw-Hill, 1999), p. 17.

40. Ibid., p. 9.

Sources for Boxed Features

a. Duane Sparks, *Questions—The Answer to Sales*, The Sales Board, Minneapolis, MN. 2005, p. vi; "CARQUEST Cares," www.carquest.com (accessed June 29, 2013).

b. Interview with and correspondence from Sybil Taylor, Communications Director, Steam Whistle Brewing, April–May, 2011.

c. Based on "Selling in Belgium," *Sales & Marketing Management*, August 2002, p. 58.

Chapter 12

1. Excerpt from "Presentation-Wise, We've Lost Our Tails," *Sales & Field Force Automation*. Published by Salesforce.com, © 1999.

2. Jan Wieseke, Christian Homburg, and Nick Lee, "Understanding the Adoption of New Brands Through Salespeople: A Multilevel Framework," *Journal of the Academy of Marketing Science*, July 7, 2007, p. 278.

3. Franklin J. Carter and Ravindra Chitturi (Winter 2009), "Segmentation Based on Physician Behavior: Implications for Sales Forecasting and Marketing-Mix Strategy," *Journal of Personal Selling and Sales Management*, 29(1), p. 81.

4. Dean A. Goettsch, "Guidelines for Rethinking Sales Presentations," *Selling*, October 2001, p. 14.

5. Ryan Kibacki, "The Changing Role of the Sales Professional," *Selling Power*, May/June 2010.

6. "Communicating Technical Ideas Persuasively." This article originally appeared in the May-June 1998 issue of the *Journal for Management in Engineering*, published by the American Society of Civil Engineers (accessed May 26, 2010).

7. Gary A. Williams and Robert B. Miller, "Change the Way You Persuade," *Harvard Business Review*, May 2002, p. 6; Renee Houston Zemanski, "Subtlety Can Sell," *Selling Power*, January/February 2007, pp. 42–44.

8. Mike Coyne, "How I Made the Sale," *Value-Added Selling*, 21, August 12, 2003, pp. 1, 4.

9. John M. Hawes, "Leaders in Selling and Sales Management," *Journal of Personal Selling and Sales Management*, November 5, 1985, p. 60.

10. Randall Murphy, "The Consultative Approach to Selling," *Selling Power*, March–April 2010, p. 32.

11. Fernando Jaramillo and Douglas B. Grisaffe (Spring 2009), "Does Customer Orientation Impact Objective Sales Performance?" *Journal of Personal Selling and Sales Management*, 29(2), p. 167.

12. Lambeth Hochwald, "Simplify," *Sales & Marketing Management*, June 1998, pp. 66–67; "Company Information," www.bellhelicopter.textron.com (accessed July 1, 2013).

13. Personal interview with and correspondence from Paul Speck, Henry of Pelham, and company website, www.henryofpelham.com (accessed January 28, 2014).

14. Cindy Waxer, "The Lighter Side," *Selling Power*, January/February, 2005, p. 91.

15. Douglas A. Bernstein, Alison Clarke-Stewart, Edward J. Roy, and Louis A. Penner, *Psychology*, 6th ed. (Boston, MA: Houghton Mifflin Company, 2003), pp. 373–74.

16. Malcolm Fleschner, "Funny You Should Say That," *Personal Selling Power*, May–June 2010, pp. 14–16.

17. James C. Anderson, James A. Narus, and Wouter van Rossum, "Customer Value Proposition in Business Markets," *Harvard Business Review*, March 2006, pp. 1–9.

18. Ibid.

19. Corbin Ball Associates, "Avoiding Death by PowerPoint," www.corbinball.com/articles/art-powerpoint.htm (accessed March 20, 2014).

20. "Communicating Technical Ideas Persuasively," This article originally appeared in the May–June 1998 issue of the *Journal for Management in Engineering*, published by the American Society of Civil Engineers, accessed May 26, 2010.

21. Gerhard Gschwandtner, "What Makes Relationships Work?" *Selling Power*, May–June 2010, p. 9.

22. Kevin D. Bradford and Barton A. Weitz (Winter 2009), "Salespersons' Management of Conflict in Buyer—Seller Relationships," *Journal of Personal Selling and Sales Management*, 29(1), p. 25.

23. Robert B. Cialdini, "Harnessing the Science of Persuasion," *Harvard Business Review*, October 2001, p. 74.

24. Ibid., p. 9.

25. Stephanie G. Sherman and V. Clayton Sherman, *Make Yourself Memorable* (New York, NY: AMACOM, 1996), pp. 58–59.

26. Willem J. Verbeke, Frank D. Belschak, Arnold B. Bakker, and Bart Dietz, "When Intelligence Is (Dys)Functional for Achieving Sales Performance," *Journal of Marketing*, 72, July 2008, p. 44.

27. John Grossmann, "Location, Location, Location," *Inc.*, August 2004, p. 83.

28. Rich Mesch, "Spinning Yarns—Seven Tips for Using Stories to Enhance Simulations and Learning," *SPBT Focus*, Spring 2007, pp. 42–46.

29. Carol Burke, "How to Create and Deliver a Winning Group Presentation," www.salesvantage.com (accessed March 20, 2104). For more information see Joann S. Lublin, "Improve Troup Teaches Managers How to Give Better Presentation," *Wall Street Journal*, February 6, 2007, B1.

30. Cindy Waxer, "Light is Right," *Selling Power*, January/February 2007, pp. 100–102.

31. Cindy Waxer, "Shine On," *Selling Power*, April 2007, p. 98.

32. Excerpt from Selling Power Magazine Article, Light is Right, by Cindy Waxer. Copyright © 2007. Used by permission of Personal Selling Power Inc.

33. Joseph B. White, "New Ergonomic Chairs Battle to Save the Backs of Workers, for Big Bucks," *Wall Street Journal*, June 8, 1999, p. B4B.

34. Rick Page, *Hope Is Not a Strategy*, p. 126.

35. Geoffrey James, "Flight to Profit," *Selling Power*, September 2004, p. 74.

36. Lambeth Hochwald, "Simplify," pp. 65–66.

37. Ginger Trumfio, "Ready! Set! Sell!" *Sales & Marketing Management*, February 1995, pp. 82–84.

38. Landy Chase, "Master the Art of Brochure Selling," *Selling*, March 2005, pp. 8–9.

39. David Ranii, "Dermabond's Debut Disappoints," *News & Observer*, July 31, 1999, p. D1.

40. "Three Guides to Using Your Catalog as a Sales Tool," *Value-Added Selling 21*, June 17, 2003, p. 4.

41. "The Presentation Paper Trail," *Sales & Marketing Management*, March 1995, p. 49.

42. Heather Baldwin, "Star Light Star Bright," *Selling Power Source Book 2002*, p. 55.

43. Heather Baldwin, "Up Your Powers," *Selling Power Source Book*, October 2001, pp. 88–92.

44. Kevin Ferguson, "Reinventing the PowerPoint," *Inc.*, March 2004, p. 42; Corbin Ball Associates, "Avoiding Death by PowerPoint"; Stacy Straczynski, "PowerPoint and Beyond," *Training*, October 2006, p. 46.

45. Gerald L. Manning and Jack W. Linge, Selling-Today.com (Upper Saddle River, NJ: Prentice Hall, 2004), pp. 26–30.

46. Cindy Waxer, "Presenting the Power," *Selling Power*, (Source Book) 2005, pp. 70–71; Cindy Waxer, "Wired to Sell," *Selling Power*, June 2007, pp. 88–90.

47. Renee Houston Zemanski, "Play It Back," *Selling Power*, September 2007, p. 43.

48. Rick Page, *Hope Is Not a Strategy* (Atlanta, GA: Nautilus Press, 2002).

Sources for Boxed Features

a. Based on Betsy Cummings, "Selling Around the World," *Sales & Marketing Management*, May 2001, p. 70.

b. Based on Chad Kaydo, "Becoming the Face of the Brand," *Sales & Marketing Management*, February 2000, p. 14.

Chapter 13

1. *Selling Power*, June 2007, p. 32.

2. Geoff James, "The Art of Sales Negotiation," *Selling Power*, March 2004, pp. 25–28.

3. Tom Riley, *Value-Added Selling* (New York, NY: McGraw-Hill, 2003), p. 17.

4. Hal Lancaster, "You Have to Negotiate for Everything in Life, So Get Good at It," *Wall Street Journal*, January 27, 1998, p. B1.

5. Joydeep Srivastava and Dipankar Chakravarti (2009), "Channel Negotiations with Information Asymmetries: Contingent Influences of Communication and Trustworthiness Reputations," *Journal of Marketing Research*, 46(3), pp. 557–72.

6. Ron Willingham, *Integrity Selling for the 21st Century* (New York, NY: Currency Doubleday, 2003), p. 154.

7. Brian Tracy, *The 100 Absolutely Unbreakable Laws of Business Success* (San Francisco, CA: Berrett-Koehler Publishers, 2000), p. 235.

8. Ron Willingham, *Integrity Selling for the 21st Century*, p. 153.

9. Brenda Goodman, "The Art of Negotiation," *Psychology Today*, January/February 2007, pp. 64–65.

10. Gregg Crawford, "Let's Negotiate," *Sales & Marketing Management*, November 1995, pp. 28–29.

11. Michael Soon Lee, *The American Salesman*, August 2007, pp. 25–28.

12. Rob Walker, "Take It or Leave It: The Only Guide to Negotiating You Will Ever Need," *Inc.*, August 2003, p. 81.

13. Robert H. Schuller, "Preparing to Negotiate," in *The Only Negotiating Guide You'll Ever Need: 101 Ways to Win Every Time in Any Situation* by Peter B. Stark and Jane S. Flaherty, Chapter 10, pp. 81–85.

14. Deepak Malhotra and Max H. Bazerman, *Negotiation Genius* (New York, NY: Random House, 2007), p. 102.

15. Klaus Backhaus, Jenny van Doorn, and Robert Wilken (2008), "The Impact of Team Characteristics on the Course and Outcome of Intergroup Price Negotiations," *Journal of Business-to-Business Marketing*, 15(4), pp. 365–396.

16. Peter B. Stank and Jane Flaherty, *The Only Negotiating Guide You'll Ever Need* (New York, NY: Broadway Books, 2003), p. 84.

17. Deepak Malhotra and Max H. Bazerman, ibid., pp. 20–23.

18. Ibid.

19. P. V. Balakrishnan, Charles Patton, and Phillip A. Lewis (1993), "Toward a Theory of Agenda Setting in Negotiations," *Journal of Consumer Research*, 19(2), pp. 637–54.

20. Peter B. Stank and Jane Flaherty, ibid., p. 79.

21. Nicholas G. Paparoidamis and Paolo Guenzi (2009), "An Empirical Investigation into the Impact of Relationship Selling and LMX on Salespeople's Behaviors and Sales Effectiveness," *European Journal of Marketing*, 43(7/8), pp. 1053–75.

22. David Stiebel, *When Talking Makes Things Worse!* (Dallas, TX: Whitehall & Norlton, 1997), p. 17.

23. For details, see Deepak Malhotra and Max H. Bazerman, ibid., pp. 59–64, p. 82.

24. Don Maruska, *Value Added Selling, 21*, April 30, 2007, p. 2.

25. Robert Wilken, Markus Corneliben, Klaus Backhaus, and Christian Schmitz (2010), "Steering Sales Reps Through Cost Information: An Investigation into the Black Box of Cognitive References and Negotiation Behavior," *International Journal of Research in Marketing, 27*, pp. 69–82.

26. Joseph Conlin, "Negotiating Their Way to the Top," *Sales & Marketing Management*, April 1996, p. 62; Neil Rackham, "Winning the Price War," *Sales & Marketing Management*, November 2001, p. 26.

27. Deepak Malhotra and Max H. Bazerman, ibid., p. 175.

28. Lain Ehman, "Not a Done Deal," *Selling Power*, November/December 2003, pp. 42–44; "Negotiate the Right Price Despite Customer Pressure," *Selling*, July 2004, p. 2.

29. William F. Kendy, "Solving the 'Friendship Buying' Problem," *Selling Power*, November/December 2001, pp. 40–44.

30. Personal interview with and correspondence from Patricia McCallum, Century 21 B. J. Roth Realty, January 27, 2014.

31. Marc Freeman, "Say It and Sell It," *Sales & Marketing Management*, November/December 2006, p. 13.

32. William F. Kendy, "The Price Is Too High," *Selling Power*, April 2006, pp. 30–33.

33. Ibid.

34. Jeff Keller, "Objections? No Problem," *Selling Power*, September 1996, pp. 44–45.

35. Adapted from Nanci McCann, "Irate over Rates," *Selling*, July–August 1996, p. 25.

36. Tom Reilly, ibid., p. 189.

37. Rick Kang, "Management by Defiance," *Profit*, June 1999, pp. 63–64.

38. Neil Rackham, *The New SPIN Selling Fieldbook*, (New York, NY: McGraw-Hill, 1996), pp. 127–45.

39. David Jobber and Jeff Lancaster, *Selling and Sales Management*, 7th ed. (Prentice Hall/Financial Times, 2006), p. 261.

40. Arnaud De Bruyn and Gary E. Bolton (2008), "Estimating the Influence of Fairness on Bargaining Behavior," *Management Science*, 54(10), pp. 1774–91.

41. William F. Kendy, ibid., p. 30.

42. Tom Reilly, ibid., p. 191–92.

43. Joseph Conlin, "Negotiating Their Way to the Top," *Sales & Marketing Management*, April 1996, p. 58.

44. William F. Kendy, "The Price Is Too High," ibid., pp. 30–33.

45. Sam Deep and Lyle Sussman, *Close the Deal: Smart Moves for Selling* (Reading, MA: Perseus Books, 1999), p. 225.

46. Roland M. Sandell, "Five Sure-Fire Methods to Overcome Objections to Price," *American Salesman*, October 1976, p. 38.

47. William F. Kendy, "Negotiation Tactics," *Selling Power*, September 2006, p. 31.

48. Based on Homer Smith, "How to Cope with Buyers Who Are Trained in Negotiation," *Personal Selling Power*, September 1988, p. 37.

49. Ibid.

50. Robert Adler, Benson Rosen, and Elliot Silverstein, "Thrust and Parry," *Training & Development*, March 1996, p. 47.

51. Homer Smith, ibid.

52. Laura Pratt, "Everyone's a Winner," *Profit*, November 2001, p. 47.

Sources for Boxed Features

a. "Getting to Yes, Chinese Style," *Sales & Marketing Management*, July 1996, pp. 44–45; Sam Deep and Lyle Sussman, *Close the Deal: Smart Moves for Selling* (Reading, MA: Perseus Books, 1999), pp. 279–81; James K. Sebenius, "Six Habits of Merely Effective Negotiators," *Harvard Business Review*, April 2001, p. 90.

b. Hal Lancaster, "You Have to Negotiate for Everything in Life, So Get Good At It," *Wall Street Journal*, January 27, 1998, p. B1; Amy Lindgren, "Want a Raise? Don't Daydream; Polish Your Negotiating Skills," *Des Moines Register*, April 26, 1998, p. IL; "The Karrass Story," www.Karrass.com (accessed July 1, 2013).

c. Mary Klonizakis, "A Class Act," *Contact*, September 2000, p. 18.

Chapter 14

1. Personal interview with and correspondence from Nadia Gelmo, Heart of Niagara, March 7–8, 2014.

2. Subhra Chakrabarty, Gene Brown, and Robert E. Widing II (2010), "Closed Influence Tactics: Do Smugglers Win in the Long Run?" *Journal of Personal Selling and Sales Management*, 30(1), pp. 23–32.

3. Ron Willingham, *Integrity Selling for the 21st Century* (New York, NY: Currency Doubleday 2003), p. 179.

4. Sergio Roman and Dawn Iacobucci (2010), "Antecedents and Consequences of Adaptive Selling Confidence and Behavior: A Dyadic Analysis of Salespeople and Their Customers," *Journal of the Academy of Marketing Science*, 38(3), pp. 363–82.

5. Gene Bedell, *3 Steps to Yes* (New York, NY: Crown Business, 2000), pp. 72–80.

6. Tom Reilly, *Value-Added Selling* (New York, NY: McGraw-Hill, 2003), p. 176.

7. Andy Cohen, "Are Your Reps Afraid to Close?" *Sales & Marketing Management*, March 1996, p. 43.

8. Michele Marchetti, "Make Process a Sales Priority," *Sales & Marketing Management*, September 2006, p. 16. See John Graham, "How to Profit From Customer Buying-Cycle Basics," *The American Salesman*, May 2007, pp. 19–23.

9. Susan Creco, "The Need for Speed—How to Rev up Your Sales Cycle," *Inc. Magazine*, April 2007, p. 38.

10. Graham Denton, "The Single Biggest Closing Mistake," Graham Denton Skills Center, www.members.fortunecity.com/salesman2/salescom/closing/thesingl.html, p. 1 (accessed September 26, 2010).

11. Ray Dreyfock, "Is the Buyer Ready?" *Selling Power*, January/February 2002, p. 52.

12. Ralph W. Giacobbe, Donald W. Jackson Jr., Lawrence A. Crosby, and Claudia M. Bridges (2006), "A Contingency Approach to Adaptive Selling Behavior and Sales Performance: Selling Situations and Salesperson Characteristics," *Journal of Personal Selling and Sales Management*, 26(2), pp. 115–42.

13. "The Closing Moment," *Personal Selling*, October 1995, p. 48; Lain Ehman, "How to Read Hidden Signals," *Selling Power*, June 2004, pp. 36–38.

14. Ron Karr, "Expert Advice—The Titan Principle," *Selling Power*, October 2001, p. 32.

15. Richard G. McFarland, Goutam N. Challagalla, and Tasadduq A. Shervani (2006), "Influence Tactics for Effective Adaptive Selling," *Journal of Marketing*, 70(3), pp. 103–17.

16. Jenny McCune, "Closing Sales with a Splash," *Selling*, September 2004, p. 15.

17. "Selling Tips," *Selling*, May 1999, p. 13.

18. Ron Willingham, *Integrity Selling* (New York, NY: Doubleday, 1987), p. 133.

19. Jeffrey Gitomer, "Did You Get the Order? If You Didn't, Here's Why," *Business Record*, May 7, 2007, p. 36.

20. Tom Reilly, *Value-Added Selling*, ibid., p. 179.

21. Ron Willingham, *Integrity Selling for the 21st Century* (New York, NY: Currency Doubleday, 2003), p. 184.

22. Jenny C. McCune, "The Brief Story of Underwear's Stupendous Success," *Selling*, March 2000, p. 15.

23. Joan Leotta, "The Management Close," *Selling Power*, November/December 2001, pp. 26–28. See Megan Sweas, "Heavyweights on Call," *Sales & Marketing Management*, December 2003, p. 14.

24. Ron Willingham, *Integrity Selling for the 21st Century*, ibid., pp. 185–187.

25. George R. Franke and Jeong-Eun Park (2006), "Salesperson Adaptive Selling Behavior and Customer Orientation: A Meta-Analysis," *Journal of Marketing Research*, 43(4), pp. 693–702.

26. Mel Siberman, *Active Training* (Toronto, ON: Maxwell Macmillan Canada, 1990), pp. 96–99.

27. T. J. Becker, "That Queasy Feeling," *Chicago Tribune*, July 21, 2002, p. W1.

28. Betsy Wiesendanger, "When a Sale Goes South," *Selling Power*, November/December 2003, pp. 65–67.

29. Betsy Cummings, "Done Deal—How One Sales Pro Closed a Big Customer," *Sales & Marketing Management*, September 2006, p. 13.

30. Personal interview, Chris Van Wiechen, Collins Nissan, March 7, 2014.

31. Personal interview with and correspondence from Nadia Gelmo, ibid.

Sources for Boxed Features

a. Barbara Hagenbough, "Economics Majors Build Brand Name with Unmentionables," *USA Today*, May 20, 2002, p. 3–B.

b. "International Snapshot," *Sales & Marketing Management*, October 2001, p. 70; Jan Yager, *Business Protocol*, 2nd ed. (Stamford, CT: Hannacroix Books, 2001), pp. 116–17.

Chapter 15

1. WFS, www.wfsltd.com (accessed March 20, 2014); Rick Thurston, personal interview, January 27, 2014.

2. Bob Johnson, "Loyalty Lessons from the Pros," *Customer Support Management*, July/August 1999, p. 115; Ranjay Gulati and James B. Oldroyd, "The Quest for Customer Focus," *Harvard Business Review*, April 2005, pp. 92–97.

3. Ibid.

4. Gary Armstrong and Philip Kotler, *Marketing: An Introduction*, 6th ed. (Upper Saddle River, NJ: Prentice Hall, 2003), p. 553.

5. Don Peppers and Martha Rogers, "Customer Loyalty: A Matter of Trust," *Sales & Marketing Management*, June 2006, p. 22.

6. Theodore Levitt, *The Marketing Management* (New York, NY: Macmillan, 1983), pp. 117–18; Tahl Raz, "The '4 + 2 Formula' for Success," *Inc.*, August 2003, p. 42.

7. Brett Boyle, F. Robert Dwyer, Robert A. Robicheaux, and James T. Simpson (1992), "Influence Strategies in Marketing Channels: Measures and Use in Different Relationship Structures," *Journal of Marketing Research, 29*(4), pp. 462–73.

8. See Tom Reilly, "Value Added Service is a Team Sport," Tom Reilly Training, www.tomreillytraining.com (accessed March 20, 2014).

9. Geoffrey Brewer, "The Customer Stops Here," *Sales & Marketing Management*, March 1998, pp. 31–32; see Ron Zemke and Chip Bell, *Service Magic* (Chicago: IL: Dearborn Trade Publishing, 2004).

10. "Why Customers Leave," *Sales & Marketing Management*, May 1998, p. 86; Tom Peters, *The Circle of Innovation* (New York, NY: Vintage Books, 1997), pp. 138–39.

11. Larry Rosen, personal correspondence, May 17, 2011.

12. Bill Gates, *Business @ the Speed of Thought* (New York, NY: Warner Books, 1999), p. 67.

13. Ruth Maria Stock and Wayne D. Hoyer (2005), "An Attitude-Behavior Model of Salespeople's Customer Orientation," *Journal of the Academy of Marketing Science, 33*(4), pp. 536–52.

14. Michael Ahearne, Ronald Jelinek, and Eli Jones, "Examining the Effect of Salesperson Service Behavior in a Competitive Context," *Journal of the Academy of Marketing Science*, Spring 2007, p. 13.

15. See Daniel H. Pink, *A Whole New Mind* (New York, NY: Riverhead Books, 2005), pp. 48–53.

16. Frederick Hong-kit Yim, Rolph E. Anderson, and Srinivasan Swaminathan (2004), "Customer Relationship Management: Its Dimensions and Effect on Customer Outcomes," *Journal of Personal Selling and Sales Management, 24*(4), pp. 263–78.

17. Steve Ham, "Oracle—Why It's Cool Again," *Business Week*, May 8, 2000, pp. 115–19.

18. Maggie Chung, personal interview, July 25, 2008.

19. Maxim Sytch and Ranjay Gulati (2008), "Creating Value Together," *MIT Sloan Management Review, 50*(1), pp. 12–13.

20. Chad Kaydo, "An Unlikely Sales Ally," *Sales & Marketing Management*, January 1999, p. 69.

21. Sally J. Silberman, "An Eye for Finance," *Sales & Marketing Management*, April 1996, p. 26.

22. Benson P. Shapiro, V. Kasturi Rangon, and John Sviokla, *Harvard Business Review*, July/August 2004, p. 162–71.

23. Daryl Allen, "Relationship Selling Is Key to Success," *Selling*, March 2002, p. 12.

24. Dave Kahle, "Protecting Your Good Accounts," *The American Salesman*, June 2007, p. 12.

25. Gary L. Frankwick, Stephen S. Porter, and Lawrence A. Crosby (2001), "Dynamics of Relationship Selling: A Longitudinal Examination of Changes in Salesperson-Customer Relationship Status," *Journal of Personal Selling and Sales Management, 21*(2), pp. 135–46.

26. Tom Reilly, "Create Satisfied Customers: Always Be Sure to Exceed Their Expectations," *Selling*, January 2001, p. 3; Mary Salafia. "Reassessment Planning," *Selling Power*, May 2004, p. 56.

27. Tom Riley, *Value-Added Selling* (New York, NY: McGraw-Hill, 2003), p. 117.

28. Personal interview, Erin Sammy, Henley Honda, January 28, 2014.

29. Andrea Nierenberg, "Eight Ways to Stay Top of Mind," *Selling*, April 1998, p. 7.

30. Queena Sook Kim, "For Sale: Super-Model Home," *Wall Street Journal*, August 6, 2002, p. D-1.

31. Melinda Ligos, "The Joys of Cross-Selling," *Sales & Marketing Management*, August 1998, p. 75.

32. Tom Riley, *Value-Added Selling*, pp. 124–25.

33. William F. Kendy, "Add-Ons Add Up," *Selling Power*, January/February 2007, p. 30.

34. William F. Kendy, "Skills Workshop," *Selling Power*, June 2000, pp. 33–34.

35. Jo Ann Brezette, "Smart Answers to Clients' Questions," *Window Fashions Design & Education Magazine*, September 2001, p. 120; Lain Ehman, "Upsell, Don't Oversell," *Selling Power*, January–February 2004, pp. 30–32.

36. John Hagedoorn (2006), "Understanding the Cross-Level Embeddedness of Interfirm Partnership Formation," *Academy of Management Review, 31*(3), pp. 670–80.

37. "Inspirations from Michele," *Inspiring Solutions*, February 1999, p. 3.

38. Jahyun Goo, Rajiv Kishore, H. R. Rao, and Kichan Nam (2008), "The Role of Service Level Agreements in Relational Management of Information Technology Outsourcing: An Empirical Study," *MIS Quarterly, 33*(1), pp. 119–45.

39. Bob Johnson, "Loyalty Lessons from the Pros," *Customer Support Management*, July/August 1999, p. 115.

40. Barry L. Reece and Rhonda Brandt, *Effective Human Relations: Interpersonal and Organizational Applications*, 12th ed. (OH: South-Western Cengage Learning, 2013), pp. 195–96.

41. Bradley E. Wesner, "From Complaint to Opportunity," *Selling Power*, May 1996, p. 62.

42. Gerald A Michaelson, "When Things Go Wrong, Make It Right," *Selling*, March 1997, p. 12.

43. Michael Abrams and Matthew Paese, "Winning and Dining the Whiners," *Sales & Marketing Management*, February 1993, p. 73.

44. "How to Diffuse a Customer Problem," *Sales & Marketing Management*, May 2000, p. 14.

45. Rick Thurston, ibid.; WFS, ibid.

Sources for Boxed Features

a. Based on Jeff Barbian, "It's Who You Know," *Training*, December 2001, p. 22.

b. "Relationships with Customers Must Be Job Number 1," *Food-Service Distributor*, July 1989, p. 74; Joan O. Fredericks and James M. Salter II, "Beyond Customer Satisfaction," *Management Review*, May 1995, pp. 29–32.

c. Jan Yager, *Business Protocol*, 2nd ed. (Stamford, CT: Hannacroix Books, 2001), p. 123; "Selling in Russia," *Sales & Marketing Management*, March 2002, p. 60; Carl F. Fey and Stanislow Shekshnia, "How to Do Business in Russia," *Wall Street Journal*, October 27, 2007, p. R4.

d. "When to Say No to a Client," *Canadian Business*, February 2014, pp. 25–26; Betsy Cummings, "You're Outta Here," *Sales & Marketing Management*, June 2001, pp. 65–66; Rhea Seymour, "Ideas That Work," *Profit*, June 2002, pp. 66–70; Betsey Cummings, "The Perfect Plan," *Sales & Marketing Management*, February 2002, p. 53.

Chapter 16

1. Paula Shannon, personal correspondence, May 2005 through March 2014.

2. Renee Houston Zemanski, "A Matter of Time," *Selling Power*, October 2001, p. 82.

3. Bernd Skiera and Sonke Albers (2008), "Prioritizing Sales Force Decision Areas for Productivity Improvements Using a Core Sales Response Function," *Journal of Personal Selling and Sales Management*, 28(2), pp. 145–54.

4. Eugene Greissman, "Seven Characteristics of High-Achieving Salespeople," *Value-Added Selling 21*, March 16, 2004, p. 4.

5. Betty Cummings, "Increasing Face Time," *Sales & Marketing Management*, January 2004, p. 12.

6. Barry J. Farber, "Not Enough Hours in the Day," *Sales & Marketing Management*, July 1995, pp. 28–29.

7. If you are interested in how to break bad habits and form good ones, see James Claiborn and Cherry Pedrick, *The Habit Change Workbook* (Oakland, CA: New Harbinger Publications, 2001).

8. See Alison Stein Wellner, "The Time Trap," *Inc.*, June 2004, pp. 42–44.

9. Brian Tracy, *The 100 Absolutely Unbreakable Laws of Business Success* (San Francisco: Berrett-Koehler Publishers, Inc., 2000), pp. 40–47.

10. Charles R. Hall, "Create Excitement, Get Motivated Through Planning," *Selling*, February 2000, p. 13.

11. Ed Brown, "Stephen Covey's New One-Day Seminar," *Fortune*, January 1999, p. 138.

12. Besty Wiesendanger, "Time to Spend," *Selling Power*, November/December 2003, pp. 28–32.

13. Hyrum W. Smith, *The 10 Natural Laws of Successful Time and Life Management* (New York, NY: Warner Books, 1994), p. 108.

14. Thomas E. Weber, "Meetings in Cyberspace May Soon Be as Routine as the Conference Call," *Wall Street Journal*, June 4, 2001, p. B1.

15. Personal correspondence, Mary Costello, Senior Salesrepresentative, Pearson Canada, January 27, 2014.

16. Ken Grant, David W. Cravens, George S. Low, and William C. Moncrief (2001), "The Role of Satisfaction with Territory Design on the Motivation, Attitudes, and Work Outcomes of Salespeople," *Journal of the Academy of Marketing Science*, 29(2), pp. 165–78.

17. Lain Chroust Ehmann, "In the Details," *Selling Power*, September 2007, p. 34.

18. Rajkumar Venkatesan, V. Kumar, and Timothy Bohling (2007), "Optimal Customer Relationship Management Using Bayesian Decision Theory: An Application for Customer Selection," *Journal of Marketing Research*, 44(4), pp. 579–94.

19. V. Kumar, Rajkumar Venkatesan, Tim Bohling, and Denise Beckmann (2008), "The Power of CLV: Managing Customer Lifetime Value at IBM," *Marketing Science*, 27(4), pp. 585–99.

20. Ibid., p. 36.

21. Ken Liebeskind, "Where Is Everyone?" *Selling Power*, March 1998, p. 35; Marie Warner, "Take Careful Steps When Redefining Territories," *Selling*, June 2001, p. 10.

22. Alison Smith, "Plan Your Territory," *Selling Power*, March 2003, pp. 37–38.

23. Daryl Allen, "Maximize Your Territory Coverage, Increased Sales and Higher Profits Will Follow," *Selling*, June 2001, p. 10.

24. Paul Clark, Richard A. Rocco, and Alan J. Bush (2007), "Sales Force Automation Systems and Sales Force Productivity: Critical Issues and Research Agenda," *Journal of Relationship Marketing*, 6(2), pp. 67–87.

25. Henry Canaday, "Automated Reports Boost Sales Productivity," *Selling Power*, June 2007, p. 13.

26. "Maintaining Perspective by Keeping Good Records," *Value-Added Selling 21*, August 20, 2007, p. 4.

27. Jeffrey E. Lewin and Jeffrey K. Sager (2008), "Salesperson Burnout: A Test of the Coping-Mediational Model of Social Support," *Journal of Personal Selling and Sales Management*, 28(3), pp. 233–46.

28. Bruce Cryer, Rollin McCraty, and Doc Childre, "Pull the Plug On Stress," *Harvard Business Review*, July 2003, pp. 1–2.

29. David Shenk, "Data Smog," *Perdid*, Spring 1999, pp. 5–7.

30. "More Useful Tips for Running Your Home Office," *Selling*, January 2001, p. 11; "Home Office Etiquette," *Sales & Marketing Management*, January 2000, p. 74.

31. Patricia Sellers, "Now Bounce Back," *Fortune*, May 1, 1995, p. 57.

32. Martin Seligman, *Learned Optimism*, (New York, NY: Knopf, 2001), p. 4; Annie Murphy Paul, "Self-Help: Shattering the Myths," *Psychology Today*, March/April 2001, p. 64; Arnold A. Lazarus and Clifford N. Lazarus, *The 60-Second Shrink* (San Luis, Obispo CA: Impact Publishers, 1997), pp. 3, 4.

33. Caleb T. Hayes and Bart L. Weathington (2007), "Optimism, Stress, Life Satisfaction, and Job Burnout in Restaurant Managers," *Journal of Psychology*, 141(6), pp. 565–79.

34. Sandra Lotzs Fisher, "Stress—Will You Cope or Crack?" *Selling*, May 1996, p. 31.

35. Husky Injection Molding Systems , "Careers at Husky," available http://www.husky.co/EN-US/Careers/Work-Environment.aspx (accessed March 20, 2014).

Sources for Boxed Features

a. Alex Pettes, *From the Flight Deck* (Bloomington, IN: iUniverse, 2010); correspondence and personal interviews, 2006–2014.

b. Based on Michael Adams, "Family Matters," *Sales & Marketing Management*, March 1998, pp. 61–65.

c. "International Snapshot," *Sales & Marketing Management*, February 2001, p. 92; Jan Yager, *Business Protocol*, 2nd ed. (Stamford, CT: Hannacroix Books, Inc., 2001), pp. 114–15.

Chapter 17

1. Jan Wieseke, Michael Ahearne, Son K. Lam, and Rolf van Dick (2009), "The Role of Leaders in Internal Marketing," *Journal of Marketing, 73*(2), pp. 123–45.

2. Robert Kreitner, *Management*, 9th ed. (Boston, MA: Houghton Mifflin Company, 2004), p. 503.

3. "Stephen Covey Talks About the 8th Habit: Effective Is No Longer Enough," *Training*, February 2005, pp. 17–19.

4. Michael R. Solomon, Greg W. Marshall, and Elnora W. Stuart, *Marketing—Real People, Real Choices*, 4th ed. (Upper Saddle River, NJ: Pearson Education, 2006), p. 444.

5. Jack Falvey, "Fly by Night, Sell by Day," *Wall Street Journal*, June 9, 1997, p. A-18.

6. Lisa Gschwandtner, "What Makes an Ideal Sales Manager," *Selling Power*, June 2001, p. 54.

7. William Keenan Jr., "Death of the Sales Manager," *Sales & Marketing Management*, April 1998, pp. 72–79.

8. Alan J. Dubinsky, Francis J. Yammarino, Marvin A. Jolson, and William D. Spangler, "Transformational Leadership: An Initial Investigation in Sales Management," *Journal of Personal Selling & Sales Management*, Spring 1995, pp. 17–29.

9. These dimensions are described in Edwin A. Fleischman, *Manual for Leadership Opinion Questionnaire* (Chicago: Science Research Associates, 1960), p. 3. The dimensions of consideration and structure are also described in Robert Kreitner and Charlene M. Cassidy, *Management*, 12th ed. (OH: South-Western Cengage Learning, 2011.), p. 399.

10. Dale Kahle, "It Takes More than Just Compensation to Unleash a Sales Force!" *The American Salesman*, October 2007, p. 5.

11. Brian Tracy, *The 100 Absolutely Unbreakable Laws of Business Success* (San Francisco: Berrett-Koehler Publishers, 2000), pp. 19–20.

12. Jared Sandberg, "Overcontrolling Bosses Aren't Just Annoying; They're Also Inefficient," *Wall Street Journal*, March 30, 2005, p. B1.

13. Sarah Lorge, "In the Box," *Sales & Marketing Management*, April 1998, p. 15.

14. Ken Blanchard, "3 Secrets of the One-Minute Manager," *Personal Selling Power*, March 1993, p. 48.

15. Robert Kreitner, *Management*, 9th ed., (Boston, MA: Houghton Mifflin, 2004), p. 508; Paul Hersey, *The Situational Leader* (Escondido, CA: Center for Leadership Studies, 1984), pp. 29–30.

16. Ron Zemke, "Trust Inspires Trust," *Training*, January 2002, p. 10; Barry L. Reece and Rhonda Brandt, *Effective Human Relations: Interpersonal and Organizational Applications*, 12th ed. (OH: South-Western Cengage Learning, 2013), p. 110; Noel M. Tichy and Warren G. Bennis, "Making the Tough Call—Great Leaders Recognize When Their Values Are On the Line," *Inc.*, November 2007, pp. 36–37.

17. Rhea Seymour, "The Mentor's Reward," *Profit*, November 2001, p. 35.

18. Kenneth R. Phillips, "The Achilles' Heel of Coaching," *Training & Development*, March 1998, p. 41.

19. Anne Fisher, "In Praise of Micromanaging," *Fortune*, August 23, 2004, p. 40; Brian Tracy, "Coaching for Success," *Sales & Marketing Management*, July/August 2007, p. 6.

20. Anne Fisher, "Essential Employees Called Up to Serve," *Fortune*, October 2000, p. 210.

21. Synnex Canada, www.synnex.ca (accessed March 17, 2014).

22. Paula Lima, "Talent Shortage? That Was Yesterday," *Profit*, February/March 2002, pp. 65–66.

23. Willem J. Verbeke, Frank D. Belschak, Arnold B. Bakker, and Bart Dietz (2008), "When Intelligence Is (Dys)Functional for Achieving Sales Performance," *Journal of Marketing, 72*(2), pp. 44–57.

24. Dana Telford and Adrian Gostick, "Hiring Character," *Sales and Marketing Management*, June 2005, pp. 39–42.

25. Andy Cohen, "What Keeps You Up at Night?" *Sales & Marketing Management*, February 2000, pp. 44–52.

26. Henry Canaday, "Search Smarts," *Selling Power*, Source Book 2008, pp. 64, 68.

27. "Sales Achievement Predictor," www.wpspublish.com (accessed June 8, 2005).

28. "Caliper Profile," www.calipercorp.com (accessed March 20, 2014.)

29. Henry Canaday, "Search Smarts," ibid.

30. Shikhar Sarin, Trina Sego, Ajay K. Kohli, and Goutam Challagalla (2010), "Characteristics that Enhance Training Effectiveness in Implementing Technological Change in Sales Strategy: A Field-Based Exploratory Study," *Journal of Personal Selling and Sales Management, 30*(2), pp. 143–56.

31. Philip Kotler and Gary Armstrong, *Principles of Marketing*, 12th Edition. (Upper Saddle River, NJ: Prentice Hall, 2008), p. 460.

32. Alan J. Dubinsky, Francis J. Yammarino, Marvin A. Jolson, and William D. Spangler, "Transformational Leadership: An Initial Investigation in Sales Management," *Journal of Personal Selling & Sales Management*, Spring 1995, p. 27.

33. Skip Corsini, "The Great (Sales) Training Robbery," *Training*, February 2005, p. 14.

34. Barry L. Reece and Rhonda Brandt, *Effective Human Relations: Interpersonal and Organizational Applications*, 12th ed. (OH: South-Western Cengage Learning, 2013), p. 148.

35. Ibid.

36. Noah Lim, Michael J. Ahearne, and Sung H. Ham (2009), "Designing Sales Contests: Does the Prize Structure Matter?" *Journal of Marketing Research, 46*(2), pp. 356–71.

37. Audrey Bottjen, "Incentives Gone Awry," *Sales & Marketing Management*, May 2001, p. 72.

38. Lain Chroust Ehmann, "A Team of Winners," *Selling Power*, November/December 2006, pp. 40–43.

39. William H. Murphy, Peter A. Dacin, and Neil M. Ford (2004), "Sales Contest Effectiveness: An Examination of Sales Contest Design Preferences of Field Sales Forces," *Journal of the Academy of Marketing Science, 20*(10), pp. 1–17.

40. Julie Chang, "Trophy Value," *Sales & Marketing Management*, October 2004, p. 26.

41. Carol Hymorwitz, "When Meeting Targets Becomes the Strategy, CEO Is on Wrong Path," *Wall Street Journal*, March

8, 2005, p. B1; Carol Hymorwitz, "Readers Share Tales of Jobs Where Strategy Became Meeting Target," *Wall Street Journal*, March 22, 2005, p. B1.

42. Michael Schrage, "A Lesson in Perversity," *Sales and Marketing Management*, January 2004, p. 28.

43. Michael Segalla, Dominique Rouzies, Madeleine Besson, and Barton A. Weitz (2006), "A Cross-National Investigation of Incentive Sales Compensation," *International Journal of Research in Marketing, 23*, pp. 419–33.

44. Eilene Zimmerman, "Quota Busters," *Sales & Marketing Management*, January 2001, pp. 59–63.

45. Christine Galea, "2005 Compensation Survey," *Sales & Marketing Management*, May 2005, pp. 24–29.

46. Dominique Rouzies, Anne T. Coughlan, Erin Anderson, and Dawn Iacobucci (2009), "Determinants of Pay Levels and Structures in Sales Organizations," *Journal of Marketing, 73*(4), pp. 92–104.

47. "Point Incentive Sales Programs," *SBR Update*, Vol. 1, No. 4; Christopher Hosford, "A Carrot That Works," *Sales & Marketing Management*, November/December 2007, p. 10.

48. Donald W. Jackson, Jr., John L. Schlacter, and William G. Wolfe, "Examining the Bases Utilized for Evaluating Salespeople's Performance," *Journal of Personal Selling & Sales Management*, February 1995, p. 57.

49. "Survey of Sales Education Process—What Works, What Doesn't," *Selling Power*, September 1999, p. 115.

50. Lisa Holton, "Look Who's in on Your Performance Review," *Selling*, January/February 1995, pp. 47–55; Barry L. Reece and Rhonda Brandt, *Effective Human Relations: Personal and Organizational Applications*, 9th ed. (Boston, MA: Houghton Mifflin, 2005), p. 195; "Customer Ratings Are Misleading," *Selling*, November 1996, p. 1.

Sources for Boxed Features

a. Personal interview with Tom Gunter, vice president of sales, ConAgra Foods, Conducted by Lisa Violo, Brock University MBA student, November 4, 2005; personal interview with H.F. (Herb) MacKenzie, August 9, 2006.

b. Douglas J. Dalrymple and William L. Cron, *Sales Management: Concepts and Cases* (New York, NY: John Wiley & Sons, 1998), pp. 344–47; William Keenan, "Time Is Everything," *Sales & Marketing Management*, August 1993, p. 61.

c. Roger Bennet (1999), "Guanxi and Sales Force Management Practices in China," in Malcolm Warner (ed), *China's Management Revolution*, (London, UK: Frank Cass Publishers), pp. 73–93; Carol Hymorwitz, "When Meeting Targets Becomes the Strategy, CEO Is on Wrong Path," *Wall Street Journal*, March 8, 2005, p. B1; Carol Hymorwitz, "Readers Share Tales of Jobs Where Strategy Became Meeting Target," *Wall Street Journal*, March 22, 2005, p. B1.

Name Index

A

Abbott Laboratories, 92
About Face Image Consulting, 132
AchieveGlobal, 23, 260
Acuff, Frank, 310
Acuff, Jerry, 171
Adams, Doug, 298
Advertising Age, 140
Airbus, 326
Air Canada, 189
Alessandra, Tony, 118, 364
Alliance Security Systems, 206
Amazon.com, 99, 100
American Institutes of Marine
    Underwriters, 427
Amgen, 16, 277–278
Amway, 18
Aramark, 42
Ashley, Darryl, 67
AT&T, 390
Atkins, Stuart, 119
Avon, 18

B

Backroads, 154
Ballmer, Steven, 115
Barauh, Jaime, 402–403
Barbaro, Ron, 329
BAX Global, 133
Bedell, Gene, 337
Bell Atlantic, 325
Bell Helicopter, 286, 298
Bellino's Italian Restaurant, 372
Bentley Motor Cars, 205
Best Buy, 55, 271
Bezos, Jeff, 99, 100
BigMachines, 271
BigMachines Express, 139
Bisignano, Jill, 372
Bixler, Susan, 86, 89, 239
BKM Total Office, 203
BlackBerry, 189, 297
Blake, Robert, 405
Blanchard, Ken, 407, 410
BlueSky Personnel Solutions, 6
BMW, 149
BNI Canada, 319
Boeing, 99, 326

Bolton, Dorothy Grover, 101
Bolton, Robert, 101
Bombardier, 326
Boston Beer Company, 21
Botello, Edith, 50–51, 74–75, 293, 322
Brodow, Ed, 314, 317
Brother International
    Corporation, 155
Busch, Ray, 345
Buseman, Greg, 423
Business Network International, 202

C

Caliper Corporation, 413
Canada Human Resources Centre, 411
Canadian Grocer, 140, 204
Canadian National Railways, 189
Canadian Professional Sales
    Association, 24, 65, 186, 327
Canadian Securities Institute, 244
Canadian Trade Commissioner
    Service, 203
C&C Market Research, 9
Canfield, Jack, 82, 92
CanTrust Real Estate, 122
Cardinal Logistics Management, 215
Carlisle, Frances, 92
Carnegie, Dale, 82, 91, 241
CARQUEST Auto Parts, 257
Carrey, Jim, 106
Casey, Jim, 32
CB Richard Ellis, 76, 97, 198, 301,
    313, 429–430
Century 21, 319
Chatter, 230, 369
Cherry, Don, 106
Chung, Maggie, 362
Cialdini, Robert, 292
Cirenza, Maryann, 423
Cisco Systems, 80, 128, 208
Citigroup Incorporated, 68
Cleese, John, 101
Clinton, Hillary, 108
ClosetMaid, 299
Closure Medical Corporation, 299
Coaching Works, 198
Cohon, Charley, 393
Collier, Linda, 373

Collins Nissan, 351
The Communication Project, 351
Concept E-Catalog, 271
Configuration Solutions, 271
Configure One, 271
Consumer Reports, 140
Cooper, Donald, 408
Corning, 44
Corporate Executive Board, 127
Corporate Knights, 156
Costner, Kevin, 110
Covey, Stephen, 39, 66, 82, 91, 404
CPSA Sales Institute, 407
Craig, John, 62
Cretney, Cliff, 356–357
Cruise, Tom, 302
Cybrant Solutions Architect, 128

D

Daley, Kevin, 260
Dataline Incorporated, 390
Davis, Stan, 4
Davis, Victoria, 12, 335, 354
Dell, 180
Dentsply International, 42
DeSordi, Sandro, 131
Diamond, Bruce, 412
Diana, Princess of Wales, 110
Direct Sellers Association, 18
Dixon, Janet, 212
Do All Industrial Supply, 243
Domanski, Jim, 132, 201
Doran, Jill, 390
Downing Displays, 299
Drake Beam Morin, 360
Drucker, Peter, 31
Dun & Bradstreet Reference Book, 213
Dunlap, Al "Chainsaw," 99
Durkee Famous Foods, 315
Durkin, Dianne, 297

E

Eades, Keith, 36, 172, 267
E. & J. Gallo Winery, 298
Eastman Chemical Company, 55
Ecolab, 280–282, 306, 436–438
Eddie Greenspan, 7

Sanders, Tim, 91
Schering-Plough, 390
Schick Technologies, Inc., 64
Schneider, Gary, 202
Schuller, Robert H., 313
Schulze, Richard, 55
Schwartz, Steven J., 132, 209
Scott Paper, 99
Scott's Directories, 203
Seligman, Martin, 247, 397
Sennett, Richard, 67
Seybold, Patricia, 39, 40
Shannon, Paula, 380–381, 400–401
Shaw, Rosado, 41
Sheindlin, Judy, 108
Shenk, David, 5
Siebel.com, 19
Siebel Systems, 417
Sierra Wireless, 373
Sim Graphics Engineering
    Corporation, 16
Simon, Paul, 110
Siskind, Barbara, 211
Siskind, Barry, 132, 209
SJS Productions, 132
Skarlicki, Daniel, 329
Slavik, Jerry, 356–357
Smith, Frederick W., 141
Smith, Homer, 327
Smith, Hyrum W., 386
Smith, Marcus, 15, 29, 48–49, 201
Smith, Stephen, 325
Smith Kline, 413
Sobeys, 174
Socrates, 260
Sony Electronics, 296
Sparks, Duane, 257
Speck, Paul, 288
Spurlock, Maria, 338
Srivastava, Alka and Mona, 341
Steam Whistle Brewing, 259
Steelcase Incorporated, 162, 166–167
Stein, Dave, 185
Stiebel, David, 316
Stoney Creek Furniture, 17
Streep, Meryl, 110
SugarCRM.com, 19
Sunbeam Corporation, 99
Sun Life Financial, 57, 156

Sutcliffe, David, 373
Suzuki, David, 109
Swartz, Jeffrey, 56

T

Taylor, Janis, 240
TD Canada Trust, 167
Teleconcepts Consulting, 132, 201
Tele-Direct Atlantic, 321
Telegraph Hill Robes, 338
Teleport Communications Group, 423
Telford, Dana, 412
Teplitzky, Burt, 290
TerrAlign, 391
Texas Monthly, 14, 124–125, 128, 146,
    299, 430–431
TFI Food Equipment Solutions, 44, 383
Theodore Kinni, 10
ThomasNet.com, 203
Thull, Jeff, 255
Tice, Steve, 16
Tilley Endurables, 160, 161
Timberland, 56
Timken Company, 158
Tindall, Paul, 198
Tingley, Judith C., 182
Todd, Ruth, 101
Tom James Company, 1–2, 27–28, 198,
    229, 425–426
Tracy, Brian, 20, 82, 384, 406
Training, 22
Tri-Ad International Freight
    Forwarding, 373
Trugreen Chemlawn, 240
Turner, Mary, 315
Twitter, 5

U

Umbrellas Plus, 41
Unisys, 99
United Technologies, 55
University, Brock, 345
UPS, 32, 80, 212

V

Vandaveer, Amy, 14, 124–125, 128, 146,
    299
Volkswagen, 187

W

Wack, Patrick, 156
Warm Thoughts Communications, 114
Webber, Alan M., 56
Weber, Mike, 370
Weinstein, Bruce, 69
Weissman, Doron, 363
Welles, Orson, 92
Wenschlag, Roger, 101, 115
Western Psychological Services, 413
WFS Ltd., 356–357, 376–377
Wheeler, Lana, 114
Whirlpool, 131
White, Colleen, 348
White, Mike, 89–90
Whites Limited, 403
Wicker Corporation, 21
Wiechen, Chris Van, 351
Williams, Mark, 323
Williams, Robin, 106
Williams Hardware, 323
Willingham, Ron, 62, 77, 118, 310
Wilson, Larry, 79
Wilson Learning, 79, 101, 112
Winfrey, Oprah, 106
WorldCom, 154
WorldCom Incorporated, 67
Würth Canada, 6
Wyeth-Ayerst International, 337
Wylie, Chris, 280–282, 306

X

Xerox, 135, 205
Xerox Learning Systems, 260

Y

Yellow Pages, 203
York University, 57
Young Electric Sign Company, 370
YouTube, 5, 301

Z

Zaleznik, Abraham, 247
Zanuto, Foster, 345
Zuboff, Shoshana, 67

Subject Index

ethics (*Cont.*)
    entertainment, 59–60
    factors influencing, 54–63
    gifts, 59
    global influences, 55–57
    influence of character, 66–68
    influence of company policies and
        practices, 57–58
    influence of sales management,
        55–57, 61
    and laws, 63
    National Business Ethics
        Survey, 68
    and partnering, 44–45, 54f
    personal code of ethics, 69
    and personal values, 61–62
    and presentation strategy, 54f
    and product strategy, 54f
    reciprocity, 58
    and relationship building, 64–65
    and relationship strategy, 52–54
    and social networking, 56
    and trust, 64
    and unethical competition, 64
    and use of the Internet, 60
etiquette, 90–91. *see also* cultural issues
evaluation of solutions, 177–178, 229
Excel, 302
excess zone, 116–117
execute, 92
expansion selling, 369–371, 371f
expectations, 359–360, 406
expected product, 160–161
expense records, 393, 394f
external motivation, 415
external rewards, 416–417
extranets, 60
eye contact, 86, 87

F

facial expression, 86–87
family, balancing with career, 390
FBR approach, 294
feature–benefit–reaction, 294
feature-benefit strategy, 141–144
feature dump, 141
features, 141, 142–143
feel–felt–found strategy, 321
Ferris wheel concept, 198, 199, 219
field salespeople, 16
fight or flight, 397
figurative language, 295–296
financial services, 14
fixed salary, 418
follow-through, 362–363, 371f

follow-up, 365–366, 371f
Foreign Corrupt Practices Act, 59
formal integrative negotiation, 310–318
four-part need-satisfaction model,
    256–258
France, 33
full-line selling, 369
functional discount, 157

G

gatekeepers, 247
general survey questions, 262
generations, 185–186
generic product, 160
Germany, 191, 220, 270, 293, 316
gifts, 55, 59
global account manager, 44
global business
    Australia, 137
    Belgium, 261
    buying process, 191
    China, 33, 57, 417
    cultural issues. *see* cultural issues
    England, 396
    and ethics, 55–57
    France, 33
    Germany, 220, 293
    India, 150
    Italy, 117
    Japan, 33, 84
    Latin America, 33, 347
    legal issues, 55
    negotiation, 316
    patience and sensitivity, 293
    relationship-focused countries, 230
    Russia, 365
goals and objectives, 384–385
goal-setting, 93
Government of Canada job bank, 412
graphs, 300
group influences, 184–187
group sales presentation, 296–297

H

habitual buying decision, 175
handshake, 86
harassment, 409
hierarchy of needs, 183–184
home office, 396
humour, in presentations, 290

I

if…then tactic, 328
illustrations, 299

immature behaviour, 115
impending event close, 347–348
implementation, 179
income, 9, 10
incremental commitment, 338
India, 150
indirect denial, 321
inducements, 361
industrial salespeople, 16
industry expert, 137–138
influencers, 232
information, 5
information-age selling, 52
information communication, 361
information economy, 3, 3–6, 19–20,
    45–46
information-gathering questions, 262
information overload, 143
information technology, 4
informative presentation, 283, 292
inside salesperson, 11
installation, 364
insurance, 14–15
integrity, 66
intensity zones, 115–117
internal motivation, 415
internal sales teams, 139
Internet, 60, 138, 412
Interpersonal Pattern Exercise, 103
investigation stage, 229
involvement, 289
Italy, 117

J

Japan, 84, 191, 316
job boards, 412
job description, 411
job interview, 413
job searches, 360

K

key account manager, 44
KISS principle, 287
knowledge workers, 19–20

L

labels, 119–120
laptop computers, 300–302
Latin America, 191, 347
Law of Direction, 384
leadership
    advice on, 409
    coaching, 408–409
    consideration, 406–407

P

paraphrasing, 269
Pareto Law, 317
partnering
    and customer relationship management, 45
    and customer service, 357–361, 362–372
    defined, 42, 79
    ethical standards, 44–45
    evolution of, 42–43
    keys to, 79
    partnership building, 372
    and relationship strategy, 51–54, 78–79
    strategic selling alliances, 43–44
    unhappy customer, 372–374
patience, 293
patronage buying motive, 189–190
peddling, 30, 42
perception, 187
performance appraisal, 406
performance data, 131
personal code of ethics, 69–70
personal digital assistant, 386
personal goals, 384–385
personal interview, 413
personality, 99
personality and skills testing, 412–413
personal selling
    and brand development, 341
    defined, 3
    evolution of, 31f
    future in, 6–11
    philosophy of, 2–3
    role of, 33
    strategic areas of, 232–233
    strategic consultative selling model, 3f
personal selling skills model, 260–261
personal values, 61–63
personal visits, 239, 366–367
perspective, maintaining, 395
persuader stage, 30
persuasion, 283
persuasive communication, 292f
persuasive presentation, 283–284, 292–296
photos, 299
physiological needs, 184
pipeline analytics, 219
pipeline dashboards, 219
pipeline management, 219
Pitney Bowes Certified Postal Consultant, 24

planning calendar, 386, 387f
plant tours, 138
The Platinum Rule, 118, 314, 349f
pleasure questions, 266
portfolio models, 217–218
portfolios, 299
positioning, 149. see also product positioning
postpone method, 323–324
postsale problems, 365
potential product, 161–162
power of association, 295–296
PowerPoint, 301
practising, 302, 349
preapproach, 228
premium approach, 244–245
presentation strategy
    adapting, 235, 285–286
    agenda approach, 242
    approach. see approach
    audiovisual presentation fundamentals, 297
    beginning and end, 295
    Business Contact Worksheet, 245t
    for buying committee, 231–232
    closing the sale, 338f
    combination approaches, 245–246
    converting the buyer's attention, 241–247
    creating the sales presentation, 254f
    creativity in, 290
    customer benefit approach, 242–243
    defined, 40, 196
    demonstration worksheet, 289f
    details in, 287
    developing, 40, 226
    group sales presentation, 296–297
    humour in, 290
    informative presentation, 283
    for need satisfaction, 282–285
    objectives of, 229
    parts of sales presentation, 303f
    persuasive presentation, 283–284, 292–296
    planning the presentation, 234–235
    preapproach, 228
    premium approach, 244–245
    preparing for presentation, 228f
    product demonstration approach, 242
    proof devices, 287–288
    quantifying the solution, 291

    question approach, 243–244
    referral approach, 242
    rehearsing, 302
    reminder presentation, 284–285
    sales call reluctance, 246–247
    sales tools, 291
    senses, appeal to, 288
    setting, 290
    six-step presentation process, 233–235
    steps in, 177f, 233–235
    strategic planning, 286f
    summarizing, 291
    survey approach, 244
    team presentation, 230–231
    telling, showing, and involvement, 289
    tools for, 298–304
    and value creation, 227, 285–291
    and value proposition, 290–291
presenting benefits, 303f
price
    versus cost, 325
    negotiating buyer concerns, 320, 324–326
    price change information, 365
    and product solutions, 133
    and quality, 325
price iceberg, 326f
price strategy, 157–159, 164
primary needs, 184
probing questions, 253, 261t, 263–264, 320, 370
problem questions, 262
problems, resolution of, 178
problem-solver stage, 30, 35
product and plant tours, 298
product buying motives, 189–190
product configuration, 128, 256, 271–272
product demonstration approach, 242
product development, 131
product differentiation, 150–151
product expert, 129
product information sources, 138–141
productivity, 419–420
product knowledge, 39, 129
product life cycle, 155
product options, explosion of, 127
product-oriented selling, 254
product positioning
    defined, 149
    and differentiation, 149–150
    essentials of, 149
    strategies, 155–164
    and value proposition, 150

products
defined, 3, 126
researching and using, 140
product selection, 270*f*, 275*f*
product-selling strategies
mature and well-established
products, 156–157
new and emerging products,
155–156
price strategy, 157–159
product positioning. *see* product
positioning
Three Dimension (3-D) Product
Solutions Selling Model,
151–154
value-added strategy, 159–163
value creation investments,
163–164
product solutions. *see also* product
strategy
company expert, 133–137
company support for product,
136–137
cost-benefit analysis, 134*t*
delivery, 133
feature-benefit strategy, 141–144
industry expert, 137–138
maintenance contracts, 132
performance data, 131
price, 133
product configuration, 128
product development, 131
product expertise, 129
product information, 138–141
product options, 127
quality control, 131
selling solutions, 126–127
service contracts, 132
specifications, 131
value adding, 125–129
written proposals, 128–129
product specifications, 131
product strategy. *see also* product
solutions
and adaptive selling, 233
defined, 39, 125
tailoring, 127
professional fees, 164
professionals, 20–21
promotional allowance, 157
proof devices, 287–288
proposals, 128–129
prospect base, 197
prospecting. *see also* account
development; business development

centres of influence, 202
cold calling, 208–209
combination approaches, 212
databases, 206–208
defined, 196
directories, 202–203
direct-response advertising, 206
educational seminars, 211
email, 205–206
importance of, 198
information, collecting and
organizing, 213–215
introduction to, 196–197
managing the prospect base,
216–220
networking, 209–211
by non-sales employees, 211–212
and planning, 198–200
prospect files, 393
referrals, 201–202
sales intelligence, 214–216
sales letters, 206
through partners, 203
with social media, 207
telemarketing, 205–206
trade publications, 203–204
trade shows and special events,
204–205
websites, 206
prospects, 196, 200
psychic income, 10
publications, 140
punctuality, 90
purchase, 178–179

Q

qualifying the prospect, 212–213, 258,
267
qualitative criteria, 420
quality, of clothing, 88
quality control, 131, 159
quantifying the solution, 133, 134*t*, 291
quantitative criteria, 419–420
quantity discount, 157
question approach
Action Selling, 257
features of, 243–244
four-part consultative questioning
strategy, 261–267
four-part multiple questioning
strategy, 253
for need discovery, 259–261
for negotiating, 322
question not asked, 259
specific survey questions, 262, 325

summary-confirmation question,
291
types of questions, 253, 261–267
questioning skills, 303*f*
questions
for closing the sale, 341
for hiring salespeople, 411
types of, 253, 261–267
quotation management, 128

R

rapport, 239–241
rational buying motive, 188, 189
rationale, 129
real estate, 14
Reality Selling Role-Play Scenarios
CB Richard Ellis, 429–430
Ecolab, 436–438
Hilti Corporation, 435–436
Liberty International
Underwriters, 426–428
Marriott International, Inc,
438–439
Mattress Firm, 428–429
Pharma Supply, 438–441
PulteGroup, 432–433
Salesforce.com, 434–435
Texas Monthly, 431–432
Tom James Company, 425–426
reciprocity, 58
recognitions, 341
recommendation strategies, 272–273
records management, 382, 392–395
recruitment of salespeople, 410–413
reference group, 185–186
referral approach, 242
referrals, 201–202, 255
reflective style, 109–110, 115, 117,
119, 349
regional account manager, 43
rehearsing, 302, 349
reinforcement presentation, 284
relationships, 5, 292
relationship selling
and communication styles, 99–102
defined, 38
in information economy, 3–6
skills for, 102
relationship strategy
adapting, 81
and adaptive selling, 232–233
conversational strategies, 91–92
defined, 38
and ethics, 52–54, 64–65
information-age selling, 52